Reading Instruction
for Today's Children

Reading Instruction
for Today's Children

NILA BANTON SMITH
New York University

PRENTICE-HALL, INC., ENGLEWOOD CLIFFS, NEW JERSEY

Grateful acknowledgment for the photographs in this book is due as follows: To Dr. Stanley Raub, Superintendent of Schools, and Mrs. Margaret L. Sucsy, Reading Consultant, Central School District No. I, South Orange, New York, for their valuable assistance in taking the photographs on pages xii, 228, 254, 304, 384, and 442.

To Mrs. Maurine H. Klein, Head Mistress, St. John's School, Mountain Lakes, New Jersey, for her gracious permission to take the photograph on page 166.

To Robert Monroe, photographer, New York City, for permission to reproduce the picture on the book jacket, and to Robert Castellucci, photographer, Mountain Lakes, New Jersey, for permission to reproduce the picture on page 506.

All photographs, except the last two mentioned, were taken especially for this book by F. H. Burrell, photographer, Palisades, New York.

PRENTICE-HALL INTERNATIONAL, INC., *London*
PRENTICE-HALL OF AUSTRALIA, PTY., LTD., *Sydney*
PRENTICE-HALL OF CANADA, LTD., *Toronto*
PRENTICE-HALL FRANCE, S.A.R.L., *Paris*
PRENTICE-HALL OF JAPAN, INC., *Tokyo*
PRENTICE-HALL DE MEXICO, S.A., *Mexico City*

Preface

This book is intended for use as a textbook in courses offered by colleges and universities and as a handbook of information for teachers in service. The chief concerns of the author in preparing the book were twofold: first, to acquaint students and teachers with all aspects of current reading theory and pertinent reading research; second, and perhaps more important, to point out possibilities of applying this theory and research to the actual teaching of children in the classroom.

In discussing the general nature of the book, mention should be made first of Part 1 which discusses "The Changing Scene." Chapter 1 reviews reading instruction in years past and leads into glimpses of what may be ahead, as discussed in Chapter 2. The modern concept of considering reading growth as closely integrated with other aspects of child development is enlarged upon in Chapter 3, "As the Child Grows." This chapter discusses reading growth as an integral part of total child growth and gives suggestions for taking advantage of our recent knowledge of child growth in teaching reading. "As Language Develops" is a chapter designed to highlight the interrelationships of reading with the other language arts and to give examples of practice in which reading instruction is intertwined with other strands in the language arts constellation. In the chapter entitled "Approaches Differ," some of the new approaches to reading which are currently under experimentation are described. Several recently implemented plans for grouping children in the classroom for reading instruction are discussed in Chapter 6, and because of the growing interest in individualized instruction all of Chapter 7 is devoted to this topic.

Part 2 is the "heart" of the book. This is the skill section dealing in four chapters with the major growth areas of skill development in reading: "Word Identification," "Getting Meanings from Reading," "Study Skills Needed in Reading Content Subjects," "Fluency and Rate." Regardless of method, material, type of children, or level of development, the teacher must teach reading skills. The "numerator" may change but the skill "denominator" remains the same. Hence nearly one-third of the book is devoted to the basic skills in reading: reviews and implications of research having to do with skill development, discussions of clusters of subskills within major growth areas, and presentations of practical suggestions which students and teachers may draw upon in implementing their skill-development programs.

Part 3 offers a contrast. While skill development is of basic importance, there is another aspect of reading growth which all too frequently receives insufficient attention. That aspect is the development of permanent ongoing interest and discriminating taste in literature. All our efforts to develop skill proficiency are of little value if students do not use reading to enrich their present and future living. In order to contribute to this objective, Part 3, entitled "Developing Interest and Taste in Literature," acquaints readers with the values of literature for children and with research in regard to children's interests in books, comics, magazines, and newspapers. In addition it contains many practical suggestions for developing wholesome reading interests, elevating tastes, and stimulating wider use of libraries—classroom, school, and public.

Part 4, "Beginning Reading Instruction," contains four chapters concerned with prereading and initial reading instruction. The placement of this section near the end of the volume is bound to evoke questions. The usual order in books on reading is to discuss "Reading Readiness" early in the book and then proceed to beginning reading, primary reading, and reading at the intermediate grade level. Beginning reading was not discussed until such a late point in this book because everything said in preceding chapters is significant to teachers of beginning reading, even during prereading periods. Since it is the teacher of beginning reading who lays the foundation, it seemed inadvisable to the author to attempt a discussion of early reading activities until the reader had become thoroughly familiar with the research, skills, and varied procedures discussed in preceding chapters.

In this connection, perhaps an observation should be made in regard to treating skills in separate chapters—an entire chapter for each growth area—rather than providing chapters for different grade levels. The former structure was followed because, first, development in any of the skill areas is continuous; and, second, grade labels do not have much significance at the present time. Each teacher must take her pupils at the stage they have reached and guide them on to higher levels of skill development. The primary teacher may have some children at intermediate grade level, and the intermediate teacher is almost sure to have some at primary level. In terms of these considerations, it seemed advisable in this book to offer a continuum of skill development activities ranging from beginning to high intermediate in each skill area, thus acquainting the college student with possibilities at all levels and leaving to teachers in service the privilege of selecting from the continuum any suggestions which might be appropriate for the level of any particular child or group of children with whom she is concerned.

Part 5 deals with "Teacher-Parent Partnerships." The full impact of parental and home influences upon success in learning to read is just beginning to make itself felt. Certainly at this time every student who is preparing to be a teacher and every teacher in service should be keenly aware of possibilities of fruitful teacher-parent interrelationships and useful procedures for promoting them.

Part 6, "Practice and Maintenance Activities," is unique. Activities were suggested in Chapters 8, 9, 10, and 11 for *introducing* various skills in each of the four basic skill areas. Most children, however, need follow-up practice after a skill has been introduced at a given school level and they also need review to maintain the skill at successive grade levels. For this reason suggestions of practical activities were assembled which the readers might use as samples in preparing their own practice materials to meet the immediate needs of the particular pupils with whom they are working. Thus, four chapters containing such suggestions were placed at the end of the book for reference purposes. Such an arrangement offers readers the advantage of having available a fund of sample practice activities, without the disadvantage of having their train of thought interrupted by encountering these numerous small·items while pursuing the content of the skill chapters themselves.

In conclusion, I wish to acknowledge my indebtedness in the preparation of this book to all those who have touched my life professionally during the many years in which I have been working in the field of reading: the children whom I have taught in public school classrooms; the teachers with whom I have worked as a supervisor in a city school system; the undergraduate students who have come to my university classes in starry-eyed eagerness to learn about the teaching of reading; the graduate students who have sometimes challenged my thinking on a point or two and who often have enriched my lectures by relating their personal teaching successes; the doctoral candidates whose dissertations I have sponsored and whose diligent searching for as yet unrevealed facts about reading has helped to keep my own research interests bright and burning. To all these I am deeply grateful, to all these I wish to express my sincere thanks.

NILA BANTON SMITH

Contents

Reading Instruction
for Today's Children

PART 1

The Changing Scene

chapter 1

As Reading Instruction Unfolded

The story of American reading instruction is a fascinating one to pursue. It is a story of old readers which have moved in long procession from the schoolroom to the garret, from noisy popularity to silent oblivion. It is a story which reflects the changing religious, economic, and political institutions of a growing and progressive country. It is a story of advancing psychologies, of broadening and more inclusive philosophies, of ever-increasing attempts to apply science to education.

Every teacher of reading should take a backward look at the evolution of reading instruction, not only to add to her cultural background in this important field, but also to serve her as a "launching pad" from which she may take off for the exciting reading adventures in the space age ahead. Toward these ends a brief review of the evolution of reading instruction in America is presented in pageant form.[1]

[1] Scenes one through four are reprinted by permission from "Historical Turning Points in the Teaching of Reading" by Nila Banton Smith in *NEA Journal*, Vol. 41 (May 1952), 280–83.

Progress in reading instruction has been marked by a succession of turning points. For a period of years reading methods and materials all over the country are quite similar—so similar, in fact, that an unbiased examiner might arrive at the conclusion that all had been turned out of the same mold, with just a slightly different crimp here and there in the contour of the pan. Then, rather suddenly, a new plan becomes popular, and reading is taught in accordance with this plan until another turning point arrives. Thus, epoch after epoch of reading instruction passes.

The epochs from 1607 to the present time are depicted in the following pageant.

Scene One: The Period of Religious Emphasis.
Time: 1607–1776.
Setting: A barren, unadorned Colonial schoolhouse.
Characters: Serious-minded children, sitting stiffly on benches. A stern-faced schoolmaster who spared not the rod, lest he spoil the child, and whose chief motive for teaching reading was to help his pupils seek salvation for their souls.
Properties: The hornbook, a hardwood board covered with a translucent sheet of cow's horn and containing the alphabet and the Lord's Prayer. The New England Primer, aptly described by Paul Leicester Ford as containing "prose as bare of beauty as the whitewash of their churches, with poetry as rough and stern as their storm-torn coast, with pictures as crude and unfinished as their own glacial-smoothed boulders, between stiff oak covers which symbolized the contents." [2]
Action: Children spelling out words, reading orally, and memorizing —procedures deemed necessary in making the best use of the religious selections in the reader. In this way the children were tutored, according to Mr. Ford, "until from being unregenerate and as Jonathan Edwards said, 'young vipers, and infinitely more hateful than young vipers' to God, they attained that happy state, when as expressed by Judge Sewall's child, they were afraid they 'should go to hell,' and were 'stirred up dreadfully to seek God.'" [3]

Scene Two: The Period of Patriotic Emphasis.
Time: 1776–1840.

[2] Paul Leicester Ford, *The New England Primer, A History of Its Origin and Development* (New York: Dodd, Mead & Co., 1879), p. 1.
[3] *Ibid.*, p. 1.

Setting: A Colonial schoolroom—still barren and unattractive—equipped with benches.

Characters: Embyro citizens of young America, faithfully pursuing their reading lessons. The schoolmaster, a strict disciplinarian, zealously bent on developing patriotic citizens for a new nation.

Properties: The cardboard-covered, blue-backed speller, containing exercises and rules for pronunciation designed to overcome diversity of dialects, patriotic selections intended to instill patriotism for America, historical and informative selections to acquaint children with America's history and resources, and moralistic selections to make them good citizens.

Action: A group of children—standing stiffly in a row, left hands held behind them, right hands holding the reader at a uniform angle—reciting to their teacher and reading orally and eloquently in interpreting patriotic selections. The teacher still has pupils spell out the words, but he is beginning to use phonics and is placing great emphasis upon oral expression.

Scene Three: The Period of German-Pestalozzian Emphasis.

Time: 1840–1880.

Setting: A classroom equipped with desks and seats with back on them!

Characters: Groups of children organized into grades. A placid, unruffled schoolmaster, living in a period of transition following post-revolutionary activities and dominated by Pestalozzian principles, advocating broader reading content and the use of the word method.

Properties: McGuffey's graded series of readers bound in cardboard, adorned with a few black-and-white illustrations, and containing selections concerned with morals, science, history, art, philosophy, economics, and politics.

Action: Children still reading orally and learning their ABC's, but also using phonics, and finding lessons easier because of controlled repetition of words.

Scene Four: The Period of Cultural Emphasis.

Time: 1880–1910.

Setting: A classroom still equipped with screwed-down desks, but with evidences of attempts to make the room more attractive with colored paper chains, children's drawings, and written work on burlap-covered wall spaces.

Characters: Children, a bit more childlike in dress than in the past,

5

memorizing and reciting in response to teacher-imposed assignments. A schoolma'am, instead of master, doling out textbook assignments and hearing recitations designed to discipline her pupils mentally and to develop them culturally.

Properties: A basic reader filled with folk-tales and excerpts from the classics designed to develop an appreciation of literature, clothbound and containing a few *colored* pictures for the first time in history. A set of supplemental readers, one per child.

Action: Children memorizing, dramatizing, reading "The Little Red Hen" during the basic reading period; memorizing lists of phonic families during a separate period; reading from a set of supplemental readers during another period.

Scene Five: Initial Period of Scientific Interest.
Time: 1910–1920.
Setting: A classroom equipped with screwed-down desks, but often having a set of small chairs in the front of the room for "the reading class."
Characters: Children dressed and acting much like children of today. A woman teacher, interested in but somewhat skeptical of scientific investigations in reading, which she is hearing about for the first time. She is also somewhat worried about new standardized tests which her superintendent wants her to give at the beginning and end of semesters to measure progress.
Properties: Literary readers, one per child to be used for basic reading; one set of supplemental readers; standardized tests in reading and other subjects; phonic charts and phonic cards.
Action: Children reading orally in the basic reader during one period, in the supplemental reader during the next period; taking a test with the use of The Gray Standardized Oral Reading Paragraphs at the beginning and end of semesters.

Scene Six: Period of Initial Application of Scientific Investigations.
Time: 1920–1925.
Setting: A classroom not much changed from the preceding period.
Characters: Post-World War I children, suddenly pulled out of education for culture and inducted into education for reality. A woman schoolteacher—enthusiastic about the new idea of teaching *silent* reading, and trying out new plans of classroom organization in order to better accommodate individual differences revealed by the widespread administration of standardized tests.
Properties: A basic set of silent readers devoted to informative and

realistic selections, each of which is followed with an exercise to check comprehension of silent reading; two or three sets of supplemental readers; seat-work of the silent reading type—quantities of it!

Action: Children reading silently, then making some comprehension response, such as acting out words or sentences, responding to true-false, completion, or multiple-choice exercises.

Scene Seven: Period of Extension of Investigations and Their Applications.

Time: 1925–1940.

Setting: A classroom equipped with tables and chairs. The low blackboards are adorned with borders and posters painted by the children. There is a library corner containing a reading table, upon which is displayed several attractive books. Children are hammering at large pieces of wood, painting with calcimine at easels, cooking simple foods, modeling lifelike figures in clay, sewing on garments for plays, building large structures which permit dramatic play—all in connection with their "unit of work."

Characters: "Activity" children working freely and spontaneously in terms of their own interests. A modern teacher with broadened objectives in reading which embrace the teaching of both oral and silent reading, and the use of materials both informative and fanciful. She hears much about "reading readiness," postponement of beginning reading for many children, and the preparation of experience charts and other co-operatively composed materials. During the last ten years of the period she is experiencing in many cases the fun of teaching school in terms of the children's interests, and is intrigued with the new "game" of trying to get her subject matter across through "units of work."

Properties: Many beautifully illustrated and interesting books, largely bearing on the topic of the "unit," but with provision also for books on other topics to stimulate independent reading. Charts and schoolmade booklets in profusion, containing cooperatively prepared reading selections growing out of children's interests. Basic reading texts used sparingly in some places, generously in others.

Action: Children reading functionally from their cooperatively prepared materials and from other materials as needed for "the unit"; also reading widely of free-choice books.

Scene Eight: The Beginning Period of the Space Age.

Time: 1940–1950.

Setting: The world at war! Birth of the atomic age! The armed forces charging that too many American youths can not read well enough to follow military instructions; mass communication threatening home reading; remedial reading clinics springing up rapidly. Children sitting in modern, attractive classrooms with movable furniture, but shifted from a more or less incidental type of reading instruction to more definitely organized skill development programs with some attention to reading in the content subjects.

Characters: World War II children, confused in the midst of stress, but intrigued with the prominence of tanks, jeeps, guns, boats and airplanes; nevertheless really wanting to learn to read, and willing and eager to be taught. A teacher hearing about studies of language arts relationships and of various facets of child growth which affect reading success. She is now providing her pupils with a series of enriching experiences rather than trying to teach all her subject matter through one large unit of work. She recognizes the need for some definitely organized practice on reading skills, but she emphasizes functional reading and free reading in ever increasing amounts.

Properties: Expanding collections of informative books which children can use functionally in meeting class and individual purposes and interests. Quantities of reading materials prepared cooperatively by children and teachers not only in the first grade but also in middle and upper grades. At the same time basic readers and workpads seem to have very general usage.

Action: Children engaging in organized developmental reading instruction, but with ample opportunities to develop skills through functional use of reading as it serves their own interests and purposes.

Scene Nine: Period of Emerging Space Age Concern.

Time: 1950–the present.

Setting: A troubled civilization; democracy threatened. School people beginning to realize the need for improved and changed reading instruction. Interest in reading instruction surging high; laymen criticizing the school's methods.

Characters: Space age children living in a mechanized world, troubled with social and political restlessness. Too many of them are not learning to read as well as they should; on the other hand many are reaching new heights of reading achievement, not only in literature but in all content subjects. High school and college students and adults beyond college are seeking reading improvement. Teachers are taking in-service or university courses in reading; receiving help in their school system from reading consultants; hearing about studies that probe to greater depths in ascertaining causes of reading difficulty, and about studies having to do with parental influences in listening, semantics, and linguistics as related to reading. They also are hearing much about individualized instruction in reading, and about teaching reading with the use of automated devices.

Properties: Most often a set of basic readers plus small sets of other readers plus quantities of trade books, one of a kind. In some cases where individualized instruction is used, the basic readers are dispensed with and only trade books constitute the substance of the reading instruction program.

Action: In most cases, children reading in small groups from a basic reader, and also reading widely of free-choice library books. In individualized classrooms, each child is reading silently from his own self-chosen trade book with opportunities at intervals to read orally to the teacher.[4]

[4] The succeeding chapters in this book will deal with reading instruction in this "Period of Emerging Space Age Concern." If the reader would like to have more details about changes that have taken place in reading since 1910, it is suggested that he refer to "What Have We Accomplished in Reading—A Review of the Past Fifty Years," an article written by the author and appearing in *Elementary English,* Mar. 1961, pages 141–50. Reprints of this article may be obtained by writing to the National Council of Teachers of English, 508 South Sixth St., Champaign, Illinois (10 cents each).

2

As the World Changes

As the world changes so must reading instruction change. We have summarized reading changes of the past. What kind of changes may we expect in the future?

Predicting what is going to happen in reading has something in common with predicting the weather—both are precarious undertakings. In both cases, however, there are some fairly reliable indications to suggest future developments.

Indications of reading change may be found in the emerging trends of our rapidly moving civilization as a whole. The winds of change are blowing with hurricane force, uprooting established tradition, sweeping away old practices, opening up new pathways. Reading is so intrinsically interwoven with life's activities and currents of thinking that it reciprocally reflects the larger trends in life itself. So this attempted prediction of things to come in reading is based upon an examination of evolving trends in our changing civilization.

Pressures Resulting from World Power
Competition

The "birth of the atomic age" is officially set as December 2, 1942, when Dr. Enrico Fermi turned on the first successful nuclear energy machine in Chicago. The first atomic bomb destroyed Hiroshima on August 6, 1945.

The atomic age and reading immediately become interactive. We didn't realize this at the time. We were too close to this earth-shaking event to sense its import for reading instruction. But we realize it now and its implications are already sketched in the unfinished scene of the future.

For one thing, pressures to increase production will affect reading. Because of competition which threatens our democratic way of living, production is being stepped up in all aspects of American life. In the future there will be increased effort to step up reading instruction, to produce higher competency in a shorter time. This trend reflects the larger motive and tempo which now is controlling and will continue to control increased production in other aspects of human endeavor.

One very healthy development which may result from the pressure influence is a vigorous scrutiny of present practices and probing inquiry into their desirability and effectiveness. Searching questions, evaluations, and investigations will be directed into presently accepted procedures and materials used in such areas as reading readiness, word identification, depth and variety of meanings, rate adjustments, contributions of other language arts to reading, parent-teacher cooperation, content, and vocabulary of reading material.

Investigators, authors, publishers will work feverishly in seeking new methods and in preparing new materials which will produce faster and better results in learning to read. The use of programmed materials, television, the augmented Roman alphabet, linguistic approaches, individualized instruction, and other new methods now emerging are harbingers of what is to come. The trend toward stepped-up reading instruction will result in a great flux of new methods and materials. The day is coming when teachers will be trained in the use of many different approaches and equipped with a great variety of materials. They will then draw upon all of these as needed in meeting exigencies of the occasion, rather than confining their teaching to just one method.

Stepped-up efforts in teacher-education in reading will ensue. Drastic modifications will probably take place in the nature of college reading courses offered to students preparing to be teachers. Lectures and textbooks will be richly supplemented with observation of excellent teachers of reading and participation in reading activities in the classroom, both as integral parts of the courses themselves. Teachers-in-service will repeatedly take in-service and college courses to keep abreast of new developments in the field.

Reading clinics will undergo change as a result of inquiry into ways in which they can better serve the strong new wave of interest in improved reading instruction. For one thing the major functions of clinics may change. Instead of trained clinicians devoting most of their efforts and specialized knowledge to the task of bringing a few children "up to grade," they undoubtedly will make broader contributions. Their most significant functions may become those of research and demonstration. Through research they will probe more deeply in attempts to find better preventive diagnostic and instructional procedures. Through demonstrations to teachers-in-service as well as to teachers-in-preparation they will show improved procedures which may be used in working with underachievers in the classroom.

Too, the personnel of those attending clinics may change. Perhaps with better teacher education there will be fewer school-age children who are in need of clinical assistance, but the age limits of those seeking clinical help may be extended. Parents of preschool children, in their eagerness to have their children become good readers, may wish to find what stage of development their child has reached in passing through the many preschool growth stages preparatory to learning to read, and what they can do in promoting his general growths in ways which will be conducive to reading competency later on. Probably increasing numbers of senior citizens will seek help in reading improvement so that they may better keep abreast of rapidly changing world events during the prolonged longevity that they anticipate.

Changes sketched above and many others would probably take place under normal conditions through comparatively slow evolutionary processes. As a result, however, of the pressures to step up production in all fields of endeavor, inquiry, investigation, and revision in reading practices and materials will be intensified and speeded up. Changes may be revolutionary.

The Explosion in School Population

The United States Office of Education predicts that by 1970 there will be 32,000,000 pupils in elementary schools (a 15 per cent increase over the number in 1960); 12,400,000 high school pupils (a 47.5 per cent increase over the number in 1960); and twice as many college students, representing 44 per cent of all 18-to-21-year-olds in the country. These staggering increases in the numbers of students to be taught in our schools and colleges result from several influences: increase in school-age population, interest of young people in having a higher education, interest of the states and the federal government in having a well-educated citizenry to combat the terrifying problems of the present civilization.

Simultaneously, with this unprecedented increase in the number of students to be taught, a scarcity of teachers is already clearly in evidence. According to authorities, there is at present writing a shortage of some 195,000 qualified teachers, more than double the shortage in 1952. Certainly the number of new teachers entering the field each year is not keeping pace with the increased enrollment of students.

What effect will the exploding school population, coupled with a scarcity of teachers, have on reading instruction? Some of the ways in which reading instruction may change in attempts to meet this problem will be discussed.

Mass Instruction

Mass instruction is one possibility. Television has already demonstrated the feasibility of having one teacher teach hundreds of students through this medium. It has been used most generally in teaching foreign languages, science, history, and geometry to students beyond elementary level. In a few places, however, reading has been taught by television in the elementary grades. If television is used more widely in teaching reading, additional reading materials must be developed for students to use as the teacher gives instructions and explanations. The television screen will not accommodate extensive passages of text in type face large enough to be read by viewers. Therefore new reading materials will probably be devised for students' use as the TV teacher guides instruction and practice, and manuals or guide books of instruction may be developed for teachers.

Mass teaching is sometimes facilitated through a plan known as team teaching. This plan has many variations. One of the most common of the team-teaching plans is that in which one teacher, in person, meets all children of about the same achievement level from different classes in a large school or from different schools in a small school system. The children gather in a large room such as an auditorium, and the one teacher teaches this large group in the same way that she would teach a smaller group in her own classroom. Other teachers usually work with the children in smaller groups for follow-up practice or explanation. In some schools teachers exchange teaching responsibilities, each one taking all pupils in both rooms for some subject in which the individual teacher is specially skilled. In all cases a "team" of teachers has mutual responsibility for planning, developing, and evaluating the instructional program for a large group of children.

For many years we have been crusading for a reduction of teacher load. Educators at the elementary level have been particularly concerned with this problem, believing that the growing elementary child needs much individual attention, companionship, and guidance from an interested and devoted teacher. Just as we have made some gains in reducing teacher load at this level it seems paradoxical that a movement has begun for teaching larger numbers of pupils at one time. Larger teaching groups may be a necessity in our approaching civilization, but perhaps mass teaching may be balanced by other arrangements in which the teacher will be relieved of some of her routine duties, leaving her time to work closely with small groups or individuals as they need her personal guidance and specialized teaching techniques.

Teacher Aids

One very promising prospect at the elementary level is that of providing teachers with aids. This is much the same plan as that used in many hospitals where trained nurses have aids to do the more routine jobs. Teacher aids may be recruited from parents or from students in education. These aids may take over such jobs as playground supervision and hall duty; take attendance, keep records, duplicate materials, and distribute supplies; check information obtained through reading or results of skill practice; supervise pupils during study, listening, and viewing periods; and perform many other duties of a nonteaching variety.

If a teacher has an aid to take care of such duties as those mentioned above, she will be free to devote herself to those aspects of instruction which require a high degree of teaching skill. She will then be able to spend more time in each school day with groups or individuals who need her personal contact and teaching ability. Under these conditions the teacher, together with her aid, might be able to handle a larger class as effectually or perhaps more effectually than one teacher can at the present time.

Pupil-Team Organization

The pupil-team organization may find wider acceptance as the population rapidly increases. In this plan children work together in small groups composed of from three to seven pupils. The group works by itself, covering content or skill exercises as fast as it can, listening to each other's reading or checking each other's responses in arithmetic, spelling, or other subjects.

Tape Recordings

For several years tape recordings have been used to measure progress in oral reading. A child's oral reading would be taped at the beginning of a semester and again at the end or perhaps at intervals within the semester. Then the tapes would be played back while the teacher and child made comparisons.

Recently, however, tape recordings have undergone experimentation as a self-teaching approach. One child or a group of children gather around a recording which tells them what to do and how to do it. They then proceed to work through an assignment, after which they again refer to the recording for answers.

More uses of tape recordings in teaching reading may be found as one way of helping to meet the problem of having an increased number of children in the classroom.

Programmed Instruction

Perhaps chief among the new devices for dealing with larger numbers of pupils will be programmed materials broken down into small learning units accompanied with answers to provide for immediate checking of each response by the child himself as he proceeds with his work. Programmed material may be provided in the form of books or tablets, or in some special format designed to fit into a teaching machine.

Programmed materials, because of their self-teaching possibilities, offer one solution to increased enrollments, and they will undoubtedly become popular. Programmed materials in the form of books, tablets, cards, answer sheets, and so on can be used in any classroom without the aid of special equipment.

Teaching machines are most frequently mentioned in connection with programmed materials. The teaching machine is used in processing the programmed material. Future uses of the teaching machine in teaching reading are possible but limited. A more complete discussion of teaching machines and an evaluation of their possible functions in reading instruction will be found in Chapter 5, pages 82–85.

Self-Learning Materials

No doubt many self-teaching materials other than programmed materials will be devised and used in elementary classrooms. These materials may consist of self-help workbooks, tablets of exercises of increasing difficulty, sets of cards, kits containing a sequence of lessons graded in difficulty, and so on. Many of these materials will carry with them some provision for self-checking.

The Laboratory Concept

The laboratory concept is concerned with a place, not a device or technique. Schools may be built so that an entire floor, designed to accommodate large numbers of children at one time, will be set aside and developed as a communication center. This center will be equipped with learning aids for use in reading development as well as with aids for use in the other facets of communication. It will contain a wide selection of printed learning materials, tapes, films, film strips, teaching machines, television on closed and open circuit—all contributing to the development of reading interest and skills. Children will work in this center individually or in groups, according to their needs. Sometimes the teacher's aid will be in the laboratory assisting with practice; at other times a skillful teacher will be there to do developmental work or to guide discussion and interpretation with an individual, a small group, or a large group. At other times children will work by themselves, using the appropriate self-teaching material, device, or medium most needed according to their own respective requirements and stage of development.

This laboratory concept combines most of the other plans, media, and devices discussed in this section. Such a laboratory would not only enable large numbers of children to develop their reading ability simultaneously, but probably would also allow for the maximum development of each individual. This concept would seem to be a feasible solution to the exploding population problem. More money allotted to education would hasten the day of its realization.

The Technological Revolution

A third influence which undoubtedly will change reading instruction in the future is the technological revolution, an influence which fundamentally is responsible for the emergence of the Space Age itself. The release of atomic energy and the conquest of space are due to technological advances, which are changing our lives in many ways. Modes of transportation and communication are revolutionized; food is refrigerated, treated chemically, dehydrated; much clothing is made of miracle fabrics—nylon, orlon, dacron; homes are constructed with new materials, air-conditioned, mechanically heated, gadget-cleaned. Cutting more deeply than these more or less surface changes is the effect of the stark, unavoidable truth that technological advances, especially in regard to space travel and war weapons, are the most generally recognized indications of world power. It is this latter implication of the technological revolution which more than any other is inciting action on many fronts, including education.

Reading in Science

It is probably largely due to this threat of technology in imperiling the American way of life that an impetus has been given to the study of science in our public schools. Educators realize that the youth of today and tomorrow must be able to understand and interpret scientific and technological trends. Furthermore, there is a critical need for more men and women who will be devoted to a life-work in science. As a corollary of these needs, it follows that students in our schools must become more interested in science, must know how to *read* science with understanding.

Special skills and approaches and the recognition of unique patterns in science writing are needed to read science effectively. More research will be done in regard to these matters, and in the future we probably shall become as much concerned about teaching children to read science as we are now concerned about teaching phonics.

Reading in Mathematics

Mathematics is closely allied to science, and much of the trouble that students have in this subject area arises from their inability to *read* problems and explanations. Many adults at the present time probably should be better versed in mathematics than they are, and undoubtedly they would be, had they been taught to read problems and mathematical symbols.

More attention, in the future, will be given to the reading skills needed in working with mathematics as well as with science. Concurrently, some specialized subject knowledge in science and mathematics will be increasingly required of teachers.

Mass Communication in Life Outside of School

Radio, television, and motion pictures are all products of the technological revolution. Radio and television have replaced the reading lamp on the living room table in many homes. The movies beckon youth to more effortless entertainment than reading. Certainly this cataclysm in communication is affecting reading, which after all is one facet in the total constellation of communication media.

17

Fortunately, some of the worries which arose when the new media first appeared have been subdued by investigations. Studies have revealed that children did not become more passive as a result of viewing television, that their eyesight was not damaged, and that their school performance was not generally affected. (See pages 85–87 for a further discussion of television and reading.)

The most imminent *danger* of mass communication lies in its potency as a molder of public opinion. The voices heard through mass media disseminate varying viewpoints, diverse opinions, differing ideologies, often with the intent to change our thinking and behavior. It is extremely urgent that listening should be accompanied with the same discriminating, penetrating, critical reactions as those employed while reading. Hence, a strong new emphasis looms up ahead on both *critical reading* and *critical listening* and their interrelationships. We use the same skills when listening critically that we use when reading critically, except that we absorb the content through the aural avenue rather than through our visual apparatus. In the future more attention probably will be given to promoting the transfer of critical reading skills to critical listening and vice versa. (See pages 263–64 for a discussion of critical reading.)

In addition to our efforts to develop more discriminating selection of and more critical reactions to mass communication in life outside of school, we shall increasingly bring the mass communication agencies into the school to use for instructional purposes, as mentioned earlier in this chapter. (See Chapter 5 for a more detailed discussion of these approaches.)

It has been observed that many children develop from television-viewing a tremendous volume of facts which enables them to talk about technical processes, distant places, and remote times with fluency and sophistication. This factual knowledge, however, is often just a veneer, lacking in genuineness and depth of understanding. It still remains for the school to supply experiences first-hand and vicariously to provide the kernels of meaning lacking in the thin shell of television communication. This being the case, does our reading content have a new function to perform in furnishing understanding and background, in helping children to sense the significance of different environments, people, and events, and in grasping their more substantial implications? If so, do we need more primary books written in natural language and dealing with subjects of more mature interest such as children enjoy viewing on television? If we had such books, might television serve as a stimulus of interest leading to a seeking for deeper meanings and clearer concepts which then might be developed through reading and discussing worthwhile context? Perhaps change will take place as such questions are pondered and explored.

Emphasis on Speed in Reading

This is an age of speed! Jet airplanes and streamlined trains whizzing over transportation lines, helicopters carrying the mail, missiles hurtling through space; telegraphs, long-distance phones, radio, television, telstar, flashing communications. These are a few examples of the Revolution in Speed which is hastening us along in its breathless celerity.

As for reading: thousands of newspapers, hundreds of magazines, dozens of books roll from presses daily, speeded by technological invention. Yet no one has enough time to read as much as he would wish. We hurry all day long—teachers and other workers hurry to their jobs in the morning, hurry through the work-day hours in an attempt to accomplish as much as possible, hurry home to get ready to hurry out in the evening to a professional or business meeting, a social function, or some one of the many fascinating recreations. More reading to be done than ever before and less time in which to do it! What is the answer? Not more *time* in which to read, but the ability to *read more* in the time we have.

This need has been felt for some time and attempts have been made to meet it. Further improvements will be made in procedures designed to develop greater speed as well as understanding of meaning, and much more concern will be shown in regard to the flexibility of speed. The day of developing just one rapid speed in reading is waning. Students will be expected to develop greater flexibility in using different rates of speed when reading different kinds of materials for different purposes. Factors which affect speed development will receive more careful scrutiny.

Revolution in Social and Political Affairs

Social and political issues are seething. Propaganda is rampant. Lack of information is much too common. Misunderstandings, faulty evaluations, and gullibility are prevalent.

Radical social and political changes have occurred in rapid succession during the last three decades. They have been accompanied with confusion arising from the inability of many citizens to understand them. Lack of understanding in turn has resulted in lowered competency to participate intelligently in the solution of these problems. Specialists in

19

current affairs predict that sharp changes will continue to occur in an equal or accelerated pace in the immediate future. An acceleration must also occur in the public's understanding of these changes.

To live dangerously in these times is unavoidable, but to live ignorantly is inexcusable. Yet, studies in America reveal that less than one-third of the population is well informed about foreign affairs, another third knows something about happenings abroad, and the other third knows almost nothing about events in other countries. The reading of high-school students indicates that, if they read at all outside of their classroom assignments, the majority of them are interested largely in articles dealing with sports, hobbies, crime, gossip, and stories of the mystery, detective, or "true-story" types.

What is being done in classrooms now? What will be done in the foreseeable future to teach students to read about the stirring issues of current life with deep understanding, with penetrating insight, with sound and unbiased evaluation?

The recent attention given to developing skills needed in reading in the content fields is helpful. Educators everywhere are becoming conscious of the need for teaching special skills required in reading in specialized areas. They know that students should not read social studies text as they would a story. In the future there will be an increase of tempo in the movement to teach students *how* to read social studies in order that they may grasp its significance and sense its impact on their own lives.

Perhaps the most important skill to use in working with social studies content is that of critical reading. Students must be taught to *think* while reading—and not only to think but to evaluate, judge, check authenticity. The lowest level of reading in social studies is that in which the student simply repeats to the teacher what "the book says." We are now beginning to emphasize thinking skills in reading; the next step will be to emphasize evaluative skills, not only in connection with reading instruction but in teaching social studies.

Developing the ability to detect and analyze propaganda is an inescapable and a mandatory duty of every teacher of social studies in this age. You and I and the students whom we teach are in the midst of a communication network which is teeming with propaganda, and there is evidence that it will increase in volume in the years ahead. Dozens of times every day we are confronted with printed or spoken messages in which someone is trying to influence our thinking and various forms of behavior. In this highly competitive age we must not permit ourselves or our students to become targets of this control. Aldous Huxley has aptly said when speaking of the propagandist, "In a land where there is no water, he digs in vain." [1]

Every medium containing printed sentences or even phrases is used as a tool by the propagandist: billboards, handbills, leaflets, pamphlets as well as newspapers, magazines, and books may serve this purpose. Teachers in the future will have the responsibility of teaching even elementary children to sense emotive language, to detect propaganda tricks, to analyze sources and purposes of propagandist writers in printed material. This is a grave need with which teachers will be increasingly concerned. (See pages 277, 561–62 for suggested classroom procedures.)

One more point: We need a citizenry that is better informed concerning public affairs, a citizen that knows what is going on *daily*. This information should not come only through a fifteen-minute newscast interspersed with commercials and restricted to the interpretation of one commentator. It should come through wide reading, in which world affairs are presented in different ways and with various interpretations. Realizing this, teachers in the future probably will be urged to spend some time daily with every group of pupils in reading, discussing, comparing accounts of important events in various newspapers and magazines. Why should children study descriptions of important *current* events years later in history books? We shall increasingly let them live history as it's happening!

Revolution of Rising Expectations

There is another world-wide revolution which will affect reading instruction in the immediate future. The revolution of rising expectations is not so obvious or so spectacular as the pressure accompanying the struggle for world power, the exploding school population, the technological revolution, or revolution in the social and political affairs of the world. Yet, it is probably more fundamental than any of these.

Aspirations of people are advancing rapidly. People the world over are expressing revolutionary drives to improve themselves, to live a better existence.

In the agrarian period of American life, man's highest expectancy was to own a piece of fertile land and to make a living by tilling the soil. In the age of the industrial revolution, the highest expectancy of common

[1] Lincoln Steffens, *Autobiography* (New York: Harcourt, Brace & World, Inc., 1931), p. 238.

21

man was to become a skilled worker in operating a machine in a factory, running a cotton gin, or driving a reaper.

In the atomic age there is a vigorous *rising* expectancy on the part of each person, an expectancy for an easier life, a fuller life, a more secure life, and a longer life. In this age of labor-saving inventions, enrichment possibilities, higher wages, and medical progress, there is promise to meet more fully these rising personal expectancies.

The farmer, the factory worker, the professional man, the business man, the manufacturer, the banker—all expect to improve in their respective working areas—they look for change, they make change come. Their personal expectancies rise accordingly.

What does this drive toward personal improvement have to do with reading?

Regardless of what job a person is doing today, he *has* to read if he expects personal improvement. Let's consider a few examples.

Jimmie was nineteen years old and he had never learned to read. Jimmie lived in the dynamic century of progress, surrounded with television, radio, movies, and picture magazines. Jimmie jostled daily with the throngs who worked and played and studied in the fastest-moving city in the world which happened to be Jimmie's home. Did reading have any role to play in Jimmie's life? Did he need reading? Did he want to learn to read? To answer these questions one must tell the story of Jimmie—a totally illiterate youth in a modern world.

When Jimmie was six years old, he had suffered deep burns about his head and chest. As a result he developed chorea, and other nervous complications. Then followed long years of invalidism during which period Jimmie was too ill to sustain the concentrated effort which was necessary in learning to read.

By the time Jimmie had reached his nineteenth birthday, however, he had recovered his health completely and had attained normal physical development. Now he hied himself out into the world in quest of a job.

Jimmie had learned to drive a truck while vacationing on a farm so he applied at a warehouse for a truck-driving position. Here he was told that he would have to have a driver's license before he could drive a truck. One must read in order to pass a driver's test. So Jimmie was obliged to abandon this plan.

Jimmie then sought and obtained a job as an assistant to a driver, one who delivered goods for a large department store. But Jimmie couldn't read the addresses on the packages or the names on the mailboxes and so he was soon without work again.

This time he went to an employment agency. In rapid succession the agency procured one job after another for Jimmie. He was intelligent and had a fine personality so that he was readily hired wherever he applied for work. But alas, in a short time, his inability to read caused him to forfeit every single position for which he was employed.

Finally he obtained a job in a factory—punching holes in leather belts. The second day that he was in the factory a typed notice was circulated. It forbade all employees to smoke while at work. The note was handed to Jimmie by the superintendent, and to relieve the strain of the "cover-up," he lighted a cigarette and virtually puffed the smoke in the superintendent's face. The result? Jimmie was fired on the spot for an apparent act of insubordination.

At this point the drive of rising expectancy seized upon Jimmie. "I must get ahead in the world," said Jimmie, "and if I get ahead I'll have to learn to read. I *must* learn to read. I'm *going* to learn to read." And he immediately enrolled in a reading clinic of which the writer was director.

Jimmie came to the clinic—a handsome, intelligent youth, eager to improve himself for life ahead in the atomic age. In conference with the writer it was revealed that not only was Jimmie handicapped in earning a living, he was handicapped socially. "I have a girl friend that I like an awful lot," he said. "And I'm in agony most of the time I am with her for fear she'll discover that I can't read. When we go to a new place on the bus I don't know where to get off because I can't read the street signs. When we walk up and down Broadway trying to choose a movie to attend, I am quite helpless because I can't read the marquees and billboards. And after the show is over, she is sure to bring up for discussion some fine point that was made in a caption—and I'm lost and embarrassed because I, of course, don't know anything that was said in the printed explanations."

Jimmie learned to read very rapidly. On the strength of his newly acquired skill the employment agency procured another job for him. One year later Jimmie came back to express his gratitude. He said that he was still holding the same job and that he had the same girl. "And I'm going to night-school and taking some courses," said he, "so I'll know something like the other boys." Jimmie was silent and thoughtful for a moment and then he continued, "It seems that all of my troubles took care of themselves when I learned to read."

Then there was the woman doing domestic work in a home on Long Island six days and nights a week who traveled ninety miles on her day off to take her reading lesson. There was the zealous, illiterate waiter in a fashionable night club who spent his forenoons in a reading laboratory, "So I can read my menus and so I can talk to my people about happen-

23

ings"; and the garage mechanic who wanted to learn to read, write, and spell "in order to improve myself so I can get a better job. I could get a promotion in the garage, if I knew how to make out bills for the customers."

The examples given are those of illiterate adults who felt the urge of self-improvement. But those who already know how to read also are participating, we might say, in furthering the revolution of personal aspirations in reading. This accounts for the thousands of adults all over the country who are flocking to reading centers to learn to read better. They do this as a result of their rising expectancy in better meeting the demands of modern life.

Another factor which is contributing to the revolution of rising expectancy is the national concern that the highest potential of each individual be developed. The larger influence in back of this concern, of course, is space age rivalry and competition among nations. Ever since the advent of Sputnik we have realized as a nation that the talent, inventiveness, thinking powers, funds of information of each citizen in our country must be tapped and freely drawn upon if, as a collective citizenry, we are able to meet, and we hope, surpass the challenges of our competitors. Reflecting this national concern the schools will take on increased responsibility for making the most of each individual child's capacity and special abilities.

What effect will the revolution of rising aspirations have on reading instruction? Surely if we meet the soaring personal desires for self-improvement, if we meet the need of the nation to develop each individual to his highest potential, than one thing is certain, the youth of America will have to *read* better than it is reading today. Changes in procedures to meet these needs will include: (1) more intensive teaching of the basic reading skills with a better understanding on the part of teachers as to what the basic skills are and how to develop them effectually, (2) wider use of visual and auditory aids, (3) new types of reading textbooks that provide for greater flexibility and make more ingenious provisions for individual differences, (4) widespread extension of reading instruction to higher grade levels, (5) more general provision for well-stocked libraries in elementary as well as in high schools, (6) new forms of classroom organization, (7) special provisions for the gifted, (8) changes in clinical services.

There is evidence that these changes are beginning to take root in some of our school systems. Progress should be and undoubtedly will be much more rapid in the future.

3

As the Child Grows

As the child grows he learns to read. Reading growth is continuous. So are other aspects of child growth continuous. The maturing child grows in many ways—and reading is just one of those ways. The reading way of growth, however, is closely interrelated with several other ways of growth. Teachers of reading need to be keenly aware of interrelationships between reading and the other aspects of child development with which reading is associated and by which it is influenced.

The concept of considering total child growth was proposed by leaders in education many centuries ago. Peter Drucker,[1] however, speaks of a new philosophy, "a philosophy of wholeness, with the whole equal to more than the sum of its parts." This is, of course, the Gestalt psychology stated simply and convincingly by a modern philosopher. This philosophy of wholeness with the whole equal to more

[1] Peter Drucker, "The New Philosophy Comes to Life," *Harper's Magazine* (Aug. 1957), pp. 37–40.

than the sum of its parts is a stimulating and useful concept for those concerned with the teaching of reading.

For centuries reading was considered to be a mental act in itself and apart from other growth factors. We are, however, now beginning to put together many facets of the wholeness of childhood in teaching this skill. When considering *reading* growth, however, it is important that we give special cognizance to those parts of total growth which investigation has revealed as being significantly related to reading development. Some factors of total growth seem to be related to reading, others do not. Certain aspects of growth which appear to be most closely related to reading will be discussed in this chapter. But first the reader may be interested in stages of growth in reading itself.

Developmental Stages in Reading

A child passes through certain stages of growth in learning to read. The first stage has its beginnings when he distinguishes between the appearance of his father and mother, and when he speaks his first word. It proceeds by degrees through early childhood and on into later years until he stands on his own as an independent reader. Stages of growth in reading are presented in regard to specific aspects of the reading process in different chapters that ensue. Perhaps a brief running account of some of the characteristics of consecutive growth stages throughout the elementary grades is appropriate at this point.

Ilg [2] gives one of the most complete sets of information available in regard to the child's growth stages in reading. A few very brief excerpts from a comprehensive address which she gave will be presented below.

When a 9 or 12 month old infant as he plays in his playpen picks out his baby books in place of other toys, one should be alerted to potential early reading and interest in being read to. . . .

The 2 to 2½ year old likes tiny things, tiny pellets, tiny cars, tiny books. You may find him walking around with a tiny edition of Kate Greenaway or Peter Rabbit not so much because he is interested in the book as in its tinyness. . . .

The sustained interest in ability to sit and listen to a story at 2–3 age offers a further clue to later good reading ability. . . .

Memorizing whole stories or especially nursery rhymes in the 3 to 3½ old period gives us a clue that good auditory recall may well be followed by good visual recall. . . .

When a 3½ year old demands to look on the page as he is being read to, he

[2] Frances L. Ilg, "The Child from Three to Eight with Implications for Reading," an address presented at a conference on *Teaching the Young Child to Read* conducted under the direction of Warren C. Cutts, Office of Education, Washington, D.C., Nov. 14–16, 1962. Reprinted by permission. See also Arnold Gesell and Frances L. Ilg, *The Child from Five to Ten* (New York: Harper & Row, Publishers, 1946).

is already beginning to relate pictures to the story. This becomes a part of his listening and enhances his grasp of the story. This same child at the later age of 5 to 5½ can move from pictures to the recognition of single words. He likes to pick out or to be shown words of strong impact such as "wow" or "oh boy." He likes to pick out proper names that he has heard in a story especially because they begin with a certain capital letter. . . .

The child's interest in recognizing sight words moves more rapidly at 5½ to 6 years. He is now beginning to recognize selected words on a page. But he is not interested in following a line on a page. His eyes prefer to move vertically. And he is interested to pick out certain words at random, ones which have meaning for him, ones that he has picked up in the content of the story as it has been read to him. He can read the word *Washington* as easily as *Jane* if the story is about Washington and he can recognize this word because it begins with W. . . .

The zest and eagerness which the truly ready first grader gives to reading is beautiful to behold. But he often has trouble keeping his place. And no wonder when we realize how unstable his visual mechanism is. . . .

Six surmounts his unstable visual mechanism by keeping his place with his fingers. Sometimes as his eyes drop to the next line he may drop too far and thus skip a line. He would profit by the use of a ruler as a marker. . . .

As six reads he often interjects words, especially adjectives he has just read even though they haven't recurred. He loves repetition and if this doesn't occur he provides the repetition himself. This is why repetitive primers are so congenial to him.

. . . Everything about six shows an interest in beginnings. He is constantly making good starts. He wants to be first. But he can't sustain very long and is very poor at finishing.

Seven is what we call a mechanical reader. His voice sounds mechanical as he reads aloud. He reads almost in a monotone with very little inflection as he links one sentence to the next, one paragraph to the next not wishing to stop and work over a word he doesn't know. Seven wants especially to hold on to the meaning of what he is reading and this might be lost if he stopped to work over a word.

The release, relaxation, and flexibility that comes at 8 years of age is a welcome change and so striking that it is as if a child had shifted to a higher gear. This change is soon evident in his reading. He develops a new capacity to attack words, new words which he has never seen. He can work them out phonetically for he now knows the sounds of letters and combinations of letters and is able to put them together. He also sees the word as a total whole in a flash. . . .

Eight reads with expression. He knows how to pause, how to drop his voice at the end of a sentence. He no longer links sentence to sentence and paragraph to paragraph the way he did at seven. He can now stop and work over a word in the middle of a sentence without losing the thread of the story. . . .

One of the outstanding forces that is operating at eight is power of attack. This leads to very real changes at 9 and 10 years. Nine is an age that makes very real demands on the growing child. His reading ability often takes great leaps. He now is more on his own. He is capable of going to the dictionary to look up meanings of new words. He comes to realize that a book is broken up into parts through the index or table of contents. He is beginning to know when he can skim and when he needs to read more thoroughly. He often prefers to read silently rather than out loud although he still needs to be checked orally. Boys who have been slow or poor readers up to now, though they have earlier shown high interest and good comprehension, may now become great readers. Nine is eager for more and more information and is definitely interested in his different subjects at school.

By ten a child should be a proficient reader. He may also be a ravenous reader, sneaking books to bed and reading under the covers by flashlight. This behavior reaches its all time peak at 11 years. Ten enjoys reading to his younger siblings and does this with good expression. He especially enjoys biographies and most of all stories about the childhoods of great men. And he is beginning to read the newspaper and to keep up with daily events.

Following this brief sketch of some of the characteristics of growth stages in reading, we shall proceed to discussions of other factors in child development which are *basic* to stages of maturation in reading.

As the Child Grows Mentally

Intelligence and Reading

Intelligence and reading have been closely associated since the advent of the earliest methods of checking mental capacity. In *The New Natura Brevium,* a law book published in England in 1534, Sir Anthony Fitzherbert suggests the ability to read as one criterion of intelligence:

And he who shall be said to be a sot and idiot from his birth, is such a person who cannot account or number twenty pence, nor can tell who was his father or mother, or how old he is, etc. so as it may appear that he hath no understanding of reason what shall be for his profit, nor what for his loss. But if he hath such understanding, that he know and understand his letters, and do read by teaching or information of another man, then it seemeth that he is not a sot nor a natural "idiot."

In other words, according to this legal statute if a person knew the simple things named in the first part of the paragraph above, and also knew his letters and could read, it was decided that he was not an idiot.

In 1797, a so-called wild boy was found wandering in the woods of Cannes in France. Itard, a physician, became interested in the boy and tried to educate him. Among other things Itard tried to teach the boy to read. While Itard made some progress with the boy, he did not learn as other children did. Eventually deciding that the boy was an idiot, Itard sent him to the Bicetre as a custodian unworthy of training.

We see that inability to learn to read was an important factor in deciding whether or not the famous "wild boy" was an idiot.

Since intelligence tests have been developed many studies have been conducted to ascertain the relationship between intelligence and reading achievement. In general these studies have revealed a close correlation between IQ scores and reading test scores. Such studies are too numerous to be quoted here, but their results can be summarized in one general conclusion: intelligence is a major factor in reading success at any level. In terms of this general conclusion, the teacher would be right "by and large" to expect that those pupils with high IQ's would make the better progress in reading.

This generality needs to be qualified in several ways, however. For one thing, we cannot assume that a high IQ necessarily will ensure reading success. Several studies [3] have shown that many bright children are not reading as well as they should and that altogether too many are seriously failing.

The implication of such studies is that other factors seem at times to overshadow the gift of intelligence in preventing children from making normal reading progress. The teacher of developmental reading who has such pupils should search deeply to discover these other factors and, if possible, remove them or have them removed, leaving the child free to achieve up to his mental capacity in reading. Such a preventive measure is more just than letting the child experience failure for several years, finally ending up in a remedial clinic as a seriously retarded reading case.

Another point to be considered: there are individual differences in reading achievement among pupils of similar intelligence even when IQ has been legitimately established. For example: in a certain class of *mentally retarded boys*, there are, among others, four boys who are very close to the same chronological age and who come from the same types of homes and environments. All four of these boys have IQ's of 60. (An IQ of 60 is supposed to be the minimum intelligence level at which a child can learn to read.) One of these boys is reading at fifth-grade level, one at fourth-grade level, one at second-grade level, and one is unable to read even in pre-primers. This may be a wider spread than is usually found in one group matched in chronological age and intelligence, but this particular example illustrates how futile it is to attempt to state a specific IQ at which an individual will or will not be able to learn to read, or to anticipate reading achievement on the basis of intelligence or mental age alone.

Still another consideration: many people believe that intelligence tests

[3] George Isaiah Thomas, "A Study of Reading Achievement in Terms of Mental Ability," *The Elementary School Journal*, Vol. 27 (September 1946), 28–33. Marian Monroe, *Children Who Cannot Read* (Chicago: University of Chicago Press, 1932). Mary I. Preston, "The Reaction of Parents to Reading Failures," *Child Development*, Vol. 10, No. 3 (September 1939), 173–79. Paul Witty and David Kopel, *Reading and the Educative Process* (Boston: Ginn & Company, 1939).

which require reading are unfair to children who do not read well. The writer gave a group intelligence test which required reading to children who were entering a clinic because they had serious reading difficulties. The same intelligence test was administered to these pupils again after eight months of corrective reading instruction had been given. In most cases, the IQ score was raised from five to fifteen points. We have rather convincing evidence that the child who is having difficulty with reading may be given a spuriously low intelligence quotient on the basis of verbal intelligence tests. A representative study that points to this conclusion was conducted by the Platters and Sherwoods [4] who used both verbal and nonverbal intelligence tests with several classes of children and concluded that ". . . low IQ's obtained by retarded readers may reflect the reading retardation rather than general inability to learn."

These considerations have an important implication for the classroom teacher. If a child isn't progressing well in reading she shouldn't be too quick in branding him "dumb" on the basis of a low IQ score. If this score was ascertained through the use of a *reading* intelligence test, it may be lower than he deserves. Under these conditions it is advisable to have him given a nonverbal or performance intelligence test. If a poor reader is branded all through school with an IQ based on a *reading* intelligence test, he may suffer a serious injustice.

In summary, the relationship between IQ and reading ability should be clarified by interpreting IQ's more broadly, applying them for reading purposes with greater care and open-mindedness, and giving consideration to the importance of other growth and endowed factors.

Mental Characteristics of Primary Children

The characteristics of mental development in primary children should be respected and utilized in teaching reading. The teacher who works with nature rather than against it will find that her reading results are more rewarding.

Intellectually, primary children have learned a great deal through their perceptual experiences before they come to school. In fact, children usually acquire one-half of their mental growth by the time they are six years old. They continue to grow intellectually all through the primary grades, although not as rapidly as during the earlier years of childhood. Their attention span is short. They have an excess of physical and mental energy which if restrained too long results in emotional upsets and be-

[4] Emma E. Platter, Stanton D. Platter, Clarence Sherwood and Sylvia Sherwood, "Relationship between Reading Retardation and the Measurement of Intelligence," *Personnel and Guidance Journal*, XXXVIII (Sept. 1959), 49–51.

havior problems. Mere retentiveness and rote memory are good. Time sense is fairly undeveloped. Children of this age seem to be unnecessarily slow in accomplishing things, and do not respond well to a rigid schedule. They need to grow in ability to live within a regular routine. Ability to reason grows through the years, and even primary children begin to show insightfulness in seeking deeper meanings and in solving problems. They are spontaneous and responsive; most of them want to learn to read and are interested in acquiring new skills in general.

In view of these characteristics the teacher of primary reading will give careful consideration to the following points:

1. She will capitalize on such assets as the child's desire to read, his responsiveness to instruction, his keenness in learning through the perceptual mediums of vision and hearing, and his increasing capacity to memorize and retain word forms.

2. She will prepare cooperatively with him reading materials based on his own experiences, and she will associate prepared reading materials with his personal experiences in meaningful ways.

3. She will guide his unfolding traits of reasoning and insightfulness through discussion of characters, situations, information, and problems encountered in the content of his reading material.

4. She will not hold the primary child for long periods of reading instruction or practice. Instead she will set aside large blocks of time in her program for reading instruction and use this time in flexible ways with groups or individuals as attention spans can tolerate and physical inactivity can endure the length of a period.

Mental Characteristics of Children in Middle Grades

Children in the middle grades continue to develop those mental characteristics prominent in the primary period, but with new accentuations and extensions. They have refined and clarified their perceptual processes. They are eager, alert, and intensely interested in developing new skills. They are keenly observant of details. Instruction and experience in reading in the primary grades has emphasized their perception of word symbols, however, oral or printed information or description does not have the same appeal to them even yet as do objects, pictures, diagrams, and other graphic representations. Concepts of time, space, and number are fairly well developed. Children in the middle grades are much more interested in people, things, and events in the world outside of themselves than are primary children. Reasoning just for the sake of reasoning seldom interests children of this age, although they have considerable capacity for reasoning if they have a motive for so doing or if reasoning contributes to a specific interest. Insight may extend to considerable depths, but it needs to be stimulated, guided, and nurtured. Somewhere during this stage—often called "The Golden Age of Memory"—the greatest relative increase of immediate memory occurs and power of prolonged retention is also on the rise. These children have seemingly inexhaustible energy and greater endurance than primary children. Their eyeballs and eye-structure have matured, so that they now can focus their vision clearly.

These characteristics have several practical implications to the teacher of reading in the middle grades:

1. Children of this age can safely do a great deal of reading, and they can remain physically passive for much longer periods of time while reading or while having practice on some aspect of reading skill. Moreover, their eyes are now ready for close reading.

2. In the light of the above combination of characteristics, the teacher may feel safe in holding these children for longer periods of reading instruction and to expect them to do considerable reading outside of instructional or practice periods.

3. Their better developed concepts of time, space, and number, coupled with their widening interests in other people, places, and times, challenges the teacher to provide opportunities for them to read a great variety of material.

4. This broadened interest in reading subject matter, together with the strong desire to develop new skills, is fortuitous for teaching the location skills in using dictionaries and other reference material, and, indeed, for teaching the whole constellation of specific study skills needed in the different subject fields.

5. The skill interest also causes the middle-grade child to enjoy practice in increasing his reading rate; in the latter part of this period such practice may well be initiated with children who are making normal progress.

6. The skill drive plus improved number concept and interest in visual materials make this an excellent period in which to teach children to *read* maps, graphs, and statistical charts.

7. Because these pupils are keen in noticing details, the teacher need not content herself merely in guiding children to follow the grosser incidents in a story, she now can hold them for detailed reading of facts in informative material. For those who wish, for example, to develop the skills of finding the main idea of a paragraph together with its major and minor details, this is the "psychological moment."

8. The high point that memory reaches at this time is valuable in in-

creasing vocabulary, remembering meanings of many new prefixes and suffixes when coping with unfamiliar words to which they are attached, and most important, recalling factual content that needs to be remembered for some purpose—a very important study skill.

9. Reasoning and insight have excellent promise of growth if the teacher will stimulate purposeful discussion of reading content through sagacious questions and pertinent remarks. All in all, this is a most propitious period for teaching reading.

As the Child Grows Physically

Physical Maturation and Growth

One of the aspects of child growth which is claiming attention in the teaching of reading at the present time is concerned with physical growth and development. The physical maturity of a child, the rate at which he is growing as compared with other children, the rhythms of growth rate at different times within the same child's life, appear to have some significance in the teaching of reading.

Here is an example to indicate how rate of growth might affect reading development: One eight-year-old boy may be growing physically and mentally like an average eight-year-old; another may be growing like a six-year-old; and another may be growing like a ten-year-old. Therefore, these eight-year-old boys may also be ready for different achievement levels in reading and for instruction which is geared to the individual growing rate of each one.

It is possible that the slowest of these three boys may spurt ahead in physical and mental growth, that the fast one may have a slowing down period, and that the average one may continue at the expected rate. If so, all three boys might be growing like twelve-year-old boys when they reach the chronological age of twelve. At this time, all three would then be ready for the same achievement level in reading even though they were two years apart at an earlier age. At this particular time, these three boys might also be able to take on new skills in reading at about the same rate of growth.

Physical immaturity as related to reading has been the subject of much investigation. Anderson and Hughes [5] compared the average growth ages of boys and girls having the same IQ in the first grade who learned to read early and late. Their conclusion was "that boys and girls who begin read-

[5] Irving H. Anderson and Byron O. Hughes, "The Relation Between Learning to Read and Growth as a Whole," *School of Education Bulletin* (The University of Michigan), XXVI (Feb. 1955), 65–68.

ing late tend to be physically less mature than boys and girls who begin reading early."

Eames [6] made a study of 80 pupils in the first six grades in which he correlated birth weight with other factors. He found that correlation "was nearly five times as great among the reading failures with birth weights being less than five pounds as among the reading failures with birth weights over five pounds." Eames [7] also made a study in regard to the effects of premature birth on reading. In a group of 100 reading disability cases he found that 15 per cent of them were children of premature birth—now retarded both in physical and reading growth.

Olson [8] reports a study in which the records of 345 unselected children were examined, and eight children of premature birth were found. Seven of the eight had an initial slow start in reading.

These and other studies strongly indicate that there is a relationship between physical immaturity and reading development, especially during the initial stages of reading.

Olson,[9] as a result of his studies, goes further, contending that reading growth throughout the elementary grades follows approximately the same growth curve as general physical development. His theory, called the *organismic-age* concept, resulted from attempts to measure a child's total development. The measure consists of averaging together a child's mental age, reading age, and age status of development in several aspects of physical growth, such as dental age, height age, weight age, grip age, and metacarpal age (development of wrist bones). Olson contends that progress in reading is more closely related to *organismic-age* than it is to mental ability. Out of this belief has grown the *seeking, self-selection,* and *pacing* theory which is being implemented through the individualized reading program, now used widely in some parts of the country.

The validity of the *organismic-age* theory is undergoing criticism by some psychologists. Blommers and Stroud [10] contend that there are neither theoretical nor empirical bases for believing that organismic age successfully predicts school achievement. They have summarized many studies in which correlations between reading ability and various aspects

[6] Thomas H. Eames, "Correlation Between Birth Weight and Visual Acuity: From the Age of Five Through Twelve Years," *American Journal of Ophthamology,* XXXIX (Mar. 1955), 375–77.

[7] Thomas H. Eames, "Comparisons of Children of Premature and Full Term Birth Who Fail in Reading," *Journal of Educational Research,* Vol. 38 (Mar. 1945), 506–508.

[8] Willard C. Olson, *Child Development* (Boston: D. C. Heath & Company, 1949), 132–33.

[9] Willard C. Olson, "Reading as a Function of the Total Growth of the Child," in William S. Gray, comp. and ed., *Reading and Pupil Development,* "Supplementary Educational Monographs," No. 51 (Chicago: University of Chicago Press, 1940).

[10] Paul Blommers and J. B. Stroud, "Note on the Organismic Age Concept," Journal of Educational Psychology, Vol. 49 (Apr. 1958), 106–107.

of organismic age were computed. They found a high correlation between reading achievement and mental age, but the addition of measures of physical growth increased the correlation only by a negligible amount. In fact they found that the larger the number of physical and anatomical scores used in determining organismic age, the poorer the correlation between it and school achievement. Anderson and Hughes also criticized the organismic theory in that they questioned the technique of averaging together various dissimilar measures into a single scale with equal weights.

From this discussion it is evident that the relationship between reading growth and general organismic maturation is a controversial matter. There is more definite data, however, in regard to relationships between reading and certain *specific aspects* of physical growth. Some of these specific aspects will now be discussed.

Sex Differences

Sex differences appear to have some significance in reading achievement. The fact that girls develop more rapidly than boys is too well-established to belabor further. By the time the girl is in the second grade, she is actually a year older physically than the boy because she is a year nearer her final development. This may mean that the second grade teacher has seven-year-old girls and six-year-old boys in the same reading class in so far as physical development is concerned. If mental development accompanies physical development as it is normally supposed to do, then the teacher of young children might expect that more boys than girls in her class would have some difficulty in learning to read. Most research on this subject indicates that this is the case. A summary of research on remedial reading cases indicates that sixty to eighty per cent of the retarded reader population consists of boys. Very few girls are found in remedial reading clinics. Durrell [11] portrayed the situation well when he stated, "Among children brought to the Boston Educational Clinic for study, the ratio of boys to girls is ten to one."

Differences in maturation may be one cause of differences in reading achievement between the sexes. Other possible reasons may be that there are physiological, cultural, and interest differences in the two sexes which cause girls to be more favorably inclined to the sedentary occupation of reading; also, there is a need for more reading materials that appeal to the interests of boys.

Some educators are urging different norms for boys than for girls on

[11] Donald Durrell, *Improving Reading Instruction* (Yonkers-On-Hudson: World Book, 1956), p. 350.

reading tests. There are also some who are advocating a second year in kindergarten or a different curriculum in first grade for boys. However, such provisions for boys in general would not seem to be practical as there are many individual differences among boys. Some are ready to start reading immediately in the first grade following one year in kindergarten; some even read in kindergarten or before kindergarten; some excel girls in reading all through the elementary grades. The best plan would seem to be that of recognizing and dealing with individual differences in all children regardless of sex.

Visual Development and Defects

Eye maturation as related to reading has been the subject of investigation. Some authorities contend that, at the first grade level, the muscles and nerves of the eyes are still immature, that the eyeball has not yet attained its final weight or shape, that the tissues of the eye are now plastic and easily molded. Moreover, several investigators have found a very high percentage of hyperopia (far-sightedness) in first grade children. For these reasons care should be taken in making visual demands of first grade children. Otherwise, it is quite possible that they may develop eye defects.

Briefly stated the developmental stages of visual skills needed in reading are as follows: at six years of age the visual mechanism is unstable and many children have difficulty in fixating at definite points and in keeping the place in reading. They make many regressive movements and are inaccurate in their return sweeps from the right end of one line to the left of a new line. At seven the child has made marked improvement in visual acuity, he can fixate his eyes at certain points on the page more effectually, and he can move them from line to line quite readily. By the time he is eight he has developed a much more flexible visual mechanism and as a result he can read faster. At nine he is able to fixate at a point with fine accuracy. From this time on his visual apparatus is almost mature in so far as visual skills for reading are concerned.

In addition to giving consideration to maturation of the visual mechanism, it is important to be on the lookout for signs of visual defects, for visual defects can affect reading growth, also. Here is an example: Bill came to a reading laboratory as a nonreader. He was eight years old, had an IQ of 140, was in perfect physical condition, was emotionally stable. Yet, he had not learned to read. During the course of diagnosis it was discovered that Bill had double vision, a fusion defect. When he looked at any object at hand he saw two objects, one superimposed slightly above the other. One can easily imagine the confusion that Bill would experience in trying to recognize a word symbol with another image of the word appearing on top of the first one and just a little above it.

Bill was referred to an eye specialist, and no reading instruction was attempted until his condition had shown marked improvement. When the eye specialist indicated that it would be safe to begin reading work, instruction was started with chart sentences printed in manuscript five inches high. As Bill's visual difficulty continued to improve, and finally reached normalcy, the size of print was gradually reduced to that of the books he should be working with at his grade level. Progress in reading was rapid, and eventually Bill was able to return to his regular school and take his place in reading with his peers.

Was a visual difficulty the major cause of Bill's reading disability? Probably so. If some teacher in Bill's regular school had suspected his visual deficiency and had had it investigated earlier in his school life, he might have been spared several years of discomfort and failure.

Mary was in the fourth grade. She had not learned to read. She wore glasses and complained that it "hurt her eyes to look at print." In exploring Mary's history it was found that she had had three eye operations in the primary grades. Undoubtedly Mary's eye trouble had been a strong contributing factor to her lack of success in reading. Would scolding, pressure, and more drill have improved Mary's reading ability? Definitely not.

These are examples of cases in which an extreme eye defect evidently was the chief cause of reading disability. However, it is important to know that visual deficiencies do not necessarily interfere with reading development.

Some children with eye defects are normal or superior readers, having compensated for this difficulty in other ways.

Between 1930 and 1940 a large number of studies appeared concerning the relationships between visual defects and reading. Several of these had contradictory results. Fewer studies have been made in recent years, but investigators seem to be reaching greater unanimity in their conclusions; namely, that large numbers of children do have visual defects; that in general these visual defects do not necessarily limit reading achievement; [12] that regardless of the relationship between these deficiencies and reading, teachers should show special consideration for children afflicted with visual defects and have them corrected if possible in the interest of general comfort and well-being.

These suggestions are offered for the teacher's guidance.

[12] An example of a representative study resulting in such a conclusion is, William H. Edson, Guy L. Bond, and Walter W. Cook, "Relationships between Visual Characteristics and Specific Silent Reading Abilities," *Journal of Educational Research*, XLVI (Feb. 1953), 451–57.

1. All children should be checked for visual defects upon entrance to the first grade or at the end of the preceding kindergarten year. Those who appear to have some special difficulty should be referred to a reliable eye doctor.

2. Teachers at all levels are urged to observe their pupils carefully for indications of eye trouble. Some symptoms to look for are watery eyes, widely dilated pupils, red or granulated lids, eye discharge, blinking or twitching lids, squints or frowns, books held too near, head held on one side. (Eye specialists usually are glad to provide a teacher with a more comprehensive list of symptoms to use in observation of pupils' visual difficulties.) Children showing indications of visual deficiencies should be examined; if a deficiency is found it should be remedied.

3. The first grade teacher, knowing that a large percentage of her pupils are probably far-sighted, is advised to confine most of their early reading work to charts and chalkboards on which the words are printed in large, bold letters. When pre-primers are introduced children should not be required to read from the book for very long at one time. It is better for them to read two or three lines, look up, and discuss; read two or three more lines, look up and discuss, and so on.

4. If the teacher knows that a child has myopia (near-sightedness) she should seat him near the chalkboard or chart when the content of the reading lesson is written on one of these mediums.

5. If a pupil above first grade level mixes letters and small words, jumbles words, loses his place, and has difficulty in following lines across the page, he should not be unthinkingly scolded for carelessness. He may not have reached that stage of maturation in reading in which such difficulties would naturally disappear; or he may have a deficiency in eye fusion. If the teacher suspects the latter, she is advised to have the child's vision checked.

Auditory Development and Defects

The child's hearing as well as his vision should be of concern to the teacher of reading.

The ear is quite fully developed at birth. At that time both the inner and the middle ear have attained nearly adult proportion. The chief difference between a child's ear and that of an adult is in the shape of the Eustachian tube, which connects the ear with the throat. In children this tube is a short, wide, straight passage. This results in the continuous threat of ear infections developing in the throat.

The consideration, however, which should be of much greater interest to teachers of reading is the large number of children with hearing defects no one has ever suspected, many of which might well affect reading success. Literature on the incidence of hearing deficiencies among school children reveals a surprising number of children with auditory deficiencies.

Ciocco [13] reported, "Approximately 5 pupils in every class of 33 have some hearing defects." In Behrens' study [14] of 203 first grade children she found that "When comparisons in auditory efficiency were made with the standard of average hearing prescribed for use with the Western Electric No. 6-A Audiometer, the group attained an average of 15 to 25 decibels below this standard." Fourth grade teachers will be especially interested in a study made by Laurer, [15] who compared the hearing loss of various age-level groups from grades three to eight and concluded that children in the fourth grade showed the greatest auditory deficiency.

Bunch, [16] Ciocco, and Behrens all found that children "tend to hear low tones to a higher degree than high tones." This is just one more reason for teachers to use low, well-modulated voices.

Many studies have been made to ascertain the relationship of auditory deficiencies and reading achievement. In general, these studies do not suggest a close relationship between auditory ability and ability to read, although some studies do show a slight relationship. Three recent studies [17] indicate that auditory acuity and discrimination do not often cause poor word recognition, but that auditory memory span might be a significant factor.

From the logical standpoint, however, it would seem reasonable to expect that hearing impairment might affect reading in several different ways, particularly in the primary grades. First, if a child lacks auditory acuity he may not have developed a sufficient vocabulary to facilitate reading, or he may have acquired faulty pronunciation, which might be a factor in word recognition. Second, he may mistake one word for another and build up wrong associations, particularly during the early

[13] Antinio Ciocco, "Observations on the Hearing of 1,930 Individuals: A Biometric Study," *Larynoscope,* Vol. 42 (Nov. 1932), 855.

[14] Minnie Sophia Behrens, *An Evaluation of Reading Readiness.* Doctor's Dissertation (Nashville, Tenn.: George Peabody College for Teachers, 1940).

[15] Frank H. Laurer, "Hearing Survey Among a Group of Pupils of Syracuse Schools," *American Journal of Public Health,* Vol. 38 (Nov. 1928), 1359.

[16] C. C. Bunch and T. S. Faidford, "Race and Sex Variations in Auditory Acuity," *Archives of Otolaryngology,* Vol. 13 (Mar. 1931), 423.

[17] Dorothy L. Poling, "Auditory Deficiencies of Poor Readers," *Clinical Studies in Reading,* Vol. 11, Supplemental Educational Monographs, No. 27 (Chicago: University of Chicago Press, 1953), 107–11. Maynard C. Reynolds, "A Study of the Relationships between Auditory Characteristics and Specific Silent Reading Abilities," *Journal of Educational Research,* XLVI (Feb. 1953), 439–49. Lester R. Wheeler and Viola D. Wheeler, "A Study of the Relationship of Auditory Discrimination to Silent Reading Abilities," *Journal of Educational Research,* XLVIII (Oct. 1954), 103–13.

stages of reading in which new word symbols are usually introduced and read orally from charts or chalkboards. Third, if his hearing is so impaired that he does not understand what the teacher is saying in her explanations of new techniques and processes or in questions she asks in giving practice on specific reading skills, his reading growth might be affected accordingly.

In view of the effect a hearing impairment may have on the comfort and total personality of an individual, in addition to the possibilities of its effect on reading achievement and progress in other subjects, it is certainly advisable for every school to have the hearing of its pupils checked in kindergarten or first grade and again at intervals throughout the other grades.

An observant teacher can often detect a hearing defect. Every teacher should be alert to such symptoms as: holding the head in a peculiar position, turning one ear toward the speaker, asking to have questions or directions repeated, unnatural tone of voice, incorrect pronunciation, earache, and frequent colds.

Some cases of hearing impairment can be remedied by otologists and physicians; others cannot. It is important that the teacher exert her efforts to refer all such cases to someone qualified to decide upon the nature of the defect and to provide therapeutic measures. For those children whose hearing cannot be improved she may make several adjustments. She may seat the child in the front of the room near the place in which she most frequently stands or sits. If the deficiency is localized or more acute in one ear, she can give consideration to the side from which he hears better. She can at all times enunciate distinctly and speak in clear, well-modulated tones.

As the Child Grows Perceptually

The original roots of perception are the sensory organs. In reading, the eyes and ears with their respective functions of vision and hearing are the most useful of these. Information concerning the psychological development of vision and hearing can be specifically applied to the teaching of reading.

Visual Perception

Visual perception begins early in the life of an infant. At six months he can perceive differences in brightness; he soon learns to differentiate between his parents and rapidly develops an ability to recognize various objects in the house. Thus his environment becomes differentiated into perceived objects.

By the time the child has entered first grade he has had a great deal of experience in visual perception. Some children have had experience in recognizing letters of the alphabet and printed words. Many, however, have not reached the stage of perceptual development in which they are able to make the complicated adjustments necessary in the perceptual processes accompanying reading.

The question of crucial significance is: how does the child first learn to recognize words? Studies have revealed various cues which may be useful to a child in the visual perception of words. Meili's study [18] indicated that children tended to perceive complex whole shapes rather than their parts when the outlines of the wholes were fairly simple and obvious. On the other hand, if certain parts of the word stood out clearly and the outline of the whole shape was rather complicated, then the parts were perceived rather than the whole. Bowden [19] found that if words are perceived by wholes, the child is aware of the presence or absence of certain characteristic letters, but without clear recognition of their position in a word. Gates and Boeker [20] reported that the word *pig* was sometimes recognized by the dot over the *i*. Wilson and Flemming [21] found that perception was influenced by certain letters, such as double-*o* in *look*. Many investigators have found that children confuse words having the same initial letter or the same final letter. There is also evidence that words of the same general length and shape may be confused with one another.

In summary it may be stated that young children may recognize words through the use of various perceptual cues, such as shape, length, and characteristic letters. None of these, however, are used in any thoughtful or systematic matter. Children need practice in perceiving both word wholes and distinctive parts.

Auditory Perception

Good auditory perception is strongly based on the physical development of hearing and the freedom from hearing defects.

The development of auditory perception evolves naturally through the

[18] R. Meili, "Les Perceptions des Enfants," *Archives de Psychology*, Vol. 23 (1931), 25.
[19] J. H. Bowden, "Learning to Read," *Elementary School Teacher*, Vol. 12 (Dec. 1951), 21.
[20] A. J. Gates and E. Boeker, "A Study of Initial Stages in Reading by Pre-School Children," *Teachers College Record*, No. V (1923).
[21] F. T. Wilson and C. W. Flemming, "Letter Consciousness of Beginners in Reading," *Journal of Genetic Psychology*, Vol. 53 (1938), 273.

early childhood period. In so far as words are concerned, the child produces speech sounds of his own during the first year of life. As a result of listening to adults, he gradually adapts his babblings to words used to represent certain meanings. In this way auditory discriminations first take place and continue to multiply.

At the time the child enters first grade, however, he is concerned only with the sounds of word wholes which he has remembered and with which he associates meaning as people speak. In reading he has a new technique to learn. No one speaks the word for him. He must figure out the pronunciation himself. With practice, he reaches a point in which he automatically associates the symbol with its pronunciation. Many children, however, need help in working out the pronunciation of symbols. The auditory perceptions which must be made in reading are well summarized by Vernon [22] who states that the child must eventually perceive: (1) that each word and its sound pattern are separate entities, with their peculiar, invariable, and universal characteristics; (2) each word's sound pattern can be analyzed into a succession of sounds, with a characteristic and invariable sequence; (3) these unitary sounds can be generalized, in the sense that they occur, in approximately the same form but in different sequences and in different words; (4) the sounds correspond to different letter shapes, visually perceived; but (5) unfortunately, in the English language, the relationships between sounds and visual percepts vary considerably from word to word.

Teaching techniques for use in the development of auditory perception and discrimination as needed in reading will be discussed in Chapter 8.

As the Child Grows Experientially

Paul was reading a story which had its setting in an old Greek school. In the course of his reading, he came to the word *stylus*. "Do you know what a *stylus* is?" asked the teacher. "Sure," said Paul. "A man that cuts women's hair."

Paul knew the meaning of *stylist*. As a younger child, he had gone to the beauty parlor with his mother and the stylist had trimmed her hair. The symbol *stylus* to him sounded the same as *stylist*, so he brought a meaning gathered from his experience to the new symbol which was embedded in an entirely different situation and had an entirely different connotation.

[22] M. D. Vernon, *Backwardness in Reading* (New York: Cambridge University Press, 1957), pp. 31–45.

This story illustrates the point that meanings are not vested in reading symbols themselves; rather, meanings spring from the mind of the reader who brings concepts to the symbols in terms of his own experience. Symbols are but empty shells. It takes experience to fill them with the meat of meaning. This being the case, one might expect that the reading process would be facilitated by building up a rich fund of meanings through first hand experiences, a reserve stock of concepts which could be drawn upon whenever the occasion demands in interpretation of reading symbols.

General Background Experience

Several interesting studies have been made in regard to the relationship of background experience to reading success. Hilliard and Troxell [23] found that children with rich backgrounds exceeded meager background children in test results of reading. McWhorter [24] enriched the experiences of children with meager backgrounds and found that this enrichment resulted in substantial gains in reading. McDowell [25] experimented in providing an "enriched curriculum" for kindergarten children and found that this enrichment was an effective way of preparing for beginning reading. Stallings [26] compared preschool experiences and reading success of urban and rural children and concluded that the varied experiences of preschool children are factors bearing in direct proportion to their reading readiness scores.

These studies and others are favorable in showing the relationship of background experience to reading. It is hoped that many more studies will be conducted in the future for the purpose of probing more deeply into this relationship.

Implications to Teachers

The hypothesis that background experience is a contributing factor to reading success is reinforced by reported studies. What can the teacher do about this important relationship?

1. Kindergarten and first grade teachers can provide their pupils with many rich background experiences designed to develop varied and ac-

[23] George H. Hilliard and Eleanor Troxell, "Informational Background as a Factor in Reading Readiness and Progress," *Elementary School Journal,* Vol. 38 (Dec. 1937), 255.

[24] Opal A. McWhorter, *Building Reading Interests and Skills by Utilizing Children's First-Hand Experiences,* Master's Thesis (Athens: Ohio University, 1935).

[25] Helen R. McDowell, *A Comparative Study of Reading Readiness,* Master's Thesis (Iowa City: University of Iowa, 1939).

[26] Robert R. Stallings, *Readiness Differences of Urban and Rural Children,* Master's Thesis. (Albuquerque: University of New Mexico, 1939).

curate concepts. Examples are: excursions, experiments, social experiences, plant and animal care, discussion of pictures, slides, filmstrips, movies, and television. While the visual aids mentioned provide vicarious rather than first-hand experience, they are useful in developing meanings which may be drawn upon in reading.

2. More specifically pointed toward success are these two suggestions: (a) analyze early books that children will use for vocabulary and concepts; (b) provide enriching experiences which will acquaint pupils with this vocabulary orally, thereby equipping them with necessary concepts before they will need them in reading. Instead of maintaining a level of over-learned concepts, reveal new horizons to them!

3. If building concepts through experience is helpful to reading growth in the first grade, it is reasonable to expect that the same principle would hold throughout the grades. One of the studies reported above indicates that this is the case, and that building experiential background is even more effective in the second, third, and fourth grades than in the first. In these and in more advanced grades rich, first-hand experiences should be continued and extended. If Paul's teacher had taken him and his classmates to a museum to see dioramas of Greek life, he wouldn't have placed a hair stylist in the Greek school.

4. Of course, teachers in the more advanced grades in elementary schools will be forced to use increasing numbers of vicarious experiences in building background for the ever-widening range of settings and topics which children meet in their reading. In addition to the direct use of first-hand experiences, the teacher in these grades may use *abundantly* still pictures, slides, story-films, movies, television, exhibits, diagrams, and conversation; and she should not hesitate to impart vivid, worthwhile information which she herself has gleaned through her own first-hand contacts with interesting people, places, and objects. It would be very stimulating and worthwhile if every teacher of reading would experiment either formally or informally in building concepts for the reading content which her pupils will use, and then check the results in order to ascertain the value of her concept-building activities.

As the Child Grows Emotionally

The Thing

T. F.

It was 12 in the nite. I was in the woods. It was very dark out. I saw something. It was a thing. I ran and ran but it ran too. I went up a tree. It came too. I

crawled to the end of a big branch. It crawled out there too and it struck me. And do you know what happened? I woke up for school.
Do not read.

The Thing was reading

So wrote Tommy during a free composition period. It requires no oracular powers to infer that Tommy was having difficulty in learning to read. Anyone reading Tommy's composition will have little doubt that this boy's fear of reading and of reading failure were causing him much distress. His attempt to run away from it in his composition is indicative of the fundamental urge to escape from danger or an unpleasant situation. His warning, "Do not read," and his technique of writing the answer upside down at the bottom of the page indicate his guilty feeling about letting others know how he felt.

Many other children like Tommy are not learning to read as well as they would like to and concomitantly are undergoing emotional stress. Many try to conceal their feelings about their inadequacy in reading, and others do not even realize that this inadequacy is a cause of their unhappiness. Nevertheless, in either case there are usually revealing manifestations which help the teacher to know that the child is experiencing emotional difficulty.

Bonnie kicks and screams when her mother asks her to do something, has tantrums at least once a week, and bites her nails and hands when asked to read. Tom is sulky, obstinate, temperamental, uncooperative, and resistant to all attempts to teach him to read. Bill is aggressive, bullies the other children, and resents suggestion and criticism. Edward is restless and inattentive and continuously clowns to attract attention. John is shy and timid, doesn't play with other children, and rarely talks. Dick —who won't even try to read—is nervous, easily distracted, frequently upset, and totally lacking in self-confidence.

This picture represents more often than not symptoms of emotional ill-health found in children who are not successfully learning to read. Certainly, not all underdeveloped readers have emotional difficulties, and results of investigations vary in regard to the percentage of those who do. All studies, however, indicate that the incidence of emotional disturbances in children who are failing in reading is alarmingly high.

The Nature of Emotional Maturation

Maturation in emotional behavior differs from maturation in many other fundamental areas of child development. Maturation is essential to physiological growth, mental growth, creative growth and any other growth that follows a natural pattern of unfolding design. Emotion, how-

45

ever, is not a concrete and orderly growth which can be characterized in stages of development. Rather is it an effect or an accompaniment of other growths. Psychologists, however, are adding to an accumulation of data which indicate that emotionality crises are more frequent at certain ages, with periods of exceptional manifestation occurring at intervals of about three years. Busemann [27] states that these ages of crisis are at three, six, nine, twelve or thirteen, and sixteen or seventeen. (The three middle ages just mentioned should be of special concern to elementary teachers.) The range of emotional behavior at any particular age, however, is still undertermined, and there is no scale of normative emotional behavior at certain age levels. Most psychologists believe that the foundation pattern of life-time emotional responses is laid in the earliest years but modified in certain respects as the individual develops physically and mentally. Emotional maturity is reached when an individual has attained the ability to respond appropriately in social-personal situations.

Reading Success and Basic Needs

Children are satisfied by those situations which fulfill their basic needs and are frustrated by those which oppose these natural needs; when frustration occurs, emotional stress develops. Learning to read is just one of hundreds of experiences that may result in satisfaction or frustration of basic drives. Which of the natural needs can learning to read fulfill or frustrate, as the case may be?

Physiologically there are two basic negative drives which success in reading can meet or which failure can aggravate: the urge to escape when frightened or injured, and the urge to get rid of painful or disagreeable substances or conditions. Tommy, frightened by reading as indicated in his composition, was trying to escape from the cause of his fright and from the disagreeable conditions with which reading was associated. In contrast, the successful reader finds reading, and all activities connected with its learning, to be satisfying. He wishes to pursue rather than flee from reading activities.

Socially, important basic needs are: approval, belongingness, similarity to others, friendship and love. The child who is reading well feels that he has the approval of parents, teachers, and classmates; he feels he is like others in his group and that he belongs to them and with them. Because he reads well he feels that those with whom he associates admire him, recognize him favorably and with affection.

From the standpoint of ego and integrative needs, the child must have

27 A. Busemann, "Die Erregunigophasen der Jugend," *Lsch. f. Kinderforsch*, Vol. 33 (1927), 115–37.

self-esteem, engage in purposeful effort, increase in self-direction. Reading well contributes to his self-esteem and enables him to work under his own direction with all school subjects that require reading and to engage in purposeful activity in connection with them.

Emotions and Reading Failure

Now, suppose that we turn over the coin and consider the child who is not achieving satisfactorily in reading.

Fernald [28] made a study of 78 cases of extreme reading disability. She found that in all cases, except four, these children had no history of emotional instability before they entered school. In all cases, other than these four, teachers and parents stated that the child had begun "his school life joyfully, eager to learn to read and write, and that the emotional upset occurred only as the child's desire was thwarted by his inability to learn as other children did."

Then Fernald discussed the social implications of these failures in reading:

So the child comes to hate or fear books, papers, pencils, and everything connected with the schoolroom. The mere mention of reading and writing will often send him into a paroxysm of fear or rage, or arouse a sullen, negative response. Since school is the first group experience for most children, these negative emotions become connected through conditioning, with the group, with the members that make it up, and with group activities. So we find the child either tending to withdraw more and more from the group and assuming a fearful antagonistic attitude toward it, or compensating for his failure by bullying or showing off. Our original case reports are full of descriptions of the "solitary child" and the "bombastic child."

Preston,[29] Newell,[30] and many others have conducted studies leading them to conclude, as did Fernald, that reading failure is responsible for emotional disturbances.

On the other hand several investigators have concluded that emotional disturbances cause reading disability. Blanchard [31] pointed out as a result of her study that emotional instability may cause reading failure. Sylvester [32] and Kunst believe that failure in reading is just one symptom of a

---

28 From *Remedial Techniques in Basic School Subjects,* by Grace M. Fernald. Copyright 1943. McGraw-Hill Book Company, Inc. Used by permission.

29 Mary J. Preston, "Reading Failure and the Child's Security," *American Journal of Orthopsychiatry,* Vol. 10 (April 1940), 239–52.

30 Nancy Newell, "For Non-Readers in Distress," *Elementary School Journal,* Vol. 32 (November 1931), 183–95.

31 Phyllis Blanchard, "Reading Disabilities in Relation to Difficulties of Personality and Emotional Development," *Mental Hygiene,* Vol. 12 (October 1928), 772–88.

32 Emmy Sylvester and Mary S. Kunst, "Psychodynamic Aspects of the Reading Problem," *American Journal of Orthopsychiatry,* Vol. 13 (Jan. 1943), 69–76.

maladjusted personality. Raines and Tait,[33] and also Missildine,[34] reviewed the literature on this subject and concluded that reading disabilities are frequently symptoms of underlying emotional illness.

While the data are equally impressive in substantiating the claim that reading failure is a cause of emotional disturbance and the claim that emotional disturbance is a cause of reading disability, the writer's studies and experience compel her to agree with Russell,[35] Robinson,[36] and Gates,[37] that emotional disturbances and reading disabilities are interactive and either one may be causal. Gates summed up the situation as follows:

All of these symptoms or forms—nervousness, withdrawal, aggression, defeatism, chronic worry—appear among cases in which the maladjustment is the cause, the result or the concomitant of reading difficulty. It is therefore not possible to tell whether they are causes or effects or an accompaniment of trouble with reading.

Regardless of whether emotional behavior is the cause, effect, or accompaniment of reading failure, one fact stands out clearly: there is a strong relationship between the two types of difficulties. Therefore, the teacher of reading should be concerned with not only the development of reading skills but also the development of emotional maturity.

Implications for Teachers

It is encouraging and challenging to know that there are things a teacher can do with children who evince symptoms of emotional difficulties—constructive things that will ease tensions, relieve strains, and possibly prevent serious maladjustment from setting in later on. The severe cases of emotional disturbance should, of course, be treated by a clinical psychologist or psychiatrist. The teacher of reading usually is not trained to give therapy to deeply disturbed children. But she who lives with the children daily can do much to help those who need to grow in emotional maturity. At the present time, it seems that almost every elementary teacher has a few children of this type in her classroom.

1. One of the first and most important steps is to discover, if possible,

33 Shirley Raines and Arthur T. Tait, "Emotional Factors in Reading Retardation," *California Journal of Educational Research*, Vol. 11 (Mar. 1951), 51–56.
34 W. H. Missildine, "The Emotional Background of Thirty Children with Reading Disabilities," *The Nervous Child*, V (July 1946), 263–72.
35 David H. Russell, "Reading Disabilities and Mental Health: A Review of Research," *Understanding the Child*, XVI (Jan. 1947), 24–32.
36 Helen M. Robinson, "Personality and Reading," *Modern Educational Problems*, ed. Arthur E. Traxler (New York: Educational Records Bureau, 1953), pp. 87–99.
37 A. J. Gates, "The Role of Personality Maladjustment in Reading Disability," *Journal of Genetic Psychology*, Vol. 59 (1941), 77–83.

the *cause* of the child's delay in learning to read. If the teacher can locate the key log or logs that are jamming the whole pile, and pull them out, perhaps the way will be opened for her reading instruction to take effect. Once instruction begins to take effect the child's reading experiences will become satisfying and pleasurable.

Don't be satisfied with such blanket platitudes as "He has a mental block" or "He isn't ready yet." Perhaps the child does have a mental block or perhaps he isn't ready yet, but these hackneyed excuses are of very little practical value. Probe deeper and find out *why*? Is it because he is immature physically, because he is experiencing a slow cycle of growth, because he has vision or hearing defects, because he is in poor health, because he has an intelligence below that of his successful classmates, because of a foreign language handicap, because of emotional stress stemming from the home? Consult with parents for leads. Enlist the cooperation of your school nurse, physician, and psychologist, and ask that they recommend sending the child to other specialists for treatment if they deem it advisable. If a nurse, physician, and psychologist are not available to your school, ask the parents to take the child to a professional person specializing in the area in which you suspect a source of difficulty. If this specialist thinks treatment is necessary ask the parents to have it given, if possible. If they cannot afford the treatment of a specialist, it may be possible to obtain help from some welfare or charitable agency in the neighborhood. To sum up: find the cause of the child's lack of development in reading if you can and remedy it. This is crucial.

2. In your own personal and teaching contacts with the underdeveloped reader let him know *always* that you are his friend. He needs your respect for him as a human being. Refrain from being impatient or irritable when he stumbles over words. Your personal disapproval will only make matters worse. Such a child may need criticism at times, but if so balance it with sympathy and understanding. Let him know that you like him just the same, even if he doesn't know how to read well.

3. Provide a child who is having difficulty with material that is easy enough to ensure him some measure of success. Competitive pressures to keep up with the good readers in the class may in itself produce emotional maladjustment.

4. Make every reading experience which you and he have together a pleasant and satisfying one, whether you are working with him alone or with a small group of children having similar difficulties. Build a bit of interesting background for the selection he is about to read; leave some purpose open for his pursuit as he reads the story. Chat and smile and laugh as small incidents are unfolded and hope that he will join you.

5. Praise him for little successes—when he recalls a previously trouble-some word, when he works out the pronunciation of a word for himself, when he answers a question on content especially well. Express your approval to him whenever you can.

6. Let him select some books to read, even if he does nothing more than look at the pictures in them. If he chooses the books himself, they will be in keeping with his interests, and this will add to his pleasure and satisfaction.

7. Give him a chance to excel in some activities other than reading. Perhaps he can draw well, maybe he would be ingenious in constructing a play radio for make-believe broadcasts, or maybe he is especially good at dramatization. If there is any area at all in which he is particularly apt, encourage him to do something in this area and recognize his work before the class as a contribution and a task well done. Such recognition will increase his self-esteem and sense of belonging to the group.

8. Keep in close touch with his parents. Advise them to remove pressure, stigma, and blame. Inform them of any small indications of reading growth that you note, and suggest that they express their approval to him. Warn them never to compare this child with other children who are reading well nor to air his handicap before guests or relatives. Very close cooperation between teacher and parents is necessary in maintaining or restoring a child's emotional morale during a period in which he is struggling for reading success.

Summary

In summarizing this chapter the profound conclusion is bound to be that reading is but one aspect of child development, accompanied and influenced by other growths. Reading development takes place as the child grows mentally, physically, perceptually, experientially, and emotionally. Truly reading growth should be considered as just one part of the wholeness of childhood.

In addition to possessing the knowledge that reading is closely inter-related with other aspects of growth, the successful teacher of reading will be stirred to do all that she can in promoting growth in all aspects of child development, for in furthering child growth as a whole she will be contributing mightily to growth in ability to read.

Additional Readings

Books and Pamphlets

Almy, Millie Corrine, *Children's Experiences Prior to First Grade and Success in Beginning Reading.* Doctor's Dissertation. New York: Teachers College, Columbia University, 1949.

Anderson, Irving H., and Walter F. Dearborn, *The Psychology of Teaching Reading.* New York: The Ronald Press Co., 1952.

Betts, Emmett A., *Foundations of Reading Instruction,* 2nd ed., Part 4. New York: American Book Company, 1959.

DeBoer, John J., and Martha Dallmann, *The Teaching of Reading,* Chap. 4. New York: Holt, Rinehart and Winston, Inc., 1960.

Dennis, Wayne, ed., *Readings in Child Psychology,* 2nd ed. Englewood Cliffs, N. J.: Prentice-Hall, Inc., 1963.

D'Evelyn, Katherine, *Meeting Children's Emotional Needs.* Englewood Cliffs, N. J.: Prentice-Hall, Inc., 1957.

English, Horace B., *Dynamics of Child Development.* New York: Holt, Rinehart and Winston, Inc., 1961.

Ephron, Beulah Kanter, *Emotional Difficulties in Reading,* Chap. 1. New York: The Julian Press, 1953.

Fuller, Elizabeth Mechem, *About the Kindergarten.* Washington, D. C.: National Education Association, 1961.

Gesell, Arnold, and Frances F. Ilg, *The Child from Five to Ten.* New York: Harper & Row, Publishers, 1946.

Goodenough, Florence L., *Developmental Psychology,* 2nd ed. New York: Appleton-Century-Crofts, Inc., 1945.

Gray, William S., *Reading and Pupil Development,* Supplementary Educational Monographs, No. 51. Chicago: University of Chicago Press, 1940.

Harris, Albert J., *Effective Teaching of Reading,* Chap. 2. New York: David McKay Co., Inc., 1962.

Harrison, Virginia, *An Evaluation of Chronological Age, Mental Age, Kindergarten Training and Socio-Economic Status as Factors Underlying Reading Readiness.* Master's Thesis. Tulsa, Okla.: University of Tulsa, 1938.

Hildreth, Gertrude, *Teaching Reading,* Chap. 5. New York: Holt, Rinehart & Winston, Inc., 1958.

Hunt, Joseph McV., *Intelligence and Experience.* New York: The Ronald Press Co., 1961.

Jersild, Arthur T., *Child Psychology,* 4th ed. Englewood Cliffs, N. J.: Prentice-Hall, Inc., 1954.

Lacey, Joy, *Social Studies Concepts of Children in the First Three Grades,* Doctoral Dissertation. New York: Teachers College, Columbia University, 1932.

Lincoln, E. A., *Sex Difference in the Growth of American School Children.* New York: Warwick and York, Inc., 1927.

Martin, William E., and Celia B. Stendler, *Child Behavior* and *Development,* rev. ed., Chap. 15. New York: Harcourt, Brace and World, Inc., 1959.

Mussen, Paul Henry, and John Janeway Conger, *Child Development and Personality*. New York: Harper & Row, Publishers, 1956.

Ohio State University, Faculty of University School, *How Children Develop*. Columbus: Ohio State University, 1946.

Prescott, Daniel A., *Emotion and the Educative Process*. Washington, D. C.: American Council on Education, 1938.

Rosenblith, Judy F., and Wesley Allinsmith, eds., *Causes of Behavior*. Boston: Allyn and Bacon, Inc., 1962.

Rossignol, Lois Josephine, *The Relationship among Hearing Acuity, Speech Proficiency and Reading Performance in Grades 1A, 1B, and 2A*. Doctor's Dissertation. New York: Teachers College, Columbia University, 1948.

Russell, David H., "Interrelationships of the Language Arts and Personality," *Child Development and the Language Arts* (A Research Bulletin of The National Conference on Research in English). Chicago: National Council of Teacher's English, 1953.

————, *Children Learn to Read*, Chap. 3. Boston: Ginn & Company, 1961.

Schonell, Fred J., *The Psychology and Teaching of Reading*. New York: Philosophical Library, 1961.

Smith, H. P., and Dechant, *Psychology in Teaching Reading*. Englewood Cliffs, N. J.: Prentice-Hall, Inc., 1961.

St. John, Charles Webster, *Educational Achievement in Relation to Intelligence*. Cambridge: Harvard University Press, 1930.

Periodicals

Bernetta, Sister M., O.P., "Relation of Vision and Reading," *Education*, Vol. 81 (Sept. 1960), 45–47.

Betts, Emmett Albert, "Visual Perception in Reading," *Education*, Vol. 73 (May 1953), 575–82.

Bevan, William, "Perceptual Learning: An Overview," *Journal of General Psychology*, Vol. 64 (Jan. 1961), 69–99.

Chandler, Caroline A., "The Importance of the Early Years," *Childhood Education*, Vol. 39 (Sept. 1962), 2–4.

Clark, Willis W., "Boys and Girls—Are There Significant Ability and Achievement Differences?" *Phi Delta Kappan*, XLI (Nov. 1958), 73–76.

Dukelow, D. A., "Building Tomorrow's Health Today," *School and Community*, Vol. 48 (Apr. 1962), 17.

Dvorine, Israel, "What You Should Know about Sight," Parts I, II, and III, *Education*, Vol. 79 (Oct., Nov., Dec., 1958).

Eames, Thomas H., "Physical Factors in Reading," *The Reading Teacher*, Vol. 15 (May 1962), 427–32.

Ebel, Robert L., "The Role of Intelligence Testing," *Education*, Vol. 81 (Oct. 1960), 76–79.

Fagerlie, Anna M., "Pupils, Problems, and Books," *Elementary English*, Vol. 38 (Oct. 1961), 406–407.

Forrest, Elliott B., "Vision and the Visual Process," *Education*, Vol. 82 (Jan. 1962), 299–301.

Goodlad, John I., "Pressures to Learn Can Be Blocks to Learning," *Childhood Education,* Vol. 36 (Dec. 1959), 162–65.

Green, Clinton Wallace, "The Relationship Between Intelligence as Determined by Intelligence Tests and the Ability to Learn as Determined by Performance on Learning Tests," *Journal of Educational Research,* Vol. 47 (Nov. 1953), 191–200.

Hollister, William G., "When Feeling Storms Becloud the Learning Process, *NEA Journal,* Vol. 51 (Nov. 1962), 18–20.

Jackson, Joseph, "A Survey of Psychological, Social and Environmental Differences Between Advanced and Retarded Readers," *The Journal of General Psychology,* Vol. 65 (Sept. 1944), 113–31.

Natchez, Gladys, "Oral Reading Used as an Indicator of Reactions to Frustration," *Journal of Educational Research,* Vol. 54 (Apr. 1961), 308–11.

Osburn, Worth J., "Emotional Blocks in Reading," *The Elementary School Journal,* Vol. 52 (Sept. 1951), 23–30.

Reed, Calvin H., "Developing Responsible Behavior," *Education,* Vol. 81 (Apr. 1961), 451–54.

Samuels, Fra L., "Sex Differences in Reading Achievement," *Journal of Educational Research,* Vol. 36 (Apr. 1943), 594–603.

Schubert, Delwyn D., "Reading and Personality Problems," *Elementary English,* Vol. 38 (Dec. 1960), 537–38.

Southall, Macie K., "How Do Children Learn?" *Childhood Education,* Vol. 36 (Dec. 1959), 151–52.

Smith, Charles A., and Myrtle R. Jensen, "Educational, Psychological and Physiological Factors in Reading Readiness," *Elementary School Journal,* Vol. 36 (May 1936).

Sterling, Blanche E., and Elizabeth Bell, "Hearing of School Children as Measured by the Audiometer and as Related to School Work," *United States Public Health Service Public Health Reports,* Vol. 45, No. 20 (May 1930), 1117–30.

Strang, Ruth, "Relationships Between Certain Aspects of Intelligence and Certain Aspects of Reading," *Educational and Psychological Measurements,* Vol. 3 (Winter 1943), 355–59.

———, "Reading and Personality Formation," *Personality,* Vol. 1 (Apr. 1951), 131–40.

Stromberg, Elroy, "The Relationship of Measures of Visual Acuity and Ametropia to Reading Speed," *Journal of Psychology,* Vol. 22 (Feb. 1938), 70–78.

Warwick, Harold L., "Hearing Tests in Public Schools of Fort Worth," *The Volta Review,* Vol. 30 (Nov. 1928), 641.

Watson, W. C., "Fostering Personal Growth in Children; The School's Role in Developing Emotional Maturity," *Chicago School Journal,* Vol. 43 (Dec. 1961), 13–21.

Wilson, Frank P., A. Burke, and C. W. Fleming, "Sex Differences in Beginning Reading in a Progressive School," *Journal of Educational Research,* Vol. 32 (Apr. 1939), 570–82.

4

As Language Develops

In this modern age we stand on the sidewalk and gaze upward with interest as a sky pilot unfolds a message in the heavens by puffing white smoke characters against a blue sky. As we gaze we marvel at this product of twentieth century genius, and perhaps it does not occur to us that this seeming innovation had its prototype in the very first composition, handwriting, and reading done by man. To be sure, primitive man had no airplane and no alphabet, but his messages were drawn in the air as they were composed and his fellowmen read them element by element as they were revealed. His hand was his writing instrument, gestures were his characters, and the air was the medium upon which they were inscribed.

The use of gestures as an early means of communication undoubtedly was supplemented or followed by the use of picture symbols. These were drawn upon sand, bark, stone, or whatever substance the exigency of the occasion demanded. Longfellow described this type in Hiawatha:

For the earth he drew a straight line,
For the sky a bow above it;
White the space between for daytime,
Filled with little stars for night time;
On the left a point for sunrise,
On the right a point for sunset,
On the top a point for noontide.
And for rain and cloudy weather
Waving lines descending from it.

Primitive pictographers were very skillful in expressing thought through pictures, and primitive readers interpreted them with keen insight. Nevertheless, the time came when picture writing was unable to cope adequately with the complexity of the languages of progressive peoples. It became necessary to represent the *sounds* of these languages; as Clodd says, "to select from the big and confused mass of ideagrams, phonograms, and all their kin, a certain number of signs to denote, unvaryingly, certain sounds." [1] Thus the alphabet came into existence, and with it the arts of writing, spelling, and reading as we know them today.

In the early development of language the acquired facets of language expression were inextricably interwoven into the over-all fabric of communication. Early school development of the language arts followed this same pattern in so far as the teaching of reading was concerned. Spelling, handwriting, reading, and sometimes composition were all tied together in the instruction that was primarily designed to teach the child to read. While we do not approve the early methods of starting beginners with work that was meaningless and unchildlike, it is interesting to note that teachers in those times did *not* pull the language constellation apart and teach each strand separately.

Wax tablets were used in the earliest teaching of reading. The tablet consisted of a wooden frame with a raised rim around it. Wax was poured on the frame to a level with the rim. Each child was provided with one of these wax tablets and a stylus. The stylus always had one pointed end for use in writing and one flat end for use in smoothing over the wax when a child wished to place new symbols on it. The child wrote letters of the alphabet, words, and verses on the tablets, usually as the teacher dictated them, and then read what he had written. In this way, listening, spelling, handwriting, and reading were all used in conjunction with one another.

As early textbooks evolved, spelling and writing were always taught as a part of reading instruction. In fact, for many years, the beginning

[1] Edward Clodd, *The Story of the Alphabet* (New York: Appleton-Century-Crofts, Inc., 1900), p. 2.

reading books were called "spellers." In some of the later readers, lined spaces were placed at the bottom of the pages. Each page contained a sentence that children were to use as a model in writing additional sentences of their own, changed by substituting various words that they had learned to read and write.

Listening was not recognized as a separate skill during these years, but children had much practice in listening as all reading was done orally and teachers often dictated content for written work.

Most certainly we would not approve the formal, stilted methods of early times which made little or no use of our present knowledge of child development and modern psychology. The interesting point to note, however, is that in early schools the language arts were taught together, each one being looked upon as a necessity in teaching the others. We hadn't gotten far enough away from the beginning developments of the language constellation to think of breaking it down into separate strands for teaching purposes.

Eventually the school curricula became highly specialized, and separate periods were instituted for spelling, handwriting, reading, and oral and written composition. Each of these skills was supposed to be taught as a separate and isolated entity. Methods are changing at the present time, however, and once again teachers are striving to teach the language arts in relationship to one another and in more natural situations. The remainder of this chapter will deal with the modern concept of teaching reading as a related part of the entire communication block.

Language and Child Development

The language development of children should be a matter of genuine concern to teachers of reading. For this reason some of the bold outlines of development of each of the language arts will be briefly sketched below.

Listening

The child learns to listen before he learns to speak. In fact it is through listening that speech is learned. A child's parents will probably try to teach him to talk, and perhaps to read, write, and spell before he comes to school (not that we would encourage this in general), but who has ever heard of parents trying to develop his listening ability? Yet growth in capacity to listen is just as important to their child's future success and welfare as the other language arts with which they are more concerned.

Stages in listening development have been stated by Strickland as follows:

1. Little conscious listening except as the child is directly and personally concerned with what is being presented
2. Easily distracted by people and things in the environment
3. Half listening while holding fast to own ideas and waiting to insert them at the first opportunity
4. Listening passively with apparent absorption but little or no reaction
5. Listening, forming associations, and responding with items from his own experience rather than reacting to what is presented
6. Listening and expressing some reaction through questions or comments
7. Listening with evidence of genuine mental and emotional participation
8. Listening with real meeting of minds.[2]

Children will be found in the elementary grades who represent each of these stages. Well-informed and conscientious teachers try to ascertain their pupils' respective stages of development in listening and provide planned experiences designed to promote growth in this skill.

Some authorities attribute the cause of reading disability in many cases to poor listening ability. Any teacher of retarded readers will agree that on the average such children are poor listeners.

Speaking

In the developmental sequence of the young child speaking follows listening. The first word usually appears sometime between the tenth and seventeenth month. From this beginning the vocabulary increases with almost incredible swiftness. New words pop up like magic, and by the time the child enters first grade he is using thousands of them with ease and understanding.

Just how many words children have in their spoken vocabularies at six years of age is unknown. Some investigators say 2,400, others say as many as 17,000. There are so many individual differences in vocabulary development that any estimate of a specific number of words at six years is not a very important consideration. The significant implication to teachers of reading is that children know how to pronounce and use a very large number of words upon entrance into first grade. This is the most valuable "stock-in-trade" which the first grade teacher has to work with in teaching beginning reading. Her job is simply that of helping children make the transition from the spoken word to the printed word by learning new printed symbols that represent known spoken symbols.

The first words spoken by a child are usually nouns or interjections.

[2] Ruth Strickland, *The Language Arts in the Elementary School*, p. 119. Copyright 1957 by D. C. Heath & Company. Reprinted by permission.

These are also the words which children find easiest to learn when they begin to read. Gradually the young child learns verbs, then adjectives and adverbs, and finally prepositions, conjunctions, and pronouns. It is no coincidence that these latter parts of speech are the most difficult ones for children to learn to read.

Young children also pick up various speech patterns by imitating the speech of adults. By the time they are six years old, practically all children use all the different patterns. The teacher of reading should consider this knowledge when making charts and other materials for her pupils to read. They are accustomed to hearing and using natural language patterns, and stilted or distorted sentences will make reading difficult for them, as will complex sentences of types which they do not use orally. If the teacher uses simple but natural speech patterns, the children will probably learn to read them with much greater ease.

The period of greatest growth in vocabulary and sentence structure takes place between two and eight years. However, teachers may expect swift progress in oral vocabulary and sentence structure all through the elementary grade years, and concurrently, progress in reading more and more "new words" and increasingly complex sentences. Children are naturally susceptible to such growth, but it takes the guidance of a wise teacher to ensure that both these types of growth may continue unabated, one feeding into the other.

Written Composition, Handwriting, and Spelling

These skills are all tied together in early child development. Almost all children pass through a scribble stage in which their crude markings may represent almost anything or nothing at all. Some bright children really pretend that they are writing a letter to someone and often can tell you what they think they have written.

Many first grade children can print their names when they come to school. If motor development permits, the first grade teacher may help the children write short greetings, salutations, or "Thank you" notes in manuscript. The first writing and spelling that one group of first grade children did resulted from receiving a beautiful bouquet of flowers from the principal. With the teacher's help, each child prepared in manuscript a "Thank you" note, and these notes were sent to the principal. As a consequence, the children recognized "thank" and "you" whenever they encountered these words in print.

Children's first experience in written composition occurs early in first grade when they compose and dictate compositions for the teacher to write on the blackboard. As she writes they note spelling, capital letters, and punctuation marks. In this way they participate in written composition ahead of the time in which they can actually write compositions themselves. Reading these compositions after they are written provides them with the valuable experience of extracting meanings from word symbols which they, themselves, have put into these symbols. This is excellent preparation for reading as well as for written composition.

Beginning with the second grade, written composition, together with its supportive skills of handwriting and spelling, usually develops rapidly. A study made by Hoppes [3] indicates the following developmental trends during the period in which children are passing through grades three to six: (1) growth in the number of sentences used in a composition; (2) growth in the length and complexity of sentences; (3) decline in the use of "run-on" sentences, although this type of error was uncommon; (4) decrease in unpleasant repetition of words and phrases; (5) growth in the use of inverted order of subject and predicate, indicative of the ability to emphasize an idea by increasing the prominence of its position; (6) increase in the proportion of abstract nouns accompanied by decrease in proportion of specific, concrete, individual nouns; and (7) decline in the number of sentences whose subject is "I," possibly marking a decline in egocentrism.

This growth in the various language skills takes place as the child grows. When he comes to his first teacher of reading he has a vast fund of "capital stock" for her to tap in initiating him into the reading processes. He has already made tremendous growth in speaking and listening, and often he has made a start at least in written composition. Having built up this rich background of language art skills, transition to the process of "listening" to what others have said or written through the medium of reading, should be an easy and pleasurable one to make. From the time that this transition is made, then, reading and all the other language art skills should grow together as school life proceeds.

Common Features of Language Art Skills

Modern educators use the term *language arts* to embrace all the language skills taught in schools. This term did not come into pedagogic nomenclature until late in our history—sometime during the 1930's—but now it is used almost as commonly as *reading* or *writing*. This term has been widely accepted and firmly incorporated into the educational vocabulary in a short time. The reason is because the term Language

[3] William C. Hoppes, "Some Aspects of Growth in Written Expression," *Elementary English Review*, X (Mar. 1933), 67–70, 121–23. Reprinted with the permission of the National Council of Teachers of English.

Arts expresses a useful concept: it connotes the idea of commonness that exists among the separate strands of language expression; it indicates that all these strands belong to the same family.

Common Purpose

Communication is the interchange of thoughts. The only reason why language developed was because human beings desired to exchange thoughts. All the different forms of language expression that have developed emanate from this same basic purpose. The generation of any one of the language arts has a two-way action: it impels a person to produce language designed for others to receive, or to receive language others have designed for him. It can automatically switch us backward and forward from one of these actions to the other with high speed, but it only works when the spring of purpose is released. That spring is the same regardless of whether we are producing thoughts through speaking or writing, or whether we are receiving thoughts through listening or reading.

Common Symbols

In language communication, interchange of thought is accomplished through the use of word symbols. Within a given national language, such as English, all word symbols, whether used in speaking, listening, writing, or reading, sprang from common origins, have undergone common modifications, and have suffered obsolescence or taken on new meanings. These symbols in our living language constitute the stuff with which we forge out any language expression. Regardless of whether we speak, listen, write, or read, we draw our word coins from the same bank.

Common Structure

The same structural patterns of sentences are used in all forms of language expression. Different words have different functions and are arranged in sentences in certain orders to express meanings. The function of a word, and consequently its meaning, may be changed by its position in a sentence. For example, note the difference in the meaning of *rakes* and *leaves* in the two sentences below:

> Tom *rakes* the *leaves* on the lawn.
> Tom *leaves* the *rakes* on the lawn.

Basic sentence patterns are of great importance; in fact they are said to be "the backbone and central nervous system" of language. Linguists state that a knowledge of word function and word order enables a pupil to analyze a sentence which he doesn't understand when someone else is speaking or when he is reading. It helps him to make his sentences understandable to others when he is writing. Sentence structure operates from a common base in all forms of language communication, and it is interoperative among them.

Common Thinking Processes and Skills

Thinking must precede or accompany all forms of language expression or reception. The mode of expression or reception may differ, but fundamentally the thought processes are the same. Thinking pre-digests, accompanies, or post-digests the raw material of language, and converts it into meanings and affectations.

The thinking processes and skill elements that reading has in common with the other language arts need to be recognized. These common elements provide many ways in which learning in all the language art mediums can contribute to and re-enforce learning in reading, and in which reading may contribute to and re-enforce learning in these related areas.

First, consider the process of obtaining meaning from language. Understanding the meaning of words is the basic factor in the efficient functioning of all forms of language expression. But something more than acquaintance with a single word in itself is needed to grasp meanings. The structural arrangement of words in a sentence, the organization of a related group of sentences, the context in which words are embedded are all significant contributors to understanding. Likewise, these factors are all significant considerations in teaching reading. They are equally important when a child is listening to the spoken words of others or when engaging in self-expression of his own, either orally or in writing.

The interpretative skills used in dealing with thought units in spoken communication are the same as those used in interpreting printed communication. In making an oral presentation, the speaker conveys a series of thoughts, each of which he expands with related details. In other words, he talks in paragraphs and uses the same structure as that found in printed or written paragraphs. To understand his message fully we need to grasp the main point in each of his thought units, and to sense the details in their relationship to this main thought. This is how children are taught to obtain meaning from paragraphs in reading. This skill, which is so important in speaking, listening, and reading, is equally important when the child is producing paragraphs of his own in written composition. It is also aided by producing other written forms, such as outlines, summaries, precis, and so on.

There are other thinking processes needed in listening to spoken communications at the present time that are just as direly needed in reading. In reading as well as in listening to the thoughts of others, the child needs to learn to think clearly and deeply in sensing meanings "between the lines," evaluating ideas expressed, discriminating between fact and opinion, noting intent to influence thinking, making generalizations, drawing conclusions. The content of language is the same regardless of whether it is spoken or printed. Therefore the thinking processes needed in dealing with this content is identical regardless of whether children are listening or reading.

A knowledge of the elements that make up a word is a prerequisite for spelling, which in turn is a necessary skill in written expression. Such knowledge also contributes to enunciation and pronunciation in oral language, and in reading, to the ability of a pupil to work out the pronunciation of an unrecognized word. Therefore, children should learn the functions of vowels, consonants, consonant combinations, and simple principles concerning them; changes in tense and number made by inflectional endings; and changes in meanings made by adding prefixes and suffixes. These skills are also necessary in spelling and writing and, to a lesser but still significant degree, in speaking and listening.

All these functions and elements common to the different language art mediums reveal the possibilities of skill re-enforcement. If teachers take advantage of the many opportunities to strengthen each of the skills through natural association with and experience in using the others, pupils should benefit accordingly.

Evidence of Language Art
Inter-Relationships

A very large number of investigations in regard to language inter-relationships has been conducted. The results of only a few samples of studies will be presented, but these brief summaries will lend credence to the basic concept advanced so far in this chapter: the desirability of taking advantage of the other language arts as supportive auxiliaries in the teaching of reading.

General English Skills and Reading

Some studies have dealt with a composite of language abilities as they relate to reading. For example, Hughes gave a battery of tests to 332 fifth grade pupils to ascertain inter-relationships among abilities in the various language arts.[4] His findings revealed high correlations among all

[4] Vergil H. Hughes, "A Study of the Relationships Among Selected Language Abilities," *Journal of Educational Research*, XLVII (Oct. 1953), 97–106.

these abilities: word meaning and language usage, reading and sentence sense, reading and paragraph organization, reading and punctuation. He concluded that a high score in one language ability or skill is accompanied by comparatively high achievement in other language areas. He also hypothesized that there might be a reservoir "of general language ability" that exerts a common influence on all aspects of the language arts.

Townsend conducted a study in which she compared reading and English scores on achievement tests given to elementary school pupils.[5] She found that there was a fairly close correlation between reading and English scores.

Gibbons gave diagnostic tests in reading to third grade pupils and found the relationships between these results and status in language skills.[6] She concluded that there was a close relationship between reading and the other language skills. She also made this observation: ability to understand the structure of sentences was closely associated with reading level, so that a lack of this knowledge proves to be a handicap in reading.

Listening and Reading

The relationship between listening and reading has been a very popular subject of investigation in recent years. Gates found that the ability to listen to a story and to supply a reasonable ending was the best single predictor of success in learning to read.[7]

Young [8] and Larsen and Feder [9] found that a high relationship existed between hearing comprehension and reading comprehension. Young drew the further conclusion that children who do poorly in listening do poorly in reading.

Nichols conducted a study to ascertain the factors in listening comprehension.[10] As a result, he concluded that in addition to intelligence and reading comprehension the factors influencing listening most significantly include recognition of correct English usage, size of the listen-

[5] Agatha Townsend, "Reading and Achievement Test Scores in the Elementary Grades," *Educational Records Bulletin No. 45* (New York: Educational Records Bureau, June 1946).

[6] Helen D. Gibbons, "Reading and Sentence Elements," *Elementary English Review*, XVIII (Feb. 1941), 42–46.

[7] Arthur I. Gates, *Manual of Directions for Gates Reading Readiness Tests* (New York: Bureau of Publications, Columbia University, 1939).

[8] William E. Young, "The Relation of Reading Comprehension and Retention to Hearing Comprehension and Retention," *Journal of Experimental Education*, V (Sept. 1936), 30–39.

[9] Robert P. Larsen and D. D. Feder, "Common and Differential Factors in Reading and Hearing Comprehension," *Journal of Educational Psychology*, XXXI (Apr. 1940), 241–42.

[10] Ralph G. Nichols, "Factors in Listening Comprehension," *Speech Monographs*, XV, 2 (1948), 154–63.

er's vocabulary, ability to make inferences, ability to sense the organization of spoken material, and interest in and emotional attitude toward the topic. According to Nichols' report, poor listeners listen for specific facts, good listeners for main ideas.

The effect of training in listening upon reading was studied by Lewis, using as experimental personnel 135 paired groups of fourth, fifth, and sixth grade pupils.[11] These pupils were trained to listen for three selected purposes and then to read for these purposes. The training in listening had a small but significant effect on their reading for these purposes.

Spelling and Reading

There have been more studies conducted to ascertain the relationship between spelling and reading achievement than between any of the other language arts and reading. Only a small sampling of these studies will be presented, but it is representative of the high correlation between these two language art subjects.

Gilbert found that pupils tend to improve their spelling through reading even when their attention is not directed to spelling.[12]

Peake reported the high correlations of .80–.85 between scores on spelling and reading tests.[13]

Townsend correlated spelling scores with aptitude and reading scores.[14] She found that there was a close relationship between spelling and both word meanings and comprehension.

Morrison and Perry gave an achievement test and a mental maturity test to 1,007 pupils and found a high correlation between spelling and general reading abilities.[15] They drew the further conclusion that there were higher correlations in the lower grades than in the upper grades.

Betts [16] Durrell,[17] Harris,[18] Russell,[19] and others have found that good

[11] Maurice S. Lewis, "The Effect of Training in Listening upon Reading" *Journal of Communication*, III (Nov. 1953), 115–19.

[12] Luther C. Gilbert, "Effect of Reading on Spelling in the Ninth Grade," *School Review*, XLII (Mar. 1934), 197–204.

[13] Nellie L. Peake, "Relation Between Spelling Ability and Reading Ability," *Journal of Experimental Education*, IX (Dec. 1940), 192–93.

[14] Agatha Townsend, An Investigation of Certain Relationships of Spelling with Reading and Academic Aptitude," *Journal of Educational Research*, XL (Feb. 1947), 465–71.

[15] Ida E. Morrison and Ida F. Perry, "Spelling and Reading Relationships with Incidence of Retardation and Acceleration," *Journal of Educational Research*, LII (Feb. 1959), 222–27.

[16] Emmett A. Betts, *Foundations of Reading Instruction* (New York: American Book Co., 1946).

[17] Donald D. Durrell, *Improvement of Basic Reading Abilities* (Yonkers-On-Hudson, N. Y.: World Book Company, 1940).

[18] Albert J. Harris, *How to Increase Reading Ability* (New York: Longmans, Green & Co., Inc., 1947).

[19] David H. Russell, "Spelling Ability in Relation to Reading and Vocabulary Achievements," *Elementary English Review*, XXIII (Jan. 1946), 32–37.

reading and good spelling go together, and that poor readers are usually poor spellers.

Handwriting and Reading

Very few studies have been conducted on the relationship between handwriting ability and reading skill. Since handwriting is largely a motor skill and reading a mental skill, any close relationship between the two probably should not be expected. One study, however, conducted by Wilson and Flemming was concerned with word recognition, phonetic analysis, and writing.[20] They found a close correlation between these skills and progress in primary-grade reading.

The effect of manuscript writing on reading has been studied by several people. These investigators found results similar to those obtained by Houston,[21] Long and Mayer,[22] and Voorhis,[23] who concluded that manuscript writing helped pupils read what they had written and also contributed to success in reading in the early grades.

Cutright's study with matched groups in the second grade revealed that children who wrote manuscript used a greater number of different words in original compositions and misspelled fewer words.[24]

Thus, there is evidence that relationships exist between reading and, respectively, general English skills, listening, spelling, and handwriting.

Examples of Reading Instruction Integrated with Other Language Art Activities

Discussions of theory, child psychology, and scientific investigations are necessary in providing background for teacher guidance, but such information needs to be supplemented with practical procedures for use in the classroom.

A good teacher rarely uses exactly the same procedure in working with two groups of children, nor the exact procedure which another teacher has used. However, some examples of practice were chosen, par-

---

[20] Frank T. Wilson and Cecile White Flemming, "Grade Trends in Reading Progress in Kindergarten and Primary Grades," *Journal of Educational Psychology*, XXXI (Jan. 1940), 1–13.

[21] Harry Houston, "Manuscript Writing and Progress in Reading," *Elementary School Journal*, XXXIX (Oct. 1938), 116–18.

[22] Howard H. Long and Willa C. Mayer, "Printing Versus Cursive Writing in Beginning Reading Instruction," *Journal of Educational Research*, XXIV (Dec. 1931), 350–55.

[23] Thelma G. Voorhis, "Relative Merits of Cursive and Manuscript Writing," *Lincoln School Research Studies* (New York: Bureau of Publications, Teachers College, Columbia University, 1931).

[24] Prudence Cutright, "Script-Print and Beginning Reading and Spelling," *Elementary English Review*, XIII (Apr. 1936), 139–41.

ticularly from the standpoint of *reading* instruction, to indicate possibilities of re-enforcing the teaching of reading with some of the other language arts.

Reading Experience Charts

The experience chart offers one of the best opportunities for providing reading instruction functionally integrated with the other language arts. In preparing such a chart, children compose a short "story," and while doing so have experience in speaking, listening, and oral composition. The teacher writes their composition on the chalkboard or on newsprint as they suggest the sentences. Thus they see the spoken words in their oral composition flow into written symbols. As the written transcription of the pupil-composed chart appears, handwriting and spelling may have functional applications. The children sense the necessity of using certain letters in a certain order in writing words. If the teacher wishes to make the most of handwriting and spelling, she may make such comments as these while writing the chart:

I must be careful to make my *t* the same height as my *k*.
All the letters in these two words are the same height. I must make them nice and even.
This new word *hat* is easy to spell. It is just *h-a-t* [saying the letters as they are written].

A Visit

The following account is representative of a first grade reading lesson in which several of the language art skills were interactive.

A policeman who was the father of one of the first grade boys visited the class. He talked to the children about being careful when crossing the street on their way to and from school and told them about the new automatic school-crossing signal that tells boys and girls when to cross. The teacher emphasized the importance of listening carefully in order to grasp all the important things the policeman had to say.

After the policeman left, the children made up a story about him (oral composition).

A policeman is a helper.
He shows us the rules.
He tells us to stop.
He tells us to go.
He helps us.

These sentences were written on the chalkboard as they were given orally by the children. While writing the second, third, and fourth copies of *He,* the teacher incidentally remarked that this little word *He* always looks the same when it comes at the beginning of a sentence because it is spelled with a capital *H* and a small *e.* She also called attention to the similarity in the successive copies of *us,* and explained that all these copies looked alike because *us* is always made up of the letters *u* and *s.* When the chart was completed, various children were given a chance to read the story as a whole, then separate sentences, and finally separate words. The reading, of course, was done orally by each child while the other members listened. This activity, then, involved oral and written composition, reading, listening, and contacts with handwriting and spelling.

After composing and reading the story, stimulation provided by the policeman's visit continued to call forth discussion. Carl began imitating a policeman while directing traffic. "He needs a *Stop* and *Go* sign," said Shirley. The idea of dramatic play came forth, and discussion and planning ensued. Oral expression and listening were involved in these activities.

The children made a traffic signal and several *Stop* and *Go* signs, incidentally learning to recognize the words *Stop* and *Go.* They planned and laid out with blocks an intersection and four street corners. Different children took turns operating the traffic signal at the general intersection and using the *Stop* and *Go* signs at the street crossings. All children participated as pedestrians. The language activities of *dramatization* and *reading* were involved in this latter activity.

Composing a Playlet

The first grade children in a certain school had been reading a simple story in which a little boy came to grief because he did not observe the basic amenities of personal grooming. After finishing the story the children went to play in their block-built playhouse. One of the girls immediately began scolding one of the boys as the boy in the story had been scolded. This led to a plan to make up a play.

The children composed the play as the teacher wrote it on the chalk board. They were not satisfied with the first version, and several revisions were made.

The only properties prepared were pictures representing different grooming activities, each bearing an appropriate label which the children composed. They took turns reading the captions and placing them under the appropriate pictures until each child was sure that he could read them well enough to place them correctly under the corresponding pictures. The labels were: "Wash your face," "Clean your nails," "Brush your teeth," and "Comb your hair."

The playlet is reproduced below:

GETTING READY FOR SCHOOL

Characters
  Mother
  Father
  Jimmy

(Scene shows Mother at stove in kitchen. Father is seated at table in kitchen preparing orange juice. Jimmy is seen in next room, lying in bed, asleep.)

Mother: (Turning toward bedroom) Jimmy! Time to get up.

Jimmy: Yes, Mother. (Jimmy yawns, stretches, gets out of bed and puts on bathrobe. Then he sits on rug on floor and puts on shoes. Next he goes into the bathroom where he washes himself, cleans his fingernails, brushes his teeth, and combs his hair. As he does each of these chores, he checks with a corresponding picture thumb-tacked to the bathroom wall, and bearing an appropriate label. After he has checked the four pictures, he goes back into the bedroom, where he goes through the motions of dressing himself. He then goes into the kitchen where the table is set for breakfast.)

Mother: Good morning, Jimmy. You look very neat.

Jimmy: Good morning, Mother. Good morning, Daddy.

Daddy: Good morning, Jimmy; here is your orange juice.

Jimmy: Thank you, Daddy. I like orange juice.

Mother: And here is your cereal. And your toast. And your cocoa. (Places each on table)

Jimmy: Oh, those are the four foods that make a one-hundred-per-cent breakfast. We learned that in school yesterday.

All: Hurrah for the one-hundred-per-cent breakfast!

The teacher reproduced copies of the playlet in large manuscript for each pupil. They practiced reading the play until each child, regardless of what part he took in repeated dramatizations, would be able to read his part "as if he were talking."

Reading, listening, oral and written composition, speaking, and dramatization were the language art skills and abilities involved in this simple activity.

Writing Informative Accounts

In some schools, primary teachers encourage discussion about an animal or object which is prominent in a selection read by the children, and then give them some additional facts about that animal or object.

For example, a group of second grade children had become very much interested in sharks while reading a sea story in which a shark was prominent. The story gave very little information about the shark, probably because to have done so would have required a vocabulary beyond the reading level of the pupils. The children, however, asked many questions about sharks. In response, the teacher said, "I'll tell you some facts about sharks. Then you write these facts and any others of your own that you want to add. Tonight each of you may surprise your mother by taking home a set of facts which you have written about sharks."

The teacher then presented these facts orally while the children listened intently:

> Sharks are called, "Tigers of the sea."
> There are 150 kinds of sharks.
> They live on other fish.
> The great white shark is a man-eater.
> It is sometimes 40 feet long.
> Sharks have long, sharp teeth.
> Sometimes one row of teeth wears out.
> Then another row grows in its place.

After giving these facts the teacher asked if there were any words the children would like her to write on the chalkboard to help their spelling. In response to the children's requests she wrote *shark, man-eater,* and *teeth.*

Each child then wrote his own story, giving as many facts as he cared to, stating them in his own way, and choosing his own order. Most children included one or more thoughts of their own, such as: "Sharks live in the ocean"; "One came near our shore last summer"; "Sharks scare bathers"; "Sometimes they tip over little boats."

When the writing was finished each pupil read his composition to the class for evaluation. In some cases revisions were made in terms of the suggestions given. The compositions were taken home and proudly read to parents to show how much information had been learned about sharks.

Through this series of experiences, children read, listened, and wrote an informative composition. Several important language art skills had been given practice.

Upper-grade teachers in schools where this plan is sometimes used have their pupils find their own facts through research in subject matter texts and reference books.

Letter Writing and Reading

The following integrated language art activities arose in a third grade classroom in New Jersey as a result of reading a story about a lighthouse. The children were very much interested in the descriptions of the storm signals and asked many questions, some of which the teacher couldn't answer. She told them that she knew some children who lived near a lighthouse and who probably could tell all about lighthouses. (The teacher had previously taught in Truro, Massachusetts, which is near a lighthouse, and she still knew teachers and children in the Truro school.) She further remarked that if they wished to do so, they might write to these children and ask them questions.

The children were delighted with the idea and immediately began to prepare letters containing their questions. Much practice on format was necessary, and care was taken in penmanship. There were many questions about spelling, for the desire to send "good letters" was strong. Standards were even developed for evaluating the letters before they were sent. Finally, a group of pupils went to the post office and mailed the letters.

The children in Truro replied with some excellent letters about Highland Light (the lighthouse), the Coast Guard, bayberries, cranberries, beachplums, and trap fishing. They also sent a collection of shells, bayberries, fish netting, and a jar of beachplum jelly. They promised to write later about the Pilgrims who landed near their town.

The letters were used as the basic material for reading lessons for quite a few days, and they also furnished leads for research. Some of the letters were read and gifts shown at a school assembly. Moreover, letters of thanks were prepared and sent to the Truro children.

At Halloween time the class sent the Truro children some masks which they had made out of paper bags as well as some samples of their craft work and paintings.

The Truro children replied with "Thank you" letters at Thanksgiving time, accompanied by a booklet which they had prepared. This booklet contained account of a trip the children had taken to the first landing place of the Pilgrims in Provincetown, and also a description of a trip they had taken to Corn Hill, where the Pilgrims first found Indian Corn. The children had copied inscriptions from tablets and statues and had written stories about the many interesting things they had seen. This booklet was eagerly read by every pupil in the room, and enthusiastic discussion ensued. The book was finally placed in the room library for the use of future classes.

The children wanted to show their appreciation by sending something worthwhile to the class in Truro. After considerable discussion they planned to make and send a booklet about Thomas Edison, who had developed many of his inventions in his laboratory in Menlo Park, which was a town near the school; many of the children's fathers work in the plant in New Jersey now known as Thomas A. Edison, Incorporated.

A rich and extensive period of reading followed. The following books in the classroom were used as a nucleus: *History Primer, New Jersey Supplement* by Q .E. Thomson, *Short Stories of Famous Men* by Reynolds and Horn, *Great Names in American History* by Gilmartin and Skill, *Edison, Inspiration to Youth* by Palmer (published by Thomas A. Edison, Incorporated, West Orange, New Jersey).

The teacher brought in a collection of clippings from magazines and newspapers resulting from the celebration of "Lights Golden Jubilee" held some years previously.

The children brought in other books from their homes and from the public library which contained information about Edison. In the process they learned to use the card catalog in the school library.

All reading was done individually, except for the reading of *History Primer, New Jersey Supplement.* Because this was considered to be the most authentic of the references, it was read and discussed by the group as a whole and used as a basis for comparison with the other books they had read.

The children increased their vocabulary, and made and used a picture dictionary containing pictures of several words and phrases whose meanings needed clarification. Such entries as the following were included: *transmitter, incandescent light, laboratory, phonograph, telegrapher, dictating machine, kinetoscope, filaments, electric light bulb, motion picture projector.*

Reading skills received a vast amount of practice through functional usage. Location skills needed in research included using tables-of-contents, indexes, dictionary, pictured encyclopedias, and card catalogs. Interpretation and critical reading were emphasized throughout the study as facts in reading materials were gathered and discussed. Word recognition skills were practiced when children needed help in pronouncing new words.

Oral reading as well as silent reading received practice as each child read to the class an incident he had found in a book and thought should be included in the booklet. The class decided whether or not the incident was appropriate for inclusion. In order that the class might make a fair judgment, the child reading orally was motivated to use a pleasant voice, good enunciation, and fluency of speech.

Finally the stories were written for the booklet. After the first writing each story was evaluated by the class and usually rewritten with improvement. The teacher typed the individual stories, and each child read his story back to the class for final approval.

Organization for the book was then decided upon: the stories were taped on the pages of a large blank book, and illustrations were made to accompany the stories. Finally the book was proudly sent to the children in Truro.

However, interest was still high, and additional use was made of reading and other language art skills in two more class activities. The children wanted to share their information about their local "hero" with another class. Personal letters of invitation were written, pictures were arranged on the bulletin board, and preparation was made for telling stories about Edison and for explaining the pictures. Much purposeful practice in oral English took place.

Finally, the principal invited the class to entertain the entire school with a program at the next assembly. Dramatizations of events in the life of Edison were prepared and enacted for this event.

The assembly program climaxed the period of rich learnings in the language arts of listening, reading, speaking, writing and dramatization, with accompanying increments in vocabulary, handwriting, and spelling.

A Reading Unit on Travel

The lesson described below is an excellent example of the functional use of several of the language arts skills in connection with a *reading* unit. This account summarizes a lesson given by Donald Nelson [25] at a Convention of the National Council of Teachers of English in Denver, Colorado. The children were sixth grade pupils, and the topic was "Let's Travel with Books."

Planning Stage

The lesson was concerned with stimulating interest in reading books with settings in different countries, and with plans in regard to efficient reading and effective sharing of content read with others.

In front of the class a large sailboat reposed invitingly on a table. A collection of attractive books dealing with other countries and representing different levels of reading difficulty was set up on another table. Several large charts which the pupils had previously composed were suspended from screens and posts in front of the space where they sat.

The teacher opened the discussion by asking such questions as:

[25] Donald Nelson is a teacher in the public schools of Denver, Colorado.

How many of you like to travel?
Have you taken a trip lately? Where?
How many of you would like to take a far-away trip in imagination?

Following the discussion, the teacher said:

"Here are some books about far-away places. You may choose a story that will take you some place that you would like to go in imagination."
"What skills will you need to use in finding your story?"

The children replied that they would need to know how to use a table of contents and an index. (In their regular classroom activity the children had had some work in using an index.)

"If you enjoy this imaginary trip very much, undoubtedly you will want to share it with the others. How can you share your reading travel trip with others?"

The children mentioned:

Telling the story	Illustrating
Writing	Using puppets
Making a Book Report	Dramatization

The teacher then asked:

"What areas of communication will be drawn upon if we use these different media of sharing?"

The following list resulted from this question:

Speaking	Reading
Writing	Listening
Illustrating	

"Take just one of the ways in which we might share our stories—story telling. Mention some ways in which you can improve your reading of the story in order that others may enjoy it as you tell it."

The following skills in reading were suggested and written on a chart. This chart was later used as an evaluation device.

1. Improve vocabulary.

"How?"
    Looking up foreign words.
    Looking up words you don't know.
    Rereading a sentence that isn't clear to see how it fits into the context.

2. Establishing a mood so we can give imaginary pictures to the audience.
3. Interpreting facts, descriptions, incidents.
4. Building atmosphere. (Think how to provide some sort of a setting.)

5. Projecting ourselves into the story. (Putting ourselves in the place of a character, imagining that we are in the situation.)
6. Getting clear concepts.
    a. Interpreting maps.
    b. Getting word meanings from context.
    c. Comparing stereotypes with realities.
    d. Analyzing geographic and historical facts.
    e. Thinking of size and time relationships.
    f. Using research skills.
7. Developing attitudes—look for moral or spiritual values.

"What oral language skills will you need? How can you make your story better than ever before?"

These skills in speaking were charted:

1. Knowing your story well.
2. Making it interesting by:
    a. Telling details.
    b. Varying sentence structure.
    c. Using varied vocabulary.
    d. Avoiding choppy sentences.
    e. Using direct quotes.
    f. Using correct connecting words—avoid "and so" habit.
    g. Using different kinds of sentences.
3. Employing good word usage.
4. Using a good beginning sentence.
5. Using a pleasing voice.
6. Giving events in sequence.
7. Save surprise for end.
8. Using an evaluation chart in telling all stories.

"What listening skills will we need?"

This list was compiled:

1. Putting yourself in speaker's place.
2. Identifying yourself with a character.
3. Helping build atmosphere—use imagination.
4. Showing interest.
5. Interpreting what you hear.
6. Avoiding interruptions.
7. Evaluating for purpose of bettering yourself.
8. Identifying a purpose for listening.

Mr. Nelson wrote additional charts composed by the children and teacher as aids in teaching language skills with emphasis on reading and speaking.

These charts were as follows:

1. Chart illustrating the four kinds of sentences.
2. Chart showing which form of commonly used pronouns to use as subject or predicate of a sentence. (No rules were learned but the class discussed why it should be "he and I" instead of "him and me" in the subject, etc.) Visual form:

Subject	*Predicate*
he	him
I	me
etc.	

3. Chart on double negatives.
4. Charts on word variables:
   Nouns: How many ways can you name the object?
   Verbs: How many ways can you say what is happening?
   Adjectives: How many words can you say to describe the object and retain the meaning? (Huge, immense, vast, enormous, etc.)

Follow-up Activities

While the lesson described above represented the planning stage only, the pupils did, of course, select individual books to read. After finishing his book each one shared the result of his reading in one of the ways planned at the beginning of the lesson.

Additional follow-up activities and materials that resulted are mentioned below.

Research activities. Each pupil selected one topic for reading research after he completed his story. For example, one boy read *Robin Hood* and became interested in English Sports. He illustrated the game of cricket on large oak tag and listed new words he had learned while reading about this game.

One boy read about the *Trojan Horse* and became interested in the Greek Gods. He did much reading about them, made a large mural illustrating many gods and goddesses, and prepared a chart of the new words learned in his reading.

After reading *Heidi,* one girl became interested in the Swiss use of goat milk and in the cheese industry. She made a large diagram showing elements in a glass of milk on a percentage basis. She did much reading of technical material. Her chart of new words was made separately.

One boy made a diorama, but most of the children made large illustrations resulting from their research of factual information suggested by the respective stories.

Bulletin Board Display. Names of characters in the fiction were placed on a bulletin board, accompanied in some cases with pictures.

Geography Activity. A large outline map of the world was hung on the wall. Each pupil put the name of a character in the book he had read on a small flag representing the country where the character lived and pinned it on the map over this country. A small group made the map as a whole, but each pupil colored the country of his character and explained to the class how the geography of the country influenced the story in which the character appeared.

Large Reading Book. A large book was prepared by the pupils showing the areas of reading covered.

Correct Usage Service. As a result of incorrect usage heard while the reading unit was in progress, a Who-Owl device was prepared and used. This device consisted of an oak-tag owl 18 x 36 inches, with two nests attached, one for boys and one for girls. Noticeable speech errors, together with their correct forms, were dropped into these nests. The figure as a whole was labelled "Who-o-o-o Said?"

Truly this was reading instruction richly re-enforced and integrated with other language art skills.

Additional Readings

Anderson, Harold A., "Teaching the Art of Listening," *School Review*, LVII (Feb. 1949), 215–24.

Artley A. Sterl, *et al. Interrelationships Among the Language Arts.* Chicago: National Council of Teachers of English, 1954.

Beery, Althea, "Listening Activities in the Elementary School," *Elementary English Review* (Feb. 1946), 69–79.

Eames, Thomas E., "The Relationship of Reading and Speech Difficulties," *Journal of Educational Psychology*, XLI (Jan. 1950), 51–53.

Goodenough, Florence, "The Reading Tests of the Stanford Achievement Scale and Other Variables," *Journal of Educational Psychology*, XVI (Nov. 1925), 523–31.

Herrick, Virgil E., and Leland B. Jacobs, *Children and the Language Arts.* Englewood Cliffs, N. J.: Prentice-Hall, Inc., 1955.

Tong, Howard H., and Willa C. Mayer, "Printing versus Cursive Writing in Beginning Reading Instruction," *Journal of Educational Research*, XXIV (Dec. 1931), 350–55.

McCarthy, Dorothea, *et al., Factors that Influence Language Growth.* Champaign, Ill.: National Council of Teachers of English, 1953.

National Education Association, *Language Arts in the Elementary School,* Twentieth Yearbook of the Department of Elementary Principals. Washington, D. C.: National Education Association, 1941.

Russell, David H., *et al.*, *Child Development and the Language Arts*. Champaign, Ill.: National Council of Teachers of English, 1953.

Seashore, Robert H., "The Importance of Vocabulary in Learning Language Skills," *Elementary English*, XXV (Mar. 1948), 137–52.

Smith, Mary Katherine, "Measurement of the Size of General English Vocabulary through the Elementary Grades and High School," *Genetic Psychology Monographs*, No. 24 (Nov. 1941), 311–45.

Smith, Nila Banton, *et al.*, *Readiness for Reading and Related Language Arts*. Chicago: National Conference of Teachers of English, 1950.

——, *Areas of Research Interest in the Language Arts*. Champaign, Ill.: National Council of Teachers of English, 1952.

Strickland, Ruth G., *The Language Arts in the Elementary School*. Boston: D. C. Heath & Company, 1951.

——, "Developing Reading Skills as Part of the Total Language Arts Program," *Reading in Action*, International Reading Association Conference Proceedings, pp. 129–30. New York: Scholastic Magazines, 1957.

The Commission of the English Curriculum of the National Council of Teachers of English, *Language Arts for Today's Children*. New York: Appleton-Century-Crofts, Inc., 1954.

Voorhis, Thelma G., "Relative Merits of Cursive and Manuscript Writing," *Lincoln School Research Studies*. New York: Bureau of Publications, Teachers College, Columbia University, 1931.

Wilson, Frank T., and Cecile White Flemming, "Grade Trends in Reading Progress in Kindergarten and Primary Grades," *Journal of Educational Psychology*, XXXI (Jan. 1940), 1–13.

5

Approaches Differ

Never have methods of teaching reading been more varied. Never have materials been more profuse. Perhaps this variety and abundance are due to the generally recognized need for improving reading instruction and the earnest desire to find more effective procedures and mediums for meeting the exigency of this situation. Whenever a pressing need is felt by many people, numerous solutions are offered. Reading is no exception to this generalization.

Abraham Fuller, an English scholar of the seventeenth century, wrote: "Marshall thy notions into a handsome method. One's work will carry twice more weight packed up in bundles, than when it lies flapping and hanging about his shoulders."

Fortunately, in America there is opportunity to develop many "handsome methods." In our educational system we have a chance to express different philosophies, to evolve different methods, to experiment with different procedures. At the present time we most certainly are taking advantage of these privileges in the field of reading. People interested in reading instruction are expressing, evolving, and experimenting as never before in our history. A book on reading instruction at this time would be remiss in its function if it did not recognize and present to its readers a variety of the approaches currently receiving attention.

Several of these approaches are subjects of controversy at the present time. The most frequent criticisms are voiced by those who disapprove the teaching of reading to preschool or kindergarten children, those who object to introducing beginning reading through the use of phonics, and those who believe that the content of any beginning reading material should be of high interest value.

On the other hand, some of the proponents of the new approaches believe that we are not making the most of the capacity of young children to read, and propose teaching reading to them at an early age. Others believe that our present methods of teaching reading should be reformed for greater effectiveness. Still others propose new mediums to use as a means of facilitating reading achievement.

Every person who is interested in the teaching of reading should be informed of these different approaches and the philosophies upon which they are based. To this end several of the approaches will be described on the ensuing pages, and ways in which they have been applied in classroom situations will be discussed briefly.

In reading these accounts the student preparing to teach reading or the teacher in practice should bear in mind that all the proponents of these approaches are motivated by a sincere desire to improve reading instruction. Regardless of personal philosophy or conviction we should keep ourselves alert to the many different developments in reading and encourage research concerning all of them. If a teacher is informed in regard to many approaches she may choose a particular approach or aspects of several approaches which seem most appropriate for the children in her classroom, and then experiment. Perhaps she may develop a new approach of her own and measure its results. In either case, the teacher of reading has an excellent opportunity to make contributions to research in regard either to using or developing different approaches to reading instruction.

The Augmented Roman Alphabet
Approach

Sir James Pitman of England has invented a new Augmented Roman Alphabet for use in teaching beginning reading. Pitman believes that while we have done much experimentation in regard to methods of teaching, we have seriously neglected to control the medium (that is, alphabet and spelling) in which beginning reading materials are printed. Therefore he has devised and augmented the Roman alphabet resulting in a new alphabet which he believes is a simpler and more consistent printed code for the English language. He proposes that this alphabet be used in materials for beginning reading until children develop sufficient skill to transfer to the reading of text in which the conventional English alphabet is used. He calls this new augmented Roman alphabet *Initial Teaching Medium* and refers to it as I.T.M.

In this alphabet there are forty-three instead of twenty-six symbols. Each symbol stands for its own and only its own phoneme (speech sound); for example the letter *o* is used to represent the sound common to such words as *on, not, odd.* This same symbol is not used to represent several different sounds as in *on, one, go, do,* and *women.* Instead these five different sounds are represented by different spellings and in some cases by different symbols [1] as

on, wun, gœ, dœ, wimen

Below is an example [2] of some of the new characters:

A.R. letter:	1. ſh	2. ſh	3. ch	4. œ
I.T.M. spelling	ſhat	ſhin	chin	tœ
Conventional} Spelling }	that	thin	chin	toe

A section of *The Little Red Hen* [3] printed in the new alphabet looks like this:

> wuns upon a tiem littl red hen livd in a barn wiſh her fiev chicks. a pig, a cat and a duck mæd ſhær hœm in ſhe sæm barn. ɛɛch dæ littl red hen led her chicks out tœ lœk for fœd. but ſhe pig, ſhe cat and ſhe duck wœd not lœk for fœd.

The new alphabet has been used experimentally in teaching four- and five-year-old children in British schools for some time and results appear to be favorable. Pitman does not recommend the use of this alphabet for

[1] John Downing, *Experiments with an Augmented Roman Alphabet for Beginning Readers in British Schools* (New York: Educational Records Bureau, 1962), p. 17.
[2] *Ibid.,* p. 17.
[3] *Ibid.,* p. 21.

any specific age level. It was used with four- and five-year-olds in British schools because those are the ages at which children enter schools in the British countries. Several schools in the United States are now experimenting with the use of this medium.

Conclusive evidence is not yet available, however, in regard to the effectiveness of teaching beginning reading with the augmented Roman alphabet, the degree with which children will be able to make the transition to reading text in conventional English, and the outcome in regard to spelling. Pitman warns that the use of this medium is undergoing only the first stage of a long-term investigation which should extend over a period of at least ten to fifteen years.

The Language-Experience Approach

The Language-Experience Approach used by several teachers in San Diego County, California, deserves recognition. For many years we have been talking about the desirability of teaching reading as a part of an integrated language arts program. Teachers in San Diego County seem to have developed practical ways of applying this theory. For a discussion of this plan see *Description of Three Approaches to the Teaching of Reading* (San Diego, Cal.: San Diego County Schools, 1962), pp. 19–25; also see *Learning to Read Through Experience* by Doris May Lee and R. Van Allen (New York: Appleton-Century-Crofts, Inc., 1963).

In the Language-Experience approach no distinction is made between the reading program and the program for developing the other language skills. At beginning first grade, the teacher encourages opportunities for creative work with crayons, pencils, and paints, as well as through the medium of language. As a child expresses himself through oral language, the teacher pulls out a sentence or two which sum up what he has said and this short composition is written by the teacher as the child watches. Group compositions are also recorded as the children look on. As the teacher writes she calls attention to items that are important to reading, such as letter formation, association of sounds with symbols, repetition of the same sound or symbol, and the function of capitalization and punctuation. These group compositions are used as a basis for discussion in which letters and words are recognized. Children read these group compositions as well as their own individual compositions.

As soon as a child makes a "commitment," that is expresses a desire to write his own language expression, he is given opportunities to do so, and the teacher now enlarges her role to facilitate growth in all the communication skills. When children become able to write independently they are provided with basic vocabulary word lists as well as with words of general interest. Thus they develop control over a basic vocabulary through their writing experiences.

As children develop in reading ability they are given increasing opportunities to read from books for interest and research purposes.

Measured results of this approach are very favorable. From an administrative standpoint the conduct of the experiment is commendable in that teachers using the plan choose to do so, in-service meetings make full use of teacher discussions, and research in regard to the approach is being made by a reading study committee composed of teachers.

The Programmed Approach

In this age of an exploding school population and emphasis upon self-learning it is not surprising that programmed instruction and the teaching machine have entered the field of reading instruction. In the flurry of excitement that accompanies this innovation, teachers and teachers-in-preparation are asking such questions as: What is programmed instruction? What is a teaching machine? What are the possibilities of programmed instruction for teaching reading at the elementary level? Each of these questions will be discussed.

Programmed Instruction

Programmed learning is achieved through the use of materials which break subject matter or skills into small learning units. Responses are called for in connection with each unit and answers are provided to which the student may refer immediately after making each response. Programmed material may take the form of separate work sheets, cards, tablets, workbooks, or textbooks.

The Teaching Machine

The teaching machine is a device which presents the individual student with a program of questions and answers, exercises to be performed or problems to be solved, together with a feed-back of answers so that he may be immediately informed of the success of his response at each step and thus be given an opportunity to correct his errors as he makes them.

In using the teaching machine the student sits at the machine and makes his responses as a preprogrammed set of questions or exercises is presented to him. After making each response the answer is flashed to him automatically, or he may pull a knob, turn a crank, push a lever or button, slide a panel or use some other arrangement for the purpose of revealing the answer.

The term *teaching machine* may be misinterpreted by some, in that the device is not a "machine" as this word is usually interpreted, any more than a pop-up toaster is a "machine." Nor does it do any actual teaching. Even the most enthusiastic users of teaching machine instruction declare that the machine itself is unimportant. What is important in programmed instruction is that information to be taught is first broken down into its fundamental units and then regrouped, or "programmed," into a logical progressive order. Programmed materials may be processed through a teaching machine or they may be used as any other material is used in the classroom in the form of books or sets of exercises.

Possibilities of Programmed Instruction in Reading

The most frequently used programs in reading are those in which questions are asked or in which true-false statements or multiple-choice exercises are presented, all based on content read. The child writes his answer to each question or responds as he is requested to do to some other type of exercise that may be used. He then immediately checks with an answer provided to him.

In some cases phonics exercises are programmed; in these the child is given practice in matching, or supplying in sentences, words containing similar elements or sounds. Exercises in supplying correct prefixes or suffixes to incomplete words in sentences are being programmed. Programs leading to increased ability in dividing words into syllables also have been used in reading instruction.

Some materials have been programmed for use at the prereading level. These consist of one-response matching exercises in which the child compares colors, geometrical figures, or letters.

No doubt the ingenuity of teachers, reading specialists, psychologists, and publishers will reveal other uses of programmed materials and will devise reading programs of several types other than those described above.

In preparing programmed materials for reading, consideration should be given to the aspects of reading instruction which especially lend themselves to this approach. Programmed instruction is best used with learnings that have to be fixed, facts that have to be memorized, and processes that have to be made automatic. The most enthusiastic proponents of programming recognize its limitations and most certainly do not advocate its use for *all* teaching. Rather, they think of programming as an effective learning device to free the teacher of repetitious tasks which take little advantage of her teaching skills and leave to her the aspects of teaching which require explanation, guided thinking, and intelligent discussion.

It is natural that the starting point in preparing frames for reading programs has been concerned with questions, true-false statements, or other objective exercises to check the child's grasp of reading content. On the whole, such exercises deal with literal comprehension; that is, the child is asked to give back exact literal information that is presented in the selection that he is reading.

Other aspects of reading for meanings, which are even more important than literal comprehension, are interpretation and critical reading. It is entirely possible to provide programs containing exercises designed to give practice on interpretation of reading content and on the critical reading of a selection, and some of this may be valuable. The interpretation process, however, doesn't always lead to one exact answer. The same passage may be interpreted in different ways, and any of several answers to a given question might be considered appropriate. The same is true of critical reading, in which each individual passes his personal judgment upon the authenticity or bias of a selection. It would seem that maximum growth in interpretation and critical reading would result from situations in which the teacher stimulates thinking with questions, remarks, and responses and in which there is interaction of the thinking of a group of pupils taking place under wise teacher guidance.

The study-skills area may be given some practice with programmed materials. Following directions, finding main ideas or certain details, organizing by means of lists or outlines, some of the location skills—all these are sufficiently objective in nature to lend themselves to programmed practice. The specific study skills needed in reading in the different subject areas are less definitive and objective. Some of these, however, do lend themselves to programmed techniques. Nevertheless, in all cases, these skills should be introduced by the teacher, and the teacher needs to insure that skill in these areas does not stop with practice exercises but rather is applied in studying subject-matter text.

Programmed instruction may have some value in giving practice on word identification techniques, provided that several considerations are respected: (1) that these techniques are carefully developed by the teacher in terms of special needs before programmed practice is given; (2) that the programs are carefully worked out so that the child has opportunity to apply the results of practice provided on each frame to the identification of words containing the elements practiced to the reading of these words when embedded in context; (3) that the child is checked by the teacher through oral response on the results of his practice.

Because sound is important in developing word identification techniques, learning such techniques involves a large proportion of auding. Auding is necessary on the part of the child to insure that he correctly identifies the *sound* of the letter elements, word structure elements, and syllabic units. Auding is necessary on the part of the teacher in finding out on which of these elements the child needs help. The only way in which she can accurately ascertain his pronunciation needs in reading is through listening to his oral reading. The most effective way of checking the results of her development and the child's practice is to listen to him as he reads orally context in which there are opportunities to apply the identification skills on which he has had practice.

The development of interest in reading and the growth of taste and appreciation are important aspects of reading instruction. These are facets which do not lend themselves to routine practice and objective testing. In the opinion of the author, programming would be of little value in promoting such growths. It is better to leave these to a wise, stimulating, artistic teacher.

The Television Approach

Educational television is being used with increasing frequency in teaching a variety of subjects. Some schools are using television as a medium for teaching reading.

The reading materials used in television reading programs are usually prepared by classroom teachers, often in conjunction with a reading consultant or studio teacher. Sometimes they are prepared entirely by the reading consultant or studio teacher.

A typical method used is as follows: The classroom teacher takes a few minutes to introduce the lesson. Then the lesson is presented by television. Often this lesson is conducted by a television teacher, while the classroom teacher walks about the room giving needed assistance to individuals. Following the television presentation the classroom teacher conducts discussion, individualizes the group presentation, and in many cases gives tests to check learning obtained while viewing the telecast.

Materials and procedure, of course, vary greatly in the television reading programs offered in different school systems. As one example the television program in the public schools of Hagerstown, Maryland, will be described briefly. The school system in this town was one of the first to initiate television instruction in reading, and it is continuing to do so with considerable success.

In the television-connected schools in Hagerstown reading instruction is given by television in grades one through six. Materials for two different programs have been prepared and are in use: the Basic Skills Program and the Controlled Reading Program.

The Basic Skills Program embraces a sequential series of lessons for the development of basic reading skills beginning with a series of twelve lessons in reading readiness. Ten controlled reader readiness film strips are projected by television as the basis of these presentations. While designed primarily for beginners, these lessons are sometimes used by immature pupils in the second grade.

Skills and understanding essential to success in unlocking words and their meanings are then developed through a series of lessons titled, respectively, Beginning Reading, Level One and Level Two. The lessons that follow the readiness phase build skills from the simplest primary level through third grade level.

Additional explanations of the Reading Skills Program are given by Velora V. Swauger,[4] television reading teacher in Hagerstown:

The *Reading Skills* lessons are of such nature that they require very little preparation for, or follow-up by, the classroom teacher. Classroom teachers find a variety of ways to incorporate the televised lessons into the language arts program. These lessons review, supplement, and reinforce skills which the pupils have been developing under the guidance of their classroom teacher.

The medium of television makes possible the use of motivational effects and devices that catch the pupil's interest and involve him in a personalized learning situation. Illustrative of this is the actuality of eye-to-eye contact, close-up of speech organs, and of "near" physical presence.

The lessons are designed to encourage pupil participation through listening, seeing, imitation, thought stimulation, imaginative play, application, and testing.

The materials used in the Controlled Reading Program consist of TV projected story films designed for use in increasing comprehension and rate. There are two levels of these materials: Level I for grades two to three, and Level II for grades four to six. Pupils who participate in this program are selected by their teachers as those who would profit most by such instruction.

The procedure used in conducting these television lessons is as follows:

1. Each filmstrip story will be introduced by the studio teacher. The vocabulary and purpose for reading the story will be developed.

[4] Velora V. Swauger, *Teachers' Guide Sheets, Basic Skills, Controlled Reading,* and other mimeographed materials (Hagerstown, Md.: Hagerstown Public Schools, 1959–60).

2. The filmstrip will be shown without interruption. The starting speed for each level is determined by the difficulty of the material and the maturity of the pupils. As the program progresses the speed will be increased.

3. Following each lesson a comprehension test will be given by the studio teacher. Each pupil will need paper and pencil. Some schools may wish to prepare answer sheets. . . .

4. Each pupil will be provided with a *TV Reading Progress Record* upon which he will record the rate in words per minute and the number of correct responses for each lesson. These records will be collected and used in the evaluation of the program.

This is a very abbreviated account of the Hagerstown materials and techniques. Perhaps, however, it will offer some idea of how reading is taught by television in this particular situation.

A very sound observation in regard to television teaching was made by Buehring [5] at the end of two years of experimentation in Hagerstown:

. . . The television set is a machine, not a teacher. . . . How the lesson is presented and what is taught depends on the teacher, since television itself does not and cannot produce or teach a lesson.

. . . Television is one process. . . . The screen lesson must be supplemented by classroom-learning situations and coordinated with other experiences of the school day. . . . How effectively television instruction is used, the rate it will ultimately attain, and its importance will depend on how intelligently and imaginatively it is used.

The Film Approach

Several schools are now experimenting with visual approaches to reading through the use of film strips and moving pictures. Some of the basal series of readers have developed film strips to accompany early books in their series. An independent series of colored films has been developed for older children by Bammon and Dawson [6] on well-chosen and significant aspects of reading such as: "Why Read?" "What Did You Read?" "How to Read?" "What's in a Book?"; and there are others. We probably shall see many additional film developments in reading in the future.

One example of the use of film strips in teaching reading will briefly describe the material and methods used in an experiment conducted at New Castle, Pennsylvania. The materials used in the New Castle study consisted of a set of film strips, one to represent each lesson in the Laidlaw

[5] *The Nation's Schools*, February 1959, by special permission. Copyright 1959 The Modern Hospital Publishing Co., Inc., Chicago. All rights reserved.
[6] Henry Bammon and Mildred Dawson, *Pathways to Reading* (San Francisco, C-B Educational Films).

basic readers. The films were in color, and a textfilm teacher's manual accompanied the films. The basic readers themselves, together with their manuals were also used in connection with this plan.

The method was as follows: a film was shown in a darkened room. This film, then, was used as a center for presenting new words, teaching phonics, word structure, comprehension, and work-study skills. Each teacher kept a notebook in which she had listed each pupil's name. As children worked with a new film, she tried to give special assistance to individuals and jotted down individual needs. In showing review films, she again provided for special practice in terms of individual needs. Following the film activities, children worked with text in the readers or workbooks themselves, as the case might be.

The author [7] of the New Castle experiment claims that the film-strip approach used produced superior results.

The Linguistics Approach

The science of linguistics has been developing rapidly in recent years. The proponents of linguistic theory and many other people in the field of education believe that linguistics has much to offer in improving language instruction in general and that there are strong possibilities of utilizing the science of linguistics to advantage in the teaching of reading. Some people are actually trying linguistic approaches and procedures in the classroom to find their effects on reading competence. Many others are theorizing about the effects of linguistics upon reading instruction.

Linguistic applications to reading is a large topic to discuss within a section of a chapter. However, due to the prominence of this subject at the present time a few linguistic terms will be defined, some theories in regard to the application of linguistics to reading instruction will be presented, and selected classroom approaches in the use of linguistics in teaching reading will be discussed.

What Is Linguistics?

The science of linguistics has not been conspicuous in its application to reading until recently, and there seems to be some confusion among teachers of reading in regard to what is meant by the term. Linguistics is a complex science with many ramifications, and to understand it fully one must study several books on the subject and if possible take some

[7] Glenn McCracken, *The Right to Learn* (Chicago: Henry Regnery Company, 1959), Chaps. 11–15.

courses in linguistics. However, in order to provide some background for those who are not familiar with the term and its meaning, a very brief and elementary explanation will be given.

Stated simply, linguistics is the study of human speech. More specifically, linguistics is a science that has to do with the origin, nature, modification, and structure of language. It is especially concerned with patterns of speech, vocal habits and systems of sound symbols.

There are two classes of linguists: the descriptive linguists who describe a language in terms of its structure at a given time, and the diachronic or historical linguists who are interested in changes through time. It is the former class of linguists who are most active currently in influencing classroom instruction.

Patterns in Sentence Structure

Linguists are concerned, for one thing, with patterns of speech, that is, the arrangement of words in sentences and the changes in function and meaning when the same word appears in different positions in a sentence.

In discussing the particular applications of linguistics to reading, many linguistic specialists emphasize the recognition of basic structural principles of word order as being fundamental in learning the reading process. They argue that, at six, children use complicated sentences, speaking them in sentence patterns which they have learned. They point out that many children's books present the language in a "baby talk" that is as unreal to the child as it is to the adult. Their practical suggestion to teachers of reading, then, is to use for beginning reading material sentence patterns which are more natural and which are already used by children in their oral speech.

According to Warfel and Lloyd,[8] the disappointment in reading in the United States ". . . arises from inability of students to find a common ground between their known readiness to speak and their need to read more and more complex thoughts. . . . This results from the failure to lift to awareness the relationship between the two codes of speaking and writing. The eye-reading methods which largely disregard research in the psychology of language operation, view reading and writing almost wholly as mechanical activities unrelated to the structuring of the language."

The authors quoted above believe that the school should focus during the first few months upon enlarging the child's speech repertory so that he can benefit by varied sense patterns.

[8] Harry R. Warfel and Donald J. Lloyd, "The Structural Approach to Reading," *School and Society* (June 8, 1957), 199–201.

Gliessman,[9] in writing about "Understanding in Reading from the Viewpoint of Sentence Psychology," urges sentence conditioning so that students will not only recognize but will develop the habit of searching within the sentence for subjects, predicates, and their modifiers in order to understand meanings in reading. To do this he says that they must know something about the ways in which sentences are formed and organized. He also states that children who are word readers do not have sentence sense, and he intimates that the development of sentence sense through the use of linguistics would not only contribute to better understanding in reading but also to fluency and rate.

A few examples of ways being used in the elementary grades to develop sensitivity to sentence patterns will be presented.

A favorite plan for use with primary children is to have them select from a book they are reading a simple sentence containing a noun and verb only, and then to invite them to add to the sentence expanding it with adjectives, adverbs, phrases, and perhaps clauses. For example: "Tommy ran. Tommy ran fast. Tommy ran fast to the florist shop. Tommy ran fast to the big florist shop." And so on until the sentence may conclude something like this. "Tommy ran fast to the big florist shop on the corner to buy some big, red roses for his mother's birthday."

In later grades children sometimes expand a simple noun-verb sentence in writing, then exchange papers and read each others expanded sentences.

Another plan sometimes used with elementary children is to have them build sentences with separate word cards, beginning with a simple pattern consisting of a noun and a verb and then proceeding to build this pattern into more complex patterns involving adjectives, adverbs, phrases, and clauses. Building sentences with cards, however, is not what is important; the emphasis is upon the position of these words in a sentence and changes in function and meanings when parts of speech are placed in different positions in the sentence, for example:

A first grade teacher, in playing a word recognition "game" with beginners in reading, gave *very simple* practice in structural linguistics. She started her description of the "game" as indicated below:

We went to our reading circle. Each child was given two or three cards with words on them that they needed in reading. The conversation then proceeded as follows:

Teacher: Does everyone know what your words say? Look at your words and say them to yourself. Would some one like to have help or do you each know your words?

[9] David Gliessman, "Understanding in Reading from the Viewpoint of Science Psychology," *The Reading Teacher*, Vol. 13, No. 1 (Oct. 1959), 22–28.

Two or three children were given help.

Teacher: Now let us see if someone has a word that he could use in starting a sentence; a sentence you know is like a line of print in your book. It tells one thing. If you find a word you think will start to tell us something, you bring your card with you and stand up here in front of the group.

Fred: Mrs. White, I do.

Teacher: What does your card say, Fred?

Fred: It says *We*.

Teacher: Good, Fred. Class, was he right? Could you start a sentence with *We*?

Children: Yes.

Teacher: Now what could we say next? "We" what? Who has a card that might help Fred's card to tell us something?

Helen: I have *like*.

Teacher: Fine, Helen. Come here and stand where you think you belong to make a sentence.

This procedure was continued until the sentence *We like cake* was completed. The teacher then asked if anyone had a word that told what kind of cake "We like." Tommy had a card with the word *marble* on it. "Could it be marble cake?" he asked. The teacher said "Yes, it could," and asked where he would stand in placing *marble* in the sentence. Tommy took his place between *like* and *cake*. The children read the sentence and those standing with cards sat down.

The teacher added *s* to the word *marble* and asked what change this made in the word. She then changed the *m* to capitalized form and asked a child to stand up with *Marbles* to be used as the first word in a sentence. Through guided discussion centered on word order, the sentence "Marbles are round" was built.

The teacher then remarked somewhat incidentally, "First we had *marble* before *cake* near the end of the sentence to tell what kind of a cake we like. Now we have *Marbles* at the beginning of the sentence because that's what we are talking about."

The lesson continued as the children made sentences with other words in different arrangements.

It is hoped that the above illustrations will reveal some possibilities of working, even at a very early level, with structural linguistics as it is concerned with word arrangement and corresponding word function.

The linguistic specialists, themselves, in working with word position and function in sentence patterns, often use formulas to stand for different parts of speech. In one set of symbols, for example, N stands for *noun;* D for *determiner,* such as *the* or *a; LV* for *verb;* I for *intensifier,* such as more, most, quite, rather; A for *adjective; av* for *adverb; AP* for *adjective phrase;* and *ac* for *adjective clause.* Thus *N LV N* would be the formula for the simple sentence *Birds are vertebrates. DIAN AP LV* would be the formula for this sentence: *The very small dog in the car is barking.*

Practice in evolving sentence patterns in the elementary grades is usually confined to oral sentences, building with word cards, or writing. Later students use formulas in analyzing spoken or printed sentences. The formulas are most frequently employed in teaching grammar in junior and senior high school, but they have been used in sixth grade and in some places as low as fourth and fifth grades.

Intonation Patterns

Linguists, however, include more than word position and function in sentence patterns. They also are concerned with intonation patterns. The understanding of a sentence entails the recognition of patterns composed of *suprasegmental phonemes,* namely, pauses, pitch, and stress, all of which signal meanings. These phonemes are combined under the term *junctures.* Junctures are combinations of pauses, changes in pitch, degrees of stress (accent) used in marking sentence ends and internal units of phrases and clauses.

Hatfield [10] explains the use of junctures in a concrete way. He states:

One of its most obvious applications is to punctuation. From his years of teaching and editing, the present writer is convinced that he has for a long time punctuated chiefly by sound; that is, he has been guided by the "junctures" in the inner speech that moves just ahead of a writer's pen or typewriter, although he did not quite realize what he was doing. And he has evidence that other practiced writers and editors do this too.

. . . Writers who watch their inner speech perpetrate fewer awkward or incoherent sentences. Many first grade teachers make use of the pupils' inner speech to implant written-sentence sense; they just ask the pupils to think each sentence through before volunteering it or writing it. Most later teachers have been afraid to trust the signals in inner speech as guides to punctuation. Now structural grammar makes it possible to see why and how this can be done. To make pupils *overtly* conscious of their inner speech and of its junctures may appear at first glance extremely difficult.

Inner speech can be brought to attention by asking pupils to think of sentences imitating a model one (a common procedure in teaching patterns); then to listen to these in imagination. Or they may be asked what they would say and how they would say it if wrongly accused of borrowing a missing book, or if congratulated upon someone else's anonymous poem.

Work on junctures begins by asking pupils to count the sentences in a paragraph read naturally by the teacher or phonograph. It may, or may not, pay to

[10] Wilbur W. Hatfield, "Will Structural Grammar Help?" *The English Journal,* XLVII (Dec. 1958), 570–75. Reprinted with the permission of the National Council of Teachers of English and Wilbur W. Hatfield.

discuss how they know where the sentences end—to bring out the *usual* pattern of a rise in pitch followed by a drop below the average level on the last syllable as the voice dies away into a short silence. If paragraphs including questions and exclamations are used, pupils may record the last word of each sentence and the appropriate punctuation after it.

The increased sensitivity to junctures, intonations, and stresses should improve oral reading, or at least facilitate instruction in that neglected art. Pupils may well be asked to prepare oral readings by first reading silently with attention to the expression the authors intended. First grade children in many good schools are asked to read each sentence silently and then to "say" it; and even we teachers do not like to read publicly any material which we have not recently read to ourselves. This greater awareness of the speech values on the printed page may be invoked to increase enjoyment of literature, especially of poetry.

In listening we all must be guided more or less by junctures and emphases, but it may well be that inadequate perception of these is often a cause of failure to comprehend. More attention to prepositions and conjunctions as markers of phrases and clauses will also aid comprehension. Of course, in normal listening the attention to these signals of structure must be chiefly subconscious.

It is apparent that attention to the structure of sentences and the function of words in sentences would help children analyze difficult sentences encountered in reading and to understand their meanings more clearly.

One of the most comprehensive sets of guidelines for a new primary reading methodology making use of sentence and intonation patterns is found in the proposals below as formulated by Lefevre: [11]

The time may have come to try teaching—first—the actual correspondence between the larger patterns of speech, structural sentence elements, and their counterparts in print and writing, *as wholes*; these could later be analyzed as much (or as little) as required for optimum control of the derivative visual and manual linguistic skills based on speech. Such a new departure would begin with a truly operational view of the reading process.

To be practical as a basis for developing a method of teaching reading operationally, as a linguistic process, an adequate description of reading American English should focus on recognition of the shapes and patterns of utterance where intonation is paramount (statements, requests, questions); on structural sentence elements (noun groups, verb groups, prepositional phrases, subordinate clauses); on the structure or function words that mark such groups (articles or determiners, auxiliary verbs, prepositions, clause markers or subordinators); and on the four form classes (nouns, verbs, adjectives, adverbs), and their regular inflections. Possibly spelling-sound relationships should be taught inductively, if needed, but such learnings in our language seem to relate more to spelling individual words than to reading. Mastering the reading process

[11] Carl Lefevre, "Language Patterns and Their Graphic Counterparts," *Changing Concepts of Reading Instruction* (International Reading Association Proceedings, 1961), pp. 245–49.

involves first of all an understanding of the relationships between the larger speech patterns and their printed counterparts; research, experimentation, and cooperation of all concerned will be required if we are to develop a methodology adequate to the task of raising reading skills to the necessary levels.

Phonemes, Morphemes, and Graphemes

While the writers quoted above would make use of the larger speech patterns in teaching reading, there are other linguists who would start beginning readers with the smaller units used in structural analysis. These units are defined below.

Phoneme—the most elemental speech sound in a particular language. Linguists vary in their opinion as to the number of phonemes in the English language, their counts ranging from 35 to 45. Some letters have more than one elemental sound, hence there are more phonemes than letters of the alphabet. On the other hand the letters *c, f, x* are not needed as other letters represent their elemental sounds.

Morpheme—the smallest unit with a relative meaning of its own, that is having a meaning when used in relation to other words to express time, place, or number relationships. The word *on* has no particular meaning in itself, but it does have a "place" meaning when used with other words in the sentence, "The book is on the shelf."

Word—the smallest linguistic unit that stands alone in conveying a meaning.

Grapheme—a letter symbol for a phoneme.

Applications

Phonemes are used as a basis for method and content in Bloomfield and Barnhart's book entitled *Let's Read: A Linguistic Approach.*[12] An example of the content of this book is given below:

had	can	cat	bag
lad	Dan	fat	nag
pad	man	hat	rag
sad	pan	rat	tag

Dan had a bat.
Has Ann a bag?
Ann had a bag.
Nat had a nag.
A fat cat had a rat.
A man had a hat.
Tab had a nap.

[12] Leonard Bloomfield and Clarence L. Barnhart, *Let's Read, A Linguistic Approach* (Detroit: Wayne State University Press, 1961), p. 2.

While recognizing the fact that phonemes are introduced scientifically in this book, many specialists in early childhood education, in reading, and in English question the advisability of using content for beginning reading which disregards children's interests, meanings, and language patterns, to the extent that is done in this book. Perhaps the greatest contribution of the book is that it is stimulating experimentation.

Goldberg and Rasmussen report that they passed through three stages in using the linguistic approach with first grade children:

1. an introductory period of formulating our point of view and searching for materials;
2. an experiment with the Bloomfield word list and materials we prepared in conjunction with it;
3. the current period during which we are developing our own word list and are continuing to prepare our own materials to be used with this list.

The conclusions of these experimenters are pertinent:

The teacher of beginning reading today cannot decide whether or not she wants to use a linguistic approach. The question now is—What is *your* linguistic approach and how do you balance the lingustic facts with the other scientific facts *you* put into *your* reading program.[13]

In concluding this section on the linguistic approach it might be said that applications of linguistic theory to reading are certainly evolving. However, major contributions in this respect have not yet been made. Linguists, reading specialists, and specialists in English need to share each others knowledge and experience. If such sharing could be done, operative frameworks might be developed which would be acceptable to all and, what is more important, which would contribute in a substantial way to reading improvement.

The Denver Approach

The public school system of Denver, Colorado, is experimenting with a new approach to the teaching of reading to preschool children and to kindergarten children.

In this approach parents are instructed how to work with their children through the use of a series of educational television programs. The parents are provided with a manual entitled *Preparing Your Child for Reading*. The manual contains suggestions for games in supplying missing words in oral sentences, in listening for similar letter sounds, and

13 Lyne Goldberg and Donald Rasmussen, "Linguistics Used to Teach Reading" presented in a paper at the Eleventh Annual Lehigh University Reading Conference, March 31, 1961; published in SRA *Insight*, Vol. 2 (Spring 1962), 14–16.

picture cards for use in matching activities, letter cards for use in teaching the alphabet, and phonic cards for teaching the sounds of letters. The television program gives further instruction and advice in the use of these materials. A Carnegie Corporation grant resulted in production of sixteen taped television programs for possible nation-wide distribution, revision of the manual, and further evaluation of the program.

A preliminary study was made in Denver during 1959–1960 concerning the effectiveness of teaching beginning reading in kindergartens. On the basis of this study Denver Public Schools received a grant from the U. S. Office of Education to continue with a five-year study.

The method used in preschool and kindergarten teaching was developed by Paul McKee and Lucile Harrison of Colorado State College. In brief this method involves giving the child practice in making use of spoken context, in distinguishing letter forms and teaching the names of letters, in listening for consonant sounds, in making letter sound associations, in using together spoken context and beginning consonant letter or letters in order to supply a word the teacher omits, in combining spoken context and the beginning consonant or blend to decide what a word says.

The Modern Montessori Approach

Maria Montessori was born in 1870 in Italy. She was graduated in medicine in 1894 after which she began to work with children of low intelligence. This work was so successful that she decided to try her methods in teaching normal children from three to five years old. Her experiments in *Casa dei Bambino* produced startling results and her system received world-wide recognition during the first quarter of the twentieth century. Interest in this method died out eventually, however, and was heard of no more until quite recently when it is being revived in a few schools. For a recent discussion of the Montessori method as applied in modern times see *Learning How to Learn, an American Approach to Montessori* by Nancy McCormick Rambusch, published by Helicon Press, Baltimore, 1962.

The Montessori Method makes use of a variety of teaching materials including blocks, beads, chains, rods of wood, and cubes which are used as a basis for giving children progressive experiences in solving problems.

Especially related to reading, the educational equipment includes a movable alphabet, sand paper letters to feel and trace, books—both trade books and readers. The teacher reads to the children a great deal, and oral language is used in placing a new word before the child for reading purposes. Short and largely individual lessons are given at appropriate moments in introducing children to new words and reading material.

It is said that through the use of this method children learn to read, write, count, and work simple sums before six years of age.

The Richards-Gibson Approach

This approach was devised by T. A. Richards and Christine M. Gibson, Language Research, Inc., Harvard University. It has been used widely in teaching English and reading to non-English speaking children and adults in foreign countries. More recently it is undergoing experimentation in some schools in which the English language is spoken. For a discussion of this method see *First Steps in Reading English* by T. A. Richards, published by Pocket Books, Inc., New York, 1962.

The basic material used in this method consists of a series of film strips. The film strips contain sentences accompanied by pictures; for example, the sentence "This is a Man" is accompanied with a stick figure picture of a man; the sentence "This is a hat" is accompanied with a line drawing of a hat.

The authors are primarily concerned that children may understand meanings. This they strive to achieve through the use of pictures and through special arrangements of sentences. All of the 500 words appearing in the material can be found in high-frequency word lists. These words are organized, however, in accordance with several controls: words are so arranged as to make it necessary for children to study how words work in context; words containing letters that make for ease of recognition are introduced first and words containing confusing letters are delayed; words are introduced in sentences in arrangements designed to promote visual and auditory discrimination in phonetic values, for example:

This is his head
This is his hand

The Delmar Experiment

An experiment in the use of the Richards-Gibson approach has been under way for some time in the Delmar Schools of Bethlehem School District, New York, under the supervision of Doris Flinton.

The Richards-Gibson film strips constitute the basic material being used in the Delmar schools. The films are supplemented, however, by mimeographed books in which a train of thought started by one of the films is furthered with social studies and science stories and arithmetic problems. Basal readers and trade books are also used for supplemental reading as soon as children gain sufficient control of the reading process to use them.

Here is an example of the way in which one first grade teacher taught a lesson. The film strip to be read contained these sentences: "This is a head. It is a man's head. A hat is on his head. Hair is on his head. Is his ear on his head?" the sentences were accompanied with illustrations of a man's head, a hat, hair, and an ear, respectively. Preceding the presentation of the film strip the children had made clay animals. At the beginning of this particular lesson, they brought their clay animals to the front of the room, told what they had made, and pointed out the various parts of the animal's body in each case, as *head, ear, hair, legs,* and so on. Following this activity they read the film strip. After reading each sentence and pointing out the picture of the word mentioned in the sentence, the children did a variety of seat work activities making use of the words in the film strips, including some writing of the words and the writing of one simple sentence.

In later grades children do a great deal of oral and written composition as extensions of topics presented in the film strips. They also read widely from other materials.

The experiment in Delmar has involved experimental and control groups. Test results have revealed that children in the experimental groups make gains in most items in standardized tests of reading, language power, composition, spelling and arithmetic.

The MacKinnon Experiment

Two experiments with the use of the Richards-Gibson approach were conducted by MacKinnon with school children in Edinburgh, Scotland, some of whom used the Richards-Gibson material and others of whom used a basal reader approach. For a complete account of these experiments see *How Do Children Learn to Read?* by A. R. MacKinnon, published by The Copp Clark Publishing Co., Limited, Toronto, Canada, 1959.

A modified form of the Richards-Gibson materials was used in these experiments. The use of film strips was not feasible in this experimental setting, so the content of the various film strips was transcribed on 15 by 11 inch, strong, nonglossy paper. The procedure used was in general the same as that used when children work with film strips themselves.

Data in regard to the experiments were gathered through record-taking activities made during classroom observations and through the administration of tests. The children using the Richards-Gibson material showed gains in reading as well as in several aspects of personal growth. The investigator found in the protocols taken while observing children that there were indications that suggest modifications of the material to make it still more effective. He stated, however, that the material would appear to warrant further investigation and he expressed belief that it might serve as a focal point in the reform of beginning reading instruction.

Individualized Instruction

Teaching reading by the individualized plan is a much discussed approach at the present time, and its use is being extended in many parts of the country. Because of the current interest in this method an entire chapter is devoted to it. See Chapter 7, "Individualized Instruction Receives Attention," pages 129–61.

The Basal Reader Approach

The approach most widely used throughout this country at the present time is the basal reader approach. Several different series of readers are in use, each of which provides reading textbooks, together with teachers' guides and supplemental materials, covering all levels from beginning reading through sixth grade and in many cases through eighth grade. Vocabulary is carefully controlled from book to book, and sequential and balanced skill development programs are provided. Authors are enriching and enhancing their programs in many desirable ways.

While basal readers have undergone many changes in recent years, no doubt they will undergo many more changes in the immediate years ahead. Some of these changes may be concerned with vocabulary enrichment, increased provisions for meeting individual needs, new types of content, and innovations in skill practice materials. The basal readers of the present, however, are being used successfully by thousands of teachers. Nevertheless, some teachers who are using this approach could use basal readers to a much greater advantage than they now are doing.

Misuses of Basal Readers

Some of the undesirable uses of basal readers are:

1. Considering the basal reader, itself, as the whole program for reading instruction.

2. Using one grade level of a basic reader with an entire class regardless of the different instructional levels of the children.

3. Setting up the goal of having children cover all pages in a certain reader as the end-point objective of a semester's work.

4. Insisting that children should not work with a reader higher than

the grade represented in their classroom so that the book for the next grade level may be fresh when he begins to work in that grade.

5. Permitting children to keep their basal reader in their desks or to take it home, thus providing them an opportunity to become familiar with stories before the teacher is ready to present them.

6. Using the teachers' guide as a detailed prescription to be followed exactly in all its aspects, or on the other hand disregarding it entirely.

7. Confining reading instruction largely to reading stories from the reader without a sufficient number of interspersed periods of skill development.

8. Failing to keep records of specific skills on which certain children need help, and providing extra practice on these skills over and above that provided for in the basic materials.

9. Using the basal reader for busy work in which the children are instructed to read from this book at their seats when they have nothing else to do.

10. Using workbooks indiscriminately with all children; failing to check workbook activities; failing to develop workbook pages with children who are not able to work independently with them without preceding explanations.

11. Simply directing children to read a story as a routine matter, without first building background and stimulating purpose.

12. Requiring purposeless re-reading.

13. Using the content of readers, which is mostly literature, as the sole basis for developing study skills needed in reading in the content areas.

Desirable Uses of Basal Readers

*Use by the Inexperienced Teacher in a
Group-Organized Classroom*

Until the beginning teacher becomes better acquainted with reading skills and techniques it is advisable for her to follow the sequence of the stories in the reader and to make careful use of the aids and instructions in the teachers' guide. It is hoped, however, that as she gains in experience she will become increasingly flexible in using the materials, more selective in choosing and following guide aids, more resourceful in creating supplemental practice materials and in providing interesting and productive practive activities of her own. From the very beginning she should, of course, extend her pupils' interests to many reading sources other than the basal reader and its accompanying materials.

Uses by the Experienced Teacher in a Group-Organized Classroom

The teacher who is highly proficient in the teaching of reading will refer to the teachers' guide as a reference for helpful suggestions as she may need them rather than slavishly following the manual page by page. She may upon occasion have children read certain stories out of order (if they are not too advanced in difficulty) as these stories carry with them possibilities for skill development needed by the children at the time. She will use numerous and varied materials and activities for skill development, many of which she personally has created and prepared. She will stimulate extensive reading from other books.

Uses by Teachers of Individualized Reading

Teachers using individualized procedures often use basal readers in such ways as these: (1) placing them on display along with tradebooks and permitting different children to select a preprimer or a story in a reader for his own individual reading if he so chooses, (2) using a certain story or section of a basal reader together with its accompanying supplemental material for development of or practice on a certain skill needed by an individual or small group, (3) using the teachers' guide for checking on skills to be developed and for examples of activities which she may prepare for use in her own skill development work.

Specific Suggestions

There are several ways in which the use of basal readers may be strengthened by some teachers, both experienced and inexperienced. Specific suggestions directed toward this end follow:

1. Request sets of readers of different levels appropriate for the reading levels of different groups in your classroom.

2. Use sets of books from different series, otherwise the slower children will hear the more advanced ones read the stories in the books at a higher level, and will already be familiar with the stories when they reach the point of working with these books.

3. Keep a record of the names of the basal readers each child reads during the year to pass on to the next teacher; also prepare a record of the instructional level of each child to pass on to the next teacher at the end of the year.

4. At the beginning of the school year refer to the records mentioned

above when procuring your basal readers from the school's stockroom and when organizing reading groups. If there are some children in your class who are new to the school or whose instructional level you question, give these children an informal test to ascertain their respective reading levels.

5. If a child or a group of children finish the reader at their grade level before a semester is over, have them use a somewhat more difficult reader at the same level from another series; or, if they are ready to read from a book at the next higher grade level in the same series, by all means let them do this. The teacher in the next grade should take pupils where they are and have them read from readers appropriate to their reading competency regardless of the label of the grade in which she is teaching.

6. Make a study of teachers' guides to ascertain the different skills to be developed, prepare a table or chart of these skills and have it duplicated, check the ones on which each pupil needs the most help, leaving space on the chart to indicate progress as it is made in each skill area.

7. If a new skill or skill element is seriously needed by several children, introduce it at the time that it is needed rather than waiting until they reach the point in the reader at which it is introduced.

8. While the children read a story from the reader for enjoyment, the chief function of having them read a story from your standpoint should be diagnosis—finding out on what skills they need practice.

9. Prepare for the reading of a new story by building informative background and pointing up a motive for reading the story as a whole. Clear the way for easy reading by clarifying new concepts and developing a few of the new words which promise to be troublesome.

10. Usually when working with children in first and second grades and often when working with slower children in more advanced grades, it is advisable to stop after they have read two or three pages or one episode and give practice on skill needs revealed while they were reading these few pages rather than waiting until they have finished reading the entire story before having skill practice.

11. Use workbooks as they are needed as a whole or in parts, the latter being more desirable. With slower children develop new workbook activities before leaving the children to work by themselves. By all means *check* the workbook results carefully after each use. Study these results to ascertain skill needs. Follow up with additional help for children whose workbook activities reveal special needs.

12. Usually have the silent reading of a part of the story done at the children's seats *following* the period in which development has been made, rather than using the seat work period as preparation for reading in class, in primary grades especially.

13. Avoid the routine "Round Robin" type of oral reading. Make the oral reading of the story interesting and enjoyable by continuously asking motivating questions and interjecting stimulating remarks as children read *out of order* in an informal, and in so far as possible, social group situation.

14. Set aside periods for extension of reading interest through such activities related to reading as painting, drawing, writing, illustrating with pictures cut from magazines, and so on. Such activities may be used to encourage children to read more carefully from their readers, and to read elsewhere for additional information. Their use is not recommended simply for purposeless "busy work" but rather for uses which contribute to genuine reading enrichment.

15. Use interesting incidents or subjects discussed in the reader as leads to further reading for research or pleasure purposes.

16. Have available a large supply of trade books dealing with different levels of difficulty. Encourage children to select books from this collection for their personal reading. Have them keep records of the books read. Check their self-selected reading by various informal methods.

Summary

Currently many different approaches to reading instruction are in use. The approaches discussed in this chapter are: the Augmented Roman Alphabet approach, the Language Experience approach, programmed instruction, the television approach, the film approach, the linguistics approach, the Denver approach, the modern Montessori approach, the Richards-Gibson approach, individualized instruction, and the basal reader approach.

Teachers are advised to keep themselves informed in regard to all of these approaches and to choose, if their school system permits, one of the approaches or aspects of several approaches which offer promise for use with the particular group of children under consideration. The hope was expressed that teachers would lend their support to continued research with these various approaches, and that they, themselves, would contribute to research efforts.

Additional Readings

The Augmented Roman Alphabet Approach

Downing, John, *Experiments with an Augmented Alphabet for Beginning Readers*. New York: Educational Records Bureau, 1962.

Downing, John, tꞷ bɛɛ *or not to be: the Augmented Roman Alphabet.* New York: Pitman Publishing Corp.

———, and W. K. Gardner, "New Experimental Evidence on the Role of the Unsystematic Spelling of English in Reading Failure," *Educational Research,* Vol. 5 (1962), 69–76.

Downing, J. A., The Augmented Roman Alphabet: *A New Two-Stage Method to Help Children Learn to Read.* London: University of London Institute of Education, 1961.

Pitman, I. J., "Learning to Read: an Experiment," *Journal of Royal Society of Arts,* Vol. 109 (1961), 149–80.

The Language Experience Approach

Allen, Van R., and Gladys C. Halversen, *The Language Experience Approach,* Ginn & Company Contributions to Reading, No. 21. Boston: Ginn & Company, 1961.

———, K. Boyd Lane, and James F. Halcomb, *Reading—The Language Experience Approach.* Sunland, California: Learning Through Seeing, Inc., 1962. (A moving picture mm bw sound: 18 minutes.)

———, and Doris May Lee, *Learning to Read through Experience.* New York: Appleton-Century-Crofts, Inc., 1963.

Description of Three Approaches to the Teaching of Reading. San Diego: San Diego County, Superintendent of Schools, 1962, 19–25.

Moving into Reading, San Diego: San Diego County, Superintendent of Schools, 1958.

The Programmed Approach

Automation and Education (Collection of articles reprinted from *Teachers College Record,* Vol. 62, No. 3. Dec. 1960). New York: Teachers College Columbia University.

Cram, David, "Explaining Teaching Machines and Programming." San Francisco: Fearon Publishers, 1961.

Davis, O. L., "Teaching Machines: New Educational Technology," *Education,* Vol. 83 (Oct. 1962), 98–101.

Dovey, Irma, "Can I Be a Teaching Machine?" *Elementary English,* Vol. 39 (Apr. 1962), 355–56.

Gates, Arthur I., "Teaching Machines in Perspective," *The Elementary School Journal,* Vol. 62 (Oct. 1961), 1–13.

Green, Edward J., *The Learning Process and Programmed Instruction.* New York: Holt, Rinehart & Winston, Inc., 1962.

Ikenberry, Nelda B., "Teaching Machines," *Elementary English,* XXXVIII (Oct. 1961), 395–97.

Lamade, Wanda, "The Teaching Machine and Its Function," *Education,* Vol. 83 (Nov. 1962), 158–62.

Lunsdane, A. A., and Robert Glaser. *Teaching Machines and Programmed*

Learning. Washington: Department of Audio-Visual Instruction, National Education Association, 1960.

Margulies, Stuart, and Lewis D. Eegen, *Applied Programmed Instruction*. New York: John Wiley and Sons, 1962.

"Mechanized Learning on Trial," *Childhood Education*, Vol. 39 (Dec. 1962), entire volume.

Schaefer, Frederic J., "Machine Teaching and the Psychology of Learning," *Elementary English*, Vol. 39 (Apr. 1962) 395–97.

Skinner, B. F., "Teaching Machines," *Science*, Vol. 128 (Oct. 1958), 969–77.

"The Teacher and the Machine," *Journal of Educational Research* (June, July 1962), entire volume.

The Television Approach

Carner, Richard L., "The Effect of Television of Reading Instruction on Attitudes toward Reading," *Elementary English*, Vol. 39 (Mar. 1962), 234–36.

———, "Considerations in Planning a Television Reading Program," *The Reading Teacher*, Vol. 16 (Nov. 1962), 73–76.

———, and William D. Sheldon, *Teaching Reading through Closed Circuit Television in the Elementary School*. Albany, N. Y.: State Department of Education, 1959.

Flierl, Nina, "Planning and Producing TV Programs in Reading," *The Reading Teacher*, II (Oct. 1957), 17–22.

Hunt, Lyman, "Teaching Reading by TV," *Education*, Vol. 8 (Oct. 1960), 118–20.

Murray, Walter I, and Karel Newman Rose, "Utilizing Television in Teaching Children's Literature," *Education*, Vol. 82 (Jan. 1962), 309–11.

Sheldon, William D., "Television and Reading Instruction," *Education*, Vol. 80 (May 1960), 552–55.

Smith, Nila Banton, "Television: A Challenging Frontier," *The Reading Teacher*, Vol. 11, No. 1 (Oct. 1957), 9–10.

The Film Approach

Allen, W. H., "Research on Film Use: Student Participation," *Audio-Visual Communication Review*, Vol. 5 (Spring 1957), 423–50.

Roshal, S. M., "The Instructional Film," USAF-NRC *Symposium on Education and Training Media*. Washington, D. C.: National Academy of Science-National Research Council, 1960.

Wagner, R. W., "The Teaching Film of Tomorrow," *Audio-Visual Communication Review*, Vol. 2 (Summer 1954), 216–19.

The Linguistics Approach

Allen, Harold B., ed., *Readings in Applied English Linguistics*. New York: Appleton-Century-Crofts, Inc., 1958.

Bloomfield, Leonard, "Linguistics and Reading," *Elementary English Review*, Vol. 19 (Apr., May, 1942), 125–30, 183–86.

Braddock, Richard, *Introductory Readings on the English Language*. Englewood Cliffs, N. J.: Prentice-Hall, Inc., 1962.

Fries, C. C., *Linguistics and Reading*. New York: Harcourt, Brace & World, Inc., 1963.

Lefevre, Carl A., "Language Patterns and their Graphic Counterparts: a Linguistic View of Reading," *Changing Concepts of Reading Instruction*, International Reading Association Conference Proceedings, Vol. 6, 245–49. New York: Scholastic Magazines, 1961.

McDavid, Raven I., Jr., "The Role of Linguistics in the Teaching of Reading," *Changing Concepts of Reading Instruction*, International Reading Association Conference Proceedings, Vol. 6, 253–51. New York: Scholastic Magazines, 1961.

Owen, George H., "Linguistics—An Overview," *Elementary English*, Vol. 39 (May 1962), 421–25.

Smith, Henry L., *Linguistic Science and the Teaching of English*, Inglis lecture series. Harvard University Press, Cambridge, 1956.

Soffietti, James P., "Why Children Fail to Read: A Linguistic Analysis," *Harvard Educational Review*, Vol. 25 (Spring 1955), 63–94.

Tabachnick B. Robert, "A Linguistic Looks at Reading: Leonard Bloomfield and the Phonemic Criterion," *Elementary English*, Vol. 39 (Oct. 1962), 545–49.

Tyler, Priscilla, "Sound, Pattern and Sense," *Changing Concepts of Reading Instruction*, International Reading Association Conference Proceedings, Vol. 6, 249–52. New York: Scholastic Magazines, 1961.

Veach, Jeannette, "Linguistics Instruction in the Teaching of Reading: Kill or Cure?" *Elementary English*, Vol. 39 (Mar. 1962), 231–33.

The Modern Montessori Approach

Burnett, Alice, "Montessori Education Today," *The Elementary School Journal*, Vol. 63 (Nov. 1962), 71–78.

"Joy of Learning, Whitby School," *Time*, Vol. 77 (May 12, 1961), 63.

Morris, Joe Alex, "Can Our Children Learn Faster?" *The Saturday Evening Post*, Vol. 234 (Sept. 23, 1961), 17–25.

Rambausch, Nancy McCormick, *Learning How to Learn*. Baltimore: Helicon Press, 1962.

——, "Montessori Reappraised," *Jubilee*, Vol. 7 (Apr. 1960), 42.

——, "Montessori Approach to Learning," *National Catholic Education Association, Bulletin*, Vol. 58 (Aug. 1961), 320–22.

Wallbank, P., "Montessori Now," *Times Educational Supplement*, No. 2184 (Mar. 29, 1957), 415.

The Richards-Gibson Approach

Everett, Richard M., Jr., *Comparison between Conventional Basic Reading*

Programs and the Language for Learning Program. New York: Washington Square Press, Inc. 1960.

Gibson, C. M., and I. A. Richards, *First Steps in Reading English.* New York: Pocket Books, Inc., 1957.

Richards, I. A., *How to Read a Page.* New York: W. W. Norton & Company, Inc., 1942.

——, *Basic English and Its Uses.* London: Routledge & Kegan Paul, Ltd., 1943.

MacKinnon, A. R., *How Do Children Learn to Read?* Toronto, Canada: The Copp Clark Publishing Co., Limited, 1959.

The Individualized Approach

See references at the end of Chapter 7, pages 129–61.

The Basal Reader Approach (Learning Series)

Alice and Jerry Basic Readers, rev., ed. Mabel O'Donnell, and others. New York: Harper & Row, Publishers.

Betts Basic Readers, 2nd ed., Emmett Betts and others. New York: American Book Co.

Developmental Reading Series, Guy L. Bond and others. Chicago: Lyons and Carnahan.

Ginn Basic Readers, David Russell and others. Boston: Ginn & Company.

Macmillan Readers, Arthur Gates and others. New York: The Macmillan Company.

New Basic Readers, Curriculum Foundation Series, William S. Gray and others. Chicago: Scott, Foresman & Company.

Reading for Interest Series, Paul Witty and others. Boston, D. C. Heath and Company.

Reading for Meaning Series, Paul McKee and others. Boston: Houghton Mifflin Co.

Sheldon Basic Readers, William D. Sheldon and others. Boston: Allyn and Bacon, Inc.

Winston Basic Readers, Russell G. Stauffer and others. New York: Holt, Rinehart and Winston, Inc.

6

Grouping Plans Take on New Forms

Mass instruction, ability grouping, chronological age grouping, IQ grouping, social preference grouping, personal interest grouping, skill needs grouping, multiple small unit grouping, individualized instruction—these and many other forms of classroom organization have been unrolled on the colorful panorama of classroom practices in American schools. Through it all the zealous quest of educational crusaders to find the *one* best form of classroom organization has been persistent and interminable. It may continue to be persistent; it surely will be interminable.

Literature dealing with research on grouping is voluminous, but results are conflicting. Research is still in the same state as that expressed by Cornell [1] many years ago when, after reviewing the numerous studies on grouping, she said, "A review of the objective results of grouping leaves one con-

[1] Ethel L. Cornell, *The Grouping of Pupils*, Thirty-Fifth Yearbook of the National Society for the Study of Education (Bloomington, Ill.: Public School Publishing Company, 1936), p. 290.

vinced that we have not yet attained any unequivocal experimental results that are capable of wide generalization."

Perhaps the chief reason why research on grouping is so inconclusive is because the real bases for grouping are too varied, too deep, and too numerous, to lend themselves to one set pattern. Individual differences in ability, rate of progress, and emotional, social, and motivational factors are too personal and unpredictable to adjust themselves to any one "formula" for organizing all children into the most productive working groups.

Proposed solutions to the grouping problem have been manifold. Dozens of plans have been introduced, only to bask in the educational limelight for a period of time and then like the Arabs, "to fold their tents and silently steal away." Reading achievement has always been, and still is, a prime consideration in these classification schemes. A child's success in reading can be strongly influenced by the classroom organization in which he lives and works. Therefore, readers of this book may find it worthwhile to review briefly some of the obsolete practices of the past and to study carefully some of the trends and arrangements of the present.

From Dame Schools to Grades

Dame schools, private tutors, schools established by religious auspices, and philanthropic societies educated a smattering of America's young in the 1600's and 1700's.

Then, in the 1800's, the Westward movement, industrialism, rapid transportation, the development of sparsely populated regions, the birth of new towns, and the mounting hordes of youth overran private and philanthropic educational facilities; public tax-supported schools were started, and mass instruction began.

At first the "Monitorial System" imported from England was hailed as the solution to the masses of youth swarming to the public schools. According to this plan, from seventy-five to three hundred pupils gathered in one room with one teacher. This larger group was divided into smaller groups, usually of nine, and each was taught by one of the abler pupils, called a "monitor."

In the 1840's rumblings came from Germany that children should be grouped in classes according to age and ability, a single teacher to a class. The idea was accepted in America, the graded system evolved, and children were taught in large groups by grades.

Thus, the lockstep developed in America.

Administrative Rearrangements Are Attempted

The years 1870 to 1910 were characterized by systematization and reorganization, new schemes of grading, new ways of classifying pupils, new promotion designs, new groupings in the classroom, and new plans for supervised study.

Each decade of this period was marked with new attempts at *administrative* rearrangement. The century of the *child* was late in dawning!

During these years, however, the complacency of educators was startled and threatened by a few strong voices vigorously protesting regimentation. Some novel plans were suggested and tried out. Some of these are described below.

Harris,[2] Commissioner of United States Education, cried out against the "Procrustean bed-of-grades." He recommended more frequent promotions. His plan divided the school year into four quarters of ten weeks each, with possible promotions at the end of each ten weeks and great flexibility in moving children from one group to another at any time.

The *Cambridge Double-Track Plan*, established in 1893, provided for two parallel courses, a regular one and one in which bright children could finish in four instead of six years.

The *Pueblo Colorado Plan* was introduced in 1888. In this plan the regular classroom organization was maintained, but group recitations were replaced with study and individual activities accompanied with help and guidance from the teacher as needed.

The *Batavia, New York, Plan* was initiated in 1898. The regular classroom organization was maintained in this plan also, but adjustments were made by providing two or more teachers for each class, one to do the regular teaching, and the other or others to supervise study periods and to give one or more hours of individual assistance to slow learners.

The *Platoon System*, introduced in 1900, embodied a departmentalized plan in which pupils studied reading and the other fundamentals in a home room, but went to other rooms and teachers, respectively, for art, music, science, library, gymnasium, shop, and so on.

These and several other plans were developed during this period as educators groped toward better types of classroom organization.

Standardized Tests Take Control

After 1910, new slogans were heard in educational forums, and new ideas were suggested on the basis of scientific findings.

2 W. T. Harris, "The Early Withdrawal of Pupils from School: Its Causes and Its Remedies," *Addresses and Proceedings of the National Education Association for the Year 1872* (Washington, D. C.: National Education Association, 1873), p. 266.

Tests of intelligence and achievement were developed; surveys were made in the schools; frequency distributions, means, correlations, standard deviations, and other statistical techniques were developed and employed.

The result: An etching of individual differences in bold relief on the tapestry of the educational scene; startling and indisputable evidence of extremely wide differences in intelligence and achievement within any one grade. These findings led to a great spurt of interest in individual differences and stimulation of new departures in class organization based on intelligence or achievement scores. Some of these are mentioned below.

XYZ Grouping

Homogeneous grouping on the basis of intelligence was introduced at this time. In 1920, Dr. Charles S. Berry [3] divided ten thousand children entering first grade in the Detroit school system into three groups on the basis of a group intelligence test. The average children, who represented sixty per cent of the pupils in any one grade, were labled the Y Group; the superior twenty per cent constituted the X Group; and the inferior twenty per cent, the Z Group. Differentiated curricula were provided each group in terms of ability. The plan was widely adopted throughout the country, but at the present time, it has been largely abandoned. There are two criticisms that are most frequently leveled against this method of grouping. Many educators think it is undesirable from social and psychological standpoints to keep all children of a certain intellectual level together in one group throughout their school years. Furthermore, it was found that there was much overlapping in achievement; that is, there were X's who did no better than some of the Y's and Z's and there were Y's and Z's who did as well or better than some of the X's.

Individual Progression Plans

Various plans for permitting each individual in a classroom to progress at his own rate sprang up close on the heels of the disclosure of wide individual differences in achievement as revealed by the new tests. The Winnetka Plan and the Dalton Plan were those most widely recognized for organizing classrooms to permit individual instruction. These plans will be discussed in Chapter 7.

[3] Charles S. Berry, "The Introduction of Homogeneous Grouping," *The Grouping of Pupils,* Thirty-Fifth Yearbook, Part I (Bloomington, Ill.: National Society for the Study of Education, 1936), pp. 37–38.

The Three-Group Plan

Several other plans were advocated but the one most frequently used throughout these years and up to the present time is the three-group plan in the primary grades and either the three-group or two-group plan in the upper grades. According to this plan, groups are organized on the basis of achievement, particularly achievement in reading. In larger schools, the highest achievers of a certain grade are placed in one classroom, the average achievers in another, and the lower achievers in another. In small schools all children of a certain grade are placed in one classroom. The teacher then usually divides her entire class into three groups: the fast-moving group, the average group and the slow group. The three-group organization often is used in all classrooms regardless of whether a teacher has a homongeneous or heterogeneous group in one grade. In fact the three-group organization within classrooms has stood as a bulwark in American schools for many years. Recent innovations, however, are beginning to gnaw at its foundation and weaken its structure.

One of the arguments advanced against this type of grouping is that there is wide variation in achievement, rate of progress, and motivational drives among the pupils in any one of these three groups and that individual needs cannot be met to the best advantage by simply labeling three groups as high, average, or low. Another argument leveled against this plan is that it is undesirable from the psychological and social point of view. Those in the average group seem to feel that they are doing as well as ordinarily can be expected. Those in the higher group, however, seem to feel that they are there because they are smarter than the others, and many of those in the lower group believe they are there because they are stupid. Mann's [4] recent study of children's own reasons as to why they were in a certain group revealed such self-pictures as these: "I happen to be smarter than the rest"; "I'm smart"; "We're smarter"; "I am in the low fift grade. I am to dom"; "I'm too dumb"; "We don't know very much."

It is not good for those in the high section to feel that they are superior to most of the other children in their classroom. As for the low group, the negative self-concept which children in this classification possess certainly does not contribute to a feeling of personal worth nor is it conducive to the development of aspiration, motive, drive—all of which are essential in reading achievement.

[4] Maxine Mann, "What Does Ability Grouping Do to the Self-Concept?" *Childhood Education*, Vol. 36, No. 8 (Apr. 1960).

Attempts have been made to conceal from children the ability level at which they are working by labeling the groups respectively with such names as "Bluebirds," "Cardinals," and "Robins," or "Brownies," "Elves," and "Pixies." This pseudo-nomenclature simply does not serve its purpose. Children know whether they are in the high, average, or low group, regardless of the name used for each classification.

The above point is neatly illustrated in an incident related to the author. Miss White, a visitor at a certain school, went out on the playground at recess time to chat directly with the children about their work. Walking up to Tommy, she asked, "What grade are you in?" "The second grade," replied Tommy. Then he added, "I'm with the 'Busy Bees.'" "What are the 'Busy Bees'?" asked Miss White. "They are the low group. We don't know anything in that group," replied Tommy. "Did your teacher tell you that the 'Busy Bees' are in the low group?" asked Miss White in shocked amazement. "Oh, no," explained Tommy, "She doesn't want to hurt our feelings." "Why don't you tell her that you know that you are in the low group?" persisted Miss White. "We don't want to hurt *her* feelings," was the surprising answer.

Fresh Viewpoints and New Patterns

The newer psychologies, philosophies, and continuing streams of scientific data concerning reading and child development combine to give us new outlooks and deeper insights into grouping practices.

New concepts of grouping embrace keen recognition of individual differences, not only in reading but also in other aspects of child development. They respect the fact that ability in reading varies widely in any one grade. There may be two or three children in third grade who are reading at primer level, some others at second grade level, many others at third grade level, a few at fourth, fifth, or sixth grade levels. Perhaps the outstanding characteristic of new grouping concepts, however, is that they recognize that children vary not only in reading ability but in intellectual capacity, rate of growth, motivational drive, experience, interests, social maturity, and social predilections. The most effective grouping plan gives consideration to all these factors. Reading is a part of total child growth and a classroom organized to respect and utilize all growth factors holds out more promise for each child's success than a classroom which uses only one factor as the basis of its organizational plan.

As an outgrowth of changed viewpoints concerning child development, several new grouping plans are being evolved. A few of these plans will be described briefly with special applications to reading instruction.

Flexibility in the One-Grade Classroom

It is not easy for a school system to depart from the conventional grade organization. It often takes time for grouping plans to change. In the meantime many teachers are making good headway in improving grouping arrangements within the one-grade classrooms in which they work. The guiding assumption underlying their changes is that their classroom organization must be flexible, moving, ever changing; therefore, they are continuously creating and disbanding groups for different purposes. There may be just one group at times that embraces all children in the classroom. At other times there may be groups of two or three, of nine or ten. No group remains permanent and fixed. Groups are ever changing in personnel in accordance with varying individual needs and interests. Moreover, each child is considered to be a unique personality, even though he is placed in a given group by the school.

The teacher has a major role in this plan. At the beginning of the school year a group, usually consisting of twenty-five to thirty, is assigned to a certain teacher and a certain classroom where the children are to work together for a year. The assigning is done by an understanding administrator who takes into consideration the general needs of the group as a whole. It is the teacher, however, who through her daily living with these children, develops a sensitivity to the needs, interests, and potential growth possibilities of each one, individually. Only she can organize, disband, and reorganize groups daily, weekly, and monthly to insure the continuous, well-rounded growth of each child.

Working with the Entire Class

Occasionally, the entire class may become a reading group. All the children in the room may meet with the teacher while preparing and reading plans for an excursion; questions in connection with a center of interest, for slides or a movie, and so on. There will also be sharing occasions in which all the children will participate: when they share the stories in books they are reading independently; when one child reads to the entire group something of interest that he has found; when one group enacts a dramatization of a story; when one group has done research reading and shares its findings with the entire class. In addition to motivating reading, such total-group situations develop a sense of togetherness, of social give and take, of being a worthy member of a larger whole.

Skill Grouping

There may be one, two, or even more groups with whom the teacher works rather consistently in skill development, probably with basic readers. However, as skill groups are continuously formed, as new skill needs are revealed, these groups will not always be intact. For example, maybe fifteen children need help in using the dictionary, and these children work with the teacher in a group while the rest of the children who don't need such help do something else. Perhaps five of the children in the entire class have difficulty in pronouncing words in which the sound of *a* is influenced by *r*. These children have one or more practice periods devoted to this need. Possibly ten minutes now and then will be devoted to one child alone to give him the special boost he needs to overcome his particular difficulty.

Skills are not neglected in this type of organization. As much and perhaps more attention is given to skill development than in the conventional program. The difference is that skill development and practice take place with smaller groups in terms of their personal needs rather than being given to all children in larger, set groups whether or not they are in need of the particular skill elements being emphasized. The teacher must be very skill conscious, however, and she must be sure that she is distributing her skill time to the best advantage.

Interest Grouping

At times reading groups are formed on the basis of mutuality of interests.

Tom, Mary, Susan, and Guy, a group of children from Miss Gray's third grade room, were strolling along together on their way to school on a bright sunny morning when Guy spied a "shining stone." Small particles in this rock glistened in the sunlight. The other children gathered around to examine the find. "Did it have gold in it?" "Maybe the glistening parts were diamonds." Thus they speculated, and interest was still high at the opening of the morning session. The children wanted to identify the composition of the stone. Miss Gray said that they might sit in one corner of the room which she designated and work on their problem. Incidentally, it might be added that as the children worked with this problem they extended their interest to rocks in general.

115

Tom, who could read at sixth grade level, procured two juvenile encyclopedias from the library. Mary, who was reading at eighth grade level, brought back two adult encyclopedias from the library. Susan, who was at third grade level, surrounded herself with all of the different science textbooks in the room. Guy, who read at first grade level, couldn't read well enough to get anything out of any of the books mentioned above. However, because he had the same interest that the other three children were experiencing, Miss Gray obtained a trade book on rocks from the librarian for him. He couldn't read the information given in this book, but it contained attractive colored pictures, usually accompanied with simple captions, and Miss Gray helped him with these. Guy spent a long time "studying" this book, after which he told Miss Gray what information he had gathered. She helped him to write his "notes," which he read to the other three children and again when the group made a report to the class.

Reading in an interest group such as this is valuable as a learning situation because of the motivation involved. Meeting the needs of children in the group who are at different reading levels often taxes the time and resources of the teacher. Many, however, feel that it is worthwhile.

Social Grouping

The above example illustrates grouping in terms of interest. There are also many occasions in which children may be grouped on the basis of social choice, those children being permitted to work together who want to be together or who want to work with a certain leader. This type of organization best lends itself to such activities as finding a suitable story to dramatize or pantomime, to use in a puppet show or mock radio or television program, or to tell or read during a story hour. It is also especially adapted to research reading in which a group decides to take charge of one aspect of a construction project, such as making the moat and drawbridge in a model of a feudal castle or preparing the miniature trees to be used in a diorama of a South American jungle.

As small groups are organized on the basis of self-selection of working companions, there may be two excellent readers and two poor readers in the same group. The good readers will probably read independently, but at the same time standing ready to give individualized help to the poor readers—and all will proceed happily because of group compatibility.

It takes a good teacher and an experienced teacher to do a highly successful job with the ever-changing, multiple-grouping plan described above. All teachers, however, new or experienced can begin gradually to loosen up their classroom organization in some of the ways mentioned. As their skill develops they will find increasing opportunities to create, reorganize, and disband groups according to individual capacities, needs, interests, and social choices.

The Ungraded School

On a July day in 1935, Dr. Robert Hill Lane [5] tossed an educational bomb into the midst of a group of listeners in Denver during the Annual Convention of the National Education Association. Dr. Lane, district principal in the public schools of Los Angeles, proposed to establish a school unit which he called the "Junior School." In this unit there would be no grades, and children would be classified as Group One, Group Two, Group Three, and so on. Reading would be the major problem attacked; a child would be "passed" only once and that would be when he made the transition to the "Upper School." Some children would be in the Junior School three years, others four years, or two years, or whatever period of time it was necessary for him to achieve such ability as would enable him to go into the "Upper School to join children for whom reading is no longer a serious problem."

Shortly after his proposal, Dr. Lane tried out his plan for an ungraded primary school with success in some of the Los Angeles Public Schools. Several years elapsed before the idea took hold elsewhere, but more recently several public school systems have adopted the plan and extended it to include the intermediate grades as well as the primary grades.

Goodlad et al. [6] offer the following advice to others who would like to start this type of organization:

1. Develop undertanding first. A year or more of study by parents and teachers before any specific change is made will pay rich dividends. Both groups need to understand the wide range of abilities and attainments represented in a first grade class. Normally, under good teaching the spread increases instead of decreases as children advance. Teachers and parents must come to undertand the barriers placed in the way of normal, continuous progress by the grade concept and its concomitants. They need to understand, too, what the removal of grades will and will not do.

[5] Robert Hill Lane, "The Junior School—Its Plan and Purpose," *Addresses and Proceedings of the National Education Association* (Washington, D. C.: National Education Association, 1935), pp. 381–82.
[6] Reprinted from John I. Goodlad, Fred E. Brooks, Irene M. Larson, and Neal Neff, "Reading Levels Replace Grades in the Non-Graded Plan," *The Elementary School Journal*, LXII (Feb. 1957), by permission of The University of Chicago Press. Copyright 1957 by The University of Chicago Press.

2. Move toward nongrading a step at a time. Teachers may first be helped to divorce themselves from their grade stereotypes by moving along with their pupils into the next grade before ungraded units actually are established. In this way the teachers come to understand more readily the tremendous grade-to-grade overlap of abilities and attainments. There seems to be some advantage, also, in removing the grade barriers a year at a time as a first-year entering group begins to advance through the school. In a relatively short time—six to eight years—only transfer pupils will know what it is to deal with grades and the accompanying externally imposed pressures.

3. Try to see an actual model early in the planning. Some persons must see to really believe and understand. If the model is common to the experience of all, it provides a discussion base from which local plans may evolve more readily.

4. Once the step has been taken, go all the way. Removing grades in name only is not enough. Grade signs must be removed from doors and replaced with "Primary—Miss Smith," "Intermediate—Miss Brown." Progress must never be thought of in terms of "promotion and nonpromotion" or "skipping and repeating." The considerations implied by these terms simply do not exist; they have no part in nongrading. This is difficult for some parents and teachers to understand—*very difficult!* Concepts of individuality, heterogeneity, continuous progress with each child moving at the rate that is best for him, must be hammered away at continuously!

5. Rigorous record-keeping and careful, periodic testing are essential. *Continuous* progress does not mean *haphazard* progress. Those persons in charge have a tremendous responsibility for assuring that each child is placed where he can profit most, where his progress in all aspects of development is optimum. Without careful observation, without periodic tests, without occasional shifting—group to group and class to class—children will be misplaced.

6. Stick to the instructional methods previously assumed to be sound. If the removal of grades suggests new and more appropriate methods, so much the better. But nongrading is an organizational, not an instructional, device.

7. Experiment. Determine what happens when children are moved through a four-year primary unit beginning with kindergarten in three rather than four years. Determine the effects of remaining in such a unit for five rather than for four years. Seek to isolate the most significant factors determining satisfactory pupil placement. Find out what areas of instruction can be taken care of best through completely individualized methods, through small groups, and through total group techniques. Nongrading in itself is little more than door-opening. With the door open, look beyond to see what comes next in finding what we need to know and doing what we know to do.

As a result of using the ungraded primary plan in Milwaukee, Kelly [7] arrives at this conclusion:

When children enter Grade IV from the ungraded primary plan, the distri-

[7] Reprinted from Florence Kelly, "New Patterns of Grouping for Reading Instruction in Kindergarten Through Grade Three," *Reading Instruction in Various Patterns of Grouping*. Supplementary Educational Monographs, No. 89 by permission of The University of Chicago Press. Copyright 1959 by The University of Chicago Press.

bution of their achievement is no wider than under the traditional plan; but reading and other limits are more clearly defined, and children's problems seem more definite. Although the pupils are often younger, they have a firm foundation for the reading program of the middle grades.

The ungraded school is highly desirable in relieving tensions aggravated by semester or yearly promotions and permitting each child to progress through the period of learning to read at his own learning rate. The chief drawback to the ungraded school is that it is difficult to administer. Several schools, however, have been able to meet the administrative problems involved.

Multiplegrade and Intergrade Grouping Plans

Multiplegrade Plan

The multigrade plan was first used in Torrance, California. It is now used in that city and in several other places.[8]

This organization groups children for a given classroom into either a primary multigrade group composed of an equal number of randomly selected children from first, second, and third grades, or an intermediate multigrade group composed of an equal number of randomly selected children from fourth, fifth, and sixth grades. The basic philosophy underlying the plan is that of recognizing children's differences rather than their similarities. The purpose is not to permit a high-achiever to pass through the school more rapidly, but rather to permit children of different ages and abilities to live together in classrooms where subgroups can be formed according to needs rather than in terms of grade levels, and in which children representing these differences may mingle and work together socially.

Each group stays with the same teacher until some of the children pass on to fourth or seventh grades, respectively; thus each teacher has two-thirds of her class remaining with her each year. During the three-year period each child has an opportunity to associate with children both older and younger than he is.

For administrative purposes, record keeping makes use of grade designations. Within the group, however, no attempt is made to classify children by grade levels. Children from the three grade levels are grouped together in subgroups according to their needs. The children in an arith-

---

[8] Walter Rehwoldt and Warren W. Hamilton, "An Analysis of Some Effects of Interage and Intergrade Grouping in an Elementary School," Doctoral Dissertation, University of Southern California, January 1957.

metic subgroup may not be at all the same children in a reading subgroup. Usually each subgroup contains children from all three grade levels, always from at least two grade levels. Teachers report that there is not as much diversity in ability levels within the three grade levels as they had expected. Often the ability levels fall into concentrated groups which makes grouping in terms of needs easier.

Parents are usually pleased with the plan. Teachers find it somewhat difficult during the first year that they try it, but adjust to it with approval after the first year.

According to this plan children have opportunities to learn from each other. It is reported that they tend to mature more rapidly because the younger ones follow the example of the older ones and the older ones seem to take on more responsibilities.

Tests have been given to the multigrade groups and their results compared with results in conventionally organized classrooms. Gains are revealed for the multigrade groups in regard to achievement in reading, arithmetic, and language, and in personal adjustment, social adjustment, social maturity, and in certain behavior characteristics.

Intergrade Plan

A plan somewhat similar to the multigrade plan is under experimentation in the William M. Stewart School at the University of Utah. This plan involves fifth and sixth graders only as they are deliberately mixed in the same classroom groups. The children remain with the same teacher for two years. Curricular areas are planned in two-year blocks. Children are taught in group units rather than in separate grades.[9]

The basic assumption back of this plan is that in providing greater flexibility in grouping, intellectual achievement and improved socialization will be facilitated; and also that undesirable conflicts can be avoided, thus releasing children to give more attention to their learning tasks, and resulting in increased learning.

In working with the groups, desirable friendship patterns and leadership and followship roles are encouraged; child-to-child and child-to-teacher conflicts are avoided by replacement in other groups. The plan tends to minimize undue fear and lack of self-confidence and the dangers of over-expectations of teachers, parents, and peer groups.

[9] George L. Miller, Jack A. McDonald, and Don A. Knight, "Interage Grouping: In the Upper Elementary School," *Toward Effective Grouping* (Washington, D. C.: Association for Childhood Education, 1962), pp. 50–53.

Teachers, parents, and pupils all like the plan. Achievement is high as measured by standardized tests.

Reading by Invitation

Two types of this organization have been reported, and each will be described briefly.

Invitation in an Assigned Three-Group Pattern

Rittenhouse reports an experiment carried on in Akron, Ohio, based on a flexible three-group pattern of fast, average, and immature readers which functioned partly as an attracting nucleus. She felt teachers would feel more secure in their initial work with the "Invitation" plan if they began with children assigned to one of three groups. It was made plain to the children, however, that they would be *invited* to be visitors to activities of other groups and that they might come to or leave at will all reading classes except the one to which they were assigned.

Rittenhouse [10] reports as follows about the visiting participation:

Children in the average group did the least amount of visiting. They seemed to need the security of their own group. Those in the average group who visited had the potentiality to move ahead.

Children on the immature level visited in large numbers during the first few weeks of the experiment. They eventually eliminated themselves because of insight into their own inadequacies. Again, those who were on the borderline in the immature group visited with the group on the succeeding level to advance. Many on the immature level found satisfaction in visiting momentarily with other reading groups. The freedom to come and go at will provided them with a feeling of acceptance which was vital to their social and emotional adjustment. This minute contact with children in upper levels was a type of satisfaction in that immature children were able to join those in other levels in all phases of the curriculum.

She [11] has this to say about the value of the plan:

Reading by invitation presents an aspect in the teaching of reading that accentuates free movement for the child to participate with the group that best meets his needs.

The child who possesses a love for reading can find satisfaction in visiting with all reading groups even if all groups are reading from the same basic series. It is more stimulating for visitors, however, if each group has access to a different series.

[10] Gloria G. Rittenhouse, "An Experiment in Reading by Invitation in Grades One Through Four," *The Reading Teacher,* Vol. 13, No. 4 (Apr. 1960).
[11] *Ibid.*

Those who have been absent are able to readjust easily in visiting with all groups. Although individual help can be given either by the teacher or a pupil-helper, individual and group instruction is as much a part of reading by invitation as it is in other methods of instruction.

The consensus of opinion of the experimenting teachers was that the most significant contribution of reading by invitation was in the children's ability to recognize both their weak and strong areas. Reading by invitation also offers the child further opportunity to assert himself in obtaining optimum growth at his level. It provides a wealth of experience in reading for all children.

Invitation in an Unassigned Group Pattern

Hester advocates an organization of reading by invitation in which the children are not assigned to a fixed group of a certain level. This plan is also described by Rittenhouse [12] as follows:

In Dr. Hester's program of reading by invitation children formulate their own reading groups as their needs indicate. According to Dr. Hester's pure form of reading by invitation, the children are told during the pupil-teacher planning period that they may join any or several of the reading groups. The children are not assigned to any particular reading group, but must be adequately motivated by the ingenious teacher to visit with one or all of the three reading groups. A child can be invited to join a group either by the teacher or by another child. Centers of interest are provided for the children who are engaged in other activities and for those who are too immature for a directed lesson. Once a week a sweep-check vocabulary test is given, and each child may tell a story he has read, or he may read a story from the blackboard which shows the new words introduced during the week.

Dr. Hester [13] says of this plan:

This plan of grouping makes it possible for boys and girls to have a common experience and at the same time to participate in reading activities suited to their different and varying needs. The flexible grouping procedure avoids the stigma accompanying segregation and has many outstanding advantages.

Team Teaching

Team teaching, mentioned in Chapter 2, connotes new arrangements in classroom organization, these arrangements changing with different teams and different groups of children.

In the interest of concrete illustration, one example of classroom organization under a team-teaching plan will be presented. Bahner [14] describes a program carried out by a team composed of a female teacher

12 *Ibid.*

13 Kathleen B. Hester, "Grouping by Invitation," *The Reading Teacher,* Vol. 11, No. 2 (Dec. 1957).

14 Reprinted by permission of the Association for Childhood Education International, 3615 Wisconsin Avenue, N.W., Washington 16, D.C. "Grouping Within a School," by John M. Bahner. From *Childhood Education,* Apr. 1960, Vol. 36, No. 8.

having a third-fourth grade combination and a male teacher having a fourth-fifth grade combination:

The typical day for this team began with a fifteen- or twenty-minute planning period during which each group discussed with its teacher the day's general plan and individual work. Reading groups then occupied the next hour and one-half. Each teacher had from two to four groups (this varied as the need arose throughout the year) composed of children with similar reading achievement levels from both rooms regardless of their grade placement.

Next came a short break for the morning fruit juice, followed by the physical education period when the two classes combined. The teachers planned this period together. Then one assumed responsibility for the total group while the other took a break, collected materials, evaluated the work of pupils, or performed other needed tasks. After the physical education period, these sixty-five children remained together for a story period, music, or art. The teacher who had the preceding half-hour away from the class assumed full responsibility now, while the other teacher had an unscheduled period of approximately twenty minutes.

From this point until lunch, the sixty-five children were divided into four arithmetic groups on the basis of achievement—again without regard to their grade placement. Each teacher worked with two groups.

The program after lunch varied considerably. Often there was some type of project going on, with the two classes sometimes combined and sometimes working separately. Special interests and abilities of the two teachers often determined just how the two classes operated. For example, both classes worked together on an electricity unit with the man assuming the major responsibility for planning the lesson, gathering the materials, and doing the group instruction. The woman member of the team performed as an aide during this project, helping individuals and small groups. Later on, the teachers reversed their roles while undertaking a unit on space.

Although sometimes taught as separate entities, social studies, science, music, and art were integrated during the afternoon period. Of course, individual work going on during reading groups was often based on the units or projects then in progress.

Raabe [15] evaluated an experiment in which four teachers worked as a team with one hundred and thirty-nine intermediate grade children as follows:

We have found the team approach to organizing for reading instruction to be very rewarding. The teachers were enthusiastic, as were the children and their parents. According to standardized tests, learning was greatly facilitated. For example, the average gain in reading made during the first semester was eight months or nearly one full school year. During the entire year, the average

[15] Reprinted from Billy H. Raabe, "In Grades Four Through Six," *Reading Instruction in Various Patterns of Grouping*. Supplemental Educational Monographs, No. 89, by permission of The University of Chicago Press. Copyright 1959 by The University of Chicago Press.

gains were approximately two grades. It is interesting to note that the greatest gains were made by the most and least able groups.

Pupil Team Grouping

Several schools are now using the plan of having children work together in groups or teams of two to seven, with a pupil leader or teacher. This plan has been the subject of considerable experimentation by Durrell who recommends three or five pupils as being the best sizes for groups.

Durrell [16] explains the way in which the pupil team organization may function as follows:

. . . At this level most of the superior readers have had considerable experience as teachers in "playing school." These teachers may replace the regular teacher in giving extra practice in many stages of reading readiness, such as letter matching and letter names. They may lead in various kinds of "games" in word recognition and word analysis and may help in oral-reading practice.

The teacher will need to observe the work of the pupil teachers and provide counsel and assistance at points of difficulty, but most pupil teachers will prove very helpful. Groups may be asked to choose a pupil teacher. Generally it is better if all of the eligible pupil teachers are given the opportunity to teach a group; so the "available" list of pupil teachers should be somewhat flexible. This small-group work should be "extra practice" and should not replace the regular contact between teacher and pupil in small-group instruction.

Pupil teachers of superior reading ability may be used in intermediate grades if the teacher is skilled in making such work acceptable. They may serve as consultants to help a group of slower pupils with difficult words encountered in silent reading. When assigned materials are much too difficult for a very slow group, the pupil teacher may present the lesson orally and explain unfamiliar words or passages. They may direct word-analysis practice or dictate spelling words to small groups. Or they may serve as "secretaries" or recorders in group study activities.

The pupil teacher is more effective in following routine activities and providing skills practice. The development of meanings and concepts is better done by the classroom teacher, although some pupil teachers will be highly effective in explaining particular meanings of words or sentences. Generally the pupil teacher will need prepared materials, such as lists of questions, lists of words, charts, flash cards, and other devices selected by the teacher. When a child or group of children is aware of the need for extra instruction, and when that instruction is helpful in attaining higher achievement, a pupil teacher is always acceptable. However, if the extra practice seems pointless or comes as a penalty, the pupil teacher will have trouble.

McHugh [17] made a study of reading results obtained in the use of this

[16] Donald D. Durrell, *Improving Reading Instruction* (New York: Harcourt, Brace & World, Inc., 1956).

[17] Walter J. McHugh, "Team Learning in Skill Subjects in Intermediate Grades," *Journal of Education*, Vol. 142 (Dec. 1959), 22–51.

form of grouping with a fourth, fifth, and sixth grade, respectively, for a year. In his particular situation, the plan showed superior results in the sixth grade but not in the fourth and fifth grades.

The plan has the advantage of allowing a maximum of pupil participation. The most frequently heard criticism is that having one pupil teach other pupils is not desirable from the social and psychological standpoint.

The Cross-Grade Plan

In a popular magazine of the late 1950's there appeared an article entitled "Johnny *Can* Read in Joplin." The article was written by Cecil Floyd, an elementary principal in the Joplin, Missouri, public school system. Although this cross-grade plan had been tried previously, it was first heard of by many people through reports of its use in Joplin and so is called "The Joplin Plan."

One school which uses the plan and approves it highly jestingly calls it their "Ring and Run Plan." This colorful appelation gives some idea of what takes place, but of course does not explain the real educational implications of the scheme. The plan, in essence, is for children in an elementary school who are at the same level in reading to go to one teacher who will teach all of them at the appropriate level. As an example, let us say that there are five children in the second grade who are reading at first semester, third grade level; nine children in third grade who are reading at this level; three in the fourth grade, two in the fifth grade, and one in the sixth grade reading at this level. At a given hour in the day and at a given signal, usually a bell, all these children would leave their regular classrooms and go to a room in which a teacher would teach reading to all of them at first semester, third grade level. Similarly, all elementary children would change rooms at this time to join others who are reading at the same level.

A preliminary study carried on by Floyd[18] in the Joplin schools indicated favorable results. A study conducted by Williams[19] of a version of the plan that had been used in the Chicago area did not reveal such spectacular results. Ramsey[20] investigated the use of the plan in the Logansport, Indiana, public schools involving fourth, fifth, and sixth grades. He concluded that it appeared to be effective in producing expected reading gains at all three levels.

[18] Cecil Floyd, "Meeting Children's Reading Needs in the Intermediate Grades: A Preliminary Report," *Elementary School Journal,* Vol. 55 (Oct. 1954), 99–103.
[19] Pauline L. Williams, "Some Group Reading Results," *Chicago School Journal,* Vol. 31 (1949), 90–94.
[20] Wallace Ramsey, "An Evaluation of a Joplin Plan of Grouping for Reading Instruction," *The Journal of Educational Research,* Vol. 55 (Aug. 1962), 567–72.

Those who are using the plan believe that it is effective in reducing retardation and that it saves time and effort for both teachers and pupils. Others feel that from the social and psychological viewpoints it is undesirable to have older children working with younger children in the same reading class. Still others believe that developmental reading should not be detached from the interests and activities of the regular classroom.

Conclusion

In concluding this chapter it is appropriate to mention a study reported by Ramsey.[21] This investigator conducted an experiment in which three matched groups of children were taught by three teachers who also were matched in ability. The classes were organized differently—one on the three-group plan, one on the individualized plan, and one on the Joplin plan. The reading results obtained by the children were about the same for all three groups and Ramsey concluded that the influence of the teacher was the most important factor. "The thought that this study indicates most clearly is that the influence of the teacher is greater than that of a particular method or special plan of organization. Given a good teacher other factors in teaching reading tend to pale to insignificance," he said.

No doubt the competence of the teacher and the way in which she relates to her pupils are vital factors. It is most important that teachers assist children to grow in terms of their individual capacities, helping them to live with themselves, to realize their strengths and weaknesses—not being overwhelmed with the latter but ever striving to improve them. Maintaining faith in the child and creating opportunities for him to experience success are more essential and hence more basic than any form of grouping.

Additional Readings

Books and Pamphlets

Betts, Emmett Albert, *Foundations of Reading Instruction,* Chaps. IV and V, pp. 35–68. New York: American Book Company, 1946.
———, "Reading for Effective Living Through Effective Class Organization," *Reading for Effective Living,* International Reading Association Conference Proceedings, pp. 30–33. New York: Scholastic Magazines, 1958.

[21] Wallace Ramsey, "An Experiment with Three Plans of Grouping," *Challenge and Experiment,* Proceedings of the International Reading Association (New York: Scholastic Magazines, 1962), p. 151.

Dolch, E. W., "Reading for Effective Living Through Effective Class Organization," *Reading for Effective Living*, International Reading Association Conference Proceedings, pp. 26–28. New York: Scholastic Magazines, 1958.

De Boer, John J. and Martha Dallmann, *The Teaching of Reading*, Chap. 14, pp. 322–27. New York: Holt, Rinehart and Winston, Inc., 1960.

National Society for the Study of Education, *The Dynamics of Instructional Groups*, The Fifty-Ninth Yearbook, Part II. Chicago: The University of Chicago Press, 1960.

——, *The Teaching of Reading: A Second Report*, Thirty-Sixth Yearbook, Part I. Norwood, Mass.: Plimpton Press, 1937. Chap. XI, especially, is recommended.

Rasmussen, Margaret, and Lucy Prete, eds., *Toward Effective Grouping*. Washington, D. C.: Association for Childhood Education, International, 1962.

Robinson, Helen M., *Reading Instruction In Various Patterns of Grouping*, Supplemental Educational Monographs, No. 89-205. Chicago: University of Chicago Press, 1959.

Russell, David H., *Children Learn to Read*, Chap. 15, pp. 489–525. Boston: Ginn and Company, 1961.

The National Elementary Principal, *Reading for Today's Children*, Thirty-Fourth Yearbook, 35 (Sept. 1955), Chap. Three, 47–110.

Periodicals

Anderson, Richard C., "The Case of Non-Graded, Homogenous Grouping," *The Elementary School Journal*, Vol. 62 (Jan. 1962), 193–97.

Barlow, Irving H., "Does Homogeneous Grouping Give Homogeneous Groups?" *The Elementary School Journal*, Vol. 63 (Oct. 1962), 28–32.

Class Size in Elementary Schools, NEA Research Bulletin, Vol. 40 (Dec. 1962).

Clausen, Robert, "Why Probe Grouping Practices?" *Childhood Education*, 36 (Apr. 1960), 352–53.

Goodlad, John I., and Robert H. Anderson, "Educational Practices in Nongraded Schools: A Survey of Perceptions," *The Elementary School Journal*, Vol. 63 (Oct. 1962), 33–40.

Crosby, Muriel, "Organizing for Reading Instruction," *Elementary English*, XXXVII (Mar. 1960), 169–73.

Dolch, E. W., "Groups in Reading," *Elementary English*, 31 (Dec. 1954), 477–84.

Hull, J. H., "Multigrade Teaching," *The Nation's Schools*, LXII (July 1958), 3–37.

Lobdell, Lawrence O., and William Van Ness, "Grouping and Enrichment," *Education*, Vol. 82 (Mar. 1962), 399–402.

Morrison, Nellie C., "Instead of Ability Grouping—What?" *Childhood Education*, 36 (Apr. 1960), 371–73.

Oakley Union School, "Providing for the Individual Pupil Through Grouping Procedures," *The Elementary School Journal*, 57 (Dec. 1956), 150–52.

Russell, David H., "Cherishing Differences in the Reading Program," *The Reading Teacher*, 7 (Dec. 1953), 66–68.

Skapski, Mary King, "Ungraded Primary Reading Program: An Objective Evaluation," *The Elementary School Journal*, 61, No. 1 (Oct. 1960), 41–45.

Stonecipher, B. L., "Grouping in the Classroom," *Education*, Vol. 83 (Oct. 1962), 77–79.

Tunley, Paul, "Johnny *Can* Read in Joplin," *The Saturday Evening Post* (Oct. 26, 1957).

7

Individualized Instruction Receives Attention

Teaching children individually in the 1600's! Individual progression in the 1920's and 1930's! Individualized instruction in the 1950's and 1960's! Thus the historical cycle has repeated itself twice in American history, but with widely differing concepts, materials, and procedures.

In order to have a backdrop against which to project the present plan of individualized instruction, the plans of the past will be discussed briefly. The bulk of this chapter, however, will be concerned with an attempt to give an objective presentation of the present-day concept of individualized instruction, of representative research concerning the plan, and of procedures teachers are using in implementing this method of teaching reading.

Changing Concepts of Individualized Instruction

In Early Times

When reading instruction was first provided for children, it was conducted exclusively on an individual basis. The child was taught as an individual by a scribe, a priest, a tutor, or some member of his family. Even in our early "Dame Schools" in America, each child was taught individually and progressed at his own rate. A small group of children would gather in the Dame's kitchen, and each one would "recite" to her from his own place in the primer or Bible as she busied herself with her household duties.

There was no particular philosophy or psychology which guided Dame School practice. The pupils who came to the Dame were at different stages of development and small in number, and there was no particular need for attempting to mold them into one achievement level for "mass production" purposes.

In the Twenties and Thirties

As indicated in Chapter 1, the scientific movement in education had its birth between 1910 and 1920. During this period, reading tests were first developed and used.

Simultaneously, intelligence tests came into wide usage in American schools. In 1908 Binet published in France an *age* expression of ability which made it possible to state crudely a child's intelligence level.[1] Goddard brought the tests to America and published a revision in 1911,[2] in 1916 the Stanford Revision of the Binet tests appeared.[3]

With the advent of reading tests and intelligence tests, educators became keenly aware of individual differences in the reading achievement of children in the same grade and class. This discovery stimulated interest in making several group adjustments in classroom organization as described in Chapter 6, but the pulsating new idea was that of breaking up class organization entirely to permit individual progression. This plan of organization received as much attention at this time as it is receiving at the present moment. Speeches, articles, and yearbooks dealt with the subject, and many school systems reported the results they had obtained from using the individual instruction plan.

The various plans, on the whole, were patterned after the Winnetka plan or the Dalton system. The Winnetka system was perhaps the plan of individual instruction most widely used in this country.

[1] A. Binet and Th. Simon, "Le developpement de l'intelligence chez enfants," *L'Année Psychologique*, XIV (1908); A. Binet, "Nouvelles recherches sur la mesure du niveau intellectual chez les enfants d'école," *L'Année Psychologique*, XVII (1911), 145–201.

[2] H. H. Goddard, "A Revision of the Binet Scale," *Vineland Training School Bulletin*, VIII (1911), 56–62.

[3] This revision was accompanied by Terman's *Measurement of Intelligence* (Boston: Houghton Mifflin Co., 1916), which gave a complete description of the tests as well as directions for administering and scoring it.

The Winnetka Plan

The individual plan of instruction that was popularized through its use in the Winnetka schools was really initiated by Frederick Burke in the elementary school of the San Francisco State Normal School (as it was called in 1913). Carlton Washburne, who was one of Burke's faculty members, later went to Illinois as Superintendent of the Winnetka Schools. While Burke's plan had been tried in a private school, Washburne put it into effect for the first time in a public school system.

The curriculum as described by Washburne consisted of two parts. In half of the forenoon and again in half of the afternoon each child worked at his own rate on assigned units covering the "common essentials." During the other half of the forenoon and afternoon the time was devoted to social and creative activities.

In discussing reading procedures, specifically, Washburne reported that beginning reading was the most difficult aspect of the curriculum to individualize. At this level, however, self-help materials were provided to enable children to do some reading by themselves. This material consisted of a picture dictionary and also of rhymes which the child had memorized and to which he would turn in finding an unrecognized sight word. From the second grade on, the reading method was as follows: the grade level of each child was determined through the administration of a standardized test; each child was given books to read silently at his particular grade level; when he had completed a book, he was given a brief test on its content.

Washburne explained that according to this plan such oral reading that was done could be done with the teacher alone rather than to the class as a whole. He explained further that it took no more time for a teacher to hear thirty or forty pupils reading to her alone, one at a time, than to hear each one read aloud to the class.

In evaluating the Winnetka plan, one finds several features to commend. It demonstrated a practical way of permitting children to progress at their own rate of learning in a public school situation, and it eliminated the undesirable practice of failing pupils. It also provided opportunities for group and creative work. On the other hand, the chief purpose of permitting children to progress individually seems to have been only that of enabling them to cover adult-prescribed increments of subject matter at their own particular rates.

Kilpatrick's evaluation of the plan in 1925 is still pertinent. In part he said:

And what now is the conclusion regarding Winnetka's plan of learning by goals? First and foremost, it tends to break the child's learning into two disconnected parts. One part, highly mechanical, belongs to the system of goals—a system too nearly complete in itself, too little connected with life. Stated psychologically, the danger is that the learning will not transfer. Stated in terms of life, the danger is a divided self—that the child will look on learning as something apart from life, something to be "learned" and then put behind him. . . . That the Winnetka plan of goals is a better way of doing many of the things the ordinary school tries less successfully to do, may well be admitted. But unless the danger of little transfer and the danger of the divided self can be better safe-guarded, the present writer, for one, does not believe that learning by goals will continue to hold its present prominence at Winnetka.[4]

The Dalton Plan

The individual method most widely known the world over was the Dalton Laboratory Plan. This plan was first introduced by Helen Parkhurst in the high school of Dalton, Massachusetts, in 1920, a few months after the individual plan had been inaugurated in Winnetka. The Dalton plan attracted practically no attention until Rosa Bassett put the system into effect in the Girl's Secondary School in Streatham, London. This experiment was received with great acclaim and wide adoption in many countries in Europe. Along with the rising tide of enthusiasm in Europe, some educators in this country became interested and introduced the plan in grade schools as well as high schools; however, it was not advocated for use in any grade lower than fourth.

In 1925 Miss Parkhurst reported that in England there were over 1500 Dalton schools; that the Dalton plan had been adopted as the official method in Holland; that there were Dalton Schools in Norway, Germany, Poland, Austria, and Spain; that 450 public or government schools in Japan were operated on this plan, 250 in China, and 50 in India. At this time she knew of 200 schools in the United States which were using the method. She also reported that her book had been translated into twelve languages, "And all this in about four years."

The philosophy and psychology of the Dalton plan is expressed in three basic principles: (1) freedom; (2) cooperation and interaction of group life, or community living; (3) the proportion of effort to attainment, or budgeting time. Freedom was translated by Miss Parkhurst as meaning freedom to pursue an interest without interruption in order to develop concentration.

Subject laboratories and specialists provided the interaction of group

[4] William Heard Kilpatrick, "An Effort at Appraisal," *The Twenty-Fourth Yearbook of the National Society for the Study of Education* (Bloomington, Ill.: Public School Publishing Company (1925), pp. 284–85.

life, or community living. Instead of confining pupils of a single grade to one room, pupils of four or five grades were permitted to go from subject laboratory to subject laboratory, "mingling and living within the school while engaged in school pursuits."

The third principle was given application through a "contract" or "job" system which permitted individual progression in the basic school subjects. A "job" comprised a certain number of "units" of work which the pupil contracted to do. A unit of work corresponded in quantity to a daily recitation in a subject. Teachers outlined the work for each job, planning for a twenty-day period in terms of what they thought a child could accomplish. Very slow children could take more than twenty days.

A pupil might do all his work, subject by subject, one subject at a time, or he could do a little on each subject each day. He was free to go to a subject laboratory whenever he wished, to plan his own time, and to use his own best methods of work.

One good feature of the Dalton plan was that the laboratory arrangement did permit social intermingling of pupils while working on their subject-matter job assignments. Of course it also permitted individual progress in the subject areas, and it gave pupils experience in planning, budgeting, and using their time. The curriculum was the same for all children, however, and the subject matter was wholly adult chosen.

Kilpatrick evaluated the Dalton method when it was at its height. He recognized its good features, but in discussing its shortcomings he mentioned what he considered to be one very grave error:

The essential error of the Dalton plan, then, is, as with all external examination schemes, that it accepts childhood as a time of storing up learnings to be used when called for at a remote day, typically in adult life. It is on this assumed theory that it sets up its series of learning stints reaching upwards from the fourth grade. It assumes that a child can learn these successive stints and hold them stored up available for use when they shall later be called for. It further assumes that it does not hurt the child to be treated in this way. Both assumptions are here denied, at least to a degree to condemn the practice. But few things, comparatively speaking, can be so learned long in advance of use to stay with one till the distant use shall come. And the hurt, positive and negative, to the ordinary child when so treated is probably very great.[5]

The Present Concept

The present concept of individualized instruction in reading extends far beyond the earlier plans permitting children to progress at their own rates. It is primarily concerned with reading as it meshes into and promotes child development in its many different aspects—physical, mental,

5 *Ibid.*, pp. 279–80.

social, emotional, linguistic, and experiential. It is interested not only in a child's reading achievement but also in his interest in reading, his attitude toward reading, and his personal self-esteem and satisfaction in being able to read.

The growing interest in dynamic psychology has called attention to the importance of motivation and levels of aspiration in learning activities. Willard Olson made several studies of growth, behavior, and development of children. He then synthesized the results of his studies and thinking into three terse terms: *"seeking, self-selection,* and *pacing."* [6] It is this crystallization of Olson's psychology which has provided the basis for most individualized teaching of reading in recent years.

Olson explained that a child is continually exploring his environment and seeking experiences that fit in with his growth and needs. These seeking inclinations, accompanied with self-selection of stimulating materials, are basic in learning. Pacing, in accordance with the child's own rate of growth, is equally important, according to Olson. Applied to reading, this would mean that the situation most conducive to reading growth would be one in which the child is surrounded with stimulating books which he can explore and from which he can select and read at his own rate.

Additional insights into the present concept of individualized reading may be obtained from a few quotations of other people who are enthusiastic about this approach.

Lazar [7] says:

Individualized Reading is a way of thinking about reading—an attitude toward the place of reading in the total curriculum, toward the materials and methods used, and toward the child's developmental needs. It is not a single method or technique but a broader way of thinking about reading which involves newer concepts concerned with class organization, materials, and the approach to the individual child. The term Individualized Reading is by no means fully descriptive, but for want of a better term most proponents of this approach continue to use it. It is actually not desirable to place a specific name to the reading program.

Garrettson [8] summarizes the concept as follows:

When a child is allowed to use material of his own choosing, move at his own pace, in an atmosphere where *how he moves is no longer public classroom concern,* he *relaxes his defenses* and begins to *feel the security of accomplishment.*

[6] Willard C. Olson, "Seeking, Self-Selection, and Pacing in the Use of Books by Children," *The Packet* (Boston: D. C. Heath, Spring 1952), pp. 3–10.
[7] May Lazar, "Individualized Reading: A Dynamic Approach," *The Reading Teacher,* Vol. 11 (Dec. 1957), 75–83.
[8] Grace Garrettson, "How One School Reads the Needs of the Slow Reader," *Nineteenth Yearbook of Claremont College Reading Conference* (Claremont, Cal.: Claremont College Laboratory, 1954).

O'Donnell [9] states:

You know and I know that when interest is aroused and opportunities for wide reading are provided, a goodly number among the average and above-average readers in our classrooms can, in considerable measure, take care of their own reading needs. With a minimum of guidance they can work out effective reading methods, sometimes more effective than those we wish upon them. . . . It is *self-propelled* if we give opportunities for self-propulsion. Why can't we bend our energies toward providing wider opportunities for self-propulsion rather than continuing our endless discussion about the intricacies and difficulties of small-group teaching? Why can't we admit, and get teachers to admit, that the presence of such a group of able readers can simplify a classroom situation immeasurably? With a minimum of skillful guidance, these pupils can be trained to proceed on their own and to teach themselves many things.

Draper and Schwietert [10] explain:

Individualized Reading recognizes, accepts, and respects the fact that children differ and that each child is an individual in his own right with his own thoughts, secrets, drives, motivations, will, wishes, desires, and learning make-up. It also recognizes that for each child reading is a personal, individual experience and often a private affair. Individualized Reading attempts to meet individual needs, in the main, by dealing with them individually. Reading guidance and teaching are tailored to the child and not the other way round. Each child is taught the reading skills when he needs them. Therefore, he sees these skills as important and worth achieving. With this motivation the child actively meets the situation head on.

Jenkins [11] gives a glimpse of the concept when she says:

Children work hard and long when they choose their own jobs. They move ahead when they have opportunity to set their own goals. They read with greater enjoyment when they choose the material. In self-selection the teacher works with individuals and knows their interests and needs more adequately than when a group works on a single book chosen by the teacher.

Terminology

Several different terms have been used for the concept of reading instruction as expressed in the section above. Some have called the plan "Free Reading"; others have called it "Recreational Reading," and still others speak of it as "Extensive Reading." These terms have all been used

[9] Mabel O'Donnell, "The Reading Maze, Our Own Creation," *Monograph for Elementary Teachers*, No. 72 (New York: Harper & Row, Publishers, 1955).

[10] Marcella K. Draper and Louise H. Schwietert, *A Practical Guide in Individualized Instruction*, ed. May Lazar (New York: Board of Education, City of New York, 1960), p. 6.

[11] Reprinted by permission of the Association for Childhood Education International, 3615 Wisconsin Avenue, N.W., Washington 16, D. C. "Here's to Success in Reading: Self-Selection Helps," Marian Jenkins, ed. From *Childhood Education* (Nov. 1955), Vol. 32, No. 3.

for several years to designate additional reading done in connection with basic reading instruction. Such terms seem inappropriate for this plan, as self-selected reading materials are the basis for teaching reading, not an adjunct to basic reading instruction.

"Self-Selection Reading" is a term frequently used to designate this concept. Some people object to this name because it seems to suggest that no teacher guidance or assignments are included and that all learning activities are left to the child himself.

In some parts of the country, "Personalized Reading" is used to designate the plan in which there is self-selected individual reading plus systematic presentation of skills on both group and individual bases. Many teachers using the plan under the name of "Individualized Instruction" claim that they also make provision for such skill development and that they often work with groups. Therefore, it would appear that a clear-cut distinction cannot be made between "Personalized Reading" and "Individualized Reading" as they are generally functioning.

"Individualized Reading" has come to be the most widely accepted term. This designation carries the connotation that reading proceeds in terms of individuals; but at the same time the word "individualized" seems to indicate that someone other than the child has something to do with shaping the instruction. In other words, this term seems to allow the inclusion of a teacher role as well as a child role in the plan as a whole.

Advantages and Disadvantages of the Individualized Plan

Opinion in regard to the use of the individualized plan varies. Most teachers who are using the method are highly enthusiastic about its values. They recognize problems attendant upon implementing the plan, but they feel that the values justify the effort expended in coping with these problems. Another group believes that children should be taught through the use of a carefully organized, sequential skill development program making use of basic readers and their accompanying materials designed for this purpose, with provision also for free supplemental reading. Still a third group believes that the answer is to be found in some combination of the two plans. One example of a combination is a plan that permits those children who are making excellent progress to proceed exclusively under the individualized method, but which provides for having slower pupils, who seem to require more carefully systematized skill practice and more developmental work and supervision, to work with the teacher in a group using organized materials. In this case, however, the basic reader instruction is supplemented by individual selection and the conference plan in a program of supplemental reading.

In the interest of presenting a completely objective picture, both the pros and cons expressed by people of varying viewpoints will be summarized.

Advantages

Some of the most frequently mentioned advantages of the individualized plan are as follows:

1. The child proceeds under his *own* motive and drive.
2. He reads at his own pace.
3. Interest is increased because the child reads material of his own choice.
4. The program permits the reading of larger amounts of material than does the grouping plan.
5. Each child is taught the skills that he needs when he needs them; thus he realizes the usefulness of skills.
6. The individual conferences promote close personal relationships between pupil and teacher.
7. There are increased opportunities to integrate reading with other language arts: vocabulary development, writing, listening, spelling; motives to communicate are strengthened.
8. The psychological effect of the program on the child is desirable. Pressures and tensions to meet grade standards are relieved, frustrations arising from failure to read as much or as well as others in a group are avoided, and the stigma of being "behind in reading" is removed. All of these concomitants pay rewarding dividends in mental health.

Disadvantages

Aspects of the plan which are considered by some to be disadvantageous are listed below. (Many teachers, however, who use the individualized plan say they are able to meet these problems.)

1. Children need to have new vocabulary and concepts developed before reading a story in order to get the most enjoyment and understanding from it. In individualized instruction the child simply plunges in. Readiness preparation is ignored.
2. Few teachers have sufficient grasp of the scope and sequence of reading skills or the necessary time to enable them to develop a completely balanced sequence of skills in each individual.
3. The values of group dynamics may be lost sight of in a highly indi-

vidualized program. The development of interpretation and critical reading proceeds best where there is mental stimulation and interaction with the thinking of several children. Children do learn and profit by working with each other.

4. The attention span of primary children is short. They get tired of working alone for long periods of time.

5. Children can't judge their reading level by looking at a book. They often choose books that are too difficult.

6. Many schools at present cannot afford the quantities of books and seatwork necessary to meet individual interests and levels, and are not able to procure them from a library or other sources.

7. With large classes it is extremely difficult to schedule the daily and weekly program so that each individual receives an adequate amount of attention.

8. Making provision for the entire roomful of children to be occupied over long periods while the teacher is working with one child poses a real problem and may result frequently in having children do "busy work" or dawdle instead of spending their time on worthwhile activities.

Teachers' Problems

The advantages and disadvantages listed above are those most frequently mentioned in educational literature. For a teacher who expects to introduce this method, statements of problems by teachers themselves may be useful in helping her to look ahead and plan constructively. She needs to recognize that there are problems in working with this plan and that she should look at them objectively and realize that they are not insurmountable.

McKillop [12] has summed up problems expressed by teachers. Her summary was drawn from observations in classrooms where the method is used and from conferences with and reports by teachers who have tried to individualize reading instruction. Excerpts will be presented.

Problems of Scheduling

Teachers reported that they had difficulty scheduling their time for individualized reading. They even had trouble finding enough time for it at all, let alone being able to choose the most desirable time of day or the most effective length of period. They expressed concern as to how their program functioned when classes became as large as thirty. They wondered how many minutes a week a teacher should strive to spend with each child.

[12] Anne McKillop, "Special Problems Encountered in Individualized Reading Instruction," *Individualizing Reading Instruction* (Newark, Del.: School of Education, University of Delaware, 1957), pp. 68–76.

Besides problems of time for the children, these teachers felt that one of their biggest problems was time to prepare the materials for children. Several reported that their program would function smoothly if they had a free period just before the reading period to prepare materials for the children who were to be working independently. . . .

Related to these problems of independent work was the problem of planning. A teacher recognized that an individualized reading program would not work unless she was free to spend her time with the child relatively free from interruptions. This, of necessity, involved planning with the other children as to their activities. . . .

Problems in the Development of Skills

One of the concerns . . . was how to ensure that specific reading skills would be taught in a systematic fashion. Part of the problem seemed to lie in the complexity of the task of remembering who was at what spot on the skill path. Was it Mary or Joe who had trouble with the "tion" ending? Had Susie been introduced to the technique of skimming? . . .

Problems with Regard to Materials

A third group of problems . . . was concerned with the choice of availability of materials for an individualized reading program. It was agreed that such a program demanded a great many materials of different sorts. If a reading program was to be based only upon one set of basal readers then children might as well be taught in reasonably sized groups. But if children were to be taught individually, the teacher would need many samples of different types of materials—readers, library books, charts, practice exercises.

How to choose the right material for the individual child posed problems. Could you rely upon him to choose his own material? What if he consistently chose material which was much too difficult for him to handle successfully? What about the bright youngster who "slid by" with easy books? . . .

Problems Beyond the Classroom

All the problems which arise in an indivdualized reading program are not to be found within the classroom, even when the classroom is expanded to include the school library. Problems arise when the children go home. Parents are accustomed to a reading program where children are divided into groups and progress smoothly from rung to rung in a basic reading series. It is difficult for them to understand why Mary is reading a library book while the boy next door is reading a reader. Sometimes, too, they do not understand the child's report that he didn't read today. They think this means he did no reading at all in the school on that day, whereas he means it was not his time to read with the teacher. He may have read silently, done several exercises, read to another child, and written and read a report in social studies, but in his terms, he didn't read today. This type of misunderstanding points up the need expressed by the teachers who reported on their experiences for time and opportunities to explain the program to parents. . . .

Underlying Problems

The first is the need for skilled teachers. This is not a program for the uncertain or the ignorant. An individualized reading program requires teachers who know the reading process, who know how children learn and who are sensitive and responsive. There is no guide book for an individualized reading program. . . .

A second and related problem . . . is the need for careful organization and planning, on the part of the individual teacher, on the part of the librarian, on the part of the administration. Time must be provided for selection of materials; funds must be available quickly; cumulative records must be in better shape than those of most schools. . . .

Another condition which seems essential for the smooth functioning of an individualized reading program is that the children themselves must carry a good deal of the burden for their own independent work. . . . They must understand the program; they must know their own strengths and weaknesses; they must be able to organize much of their own practice. Fortunately, with skillful teachers, with suitable materials, with a careful plan, the children can be remarkably responsible and independent. It is our task to give them a chance.

As indicated in the above quotation, this approach calls for a high level of teacher performance. There are, of course, concomitant problems, but they can be met by a skilled teacher and accompanying satisfactions are high.

Preparing to Teach by the Individualized Plan

If the reader is thinking of trying out an individualized program in her own classroom perhaps the suggestions below will be helpful.

Examine Your Own Image

First, examine your own image to see if you possess the personal qualifications for teaching reading in accordance with this plan. Are you strongly convinced that the philosophy and psychology upon which this plan is based are sound? Strength of conviction is of fundamental importance. Are you the adventurous type who can enter upon this new undertaking with courage, stamina, and enthusiasm? You will need all these qualities. Have you a boundless supply of energy? Individualized teaching of reading requires hours of planning, testing, evaluating, record keeping, collecting. It's no job for an enervated person. Do you have a world of patience? This trait will be essential in breaking the group down to individual levels, in teaching children to work by themselves, in letting them mull around while selecting their individual books, and in many other situations. Are you an *excellent* organizer? Surely this ability will be necessary in planning time allotments and in forwarding a program of reading instruction in an ever-changing classroom with highly diversified individual needs.

Prepare Yourself Professionally

Make a careful study of the individual plan. Read many of the references at the end of this chapter and others. Attend lectures and panel discussions on this subject scheduled in the programs of educational meetings. If possible, visit classrooms in which the individualized plan is being used and talk with teachers who are using it.

By all means make a careful study of skills in reading. There is much more involved in teaching reading skills than merely helping children to use phonics and asking comprehension questions. If you are going to dispense with an organized skill program planned by reading authorities and provided for in the materials of a basic reading system, and depend solely upon yourself to develop well-rounded skill competency in each individual, then you must know a great deal about skills.

In the interest of informing yourself on reading skills study the skill development chapters in this book (Chaps. 8, 9, 10, 11). Be sure that you have the content of a reading skill program clearly in mind and that you know what the reading skills are that should be developed in each of the growth areas. Furthermore, be sure that you have some clear ideas on how to develop these skills and the kinds of content and reading situations especially appropriate for teaching different types of skills. Keep these objectives in mind while studying the skill development chapters that follow. Read other references on skills, also. Take one or more currently given courses in reading. A heavy responsibility will rest upon you if you depend upon yourself to develop competency in all the reading skills. Prepare as well as you can by highly sensitizing yourself to the various reading skills and ways of promoting their respective growths.

Assemble a Collection of Books

If the practice of self-selection is to ensue, then it is obvious that there must be a large collection of books from which to select. Most advocates of the individualized plan state that a teacher should have 100 or more titles available during the course of a year. A few copies each of pre-primers, primers, and readers from basic reading series usually are included. The majority of the books, however, are trade books of realistic fiction, fanciful stories, or nonfiction. Many different levels of difficulty are represented.

The teacher usually has books of several different titles in her classroom which she can use under the new organization. To these she adds as many additional titles as she is able to purchase within the limitations of the school's budget. She may then borrow from central school libraries, public libraries, and bookmobiles. These sources usually will loan a teacher twenty to thirty books a month. The children may also borrow from libraries and bring books from their own collections at home. Many parents are willing to buy one book to add to the classroom collection.

Supply Material for Independent Work

Not all children will want to read in books *all* the time you are working with different pupils individually. Furthermore, for skill development purposes children need to engage in reading activities other than reading a selection in a book. To meet these needs, a teacher who plans to try individualized instruction should have at hand a quantity of worthwhile material with which children can work independently at their seats. Many of the maintenance activities given on pages 540–80 are examples which may be used in preparing materials for independent work.

Conducting an Individualized Reading Program

Briefly the procedure used in individualized classrooms can be summarized as follows:

Each child selects a book that he wants to read. During the individual conference period the teacher sits in some particular spot in the room as each child comes and reads to her. As he does so, she notes his individual needs and gives him appropriate help. Finally she writes what the child is reading, his needs, and strengths on his record card. Then another individual conference is held, and so on. If several children need help on the same skills, they may be called together in a group for such help.

This general characterization of the procedure will now be expanded with a more detailed discussion of its various aspects.

The Conference Period

The conference period coincides with what is called the "reading period" in conventional programs. It is usually forty-five minutes to an hour in length. Often the teacher spends the beginning part of this period planning with the children how they will occupy themselves while she is working with individuals.

When she is ready to work with individual children she may place herself in any one of several different spots in the room. Some teachers prefer to sit in one corner of the room or in the back of the room where they can be somewhat secluded while working with pupils individually. Some sit at the teacher's desk in the front of the room, feeling that they can better look after the children at their seats from this vantage point. Others circulate about the room stopping to work with individual children who are ready for a conference. Still others sit in a chair which they slide up and down the aisles, pausing here and there for individual conferences. Some vary their positions in the room from day to day; others use a fixed spot continuously.

The length of the conference with each child varies from two to ten minutes. During this time the teacher checks the number of pages the child has read and perhaps chats with him briefly about what he has read. She may have him read parts of the story orally, ask him questions on these parts or other parts, check his word recognition by asking him to pronounce certain words, give him help on some skill element he especially needs, or discuss and plan follow-up activities with him. Thus during the conference period the teacher checks, diagnoses, teaches, evaluates, and extends the pupil's interests and activities.

Record Keeping

Keeping individual records is essential in the procedure for teaching reading by the individualized plan. Each time a child has a conference with the teacher she records the name of the book and the number of the last page which he read up to this time, his special progress, his special needs, the specific help given, and notes on his interests and attitudes.

Some teachers have a six-by-nine-inch card for each child; others have a large notebook in which one or more pages are used in recording information about each pupil. A simple format is helpful in organizing information. An example of such a format is given below.

JOHN MORRIS					
DATE	BOOK AND PAGE	PROGRESS	SPECIAL NEEDS	INTEREST AND ATTITUDE	OTHER REMARKS
Nov. 17	*Mr. Popper's Penguins,* p. 84.	Reads more smoothly.	Missed several words having *a* followed by *r.* Gave him help on this.	Keenly interested in this story. Delighted that he had read so many pages.	Behavior problems subsiding.

Group Sessions

Some people make the mistake of thinking that the teacher using the individualized plan always works with a pupil individually, that there is never any instruction given to groups. This is not true. It is possible and desirable upon occasion to make use of each of the different types of grouping described in Chapter 6, pages 108–28. Many teachers of individualized instruction find frequent opportunities to have group work of all of these different types as a supplement to their individualized procedures.

Total Class Grouping

In an individualized classroom providing for rich child experiences, there are many times in which the entire class can join in reading activities. Charts evolving from a mutual experience or based on plans for activities, questions to which answers are sought, directions for going somewhere or doing something—all such mutually prepared charts call for whole-group participation and provide opportunities for whole-group reading. Notices placed on the chalkboard or bulletin board are read by the entire group.

The whole class may also be involved in planning activities, such as planning procedures for book selection or for individual conferences, planning what to do for independent work, and planning sharing experiences in which one child or a group will share their reading with the class as a whole. Sometimes a new reading skill is introduced to the group as a whole. Whenever there is a need or a reason for the entire class to work together, whole-class grouping may ensue. It's up to the teacher. There is nothing in the philosophy of the individualized plan itself which precludes functional whole-group participation in a reading activity.

Small Group Arrangements

Sometimes children who are reading or have read the same book gather in a group to "talk it over." Such discussion may lead to plans for some sharing activity, such as a dramatization, puppet show, or mock radio or television program. At other times, children reading the same book may work with the teacher as a group during the usual individual conference period.

Now and then two or three children who like to be together socially gather in one spot when reading from their individual books. Usually there is considerable oral reading to each other in such a group, and often the children help each other with unrecognized words.

Interest groups emerge at times. Four or five children may become interested in elephants, for example. Regardless of their different levels of ability they may work together, each sharing information and interesting incidents from the book or story he is reading at his own ability level.

Skill groups are frequently formed to meet individual needs. If two or three or several children need help on the same skill, these children meet as a group with the teacher for development of and practice on the skill. This group is disbanded one by one as children master the skill, and new groups, possibly composed of some of these children and others, assemble to meet other skill needs.

Thus group work proceeds on many different bases: common purpose, common social preference, common interest, common skill needs. Proponents of the individualized plan stoutly proclaim that no teacher who fully understands the broader concepts of the individualized plan would deny children the opportunity for group work motivated by some of the common purposes mentioned above.

Examples of Practice

In the interest of concreteness and practicality some first-hand accounts of classroom procedures will now be presented. These accounts are given in the words of teachers who have taught reading by the individualized method or in the words of those who have worked closely with teachers in a supervisory or research capacity.

Beginning Reading

Beginning reading is considered by many to be the most difficult stage in which to use the individualized plan. Considerable experimentation has been carried on in the New York City Schools in using this plan in beginning stages as well as at other levels. Draper, Schwietert, and Lazar, of the City Schools Research Department, discuss the procedure used at this level in their monograph, *A Practical Guide to Individualized Reading*.[13] An excerpt from their treatment of this subject is given below:

The child is led naturally and functionally into symbolization. Many of the classroom experiences are increasingly translated into written or printed symbols. Introduction to symbolization through the children's own experiences

[13] Marcella K. Draper and Louise H. Schwietert, *A Practical Guide to Individualized Reading*, ed. May Lazar (New York: Board of Education, City of New York, 1960), pp. 97–99.

145

conveys the idea that reading "says something" and, therefore, is meaningful. Symbolization in this fashion shows that words and sentences are so tied up with the experiences that the child knows that the symbols tell about the experiences even though he cannot read them. This supplies natural content for the child's first reading. The following are some "experience" records which may be used for "reading" in the first grade:

Children's names on their work or belongings—captions and names on their paintings, finger paintings, drawings.

Class Diary of the children. Each child tells some interesting item about himself which he wishes to appear on his page of the diary—"I have a pet hamster named Oscar."

Provocative news items on the blackboard—"Hurray! Hurray! Our party today."

Picture and phrase weather chart—"The sun is playing hide-and-seek with the clouds."

Highlights of the day's planning on the blackboard or the bulletin board— "Today we will visit the farm at the Bronx Zoo."

Class log of a day's unforgettable experience—"The Day the Cocoon Opened."

Charts of ongoing activities and experiences. Effective in-class and out-of-class living provides the impetus for discussion and reading.

Directions on the best places to keep equipment—"Trucks rest here." "Blocks are stacked in this section."

Personal items on the blackboard or bulletin board—"Joseph, how well you said, 'Good morning' today."

A special individual note to the child—"Dear Linda: Thank you for bringing your bunny, 'Suzy.' The children loved to touch her soft fur."

In addition to the many suggested experiential materials listed above, the teacher, at all times, encourages the child to dictate his personal ideas and stories. She may prepare booklets of these stories for rereading. This activity is one of the major bridges between the child's spoken ideas and the printed word.

At first the teacher reads these experience records to the children. Interest is usually high because the items are about the children themselves. The child enjoys having his experiences personalized and recognized. He likes to read things about himself, his interests, his family, his friends, his ideals, his longings, his aspirations. Soon individual children will begin informally to read some of the items in the printed records. The teacher gives help in recognizing words and phrases in order to give the child any necessary support to get at the ideas.

Through the experiences outlined above, some of the children will have begun to acquire certain reading knowledges and essentials. For example, the child might have acquired—

some sight vocabulary.
the ability to read from left to right.
the ability to move his eyes from line to line in orderly progression.
some powers of auditory and visual discrimination.
some ability to use configuration and contextual clues.
some ability to apply simple word analyses techniques.

increased power of sustained attention.
ability to organize ideas and develop a sense of sequence of ideas and events.

When the teacher thinks the child has reached the "teachable and learnable" moment for faster development of reading and of more complex skills, he is encouraged more and more to read his dictated stories on his own. It is important that a child's first books should be outgrowths of his experiential learning; that is, booklets of his own dictated stories. Such booklets will be building upon words he knows and already uses casually. This provides better continuity of experiences for the child than do the so-called "stories" in the pre-primer or primers of the basic-reading series. One first-grade teacher said, "I use the children's writing as their first reading materials. I can't emphasize enough the worth of this experience. It is the easiest way to develop sight vocabulary. Moreover, it soon leads to children's writing by themselves."

Along with reading the experiential materials, the child is gradually introduced to the simple books in the classroom. It must be clearly understood, however, that these first simple books should be familiar to the children. The first commercially printed books, through which the child does independent reading (giving the symbols back), should have been part and parcel of his interest experiences and classroom living all along. These books should have been read to the children. The ideas and pictures should have been discussed, the content dramatized where possible, and the words explored from a conceptual standpoint. Knowing the content of a story helps the child with symbolization and word recognition—it is the "crutch" to unlocking the words. Knowing the content gives continuity of experience because it is going to symbolization from ideas.

Furthermore, knowing the content gives the child self-confidence because selection can be made on a sound basis. The child is building on familiarity of previous experience. One teacher expressed it in this way, "As all the language and first-hand experiences are going on, I begin to introduce simple books. I read each one to the children. They discuss it and dramatize it before it is put on the library shelf. The child must know what the book is about in order to tell whether or not he wants to go to it. The children begin gradually to gravitate toward these books, tell each other the story from the pictures, and begin to read the simple text."

The books are easily accessible to the children. The children are given ample time to browse through them, to recall their content, and to choose one they might wish to read. When the child is reading his first books (first in terms of expecting him to uncode the symbols in order to read them back), the teacher sits with him or with a small group of children, each reading his individual book. She gives each one any necessary help, guidance, and encouragement. She supplies some words quickly; eases over other words; helps with recognition, pronunciation, and meanings.

The child may read all of one book or a selected story from a collection of stories within a book. As he finishes one book, he discusses it with the teacher or the children and is encouraged to take another. One teacher described her early practices thus, "I feel that children should know how to recognize a number of words before they are set free to read on their own. As my children show the spark for reading, I say directly to them, 'Take a book you like. There will be plenty of words you won't know. *Don't feel afraid* to ask about those words.'" Another first-grade teacher said, "Young children set up their own means of selecting books. Here are their criteria: 'Can I read it? Am I interested in it?' At first, all independent reading is done under the watchful eyes and keen ears of the teacher so that the child will not be discouraged by some of the hurdles he will necessarily meet."

From this description, teachers can readily see that Individualized Reading makes definite provision for "Readiness." Children certainly are not "plunged" into reading without preparation, and great effort is made in advance to deal with unknown words and their meanings.

As the child continues to read, the teacher notes individual growth. She checks on the child's reading and evaluates how and what he reads. She keeps track of and helps him with the words he asks for and the skills he needs. If she finds that there are common words and skills needed by a number of children, she forms a temporary group who will work together. She also provides for numerous and happy class sessions in which the children discuss the varied words, ideas, and stories they have read. As the children continues to read on his own under the careful scrutiny of the teacher, he gains more and more power to read simple books. Soon he reaches for a book whose content is not wholly familiar to him. He begins to read it because he is not afraid and knows that the teacher is there to give him the help he needs.

Second Grade

The teaching activities used by four teachers in teaching second grade children with the "Self-Selection" plan is described by Jenkins, a consultant in the Los Angeles County Schools, and by the principals in whose schools the second grade teachers worked. Excerpts from their description are given below:

The self-selection or individualized approach to the reading process has been tried by four teachers in our school during the past two years. The results obtained indicate that there is enough merit in it to warrant further study and experimentation.

Careful Planning Precedes Introduction of Self-Selection

Careful plans were made by these four teachers before they introduced self-selection to their pupils. Their plans included: studying what has been written regarding it in the literature; preparing charts of comprehension and word attack skills to be developed; arranging for a large classroom collection of reading textbooks with a wide range of difficulty; arranging to have a large collection of trade books of many types and subjects and of a wide range of difficulty; preparing a plan for recording detailed information for each child concerning skill development, vocabulary development, and books read; outlining how self-selection would be introduced to the pupils and to the parents; and selecting and organizing practice materials.

With this careful preparation, each teacher was ready to introduce the new approach with the assurance that he would be conducting a systematic and comprehensive program of instruction in reading which would differ in two main ways from our regular program. First, the children would be permitted to select their own reading materials rather than follow the basic series textbooks.

Second, the skills program would be developed primarily on an individual basis rather than within the three customary ability groups. . . .[14]

Arranging the Environment

Books, and more books seemed to be the keynote in the experimental classes. Prior to the actual initiation of self-selection, two or three days were spent by each teacher in setting up the classroom library. The children, with the teacher's guidance, worked out plans for the display of the reading materials. Each class developed the room environment which best suited its needs. However, one basic practice was common. The books were invitingly arranged and easily accessible to the children. Then children had time to browse and choose, each his own book.

Grouping

It was thought that children in primary grades would feel more comfortable about their reading if they could gather around the teacher and be assured of her immediate help. In order to keep this intimate contact between the children and teacher, some sort of grouping was planned.

The teachers using self-selection wished to avoid any grouping based upon the reading proficiency of the pupils, since this would counteract the very environment which they were striving to create. Also, more equal distribution of the teacher's assistance could be given if groups were composed of approximately equal numbers of slow, average, and fast readers. With these factors in mind, each teacher developed her own method of grouping. In general, groups were formed on the basis of friendships, common interests, or common problems.

One teacher decided to base her groups on the results of a simple sociometric test. She asked each child in a casual manner the following question: "Whom would you like most to sit near at reading time?" On the basis of the children's choices, three groups were formed. A chubby second grader explained to a visitor, "We don't have a 'dumb' group, we just read with our friends." Friendships were being strengthened and good attitudes toward reading were growing while children chuckled over the funny part of a story or helped one another with the hard words in their chosen books.

[14] Marian Jenkins, "Self-Selection in Reading," *The Reading Teacher,* 11 (Dec. 1957), 88–90.

Measuring Results of Growth in
Reading Skills

The individualized groups met with the teacher on a daily basis. Each child in the group had his "special time" with the teacher for individual instruction. His particular reading problem was brought into sharp focus and reading skills were reviewed, developed, and refined at the time of immediate need.

A detailed reading record card was kept for each child. Daily reference was made to this record in order to ascertain whether the difficulties of yesterday had been mastered or if they still persisted. This practice gave continuity to the instruction and kept both child and teacher aware of just what the problems were and what progress had been made. . . .[15]

Fifth Grade

Young, a fifth grade teacher, tells how she proceeds in using the individualized plan:

I introduce my selective reading plan by allowing the children to browse through the books on display in the room, finally selecting one they wish to take to their seat and read. I make a card for each child, then divide the cards, in no particular way, into four groups. I then ask each group of children to decide on a name for themselves, such as Explorers, Pioneers, Sea Hawks. The next step is to make a contract or plan whereby each child agrees to read from beginning to end the book he has selected. If a child feels a need to break his contract, he must discuss the reason with the teacher. If the selection was a poor one or too difficult, he may select another book with the help and consent of the teacher. At the time the contract is made, I record on the child's card the name of the book selected and the date. Children also keep individual records of books read and their chosen method for reporting. When a book is finished, I complete my record by noting the date and method of reporting. I also note the individual's needs as they arise and any other details that need attention.

Daily Procedure

On Monday I call two groups to the reading table, one at a time, and listen and talk to each child individually, a little apart from the group. The other children at the table continue to read until each one has had an opportunity to read to and talk with me. Each has his "Own Dictionary" containing words with which he needs help. During the individual discussion these words are studied. On Tuesday I follow the same plan with the other two groups.

On Wednesday we have book chats; some of the children tell a little about the book they have chosen, the author, some of the characters, the setting, and why they chose the book. The helpers volunteer, so they do not feel obligated

[15] Marian Young, "A Report on Self-Selection in Reading," *Elementary English*, 35 (Mar. 1958), 177–78. Reprinted with the permission of the National Council of Teachers of English and Marian Young.

to spend this time helping if they are reading or preparing a book review that is important to them.

Thursday is book reviewing day. Each child has in his reading folder a list of various ways to review a book, which was made up by the class. The method most popular with this group is dramatization, although we have many flannel board stories, experiments, and stories told through the use of puppets. The story is never completed but enough is told to encourage the rest of the class to want to read the book. The book of the week is then chosen, using standards set up by the class. Consideration is given to book selection, organization of the report, and interesting presentations. The names of the children who gave reports and the title of the book of the week are recorded on a wall chart.

When a child finishes reading his book, he is encouraged to work on his plan of reporting. It may involve art, working with science equipment, making puppets, or planning a dramatization with the help of others.

Friday is used for reading "Weekly Readers," "News Time," and remedial work. If two or three children are reading the same book, they sometimes read to each other. Other children study their dictionary words; some make book jackets. Each child fills out a book review question sheet on each of the books he reads. This is for his own record and should be checked by the teacher at intervals.

In my daily lesson plan, time is allowed for word study before each reading period. This consists of various ways to attack words, dictionary work, root words, suffixes, prefixes, phonics, and other needs as they arise. I also give a list of "added vocabulary words" to my fast learners. I feel all the children have been well prepared for independent reading before the period begins. The interest in reading is great because each child has selected the book of his choice. . . .

Sixth Grade

Kingsley, of the Bellingham City Schools in Washington, tells how she conducted an individualized program with sixth grade children: [16]

General Planning and Discussion

As is desirable in any activity undertaken with youngsters, the plan was discussed with the children before an attempt was made to inaugurate it. This initial discussion centered around four major items. *Would they enjoy reading library books of their own choosing rather than series of readers or specified books related to their social living?* Although some were a bit suspicious of this innocent-sounding plan, nearly all thought it would be wonderful. The only ones not whole-heartedly in favor fell into two categories: the folks who thought that reading, to be really worthwhile, must be hard, and the group that never had liked reading, anyway. However, all were willing to try it out.

[16] Marjorie Kingsley, "An Experiment in Individualized Reading," *Elementary English,* 35 (Feb. 1958), 113–16. Reprinted with the permission of the National Council of Teachers of English and Marjorie Kingsley.

How would they keep track of the books read? This was discussed at some length, and the details may be found in the section on "Record Keeping." *What about words with which they had trouble?* It was decided that word lists would be kept by the individual youngster. He would use a dictionary or ask a neighbor, depending on what was appropriate at the time of the difficulty. The word list was later abandoned as a requirement, although some of the children continued to keep them, anyway. This change in the plan was made because the poorer readers found that listing and looking up every unknown word defeated the purpose of the reading—that of learning to enjoy books. It was felt that if the child could get the gist of the idea, he wasn't to worry about every single word. . . . The last thing talked over was *the responsibility which must be assumed by the individual in keeping himself supplied with suitable reading material.* Some of the poorer readers, though not all, of course, were among the least mature children in the group. Naturally, these immature folks were the ones who were most likely to find the assumption of such a responsibility a rather large order. It involved making the effort to go to the library, the ability to choose suitable material, having the books at school when needed, and seeing that they got back to the library on time. All of this assumes an interest in reading as an activity which a number of the children didn't have at that point. This area was the single biggest problem encountered in the course of the year.

Individual Conferences with Children

Following the general discussion, parts of several days were spent in individual pupil-teacher conferences for the purpose of going over the results of the Gates Survey. Since the philosophy of individual differences was basic to the program, an effort was made to help each child understand where he stood in vocabulary, comprehension, and speed, as measured by this instrument. The most difficult part of the process was helping the child to accept the fact that he read at a certain level and that it was all right. So much of both status and stigma has been attached to "how well you read" that this acceptance was not easily achieved. . . .

Trip to the Public Library

The next step in the initiation of the program was a group trip to the public library. The children's librarian presented an informal orientation talk, gave general location of books, took applications for new cards, and straightened out a number of old library fines! The children spent about half an hour browsing and selecting books. A number of the children already knew how to use the card catalog and instructed those who had not used it previously. Most of them chose material that was appropriate in terms of both difficulty and interest. Those who didn't choose wisely that first time did a much better job when the class returned two weeks later. And then they just plain read.

For the first few days following the trip to the library, the children just read —about forty-five minutes in the morning and thirty minutes in the afternoon.

There were no interruptions from the teacher—the only requirement was that they should read, which nearly all did with obvious enjoyment. Those few youngsters who had chosen unwisely were helped to locate more suitable material in the school library. With two boys, this help was difficult to give— they liked jet planes and science fiction and there just weren't any available at the second and third grade levels. Anyone wishing to make a fortune and retire early should write more such books. They'd sell like wildfire. . . .

The Child's Written Record

The first record kept of any reading was made by the youngster in his own notebook. This record included the title of the book, author, date begun, date finished, and comments about the book sufficient to identify it to the reader for the purpose of telling another individual about it. This excerpt came from the notebook of a girl who read at the sixth grade level:

Kay Everett Calls CQ by Amelia Lobsenz
Date started: Sept. 14, 1953
Date finished: Sept. 17, 1953
Kay Everett and two other girls join Jane Carton, a girl ham operator, to spend a summer touring the New England country in a trailer. Their adventure starts with the discovery of some stolen jewels in an old cabin. When their own belongings are ransacked, they decide to go after the thief themselves.

There was a tremendous range in both quality and quantity, depending upon the reader and the material read. On the whole, the group kept excellent records of the books read.

The Teacher's Written Record

At the time of a child's individual conference with the teacher, held while the remainder of the class was reading, the youngster brought his reading notebook and the book being read currently. These conferences began about the fourth day after the actual reading was started. During the conference the child gave the names of the books read, together with general information about each. He picked out one favorite book to discuss in considerable detail. Comments were encouraged through questions, which varied with the reader. Who was the most important person in this book? Why do you think he was so important? Who would you like most to be in the story? Why? What was the main idea in the story—what was the author trying to get across? What new thing did you learn from the book? What made this book special for you? How did the author make it so enjoyable? Were there any ideas in the story with which you had trouble? Did you have special difficulty with words? The variety of questions is unlimited. They were selected in terms of the youngster whose reading was being discussed.

As the next step in the conference, the child picked out a good spot in the book he was currently reading and told what had happened in the story up to that particular point. He then read aloud the part he thought especially good or exciting. With careful watching and listening, the teacher learned most about the way the child read and was able to make helpful suggestions for improvement. Sometimes the conference was over in ten minutes and other times it lasted a half hour. At the beginning of the year, about four conferences were held a day. This varied from day to day, depending upon other parts of the program. As time went on, some youngsters did not require as many conferences and others needed more. . . .

Research Findings

Individualized instruction is a subject of such strong current interest and the research findings are so controversial that it seems advisable to provide the reader with an objective presentation of representative samples of studies in this area.

Most of the studies have evolved from the desire to compare the relative effectiveness of the individualized plan and the group basal reading plan. An over-all perusal of the sample researches summarized below indicates that as yet there is not enough definitive data from which to draw generalizations. This is partly due to the fact that the individualized plan has not been used long enough for several tightly controlled studies to have been conducted. When a great preponderance of studies carried on in different parts of the country point to a superiority of one method over another, then there is decisive evidence of the relative effectiveness of the two methods. Such a preponderance of evidence has not yet accumulated in regard to the relative merits of individualized instruction and group basal reading methods.

Another point to be considered is the large number of variables present in any two of these reading situations under comparison. No highly satisfactory technique has yet been devised for equating teachers for general competence; but even if we accept the premise that teachers have been well-matched for general competence in some experiments, then such factors need to be considered as the attitude of the teacher toward the method she is to teach, the length of time that she has taught by this method, the amount of training taken or supervisory help given in the method to be used. In the case of the carefully organized method, does the teacher slavishly follow teacher's guides and spend her whole time on a basic reader with two or three different groups? Does she use multiple readers? Does she teach small groups at different levels? Will she give more or less help on skill development and practice according to needs? Will she have periods for free-choice reading and keep a record of the number of books each child reads in addition to the core basic instruction? These and many other variables must be considered in order to ascertain the kind of basic program with which individualized instruction is being compared. Similarly, many details about the individualized program under comparison must be known. Both basic reader programs and individualized programs vary greatly. We must be cautious about accepting information drawn from *surface* descriptions of experiments as conclusive. We need to know *what kind* of an individualized program is being compared with *what kind* of a basic reader-program; and we need to know how a large number of variables were controlled in each situation.

A few very good experiments have been conducted, but many more are needed. A number of thoroughly scientific studies are under way. Some of these are longitudinal in nature and will require several years for completion. Others are short-term studies, but nevertheless, are being carefully controlled and well-handled statistically. With these prospects in view the results of a wealth of worthwhile studies should accumulate rapidly.

Studies Favoring Individualized Instruction

A doctoral study conducted by Acinapura involved children in fourth, fifth, and sixth grades who were matched in reading ability, IQ, and socio-economic status. The experimental group was taught by the individualized plan; the control group, by the three-ability grouping plan. Test results showed the two groups to be equally efficient in vocabulary. The individualized group was statistically significant in their superiority over the other group in silent reading comprehension and in total silent and oral achievement.[17]

Cyrog conducted a study in which individualized instruction was introduced gradually over a three-year period. The investigator reports that after three years, a fifth grade class achieved a median reading score of 6.2 on the California achievement test although the pupils mental-grade equivalent on the California Test of Mental Maturity was 5.2. He drew the conclusions that "individualized reading over a two or three-year period produces better than average results," and that "individualized reading can be used successfully in first grade." This is one of the better action-type studies reported. It must be pointed out, however, that no control groups were used in the study and that statistical data for four of the five participating groups was not given.[18]

[17] Philip Acinapura, *A Comparative Study of the Results of Two Instructional Reading Programs*. Unpublished doctoral dissertation (New York: Teachers College, Columbia University, 1959).

[18] Francis Cyrog, "A Principal and His Staff Move Forward in Developing New Ways of Thinking About Reading," *California Journal of Elementary Education*, 27 (Feb. 1959), 178–87.

Duker carried on an experiment in grades four, five, and six, in which the pupils were randomly assigned to experimental and control groups; five of the groups were taught by the individualized plan and the other five were taught by the conventional reader program. This study is unique in that student teachers carried on the individualized program under the supervision of experienced teachers, while the basic reader groups were taught wholly by experienced teachers. The individualized groups were at a disadvantage in being taught by student teachers. This disadvantage may have been overcome, however, by two other factors: both the regular teachers and student teachers were present in the individualized classrooms in many cases, and longer periods were devoted to reading in the individualized rooms than in the basic reader rooms. Test results showed an average of six month's gain for the individualized groups as compared with two month's gain for the basic reader groups. The differences in favor of the individualized reading group were statistically significant at the .01 level.[19]

McCristy matched eight second grade classes in year's attendance; age; mental status, socio-economic class; reading grade status; and teacher background, experience, and competence. The experimental groups were taught by the individualized plan and the control groups were taught by the three-ability-grouping plan with the use of basal readers. The latter group also had access to well-stocked classroom libraries for supplemental reading. The control group averaged 1.14 years in total reading gains while the experimental group averaged 1.41 years. In vocabulary growth the control group averaged 1.09 and the experimental 1.96 years. In comprehension fifty-nine per cent of the experimental group gained two years or more, while twenty-four per cent of the control group scored in this range.[20]

Studies Favoring Group Instruction

Anderson, Hughes, and Dixon used for their experimental population pupils in a laboratory school having individualized instruction as compared with pupils in a neighboring school having group basal reading instruction. The pupils in this latter group had an average IQ that was ten points below the laboratory group. In spite of this handicap a far greater percentage of the basal reader group "achieved a reading age of

[19] Sam Duker, "Research Report: Effects of Introducing an Individualized Reading Approach by Student Teachers," *Research in Action*, Proceedings International Reading Association (New York: Scholastic Magazines, 1959), p. 59.

[20] Antoinette McCristy, *A Comparative Study to Determine Whether Self-Selection Reading Can Be Successfully Used at Second Grade Level.* Unpublished Master's Dissertation (Los Angeles: University of Southern California, 1957).

eighty-four months at or before a chronological age of eighty-four months."[21] The brighter group did not overtake the basal reader group until they were 132 months old on the average.

Safford made a study of seven classes of pupils in a California district, who had been taught by the Self-Selection method during the past three years, and compared their reading achievement with the district mean. He concluded that:

(1) For the majority of the individual pupils in the seven classes, the use of individualized reading techniques resulted in lower gains in reading achievement over a period of one calendar year, when contrasted with the results of other methods of reading instruction that are currently being used in this district and throughout the nation. (2) The use of self-selective reading methods achieved no significantly different results with the superior students than with average students. (3) The use of individualized reading techniques resulted in no significant difference in growth between reading vocabulary and reading comprehension.[22]

Karr's study was concerned with third grade classes. The achievement of groups having individualized instruction for six months was compared with the achievement of groups in a different community taught by the basal group procedure. The latter groups made slightly higher gains in vocabulary and comprehension than did the individualized groups. The teachers of the individualized groups, however, were satisfied with that plan of teaching.[23]

Studies Revealing No Difference

Walker experimented with two equivalent groups of children matched in reading ability, IQ, and socio-economic status. One group was taught by the individualized reading program, the other by group basal reader procedures. As was the case in Duker's study the teaching was done by student teachers, supervised by critic teachers. The student teachers gave the usual report that the children in the individualized group were more interested in reading and read more books. The data, however, showed no significant difference between the two groups in reading gains.[24]

The fact that these groups were taught by inexperienced students may

---

[21] Irving H. Anderson, Byron A. Hughes, and W. Robert Dixon, "The Relationship Between Reading Achievement and the Method of Teaching Reading," *University of Michigan School of Education Bulletin*, 27 (Apr. 1956), 104–108.

[22] Alton L. Safford, "Evaluation of an Individualized Reading Program," *The Reading Teacher*, 13 (Oct. 1960), 262–65, 270.

[23] Harold Karr, "An Experiment with an Individualized Method of Teaching Reading," *The Reading Teacher*, 7 (Feb. 1954), 174–77.

[24] Clare Walker, *An Evaluation of Two Programs of Reading in Grades Four, Five and Six in the Elementary School*. Unpublished Doctoral Dissertation (New York: School of Education, New York University, 1957).

have some influence on its validity, since all other factors were controlled.

An experiment conducted by Bohnhorst and Sellers involved five teachers in grades one, two, and three. Their most capable groups were taught by the individualized plan for a period of eight weeks. These same groups had been taught by the basal textbook plan for the preceding eight weeks. Test results for each of the two eight-week periods were compared. This comparison gave a suggestion of better progress for the experimental group, but the differences were not significant.[25]

Burdette experimented with the individualized plan in George County, Maryland. She compared the progress of elementary pupils under the individualized system with those under the three-group method and found no statistical differences in results. She reported, however, that many teachers using the individualized plan were enthusiastic about this method of teaching.[26]

Hilson and Thomas taught individualized reading to a first grade class and compared the results with those of two other classes where reading was taught by group procedures. Results of tests revealed no real difference in the achievement of children taught under the two different plans. As is true in many cases, it was reported that the children in the individualized group were more enthusiastic about reading.[27]

A Study Favoring a Combination

There are some studies whose results indicate that the individualized approach should be used with some children, and the group-basal reader approach with others. A well-conducted study made by Sartain involved ten second grade classes chosen at random. During the first three months of the experiment, five of the classes were taught by the individualized plan while the other five were taught by the group-basal reading plan plus supplemental reading. The same types and quantities of books were provided to each classroom. At the end of three months all classes rotated to the opposite method and the same teachers continued for three months with the same children; but they used the method having basal reader periods with groups and added the individual conference plan to self-selected supplementary reading. Comparisons of achievement revealed that pupils with lower IQ's made greater gains in word recognitions when using the group-basal reading plan. The investigator recom-

---

25 Ben A. Bohnhorst and Sophia N. Sellers, "Individual Reading Instruction vs. Basal Textbook Instruction: Some Tentative Explorations," *Elementary English*, 36 (Mar. 1959), 185–96.

26 Eunice E. Burdette, "What Research Says," *The Reading Teacher*, 11 (Dec. 1958), 119.

27 Helen H. Hilson and Glenn G. Thomas, "Individualized Reading in First Grade," *Educational Leadership*, 16 (Feb. 1959), 319–22.

mended using the group-basal reading plan with such children, adding to it the individual conference plan in connection with their supplemental reading.[28]

This experiment should be repeated and extended over longer periods of time. Three months is a relatively short time in which to measure reading growth. It would be desirable if the same groups could be rotated through the first and second years of instruction, even more so if the two methods might be rotated through four or six years of reading instruction.

Additional Readings

Books and Pamphlets

Blake, Howard E., *et al.*, "Here's to Another Way," *Creative Ways in Teaching the Language Arts,*" No. 15. Champaign, Ill.: Subcommittee of the Elementary Section Committee of the National Council of Teachers of English, 1957.

Burrows, Alvina Treut., *Teaching Children in the Middle Grades,* Chap. X. Boston: D. C. Heath & Company, 1952.

Conroy, Marie R., "Using Individual Reading Materials Instead of Sets of Class Readers," *New Practices in Reading in the Elementary Schools,* 319ff. Washington, D. C.: 17th Yearbook, DESP, NEA, 1938.

Gans, Roma, *Guiding Children's Reading Through Experiences* (Booklet). New York: Teachers College, Columbia University, 1941.

Garrettson, Grace, Beatrice Termeer, and Irene Whitcomb, "Through Self-Selection—Progress Unlimited," *Reading,* Bulletin No. 98, pp. 23–27. Washington, D. C.: Association for Childhood Education International, Nov. 1956.

Miel, Alice, ed., *Individualizing Reading Practices.* New York: Bureau of Publications, Teachers College, Columbia University, 1958.

National Council of Teachers of English, "Reading," Chap. VI in *Language Arts for Today's Children,* pp. 165–66. New York: Appleton-Century-Crofts, Inc., 1954.

Olson, Willard C., "Child Growth and Development," *Reading,* Bulletin No. 98, pp. 2–5. Washington, D. C.: Association for Childhood Education International, Nov. 1956.

Sartain, Harry W., "In Combining Sequential and Individualized Reading," *Sequential Development of Reading Abilities,* Supplemental Educational Monograph No. 90, pp. 187–90. Chicago: University of Chicago Press, 1960.

Stauffer, Russell G., ed., *Individualizing Reading Instruction,* Proceedings of the 39th Annual Education Conference. Newark: University of Delaware, 1957.

Veatch, Jeannette, *Individualizing Your Reading Program.* New York: G. P. Putnam's Sons, 1959.

[28] Harry W. Sartain, "The Roseville Experiment with Individualized Reading," *The Reading Teacher,* 13 (Mar. 1960), 277–81.

Washburne, Carleton W., *Adjusting the School to the Child,* 68ff. New York: Harcourt, Brace & World, Inc., 1937.

Periodicals

Barbe, Walter B., "Personalized or Individualized Reading Instruction," *Education,* Vol. 81 (May 1961), 537–40.

Crossley, Ruth, and Mildred Kniley, "An Individualized Reading Program," *Elementary English,* Vol. 36 (Jan. 1959), 16–20.

Dickenson, Marie, *et al.,* "Through Self-Selection to Individualized Reading Procedures," *California Journal of Elementary Education,* Vol. 27 (Feb. 1959), 150–77.

Evans, N. Dean, "Individualized Reading—Myths and Facts," *Elementary English,* Vol. 39 (Oct. 1962), 580–83.

Fox, Lorene K., "Opinions Differ on Individualized Reading," *NEA Journal,* Vol. 47 (Mar. 1958), 162.

Gray, William S., "Role of Group and Individualized Teaching in a Sound Reading Program," *Reading Teacher,* Vol. 11 (Dec. 1957), 99–104.

Greenman, Ruth, and Sharon Kapilian, "Individual Reading in Third and Fourth Grades," *Elementary English,* Vol. 36 (Apr. 1959), 234–37.

Haskell, Charlotte L., "What Research Says," *Reading Teacher,* Vol. 12 (Dec. 1958), 119.

Hilson, Helen H., and Glenn G. Thomas, "Individualized Reading in the First Grade," *Educational Leadership,* Vol. 16 (February 1959), 319–22.

Hunt, Lyman C., Jr., "Individualized Reading: Teaching Skills," *Education,* Vol. 81 (May 1961), 541–46.

Jacobs, Leland B., "Reading on Their Own Means Reading at the Growing Edges," *The Reading Teacher,* Vol. 6 (Mar. 1953), 27–30.

Kingsley, Marjorie, "An Experiment in Individualized Reading," *Elementary English,* Vol. 35 (Feb. 1958), 113–18.

Largent, Mary, "My Third-Graders Are Eager Readers," *NEA Journal,* Vol. 48 (Mar. 1959), 64–65.

Lazar, May, "Individualized Reading: A Dynamic Approach," *Reading Teacher,* Vol. 11 (Dec. 1957), 75–83.

——, "Individualized Reading," *Education,* Vol. 78 (Jan. 1958), 281–87.

Mackintosh, Helen K., and Mary Helen Mahar, "Teaching Reading the Individualized Way," *School Life* (May 1958).

Mays, Viola, "What Research Says," *Reading Teacher,* Vol. 12 (Dec. 1958), 120.

McCullough, Constance M., "Opinions Differ on Individualized Reading," *NEA Journal,* Vol. 47 (Mar. 1958), 163.

McNabb, Isabel, "What Research Says," *Reading Teacher,* Vol. 12 (Dec. 1958), 122.

Sartain, Harry W., "A Bibliography on Individualized Reading," *The Reading Teacher,* Vol. 13 (Apr. 1960), 262–65, 270.

Sartain, Harry W., "Research on Individualized Reading," *Education,* Vol. 81 (May 1961), 515–20.

Smith, Lois, and Jane Becher, "Self-Selection with Intermediate Children," *The Reading Teacher,* Vol. 14 (Nov. 1960), 83–88.

Smith, Nila Banton, "Individualized Instruction: Concepts Old and New," *Education,* Vol. 81 (May 1961), 527–29.

Veatch, Jeannette, "In Defense of Individualized Reading," *Elementary English,* Vol. 37 (Apr. 1960), 227–33.

Warford, Phyllis, "Individualized Reading in First Grade," *Elementary English,* Vol. 37 (Jan. 1960), 36–37.

Wilson, Harriet, "Stop Reading in Ability Groups," *Instructor,* Vol. 65 (Apr. 1956), 35, 74.

Witty, Paul, with Ann Coomer and Robert Sizemore, "Individualized Reading—A Summary and Evaluation," *Elementary English,* Vol. 36 (Oct. 1959), 401–12, 450.

————, "A Forward Look in Reading," *Elementary English,* Vol. 38 (Mar. 1961), 151–64.

PART 2

Skill Development

GROWTH AREAS IN SKILL DEVELOPMENT

WORD IDENTIFICATION	MEANINGS	STUDY SKILLS	FLUENCY AND SPEED

What are the reading skills? The cover-all term "reading skills" rolls glibly off our tongues in clichéd repetition. It sounds practical and useful and "professional." But do we really know what we are talking about? Are we fully cognizant of the different kinds of reading skills and how to develop them? Or do we teach reading more or less as a "lump-sum?" These are some of the questions that we, as teachers, need to ask ourselves, searchingly.

The writer sometimes startles her graduate students, most of whom are experienced teachers, by asking at the beginning of a course, "What are the reading skills?" The replies that come back immediately are: "Word Recognition" and "Comprehension." Then they begin to strain, and give such answers as "Eye-Movements" (which is a physical adjustment, not a reading skill, per se), "Silent Reading" (which is not a particular skill but a composite of many skills), and so on. If we don't have a clear-cut idea of what the reading skills are, how can we develop them adequately?

Regardless of whether a teacher is using an integrated language-arts approach, a television approach, a linguistics approach, an individualized instruction approach, or a basal reader approach, it is essential that she should have a comprehensive grasp of reading skills. The "numerator" may change but the skill "denominator" remains the same. In basic reading systems authorities have planned a skill development program with scope and sequence, but even in using such a program, as well as others, a teacher needs to be perceptive, discriminating, and resourceful in recognizing the different skills, in sensing which children need additional help in certain of them, and in providing this additional help. A teacher who is thoroughly informed concerning the skills and sensitive to them and who is ingenious and creative will find opportunities for pupils to practice these skills functionally in reading situations many times each day.

Perhaps nothing would contribute more to the improvement of reading instruction in American schools than a keen awareness of the various reading skills on the part of teachers and a dedicated attempt to provide for their well-rounded development throughout the elementary grades.

First of all we need to have a distinct and concise grasp of the major growth areas in reading skill development. Just visualizing the major areas in which we are to develop skills helps to add wholeness and balance to our viewpoint. All of us are highly sensitive to fundamental skill areas in arithmetic. When asked what they are we immediately reply, "Addition, subtraction, multiplication, and division." And we are right, for regardless of what we do in arithmetic we use some skill under one of these categories or a combination of skills from two or more of them. In reading there also are basic skill areas which we draw upon singly or in combination, usually in combination. These basic skill areas are: (1) word identification, (2) getting meanings from symbols, (3) study skills, and (4) fluency and speed.

But we must go further than recognizing and being concerned about these large skill areas just as generalities. Each of these major areas has many subareas of skills which contribute to the large area but which differ from one another. It is not enough, for example, to know that there is one big skill called "Word Identification." We must know what the several different skills are that prove helpful to children in identifying unrecognized words and what we can do in developing each of these different skills.

The reading process is extremely complex. How very simple it would be to teach reading if there were nothing more to it than spelling and pronunciation, which was the concept of reading instruction for several centuries. In this age we see reading as a many-sided process with innumerable facets which work together in continuously changing combinations. Each reading act is a composite of skills interwoven, interlaced, intertwined. New knowledge comes to us daily about this amazing process. The purpose of Part II of this book is to indicate the results of some of the research in regard to the reading process, to point out the more important subskills that cluster under the larger growth areas, to differentiate between them, and to offer suggestions of practical ways of developing them.

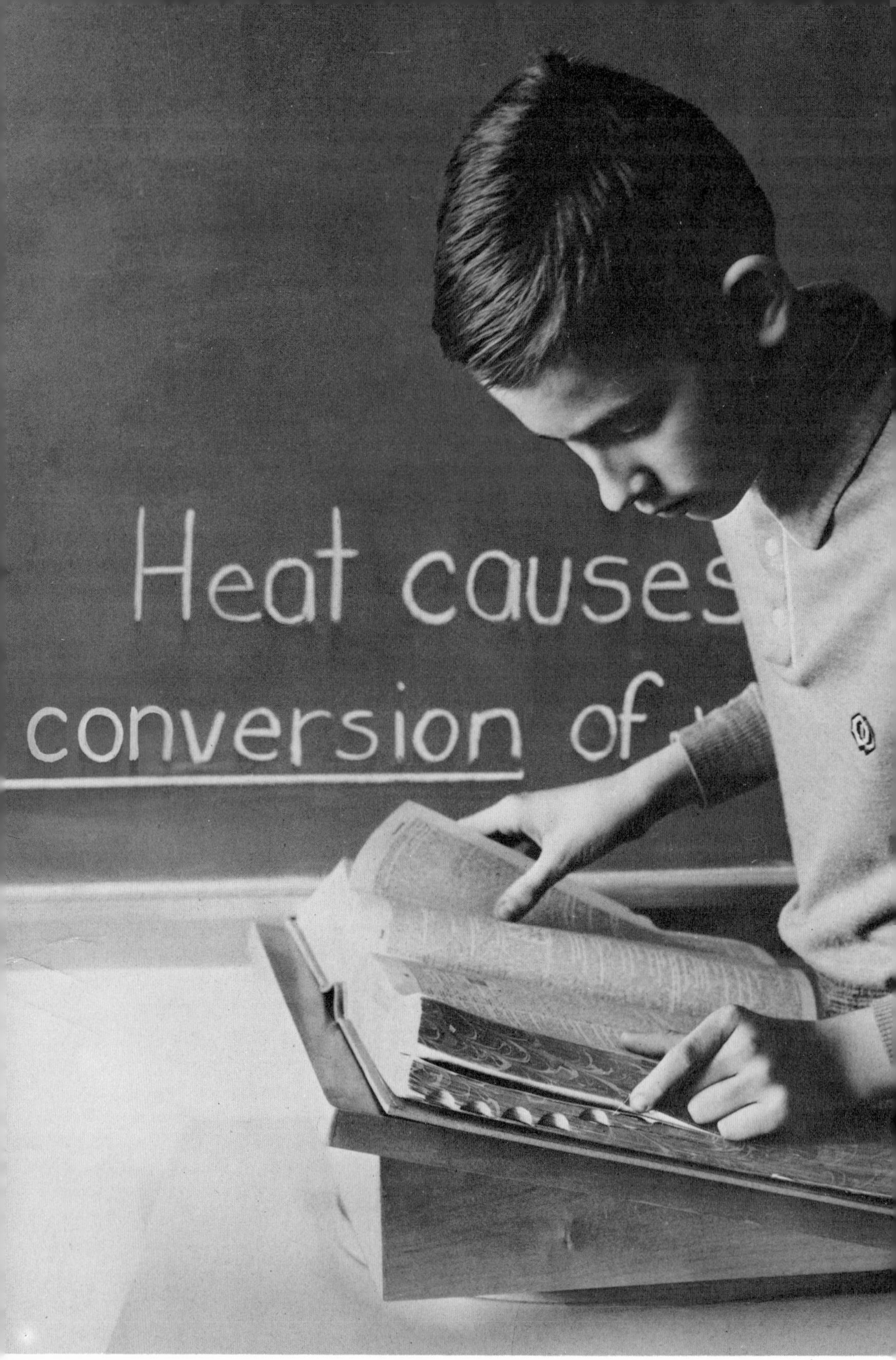
Heat causes
conversion of

8

Word Identification

The growth area of word identification is the most basic of all the skill areas. It is the foundation upon which the skills in all other growth areas are laid. Unless a child can recognize the words for which printed symbols stand, he can't read—period!

There are many different ways in which children may work out the pronunciation of words. None of these ways are foolproof. One technique may be effective in one situation, and a different technique in another; or it may take a combination of two techniques to work out a certain pronunciation, or perhaps one technique will be needed to check another. Therefore, the judicious thing to do is to teach children several different methods of attack. Flexibility is the watchword!

The techniques represented in the diagram on page 168 are the principal ones to teach children in developing their word identification ability. The use of picture clues and recognition of sight words are techniques which children usually

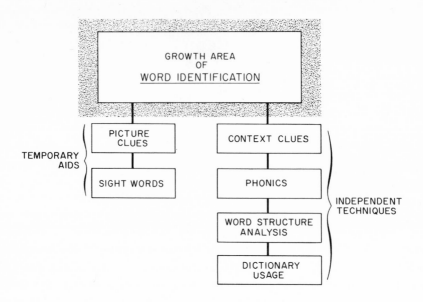

are taught in the earliest stages before the other methods of attack are introduced. These techniques have some use throughout the grades, and the technique of recognizing sight words is used almost exclusively by mature readers. However, the techniques that are of real value to children in successfully attacking unrecognized words *independently* are the use of: (1) context clues, (2) phonics, (3) structural analysis, and (4) the dictionary. All of these techniques will be discussed in detail.

USE OF PICTURE CLUES

The use of pictures as clues to word identification is most appropriate during the beginning stages of reading. Pictures provide interesting and attractive media with which to work, and they offer the child valuable assistance in making the transition from recognizing an object and naming it to recognizing a symbol which stands for an object and naming it.

Picture Clues in Books

The first books that children use for reading are really picture books with a few words appearing beneath the pictures here and there. The skillful teacher helps children to deduce the names of the symbols from the pictures. Perhaps before reading a book the teacher will give the names of the characters as she shows the children the character's pictures in the book, explaining as she does so: "The girl's name is Nancy, and this word under the picture says *Nancy*," and so on. Later, the children being taught read the words, referring to the picture to find out what each word is. Thus they have experience in using their first self-help technique in identifying new words.

While the picture clue technique is more valuable at beginning stages than later, it is of use throughout the elementary school. Books today are beautifully illustrated and great strides have been made in recent years in providing pictures that supplement information given in the context and that help children to visualize the concepts presented. Good teachers make the most of illustrations in serving these purposes and also in aiding word identification. As an example of such use of pictures consider the third grade children who were reading a story with its setting in a mid-western wheat field at harvest time. *Combine* was a new word on the page and also a new concept in its use as a machine. These children lived in a city where they were totally unfamiliar with harvesting procedures. So before reading the selection, Miss Steele, the teacher, asked them to look at the picture on the page and to see if they could tell what the machine was and what it was doing. Interest was aroused but answers were quite befogged. Miss Steele then explained that farmers formerly cut their wheat with a machine called a reaper, then hauled it to a barn where another machine, called a threshing machine, separated the kernels of wheat from the chaff. She further explained that, at present, farmers have one machine that does the work of both of the machines of former times, that this machine combines both operations, and so is called a *combine.* She then wrote on the chalkboard *com'bine, com bine',* with the accent mark in different places. Discussion followed in regard to the meaning of *combine* in the two situations. Finally, the generalization was drawn that the word was pronounced *com bine'* when it was an action word and *com'bine* when it was used as the name of something such as the machine in the picture.

In a few minutes John was reading the story orally when he encountered the word *combine,* and in spite of preceding development and discussion he didn't recognize this word. "It's the name of the machine in the picture," suggested Miss Steele. John glanced at the picture and came through with the pronunciation *com'bine.* Thus a third grader made good use of a picture clue in identifying an unrecognized word.

Pictured Vocabulary Cards

Children enjoy playing games with pictured vocabulary cards which are prepared by the teacher or which can be bought commercially. Several different companies have available packs of pictured word cards, which have a picture and the word that represents the picture on one side, and the word alone on the other side. One way to play a game with such cards is as follows: Each of two children take a few of the cards, perhaps six or eight, and study them by looking at the picture side of each one and reading the word, then turning the card over and reading the word on the unpictured side. After studying the cards they take turns testing each other. One of the children holds the other's cards up for him to recognize. The child holding the cards keeps the pictured side toward himself and holds the unpictured side toward the one who is trying to recognize the words. If a child misses a word, the card is laid in a certain place. After the trial at reading all the cards in the pack, the child who has been tested then tests the other child. The child who reads the most cards correctly wins the game. Then each one studies the cards he has missed, and each tests the other again.

Working with pictured word cards, of course, does not give the child facility in attacking new words independently, and it provides practice only on picturable words which are the easiest ones for children to recognize. Pictured cards do, however, often enable children to learn to recognize several words rather rapidly, and these words are meaningful to them because of the accompanying picture.

The use of picture cards is often especially effective as a first step in working with older pupils who are seriously retarded in reading. If such a child has reached the middle grades with extremely low word identification ability, then work with pictured word cards often enables him to build up a small stock of recognized words rather quickly. This gives him a sense of accomplishment at the outset of his corrective work in reading, which is, of course, a valuable asset in continuing reading improvement activities.

One example will be given of the use of pictured cards with an older pupil. Philip suffered an injury when he was six years old which prevented him from attending school for several years. Eventually he recovered, and at twelve he came to the writer for a conference about learning to read. Philip required careful diagnosis, of course, but during this first conference it was learned that he knew just one word, *the*. In order to give him something constructive to do immediately, the writer provided him with twenty pictured word cards to take home, explained to him how he could work with them himself, and told him to see how many words he could learn before coming back again. To her surprise, Philip knew all twenty words when he arrived for the next session. He continued working by himself and in this way built up a vocabulary of seventy-five pictured words. As he learned these words they were woven into compositions which he dictated, and the other word identification techniques discussed in this chapter were developed in connection with the reading of these self-dictated stories and later in connection with reading from books.

The use of picture clues is limited, but it does have a place in the word identification program. Its most important functions were discussed above.

Pictured Dictionaries

Pictured dictionaries also fall within the category of recognizing words through the use of picture clues. Learning new words through meaningful association, developing self-helpfulness, and establishing dictionary habits are all products of using picture dictionaries. Several published picture dictionaries are available even for the early primary grades.

The subject of pictured dictionaries and their uses is discussed further under "Picture Dictionaries," pages 326–28.

USE OF SIGHT WORDS

The term *sight words* is used to denote those words that children learn to recognize by sight without aid of any of the other identification techniques represented in the diagram on page 168.

While learning to recognize words by sight doesn't develop "power" in children to attack unrecognized words by themselves, it does serve certain purposes which are sufficiently significant to justify including the learning of sight words in the word identification program. Most children who learn to read at home naturally and at their own request learn whole words. Modern psychology and philosophy support the contention that it is advisable for beginning readers to work with meaningful word wholes rather than to memorize phonic elements. There is some diversity from this point of view by a small minority, but the great majority of reading authorities believe that meaningful word wholes should be used at the starting point in reading instruction. In this capacity, recognizing words by sight may serve its largest function during the early stages of learning to read.

Sight recognition has another service to render, however, at other levels of development. There are several frequently recurring words which do not lend themselves to phonic analysis or other methods of attack, such as *what, where, would,* and *was.* Unless a child can recognize such words instantly by sight, he is apt to be quite frustrated in reading almost any page of print. Underdeveloped readers, and even average readers in second and third grades and higher, often can't "see the woods for the trees" because they are unable to recognize many of these common words. In such cases concentrated effort to fix recognition of these words by sight "opens up" the pages of print for them immediately. Under these conditions teaching such words by sight is justifiable at higher levels as well as at the beginning stage.

Cues and Clues to Visual Perception

The child accomplishes his first recognition of sight words through the use of various cues and clues. Several studies of children's word perception have been made. Results of these studies which may be of interest to teachers will be mentioned briefly. Detailed discussions of the studies will be found in the references cited at the bottom of the page.[1]

Configuration

Some authorities consider configuration to be one of the important methods of word attack, in addition to the other techniques, such as picture clues, sight words, context, phonics, structural analysis, and so on. The writer prefers to classify configuration as just one of the cues to recognition of sight words rather than as an important general technique in itself.

The configuration of a word means, of course, its general contour or shape. This word shape has been found to be the strongest cue to recognition. A child may have little or no difficulty in learning to recognize *Grandfather* because of the characteristic shape of the word, while he may have a great deal of trouble in recognizing *is* because it does not have a distinctive shape. The longer words are at an advantage from the perception standpoint.

As an interesting sidelight the writer will describe a small informal

---

[1] Arthur I. Gates, "Implications of the Psychology of Perception for Word Study," *Education*, Vol. 75 (May 1955), 589–95. Jean T. Goins, "Visual Perception Abilities and Early Reading Progress," Supplementary Educational Monographs (Chicago: University of Chicago Press, 1958), p. 81. Albert J. Harris, "Visual and Auditory Perception in Learning to Read," *The Optometric Weekly*, Vol. 50 (1959), 2115–121. Sister Mary James Harrington and Donald DeWitt Durrell, "Mental Maturity Versus Perception Abilities in Primary Reading," *Journal of Educational Psychology*, Vol. 46 (Oct. 1955), pp. 375–80. Robert E. Mills, "Evaluation of Techniques in Teaching Word Recognition," *Elementary School Journal*, Vol. 56 (Jan. 1956), 221–25. Ross L. Mooney, "The Perceptive Process in Reading," *The Reading Teacher*, Vol. 13 (Oct. 1959), pp. 34–39. Muriel C. Potter, *Perception of Symbol Orientation and Early Reading Success*, Contributions to Education, No. 939 (New York: Teachers College, Columbia University, 1949). Magdalen D. Vernon, *Backwardness in Reading: A Study of Its Nature and Origin* (New York: Cambridge University Press, 1957). Joseph Wepman, "Auditory Discrimination, Speech, and Reading," *Elementary School Journal*, Vol. 60 (Apr. 1960), 325–33.

experiment which a teacher and herself carried on one morning with a group of first grade children. Upon entering the classroom, the teacher was found to be flashing word cards for the children's identification (a practice which is now frowned upon). One of the words in the pack of cards was *grasshopper*. The teacher was asked to take this word out of the pack, trace its shape on a card, and place this shape rather than the word itself in the pack. This was done, and then the children were called up individually to read the words. When a child came to the *grasshopper* configuration, the teacher would ask, "What would the word be if all of the letters were filled in?" Nine out of thirteen children recognized the word from its shape.

Letter details

Letter details have an influence on recognition. As an example of this influence children have been found to recognize *pig* because of the dot above the *i* and *look* because of the double *oo*. Letters at the beginning and end of words give cues more often than letters in the middle unless the middle letters have something distinctive about them.

Some teachers try to call attention to letter characteristics by making associations between them and objects. According to this practice the children may be told that they will have no difficulty in remembering *orange* because "there is a little orange at the beginning of the word," or that *rabbit* will be easy for them "because they can see a rabbit's ears sticking right up in the middle of the word." This is a very fallacious practice. An association should not be built up in connection with a letter or a group of letters in any one word when the same letter or group of letters appear in many other words. The "little orange" (*o*) may help them to remember *orange* but what about *old, open, owl, ocean?* Thinking of "the little orange" at the beginning of these words is not going to give a cue to recognizing them. And what about *pebble, robber, sobbed?* Would associating the double *b* with rabbit ears help here? Instead of building up inappropriate associations, let the children discover "what is interesting" or "what is different" about a word. It is perfectly all right at times to call attention to distinguishing characteristics yourself; for example: when discussing *baby*, the teacher may say "This word has two letters that are just alike"; or in discussing *stop*, "This word has one letter that rises up above the others, and one that extends below the others," pointing out the letters in each case, saying the names of them if the teacher wishes to do so.

The interest cue

Interest and pleasant association are aids to recognition. Other things being equal a child would probably be able to recognize *candy* more readily than he would *table*. In beginning work interest cue words are especially important.

Meaning clues

Meaning is a very important clue when recognizing a sight word in a sentence. This process will be discussed in the next section under the heading of Context Clues.

Word Recognition Games

Is it desirable to play games with children to help in fixing sight words?

Focusing pleasurable attention on word forms through the use of games in which the words are repeated orally is a method widely used by primary teachers in fixing sight words. Of course, such games are used more extensively in beginning reading classes than elsewhere because children at this stage have not yet developed ability to attack words independently and are largely dependent upon memory. The value of such games depends upon the type of game, its content, and the way in which it is played. A teacher should choose these games with care.

Avoid contrived games

Many devices widely used in the past for sight word practice are artificial and far-fetched. Reference is made to such devices as these: The teacher draws an apple tree on the chalkboard, prints a word on each apple, and lets the children pretend they are picking apples; that is, each time a child names a word he has "picked an apple." Or a brook is drawn on the chalkboard, with stones placed at intervals across it. The words to be given practice are written on the stones. The child tries to walk across the brook by stepping on the stones; that is, each time he pronounces a word correctly, he is supposed to have taken another step across the brook.

There are several reasons why it is not desirable to use such devices as these. In the first place, while they are taken from real life situations, their application is so far removed from the original activity that it seems almost an insult to the intelligence of any child to resort to such pretense in order to give him practice on words. Probably the more serious objections, however, have their roots in modern psychology. In the first place, the use of such devices builds up wrong associations. Suppose one of the words is *fly;* is there any reason why connections should be built up between *fly* and picking apples or walking across a brook? It is better not to associate a word with anything at all than to build up a wrong association. Another objection is that attention is divided between concentrating on the words and enjoying a vivid play experience. For this reason practice probably is not so effective as it would be if the attention were sharply focused on the words to be fixed, rather than being diluted and overshadowed by a play activity.

Avoid presenting words in isolation

There is another very undesirable feature in practically all contrived games and in far too many games in current use that do concentrate on the words themselves without contrived "trimmings." This highly objectional feature is that the words are presented in isolation, entirely apart from context. Flash card games, games played with lists of words on the chalkboard, spinning disk games in which the child is to pronounce the word pointed to when the hand stops spinning are examples of the isolated-word type of game. Practice in word recognition should be directed not only toward ability to pronounce a word but also toward recognizing its meaning. Words have many different shades of meaning, and the particular shade of a certain word meaning is apparent only when the word is surrounded with other words. The word *can*, a very common word in beginning reading, may mean one thing in the sentence, "I can help Mother," and another thing in the sentence, "Tom has a can of dog food." It is the words which surround any particular word which give that word its meaning. Games involving isolated words that are pictured, of course, are not open to the same "meaning" objection that other games are because the meaning is represented pictorially.

Keep the content close to life's setting

Aside from considerations of meaning, any developing skill should be kept close to the setting in which it is used in life. We don't read separate lists of words in life; we read words embedded in context. In the light of this observation, children should learn to recognize sight words in contextual settings. We can be more sure of a transfer under these conditions.

Many experienced teachers have heard a parent say something to this effect: "I can't understand why Tom isn't able to read. I have had him memorize all of the words in the vocabulary lists at the back of his reader, but he doesn't know them at all when he reads stories in the book." Abundant reports of this kind from parents and teachers, too, bear evidence to the lack of transfer to the reading situation when children are given practice in memorizing isolated words apart from context.

Ensure maximum participation

Another objection to many word recognition games is not intrinsically bound up with the content of the game but is concerned with its organization and operation. Games in which the teacher plays the game with just one child when several in a group need the same practice is an inefficient use of teaching effort. In such cases the other children in the group may look on; perhaps some do not even look on, and we don't know how many of them or whether any of them are actively participating mentally in the practice. Spectator practice can't be depended upon for as effective results as personal participation. Therefore, in order to make maximum use of teacher effort and pupil time, it is advisable to choose games in which all the children needing practice make responses during each round of the game rather than games in which just one child has the benefit of playing with the teacher.

Use a variety of games

Some teachers have one or two favorite games in their "bag of tricks" which they pull out and use daily during comparatively long periods of time. While the teacher may feel secure and comfortable in using games that she is accustomed to, the children may become tired of playing these same games repeatedly for fifteen or twenty minutes at a time, as is frequently the case.

Interest is a strong factor in acquiring new words in a reading vocabulary, and variety in game-playing keeps interest high. Teach the children how to play several worthwhile games. Play one for a few minutes one day, another for a few minutes the next day, and so on, all as a part of and we hope tied in with current reading experience and the needs of participating pupils. If an entire period is devoted to game-playing, change to a different game every few minutes rather than devoting the entire period to one game. The same words may be given practice in each of the different games, and practice results should be enhanced by this variety.

Sample games

Two sight word games are described which avoid the objectionable features and incorporate the desirable features mentioned in the discussion above. They are not contrived, they give practice on words in meaningful context, and they provide for maximum participation of all pupils. The creative teacher and perhaps the pupils themselves, often may make up other games which include these features.

The guessing game

The teacher prepares some sentences containing sight words which are giving trouble to certain children in the classroom. For example, the words causing the most difficulty with children in a certain second grade were *said, here, is, my, you,* and *can.* The teacher made up these sentences:

Susan said, "Here is my cake, Bill.
You and I can eat my cake."

If possible the sentences should be tied in with some experience the children are having or have had recently or with something they are reading. In this particular case, Susan, one of the pupils in the group needing help, had told about a little cake she had made the day before that she had shown to her brother Bill and had invited him to eat with her. The sentences above were meaningful because they related to Susan's personal experience.

If it appears that sentences containing the sight words on which practice is desired cannot be an outgrowth of current experience or reading, then the teacher may make the sentences more meaningful by preparing a short background story leading up to the sentences and telling it to the children when they are about to work with the sentences. In some cases the children are able to make up sentences containing words on which they need practice.

Just one short sentence may be used in beginning reading stages. In later stages several sentences may be used in one composition, and several different groups of sentences may be used if it seems advisable.

After the sentences are composed the teacher manuscripts or prints them on tag-board, cuts the sentences and words apart, and places them in the pocket chart. (If a pocket chart is not available she may write the sentences on the chalkboard.)

In playing the game one child goes out in the hall. Another child in the group selects a word for the child in the hall to "guess." He pulls out the card for this word, shows it to the other children, and they read the word orally. This ensures that everyone in the group knows what the word is that the child in the hall is to "guess," and it also offers everyone a chance to have some initial practice in recognizing that particular word.

The child who is in the hall is then called back to the classroom. He pulls each card up in turn, but doesn't take it out of its context. (He shouldn't be permitted to point to a card.) As he pulls a card up, he asks, "Is it *Susan*?" "Is it *is*?" "Is it *my*?" and so on until he mentions the word that was chosen. Each time he asks a question all the children in the group reply, "No, it is not *Susan*," "No, it is not *is*," and so on. Thus, not only the child who is trying to find which word was chosen has practice in associating the spoken word with the sight word symbol, but all the children in the group actively participate in the practice.

After the child who is trying to "guess" which word was chosen finds the word, another child goes out in the hall and the game continues. When first playing the game it is desirable for the child who is guessing to pull up the cards in order. Later, it adds to the interest if he is permitted to skip about, selecting words out of order.

The clap game

This game may be played with sight words in an experience chart or with words in specially prepared sentences as suggested in connection with the "Guessing Game" described above.

The teacher tells the group that they may clap *once* when she pulls up or places the side of her hand beneath a card that she is thinking of and has named. Emphasize that there is to be only *one* clap, otherwise they may enter into prolonged applause each time the teacher takes a turn in having them recognize a word.

Using the sentences presented in the "Guessing Game" as an example, the teacher might say, "I am thinking of the word *my*. You may clap once when I pull up the card with *my* on it." The children sit with hands in readiness to clap. The teacher begins by pulling up the card with *Susan* on it and continues silently to pull up the other cards in order until she comes to *my*, when the children clap.

Throughout the game all children watch intently, for who would miss a chance to clap? The game is diagnostic in that some children clap ahead of time. This indicates that they need practice in recognizing the word for which they clapped, as well as the one the teacher named to be recognized. These children can be given additional practice in recognizing the words for which they gave the wrong clap.

The context may be made simpler or more difficult, ranging from one simple sentence to several more complete sentences according to the ability level of the children.

The game itself may be varied by having different pupils take turns at thinking of words and pulling up cards until they come to the right one. After pupils have had some experience in playing the game, the cards may be pulled up out of order instead of following the order of the words in the sentences.

Self-Help References

Supplying self-help references for children's use in finding out sight words for themselves is one of the most commendable provisions a teacher can make. Both the attitude toward and the habit of finding out unrecognized words by one's self are important assets in learning to read. Furthermore, when a child uses his own initiative in finding out a word, and the activity is reinforced by success and he is able to continue with his reading unimpeded with word recognition difficulty, the word is more apt to "stick." It is, according to psychology, "more firmly impressed in his mental grooves."

With these thoughts in mind a few suggestions of self-help references will be made.

A chalkboard dictionary

Some teachers prepare a chalkboard dictionary for use during the early stages of reading instruction. While this dictionary usually is placed on one section of the chalkboard, it can be placed on a large tagboard chart. To make the foundation for the dictionary, the teacher draws horizontal lines about four inches apart, one for each letter of the alphabet, except that only one line is allowed for *XYZ*. The appropriate letter, both in capitalized and lower case forms, is placed at the left of each line. Whenever a new picturable word comes up in reading, the teacher pastes the appropriate picture for the word on the line containing its beginning letter and writes the name in manuscript beside the word in both lower case and capitalized form. Sometimes the teacher draws the pictures of the words. Stick figures are especially appropriate for action words such as *run,* *hop,* and *jump.* Sometimes the children find pictures to illustrate the words.

The section of the chalkboard dictionary for *a, b,* and *c* might look something like this:

a		apple Apple					
b		baby Baby		ball Ball		bed Bed
c		cake Cake		cat Cat			

The teacher and children read the words together as new ones are added to the dictionary. If a child fails to recognize one of these words while reading in a book, he refers to the picture dictionary on the chalkboard or chart and finds it for himself.

A class dictionary booklet

A dictionary booklet may be built up for use by all children in the class in any of the primary grades. To prepare a class dictionary the teacher may procure a large notebook together with a set of alphabetical tabs to be attached to the edges of the leaves. As a new word comes up that the children wish to record for future reference, they find the place for it in the class dictionary, and the teacher (or a child in second or third grade) manuscripts the word in the appropriate spot. Children and teacher then search for a picture to illustrate the word. They may look in old catalogs, magazines, newspapers, and discarded books for an appropriate illustration. When a good picture is found it is pasted above the word in the class dictionary. Sometimes children draw or paint pictures of a word, and the best one is chosen for the dictionary.

As the dictionary develops children are free to go to this reference and look up a word at any time while reading.

Labeled pictures

Not all words that children need can be pictured. In fact the most difficult sight words are those that do not lend themselves to picturization, such as *was, here, their, of,* and so on. Labels beneath pictures can be used as self-help references for such words.

In preparing material to use in connection with this activity the teacher makes a collection of attractive colored pictures. She also jots down the unpicturable words that are causing the most trouble. She then selects a picture which she thinks lends itself to a label that will include some of these difficult sight words. The class discusses the picture and composes an appropriate label to be pasted beneath the picture or attached to it. With skillful guidance the label may be one that contains several of the difficult words.

For example, several children in one second grade group were having difficulty with the words *these, their, were, was,* and *while.* It was during the maple sugar season, and the children were interested in the process of making maple sugar and were engaged in some language activities in connection with this topic. The teacher brought out a picture showing some children in the woods tending a pan of maple syrup as their father was disappearing far down the road. After some discussion the pupils in the classroom made up this label for the picture: "These children were making maple syrup while their father was away." The teacher manuscripted the sentence on a strip of tagboard, attached it to the picture, and hung it up in the classroom. The children found the hard words (*these, their, were, was, while*) in the sentence, and the teacher drew a "box" around each of these words to make it stand out. The children referred to the label whenever they had trouble with one of these words.

A few labeled pictures of this sort can take care of nearly all the unpicturable sight words that cause trouble.

Key sentences

Some teachers have found it valuable to prepare a group of key sentences containing each of the sight words giving difficulty, printing each group of key sentences on a separate chart and assembling all the key sentence charts in one place for permanent reference.

The key sentences should be given by the children themselves. For example, the teacher tells the children that she is going to manuscript several sentences on a chart with the word *where* in each of them and place the chart beneath the chalkledge in the front of the room so that when they forget *where* they can look at the chart, read the sentence, and thus find out the word. She then asks them to give her several sentences with *where* in each one. She manuscripts the sentences on the chalkboard and transfers them to tagboard later. The suggested sentences might be the following:

where
Where is your hat?
Where is your book?
Tell me where your mother is.
Where is your pencil?

Individual word booklets

Each child may have a little notebook in which the words causing him difficulty are recorded by the teacher. Each word may be followed by an appropriate sentence suggested by the child, such as: "*How*—How old are you?" The child studies these sentences by himself, and during certain times set aside for the purpose he may read them to the teacher or another pupil. His goal will be to beat his own record each time by recognizing more and more of the words.

Charts previously read

Some teachers save experience charts which the children have composed and read, attach wooden fasteners to them, and suspend them from a wire extending across one side or one end of the room. Frequently, when a child does not recall a word while reading from a book, he refers to one of the old familiar charts in which it appears and thus finds it out for himself.

USE OF CONTEXT CLUES

"What word would it have to be to make sense?" Teachers up and down and around the countryside have been asking this question of their pupils for years. In so doing they have been encouraging the use of context clues in finding out an unrecognized word. This method is fine, but teachers need to do more, much more, in developing ability to use the context skill. This is an important word-getting technique and one that should be developed through planned, thoughtful, and intelligent guidance, just as the ability to use phonics or structural analysis are developed through carefully planned instruction.

Perhaps it is the context clue technique that aids the mature reader most often in recognizing a word which he sees for the first time in print. Suppose that you, the reader, had never seen the printed symbol for *podium*. You had, however, heard a radio announcer say that James Whitehall, the conductor, had just ascended to the podium, and that you were about to hear the strains of the Strauss Waltz. Suppose further that while watching television you heard the person in charge of a program say, "Henry Bedell is now mounting the podium. He will lead his orchestra in playing *Il Trovatore* for your entertainment," and you watched as Mr. Bedell stepped up on a raised platform above the level of the musicians in the orchestra. During experiences such as these you had learned the pronunciation of *podium* and its meaning when used in a context having to do with the conductor of an orchestra. Then one day it happens that for the first time you encounter the word *podium* in print. You read that "the famous orchestra leader, Jacob Heindrich, suffered a heart attack just as he climbed up on the *podium*." You don't hesitate for one moment in pronouncing this word which you have never seen before as a printed symbol. You don't read it as pŏd'ium or po dī' um or with any other pronunciation except the right one. You call the word pō'dĭ ŭm just as you have heard it called when used verbally in similar context. No phonetic analysis was necessary; context clues came to your aid so swiftly and automatically that it didn't occur to you that you were pronouncing a new word symbol for the first time. As adults we probably use context clues so frequently and effectually that we are not aware of this valuable aid. We should help children to take steps toward this stage of maturation.

Not many studies have been made in regard to children's use of context clues as a word identification technique. McKee,[2] however, arrived at an important conclusion as a result of research. His conclusion was that the average child in fourth grade can use context clues to identify the meaning of an unrecognized word in his textbooks about once in three times. This finding gives us reason to believe that it is advisable to give more guidance in the use of the contextual technique.

[2] Paul McKee, *The Teaching of Reading* (Boston: Houghton Mifflin Co., 1948), p. 73.

Types of Context Clues

Attempts have been made to analyze text in order to find out what kinds of context clues can be utilized in reading. As a result, there is one classification concerned with the nature of the text itself and another concerned with typographical and structural aids. The results of each of these types of analysis will be given.

Analysis of the nature of text

McCullough [3] states several different situations in which the nature of the text could lead to the recognition of a word. It is useful for the teacher to have these situations in mind, although it would not be at all advisable for her to have children learn these types and try to identify them in working out words. Perhaps some acquaintance with the types might be given to children in the upper grades, but in general it is the teacher who will make use of these types in the kinds of questions she asks while guiding children to use context clues.

Some types of clues discussed by McCullough are listed below together with brief explanations and examples prepared by the writer.

1. *Experience.* The child supplies the word because it makes sense in terms of his own experiences. For example: The postman brought a (letter) from Aunt Mary.

2. *Comparison or contrast.* The unknown word may be supplied because it is evident in a contrast or comparison. For example: Rabbits have short tails and cats have (long) tails.

3. *Familiar expression.* Sometimes a word is supplied because it just fits naturally into a cliché which has been heard so often that it is familiar as: The popcorn was white as (snow).

4. *Definition.* Sometimes an unknown word is defined in a passage and the definition gives a clue. For example: Tommy was the largest animal in the zoo. He was an old gray (elephant).

Analysis of typographical and structural aids

Artley [4] lists several aids which can be used as clues to word meanings. His classification embraces: (1) the typographical aids of quotation marks, italics, bold face type, parentheses, and footnotes and glossaries; (2) structural aids such as appositive phrase or clause, nonrestrictive phrase or clause, interpolated phrase or clause; (3) the substitute words —synonyms and antonyms; (4) word elements—roots, prefixes, and suf-

---

[3] Constance M. McCullough, "Context Aids in Reading," *Elementary English Review,* Vol. 20 (Apr. 1943), 140–43. Reprinted with the permission of the National Council of Teachers of English and Constance M. McCullough.

[4] Sterl Artley, "Teaching Word Meaning Through Context," *Elementary English Review,* Vol. 20 (February 1943), 68–74. Reprinted with the permission of the National Council of Teachers of English.

fixes; (5) figures of speech—similes and metaphors; (6) pictorial representations—pictures, diagrams, charts, graphs, and maps; (7) inference; (8) direct explanation; (9) background experience; (10) subjective clues —tone, mood, and intent.

While some of these devices are too advanced for use with elementary pupils, most of them are applicable at this level. Formal teaching of this set of aids as a context syllabus is not advisable. Children should, however, be made aware of such of these devices as are appropriate at their respective levels, and they should have pointed out to them the effect which the devices have on meaning. Upon many occasions a child will be able to supply an unrecognized word in context if his attention is called to one of these clues which offers an appropriate lead to the word concerned.

Procedures for Developing Skill

There are several different ways in which a teacher can develop and give practice in the use of contextual clues. A few practical suggestions are given below:

Teacher instruction, comments, and questions

Perhaps the most effective way to develop contextual sensitivity and ability is to make the most of each functional opportunity while children are reading, that is, to give them help in finding out an unrecognized word through the use of context clues whenever they meet a new word that is appropriate for this method of attack. Much more is involved in giving this help than merely saying "Guess the word," which really does little to develop skill and which in many cases proves to be a dangerous procedure.

The first time there is trouble with an unrecognized word which plainly can be gotten through context, the teacher may use this situation as an example in explaining to the children that they can often find out what an unrecognized word is if they will just go on and read the rest of the sentence and then come back to the unrecognized word. The teacher should frequently talk to them about the help which such a procedure will offer and encourage them to use it.

It is particularly necessary to emphasize to first grade children that it is all right to go on and read the rest of a sentence when they come to a word within the sentence that they don't know. Those of us who have worked with first graders know that when they are reading by themselves and come to a word they don't recognize they are "stuck." There is no further reading until they find out what the one word is. While accuracy in reading is a great virtue, it also is of benefit to teach children to try and find out the word by reading the rest of the sentence.

As for guiding comments and questions, these, if skillfully worded and propitiously given, will be of great benefit. Below are a few examples of what is meant by guiding comments and questions. These examples are drawn from different levels—grades one through six.

Daddy flew away on a big airplane.

Jane read this sentence through until she came to *airplane.* She stopped, puzzled, because she didn't know this word. "Think what the sentence tells you up to this word," said Miss Griffin. "Daddy flew away on a big _____. Daddy couldn't fly away on a big train or a big bus. Daddy flew away on a big _____," and at this point Jane supplied "airplane."

Tom was six years old.
He had a birthday party.

Jimmy read these two lines very well until he came to *birthday.* This word he didn't know. "Read the next word," said Miss Jones. Jimmy promptly read *party.* "Now you'll have no trouble getting the word before party," said Miss Jones. "Let's start over again, beginning with *Tom.*" Jimmy read the two sentences again, this time readily supplying the word *birthday.*

Fred and Uncle Bob were up early. Fred helped to wash the breakfast dishes.

Ted failed to recognize *breakfast* while reading the above paragraph. "Well, if they were up early, what meal would they have had at which dishes were used?", asked Miss Bellam. "Breakfast" replied Ted and continued with his reading.

The drivers rushed after the elephant, and the noble Lords and Generals hastened to place themselves between the King and the raging beast.

Sue read the last part of the sentence, ". . . and the *ragging* beast." "Think what you said," directed Miss Withers. "Does *ragging* beast make sense? According to this story was the elephant angry? Could we have said that the elephant was in a _____?" Miss Withers wrote *rage* on the chalkboard and Sue read it. "Now look at the word before beast. What kind of a beast was it?" Sue now read *raging* beast with confidence.

With the uses of such activities teachers may continuously help children to use context clues all through the elementary grades.

Additional Practice

There are some children who "catch on" to the use of context clues very quickly, as is the case with other methods of attacking words. Others benefit from some direct practice; still others require a great deal of practice before they become adept at using this skill. Several aids to use for this purpose will be found in Chapter 21, pages 541–44.

Dangers in the Context Clue Approach

The first danger in developing the context clue approach arises from indiscreetly instructing the child to "Guess the word." According to Webster *guess* means "to form an opinion without evidence; conjecture." The term *guess* can be used acceptably in a simple little game, such as the one described on pages 176–77 in which *guessing* which word card someone has pulled up in a wall chart is just a matter of chance. Finding out an unrecognized word through the use of context is different. In this case the child carefully considers the meaning implied in a sentence or paragraph as a whole, and in the light of this meaning he reasons what the unrecognized word might be and deduces it as a result of his reasoning. The meanings conveyed by a combination of other words in a passage constitute the evidence on which the child bases his conclusion in supplying the unrecognized word.

Surely this process of examining meanings, reasoning, and deducing an unrecognized word is not just a matter of chance guessing. Telling a child to "guess" an unknown word in context is placing before him a superficial and erroneous concept of the process of finding out words through contextual clues. Rather, instructions should be given which will guide the child through the thinking processes necessary in using such clues intelligently. The section under "Teacher Instruction, Comments, and Questions" pages 184–85 contains suggestions for giving this type of help.

Another danger is that some children who are already wild guessers in reading will be so stimulated by the teaching and learning activities in connection with the use of contextual clues that they will become even wilder and more prolific guessers of words. Such children should be held to accuracy in reading and shown the fallacy of "sticking in" a word when it doesn't make sense. Strong emphasis also should be placed on other methods of attack in working with such children.

A third danger is that an overemphasis on the use of context clues may cause some children to look upon this procedure as an easy way to get all words, and may result in retarding or diminishing their attempts to use other techniques.

To avoid this state of affairs the teacher should continuously emphasize to children the need of having "several different tools to unlock new words," so that if one doesn't work they will have another one to use or to serve as a check. When context clues are tried and fail, the teacher would do well to remind the children of the possibilities for failure by saying something to this effect: "You see, trying to get a word from meanings in a sentence doesn't always work. We need to know other ways of getting unknown words, such as using phonics, examining the structure of a word, and referring to the dictionary." In discussing the particular word under consideration, suggest or ask the children to suggest which method of attack or combinations of methods of attack could be used to advantage in working out the pronunciation and meaning of that particular word. Continuously encourage versatility of attack.

Words of warning in regard to teaching the use of context clues are important and need to be observed carefully. If the precautionary measures mentioned above are observed, however, the teacher may proceed in her development of this technique with confidence that her efforts will be richly rewarded.

USE OF PHONICS

Phonics has been the subject of rabid criticism or enthusiastic approval off and on throughout nearly two hundred years of reading instruction. It still is not only a controversial subject, but one which is very much misunderstood, particularly by laymen.

Popular magazines carry articles by recognized writers and well-known individuals in fields other than reading who state that all would be well if the schools would teach by the phonics method instead of by the word method. Prominent men including some learned professors in the arts and sciences denounce "the school's word method versus phonic method" in radio, television, and forum interviews, in speeches, and in discussions.

This criticism which is being leveled against our schools is so serious that the writer feels an obligation to clear up the matter before proceeding with *teaching* considerations concerning phonics.

Phonics Versus Word Method

Both phonics and word method have had peripatetic existences in American history. First one is in and the other is out and vice versa. This is an old, old story. Perhaps a recounting of this old story will lead perspective to the present-day student or teacher who is concerned with reading.

Phonics Takes Root in America

Previous to the Revolution reading was taught throughout the colonies by the ABC method. Children first learned their ABC's, then as each new word was presented to them they were taught to spell it. "*C-a-t cat*" was the accepted order of procedure in colonial reading instruction.

Following the Revolution, American teachers decried the use of the English reading texts which had been used exclusively in our schools up to that time. And one of these teachers—Noah Webster—prepared the first reading texts to be authored by an American citizen. In these texts Webster introduced phonics, not as an aid in learning to read, but as a medium for unifying American language.

In the preface of his famous speller Webster [5] expressed his foremost aim in this way:

> To diffuse a uniformity and purity of language in America—to destroy the provincial prejudices that originate in trifling differences of dialect, and produce reciprocal ridicule—to promote the interest of literature and harmony of the United States—is the most ardent wish of the Author; and it is his highest ambition to deserve the approbation and encouragement of his countrymen.

The medium which Webster proposed to use in accomplishing this aim was to begin "with the elements of the language and explain the powers of the letters." This he did in his "Speller" which really was the first reader that children were to use when they entered school. They were still to learn the alphabet as a starting point, but in addition to learning the names of the letters they were also to learn the sound of the letters and of letter combinations. The learning of these sounds was supposed in turn to unify and purify American language.

Although Webster's aim for introducing phonics into American schools was a lofty and patriotic one he came precariously close to failure in realizing it. His books did not receive the immediate "approbation and encouragement" of his countrymen.

He had prepared three books: a spelling book, a treatise on grammar, and an advanced book on "Lessons in Reading and Speaking." All three books were bound together in one volume and titled *Grammatical Institute,* [6] a name advised by the President of Harvard University whose learned counsel had been sought by the author. Furthermore, Webster's picture appeared on the first page of the volume. Since the art of engraving was practically undeveloped at that time, the picture had been reproduced by a wooden plate which was not suitable for depicting anything so intricate as a mass of tiny strands of hair. Hence the picture showed a man with pointed, hornlike spikes standing upright on his scalp.

Newspapers and magazines of the time were filled with a flood of criticisms concerning the new books. Most children attended school only long enough to master one reader, and "Why should they be forced to buy

[5] Noah Webster, *The American Spelling Book* (Boston: Isaiah Thomas and Ebenezer Andrews, 1798), p. 1.
[6] Noah Webster, *Grammatical Institute* (Hartford, Conn.: Hudson and Goodwin, 1782).

three books to get one?" parents asked. They thought the title of the book was "high-filutin," and did not fit in with the ideals of the common man in the new democracy." The photograph of "the author with horns on his head" was the object of widespread derision and fun-poking.

After seven years of gloomy failure the books were taken over by a different publisher and revised. This time the horn-headed portrait was omitted and the books were bound in three separate covers. Each book was then given its own distinctive name. The first book in the series appeared as *The American Spelling Book.*[7] This beginning book was encased in brown cardboard covers concealed with a coating of pale blue paper—and it was this volume that was destined to become the famous old "Blue-Back Speller."

Gradually this book became popular. Finally its widespread acceptance caused it to enact in this period the stellar role which *The New England Primer* had enacted in the preceding period. Royalties from this "Speller" enabled Webster to support his family for twenty years while he was writing his dictionary. In writing to a friend, Webster [8] said,

. . . for nearly thirty years, returns of the numbers printed, enable me to state, with tolerable certainty, that the whole number published cannot fall much short of ten millions of copies.

So we may know that at least ten million American boys and girls learned to use phonics while working with the old Blue-Back Speller. For several years, however, the phonic method was not used for the purpose of aiding children to work out the pronunciation of unrecognized words which they met in reading. It was used in realizing Webster's patriotic aim of unifying spoken language in America. As the years rolled by, however, patriotism and phonics parted ways. Phonics then continued under the sponsorship of pedagogy. Pedagogy gave phonics its new function—that of helping children to attain independence in attacking new words while reading. In this role phonics has continued its long trek through American classrooms from post-Revolutionary days to the present time.

The Word Method Is Initiated

During the 1840's many American educators visited experimental schools in Prussia and Switzerland and returned with enthusiastic reports of what they had seen. These experimental schools were largely

[7] Noah Webster, *The American Spelling Book* (Boston: Isaiah Thomas and Ebenezer Andrews, 1798).

[8] Noah Webster, *The New England Magazine*, IV (Boston: J. T. and E. B. Buckingham, 1833), p. 475.

under the influence of Pestalozzi, and Pestalozzi advocated teaching reading by presenting an object or a picture together with a word which represented it. Our educators who saw this method in use thought it was much more sensible than starting children out with the ABC's, and they said so in no uncertain terms in speeches and articles upon their return to America. Thus the idea of the word method started to filter through in the United States.

It was during this period of agitation that readers based on the word method began to appear. In John Russell Webb's primer, *The New Word Method* (1846),[9] we find this amusing account:

The Origin of the Word Method

On an early summer morning of 1846, a young man, barely twenty-one years of age, was reading a newspaper in the sitting-room of his boarding place. He was the teacher of the village school.

From early boyhood he had been regarded as "odd." He did not do, he did not think, as boys of his age generally did. Often he was reproved for finding fault with what others considered "well enough." He would reply: "If we could see no defects, we would make no improvements." Many were the little devices, to save labor and give better results, seen on the home farm.

While awaiting breakfast, as already mentioned, a little girl, four or five years old, climbed into his lap as she had often climbed before. Her mother was in the kitchen preparing the breakfast; her father, in the yard milking the cow.

The teacher laid down his paper and began to talk to the child. The father was mentioned, what he was doing, and the cow was talked about. Just then his eye caught the word *cow*, on the paper he had laid down. He took it up and pointed out the word to the child, again calling attention to the cow, and to this word as the name of the animal her papa was milking. Soon she looked up into the teacher's face; her eyes kindled with intelligence; she caught the paper, jumped out of his lap and ran to her mother, exclaiming as she ran: "I know what it means; I know what it means. It is a cow, just like what papa is milking!" and she pointed out the word to her mother.

Many a boy and many a man before Newton had seen an apple fall. It may be that many a teacher had done just what this teacher did; but into him the circumstances had flashed an idea. He at once began to experiment, not only with the little four-year-old girl, but with the beginners in the school. The lessons were prepared in the evening, and in the morning printed on the blackboard, and he, himself, taught them to the children with the most marked—the most wonderful success. There were no unpleasant tones, no drawling. On the contrary, the children read in pleasant natural tones, giving the emphasis and inflections of the playground.

From time to time these lessons were printed and formed page or hand

[9] J. Russell Webb, *Webbs' Normal Reader*, No. 1 (New York: Sheldon, Lamport, and Blakeman, 1855).

cards. The children became very much interested in reading them. They read them in and out of school. They read them anywhere—everywhere one would listen. They took their cards with them to the table—to bed, as little girls sometimes do their dolls.

At first all the parents were very much pleased. But, alas! there was trouble ahead. It was soon discovered that the children could not spell the words— that they did not even know the names of the letters! Some of the parents "waited on the teacher," and left with him unpleasant memories. Others had faith that "That teacher knows what he is about." There was a good deal of talking, and what "the teacher" was doing became noised abroad.

That fall a Teachers' Institute was held at Watertown, twelve miles away. Our teacher was sent for. They wanted to know what the "new thing" was. For a week it was explained, illustrated, discussed. Then the following resolution was passed:

Resolved, That having heard an exposition of a new method of teaching children to read, by J. Russell Webb, we are of opinion that the interests of our schools require its publication, and we pledge ourselves to use efforts to introduce its use into our schools should it be published.

Resolved, That a copy of this resolution be signed by our chairman and secretary and presented to Mr. Webb.

E. S. Barnes, Chairman
J. L. Montgomery, Secretary

Watertown, N. Y.,
October 20, 1846

A Watertown bookseller (Joel Greene) was present. He offered to publish an edition at his own expense—and he did, that fall, 1846. This edition bore the title: "John's First Book; or, The Child's First Reader."

The New York *School Journal* says: "That book was the means of a great reform. Millions of children have been saved years of drudgery by the use of the method it proposed, and Mr. Webb is entitled to unlimited praise."

And this is how the Word Method originated, and how it was born into the world. Since then it has written its own history.

Webb was not wholly deserving of the great distinction which "the nephew of the man after whom he was named" confers upon him. Worcester had previously advocated the word method and Bumstead had already published his primer based on this method. Webb may have developed his ideas independently of the others, but at least he did so contemporaneously with them. The account, nevertheless, is enlightening in that it shows the seriousness with which this change of method was regarded.

The word method was used widely for about forty-five years. This was the only period in American history in which the so-called word method was ever advocated by editors and authors of readers as a general method of teaching reading.

Phonics Is Re-Emphasized

But the word method as such was not to endure. In the 1890's, phonics came back again with renewed emphasis. A growing dissatisfaction arose because many children were not reading, and this deficiency was laid to the word method.

As an example of such criticism, here is a quotation from a publication of 1889.[10] This is similar to some of the criticisms that are heard at the present time.

There is quite a general complaint among teachers, principals, and superintendents that pupils in the higher grades are not able to read with ease and expression; they have so little mastery over words that an exercise in reading becomes a laborious effort at word-calling.

We are inclined to think the inability of pupils in the higher grades to call words is the legitimate outgrowth of the teaching of the word method. By this method the word is presented to the child as a whole, and the teacher either tells the child the word, or by skillful questioning leads him to use the word. Later, when phonics have been introduced, the teacher writes the new and difficult words on the blackboard and marks them. The general results of these methods on the mind of the pupil are about the same. He soon learns to think he can do nothing with a new word without the help of the teacher in some way. While he should be learning independence in making out his words, he has learned dependence, and his dependence increases with the increase of difficulties.

So educational thinking changed in regard to the word method, and the learning of phonic elements and organized systems of phonics came back again as the most widely approved method of approach to reading. The Ward readers, the Beacon readers, and the Gordon readers were the most popular reading series used between 1890 and 1920. In using these readers, children were started out immediately upon entrance into first grade with the memorization of the sounds of letters and groups of letters. Later they read content entirely subservient to phonic elements—the "Kate ate a date" sort of thing.

Phonics Is Practically Abandoned

This extreme emphasis on phonics lasted for several years but eventually phonics again came under criticism—this time as a result of newly devised tools of scientific investigation and freshly formulated psychologies and philosophies concerning reading method.

The scientific movement in education developed between 1910 and

[10] Rebecca S. Pollard, *Pollard's Synthetic Method. A Complete Manual* (Chicago: Western Publishing House, 1889).

1920. Scientifically standardized tests appeared for the first time and among these were tests of reading. When administrators began giving school-wide reading tests they discovered how very poorly thousands of children were doing in reading. Many couldn't even pronounce the words and those that could call word symbols by names weren't getting the meaning. They didn't know what they were reading about.

This appalling situation was blamed on phonics. Educators reasoned that teachers had been emphasizing the skill of juggling with phonetic elements at the expense of teaching children to get meanings from reading. So a strong new emphasis came in, emphasis on silent reading accompanied with checks of understanding.

Coordinately with the new emphasis on reading silently for meanings, the method by which phonics had been taught was held up as a horrible example of skill development technique. Educators could not reconcile the teaching of meaningless, isolated phonic elements with the new psychologies and philosophies which maintained that any developing skill should be kept close to the situation in which it is used. The method of teaching phonics at that time was sometimes compared to the process of knitting without yarn in the needles.

With the new emphasis on meanings and severe criticism of the method of teaching phonics, the whole area of phonics teaching fell into disrepute. This subject was considered old-fashioned, out-moded, behind the times. Phonics was practically abandoned throughout the country.

If this were the period in which the present-day critics were making their complaints against the schools for not teaching phonics, their criticisms would have been well-grounded and entirely justifiable. But this era has already receded into the annals of reading history.

Phonics Comes Back

Eventually the itinerant phonics came back! In the latter half of the thirties the schools were still plagued by a large number of children who were not reading up to expectancy. So phonics was re-examined. Many educators argued that any aspect of teaching which had had so long a history as phonics must have some value. Furthermore, several studies [11]

[11] Donald C. Agnew, *The Effect of Varied Amounts of Phonetic Training on Primary Reading*, Duke University Research Studies in Education (Durham, N. C.: Duke University Press, 1939). Dorothy M. Browne, *Phonics as a Basis for Improvement in Reading* (Washington, D. C.: The Catholic University of America, 1939). S. C. Garrison and Minnie T. Heard, "An Experimental Study of the Value of Phonetics," *Peabody Journal of Education*, Vol. 9 (July 1931), 9–14. Arthur I. Gates and David H. Russell, "Types of Material, Vocabulary Burden, Word Analysis and Other Factors in Beginning Reading," *Elementary School Journal*, Vol. 39 (Sept. and Oct. 1938), 27–35, 119–28. Raymond M. Mosher

had recently been carried on which revealed that phonics was effective.

So phonics began coming back gradually in the late thirties, and it has been coming back ever since. Phonics is now being taught more generally than at any time since the early nineteen hundreds. Two nation-wide studies [12] which are just now being completed reveal that teachers "overwhelmingly believe in Phonics" and that phonics is being taught in classrooms throughout the country. Both of these studies indicate, however, that teachers reinforce phonics by teaching children other methods of "figuring out" how a new word is pronounced. Phonics is not fool-proof as a tool to use in ascertaining pronunciation. This method needs to be supplemented and checked by other word attack methods: using context clues, analyzing the structure of words, and using dictionary skills. Present-day teachers are teaching phonics plus these other word-getting techniques.

Phonics usually is also taught now with a different timing, a different method, and a different distribution.[13] Most schools today do not start children out juggling with phonetic elements, nor do they give them almost all their phonics in one dose when they enter first grade. The preferred method is an eclectic approach in which an attempt is made to develop interest in reading; to develop the attitude that reading is a process of getting meanings; and to develop some facility in applying the concept of reading in larger thought units rather than reading one letter or one word at a time, a concept which is a basic consideration in laying the foundation for fluency and rate. The medium used to accomplish these initial goals are stories based on children's own experiences. As soon as the initial attitudes are developed, children are taught phonics *in the first grade* and in *all of the other grades*, plus several other techniques to use in identifying unrecognized words.

and Sydney M. Newhall, "Phonic Versus Look-and-Say Training in Beginning Reading," *The Journal of Educational Psychology*, Vol. 21 (Oct. 1930), 500–506. Maurine V. Rogers, "Phonetic Ability as Related to Certain Aspects of Reading at the College Level," *Journal of Experimental Education*, Vol. 6 (July 1938), 381–95. Elmer K. Sexton and John S. Herron, "The Newark Phonics Experiment," *The Elementary School Journal*, Vol. 37 (June 1937), 752–63. Harry L. Tate, "The Influence of Phonics on Silent Reading in Grade I," *The Elementary School Journal*, Vol. 37 (June 1937), 752–63. Harry L. Tate, Theresa Herbert, and Josephine K. Zeman, "Non-Phonic Primary Reading," *Elementary School Journal*, Vol. 40 (Mar. 1940), 529–37. Joseph Tiffin and Mary McKinnis, "Phonic Ability: Its Measurement and Relation to Reading Ability," *School and Society*, Vol. 51 (Feb. 10, 1940), 190–92.

[12] Alvin Barclay, Report given at "A Policy Conference on Reading Instruction," directed by James Conant (New York: Sept. 22–23, 1961). Mary Austin, "Harvard-Carnegie Study—A Preliminary Report," presented at the Conference of the International Reading Association (San Francisco: May 5, 1962).

[13] For exceptions see Chapter 15, "Beginning Reading Instruction," pages 450–51.

A recent study offers evidence that a multiple approach is effective. Frederick B. Davis of Hunter College, New York, reports that systematic phonic instruction had been tried out for several years in the Philippines with children using Tagalog, a perfectly phonetic language. At the same time other groups were taught by the modern multiple approach. Children of the two groups were paired in regard to ability, mental age, and other factors, and teachers were paired according to ability. Test results revealed that the multiple approach excelled the exclusive formal approach in learning to read Tagalog. At the beginning of the third year, English was introduced. At the end of the third year, test results showed that children who had been taught by the multiple approach made the transition to reading English better than those who had been taught by the phonic approach alone.

This study provides convincing evidence that the multiple approach is superior to the exclusive use of phonics.

What Phonics Content Should Be Taught?

Phonic elements

If we think of phonics content in general terms, it is apt to appear as a confusing mass covering a multitude of sound elements. The writer has asked classes of graduate students with teaching experience, "How many different sounds do you think we need to teach to children in the elementary grades?" "Two Hundred." "Five Hundred." "A Thousand." And so the answers come. Unless we have some organized picture of the content of phonics we are apt to think that it is much more expansive than it really is. To clarify and simplify this concept a chart of basic phonic elements is presented. There are, of course, several additional sounds of each vowel and some exceptional and unusual sounds of some of the other letters and combinations which are not represented on the chart. These can be gleaned through dictionary usage. If, however, a child in the elementary grades learns to recognize all the sounds listed in the chart, he will have an excellent *basic* knowledge of phonics.

Some studies have been conducted to determine the relative frequencies of phonic elements, the assumption being that those elements having the highest frequencies in printed material are the most important ones to teach. The pioneer study was made by Vogel, Jaycox, and Washburne [14] who analyzed the vocabularies of readers and standard vocabu-

---

[14] Mabel Vogel, Emma Jaycox, and Carleton W. Washburne, "A Basic List of Phonics for Grades I and II," *Elementary School Journal*, XXIII (Feb. 1923), 436–43.

lary lists to find out which letter groupings occur most commonly. An early study by Cordts [15] also analyzed primary reader vocabularies for

A BASIC PHONICS PROGRAM

CONSONANTS				
SINGLE CONSONANTS		CONSONANT BLENDS	SPEECH SOUNDS (CONSONANT DIGRAPHS)	
ONE SOUND	TWO OR MORE SOUNDS		ONE SOUND	TWO SOUNDS

b   m
c   n
d   p
f   r
h   t
j   v
k   w
l   x
    y
    z
	c (came
	   face)
	g (go
	   gem)
	s (hiss
	   rose
	   sugar)
	x (box
	   exit
	   xylophone)
		bl sc
		cl sk
		dl sm
		fl sn
		gl sp
		pl st
		sl sw
		br tw
		cr wr
		dr scr
		fr spr
		gr str
		pr shr
		tr spl
		    sch
		    thr
			ch
			gh ng
			ph nk
			qu
				th (those
				   thin)
				wh (what
				   who)

VOWELS					
SINGLE VOWELS *			VOWEL COMBINATIONS		
LONG OR SHORT	FOLLOWED BY R	A FOLLOWED BY L OR W	EQUIVALENT VOWEL DIGRAPHS	VOWEL BLENDS (DIPHTHONGS)	
				ONE SOUND	TWO OR MORE SOUNDS

a   o
e   u
i   y (some
    times)
	a (star)
	e (her)
	i (stir)
	o (for)
	u (blur)
	y (syrup)
		aw (awe)
		al (all)
			ai (tail)
			ay (say)
			ea (each)
			ee (keep)
			ei (receive)
			oa (coat)
			oe (Joe)
				oi (boil)
				oy (boy)
				ue (blue)
				ew (few)
					ow (cow
					   show)
					ou (bough
					   journey
					   though
					   through
					   touch)

* There are several sounds of the single vowels other than those represented in the chart. Recognition of these sounds, however, becomes useful only after the child learns to use the dictionary and to interpret diacritical markings. This is true, also, of exceptions and rarely used sounds.

15 Anna D. Cordts, and Maude Mary McBroom, "Phonics," *Classroom Teacher,* II, 427–29. Chicago: Classroom Teacher, Inc., 1927.

phonetic elements. Two studies reported by Black [16] and Oaks [17] were concerned with frequency of consonant and vowel sounds, respectively, in primary reading vocabularies. The resulting lists are too long to include in this book. The studies are mentioned, however, so that the reader may refer to them directly if he or she so desires.

Phonic terms

In connection with the discussion of phonics and phonic content, a few explanations of terms may be appreciated.

Phonetics and *phonics* are often confused. *Phonetics* is the science of speech sounds and is the appropriate term for speech specialists to use in connection with their work. *Phonics* is the application of phonetics to the working out of word pronunciations while reading. *Phonics,* then, is the word that we should employ when discussing the use of sounds in helping children to pronounce unrecognized words while reading.

A *consonant blend* is a group of two or three consonants which are blended together to make one sound but which do not lose their separate identity. For example, *Cl* is a blend in the word *clean;* but while c and l are blended to make one sound, a little of the c and a little of the l can still be heard.

A *consonant speech sound* is one in which a group of two consonants produce one sound, but the sound is a new sound entirely; both of the separate letters lose their individual identities. In the word *children,* ch gives one speech sound, but neither the sound of c or h is heard as a separate letter.

Consonant Digraphs is another phrase having the same meaning as *speech sounds* discussed above. *Consonant digraphs* and *speech sounds* are synonymous terms.

Vowel Digraphs are made up of two vowels that represent one sound, as *ai* in *hail.* The a and i together have only the sound a.

Diphthong is the term used for a combination of two vowels which produce a single blended sound, as *oi* in *soil* or *ue* in *blue.*

Phonic principles

In addition to phonic elements and their sounds, there are certain guiding principles concerning the pronunciation of word elements that usually are taught to children in the elementary program.

[16] Elsie Benson Black, "A Study of the Consonant Situations in a Primary Reading Vocabulary," *Education,* LXXII (May 1952), 618–23.

[17] Ruth E. Oaks, "A Study of the Vowel Situation in a Primary Vocabulary," *Education,* LXXII (May 1959), 604–47.

A recent study [18] indicates that teachers and teachers in preparation are not as familiar with these principles as we would expect them to be. Aaron checked the knowledge of phonic generalizations with 293 subjects embracing the two categories—experienced and prospective teachers. Their mean score of correct items was about 57 per cent. Primary teachers were no more familiar with the principles than were teachers at other levels. It is hoped that readers of this book, whether experienced or inexperienced teachers, will become acquainted at least with the most common of these principles. These common principles are listed below.

1. When a one-syllable word contains two vowels, one of which is the final *e*, the first vowel is usually long and the final *e* is silent, as in *pine, note*.

2. When there is only one vowel in a word and that vowel does not come at the end of the word, the vowel is usually short, as in *pin, not*.

3. When two vowels come together in a one-syllable word, the first vowel is usually long and the second vowel is usually silent, as in *boat, hail*. (There are some exceptions, of course, such as *bread*.)

4. If *y* is the final letter in a one-syllable word it is usually long, as in *fly, cry*; if it is the final letter in a two-syllable word, it is usually short, as in *baby, happy*.

5. The letter *c* has the soft sound when followed by *e, i*, or *y*, as in *center, city, cypher*; it has the long sound when followed by *o, a*, or *u*, as in *cold, cage, cure*.

6. The letter *g* has the soft sound when followed by *e, i* and *y*, as in *gentle, giant, gypsy*.

7. When *ght* appears in a word, *gh* is silent.

8. Usually a consonant is silent in these cases:
   k when it comes before *n*, as in *knee*.
   w when it comes before *r*, as in *write*.
   c when it is joined with *k*, as in *kick*.
   gh when it comes at the end or close to the end of a word, as in *though*.
   t when it comes in the middle of a one-syllable word, as in *hatch*.

9. The vowels *a, e, i, o* and *u* all have a soft, short sound which is the same, as in *balloon, garden, April, cotton*, and *circus*. This sound always occurs in an unaccented syllable and is called the *schwa* sound.

How Should Phonics Be Taught?

There are dozens of approaches to the teaching of phonics at the present time. All approaches, however, fall within two general categories: (1) those that start out the beginning reader directly in learning the sounds of letters and letter combinations, and (2) those in which the child is taught to recognize whole words for a short time as a preliminary to teaching phonics. The majority of reading authorities support the latter

[18] I. E. Aaron, "What Teachers and Prospective Teachers Know about Phonics Generalizations," *Journal of Educational Research*, LIII (May 1960), 323–30.

method and we have some evidence that it is the more effective of the two methods.

An early study made in England is pertinent to this subject. Gill [19] found that a sentence method produced better results than the phonic method in two groups of beginning readers.

In the United States Sparks and Fay [20] compared groups who used reading material which introduced phonics at beginning of grade one with those who used a basal reading program in which sight words were taught first and then followed with phonics. At the end of first grade the phonics group was somewhat superior to the other group. This may have been due to the tests, one of which had three sections out of six on phonic skills. In the second and third grades there was little difference in the two groups. In the fourth grade the basal reader group was superior.

Bloomer [21] found no significant advantage in teaching reading by a modified phonetic method over the conventional procedure. See also the discussion of the recent study made by Davis, page 195.

Several researches have been made similar to the ones mentioned above, in which modern psychology and philosophy and experience have combined to yield a body of convictions in regard to sound method in teaching phonics, convictions which are approved overwhelmingly by reading authorities. The considerations given below express these convictions.

Functional phonics is recommended

Instead of giving only isolated drill on phonics elements, as was done almost exclusively in years past, most authorities now advocate the practice of teaching children the phonics they need in connection with words that give them difficulty in their daily reading. This practice removes phonics from the category of the much criticized method in which children simply memorize phonic elements as an exercise in itself. In modern methods, phonics becomes an integral part of natural reading situations in which it is functional and meaningful.

Several studies have been conducted which show that better results are obtained when phonics is taught in moderate amounts in terms of children's needs. Gates and Russell [22] experimented with three groups, one

[19] Edmund J. Gill, "Methods of Teaching Reading," *Journal of Experimental Pedagogy*, Vol. 1 (1911–1912), pp. 243–48.

[20] Paul E. Sparks and Leo C. Fay, "An Evaluation of Two Methods of Teaching Reading," *Elementary School Journal*, Vol. 57 (Apr. 1957), pp. 386–90.

[21] Richard H. Bloomer, "Reading Methodology: Some Alternative Organizational Principles," *The Reading Teacher*, XIV (Jan. 1961), 167–71.

[22] A. J. Gates and D. H. Russell, "Types of Materials, Vocabulary, Burden, Word Analysis, and Other Factors in Beginning Reading I and II," *Elementary School Journal*, Vol. 39 (Jan.–Mar. 1938), 27–35, 119–28.

of whom had no phonics, one of whom had large amounts of conventional phonic drill, and one of whom had moderate amounts of informal, newer-type word analysis. The third group exceeded each of the other groups, both in word recognition and in comprehension. House [23] conducted a study in the middle grades. Among other conclusions he stated that word analysis skills may be taught most effectively "when the functional use of what is taught can be integrated with such instruction." Tate, Herbert, and Zeman [24] found that incidental phonics taught in connection with children's needs in attacking unrecognized words in their reading was superior either to isolated phonics or to no phonics.

Thus research, as well as modern educational psychology and philosophy, back up the type of phonics instruction which is widely used at the present time. This is the type in which children learn and apply phonics as required to meet their immediate needs in functional, integrated, meaningful reading situations.

Certain psychological principles usually observed

One principle, simply stated, is that teachers should start with something within a child's experience and build upon that in proceeding to a new and unknown learning element; that is, proceed from the known to the unknown. Another principle, again simply stated, is that it is better to start with a meaningful unit as a whole and then break it down into its parts than to start with small meaningless parts and put them together to make a meaningful whole.

The conventional methods of teaching phonics in years past proceeded in direct opposition to these principles. The child was first taught the sounds of the letters of the alphabet. These sounds or letters certainly were not within his experience, nor did they have any meaning for him. Once these smallest of language units were learned, they were put together to make a word, and the words in turn were put together to make a sentence. This was the analytic approach.

Today most reading authorities feel that it is advisable to have a child start his reading experience through the use of an entire composition based on one of his experiences and then to break it down into sentences, phrases, and words. This is usually accompanied with other experiences with whole words seen as labels on familiar objects, as pictured words, and then as words in simple meaningful sentences in books. Visual and auditory perception also are given practice from the beginning. Follow-

[23] Ralph W. House, "The Effect of a Program of Initial Instruction on the Pronunciation Skills at the Fourth Grade Level as Evidenced in Skills Growth," *Journal of Experimental Education*, Vol. 10 (Sept. 1941), 54–56.

[24] H. J. Tate, Theresa M. Herbert, and Josephine K. Zeman, "Nonphonic Primary Reading," *Elementary School Journal*, Vol. 40 (Sept. 1940), 529–37.

ing experiences of this sort, children are taught the sounds of separate letters or letter groups, drawn from the word wholes that they already know. This is an approach beginning with larger meaningful units based on children's experiences and proceeding to the smaller letter units drawn from the larger known word units.

Phonics ability is a composite of several skills

The use of phonics is a complex matter. There is much more involved in phonic competence than simply recognizing the sounds of letters or letter groups. There are at least four separate skills involved in the total phonic process.

One distinct skill is that of *visual discrimination,* becoming keenly adept at seeing likenesses and differences in word elements. Many children are not conscious of letters within words. They don't see the *b* in *boy,* nor the *an* in *can.* The ability to note specific letters and letter groups within words and their similarities and dissimilarities must be developed. Hence visual discrimination is the basic component in the total phonic process.

While being able to perceive elements within words is a first essential, it does a child no good simply to *see* likenesses and differences in word elements unless he also knows the sounds of these elements. So he must learn the skill of *auditory discrimination,* that is, recognizing and distinguishing between the sounds represented by different letters and groups of letters. This ability is another important component of the total phonic process.

Unfortunately a great deal of phonics teaching ends with development of the two abilities described above. As a result there are many children who are adept at perceiving word elements and who can glibly give their sounds, but who are totally unable to apply these skills in working out a new word that they meet in context. This deficiency is probably due to the fact that their instruction stopped with visual and auditory discrimination only. They need to develop two additional skills in order to have their phonics ability really function. One of these skills is that of *blending,* that is, running the sounds together smoothly in the natural pronunciation of a word. This is sometimes a difficult process to teach, and it usually requires a great deal of practice.

If a child does acquire all three of the skills above, they still may not be of much use to him unless he has learned to combine and apply them to a new word in a contextual situation. *Contextual application* is the fourth important skill. It is one thing to learn to juggle phonic elements as separate entities and another thing to integrate and apply these skills when meeting an unrecognized word in the midst of reading a sentence. Yet, if a child is unable to do this, all the teaching and learning effort involved in acquiring the other three skills is lost. Teachers need to give *much* more attention to contextual application.

Avoid misrepresentation of natural sounds

Sounds are frequently exaggerated in classroom instruction, especially when the children try to verbalize the isolated sound of a consonant or consonant combination. In such cases the children give the sound of *c* as "cuh," *b* as "buh," *k* as "kuh," *l* as "e-e-ell," *r* as "errr" and so on. One cannot articulate the sound of a separate consonant unless a vowel is added, and when a vowel is added the result is a syllable, not a consonant sound. When a child tries to blend this syllable with other elements in a word he meets with difficulty. Thus, the practice of having children verbalize separate consonant sounds may do more harm than good.

Here is an example: Marilyn, a third grade pupil who couldn't read very well, was reading orally to me when she came to the word *Pam*, the name of the girl in the story. Marilyn couldn't pronounce this word, and since it was entirely phonetic I wrote it on the chalkboard and asked her to try to work it out from the sounds. She readily identified *am*, then began saying "Puh-am," "Puh-am," "Puh-am" over and over again. In sounding *p* as the syllable *puh* she was trying to make a two-syllable word out of *Pam*, and she never did arrive at the correct pronunciation. All the meticulous work of the primary teachers in teaching Marilyn "the sounds of the letters" militated against Marilyn's ability to attack new words successfully. Her past instruction and practice stood in her way rather than helping her because she was sounding consonants as if they were syllables.

Generalize phonic sounds and principles

According to the principles discussed above, the child should have accumulated a stock of sight words before he is taught the sounds of separate letters. Furthermore, he should have accumulated three or four or more sight words containing the same letter element before that element is taught. In other words, if the sound of initial *b* is to be taught, the child should perhaps have learned as sight words: *boy, big, ball*. These known sight words are then used as a basis for teaching the sound of *b*.

Similarly, when the time comes for teaching the "principle of a final *e* in a one-syllable word" it is advisable to place on the chalkboard several final *e* words that the children already know (as *ate, bite, cute, note*) together with their known counterparts (as *at, bit, cut, not*) that do not end in final *e*. Through discussion of these samples representing the rule, the children are guided to generalize the effect of the final *e* on the preceding vowel.

Avoid the fallacy of "family words"

"Family words" are words that include the same "family name," or "phonogram." A phonogram is a word element, a letter, or a group of letters forming a speech sound. Examples of family names or phonograms are *all, at, an, ill, it, am, is, as, et, ick, ack,* and so on.

According to former methods of teaching phonics, children memorized the "family" names and were then drilled in reading lists of words made by attaching different initial consonants to each "family" name. For example, *all* is a family name; in working with this word element, pupils went through the ritual of reading these words repeatedly until they knew them "by heart": *ball, call, fall, gall, hall, mall, pall, tall, wall.*

Modern authorities frown upon the practice of using the "families" as the basis of phonics instruction. One reason for the objection to such a practice is that these phonograms occur in such a small percentage of words in the English language. Dolch [25] investigated the value of "important" phonograms which are commonly taught in the primary grades as a means of sounding polysyllables. This study indicated that the twenty-six phonograms commonly considered as "important" corresponded only to 11.6 per cent of the 8,509 syllables in a sampling of fourteen thousand running words in elementary textbooks in arithmetic, history, and geography; that 6.8 per cent of these were accounted for by the endings *-ing, -er,* and *-ed,* and that therefore only 4.8 per cent corresponded to the remaining phonograms. This study implies that teaching the twenty-six phonograms in themselves is of small value.

After finding that the number of phonograms was too limited to be of much use as phonic content, Dolch [26] conducted another study in an attempt to discover what common syllables might be taught in the phonics program.

In this study he analyzed the words used in the preceding study and tabulated these words in two different ways. His conclusions from this study were as follows:

Two methods of tabulation give different results, and frequencies, no matter how computed, range from high to very low and yield no satisfactory basis for drawing a line between common and uncommon. . . .

[25] E. W. Dolch, "Phonics and Polysyllables," *Elementary English Review,* Vol. 15 (Apr. 1938), 120–24.
[26] E. W. Dolch, "Sight Syllables Versus Letter Phonics," *Elementary School Journal,* Vol. 36 (June 1937), 752–63.

. . . Perhaps a well-developed skill in working out any syllable, common or uncommon, will give the child the best aid in attacking the host of polysyllables which he will always meet in his reading.

This conclusion points to the desirability of teaching the child to work with the sounds of all the letters in whatever situation he may find them, rather than concentrating on a few phonograms which do not occur with high frequency in polysyllabic words. Phonics instruction which teaches children to blend consonants and consonant combinations only with family names is extremely limited. The present consensus seems to be that children should be taught to blend consonants with any combination of letters which they may encounter in words that give them trouble. The "family names," under these conditions, enter in, but children also have experience in blending many other elements. They are not restricted narrowly to a few "family names" which they memorize in isolated drill situations.

Children's phonic needs differ

Some children don't need phonics. A conclusion reached in one of the earliest phonic studies [27] was: "Phonetic drills have a very real value but are not essential to every child. . . ." Anyone who has taught elementary children realizes that this is true. Some children develop a natural phonic sense of their own, and are able to pronounce practically any word they find in reading. In such cases it would be unwise to attempt to teach these children other ways of finding out words. On the other hand, among the many who do need phonics there may be some who are particularly weak in auditory discrimination and especially need practice in listening to sounds; others may be especially weak in visual discrimination and need practice particularly in developing keenness in *seeing* word elements, and so on. Occasionally there is a child who simply doesn't grasp phonics instruction at all. As an interesting illustration of such a case, the experience of the reading consultant who was giving a demonstration before a large audience at a reading conference will be related.

The third grade children with whom the reading consultant was working had been given phonic instruction from the late first grade up to the end of their third year, at which time the demonstration was given. The demonstration proceeded very successfully until Sammy came to the word *stick*, which he didn't recognize. "That's an easy word," said Miss Stark. "You can get that by sounding." But Sammy made no response. Miss Stark then wrote the word on the chalkboard, underlining its elements as

[27] Lillian B. Currier, "Phonics or No Phonics," *Elementary School Journal*, Vol. 23 (Dec. 1923), 286–87.

follows: _st ick_. "Work out the first part, then see if you can get the second part," instructed Miss Stark. But Sammy only looked on in puzzled silence. Miss Stark then wrote on the chalkboard:

$$stop \quad sick$$
$$stick$$

She asked Sammy to pronounce the word _stop_ and _sick_. These evidently were known sight words and Sammy happily read these words. "Now put together the first part of _stop_ and the last part of _sick_," said Miss Stark sweeping her hand quickly under the _st_ in _stop_ and the _ick_ in _sick_. She did this repeatedly but Sammy only looked on in troubled silence. Miss Stark now began to look troubled herself. The purpose of her demonstration was to show teachers how to help children work out words by themselves. Was _she_ to fail, as well as Sammy? As a last resort Miss Stark pronounced the two elements for Sammy as she quickly swept her hand from one to the other saying "st-ick, st-ick, st-ick; what have I?" A great light dawned on Sammy's face as he looked up and answered "hiccups."

Sammy was one of those children with whom phonics just doesn't "take." Teachers find such children in their classes occasionally. Such a child should be sent out for special diagnosis—to an otologist to see if there is a hearing difficulty; if not, then to a neurologist to see if there is some neurological basis for a lack of phonic sense.

The intent of the discussion in this section is to place before the teacher or prospective teacher the urgency for keeping herself alert to the individual needs of her pupils, and to provide assistance in accordance with these needs, rather than having an entire group participate in phonics instruction when perhaps some of them don't need the particular kind of instruction which is being given.

Introducing a New Phonic Element

There are several different ways of introducing phonic elements. Regardless of the procedure, however, it is advisable to make use of the fundamental considerations discussed above. If a teacher has been using a method of her own, she would do well to check it with the fundamental considerations to see whether or not her procedure makes use of these principles. If not, or if she has never had experience in teaching phonics, she would find it advantageous to use some of the procedures, in whole or in part, described below. All these procedures are simple to use, each one makes use of the fundamental considerations, and all have been found through experience to yield excellent results.

Incidental development "on the spot"

Perhaps one of the most effective ways of developing new phonic elements or generalizations is to capitalize upon opportunities as they arise.

For example, the children were reading about Uncle Leamy and his pet seal. "Uncle Leamy usually kept the seal on the boat with him but one day he let the seal out on the beach," and so on. The children had difficulty in pronouncing *Leamy*. The teacher explained, "That word has two vowels together in it," as she wrote *Leamy* on the chalkboard. "What are other words in these sentences that have two vowels together in them?" She wrote *seal, beach, boat* on the chalkboard as the children mentioned them and underlined the vowel combination in each word. "You already know these words. When you pronounce them, which of the two vowels do you hear? Yes, you hear the first one. That is usually true. Can you make up a sentence about this?" The children arrived at this conclusion "When two vowels come together in a word, the first one is usually long." "Now," said the teacher, "with this in mind, what is the name of the man in the story (placing her hand under *Leamy* on the chalkboard)?" The children pronounced the word. "How do you know you are right?" They applied the principle. As they continued with their reading they had no further difficulty in pronouncing *Leamy*.

In another case, the children read about a boy "who had a bowl of soup. He sat down to eat it." John pronounced *bowl* with the same sound of *ow* as in *down*. The teacher wrote *bowl* and *down* on the chalkboard and asked John to underline the *ow* in each. Then she explained, "*ow* has two sounds, one as in *cow*, another one as in *own*. She wrote the two words on the chalkboard, and added other words as the children mentioned them and told her under which heading to write each one. The words so classified were: *now, brow, owl, fowl, clown; show, blow, crow, snow, slow*. The teacher then explained that they could be more sure of an *ow* sound in a word if they would try it both ways and see which sound makes sense. She continued, "Which sound did John use for both of the *ow* words? Did it make sense? John do you want to try the other sound in this word (pointing to *bowl*)? Read the sentence pronouncing the word that way. Does it make sense?" Thus John worked out the pronunciation of *bowl* and checked it with context, and everyone learned about the two sounds of *ow*.

Warning: The teacher must use judgment in regard to the amount of time that it is expedient for her to use in working with "on the spot" phonics. It isn't advisable to interrupt a strong flow of interest in a story to engage in extensive phonic work. If the need arises at the beginning of a story before the plot thread has become engrossing, a longer development may be justifiable; or if a child can be helped to get a word quickly through a phonic suggestion while he is reading, it is advisable to give him such help at that time. If, however, a suggestion or a chalkboard development threatens to cut into the interest flow to any great extent, the child should be told the word so that he can proceed with his reading, and then the phonic development or practice should follow directly afterwards while the child's need for having help with the particular word is still fresh in his mind.

Planned development

In this procedure the child meets difficulty in recognizing a word in a sentence. This word is one he is about to encounter in reading a story in a book. An element needed in recognizing this new word is pulled out for development through the use of known sight words from which the new sound is deduced. As a result of this practice children return to the original sentence and read the previously unrecognized word. They then apply the results of all this practice when encountering the word in reading story context in their books.

Perhaps the best way to explain this procedure is to give an example. Developing the initial consonant *h* will be used for this example, but the same general procedure is equally effective when used in developing a final or medial consonant, a blend, or a speech sound.

1. *Providing a contextual setting.* The teacher selects from context which is about to be read a sentence containing a new word that begins with *h* and that lends itself to phonic treatment. An example of such a sentence is "Nancy took the kitten in her hand." *Hand* is a new word and is appropriate for use in developing the consonant *h*. She manuscripts the sentence on the chalkboard.

This part of the procedure enables the teacher to introduce the new consonant in a contextual setting rather than as an isolated letter, and it provides for immediate application in reading context following the introductory practice. Explanations to the children follow.

2. *Meeting a need in context.* The teacher explains that this is a new sentence which they will soon read in a story and that it contains a new word. She adds, further, that she will show them a way to find out what this word is when they try to read it for the first time in their books.

She asks the children to read the sentence. They have difficulty with the word *hand*. (Supplying the word through context won't help because the word could be *basket, doll-buggy, car,* and so on). At this juncture she explains that she will show them how to find out this word all by themselves, whenever and wherever they see it.

3. *Visual discrimination.* Children need to become sensitive to the appearance of *h* at the beginning of words, to *see* that many words begin

with *h*. Practice designed to develop this sensitiveness might be as follows: The teacher lists vertically known sight words beginning with *h*. The list might look something like this before and after the children work with it.

Before	After		
hen	h|en	(h)en	hen
home	h|ome	(h)ome	home
help	h|elp	(h)elp	help
have	h|ave	(h)ave	have
him	h|im	(h)im	him

She explains that there is something that is alike in all these words. She then asks a child to draw a long box around the letter that is the same in all of them. Others may have a turn, some drawing a circle around each copy of *h*, others underlining each copy of *h*, and so on.

4. *Auditory discrimination.* Not only must the child be able to *see h* in a word, he must be able to *hear* its sound. Practice in hearing the *natural* sound of a phonic element can be given only when the sound is embedded in a word whole; therefore the procedure described below is suggested.

The teacher explains: "This letter *h* has a sound all its own. If you know what this sound is it will help you many times in figuring out the pronunciation of a new word. Listen to see if you can hear this sound as I pronounce the words on the chalkboard."

She reads the words, slightly emphasizing but not isolating the sound of the initial consonant *h*. Different pupils are asked to read the words, emphasizing the sound of *h* in each, so that the others can hear this sound.

An auditory perception game is played. The teacher may say several words which begin with different letters, including some that begin with *h*. The pupils clap *once* whenever a word is said beginning with the sound of *h*. An example of a list of words which might be used for this purpose is:

girl	have	table	chair
hat	told	flower	tick
home	head	hands	fall
boy	house	horns	hall

In addition to serving the practice function in auditory discrimination, this game is diagnostic. Children who clap at the wrong time are in need of further practice. This practice may be given through the use of some of the other procedures described on pages 545–47.

5. *Blending.* After children have had practice in recognizing the initial consonant *h*, both visually and aurally, they are ready for blending this sound with other vowels or letter combinations. One of the most satisfac-

tory ways of doing this is again to proceed from the known to the unknown.

The teacher writes a known sight word such as *top* on the chalkboard. She asks the children to read the word. Then she explains, "I am going to take the first letter off *top* and write the letter *h* in its place to make a new word. She erases the *t* from *top* and adds *h*, making the new word *hop*. The children are asked to read this word.

In a similar fashion *h* is substituted for the initial consonant in other known sight words such as: told (hold), fall (hall), catch (hatch), mouse (house), corn (horn), good (hood), say (hay).

Finally, the teacher presents a known word which can be changed into *hand*, the new word needed in the original sentence written on the chalkboard. As an example, suppose that the children know *sand* as a sight word. Then the teacher would explain, "Now, you will be able to read the new word in the sentence that I wrote on the chalkboard. What is this old word that you already know (writing *sand* on the chalkboard). Now I am going to take the *s* off this word and replace it with the new sound of *h* (erasing *s* and replacing it with *h*, making the word *hand*). What is this new word?"

6. *Contextual application.* At this point the children may be asked to read sentences containing the new words that they have made by substituting *h* for the other initial consonants; that is, they are given a chance actually to apply the results of their practice while reading words in contextual situations.

Some sentences which might be used for this purpose are as follows:

Mary saw the robin $\begin{cases} \text{top} \\ \text{hop.} \end{cases}$ Chickens $\begin{cases} \text{hatch} \\ \text{catch} \end{cases}$ out of eggs.

The bowl was
   not large enough to $\begin{cases} \text{told} \\ \text{hold} \end{cases}$ the milk.   David can blow his new $\begin{cases} \text{corn} \\ \text{horn.} \end{cases}$

Ralph walked down the $\begin{cases} \text{fall} \\ \text{hall.} \end{cases}$ Mildred has a new red $\begin{cases} \text{hood} \\ \text{good.} \end{cases}$

Sylvia lives in a big white $\begin{cases} \text{house} \\ \text{mouse.} \end{cases}$ Horses like to eat $\begin{cases} \text{say} \\ \text{hay.} \end{cases}$

In later stages the multiple-choice word may be omitted, and the new word may be written directly into the context of the sentence.

7. *Applying practice to an immediate reading need.* The teacher refers to the sentence written on the chalkboard at the beginning of the developmental activity: Nancy took the kitten in her *hand*. "Now you can read this sentence and get the new word without any trouble, I'm sure." The children read the sentence. "We shall see if you can read the new word that well when you find it in the story that we soon shall read."

The result of all this practice is applied in reading the story in which *hand* is a new word. It also is applied in working out any other unrecognized words beginning with *h* in the immediate story and in successive stories.

Using contextual charts

Some teachers prepare charts with a series of sentences, one of which asks a question to be answered with a word selected from multiple-choice words. The chart is used as a basis for developing new phonic elements. These charts also make use of picture clues and context clues.

Two sample charts are presented together with a stenographic report of the way in which a teacher worked with each of these charts.

Chart 1

Tom found something with which to run and jump.
Mary turned it for Tom.
What was it? _____ rope, joke, hope.
                    (picture of a rope)
Note: Familiar words are *joke, hope*. New word is *rope*.

Teacher: Tom found something nice to play with. This story will tell us what it was.
Charles: I can read the story.
Teacher: Do you know what Tom found?
Charles: Yes.
Teacher: You may read the story and tell us what it was.
Charles: (Reads correctly.) It had to be rope because here is a picture of a rope. I know all these other words, too.
Teacher: You may tell us what they are.
Lois: I know one of those letters.
Teacher: You may show us. (Points to *h*.) What letter is this?
Lois: It is an *h*.
Teacher: Do you know how *h* sounds in a word?
Lois: No.
Teacher: (Pronounces *hope*, emphasizing the sound of *h*.) "Did you hear the *h* sound? Can you make the rest of us hear it?
Lois: (Pronounces *hope* emphasizing the sound of *h*.)
Fred: There is a round letter in all the words.
Teacher: Yes, Fred, that is an *o* and it sounds just like its name in these words. This letter (pointing to *r*) is *r*. Can you hear the *r* and *o* when I say *rope*?
Children: (All the children said *rope* so that the teacher could hear the sound of *r* and of *o*.)

Practice and Maintenance Activities

The development of a new phonic element is sufficient for a few children, but the great majority require continued practice throughout the primary grades and frequent review and maintenance in the upper elementary grades.

Most children will need special practice, particularly on some one of the phonic processes: visual discrimination, auditory discrimination, blending, or contextual application. Their needs vary also in terms of phonic elements. One child may need more practice on certain vowel sounds, another on certain consonant blends, and so on. Practice should be given in accordance with the need. It isn't necessary to continue giving equal practice on all four of the processes if a child needs more help on only one of them, or on a miscellaneous group of phonics elements if he needs practice only on certain of them.

After a pupil has had initial development of a new element and knows the meaning and function of phonics, it is entirely permissible to use separate words in practice activities to promote further development of visual or auditory discrimination or of blending. These are pronunciation techniques, not meaning techniques. Visual and auditory discrimination are concerned with seeing and hearing, while blending is a knack of running word sounds together; therefore, it is not essential that after the developmental stage words used for identification practice of these types always should be presented in context as is the case when working with the initial development of a phonic element or when working with a whole word in developing sight word recognition in which meanings are important. Whenever it is possible, however, to have sentences read that contain words calling for use of the practice given, it is highly desirable to provide such sentences. The teacher should also be continually vigilant in helping the child apply the result of his practice in working out unrecognized words in his regular reading activities, for the end function of teaching phonics will be lost unless the child makes use of it in his reading.

Many examples of practice and maintenance activities to use in establishing phonic skills are offered in Chapter 21, "Suggestions for Maintenance and Practice," pages 544–50.

When Should Phonics Be Taught?

No definite statement can be made in regard to the time in a child's life at which we should begin to acquaint him with phonics. Readiness for phonics instruction is an individual matter depending upon many factors.

As indicated earlier in this chapter, it was customary in the past to teach the alphabet immediately when the child entered first grade, to follow by teaching the sounds of the letters of the alphabet, and finally to put these sounds together to make words. The major emphasis from the first day in first grade throughout the year was on sounding phonic elements. Some critics of present-day reading instruction are urging that we return to this practice.

The overwhelming majority of reading authorities, however, believe that the following criteria should be observed in regard to the time at which children should begin to sound letters as a means of working out word pronunciations:

1. Children should develop an interest in reading and a desire to read before working with such technical aspects of reading as sounding letters.

2. Children should acquire the attitude of reading for meanings in sentence, phrase, and word wholes before having their attention directed to the analysis of words into sound elements—an activity which might distract temporarily from their meaning concepts.

3. Children should have practice in visual and auditory perception which skills are fundamental to the use of phonics.

4. Children should first acquire a reading vocabulary of word wholes sufficient in size to represent the letter sounds which are later to be taught so that they may generalize from known words those sounds needed in unlocking new words. For example, if we are to teach the sound of the consonant *f*, the child should previously have had experience in recognizing a few words beginning with *f*, such as *fox, fat, for*.

5. It is important to make a start in the type of reading which is conducive to the establishment of good eye-movements before having the children concentrate on the smaller units within words.

In addition to the opinion of experts, a few studies have been conducted which have yielded data in regard to the maturation level at which children can best make use of the total process of using phonics. "The Newark Phonics Experiment," as reported by Sexton and Herron,[28] has special significance in regard to the time of introducing phonics. This investigation involved several hundred children who were followed in their progress from the 1B grade through the first half of the second grade. The conclusions drawn were to the effect that the teaching of phonetics functioned very little or not at all during the first five months of reading instruction, that phonetics instruction began to be of some value in the second five months, and that it was of great value in the second grade.

The investigation cited above and others would indicate that the child reaches the maturity level at which he can most successfully make independent use of formal phonics and all the processes involved when he is seven years old mentally. This period normally falls in the latter part of first grade or at the beginning of the second grade, but there are vast individual differences. Some children who have been reading before

28 Elmer K. Sexton and John S. Herron, "The Newark Phonics Experiment," *Elementary School Journal,* Vol. 28 (May 1928), 690–701.

they come to first grade might be ready to use phonics immediately. Others might not be ready to make use of phonics until third grade.

Normally, however, the first grade child needs to be nurtured to a maturity in phonics. Phonics is such an important and complex skill that a strong foundation program should be provided throughout the first grade, a program which will bring the child to a state of maturation in respect to phonics that will enable him to make wide and independent use of his knowledge of letter sounds in attacking new words as soon as possible. Much should be done during the beginning first grade period.

Such a program entails much practice in visual discrimination not only of pictures of objects and forms but also of words, their beginnings and endings and elements within; and of auditory discrimination, not only of rhyme words but of sounds of consonants and vowels.

In the second half of first grade it is of course advisable to continue all visual and auditory experiences used during the preceding months. But at this level children are ready for still more intensive work in identifying consonants and consonant combinations visually and in recognizing their respective sounds. They can do some substitution work in the interest of blending.

When the child has reached the maturity level at which he can make the best use of formal instruction in phonics, certainly no time should be lost in launching an extensive and carefully organized program to promote the wide and independent use of phonics in attacking new words, regardless of the grade or the time in the school year when this occurs.

The second grade seems to be a strategic point in phonics instruction. Most children at the second grade level are ready to make wide and successful use of all four aspects of phonics instruction: (1) visual discrimination, (2) auditory discrimination, (3) blending (through word building experiences), and (4) contextual application (or experiences in which they apply all their phonic knowledge in attacking new words in context). Extensive practice should now be provided in all these aspects of phonics, and the child should be expected to apply them independently whenever he meets in his reading new words which lend themselves to phonetic analysis.

All phases of this work should be continued in the third grade. Children in this grade usually have not yet learned formal dictionary techniques; they must depend more upon phonics in attacking new words now than they will have to later, and they, like second grade children, are at a maturity level at which they are able to make extensive use of phonics. All the phonic knowledge developed in the preceding grades should be reviewed, maintained, and continually applied at this level; and some of the more difficult phonic elements should be delayed for introduction at this point.

Phonics instruction should still continue throughout the middle grades, at least in two capacities. First, there are usually some children in the fourth, fifth, and sixth grades who are poor readers and who have difficulty in word recognition. If these children have not yet learned to use the tool of phonics in attacking new words independently, then they should be given both developmental and maintenance work in phonics at whatever level is appropriate for their respective stages of maturation in phonics growth.

In addition to providing phonics instruction for poor readers, the upper grade teacher should keep phonics usage alive with all her pupils, and also carry it forward in at least two new steps. One of the new developments in phonics at this level is that of applying phonic techniques to polysyllabic words. In the primary grades most of the phonic work is concerned with words of one syllable. When children try to use phonics in pronouncing the longer words of two, three, or four syllables at the fourth grade level they often experience difficulty. One of the first responsibilities, then, of the fourth grade teacher is to teach children to divide words into syllables and then to apply phonics to each syllable as they have been accustomed to applying phonics to one-syllable words in the primary grades. Fifth and sixth grade teachers should continue and encourage this combined application of phonics and syllabication in cases in which children still have difficulty in pronouncing new polysyllabic words.

The middle-grade period is, of course, the one in which children should develop facility in using the dictionary. Phonics is basic to one phase of dictionary work—that of learning to interpret diacritical markings. If in the primary grades children have learned the different sounds of some elements, such as the long and short sounds of vowels, the two sounds of *g*, the two sounds of *c*, and so on, then the upper grade teacher has only to explain the markings for these sounds and to give practice in interpreting them. After having capitalized upon the knowledge which children already possess of the most commonly used sounds, she will proceed to teach additional new sounds and interpretation of their markings until all children possess ready facility in interpreting diacritical markings in the dictionary.

Therefore, in answer to the question "When should phonics be taught?" we might well reply, "All through the elementary school, with continuous adjustment of instruction to meet maturity levels and individual needs."

USE OF STRUCTURAL ANALYSIS

Why Teach Structural Analysis?

Recognizing word structure elements poses a problem for children
"Say the *ed* part of the word."
"There's an *s* on that word. Let me hear you read it with *s* at the end."
"Add the *ing*. You left that off."
"See that *ly*? Read the word again and put *ly* on it."

Any teacher who has had experience in the elementary grades probably has had occasion to make remarks similar to the ones above countless numbers of times. The inexperienced teacher will be amazed to find how often children do not include word endings, and often beginnings, in their reading. In other words, inability to recognize word structure elements in reading is a persistent problem with many children in the elementary grades. This should be a challenge both to experienced and inexperienced teachers to *teach* children to recognize word structure elements while reading, rather than leaving this important aspect of word recognition to chance.

Structurally changed words occur with high frequency

There is a strong trend in all out-of-school reading materials to use increased numbers of modified words (see Chapter 9, pages 281–87, for a discussion of this trend). An increase in the number of modified words is also apparent in textbooks. In randomly selecting one page in a third-grade geography the following modified forms were found: *railroad, rainfall, mountainous, descendants, irrigated, irrigation, reservations, canneries, agricultural, specializes, tropical, population, grassy.* If children are to meet changed word forms in large numbers in the content fields, as well as in literature, it is especially urgent that they should be taught to recognize the pronunciation and meaning of these modified forms.

The content of readers is no exception to an increased usage of modified forms. Teachers need to be alerted particularly to the fact that after a structural element has had initial development in a reading program, it is added to other words throughout the readers; and words so modified are not counted as new words in the vocabulary. For example, the vocabulary list in the back of the book for one page in a certain beginning third reader listed two news words: *thin, soup.* An examination of the text for this page, however, disclosed the use of these changed forms: *helping, boxes, hardly,* and *scared.* Many of the children who read this page had difficulty with these words. They knew *help* and *box* and *hard,* and the teacher had developed the inflectional endings *ing, ed,* and *es* through one presentation for each, but the pupils were not ready to add automatically these endings to any word they met. Similarly, they had had general practice in recognizing two separate words in a compound word, and in an earlier story they had had the word *scarecrow;* but they were not able to recognize *scared* when they came to it just because they had had *scarecrows* in a preceding story. All things considered, for these children, this was not a simple page containing two new words only; it contained six words which should have been given special attention by the teacher.

It is good that opportunities for additional practice are provided in reading materials, but there is no assurance that children will recognize a word to which a structural element has been attached just because they have had it presented to them once. The teacher should be continually on the lookout for changed word forms and should be sure to use them for review and application purposes.

Structural analysis is faster than phonic analysis

Structural analysis and phonic analysis are frequently confused. They are, however, quite different in content and application. Phonics is concerned with the sound elements in words; structural analysis, with the units that make up the structure of a word or that change the meaning of a word. Structural analysis can be put into effect more rapidly than phonic analysis; it doesn't take as long to perceive whole structural units in a word as it does to sound out letters or letter combinations. Structural analysis is most useful from third grade on where children frequently need to pronounce new words of two or more syllables. When this stage has been reached, pupils should be encouraged to use structural analysis first in attacking an unrecognized word, and if that doesn't work, then to use phonics. The two should be combined frequently.

Definition of Terms

This area of study carries with it its own specialized terminology. Some of its terms will be explained.

Root and *stem* are generally used interchangeably to denote a word base which is not compounded or modified by a prefix, suffix, or inflectional ending, and which remains unchanged through such modification. *Stem* is more often used for an English word, and *root* is more often used for a word part taken from a foreign language. An example of a *stem* is *bound* in *bounding, bounded, rebound;* an example of a *root* is *celer* as in *acceleration, celerity.* For structural analysis purposes in the elementary grades, the term *root* will be used in this book to cover both situations.

Inflectional forms are words that have undergone change by the addition of an ending for grammatical purposes, such as case, gender, number, tense, person, mood, or voice. Examples are *boys,* in which *boy* is changed to the plural form by adding *s; walked,* in which *walk* is changed to the past tense by adding *ed.*

A *derivative* is a word derived from another word by adding a prefix or suffix; for example, *basketful* is a derivative of *basket.*

A *word variant* is made up of a root or stem and an inflectional ending, such as *talking.*

A *prefix* is one or more letters or a syllable combined or united at the beginning of a word to change its meaning; for example: *a* as in *aloud, pre* as in *preview.*

A *suffix* is an element added to the end of a word to change its meaning, as *ward* in *westward.*

An *affix* means "that which is attached"; it may be either a prefix or a suffix.

A *syllable* may be one or several letters taken to make one uninterrupted unit of utterance as: *pic to graph.*

The Content of Structural Analysis

The content of structural analysis, like phonics, is made up of several elements that lend themselves to classification. A total graphic picture of word structure elements and processes from the teaching standpoint, together with examples, is presented in the chart on page 218.

It isn't possible, of course, to list all the root words, compound words, contractions, and possessive forms which youngsters will meet in their reading in the elementary grades. The common inflectional endings are established by the grammar of the English language as *s, es, ing, er,* and *est.*

Studies which have been made of the frequency of *prefixes* and *suffixes* offer some, but not complete, guidance in regard to the teaching content of these elements.

According to Stauffer's study [29] of Thorndike's *The Teacher's Word Book,* the following prefixes appear with the highest frequency: *ab, ad, be, com, de, dis, en, ex, in* (into), *in* (not), *pre, pro, re, sub, un.*

Thorndike [30] made a study of suffixes appearing in his word list. He found that "Among the three thousand commonest words, the following suffixes appear with a frequency of twelve or more: *-ion, -tion,* and *-ation*

[29] Russell G. Stauffer, "A Study of Prefixes in the Thorndike List to Establish a List of Prefixes that Should be Taught in the Elementary School," *Journal of Educational Research,* Vol. 35 (Feb. 1942), 453–58.

[30] Edward L. Thorndike, *The Teaching of English Suffixes* (New York: Bureau of Publications, Teachers College, Columbia University, 1941).

CLASSIFICATION OF WORD STRUCTURE ELEMENTS TOGETHER WITH EXAMPLES AND WORD RECOGNITION PROCESSES

WORDS IN A COMPOUND WORD	STEM OR ROOT WORD	INFLECTIONAL FORMS	PREFIXES	SUFFIXES	POSSESSIVE FORMS	CONTRACTIONS	SYLLABLES
Example: *snowman* Children learn to identify the two separate words in a compound word as *snow, man,* when having difficulty in reading a compound word.	Example: *joy* Children learn to look for the stem word in words changed by adding affixes as *joyful, enjoyed, enjoyment* as needed when meeting unrecognized words.	Examples: Words changed by adding *s—cats* *es—boxes* *ed—walked* *ing—walking* *er—sweeter trainer* *est—sweetest* Children learn to recognize and pronounce these endings when encountered in reading words.	Examples: *re—return* *dis—disappointed* Children learn to recognize prefixes and their meanings when encountered in reading words.	Examples: *ment—amusement* *less—helpless* Children learn to recognize suffixes and their meanings when encountered in reading words.	Examples: *John's* hat the *girl's* doll Children learn to identify possessive forms by noting apostrophy *s* in reading words.	Examples: *didn't* *aren't* *haven't* Children learn that the one word stands for two words, and that the apostrophy shows where a letter was left out.	Examples: *dan ger* *wis dom* Children learn the concept of a syllable, and learn several ways of dividing words into syllables, when reading words.

(31); *-er* (22); *-y* (21); *-al* (21); *-ent* (15); *-ful* (15); *-ity* or *-ty* (13); *-ure* (13); *-ous* (12)."

Thorndike also found that "Among the five thousand commonest words, the following suffixes occur with a frequency of twelve or more: *-ion, -tion,* and *-ation* (107); *-er* (69); *-y* (61); *-al* (45); *-ous* (40); *-ment* (39); *-ful* (37); *-ity* or *-ty* (34); *-ent* (31); *-ure* (27); *-ness* (25); *-ence* (23); *-ance* (21); *-en* (21); *-ly* in adj. (19); *-ary* (17); *-ive* (17); *-ant* (16); *-able* (15); *-an, -ian, -n* (14); *-ic* (12)."

The teacher will not necessarily teach the prefixes and suffixes in the order of frequency indicated above; nor will the elementary teaching program as a whole be confined to those elements listed. While all of these commonest elements should be included in the total elementary program, specific ones should be taught in relation to children's needs and maturity; and if a particular prefix or suffix not in these "commonest" lists appears in children's reading it may well be given attention.

Procedures for Teaching Structural Analysis

Compound Words

Introduction and Development

One of the easiest beginnings in structural analysis is that of helping children to see the two word units in a compound word. Even in the earliest stages of reading, children meet such compound words as *playhouse, something, into, policeman, grandfather.*

In chart and chalkboard activities the teacher may call attention to the two separate words in a compound word in some such way as this: "This word *playhouse* has two words in it (placing her hand over *house*). You see if I cover up *house* I have *play;* if I cover up *play* I have *house* (covering *play*). Show me *play* in this word, Jane. Mark it off with the sides of your two hands, placing one hand on each side of *play*. (Jane does as directed.) What word did you show me?" (Jane answers *play*.) Similarly the teacher may have *house* marked off with the sides of a pupil's hands or indicated in some other way.

An example of the use to which a child may put a knowledge of a compound word even after its first introduction will be given. Miss Hill had called attention to the *in* and *to* in the new word *into* with the use of a procedure similar to the one described above. Cathy met this word *into* in her book soon afterwards and didn't recognize it by sight. "Don't tell it to me. Don't tell it to me!" she cautioned the teacher. "Wait a minute till I part it." Cathy covered *to* with her index finger, and looking at the remaining word said, "This is *in*"; then she covered *in* and read *to*. Removing her finger she victoriously announced "into!"

It is helpful to synthesize as well as to analyze compound words. For example, a new word which the children may meet is *bird*. They have already had the color words *black* and *blue*. The teacher writes *bird* on the chalkboard saying, "I can make a big word with bird in it." She then writes *black* on the chalkboard. "Now watch while I run these two words together to make one big word." She writes *blackbird* and the children read it. Similarly she combines *blue* with *bird* to make *bluebird*. They thrill with achievement at being able to read "big words" like this.

Auditory perception of two words within a compound word may be developed by having children listen to the teacher say a new compound word and then tell what two words they hear. At other times the teacher may ask some of the children to give compound words orally and may then ask the other children what two words they hear in each compound word.

As pupils progress through the grades they will meet increasing numbers of compound words, the development of which should be a continuous process. As needs arise, the teacher may place sentences containing compound words on the chalkboard and discuss their component parts and meanings. Whenever a child has difficulty in pronouncing a compound word, he should be asked first to find and read the two separate words that make up the total word. Thus the development of ability to perceive the two word units within a compound word and to sense the meaning of compound words should be functional and continuous all through the grades.

Review and Maintenance

Some children will "catch on" to the technique of analyzing compound words as a result only of introducing the procedure described above. Others will need practice in order to develop a keener sensitiveness to the use of this technique. Some ways of providing additional practice are suggested in Chapter 21, "Suggestions for Maintenance and Practice," pages 551–52.

Little Words in Big Words

The practice of having children look for "little words in big words" is highly questionable and should not be considered as part of a word structure program. This is such a widely used and misused technique, however, that it warrants discussion in the interest of clarification.

One way in which teachers make use of this technique is to teach children to "look for the little word" when they have trouble in pronouncing a new word, such as *at* in *pat*. It might work in this case, but what about *at* in *what?*

Some children who had been taught always to look for a little word first in working out a new word were reading silently about *Timmy, the Toad.* In the midst of the story, Jane burst out with this inquiry: "Miss Anderson, what is a *to ad?*"

The little word technique misleads very often in the pronunciation of one-syllable words, and even more often in the pronunciation of polysyllabic words. Imagine a pupil trying to pronounce *dynamite* by first looking for *am, Jonathan* by looking for *at, territory* by looking for *it,* or *recreation* by looking for *eat.*

In addition to the practice mentioned above, a favorite activity in some classrooms is to have children see how many words they can find in a given word, such as *father.* They find *fat, at,* and *her.* This activity violates several things commonly taught in phonics and word structure. First, the vowel *a* has a different sound in *fat* and *at* than it does in *father;* second, children are taught that the two letters of *th* when together make one speech sound and are not pronounced separately; third, the syllabic units in this word are *fath* and *er,* each having one vowel sound. From all these standpoints, having children see how many words they can find in *father* is misleading and undesirable, as it is in most cases.

However, this "little word" technique has two "legitimate" uses if they are not overworked. In the beginning stages of reading, before children have developed sensitivity in seeing elements within words, it is helpful for the teacher upon occasion to point out a known word in another word, as "The little word *at* that you already know is in the word *cat.*" But she shouldn't go so far as to teach the children to make use of this technique as an independent word-getting process.

Another use of this technique is finding root words in words modified by inflectional endings, prefixes, or suffixes, such as finding *walk* in *walking, load* in *unload,* and *sweet* in *sweetness.* In these cases children are perceiving whole word units, which is an excellent structural analysis technique.

Root Words

Introduction

In this discussion reference is made to procedures used in identifying the basic meaning element in a word modified by inflectional endings, prefixes, or suffixes. Thus, in the word *unskillful* children should be taught to look for *skill* (not *ill*); in *information,* they would look for *form* (not *or*). Teaching children to search for the root word as a first step in working out the recognition of a modified word is an important part of the word structure program.

The development of sensitivity to root words is necessarily related to the development of inflectional endings, prefixes, and suffixes and will be discussed in connection with these topics.

At this point, however, a word might be said about initial auditory and visual discrimination. A beginning in auditory discrimination of root words can be made very early. Suppose that the children have the new word *playing*. The teacher may say, "What whole word do you hear in *playing;* if we left off the *ing* part what word would we have left? Can you tell me the main word in these other words as I say them: *hunted, walking, shouted, sleeping* . . . ?" and so on. Continue in this way when other new modified words come up in reading situations.

Visual discrimination of root words may be developed first by pointing out the root word and separating it from its inflectional ending whenever such a word comes up in reading context, as: "The word *holding* is a new one (writing it on the chalkboard). What is the main word in this word? Yes, it is hold" (boxing or underlining *hold*).

Review and Maintenance

Suggestions for continued practice in detecting root words will be given under the discussions of "Inflectional Endings" and "Prefixes and Suffixes" that follow.

Inflectional Endings

Introduction

An introduction to inflectional endings and their functions may be made informally as the children meet words modified by these endings.

Perhaps the first inflectional ending that a child will encounter in his reading is *s*, added to make plurals. Some classroom situation may be used to develop this concept. For example, the first word of this type to come up might be *boys,* with *boy* having been learned previously as a sight word. When the word *boys* is encountered, the teacher may write both *boy* and *boys* on the chalkboard explaining that when we want to talk or read about more than one boy we add an *s* to the word. She might then have one boy stand near her and write *one boy,* then have two boys stand near her and write *two boys,* then have one girl stand near her and write *one girl,* and so on. The children may then read the phrases (with help on the number words) and finally be given turns in circling the *s* in a word that names more than one.

Similarly, when an *ing* ending first appears in reading, the teacher may develop this element through a classroom situation; for instance, let us suppose that the new word is *walking,* and that it appears in the sentence "Tom was walking to the store with Daddy." The teacher may write this sentence on the chalkboard, call attention to the word *walking,* and say that she will explain something about this word. She may then ask different children to dramatize such actions as *walk, laugh, jump, pull, push,* and so on. While the children are performing these actions, sentences similar to the following may be written.

John is walking.   Bob is pulling.
Dick is laughing.   Charles is pushing.
Mabel is jumping.

The children may read the sentences, with help if necessary on any of the proper names or verbs. The teacher may ask what is alike in all the words that tell what the children did. The *ing* ending may be underlined in each word and the sentences read again, making sure that everyone can hear the *ing.*

The *ed* ending might be introduced in the same way, except that each sentence would be written after the action had taken place rather than while it was in progress, as was the case with the *ing* words.

Development

After the pupils have had a few sight words containing one of the endings, an organized development may take place. All the principles applied to the development of phonic elements should also be applied to the development of inflectional endings. An example of one way in which these principles may be applied is described below.

Suppose that the children had met the word *standing* in a sentence and had experienced difficulty with it. The teacher might write the sentence on the chalkboard: *The man was standing on the walk,* and explain that she would help them with the word that gave them trouble.

Visual discrimination might be sharpened by listing in a vertical column known sight words ending with *ing,* such as *looking, walking, going.* The children might find the part that was the same in each word and box or circle it.

For auditory discrimination the children might listen as the teacher pronounces words and clap or stand each time she says one ending in *ing.* She might say words of this type: *quickly, helping, eating, waited, standing, shouted, falling.*

Known root words might then be written on the chalkboard and the children asked to add *ing* to each and to pronounce the word so modified: *help (helping), play (playing), sleep (sleeping), stand (standing).*

After the word-building experience, the children might read sentences containing the new words they had built and choose the right word from multiple-choice endings, as:

> *help*
> Susan was *helped* her mother with the dishes.
> *helping*
>
> *playing*
> Baby was *played* with a ball.
> *play*
>
> *sleep*
> Harry found the kitten *sleeping* on his bed.
> *slept*
>
> *stand*
> Billy was *standing* out in the rain.
> *stood*

Finally, application could be made to the original need by having the children read the sentence in which the word *standing* originally gave trouble.

Review and Maintenance

There are some children who may need review and maintenance of inflectional endings all through the elementary grades. A few structural analysis, word-building, and classification activities are suggested for this purpose in Chapter 21, "Suggestions for Maintenance and Practice."

Principles To Be Generalized

There are certain principles concerning changes in the structure of words which occur when inflectional endings or suffixes are added. Some of the most important of these principles are presented for the teacher's information. These principles should be *generalized* by the children, *not memorized*.

When pupils have had several sight words which represent a certain principle, these words may be written on the chalkboard, with the root word opposite each inflected or suffixed word. Through discussion the teacher may guide the children in discovering and formulating the principle for themselves.

1. In many cases the word is unchanged when an inflectional ending or suffix is added, as *talking, basketful*.
2. The final *e* is usually dropped when adding an ending beginning with a vowel, as *hoped, biting*.
3. When a word ends in a single consonant following a single vowel, the final consonant is usually doubled when adding an ending, as in *running, dropped, winner, soggy*.

4. When a word ends in *y*, following a consonant, the *y* is usually changed to *i* when adding an ending as in *cried, ponies, tinier, happiest, happily.*

5. When a word ends in *f*, usually the *f* is changed to *v* when *es* is added, making the plural form, as in *calves, wolves.*

Prefixes and Suffixes

Prefixes and suffixes should be taught in accordance with the same general procedures suggested for inflectional endings, but with increased emphasis upon the effect of these elements in changing word meanings.

Introduction

Discussion may take place whenever children first encounter a word containing a new prefix or suffix. Call attention to the prefix or suffix. Have the pupils find the root word and see if they can tell in what way the prefix or suffix changes its meaning.

Development

When it is time to give organized development of a new prefix or suffix, it may be done through generalization from known sight words containing the prefix or suffix.

1. A sample procedure for generalizing a prefix meaning is given. Suppose the youngsters have had the word *retold* and *return,* and the new word *repaint* appears in their reading. Write on the chalkboard the words *return* and *retold* in a vertical column. Have children tell what is alike in both words. Erase the *re* in each word and ask what the word means. Add *re* again and ask how the meaning is changed. Write several roots, including *paint,* as *paint, write, tell.* Discuss their meaning. Have *re* added to each one and discuss the changed meaning. Ask children to give sentences using first the root word and then the changed word. Have them read sentences containing the root words, as:

John will paint the doghouse.
Mary plans to write a letter to her grandmother.
Jean, will you tell your story?

After pupils have read each sentence, erase the verb and write in its place the same verb modified by the prefix *re.* Discuss the change in meaning.

2. Another way of developing a prefix might be as follows: Write on the chalkboard a sentence such as *Lillian told her story a second time.*

After having the sentence read, ask the pupils if they can think of a shorter way to say the same thing. Write *Lillian retold her story.* Explain that the prefix *re* means repeating, doing again. Have them circle or underline the prefix *re.* Write additional sentences containing root words prefixed by *re.* Have the children read the sentences, underline the prefixed words, and tell their meaning.

Suffixes may be developed in the same ways as prefixes. In developing suffixes, as well as prefixes, it is desirable not only to have children visualize the element but to understand how it affects the meaning of a word. Emphasis should be placed upon discussion of changed meaning and the reading of sentences in which root words have been modified by adding the prefix or suffix under consideration.

Review and Maintenance

Many children need to refresh their knowledge of prefixes and suffixes previously developed and review the function of these elements in helping with their word recognition ability. Several of the suggestions offered for reviewing inflectional endings may be used also for reviewing prefixes and suffixes. Additional suggestions are given in Chapter 21, pages 552–54.

Possessive Forms

Reading possessive forms is no problem for many children; however, there are usually some pupils in first and second grade who need to have the concept of the added *apostrophe s* developed.

Development

For the benefit of children who fail to pronounce the *s* in possessive forms, the procedure might be as follows: pick up a child's book and ask, "Whose book is this?" Then write the response on the chalkboard, as *Mary's book.* Repeat the procedure with another child's book, but omit the apostrophe and *s* from the child's name, as *Tom.. book.* Ask the children to read the sentence and lead them to discover what is wrong. Add the apostrophe and *s,* calling these symbols by their names. Then have the phrase read again. Repeat with the books of other children. Vary the procedure by holding up pencils, crayons, tablets, or other possessions of the pupils.

At other times pupils might underline the correct word in phrases of this type:

Helen's	Ned	Tom's
pencil	book	crayons
Helen	Ned's	Tom

The teacher may write on the chalkboard possessive and nonpossessive forms of the names of children who possess certain articles which she will name later.

Bill	Susan's	Roger's	Janet
Bill's	Susan	Roger	Janet's

Then she may ask questions of this type: Whose raincoat is yellow? Whose hair-ribbon is red? Whose sweater is blue? Whose dress is green? Different children indicate and read the appropriate answer in each case.

Contractions

Two words that have been shortened to make one word by omitting certain letters represent a change in word form and so belong to the teaching category of structural analysis. Some of the more common contractions are: I'll, we'll, aren't, don't, doesn't, can't, couldn't, woudn't, it's, she's, he's, how's, where's, that's, what's.

One teacher developed contractions as described below. The children had already learned *don't* as a sight word, and *I'll* had been introduced as a sight word in the story they were reading. Therefore, these two words were used as a basis for initiating work with contractions.

"I noticed that some of the boys got paint on their suits this morning, so I am going to tell you this," said Miss Evans. She wrote on the chalkboard, *Do not get paint on your suits.*

Tommy read the sentence. He was able to supply the new word *paint* from context.

"There is a shorter way of saying this," continued Miss Evans. "Instead of saying, 'Do not get paint on your suits,' I could have said, 'Don't get paint on your suits.'"

She erased *Do not* and replaced it with *Don't*. Ann read the sentence. Then she wrote these sentences on the blackboard:

Do not get mud on your shoes.	Do not let your dog go hungry.
Do not get your feet wet.	Do not play on the way home.

In each case she had the sentence read, then replaced *Do not* with *Don't* and had it read again.

Maintenance and Practice

Other ways a contraction may be reviewed or practiced are suggested in Chapter 21, page 554.

Syllabication: Developing the Concept of a Syllable

A syllable is a pronounceable unit in a word. It must contain a vowel sound either alone or combined with one or more consonants. The ability to recognize syllables in words is a valuable economy. Often skill in dividing a polysyllabic word into syllables is all a pupil needs in working out the pronunciation of a new word. If this technique works for him, he is then saved the more laborious process of applying phonics to smaller elements.

Introduction

The first step in introducing the child to syllabication is to develop in him the ability to identify the sound of separate pronounceable units in a word. As early as the second grade, the teacher may begin developing sensitivity to syllables incidentally and casually. For example, when the new word *wonderful* is being discussed, the teacher might say something like this: "This long word has three parts in it. Count them (pronouncing *won der ful*). Some words have two parts, as *princess*. Count them (pronouncing *prin cess*). And some only have one part, as *spot*. Count how many parts you hear in *spot*."

Organized Development

When it seems advisable to develop the true concept of a syllable, both auditory and visual discrimination should be given attention. As in the case of the development of other word elements, familiar words should be used as a working basis. The concept that a syllable contains one sounded vowel should be *generalized* by the children.

An example of one type of procedure that has been used for this purpose is given below.

The teacher first developed ability to *hear* two syllables in a word. This was introduced as follows: "Some words have two parts. Listen while I say *darkness*. One part of the word is *dark* and the other part is *ness*. Can you hear two parts in *surprise*? What are the two parts?" She continued this procedure with the words *Johnson, watchman, grinding, blanket, Sunday*.

She explained that she would say some words which have only one part, and some which have two parts. She asked the children to clap once every time she said a word which had one part, and twice each time she said one which had two parts. She pronounced words such as *rang, shallow, morning, Ray, wife, happen, mutton, top, garden*.

After the children were able to hear the difference between one-syllable and two-syllable words, she introduced the term *syllable*. "Each part of the word which you can hear separately is called a syllable. In *darkness, dark* is a syllable and *ness* is a syllable." She wrote *syllable* on the chalkboard and had the children read it.

Following this introduction, she developed the true concept of syllables as determined by vowel sounds. She wrote on the chalkboard several one-syllable words, as: *big, top, rich, bell, had*. "How many vowel sounds can you hear in *big*? How many syllables are there in *big*? Let's make a note of that." She wrote on the chalkboard the headings below, together with *big*. She asked the children to tell her the number to write under each heading:

	Vowels	*Syllables*
big	1	1

She then added other one-syllable words, and the number of vowels and syllables in each were written.

She wrote two additional headings—*Vowels, Syllables*—and repeated the procedure using two-syllable words, as *river, stupid, broken, farmer, basket*.

As a result of this experience, the children arrived at these generalizations: (1) Every syllable has one vowel sound. (2) There are as many syllables in a word as there are vowel sounds.

A similar procedure may be used in extending the development to three- and four-syllable words when it seems practical to do so.

Developing the sound of a single vowel in a one-syllable word is another consideration in teaching syllabication. This is a phonic principle but it needs to be reviewed again in its special application to syllabication. One suggestion for such a development is given below.

Write on the chalkboard some one-syllable words and questions as indicated below. Have the children answer the questions for each word in the two groups of words.

red	best	so	my
hat	met	he	me
fun	sat	go	be
hill	with	she	no

How many syllables are in the word?
How many vowels are in the word?
Is the vowel at the end of the word?
Is the vowel long or short?

Guide the children to awareness of this fact: when there is only one vowel in a one-syllable word, it is usually short unless it is at the end.

Another phonic principle which should not be disregarded when developing syllabication has to do with a silent vowel in a one-syllable word. One way in which this concept may be developed is as follows:

Write on the chalkboard one-syllable words containing a silent vowel, as in *foam, each, wife, real, load, white, rope.* Ask the children the following questions about each word: (1) How many syllables does it have? (2) How many vowels does it have? (3) Is the first vowel long or short? (4) Is the second vowel sounded or silent?

Guide the children to awareness of this fact: (1) when there are two or more vowels in a word of one syllable, the first vowel is usually long and the other is silent; (2) such words contain only one syllable because they contain only one *sounded* vowel.

Review and Maintenance

Review of ability to identify a syllabic unit should be given in terms of the needs of certain children and with the use of words which the children are currently meeting in their reading. A few samples for the teacher's use in preparing material for such activities are presented in Chapter 21, page 555.

Syllabication: Dividing Words into Syllables

Once the concept of a syllabic unit has been developed, the children are ready to begin the breaking up of words into syllables. They should learn several different procedures for doing this.

Some of the most useful syllabication procedures are mentioned below.

Dividing Compound Words

An easy first step evolves from the preceding work that children have had in recognizing the two words in a compound word. For practice activities see Chapter 21, pages 555–56.

Dividing Double-Letter Words

This also is one of the easiest beginning guides to apply in syllabication. For suggested practice activities see Chapter 21, page 556.

Dividing Affixed Words Between Root and Affix

Another easy technique to develop is that of dividing a word between its affix and root. Practice activities for use in connection with this procedure are given on pages 556–57 in Chapter 21.

Generalizing the Principle of Dividing Between Two Consonants

After having experiences of the types above pupils are ready for the development of the important principles of syllabication. They should be guided to discover these principles through generalization. One way in which this can be done is to write on the chalkboard words, familiar to the children, in which two consonants appear between two sounded vowels, such as: *center, person, perhaps, circus, compare, order, certain.*
Explain: "Here are some words that you already know. You can tell where to divide the words into syllables just by saying them to yourself. Draw a line between the two syllables in each of these words."
After the words have been divided, discussion may take place in regard to the sounded vowels in each word, the two consonants between the sounded vowels, and the point at which the words were divided.
As a result of discussion the children may be guided to a generalization which will enable them to fill in the blank words in the principle below, which the teacher writes on the chalkboard.

Principle No. 1: When two _____ come between two sounded _____, the word is usually divided between the two _____.

Following the generalization of the principle, the teacher may select words from reading material that the pupils have not yet covered and to which the principle can be applied. She writes these new words on the chalkboard and gives the pupils an opportunity to use the principle in dividing these words.

Generalizing the Principle of One Consonant Appearing Between Two Vowels

A procedure similar to the one described above might be used in this case.
Known words which pupils might divide simply because they already know how to pronounce them might be of this type: *divide, total, decide, travel, polar, locate, human, climate.*
Following discussion, a generalization may be drawn which will enable the pupils to supply the missing words in this principle:

Principle No. 2: When one _____ comes between two sounded _____, the word is usually divided just before the _____.

After the generalization has been made the children may be asked to apply the principle to new words which had not appeared in their previous reading material, such as *design, canal, storage, Pluto, Venus,* and so on.

Developing the Principle Concerning *le*

This principle may be generalized as suggested for the other two principles above. Children may first divide known words ending in *le* because they already know how to pronounce the words. Words of this type may be used for the first dividing activity: *table, able, circle, marble.*

Through separation of syllables and discussion, the children may be guided in arriving at the principle below, which they should be able to complete:

Principle No. 3: When a word ends in _____ and a _____ precedes the _____, then that _____ goes with the _____ syllable.

After generalizing the principle pupils may apply it to such words as: *bridle, Bible, maple.*

Generalizing the Principle Concerning *ed* as a Separate Syllable

The children may read several root words to which the *ed* ending has been added. Among these words there should be several whose roots end in *d* or *t*. An example of such a list might be:

played	sailed	rained	pulled
worked	planted	helped	waited
sounded	needed	wanted	loaded

Have the children read the words and underline those in which they hear the *ed* as a separate syllable. Ask them to study the words to see if they can find anything which they have in common. Guide discussion to a generalization which will enable the children to supply the missing words in this principle:

Principle No. 4: When _____ is added to a word ending in *d* or *t*, it is pronounced as a separate syllable.

Have the children find several other words to which the principle applies.

Recognizing a Blend or a Speech Sound as Representing Just One Consonant

For syllabication purposes the principles above often fail to work because pupils consider such elements as *st* or *th* as "two consonants." An example of a possible procedure to use in these cases is suggested below. The teacher writes the syllabicated words on the chalkboard as the explanation proceeds.

Principle No. 1 does not apply when a blend or speech sound falls between two sounded vowels. We never split a blend or a speech sound.

The word *father* has two consonants between two sounded vowels, but we do not divide the word this way: *fat her.* Since *th* makes just one sound, it is considered in the same way that one consonant would be considered. So Principle No. 2, applies, and the word is divided in this way: *fa ther.*

It is sometimes puzzling to know where to divide a word which has three or more consonants between two vowels.

The word *instrument,* for example, has four consonants between two sounded vowels. The letters *str* make up a blend, however, which cannot be split. So the divisions in the word are made as follows: *in stru ment.*

This discussion may be followed by having the children underline the blend or speech sound in several words of two or more syllables, and then having them divide the words into syllables. Words of this type may be used for practice: *describe, author, improve, farther, complete, extreme, progress, degree.*

Review and Maintenance

Syllabication skills can best be reviewed and maintained through continuous application to words met currently in reading context. The teacher should repeatedly encourage and supervise children in attacking new words as follows: (1) examine the word form carefully, (2) separate the word into syllables using any of the syllabication guides that can be applied, (3) if the word isn't recognized by this time use phonics to help with the pronunciation, (4) try fitting the word into the context to see if it makes sense.

Syllabication, however, is such a complex and at the same time such an extremely important word identification skill that it is advisable to provide direct practice in establishing it. Suggestions for use in giving practice on a wide variety of syllabication techniques are provided in Chapter 21, pages 555–56.

Accent

Accent is the stress given to a syllable in a word. In addition to knowing how to identify syllables in words, children need to understand what an accent is and how to interpret accent marks in pronouncing words.

There are no hard and fast "rules" in regard to accent, but there are a few trends or inclinations about which the teacher should be informed. She may pass the information on to the pupils through the generalization process, if and when she thinks it is desirable.

In two-syllable words the accent usually falls on the first syllable unless that syllable is a prefix, as *carbon, forest.*

Usually the root of a word is accented, as *departed, recalling.*

When a word ends in *tion* or *sion*, it is accented on next to the last syllable as *condensation, declension.*

Accent affects vowel sounds. The vowel has the long sound when accented in *a'ble* but a different sound when unaccented in *a part.* The vowel principles apply to accented syllables but they usually do not apply to unaccented syllables.

Introduction of Primary Accent

Information about accent and accent marks usually is presented to a group of pupils when the teacher thinks that they are approaching readiness for the use of dictionary pronunciation skills.

One approach to the development of accent might be for the teacher to look out for words which the children mispronounce in reading or discussion because of accenting the wrong syllable. She won't interrupt the interest in pursuing a story plot or a spirited discussion with a development of accent; rather she will correct the pronunciation at the time and say something to this effect: "I'll tell you an interesting thing about that word later."

At a later period she may use the misaccented word, and others that she has collected from the children's speech, as a basis for telling them that in all words of two or more syllables one syllable is pronounced more forcibly than the others. She may then pronounce some words, such as *wonder, consonant, exception, departure,* and call attention to the syllable of special stress. Next she may say several words containing one accented syllable, and ask the children to tell her what the accented syllable is in each case.

As a follow-up, some words with which the children are familiar may

be written on the chalkboard. The teacher may explain that a mark like '
is used after a syllable that is to be accented to indicate that it is the one
to be stressed. She may place the accent mark after a syllable in each of
the words on the chalkboard and have the children read the words to
try out its application.

Finally, she may write familiar words on the chalkboard and have the
children divide the words into syllables, discover the accented syllable in
each one, and place it appropriately. The example words which children
have been mispronouncing because of wrong accent might be added to
this list.

For practice suggestions to use in follow-up work see Chapter 21,
page 557.

Introduction of Secondary Accent

When need arises in connection with the wrong pronunciation of a
word containing three or more syllables, the children may be given information concerning the secondary accent. The teacher's explanation may
consist of information of this type:

Many words have two syllables that are accented. Equal stress is not placed
on both accented syllables, however. One is stressed more heavily than the
other. The one heavily stressed is called the primary accent. The one less heavily stressed is called the secondary accent. In a word such as *conservation*
(write the word that has been mispronounced as an example) the syllable
va is stressed heavily. The syllable *con* is stressed lightly. The syllable *va* has
the primary accent, and the syllable *con* has the secondary accent. In *Webster's Dictionary*, the primary accent is marked with a large, bold accent mark
like this ', and the secondary accent is marked with a short, light line like this
'. In some other dictionaries the secondary accent is indicated by two light
marks like this ".

This introduction may be followed by having pupils mark the two
accents in familiar words and pronouncing new words in which they
make use of primary and secondary accent marks.

Dictionary Aids to Pronunciation

I heard a man on television last night say "ăl'mŏnd." I have always thought
the word was pronounced ä'mŭnd. Have you heard people say ăl'mŏnd? Do
you suppose they are right? How can we find out for sure?

Miss Hughes followed this discussion by looking up the word in the
dictionary in front of the pupils and placing the main entry and the

respelling with its diacritical markings on the chalkboard. She asked the youngsters to help her to work out the pronunciation with the use of the dictionary aids, some of which she explained briefly as she followed up with later development.

It is in ways like this that the astute teacher develops attitudes toward the use of a dictionary as a source of reference for, and final authority on, word pronunciation. And attitude is of great importance in developing dictionary skills, as well as other skills! Of what avail is effort expended in developing word attack skills unless a positive attitude toward using these skills is developed simultaneously?

Both attitudes and skills in dictionary usage are developed most effectually in "on the spot" situations in which a doubt about a word exists. This might happen during discussion any time in the day; it might happen while reading in any subject area. Take advantage of every opportunity to encourage pupils to develop their dictionary attitudes and skills and to apply them in functional situations.

Dictionary skills, however, cannot be left entirely to chance. They are too numerous and complex. Their development needs to be carefully planned in terms of specific clusters of skills. One cluster consists of those skills necessary in locating a word in the dictionary, another is concerned with working out pronunciation of words, and a third is concerned with getting meanings from words. Not all of these skills should be "thrown at" pupils at one time. Ordinarily the location skills should be developed first, then the meaning skills, and finally the pronunciation skills, the first two clusters, and then the integration of all three clusters as fast as possible.

Children usually develop some ability in using rudimentary location skills and rudimentary meaning skills in the primary grades. Each of these clusters need further development and refinement in the upper grades. (See Chapter 10, pages 325–31, for a discussion of dictionary location skills and pages 331–32 for a discussion of dictionary meaning skills.) Because the pronunciation cluster is a hierarchy built upon all the phonic and word structure skills discussed in this chapter, it is usually the last of the dictionary skill clusters to be developed. Fortunately, pupils usually have had acquaintance with several of the pronunciation skills through their phonic and word structure activities preceding the use of pronunciation aids in the dictionary.

Pupils must realize that sounds of the language are represented by letters, and that sometimes two or more sounds are represented by the same letter. This they have learned through phonics instruction.

They need to have skill in identifying a root word and in recognizing it in its changed forms when modified by inflectional endings. This they have learned through structural analysis.

Many words do not appear in the dictionary in all their inflected forms, and the child cannot find the word in the dictionary unless he knows its root. As an example of such a handicap, suppose that a pupil pronounces *hurries* as "hûr′ rĭ ĕs" and attempts to look it up in the dictionary to ascertain its meaning; he wouldn't find the word; but if he realizes that the root is *hurry* and that it has been changed by an inflectional ending, the word will give him no trouble.

Another preparation for using pronunciation aids in the dictionary is a knowledge of syllabication. Through syllabication instruction children have learned that a syllable is a pronounceable unit, and that words can be made up of one, two, or several of these pronounceable units. This is an essential dictionary readiness activity.

A fourth essential in making use of dictionary aids to pronunciation is an understanding of accent and the use of accent marks. Pupils should have had experience with accents in connection with their work in syllabication.

Equipped with a knowledge of phonics and structural analysis, including syllabication and accent, the child has an excellent stock in trade to capitalize upon in developing the additional skills that he needs in learning to use pronunciation aids in the dictionary. These additional skills include the use of diacritical marks and respellings.

Diacritical Marks and Respellings

There was a time, some years ago, when primary children were given extensive practice in the use of diacritical marks. Even the words in primers were liberally marked with macrons, carets, dots, and other symbols of like nature. It was not uncommon to find passages such as the following in beginning readers:

Rōşé is a good mĭtt̸ māk er.
What is she k̸nit t̸ing now? That is not a mĭtt̸. See, it has a hee̸l. What a k̸nĭt ter you are, Rōşé! [31]

From many standpoints this was an exceedingly undesirable practice and was abandoned about half a century ago. According to present thinking, diacritical marks should be taught at the time that a child has

[31] Edward G. Ward, *The Rational Method in Reading, Primer* (Newark, N. J.: Silver Burdett Company, 1894), p. 103.

a functional need for them in connection with his dictionary work. Even then, it is not necessary for him to memorize *all* the markings and their sounds. He can always turn to the key at the bottom of the pages or in the front of a dictionary to identify any of the less frequently used sounds. If he can *interpret* these markings in the successful pronunciation of words, then the objective for teaching diacritical marks has been achieved.

Introducing Diacritical Marks and Respellings

Diacritical marks and respellings must of necessity be developed together, for it is in the respellings that diacritical marks are most frequently used.

No doubt the children will ask about respellings in their contacts with glossaries and dictionaries. If so, the function of respellings and diacritical marks may be explained at that time. If not, the teacher may make such an explanation at a time when she and the group together are looking up a new word in the dictionary.

The pupils may be told that when they look up a word in a glossary or dictionary they will find after the word a second spelling in parentheses. This second spelling tells them how to pronounce the word by showing the syllables, the accent mark, and the sounds of the vowels. But in some cases the second spelling is different from the one used in the text of the story, for example, *English* (ĭng′glĭsh), *pygmy* (pĭg′mĭ), *dense* (dĕns), *curds* (kûrds). The teacher may explain that many of our words are not pronounced just as they are spelled; thus, in a glossary or dictionary, words are often respelled just the way they are pronounced. The children should be urged always to look for the spelling in parentheses as an aid in working out the pronunciation.

Then the diacritical markings may be taken up as applied to the word in question, which for the sake of illustration we shall say is *archive* (är′kīv). The teacher may explain the markings in some such manner as this: "Vowels have many different sounds. You have learned the long and short sounds of vowels, and the sound when a vowel is followed by *r*. There are also several additional sounds. In order to help you know which sound a vowel has in a certain word, a marking scheme has been developed and is used in glossaries and dictionaries. You will find it at the beginning of some glossaries, always at the beginning of dictionaries, and in large dictionaries at the bottom of the pages." At this point it would be advisable to let the pupils turn to these sources to get an overview of the entire marking system. The children should be told that marking keys vary somewhat from one glossary or dictionary to another, and that they will need to make use of the system appearing in the particular glossary or dictionary that they are using.

If there are not enough dictionaries or glossaries to accommodate each child in the group, the teacher may place the entire key for diacritical marks on the chalkboard. To follow up with illustrations it is advisable to read the key through, with the children stopping, of course, to work out the pronunciation of *ar* in *archive* when discussing the *a* so marked in the key, and the *i* in *kiv* when discussing the *i* so marked in the key. (The word, of course, should be one with which the children have had trouble, not necessarily this particular one.)

After the general introduction of the key the teacher will probably wish to concentrate on just a few of the sounds until the children have become thoroughly familiar with them. Then she will concentrate on a few more of the sounds at another time, and so on, until the children can interpret diacritical marks when looking up any word in the dictionary.

Suggestions for additional practice will be found in Chapters 21 and 23, pages 557, 559.

Maturity Levels and Sequence

Word structure elements cannot be assigned definitely to certain grade or age levels. The time at which a certain element or a certain type of element is introduced depends upon:

1. The frequency with which this element appears in the child's reading.

2. The child's need for having development of and practice in using this element in attacking unrecognized words. Has he already mastered the element through experience in reading and his own generalization, or would he profit by having help in identifying and using the element?

3. The child's stage of maturity in reading. Has the child reached a stage in his development which will enable him to profit by instruction in regard to this element?

We always must bear in mind, however, that reading is a continuous growth process and that the foundation for most of the skills should be laid in first grade and reviewed, built upon, and expanded at successive levels all through the elementary school.

Furthermore, we must ever keep strongly before us the fact that there are always vast individual differences. We usually think, for example, of the fourth grade as the stage at which children should learn all the dictionary skills. While this generally seems to be the appropriate level for children of normal maturation to acquire these skills, there may be some who are ready for them in second or third grade; others may not be ready until fifth or sixth grade. So the time at which a child reaches a maturation level appropriate for a certain word structure skill depends upon the stage of development of the child himself, not upon the grade label which he happens to bear.

With these considerations and exceptions in mind, some general statements may be ventured in regard to maturity levels and sequence in structural analysis.

At the first grade level, children may become aware of and gain some skill in using structural analysis of compound words and of words ending in *s, d, ed,* and *ing.* They may learn some possessives and contractions as sight words.

When the children have progressed to the normal stage of second grade development, they may be expected to increase the abilities developed in first grade and to add to them several of the variant endings —such as *es, er, est, ly*—and the generalizations concerned with the changes in word form made by adding these endings to certain vowel and consonant situations. The concepts of contractions and possessives can be understood at this level, and children should become skillful in recognizing word forms changed by contractions or by adding apostrophe *s.* At this stage they should be able to make considerable use of structural analysis along with phonic and context clues.

Many prefixes and suffixes appear in words encountered in third grade reading material, and childen of normal development can understand changes made in meaning by the addition of these affixes. Therefore, this is a time when some of the more commonly used prefixes in third grade material (such as *a, re, in, un, be, dis*) and commonly used suffixes (such as *ful, y, less, ness*) may be developed. Orientation to syllabication, accent, and dictionary skills may also be made at this level. In addition to these new developments, children should continuously grow in ability to apply all word structure knowledge and skills developed at preceding levels.

New word structure skills that may be given emphasis in grades four, five, and six are syllabication and skills in detecting accent. These skills may be introduced at the fourth grade stage and carried to higher levels of competency through grades five and six. Because prefixed and suffixed words increase in numbers and variety in intermediate grade material, marked advances should be made in developing the identification and meaning of these affixes. Work with compound words whose meanings

241

are substantially changed in compounding is needed at these levels. Inflectional endings may still need review. This is the period when children should become highly efficient in combining and integrating all these skills with the other word recognition skills in attacking polysyllabic words independently and accurately. Versatility is the watchword!

INTRODUCING NEW WORDS

This chapter should not close without offering some helpful suggestions on introducing new words in preparation for reading a selection for the first time.

Some teachers do not develop new words previous to reading a fresh selection. Instead they jot down unrecognized words as children read silently, then develop and give practice on these words later. The most common practice, however, is for the teacher to introduce the new words before reading. Probably both practices are necessary. Rarely can a teacher anticipate all the words which children will fail to recognize in reading a new selection. She can, however, select those which she feels certain will cause difficulty and "clear the woods of some of the trees" ahead of the reading of the selection. Then after the reading she may give additional practice on any other word difficulties that arise while the children are reading. Practice at both times is usually necessary when working with children in the primary grades, or with those in upper grades who have not attained independence in word recognition and the use of dictionary techniques.

The all too-common practice of the past has been one in which children are drilled on lists of isolated words. In introducing new words for a reading lesson the teacher would write a list of words on the chalkboard and have the children say the words forward, backward, and out-of-order as a preliminary to reading the selection in which the words appeared.

According to modern psychology and the science of semantics, it is not desirable for a teacher to introduce the new words in a selection by placing a list of these isolated words out of context on the chalkboard and drilling on them. Psychologists tell us that any new skill should be kept close to the meaningful situation in which it is used; semanticists tell us that it is the context which surrounds a word that gives it its meaning. Investigations in reading have shown that context aids both recognition and understanding of meanings. English specialists and reading specialists also believe that it is highly desirable for pupils to use a new word in oral context before reading it in printed form.

In consideration of the reasons given above it would seem advisable to introduce new words in contextual settings which make use of the words in the sense in which each is used in the material which children are about to read. While this philosophy sounds sensible, many teachers ask, "How can you do it?" "How can you introduce new words in context?"

In answer to the above questions some suggestions of procedures will be given. Not all suggestions appeal to all teachers. All teachers, however, are continuously searching for effective ways of adding variety to their teaching techniques. Possibly some of the following ideas of introducing new words will contribute to this purpose.

Using Sentences Growing Out of Children's Experiences

The teacher may guide children's conversation in ways which will elicit sentences growing out of their experiences and which contain the new words. These sentences may be manuscripted or written on the chalkboard and used for discussion and practice purpose.

Here is one example of this procedure: As a supervisor, the writer was about to visit a second grade classroom. The teacher had written *woman, met,* and *pocketbook* on the blackboard in a vertical list and had planned to introduce these new words for a reading lesson. She asked me to teach the lesson, and, challenged by having an opportunity to attempt an introduction of these new words through context, I agreed.

After asking the teacher to write each child's name on a large strip of paper and place it on his desk, I began the development by saying, "As I was driving to your school this morning I met several interesting people. I met some firemen. They had a fire truck. I met a school bus driver. He had a bus-load of children. I met a man driving a delivery wagon for a grocery. I imagine he had many good things to eat in his wagon."

"Did you meet anyone on your way to school?"

"I met the milkman" responded Shirley.

"Good," I responded as I wrote on the chalkboard, *Shirley met a milkman.* "Who else met someone?"

"I met a big Newfoundland dog," volunteered Henry.

"That was interesting," I remarked as I wrote, *Henry met a Newfoundland dog.*

After receiving and writing on the chalkboard three or four sentences which gave practice on the new word *met,* Jean fortunately volunteered, "I met a woman." This sentence gave the opportunity to introduce the reading symbol for *woman.*

"Did she have anything in her hand?" I asked. "Yes, a shopping bag," Jean answered. While the answer didn't include the pocketbook that I had hoped for, it was written on the chalkboard.

Time was passing, so I hastened the process of eliciting experience sentences by remarking, "What is that on your desk, Mary? Is it something new?" "It's my new pocketbook," replied Mary, and the sentence *Mary has a new pocketbook* was added to the others on the chalkboard. (As an alternative, I might have gotten something out of my own pocketbook, and the children could have given a sentence about this.)

The sentences on the chalkboard were read through as a whole. All sentences containing *met* were found and the word underlined, similarly sentences containing *woman* and *pocketbook* were read and these words were underlined. Some quick games (such as those described on pages 176–78) were played, concentrating upon *met, woman,* and *pocketbook.* The sentences were left on the chalkboard for reference, and the new pages in the selection were read with the greatest of ease.

Teachers can frequently use a similar procedure in introducing through context all or at least part of the new words to be read in an ensuing selection.

Discussing an Introductory Picture

Often a picture at the beginning of a selection can be used for discussion which results in sentences or phrases in which the children use the words orally and through which they gather meaningful concepts of the words. The teacher may write useful phrases on the chalkboard as they are mentioned, and use these for quick practice later if she desires.

For example, a full-page colored spread preceded a story in which the first two pages contained these new words: *sweater, deer, fawn, twins,* and the names of three characters, *Mary, Janet,* and *Jim.* The illustration showed the three children near the edge of a woods and showed a deer and a fawn in the woods.

"Here is a picture of the children about whom we shall read," explained Miss Skinner. "Two of them seem to be exactly the same size and same age. What do we call two children in a family who are exactly the same age?" "Twins" came the reply. "That's right," said Miss Skinner as she wrote on the chalkboard, reading aloud as she did so: *These children are twins.*

"The twins have names that begin with the same letter. The girl's name is *Janet* and the boy's name is *Jim.*" The names were written on the chalkboard and the children read them. (Proper names usually gain nothing from context and it is all right to present them as separate words.)

"The twin's older sister is with them. Her name is *Mary.*" Miss Skinner wrote the name and the children read it.

"It must have been a cool morning. Each of the children has on a sweater. What color is Janet's sweater?"

"Yes, *Janet's sweater is yellow*." The sentence was written as were additional sentences telling the color of the sweaters of the other two children.

"What is the large animal that you see in the woods?"

"*It is a deer*." The sentence was written and some discussion of deer followed.

"What is the small animal that is lying beside the deer?"

"It's a baby deer."

"What is a baby deer called?"

"It's a fawn."

"Yes, *A baby deer is called a fawn*," replied Miss Skinner as she wrote the sentence on the chalkboard.

Some quick practice followed in reading the sentences on the chalkboard before the reading of the new story was undertaken.

Supplying Missing Words

The attention of the children may be concentrated upon a new word by letting them supply this word orally in an incomplete sentence written on the chalkboard, as "Tom caught a bird in the orchard. He kept his bird in a ———." When the children supply the word *cage* orally, the teacher may write the word in the blank and have them read the complete sentence.

This procedure for introducing new words has the advantage of giving children practice in supplying words in context.

Using Key Sentences

Some of the new words in a story may be developed through the use of key sentences written on the chalkboard.

Tom threw some bread on the ground, and a parrot *swooped* down to get it.

The teacher may help the children read the sentence by telling them the word *swooped*, if necessary, and emphasizing it by drawing a line under it. The sentence should be left on the chalkboard, and if a child fails to recognize the word while reading he may refer to this key sentence and find it out for himself.

Using an Experience of the Teacher

Sometimes the teacher may tell about an immediate experience which she has had and which results in a group of sentences designed to introduce several new words. For instance, one teacher needed to develop the new words *crowd, moment, danger,* and *signal* for a new reading lesson. She told and wrote the following experience of her own on the chalkboard and had the children read it.

This morning a *crowd* of boys and girls stopped at the corner for a *moment*. Do you know why they stopped? The red light meant *danger*. They were waiting for the policeman to give them the *signal* to cross the street.

In composing sentences based on such experiences it is not necessary that all the words other than the ones to be introduced should be familiar to the children. If there are some other words that they do not know, the teacher may tell these words to them so that they will be free to concentrate on the new words to be developed for immediate use in reading.

Questioning Directly to Develop Meanings and Concepts

This procedure may best be described by giving an example. Suppose that the new words are *market* and *traders*. The teacher might ask, "What do we call a place where people take things to sell and other people go to buy these things?" When some child suggests *market* the teacher may write on the chalkboard, "*People buy and sell things in a market*," and have the children read the sentence.

Similarly, to develop the word *trader*, the teacher may say: "When we go to market we pay money for what we buy. In some parts of the world people do not use money to pay for the things they get at the market. They bring something to the market to exchange for the things they want. This is called *trading*."

She may then write on the chalkboard, "*People may trade furs for cloth*. People who trade are called *traders*," and have the children read the sentences.

Using Teacher-Prepared Background Material

The teacher may write a few paragraphs designed to introduce new words and develop concepts. She reads or tells this selection to the class, writing new phrases or sentences on the chalkboard as she comes to them.

An example of such background material is given below. The italicized words were written on the chalkboard and read by the children.

Did you ever go to a movie which showed pictures of a *jungle*? (Encourage free discussion if several have seen such a picture. Make sure before going farther that all members of the class have at least an elementary concept of what a jungle is.)

We are soon to read some stories about children who live in jungle lands. But before we do this, let us find out just where these jungles are. The two largest jungle lands are along the *Congo* (kong' go) *River* in *Africa* and along the *Amazon* (am' a zon) *River* in *South America*. (Let the children locate these rivers on a globe or wall map or in their geographies. Let them trace the course of the rivers and their tributaries, and notice their length.)

These jungle lands are quite different from the land in which we live. In the first place, both of them are in the very hottest part of the world. The sun is almost directly overhead at noon, and it is hot in winter as well as in summer. During certain parts of the year it rains almost every day. (Discuss with the children the effect of excessive heat and abundant rainfall upon vegetation.)

Now that we all have some idea of what a jungle is like, let us pretend that we are fortunate enough to take a trip to the Congo country. As we sail up the river, we see *lazy crocodiles* asleep in the mud along the banks. Now and then our boat passes a *hippopotamus* lounging in the sun. *Monkeys* chatter in the trees.

Discussing Children's Experiences Related to Story Characters

Sometimes the preparation for a new story may be built through a discussion of children's own experiences which are related to the experiences of the characters in the story. For example, a group of children were to read a story about an American family who went to Iraq to dig relics. The teacher introduced the story as indicated below. The italicized words were some new words in the story which she thought might cause the children trouble. She wrote each of the words on the board as she said it.

Have any of you ever found Indian arrowheads (or other relics) buried in the ground somewhere? (Let the children discuss freely what they have found.) Do you know why these Indian arrowheads are useful to us? What might they tell us about the Indians? Yes, we know many things about the Indians of our country who lived long ago, because men have dug up from the ground many articles that the Indians used in early times.

Some men spend years and years *digging among ruins for objects* which will help to tell about people who lived long ago which have been buried in the sands of Iraq. *Ned* and his family lived in the *United States*. The story tells of their *trip to Iraq*. They traveled up the *Tigris River*. (The children were asked to locate this river on the map.) While Ned and his father went out to the excavation camp, Ned's mother and sister stayed in a *hotel in Baghdad*. (The children were asked to locate this city on the map.)

Using Phonics and Structural Analysis

If the children who experience difficulty in recognizing new words are sufficiently advanced as to have had phonics and structural analysis or are being taught these techniques, the techniques should be applied functionally during the course of using any of these procedures for introducing new words.

EVALUATION OF ACHIEVEMENT IN WORD
IDENTIFICATION

New Concepts of Evaluation

Just a word about evaluation of reading achievement which seems to be taking on new forms. For many years, we measured effects of reading instruction formally with standardized tests given at the beginning and end of each semester. We still are doing this and it is desirable to do so, providing the test results are interpreted in terms of the personal equipment, opportunities, and abilities of each individual child.

In addition to using standardized tests, teachers have evaluated each child informally each time he has read by answering such questions as "Is he able to successfully attack and pronounce more new words by himself?" "Is he growing in ability to answer questions on the content?" "Is he reading with greater fluency?" We are still noting these evidences of growth in the mechanics of reading and it is important that we continue to do so. But new concepts of evaluation of reading growth are emerging —concepts which are broader and deeper than those only concerned with mechanics of reading. Many teachers are now evaluating the reading of a pupil not only in noting such items as mentioned above but also with such concerns as these:

Was this reading experience sufficiently satisfying to aid in developing in this child a sense of personal dignity and worth and achievement?

Have new interests arisen which will lead on to further reading?

Has worthwhile information been acquired from the reading content?

Has the child done some real thinking in connection with the reading content?

Have deeper insights into human living and deeper understandings of human relationships been developed from the import of the content read or from the discussions concerning it?

Is this child increasing his ability to evaluate his own growth in reading?

And certainly in this searching for evidences of child growth the teacher will include the question: "Is he extending and refining the reading skills that he will need in realizing his goals in school, in his life's work, in his recreational pursuits?"

And as for the teacher herself, in applying the newer ideas she needs continuously to evaluate herself in new ways. She needs to search intensively for the answers to such questions as these:

Am I deepening my own insights in regard to the total growth of each child as well as his reading growth?

Am I providing reading experiences which are simple and interesting enough to be satisfying but difficult enough in learning elements to enable each one to stretch toward higher realization of his abilities?

Am I willing to permit each child to be his own age and to do what he is ready to do?

Am I looking for weaknesses as well as strengths in children's learning to read?

Am I seeking the causes of the weaknesses?

Am I improving my own skills of evaluation?

Am I frankly acknowledging the fact that some of the child's weaknesses may be due to my teaching?

Am I examining both my strengths and weaknesses objectively, and facing my weaknesses with renewed efforts to improve?

The teacher who evaluates herself continuously in regard to the deeper growths of human beings as well as growth in reading achievement will probably be successful in applying any of the new ideas which are in our midst at the present time or which are likely to develop in the future. She will dare to try new ideas, she will know how to judge their worth, she will be able to adjust them in ways most conducive to growth in the particular children with whom she is working.

Informal Inventories

Many teachers believe that oral reading provides the best check of ability in word identification. Informal inventories in which individual children read orally to the teacher are often used in locating the child's instructional level. Some inventories of this type may be used.

Using a series of readers

In conducting such an inventory the teacher procures a series of readers. She chooses one which she judges to be fairly close to the child's reading level and asks the child to read orally a selection in the early part of the book. As he reads she jots down the words that he misses. Following the reading she asks some questions, usually ten, to check his grasp of meanings. The instructional level of the child is usually the one at which he makes an approximate pronunciation score of eighty per cent to eighty-five per cent in the primary grades; and a score of eighty-five to ninety per cent in answering questions on content both in primary grades and in middle grades.[32] If a child scores below these percentages she tries having him read in a book at the next lower level. If he scores

---

[32] Authorities vary in the percentage scores used. The percentages advocated by Emmett A. Betts, *Foundations of Reading Instruction* (New York: American Book Co., 1960), p. 449, for instructional level are "a minimum comprehension score of at least seventy-five per cent, and accurate pronunciation of ninety-five per cent at all levels."

above them she has him read from a book at the next higher level and so on. Usually readings should be done with samplings at the beginning, in the middle, and at the end of each book until the child's level is found.

Botel reading inventory

This is an inventory prepared by Morton Botel which checks word recognition, word opposites, listening, and phonic mastery in oral reading of lists of words and word elements. (Follett.)

Graded selections for informal diagnosis

This material was prepared by the author and others. There are two books, Volumes I and II, designed for checking levels from preprimer to end of sixth grade. It consists of sample selections from a basal series of readers. Each selection is followed by (1) a set of literal comprehension questions, (2) a set of interpretation questions, (3) lists of words that appear in the selection organized in groups representing different phonic and word structure elements so that the teacher, by locating words a child misses, can ascertain the types of word identification elements on which he needs practice. (New York University Press.)

Standardized Tests

There are several excellent standardized reading tests on the market. Many of these contain sections which check aspects of reading other than word identification. All the tests mentioned below either test word identification solely or include this skill as a part of their total contents.

California reading tests

These tests check vocabulary and comprehension. There are different levels for lower primary, primary, and upper level grades. (These tests are also published as a part of the *California Achievement Tests*, California Test Bureau.)

Gates reading tests: 1958 revision

Primary test for grades 1 and 2 includes word recognition, sentence reading, and paragraph reading. *Advanced Primary* for second half of grade 2 and grade 3 includes word recognition and paragraph reading. *Basic Reading Tests* for grade 3 through 8 include various types of comprehension and interpretation skills and reading vocabulary. (Teachers College Bureau of Publications, Columbia University.)

Gilmore oral reading test

This is an individual test containing ten paragraphs of increasing difficulty for oral reading. A record form is provided for checking errors in pronunciation and comprehension responses. (Harcourt, Brace & World, Inc.)

McCullough word analysis test

This test checks ability to recognize and apply various types of phonic elements. (Ginn & Company.)

Roswell-Chall diagnostic reading test

This test consists of a series of exercises for analyzing word recognition and word analysis skills. (Essay.)

SRA achievement series: reading

Tests for grades 1 and 2 test verbal-picture association, language perception, comprehension; tests for grades 2–4 test comprehension and vocabulary; tests for grades 4–6 test comprehension and vocabulary. (Science Research Association.)

Stroud-Hieronymus primary reading profiles

There are tests for grade 1, also for grade 2. Each set includes tests of aptitude for reading, auditory association, word recognition, word attack, and reading comprehension. (Houghton Mifflin Co.)

ADDITIONAL READINGS

Books

Betts, Emmett A., *Foundations of Reading Instruction*. New York: American Book Company, 1946.

Bond, Guy L., and Eva Wagner, *Teaching the Child to Read*, 3rd ed. New York: The Macmillan Co., 1960.

Burrows, Alvina T., *What About Phonics?*, Bulletin No. 57. Washington, D. C.: Association for Childhood Education International, 1951.

Dawson, Mildred A., and Henry A. Bamman, *Fundamentals of Basic Reading Instruction*. New York: Longmans, Green & Co., Inc., 1959.

De Boer, John J., and Martha Dallmann, *The Teaching of Reading*. New York: Holt, Rinehart & Winston, Inc., 1960.

Durrell, Donald D., *Improving Reading Instruction*. New York: Harcourt, Brace & World, Inc., 1945.

Gates, Arthur I., *The Improvement of Reading*. New York: The Macmillan Co., 1947.

Gray, William S., *On Their Own in Reading*. Chicago: Scott Foresman & Company, 1948.

———, "Reading: IV The Teaching of Reading," in ed. C. W. Harris, *Encyclopedia of Educational Research*, 3rd ed. New York: The Macmillan Co., 1960.

Harris, Albert J., *Effective Teaching of Reading*. New York: David McKay Co., Inc., 1962.

Hester, Kathleen B., *Teaching Every Child to Read*. New York: Harper & Row, Publishers, 1950.

Hildreth, Gertrude, *Teaching Reading*. New York: Holt, Rinehart & Winston, Inc., 1958.

McKim, Margaret, *Guiding Growth in Reading*. New York: The Macmillan Co., 1955.

Russell, David H., *Children Learn to Read*. Boston: Ginn & Company, 1961.

Smith, Nila B., *Sailing into Reading*. Washington, D. C.: National Education Association, 1955.

Trabue, M. R., "Special Tools that Facilitate Expression: Use of the Dictionary," *Forty-Third Yearbook Part II*, National Society for the Study of Education, pp. 187–93. Chicago: University of Chicago Press, 1944.

Periodicals

Aaron, I. E., "An Informal Reading Inventory," *Elementary English*, XXXVII (Nov. 1960), 457–60.

Artley, Sterl A., "Phonic Skills in Beginning Reading," *Education*, Vol. 82 (May 1962), 529–32.

Betts, Emmett A., "Phonics: Consonants," *Education*, Vol. 82 (May 1962), 533–36.

Breen, L. G., "Vocabulary Development in Teaching Prefixes, Suffixes and Root Derivatives," *The Reading Teacher*, Vol. 14 (Nov. 1960), 93–97.

Crosby, Muriel, "Words Can Make a Difference," *Elementary English*, Vol. 37 (Feb. 1960), 81–85.

Dolch, Edward W., "How a Child Sounds Out a Word," *Elementary English Review*, Vol. 22 (Nov. 1945), 275–80.

———, "Am I Teaching Phonics Right?" *Elementary English*, Vol. 34 (Apr. 1957), 227–34.

Glass, G. G., "Look at the Teaching of Word Analysis," *Elementary School Journal*, Vol. 53 (Oct. 1958), 35–38.

Hildreth, Gertrude, "New Methods for Old in Teaching Phonics," *The Elementary School Journal*, Vol. 52 (May 1957), 436–41.

McCullough, Constance M., "Context Aids in Reading," *The Reading Teacher*, Vol. 12 (Apr. 1958), 225–29.

———, "Flash Cards—The Opiate of the Reading Program?" *Elementary English*, Vol. 32 (Oct. 1955), 379–81.

Nephew, Ervin, "Evaluation of a Reading Program," *Education*, Vol. 81 (Jan. 1961), 291–92.

Roswell, Florence G., and Jeanne S. Chall, "Helping Poor Readers With Word Recognition Skills," *The Reading Teacher*, Vol. 11 (Apr. 1957), 200–204.

Sister Mariam, OP, "Context Clues in Primary Reading," *The Reading Teacher*, Vol. 12 (Apr. 1958), 230–33.

Smith, Nila B., "Phonics in Beginning Reading: Review and Evaluation," *The Reading Teacher* (Dec. 1955), 73–80.

———, "What Research Says about Phonics," *Journal of Educational Research*, Vol. 51 (Sept. 1957), 1–9.

———, "Phonics and Word Method: Origin and Development," *Education*, Vol. 78 (May 1958), 515–20.

———, "What Research Tells Us About Word Recognition," *Elementary School Journal*, Vol. 55 (Apr. 1955), 440–46.

Smith, Nila B., "What Have We Accomplished in Reading?" *Elementary English,* Vol. 35 (Mar. 1961), 141–50.

Staiger, Ralph C., "Teaching Pronunciation Symbols," *Education,* Vol. 82 (May 1962), 537–39.

Transberg, Josephine, "The Place of Phonics in Basal Reading Instruction," *The Reading Teacher,* Vol. 8 (Oct. 1954), 18–20.

Witty, Paul A., and Robert A. Sizemore, "Phonics in the Reading Program," *Elementary English,* Vol. 32 (Oct. 1955), 355–70.

9

Getting Meanings from Reading

Getting meanings from printed symbols is equally as important as pronouncing words, for what use would the pronunciation of word symbols serve an individual if these symbols had no meaning for him?

To illustrate this point an amusing example is given below. The example is concerned with a fifth grade boy who could pronounce word symbols glibly, but was at a loss to understand the meanings which these symbols conveyed.

Here is Lincoln's *Gettysburg Address* as read by this boy. The interpolations in parenthesis express the thoughts that passed through the boy's mind as he perused this piece of literature.

Fourscore (a score is what we have after a baseball game is played) and seven years ago our fathers (this must mean our own and our step-fathers) brought forth on this continent (that's North America; we had that in social studies) a new nation (that's America or the United States, I think), conceived (I wonder what that means) in liberty (that's what a sailor gets), and dedicated (that's what they did to the building on the corner) to the proposition (that's what they voted on to give the teachers

255

more money) that all men (what about the women) are created (we had something about that at Sunday School) equal (we use that in arithmetic problems). Now we are engaged (Marge is engaged to Bill and they're going to get married soon) in a great civil (civilians are people that aren't in service) war, testing (they say that when they try the microphone) whether that nation (I wonder which one this is), or any nation (I guess it doesn't matter which one) so conceived and so dedicated, can long endure (that's what the dentist said I'd have to do when he fixed my tooth). We are met (by whom?) on a great battlefield of that war. We have come to dedicate a portion (that's the amount of food I get for supper) of that field (like where we play games when we go home) as a final resting place (that's where we stop to rest when we go hiking) for those who here gave their lives that that nation might live (people live, but I didn't know that nations lived). It is altogether (everybody says it at once) fitting and proper (right) that we should do this (what?). But, in a larger sense, we cannot dedicate—we cannot consecrate—(that means to think a lot about something) we cannot hallow—(nothing in the middle) this ground. The brave men, living and dead, who struggled here, have consecrated it far above (that means over the top of something) our poor (without money) power (electricity) to add (2 plus 2) or detract. The world will little note (on the staff in music) nor long remember what we say here, but it can never forget what they did here. It is for us, the living, rather, to be dedicated here to the unfinished work which they who fought here have thus far so nobly advanced (my father sometimes gives me money in advance). It is rather for us to be here dedicated to the great task remaining before us—that from these honored dead we take increased (that's what the cleaner did to dad's pants) devotion (part of a church service) to that cause for which they gave their last full measure (a ruler or part of music) of devotion; that we here highly resolve (to work a problem again) that these dead shall not have died in vain (a blood vessel); that this nation under God, shall have a new birth (a baby is born) of freedom (prisoners get that when they come from jail), and that government of the people, by the people, for the people shall not perish (a district of the church) from the earth (the world or soil).

This boy could pronounce the words; he could memorize this address and recite it with his classmates; but because of his limited understanding of meanings the entire selection to him was more or less just a confused jumble of words. Its deep significance was lost.

If we could take a peep at what goes on in children's minds while reading, we probably would be surprised to find how often their understanding is as foggy as was that of the boy who read the *Gettysburg Address*. Teaching children to get meanings from reading is a major responsibility.

"Comprehension" Is a Blanket Term

There are different types of meaning-getting skills, just as there are different types of word-identification skills. Meaning-getting skills may be distinguished from one another in terms of the thought processes that are involved. For many years teachers made the mistake of laboring under the misconception that all they had to do to teach children to get meanings in reading was to give them some "comprehension" questions and exercises—the word "comprehension" connoting one big skill to be taught as a "lump sum."

This general concept of meaning-gathering probably was due to the fact that attention to meanings in teaching reading came very late in our history. From the beginning of reading instruction, oral reading held an undisputed claim over other classroom methods. The one objective for teaching reading was to enable the child to call reading symbols by their right names. It was not until the decade of 1915–1925 that any attention at all was given to teaching children to glean meanings from reading. During this period there was a new emphasis upon meanings in all subject areas. Simultaneously, reading tests were developed and given for the first time, and it was found that many children didn't understand what they were reading. There was a great dawning of the truth that teachers should be teaching children to get meanings from printed symbols as well as to pronounce words. Suddenly, teachers found themselves immersed in the new technique of teaching *silent* reading for the purpose of getting the thought. This extreme emphasis was later ameliorated and subdued, with the result that a more sensible balance was established between oral and silent reading.

It was, however, during this first period of emphasis upon silent reading as a thought-getting process that the new word "comprehension" first entered the reading vocabulary. It has been with us ever since and no doubt has stood in the way of giving attention to several different and specific meaning skills which should be developed if reading is to be taught effectually.

"Comprehension" is just a big blanket term that covers a whole area of thought-getting processes in reading. Teachers need to be fully aware of the different mental processes involved in reading for meanings and to stand ready to aid their pupils in developing all of them.

The Thinking Skills in Reading

The emphasis at present is upon the *thinking* skills in reading. What are the thinking skills? And what do we know about them?

There are three sources to which we may turn in seeking answers to these questions: (1) reasoned analyses of experts, (2) experimental research, and (3) statistical analyses. Samples will be drawn from each of these sources in giving some tentative answers to the questions in the paragraph above.

Reasoned Analyses of Experts

Gates [1] names several mental processes involved in meaningful reading when he states, "The reading program should make careful provision for contributing as fully as possible to the cultivation of a whole array of techniques involved in understanding, thinking, reflecting, imagining, judging, evaluating, analyzing, and reasoning."

DeBoer [2] describes critical reading as involving ". . . the search for relevant materials, the evaluation of the data, the identification and comparison of sources, and the synthesis of findings. It involves the capacity for suspended judgment and the interpretation of the writer's motive. But chiefly it involves a sufficient background of knowledge to provide a sound basis for judgment."

Traxler [3] states, "Any conception of reading is inadequate that fails to include reflection, critical evaluation, and clarification of meanings."

Guilford [4] presents an easy-to-grasp organization of intellectual activities. It is assumed that the "intellectual activities" used in any thinking are the same ones that are used in reading. In discussing this organization of intellectual activities Guilford says:

During the past twenty years numerous investigations by the methods of factor analysis have brought to light some sixty different abilities having to do with intellectual activities. The large number is rather overwhelming to those who have been accustomed to the simple idea of one ability—intelligence— or at the most, the few primary mental abilities of Thurstone. Fortunately, it has been possible to find a definite system in which to organize the intellectual abilities, with some interesting new principles. The system is known as the "structure of intellect."

There are five classes of abilities depending upon the basic kind of operation or activity involved. A group of cognitive abilities have to do with discovery or recognition of information. They are ways of understanding or comprehension. A parallel group has to do with retention of information. Two parallel groups are concerned with productive thinking. Given certain information, we not only understand it but we can generate from it some new information. An important new distinction is that between divergent production and convergent production. In divergent production the goal is to produce a

---

[1] Arthur I. Gates, *Reading in the Elementary School*, Forty-eighth Yearbook of the National Society for the Study of Education, Part II, Chaps. 1, 2 (Chicago: University of Chicago Press, 1949), p. 3.

[2] John DeBoer, "Teaching Critical Reading," *Elementary English*, Vol. 23 (Oct. 1946), 251–54.

[3] A. E. Traxler, "Problems of Group Remedial Reading in the Secondary School," *High Points*, XX (1938), 5–18.

[4] J. P. Guilford, "Frontiers in Thinking that Teachers Should Know About," *The Reading Teacher*, Vol. 13 (Feb. 1960), 176.

variety of ideas, all of which are logically possible in view of the given information. In convergent production the conclusion is completely determined by the given information, or at least there is a recognized best or conventional conclusion. A fifth group has to do with evaluation, which, in more familiar ways of speaking, means critical thinking. We continually evaluate what we know, what we recall, and what we produce by way of conclusions.

Experimental Research

Gans [5] arrived at this very sound conclusion as a result of her study of critical reading:

Reading is not a simple mechanical skill; nor is it a narrow scholastic tool. Properly cultivated it is essentially a thoughtful process. However, to say that reading is a "thought-getting" process is to give it too restricted a description. It should be developed as a complex organization of patterns of higher mental processes. It can and should embrace all types of thinking, evaluating, judging, imagining, reasoning, and problem-solving.

McCullough [6] made a study of the interrelations obtained from scores of various types of comprehension in first, second, and fourth grade children. She concluded that children at all these levels are able to think about story material in the four ways examined: main idea, details, sequence, and creative reading (seeing relationships, drawing conclusions, passing judgments, and the like).

Among the abilities singled out by Sochor [7] in her study were: ability to make inferences, to identify a generalization, to apply information derived to a problematic situation, to sense relationships among ideas, to determine the relevancy of ideas, to distinguish the central theme of a selection, to identify the author's purpose, to sense semantic variation among words.

Piekarz [8] found that the type of comprehension used by a group of sixth grade pupils depended upon their reading competence. The poorer

[5] Roma Gans, A Study of Critical Reading Comprehension in the Intermediate Grades, Teachers College Contributions to Education, No. 811 (New York: Teachers College, Columbia University, 1940).

[6] Constance M. McCullough, "Responses of Elementary School Children to Common Types of Reading Comprehension Questions," Journal of Educational Research, Vol. 51 (Sept. 1957), 65–70.

[7] Elona E. Sochor, Literal and Critical Reading in Social Studies. Unpublished Doctor's Dissertation (Philadelphia, Pa.: Temple University, 1952).

[8] Josephine Piekarz, "Getting Meaning from Reading," Elementary English, Vol. 56 (Mar. 1956), 303–309.

readers confined their answers largely to literal comprehension, while the better readers made a greater variety of responses fairly equally divided into literal meanings, implied meanings, and evaluations.

The above investigator also found that high intelligence was not a factor which would assure ability to get deeper meanings. The responses of a boy with an IQ of 129 and a girl with an IQ of 127 were analyzed. It was found that the boy was one of the highest of a group of twenty-two pupils in ability to derive accurate understanding from and to make critical analysis of reading content, while the girl ranked as one of the lowest. This and other studies indicate that the various abilities needed in getting meanings from reading may respond to development, that they do not always bud out spontaneously from the matrix of a high intelligence. Most studies, however, do show a high relationship between intelligence and use of the various thinking skills in reading.

Some Statistical Analyses

Thorndike [9] has given us the shortest and perhaps most cogent definition of reading. He said simply: "Reading is thinking." No doubt he reached this conclusion as the result of his analysis of errors which children made in reading a paragraph. This analysis revealed that comprehension in reading involved the same kind of "organization and analytic action of ideas as occurs in thinking of supposedly higher sorts."

Among the statistical analyses of reading skills mention should be made of Holmes' [10] "sub-strata factor theory." Holmes developed this theory through use of factoral analysis of an orderly arrangement of causal factors in speed and power of reading. At the first level of depth he found that the factors of word discrimination, word sense, and span of recognition contribute fifty-six per cent of the variance in speed and power of reading. Seventy-seven per cent of the variance found in power in reading was attributed to such factors as vocabulary in context, intelligence, and understanding of verbal relationships. His additional analyses show much overlapping and the dependence of one factor upon another, all of which serve to point up the complicated interrelationships of factors which make up the complex act of reading.

Several other statistical analyses have been made, one of which listed two hundred and fourteen reading skills that had been mentioned in

[9] Edward L. Thorndike, "Reading as Reasoning: A Study of Mistakes in Paragraph Reading," *Journal of Educational Research,* Vol. 8 (June 1917), 323–32.
[10] Jack A. Holmes, *The Sub-Strata Theory of Reading* (Berkeley, Cal.: California Book, 1953).

educational literature. This study was made by Burkart,[11] who followed her listing of these many skills by having reading specialists rank the items for importance. Space does not permit a ranked list of abilities resulting from this study. It may be of interest, however, to note the headings which the investigator used for grouping her "Major Reading Abilities Constituting the Generic Reading Abilities." These headings were "Observation," "Research Abilities," "Aesthetic Abilities," "Hygienic Abilities," and "Oral Reading Abilities." The lists have to do with many items that are not thinking skills, per se.

As a general conclusion to this discussion it might be stated that regardless of the technique used to ascertain thinking skills in reading all results point to the fact that the reading process is a very complex one, making use of all thinking skills of which the human mind is capable.

What Can Be Expected of Children in the Use of Thinking Processes

While considering the skills of interpretation and critical reading this question frequently arises: Are children able to do the kind of thinking necessary in obtaining deeper meanings in reading?

In discussing the mental characteristics of children in Chapter 3 (pages 30–33 it was pointed out that primary children grow rapidly in reasoning ability, insightfulness, and problem-solving skill. These characteristics are extended and accentuated in the middle grades, as are concepts of number, time, and space. Broadening of interests in subject matter, a strong desire to achieve in skill areas, increase in organizational ability and in imaginative powers are characteristics of middle-grade children. All these characteristics of childhood contribute valuable stock in trade in guiding pupils' growth in the use of thinking skills in reading.

Development of the *thinking* process in young children is receiving much more attention now than formerly. Recent researches in the field of early childhood are stimulating fresh approaches in this direction. The depth studies of Wamm [12] reveal that even at three and four years of age children *think* during most of their waking hours. They classify within their limits, they make discriminations and differentiations, they generalize in so far as they can, they integrate information to higher

[11] Kathryn H. Burkart, "An Analysis of Reading Abilities," *Journal of Educational Research,* Vol. 38 (Feb. 1945), 430–39.
[12] From reports of research conducted by Kenneth Wamm and associates, Teachers College, Columbia University; to be published in the new Putnam series of Depth Studies in Education.

levels, they test their learnings on others. All these types of thinking they do in trying to make sense out of this world in which they find themselves. Studies at Ohio State University [13] are revealing that first and second grade children when freed of dealing with the new language of *number symbols* can reason far beyond our usual expectations of them. Studies of Huck,[14] Navarra,[15] and others of what children know when they come to school are increasing and are revealing astonishing amounts of information. Masland, Sarason, and Gladwin [16] produce evidence to show that even mentally retarded children *think;* therefore, there is no reason to confine even their learning experiences to routine drill.

The numerous studies which have been made of children's ability to use the higher mental processes in thinking reassure us in believing that pupils of average intelligence are capable of doing all the kinds of thinking that we would like them to do in getting deeper meanings in reading.

Definition of Terms

A new vocabulary has been developed in regard to meaning skills in reading. Once a departure was made from the cover-all term of "Comprehension" a new nomenclature was developed to classify the more specific skills included under the general term.

Literal Comprehension

The term *literal comprehension* is widely used at present to name the skill of getting the primary, direct, "literal" meaning of a word, idea, or sentence in context. Reading authorities are generally agreed on the connotation of this term.

Interpretation [17]

The term *interpretation* of reading matter eventually was introduced and is now heard more often than the general term of *comprehension*.

[13] From studies being conducted at University School, Ohio State University, Columbus, Ohio.

[14] Charlotte S. Huck, *The Nature and Derivation of Young Children's Social Concepts.* Unpublished doctoral dissertation (Evanston, Ill.: Northwestern University, 1955). Some of the findings are summarized in Charlotte S. Huck, "Children Learn from Their Culture," *Educational Leadership*, XIII (Dec. 1955), 171–75.

[15] John G. Navarra, *Development of Scientific Concepts in a Young Child* (New York: Bureau of Publications, Teachers College, Columbia University, 1955).

[16] Richard L. Masland, Seymour B. Sarason, and Thomas Gladwin, *Mental Subnormality: Biological, Psychological, and Cultural Factors* (New York: Basic Books, 1958); also Samuel Kirk, *The Early Education of the Mentally Retarded* (Urbana, Ill.: University of Illinois Press, 1958).

[17] David Russell and some others use the term *Creative Reading* to include most of the skills and abilities described in this definition of *interpretation.* See David H. Russell, *Children Learn to Read* (Boston: Ginn & Company, 1961), pp. 454–88.

It has been used to include those skills necessary in getting deeper meanings in addition to those obtained by simple *literal comprehension.* Such skills are those that are concerned with supplying or anticipating meanings not stated directly in the text, such as drawing inferences; making generalizations; reasoning cause and effect; speculating on what happened between events; anticipating what will happen next; detecting the significance of a statement, passage, or selection; making comparisons; identifying the purpose of the writer and the motive of characters; associating personal experience with reading content; forming sensory images; experiencing emotional reactions.

In this book the definition and skills mentioned above are included under the classification, *interpretation,* as representing a level of the understanding of meanings which includes the literal comprehension level but advances beyond this level in its involvement of numerous *thinking* skills.

Critical Reading

Currently the term *critical reading* is in high favor. Many writers and investigators are including so many skills under this heading that the term is becoming almost as blanket-like in its concept as the former general term, *comprehension.* One thing that those who discuss critical reading have in common is that all exclude *literal comprehension.* With this exception, however, one finds that many discussions of critical reading embrace practically all the *interpretation* skills mentioned above, as well as many of the study skills and evaluative skills. So conceived, *critical reading* implies any reading in which thinking is done.

In the interest of helping teachers obtain a clearer perspective of the different levels of meaning skills, this chapter treats critical reading as the third level in the hierarchy of reading-for-meaning skills. According to the writer's thinking, *critical reading* includes *literal comprehension* and *interpretation* as defined above, but it goes further than either of these in that the reader evaluates, that is, passes personal judgment on the quality, the value, the accuracy, and the truthfulness of what is read.

This distinction is appropriate in terms of the meaning of the word *critical,* an adjective derived from the noun *critic,* which in turn had as one of its foreign sources the Greek word *krinein*—meaning "to judge, discern." One dictionary definition of *critical* is "exercising or involving careful judgment; exact, nicely judicious as a critical examination." Another dictionary defines critical as "to judge with severity."

Definitions of *critic, criticism,* and *criticize* add to our understanding of the term *critical. Critic* is defined as "one who expresses a reasoned opinion . . . on any matter . . . involving a judgment of its value, truth or righteousness. . . ." *Criticism* is defined as "A critical observation or judgment"; and *criticize* is defined thus: "to examine and judge as a critic."

In consideration of the meaning of *critical* it would appear that we are stretching things a bit too far when we include almost all the skills that make use of *thinking* processes in reading under the present popular term *critical reading*. In this chapter critical reading is restricted to the kind of reading done when *personal judgment* and *evaluation* are involved.

Specific Word Meanings

Sensing the semantic implications of words is a very important growth area to be developed in helping children get meanings from reading. This area involves working with specific word meanings: primary meanings, multiple meanings, abstractions, meanings of variant word forms, synonyms, antonyms, similes, and metaphorical language. Attention should be given to these skills regardless of whether a child is engaging in literal comprehension, interpretation, or critical reading.

In keeping with the definitions and explanations above, a diagram is presented to represent graphically the sub-areas of skill development in the larger growth area of getting meanings from reading.

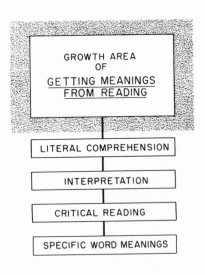

Literal Comprehension

Literal comprehension is the process of getting obvious and direct meanings from symbols as they appear on the printed page.

Consider the paragraph below as the opening paragraph in a story:

The sun had sunk in the West. It was growing dusky. The car was filled with shadows.

If a reader did nothing more than to comprehend this paragraph *literally* he would simply gather the "face" meaning from each sentence. In reading the first sentence he would understand that the sun had gone down in the West. If he understood the meaning of *dusky,* the import that he would gather from the second sentence would be that it was growing sort of dark; and he would understand from the third sentence that there were some shadows in the car. So far he has been picking up apparent, surface meanings only; he has been engaging in "literal comprehension." But suppose that as a result of reading all these sentences he gathers the impression that *night was falling;* then he has *interpreted* what he has read; he has used the interpretation process in gleaning meaning not stated directly in the paragraph. The author didn't say "night was falling" in so many words, but all the sentences combined were intended to create atmosphere, to convey the feeling of approaching nightfall.

This is one illustration of the difference between *literal comprehension* and *interpretation.* In literal comprehension the individual gets the literal meaning of words; in interpretation he reads between the lines or combines several sentences, making inferences, drawing conclusions, arriving at generalizations, or perhaps experiencing emotional reactions.

Overemphasis of Literal Comprehension

Reading content is one of the most productive mediums to use in developing thinking abilities through discussion. Are we making the fullest use of this medium for this purpose? Are we conducting discussions at a level which is too low, in many instances, to stimulate real thinking on the part of boys and girls? Are we, too often, simply asking them to repeat, parrot-like, what is said in the book rather than guiding discussion in ways which will encourage them to probe for deeper meanings and to evaluate critically?

Guidance directed toward literal comprehension is the lowest rung on the ladder of possibilities in so far as stimulation of thinking is concerned.

For example: The children are reading a story about two children and their toys. "With what was Ann playing?" asks the teacher. "Ann was playing with her doll," comes the answer. And this statement is given in so many words in the text. "What was Jack doing?" And the text says quite definitely that "Jack was playing with his rocket."

Questions of this type require only slight mental activity on the part of the teacher and little or no thinking on the part of the pupils. Such questions undoubtedly give children practice in recalling and reproducing statements or facts and have a place in detailed factual reading. It is doubtful, on the other hand, whether this form of questioning helps children develop the ability to glean the types of meanings from reading that they need to enrich their lives to the fullest extent.

Through continued practice, however, children often become so glib in answering this reproduction type of question that they convey the impression of having achieved a high degree of excellency in "comprehension."

A thirteen-year-old boy named Larry was recently sent to the writer for diagnosis. He had above-average intelligence and was considered a "very good reader," but he was failing in other studies. As a part of the diagnosis, the boy was asked to read *Johnny Appleseed*. A class of graduate students read the story also and observed Larry's responses. When Larry had finished, he was asked several questions which could be answered by restating what had been said directly in the text:

"How long ago did Johnny Appleseed live?"
"More than a hundred years ago."
"What was his real name?"
"Jonathan Chapman."
"How did he spend his time?"
"He planted apple trees."

These and additional questions of the reproduction type were asked, and Larry answered all of them unerringly in the words of the book.

"Do you think Larry needs help in comprehension?" the graduate class. was asked.

"No," came the unanimous response, "his comprehension is perfect!"

Larry had been checked on his *literal comprehension,* but the discussion had been extremely limited. What happened when he was asked some questions at a higher level of comprehension—in other words, questions which called for interpretation of meanings not stated directly in the text?

"Why did Johnny choose to plant his trees deep in the wilderness where the settlers had not yet come?"
"He wanted to be alone while he was working," Larry replied.

Larry had missed an important implication in drawing this conclusion. Johnny's real reason for planting the trees before the settlers arrived was, of course, so that the trees would grow and bear fruit by the time the settlers moved in. Larry's answer made Johnny an unsocial person who didn't want anyone around him while he was working.

Several other questions of the thinking type were asked. Larry's replies to all of them were equally faulty, and all of them failed to evoke any give-and-take discussion.

Larry is only one out of hundreds of intelligent pupils who learn the superficial knack of giving back what the text says, but who never tap the significance of meanings which can be gleaned only through the use of mental processes of a higher type.

Techniques for Literal Comprehension

While the preceding discussion highly favors the aspect of reading instruction which places emphasis upon the use of the thinking processes in reading, the point must be made that there is a place in the meanings area of growth for teaching literal comprehension. Perhaps at beginning stages a considerable amount of literal comprehension is necessary, even in working with story materials; but it is hoped that encouragement is given to children to respond in their own words, rather than to parrot the exact words of the text. Literal comprehension, even to the extent of using the exact words of the text, is often necessary in reading in the curriculum areas of science, arithmetic, geography, and history. Thus, literal comprehension does have certain functions to perform, and children should be given some experiences directed to their growth in the use of this reading skill.

The techniques which lend themselves best to practice in literal comprehension are those most frequently used in objective tests in which one absolutely accurate response is expected: a factual question, a true-false statement, a completion statement, or a multiple-choice sentence.

The synopsis of a story will be given as an illustration.

The story is about Bob and Nancy, two children who lived on a desert. Another character in the story is Borroboy, the children's donkey. One day the children went out on the desert to look for wood. They took Borroboy along to carry the pieces of broken bushes they found. Nancy saw a rabbit and the children ran off to catch it. When they came back they found that Burroboy was gone. At the same time something else happened. Suddenly a great yellow cloud came rolling toward them. It was a desert sandstorm. After a struggle the children reached their home safely. Burroboy was standing by the porch with the wood on his back.

Examples of literal comprehension checks based on direct statements in the text might be as follows:

Factual question: Who was Burroboy?
True-false statement: The children went out on the desert to gather flowers.
Multiple choice sentence: Nancy saw a $\begin{array}{l}\text{bear}\\\text{squirrel}\\\text{rabbit.}\end{array}$
Completion statement: Suddenly a great yellow _____ came rolling toward them.

Additional Literal Comprehension Activities

Many other types of questions and instructions may be used in giving practice in the use of literal comprehension. For readers who would like some additional ideas in regard to this matter some suggestions are given under "Additional Practice and Maintenance Activities in Getting Meanings," pages 559–60.

Interpretation

Suggestions for Developing Interpretation

One of the most productive ways of developing ability to derive deeper meanings in reading is through discussion in which the teacher makes a special contribution by throwing in questions here and there to stimulate cause-and-effect reasoning and to point up the necessity for supplying details "between the lines," making comparisons, drawing inferences, and gathering generalizations.

In a third-grade classroom recently, such a discussion took place. The children had read a story about Fred. Here is the synopsis:

A boy named Fred visited his Uncle Bill, a sheepherder who lived in a covered wagon in the foothills. Two horses were eating grass beside the wagon. During the first few days of his visit, Fred was concerned with his uncle's shepherd dogs, who stayed out with the sheep at night, even in bad weather. One night, Uncle Bill took Fred out to the herd while a storm was raging. He called the dogs. They appeared from the midst of the herd of sheep, but they "did not want to leave their woolly hiding place." Fred said, "All right. I won't worry about them anymore."

The children and the teacher discussed the story as they went along and also after they had finished. Everyone entered into the plot with interest and enthusiasm and relived the experiences of the characters. As all of this was taking place, however, the teacher kept uppermost in her mind the importance of stimulating children's thinking in working with meanings derived from their reading. Now and then, at appropriate times, she asked questions to which there were no answers directly in the text—questions which called for *thinking*, not just for a regurgitation of statements in the story.

"You have just read that Uncle Fred *lived* in his sheep wagon. What do you think the inside of the sheep wagon was like? Can you picture it in your mind and describe it?" (Reasoning about details not given.)

The children reasoned he must have had: a stove, probably fueled by wood that he picked up; cupboards; dishes; at least two bunks for beds; table and chairs.

"Of what use were the two horses eating grass beside the wagon?" (Inference.)

Answers volunteered were: "Uncle Fred needed them when he wanted to go to town and get groceries." "He used them to move his wagon when he had to take his sheep to a fresh pasture."

"Why do you suppose one of the dogs was called Taffy?" (Cause and effect.)

None of the children ever had seen warm taffy pulled nor noted its golden-brown color when it is in this elastic state. The colors they associated with taffy were greens, blues, pinks, and yellows, which they found in the salt-water-taffy boxes that their parents had brought from the seaside. The children lacked the experience necessary for this concept; therefore, the teacher told them about taffy in its natural state and compared its color with Tom's sweater and Jan's hair. The children then easily decided why one of the dogs was called Taffy.

"Can you think of anything interesting that Fred might have done between the time that he arrived and the night of the storm?" (Supplying happenings between incidents.)

The leading character became a living boy, having real experiences, as the children speculated upon things that he might have done during the gap between events in the story: "Probably he went for a ride on one of his Uncle's horses." "Maybe he caught a rabbit to take home for a pet." "He might have met a bear and the dogs chased the bear away and rescued him."

"Compare the way that Fred felt at the beginning with the way he felt at the end of the story. Why did he change?" (Comparison, cause, and effect.)

At no point in the story does the author tell how Fred felt, nor is there any statement in regard to why he changed. The children, however, were able to find telltale words and phrases that indicated how worried Fred was all through the early part of the story, and other words and phrases which revealed his satisfaction and peace of mind toward the end of the story. It simply required one major decision on their part to uncover the cause of this change in the boy—the dogs were happy out with the sheep.

"In what part of the country do you think this story took place?" (Generalization.)

The children examined the pictures, gathered bits of information here and there throughout the text, and after putting all these together decided that the story took place in the Rocky Mountains.

Thus a wise teacher can guide discussion fruitfully in connection with children's reading dozens of times every day; thus, deeper meanings emerge from the page, and the real signficance of the printed symbols becomes fully apparent.

Additional Examples of Interpretation Questions

There are many different types of questions which may stir pupils to *think* about content read and to make their own interpretations.

For the teacher of reading who would like to have suggestions of questions of this type, several samples are provided under the heading, "Additional Practice and Maintenance Activities in Getting Meanings," pages 560–61.

Critical Reading

This section will discuss the highest level of mental activity in understanding meanings, that of *critical reading* which, as defined on page 263, is at the top of the reading-for-meaning hierarchy. In doing critical reading we do need to *comprehend literally*, we do need to *interpret* the author's unwritten meanings, but we need to go still further than either of these meaning-getting processes can take us. In critical reading we need to read with an attitude of inquiry, a desire to seek the truth, and a will to search further, if necessary. We need to evaluate, challenge, decide upon truthfulness, bias, authenticity. In critical reading the individual needs to react personally in agreeing or disagreeing with the author as a result of personal judgment based upon experience, facts gleaned from various sources, or possibly as a result of clear-cut reasoning.

Critical reading is of tremendous importance at the present time. Because so many people are trying to influence our thinking, it is urgent that young Americans learn to evaluate critically. We should be emphasizing critical reading much more than we are doing at the present time.

Procedures for Teaching Critical Reading

Utilizing Incidental Opportunities

Critical reading is not of such a nature that procedures can be planned "step by step." Rarely should a teacher plan "to give a lesson" in critical reading, particularly in the primary grades. More direct work can be done at times in the upper grades. Leads into critical reading activities usually arise from discussion of reading content. Children themselves often offer leads to critical reading. The wise teacher keeps herself ever on the alert for such leads, encouraging them with commendation for good thinking and stimulating further search for facts with tactful questions or remarks.

Perhaps the most helpful way of suggesting procedures will be to describe some incidents which have actually occurred in classrooms.

Jean was reading in a preprimer. On the page there was a picture of two chairs, backs toward each other and a space in between. A newspaper was spread over the tops of the two chairs to make a roof for a playhouse. A kitten was playing on top of the newspaper. Jean said, "There is something wrong here. A kitten couldn't stand on top of those papers. The papers would fall through with him." This was critical reading at the preprimer level. It was critical reading of a picture, to be sure, but the same mental process was used as would have been used had Jean passed judgment upon the content of printed text. Jean was praised for noting the flaw in the make-up of the picture.

Billy was reading in a second grade arithmetic book which had been written several years ago. He read a problem that said, "Mary went to the store to buy two quarts of milk. If she paid 12 cents a quart, how much did the milk cost?" Billy said, "There is something wrong here. I went to the grocery store this morning and bought some milk for my mother, and it was 20 cents a quart." Critical reading you see; passing judgment! Critical reading can take place in arithmetic or it can take place in literature or in any subject field. Incidentally, it should be added that Miss Evans had the children find the copyright date in the book, and this explained the low price of milk in this particular case.

The first grade children were reading a story about some other children who used empty pea-pods for boats. They sailed the boats in the bath. One of the boys made the boats go fast by splashing the water backward and forth with his hand. They supposedly played in this way all morning. "I don't think they sailed the boats all morning," volunteered Stephen. "If they splashed the water enough to make the boats go fast, they would have tipped them over." Stephen was questioning the author's statement. "Good thinking," reassured Miss Baker. "You probably have thought of something that the author didn't. Try floating some pea-pods in the bathtub at home. Splash the water and see what happens. Then you'll know whether you or the author of the story is right."

The third grade children read a story in which grasshoppers were named as one of the foods which the Indians ate at a feast. "I don't believe they ate grasshoppers," said Susan. Several other children agreed with her. "How could you find out?" asked Miss James. They searched through many books containing Indian stories to see if they could find any evidence of grasshoppers having been used for food. Miss James finally brought in the IJ volume of Compton's *Encyclopedia.* The children found the section on Indians and "poured over it." Much of it they could not read. During the search through the pages, however, Jean ran across this statement which she excitedly read to the class: "The Seed Gatherers ate quite a few things which many people would think unpleasant. These included crickets, grasshoppers, insect larvae, ants ground into flour, and certain lizards and snakes." The author of the story was right. The doubting third-graders were wrong.

Tom, in the sixth grade, brought in a short article about Mars. It included a description of the canals on this planet. After Tom read the story to the class, Jim, another pupil, said, "I heard a man say over the radio that scientists no longer believe that there are canals on Mars. This author evidently isn't up-to-date on his information." "Who is he?" asked Miss Steele. "Do you know if he is a scientist whose information could be trusted?" Tom didn't know. Research followed making use of "Who's Who" references, a letter of inquiry to the publisher, science textbooks, periodicals, encyclopedias. As a result the pupils concluded that the man who wrote the article was not a scientist but rather a free-lance writer who wrote on many popular subjects. They also found that most scientists at present do not believe that there are canals on Mars.

Planned Activities for Critical Reading

While on-the-spot discussion is undoubtedly the most fruitful way of developing critical reading, there are several planned activities which may well be used for this purpose. See "Suggestions for Practices and Maintenance Activities" on pages 561–62, for additional suggestions.

Critical Reading of Propaganda

In this age of multitudinous attempts to influence our thinking through the use of printed material, much more emphasis should be placed upon detection and analysis of propaganda. Youth should be taught to look for slants and biases and tricks of propagandists so that they will be in a position to judge the validity of statements which they read in all printed material.

Experiences designed to teach pupils how to read propaganda do not have to wait until the high school years. Much can be done in the upper elementary grades, beginning as low as the fourth grade, and in some cases, the third grade. Some background information will be given to the teacher, after which teaching procedures will be suggested.

Background Information

Propaganda may be defined as a deliberate attempt to persuade a person to accept a point of view or take a certain line of action. Propaganda always has been a strong force in shaping the affairs of man, and it still is. You will find propaganda in all types of reading material: billboard ads, handbills, pamphlets, newspapers, magazines, books. Pupils at the elementary level should be taught to recognize this propaganda in some of its more simple forms.

Effective propaganda makes a strong appeal to human needs, interests, curiosities, loves, hates, prejudices, fears, lusts, cupidities, or amusements. Your first step is to identify the technique used in making the appeal.

To make a list of human interests and desires and ways in which the propagandist appeals to them would be an involved task. Different schools of psychology have compiled such lists, and they vary. In any event, no such list would be sufficiently inclusive. The propagandist doesn't care whether motives are innate or the result of environment. All he cares about is that they exist in the people to whom he wishes to appeal.

There are some propaganda techniques which are so inclusive that they appeal to whole clusters of interests. Seven of these techniques are generally recognized as basic.

Bad Names

One of the propagandist's most usual techniques is that of using disagreeable words to arouse our fear, hate, or disapproval, without giving any evidence to support the point he is making. The "bad word" technique is used in some political campaigns: mud-slinging, name-calling, innuendos.

This technique is also used with high frequency in advertisements in which the propagandist tries to cause the reader to apply several unpleasant words to himself, personally, and thus to be so moved that, in order to overcome the disgusting state of affairs, he will purchase the product the advertiser is trying to sell. One ad for tablets to increase weight was headed, "Why Be *Skinny*?" There was a picture of a very thin girl in a bathing suit, while a man looking at her was saying, "No *Skinny Scarecrow* for me!"

Some of the text in the ad read as follows:

Why should you *dread* going to parties and socials, simply because you look *scrawny* and *spindly*? Why ever feel *self-conscious* about your body again. If you're *underweight* or just a little on the *thin* side, due to *faulty* appetite or *bad* dietary habits, you can put on up to a pound a day of attractive weight without exercise, *dangerous* drugs or *special* diet. Don't be a *wallflower* because you have a figure like a *broomstick*. Gain more weight!

Glad Names

Quite the opposite is the "glad name" or "glittering generalities" technique. With the use of pleasant words, a halo of desirable associations is built around a person or thing to such an extent that the reader is moved to adore, respect, and vote for the person, or to buy a product in order to have all the desirable qualities mentioned.

In advertising, the "glad name" technique is used more frequently than the "bad name" technique.

This cream truly works *miracles* on your skin. Pat a small amount on at night. In the morning you'll be *amazed* to see how *lovely* you are. Skin *smooth* and *fresh! Soft* as *velvet! Glowing* and *radiant!* A *new, beautiful* you!

The use of these glad words appeals to a woman's desire to be beautiful and is supposed to cause her to buy the cream.

Transfer

Another commonly-used technique is that of transfer, by which the propagandist tries to get the reader to transfer his respect, admiration, or reverence from something to which he has already attached one of these attitudes to something else. A candidate for office may be played up as a "typical American." Or the leaders of a cause may make a strong point of having God's sanction, in the hope that the public will transfer reverence for God to the cause. The flag, Uncle Sam, or a cross is frequently pictured in conjunction with a printed message in which the propagandist wants us to transfer our respect for the government or the church to his idea.

In advertisements, famous people in show business, sports, or society are frequently used for transfer purposes. For example, a well-known television person is pictured examining crocheted articles in a full-page ad of manufacturers of crochet thread. The two-line heading reads, "Delighted with the pretty things you can crochet with top quality thread for only 98¢."

The ad doesn't state that the woman in the picture crochets or that she uses the thread or that the crocheted articles shown are in her home. There is no connection between her and the crochet cotton advertised. She is pictured in the ad purely for transfer purposes.

Testimonial

This method of appeal is very much like transfer, except that in this case some noted person goes so far as to say that he uses the object of the propaganda. A famous tennis champion may say that he is going to vote for Mr. So-and-So. The readers should inquire, "What difference does that make to me?" What motive or reward prompted the tennis player to let himself be quoted? What qualifications has he for judging candidates?

The picture of a famous movie actress appeared in an ad for a low-caloried drink.

Movie actresses must have slim, attractive figures.
I keep my figure trim by drinking No-Weight beverages.
(Signed) Shirlene Lovely

Probably the actress rarely or perhaps never drinks No-Weight beverages and keeps her figure trim through exercise and diet. Yet without a doubt untold numbers of girls rushed to their grocer for a case of "No-Weight" as soon as they finished reading the ad.

Plain Folks

Admiration of the humble, unpretending, common man is an American tradition. The Pilgrim fathers despised anything that was "hi-falutin'" or smacked in any way of artificiality or affectation. One reason Lincoln has been idolized is that he came from a lowly family. Propagandists often go to great lengths in painting a word-picture of the person they wish to promote to convince the public that he is just an ordinary man. The candidate for office may be shown driving a tractor, shoveling snow off the walk in front of his home, playing with his dog, coming home from Sunday School, and so on.

A recent article about a young baseball player stated that he mowed the lawn and walked the dog and helped his wife by drying the dishes and caring for the baby. It was hoped that readers would develop a deep admiration for him as a common man.

The Band-Wagon Technique

The band-wagon technique is used to get the reader to accept something because everybody else is enthusiastic about it. It is based on the theory that the reader will want to think, vote, or buy what the great majority favors. If everybody else is doing it, then the reader should do it too. The reader wouldn't want to be different from other people.

The hat salesman uses this technique when he says, "They're all wearing the narrow brim this year." If the customer has already built up resistance to band-wagon propaganda, he will probably reply, "Well, show me something less common."

In using the band-wagon technique, the propagandist frequently directs his appeals to groups of similar religious belief, groups of similar racial descent, groups engaged in the same type of work, and so on: "All of us farmers want prices raised, and we know that Davis is the man that will do this for us."

Or he appeals to the desire of the masses to be on the winning side. "Don't throw your vote away. Vote for Gregory. He's sure to win anyhow."

In advertising, this technique is used very frequently. "Nine out of ten use Gribber's Shaving Cream." "Cigs outsell all other cigarettes in America." "10,000 Americans switched to Best Ever Coffee last month, why not you?" "Everybody's doing the Mumbo. Let us teach you how."

Card Stacking

This is the most subtle and probably the most dangerous of the propagandist's techniques. Even though the reader is acquainted with propaganda procedures he will be tricked with this every once in a while—unless he is very careful.

A cardsharp can cheat his victim by arranging the cards in the deck in such a manner that he will receive the winning combinations when the cards are dealt. Similarly the politician or ad writer may show only what is favorable to his purpose. He glorifies points which contribute to his ends but omits or misrepresents those which might influence the reader in the opposite direction. By card stacking an ordinary candidate for office may be built up as an intellectual giant, a wise administrator, and a benevolent leader. His detrimental qualities are concealed.

Nowhere is this technique more frequently used than in advertisements. In reading about one cigarette the reader is told that it "lasts longer, tastes better, contains finer tobacco." Lasts longer—than what? Tastes better—than what? Contains finer tobacco—than what?

Analyzing Propaganda

Having an initial awareness of propaganda is not sufficient. A person should be able to analyze it as well.

As a frame of reference for analysis of propaganda found in printed material, five leading questions are offered:

1. Who is the propagandist?

2. Whom is he serving?
3. What is his aim in writing on this subject?
4. To what human interests, desires, emotions does he appeal?
5. What technique does he use?
6. Are you or are you not going to permit yourself to be influenced through the tactics of this propagandist?

Procedures for Working with Propaganda

One very effective procedure for use in elementary grades is that of identifying tricks used in colorfully pictured advertisements cut from magazines. The teacher explains one of the basic propaganda tricks, then shows and reads (or has pupils read) several different advertisements to see if the pupils can recognize the trick in any of them.

This continues, accumulatively, until all seven basic tricks have been introduced and practice has been given in recognizing them.

After children have had some experience as indicated above, they may be invited to bring in advertisements themselves, show them to the class, and tell what trick or tricks they think have been used in each one. The writer has seen these activities in connection with advertisements used very successfully with third-grade children.

In later grades the identification of the basic propaganda tricks may be extended to clippings of text (without pictures) from newspapers and magazines. With some classes it may be possible to have pupils analyze examples of propaganda with the use of the questions suggested above. Question number 4 should be omitted when working with elementary children.

Another plan for providing practice in recognizing propaganda tricks is for the teacher to prepare or collect samples of text representing the different tricks. She then may reproduce these samples by multigraph, thermafax, or some other facility. Pupils study the sections of text, decide what tricks are used, and write the appropriate name above each sample.

Specific Word Meanings

The fourth sub-area of growth in getting meanings from reading is concerned with semantic implications, or in more simple phraseology, with specific word meanings. This is a fascinating and significant aspect of reading instruction.

Words are jewels with many facets, and sometimes these facets reflect in amusing ways. An illustration of this is revealed in the following incident.

Professor Brown had a young son who was ready to enter kindergarten. This youngster loved to do woodwork, and his father had fitted up a corner in the garage at home in which Tommy might pound and hammer and saw. When Dr. Brown took Tommy to the kindergarten the first morning they found that the kindergarten teacher had arranged various centers of interest. There were blocks in one corner, clay in another, and so on—and there was one corner that was given over to woodwork. Of course, Tommy immediately went to this corner and began sawing a lath. He couldn't hold it very steadily, so the teacher brought out a vise, put the lath in the vise, and screwed it down. The little gadget held the lath securely as Tommy sawed and sawed. Others asked for a vise. The teacher brought out several of these gadgets, and the little boys had an exciting time that forenoon in the woodworking corner. In the afternoon, when Dr. Brown arrived home, his little son came running to meet him. Dr. Brown said, "Well, did you enjoy your first day at school?" And Tommy replied, "Oh, yes. I had a good time, an awfully good time." Then Dr. Brown asked, "What did you like best of all this morning?" Surprisingly Tommy replied, "Well, I liked the teacher best of all because she has so many vises."

Specific word meanings are not only amusing at times but attention to them yields rewarding results in the teaching of reading. For many years after teachers began to think about getting meanings from reading symbols they were concerned only with the meaning of a paragraph or of a whole sentence or of a whole selection. It is only recently that they have become seriously concerned with teaching children to get specific word meanings. Sometimes the whole plot of a story or the heart of a selection in science or social studies hangs upon one word, and if children give this one word the wrong meaning they misinterpret the entire selection. The paraphrased poem below makes this point quite vividly:

Words Words Words

For want of a word,
the phrase is lost.
For want of the phrase,
the sentence is lost.
For want of the sentence,
the paragraph is lost.
For want of the paragraph,
the selection is lost.
All meaning is lost for
want of a word.

This probably is the case in reading more often than most of us would suspect.

Influences Affecting Emphasis on Word Meanings

Teachers' Experiences

The recent emphasis upon teaching specific word meanings as an integral part of reading instruction is probably due largely to three causes: teachers' experiences, the urgings of the semanticists, and scientific studies. Every teacher of reading has often experienced situations in which a child has misinterpreted a story or part of a selection because he attached the wrong meaning to some one word. For example, one teacher told of such an incident in connection with the reading of the Cinderella story. After reading the story she told her pupils that they might draw a picture of some part of the story. Later one little boy came up to show his picture to the children. There was Cinderella in all of her finery trailing across the diamond in a baseball field with the big amphitheatre surrounding it. The teacher said, "Why do you have Cinderella out on a baseball diamond?" The youngster replied, "Well, the story said she went to a ball." This child's concept of going to a ball was to go to a baseball park. His parents probably go to a "party" or a "dance" occasionally, but they no longer call the party or dance "a ball." Because the meaning of the word *ball* as used in this story was entirely outside the child's experience, he missed the point of the story or at least a very important point in the story.

In the light of such experiences, thinking teachers have come strongly to realize that a heavy responsibility rests upon them to teach specific word meanings as a part of their instructional program in reading.

Semantics

Semantics is a comparatively new term in the field of reading instruction, yet neither the word *semantics* nor the science for which it stands is new in the history of languages. While the early students of linguistics were chiefly concerned with the origin, nature, structure, and modification of language forms, some attention always has been given to meanings. It is only recently, however, that the semanticists, those primarily concerned with the significance of words, have brought sharply to our attention inadequacies in the use of words and in the interpretation of word meanings. The analyses, examples, and principles which the modern semanticists are placing before us are so impressive and convincing that we in the teaching profession are moved to a re-examination of the entire curriculum in search of fresh possibilities for aiding children to express themselves more effectually and to interpret language symbols more exactly.

Scientific Studies

Several studies have appeared in regard to the relation of word meanings to reading. Sanderson [18] reported an experiment to determine the effect of direct instruction in the development of meaning vocabularies. She reported a rise in vocabulary power as a result of instruction. Thorndike,[19] Traxler,[20] and Wesman [21] found that there was a positive relationship between size of vocabulary and achievement in school. A comparison of early and later studies [22] of the size of children's vocabulary reveals a rise in the number of words known at different age levels in more recent times. This may be partly due to television and other widening of experiences, and partly due to the testing techniques used.

A few studies have been made of the multiple meanings of words. Lovell [23] conducted a study to ascertain the likelihood that an individual who knows the commonest meaning of a word will also know additional meanings of it. He concluded that richness and intensity of knowledge can be estimated from tests that require knowledge of the single commonest meaning. Zipf [24] conducted a statistical study of definitions in the *Thorndike-Century Senior Dictionary* and concluded that the number of meanings of words and their frequency of usage are directly related. Howards [25] investigated knowledge of meanings of high-frequency, monosyllabic, multiple-meaning words in grades 4, 5, and 6.

[18] Marion Sanderson, "An Experiment in the Development of Meaning Vocabularies," *Studies and Summaries* (Prepared by Hugh H. Bonar) (Manitowac, Wisc.: Manitowac Public Schools, 1941), pp. 31–55.

[19] Robert L. Thorndike, "Two Screening Tests of Verbal Intelligence," *Journal of Applied Psychology*, Vol. 26 (1942), 128–35.

[20] Arthur E. Traxler, "The Relationship Between Vocabulary and General Achievement in the Elementary School," *Elementary School Journal*, Vol. 45 (Feb. 1945), 331–33.

[21] A. G. Wesman, *A Study of Transfer of Training*, Teachers College Contributions to Education, No. 909. (New York: Bureau of Publications, Teachers College, Columbia University, 1945).

[22] Madorah E. Smith, "An Investigation of the Development of the Sentence and the Extent of Vocabulary in Young Children," *University of Iowa Studies in Child Welfare*, Vol. 3, No. 5 (1926). Noel B. Cuff, "Vocabulary Tests," *Journal of Educational Psychology*, Vol. 21 (Mar. 1930), 212–20. Olive J. Grigsby, "An Experimental Study of the Development of Concepts of Relationship in Pre-School Children as Evidenced by Their Expressive Ability," *Journal of Experimental Education*, Vol. 1 (Dec. 1932), 144–62. R. H. Seashore and L. D. Eckerson, "The Measurement of Individual Differences in General English Vocabularies," *Journal of Educational Psychology*, Vol. 31 (Jan. 1940), 14–38. Mary K. Smith, "Measurement of the Size of General English Vocabulary through the Elementary Grades and High School," *Genetic Psychology Monographs*, Vol. 24 (1941), 311–45.

[23] George D. Lovell, "Interrelations of Vocabulary Skills: Commonest Versus Multiple Meanings," *Journal of Educational Psychology*, Vol. 32 (Jan. 1941), 67–72.

[24] George Kingsley Zipf, "The Meaning Frequency Relationship of Words," *The Journal of General Psychology*, Vol. 33 (Oct. 1945), 251–56.

[25] Melvin Howards, *Measuring Children's Understanding of Selected Multiple-Meaning Words as It Relates to Scientific Word Lists*, Unpublished Doctoral Dissertation, New York University, 1962.

His findings revealed that no child tested knew all meanings of the common multiple-meaning words tested, but there was growth in knowledge of these meanings from grade to grade.

Bloomer [26] made a study which resulted, among other things, in this conclusion: "The relationship between concreteness and reading difficulty is stronger than the relationship between concreteness and spelling difficulty; and the relationship is in the direction expected; that is, more concrete words seemed to be easier to read and to spell."

Several other studies of word meanings as related to reading are now in progress. Because of the significance of this aspect of linguistics, probably many additional studies will be conducted in the near future.

Types of Word Meanings

In the discussions of the semanticists they mention different types or classes of words to which special consideration should be given. Many teachers find it helpful to have these classes in mind while teaching reading.

Polysemantic Words

The chief trouble-makers are the polysemantic words. A polysemantic or multiple-meaning word is one that is capable of shifting its meaning many times from one thing to another, each time having a connotation which is quite different from the others. As an example, consider the word *note:* In a selection about music, the word *note* would probably mean an elliptical character placed in a certain position on the staff. If the context referred to *note* in connection with a business transaction or arithmetic it might mean "a written promise to pay." If *note* were encountered in text having to do with English, it might mean an informal communication; or on the other hand, if it appeared in social studies it might mean a formal communique between the heads of two nations. In the directions for an experiment in science the reader might be told to carry out certain directions and then to *note* results, meaning to observe; while, in a selection in literature, he might read about a character who was of great *note* in his community.

So many words in the English language have multiple meanings that children are often confused and unable to make the transition from one meaning to another. A mother tells of such an incident that led to a very erroneous interpretation. She told her young son, Jimmy, a story about the Garden of Eden, after which she explained that he might draw a

26 Richard H. Bloomer, "Concepts of Meaning and the Reading and Spelling Difficulty of Words," *Journal of Educational Research,* Vol. 54 (Jan. 1961), 178–82.

picture of the story if he liked. Jimmie proudly showed the resulting picture with lush flowers and trees, a man and a woman, and a box-like object in one corner of the sheet of paper. "What is that?" asked the mother. "It's the car" replied Jimmie. "I didn't say anything about a car when I told the story," remarked the puzzled mother. "Well, you said God drove them out of the garden." The only meaning of *drove* which Jimmie knew was the one associated with manipulating an automobile while in motion. *Drove* in this sense is, of course, derived from *drive*, meaning to "impel forward," but Jimmie hadn't made that generalization yet. He would probably have been quite nonplussed upon hearing someone talk about a farmer who "drove his cattle to pasture," or a rancher who had "a drove of cattle."

It is surprising to note the number of multiple-meanings found even in reading material used at the first grade level. The following sentences were copied from a first reader:

The dog went away and never came *back*.
John put a little saddle on the dog's *back*.
Mr. Jones *backed* his car into the garage.
Mr. Nichols *backed* the baseball team.
Mrs. Brown *backed* the rug with rubber.

In these cases the context is the only clue to the meaning of *back*.

In dealing with multiple meanings in reading, it is advisable for the teacher to check frequently upon the new use of a multiple-meaning word and explain its meaning, guiding children to make the transition from one meaning to another. The goal should be to help each child build up a constellation of multiple meanings for polysemantic words so that he can pull out any one meaning in bold relief whenever it is needed in interpreting a particular context.

Changing Functions of Words

The various functions which one word may perform in speech is another aspect of multiple meanings and one in need of special attention. We encounter *sound* as a noun, the subject of a sentence in the statement, "The sound of thunder was not pleasant to Jane." It has a different meaning when it is used as a verb in "Sound the chimes, Mary." And still a different meaning when used as a modifier in "Uncle Fred was sound asleep."

The writer was in a classroom one day when the teacher wrote a sentence from a selection the children had read on the chalk board, telling them to draw a picture of the sentence. The sentence was, "The great golden sun rose high above the mountains." Seven of fifteen children drew a picture of high mountains, a blazing yellow sun, and a red rose. They knew the meaning of rose in its noun function, but they did not recognize it in its verb sense. Because of this deficiency they misinterpreted the meaning of the sentence.

In promoting reading interpretation teachers should help children in sensing different meanings according to the functions of the word, and assist them in becoming aware of any differences in pronunciation or spelling which may accompany these changing functions.

Similes and Metaphorical Language

The use of similes and metaphorical language should be singled out for special consideration, and this doesn't apply just to high school teachers by any means. Here are a few samples taken from a beginning second grade reader: "The little house sitting high up on the hill was shining like a new penny." How could a house shine like a new penny, children might wonder. "They found little Sally curled up in a ball." The writer asked some children what this sentence in the reader meant. They thought it meant that Sally was curled up inside of a big ball. They didn't understand that she was curled up in the shape of a ball. "Tom found a brown flint arrowhead in a cup of sand." Several children thought that the arrowhead was found in a tea cup filled with sand. They didn't understand that the "cup of sand" was a small depression in the soil. Many similes and many examples of metaphorical language can be found in books for elementary children even very early in the primary grades. The frequency of such comparisons increases and becomes more abstract, of course, as children read books at successively higher levels. Teachers don't know how much such comparisons mean to children unless they ask them. Children's answers usually are quite convincing of the need for giving special attention to passages of this type.

Changes in Word Structure

The increasing need for giving more attention to the analysis of word elements in interpreting meanings is importunate. In our frantic search for words to express new meanings in this rapidly changing world, and in our haste to say everything in the quickest possible way, we are adding suffixes and prefixes to thousands of words which heretofore have not been so modified. If we are feeling low we seek a *pepper-upper* in the way of an *enriched* food which might contain *flavoprotein.* In the laundry, we use a *wonder-working soapless* powder to *activate* the water, which in turn has a *super-wetting* effect on our *washables.* In years past we might have said "I am going to take a tonic to pep me up," or "I am going to use some Scrub-Clean soap in washing my soiled clothes." But now verbs and adverbs become nouns, nouns become verbs and adjectives—all with the aid of prefixes and suffixes.

If the reader wishes convincing evidence of the prevalence of modified words in modern reading text, let him try the experiment of counting the number of variant forms in a paragraph or two of reading matter in a current newspaper, magazine, or novel.

Here are a few examples clipped from newspapers:

NEW YORK, Dec. 28—*American military personnel* were *restricted today* to stay *within* the Saigon city *limits. Military officials also urged* the *soldiers* to travel with *companions whenever* possible.

The *action followed official confirmation* by the *military advisory* group that a *26-year-old American* army *specialist* was *missing.*

In these short paragraphs there are twenty- four words that have been changed in some way from their root form, and nineteen which remain unchanged. More than half of the words in the paragraph have been modified.

The above example is typical in illustrating the large proportion of words which are being modified in modern text by adding different beginnings and endings.

Another manifestation of this same trend is seen in the rapidly increasing use of hyphenated and compounded words. If the reader should doubt the prevalence of such words in recent writing, let him turn to any selection of his choice in a current newspaper or magazine and count the number of words of this type which he can find. If he starts with a page of fiction, he may find himself reading about a *streamlined* bit of femininity with an *upswept hair-do,* wearing an *eye-catching, waist-hugging* gown of *sharkskin* with a *pencil-slim* skirt and a *figure-flattering* bodice.

If news items are selected, he may read that "*Freeholders* voted this *afternoon* to guarantee $15,000,000 in *short-term* notes to establish a *wholesale* food center in the *Meadowlands*"; or that "Losses stemming from the *nationwide* steel strike *sky-rocketed into* billions as the labor dispute hit the *100-day* mark"; or that "There was an *all-out* drive to subdue the reign of terror *shape-up.*"

Turning to advertisements the reader may find such highly compressed statements as "*wet-weather raincoats* that can be *home-dried* or *dry-cleaned*"; or a "Jacket for young *on-the-go* life from morning till *date-time, zephyr-light, sheer-wool, high-lighted* with satin trim"; or "*anti-gray-hair* vitamins," a "*magno-low writing-ring* with *ruby-red* setting," a *"performance-engineered* radio," and a *"medically-proven* cough syrup" —all of which can be procured in a local *budget-tailored* store.

This extraordinary trend toward increased use of variant forms is not limited to reading materials in life; school texts also are moving in this direction. Geographies, history books, science texts are all using modified forms more freely. Reading textbook vocabularies pose a special problem in this respect for teachers not acquainted with the policy of including or excluding variant forms in the vocabulary lists in the back of the books. (See discussion pages 215–16.)

Since textbooks include large numbers of modified words, and since variant forms are not included in the vocabulary lists of basic readers after they have once been introduced, it is desirable for the teacher to look ahead in any material that the children are about to read to see if there are words in modified forms which may give trouble. If so, he or she may then plan to clarify the changed meaning of these words (and pronunciation also, if necessary) through discussion or chalkboard explanation.

Concluding this section we might ask, "What is the general implication to the teacher of reading in regard to this phenomenal trend toward increased usage of words in modified forms? It means that we, as teachers, must spend more time in helping children analyze words into their elements, deciding upon the root word and its meaning in each case, discussing the changes in meaning made by modification, and finally drawing conclusions about the total meaning of the modified words as they appear in the particular context under consideration. This is a must!

Stereotypes

Stereotypes are trite expressions which some one has originated at some time but which we have adopted, using them over and over again instead of saying what we have to say in original language which better conveys our own personal experience. "The winding river"; "the rosy dawn"; "a snow-white horse"; "the executive in a swivel-back chair"; "the student in horn-rimmed glasses." Such hackneyed phrases may represent generalizations which someone else has made at some time as a result of his experiences, but they do not necessarily describe what every individual has experienced in these same situations. As an example of the use of stereotype, an English teacher relates this incident: She had asked her students to write a composition about meeting someone at the airport, railroad station, or bus depot in their town. When one boy read his composition he told how excited he was when he "saw the train come slowly winding round the bend." "There is no bend in the track approaching our railroad station," interrupted the teacher. "Why did you say 'slowly winding round the bend?'" "I thought it sounded more literary," replied the youth.

In so far as *reading* is concerned, children should be aware of stereotypes and asked to tell what their own concepts are of things stated in stereotypic forms.

Need for New Words

One other consideration in regard to words and concepts might be mentioned—that is the need which some people are feeling for new words. There are those who are urging that it would be better to coin some words for new concepts rather than trying to fit our new concepts into old words which have had a long history of established meanings.

Some new words are emerging, particularly in the scientific fields of medicine, physics, chemistry, invention, and to some extent in the fields of industry. Examples of such words which have recently come into wide usage are *penicillin, barbiturates, radar, electronics, telegenic, Sanforized, Quonset Hut, launching pad.*

It seems to be in the field of social studies that new words are most needed for new concepts or vice versa. Some people are saying that the new patterns of world crisis require new forms of expression, new words, if misunderstanding is to be eliminated. For example, consider the word *Americanism:* many verbal and even legal battles have been fought over this word, yet who can define this term definitely and specifically? Webster states that *Americanism* is "attachment or loyalty to the United States and its traditions, interests and ideals." Here we are confounded with five more abstract words, each of which is subject to wide variation in interpretation: *attachment, loyalty, traditions, interests,* and *ideals.* Each of us brings to bear upon such words concepts arising from our own personal experience, and while we have a hazy impression of what each of these words means to us personally, we would have difficulty in stating it concretely. We really haven't thought through these meanings as carefully as we should.

Raymond B. Fosdick,[27] retired president and trustee of the Rockefeller Foundation, says:

All the words that we use today, like "nationalism" and "sovereignty" and "patriotism," and subtler words like "prestige" and "ambition" and "power"

---

[27] Raymond B. Fosdick, "We Need New Words and New Faith," *New York Times Magazine* (Dec. 1948), p. 7. Copyright by The New York Times. Reprinted by permission.

were in the dictionary of 1901, and in our current dictionaries there are few if any new words that have been coined to represent new devices and methods for harnessing to universal social goals the forces which physics and chemistry have unleashed in the last half century. Unfortunately, for this purpose we have to rely on the old dictionary.

We need more words in the dictionary that deal with concepts like social adaptation and adjustment, and with adventurous ideas that have to do with the art of human relations. Our vocabulary is poverty-stricken in this whole range of thought, because we have found so few tangible and workable principles and techniques that can be defined. We are trying to get along as best we can with the old words and meanings which we spell out in the dictionary of 1901, although we have to live our lives in an environment that often has little relevancy to those words and meanings.

Perhaps some of the children with whom we are working in the schools of today, if encouraged, will make contributions to human relations by coining new words and new definitions for new social concepts which will help to clarify and unify thinking and promote international understanding.

Concepts Related to Reading
for Meanings

What Is a Concept?

Possibly the first response to the question above might be, "it's an idea" or "it's a meaning" or "it's an understanding." A concept might be any one of these. For our purposes, however, in considering the many-sided relationships between reading and concept building, we need to amplify, extend, and qualify such a definition in many different ways.

It may be useful to think of a concept as "crystallized experience." The word *experience* is significant in this definition because experience is the very substance out of which concepts are made. A concept is the residue left as a result of experience; it is the condensation of experience which takes definite form in the mind. The word *crystallized* is used as a qualifier of experience because, metaphorically speaking, a crystal possesses many of the same qualities as those which are inherent in concepts.

Building Concepts

Because concepts play such a versatile role in reading, it is important that teachers of reading be fully aware of the processes by which concepts are built. The first step in building a concept is that of having experiences. Experiences are the self-starters of concepts, but concepts do not necessarily result from experiences; just experiences are not enough.

There must be a second step, that of drawing conclusions from the experiences and later classifying and summarizing conclusions from several experiences. These classifications or summaries derived from experiences are called concepts. These concepts may be sound or faulty, full and complete or meager and inadequate. Regardless of their state of perfectness we use them in interpreting words verbally or as they appear in text. Concepts constitute the medium which makes experiences usable in interpreting reading symbols. So the third step in concept building, in so far as reading is concerned, is that of applying concepts to new experiences which are encountered on the printed page.

John Dewey [28] has said:

> Concepts enable us to generalize, to extend and carry over our understanding from one thing to another. . . .
> Conceptions standardize our knowledge. They introduce solidity into what otherwise would be formless, and permanence into what would otherwise be shifting. . . .
> It would be impossible to overestimate the educational importance of arriving at conceptions: that is, of meanings that are general because applicable in a variety of instances in spite of their difference: that are constant, uniform or self-identical in which they refer to, and that are standardized, known points of reference by which to get our bearings when we are plunged into the strange and unknown. . . .
> Without this conceptualizing or intellectualizing nothing is gained that can be carried over to the better understanding of new experiences. The deposit is what counts, educationally speaking.

The above quotations from Dewey are highly charged with valuable meanings, but there is one statement which seems to stand out above all the others in its significance. It is this simple statement: "The deposit is what counts. . . ." We, as teachers, must not only provide children with varied, abundant, and rich experiences, but we must guide them in classifying their ideas derived from experience into wholesome and well-rounded concepts. In reading interpretation as elsewhere, "The deposit is what counts."

Confusions Due to Faulty or Inadequate Concepts

What happens during the process of reading interpretation if concepts have not been well built? What happens if concepts are meager, lacking, or inaccurate, and are still in isolated strands instead of classified and generalized?

Perhaps a concrete example will answer this question better than a discussion. Let's consider the case of a class of first grade children who

---

[28] Reprinted from *How We Think* by John Dewey by permission of D. C. Heath and Company. Copyright 1933, 1961.

were reading a farm story. The story had its setting in a vegetable garden, a typical large farm garden in which vegetables were grown in sufficient quantities, not only to supply the immediate needs of the family, but also to feed the hired men and to can or store for winter.

The children who were reading the story lived in Los Angeles. Few of them had ever seen a vegetable garden; none of them had ever had any contact with an acre garden plot, such as one finds on Midwestern farms, or with many of the other objects mentioned which had to do particularly with farm life in the Midwest. The new words in the story were: *garden, plant, earth, vegetables,* and *row.* The teacher developed the pronunciation of these words before the class read the selection, but she did not discuss their meanings.

As the children read, they had a great deal of difficulty. They hesitated and repeated, and stumbled and stopped—not because of pronunciation difficulties but because of confusion resulting from faulty or inadequate concepts. A check-up revealed the following disparities in interpretation: A *garden* to these children meant a small round space in the backyard in which pansies and forget-me-nots were blooming. *Plant,* which was used in the story as a verb, to these children meant the philodendron which grew in a container placed on a table in the living room. *Earth* to them meant the place in which we live, rather than the soil in which the garden seed had been planted according to the story. *Vegetables* to them meant several grown edibles such as corn, peas, oranges, carrots, figs, avocadoes, and so on. They had not yet arrived at generalizations to guide them in distinguishing between vegetables and fruit.

The word *row,* which was used in the context as "a row in the cornfield," was a universal source of difficulty. It was found that all the children could pronounce this word, but as with the other words, they were confused about meaning. The school was near a small lake. Nearly all the pupils had gone for a row with their fathers in a rowboat on this lake. When they read about "a row in the cornfield" they thought they must have made a mistake, and at this point the reading process broke down.

This example illustrates a very important consideration, namely: words have different meanings in terms of the experience of the author, in terms of the experience of the reader, and in terms of the contextual setting in which they are found. Teachers have a tremendous task in attempting to bridge the gap among these important factors. They not only need to bridge the gap between authors and reader, they also need to provide new experiences where concepts are lacking and to help children generalize and classify ideas gathered from both old and new experiences.

In these ways, they can assist their pupils to form flexible, versatile, usable concepts, which, again metaphorically speaking, will not refract rays of light into distorted images, or flood meanings with a gloss of false colors, but which will enable pupils to see through the crystal-clear substance of experience to the full meaning behind reading symbols.

Research

Numerous studies have been made in regard to the development of children's concepts in general. These many studies will not be reviewed here, but some references to them will be made in the bibliography at the end of the chapter. In general these investigations indicate that children grow in conceptualization from infancy throughout the period of childhood. As examples of studies of age changes in concept, reference might be made to an investigation conducted by Feifel and Lorge.[29] They found, as would be expected, that there are qualitative differences between concepts of young and older children. Kruglov [30] also found that the trend was toward more qualitative concepts in older children. Russell [31] summed up research in regard to concept development as follows: "Concepts change from immediate to remote, concrete to abstract, simple to complex, egocentric to social, diffuse to focussed, vague to specific, and contradictory to consistent."

Some studies that are of particularly pertinent interest in the teaching of reading will be mentioned briefly. Reichard, Schneider, and Rappaport [32] identified three sequential levels of concept development: (1) the concrete, (2) the functional, and (3) the conceptual or abstract meanings. Gerstein [33] constructed a multiple-choice test based on the pattern of these three levels. She hypothesized that individuals on a level of concrete concepts would select concrete meanings and so on with the other levels. The results showed a definite trend in this direction. Chase,[34] using Gerstein's technique of measuring the three levels of concepts, tested fourth, fifth, and sixth grade pupils' concepts associated with verbal

29 Herman Feifel and Irving Lorge, "Qualitative Differences in the Vocabulary Responses of Children," *Journal of Educational Psychology*, Vol. 41 (1950), 1–18.
30 Lorraine P. Kruglov, "Qualitative Differences in Vocabulary Choices of Children as Revealed in a Multiple-Choice Test," *Journal of Educational Psychology*, Vol. 44 (1953), 229–43.
31 David H. Russell, "Concepts," in ed. C. W. Harris, *Encyclopedia of Educational Research*, 3rd ed. (New York: The Macmillan Co., 1960), p. 328.
32 S. Reichard, M. Schneider, and David Rappaport, "The Development of Concept Formation in Children," *American Journal of Orthopsy* (1944), 156–61.
33 Reva A. Gerstein, "A Suggested Method for Analyzing and Extending the Use of Bellevue-Wechsler Vocabulary Responses," *Journal of Consulting Psychology*, Vol. 13 (1949), 366–70.
34 Clinton I. Chase, "An Application of Levels of Concept Formation to Measurement of Vocabulary," *The Journal of Educational Research*, Vol. 55 (Oct. 1961), 75–78.

symbols in arithmetic. From the results of his study the investigator concluded that students' responses "illustrate a preference for definitions at one level of concept formation over other stages, the preferred level corresponding with progress in the development of concepts." He hypothesized that this approach could be of value in measuring the status of children's concepts associated with terms specific to other academic areas as well.

These studies offer stimulating leads to teachers of reading. They suggest the possibility of attempting, through informal observation and checking, to ascertain concept levels of different children, and then attempting to develop children who are at lower levels to higher levels of conceptualism.

A few studies have been made which show the direct effect of experience upon reading ability. While it is generally recognized that reading is essentially a process of gleaning meanings from printed symbols, it has been pointed out on page 43 that these meanings are not vested in the symbols themselves; rather these meanings spring from the mind of the reader who brings meaningful concepts to the symbols in terms of his own experience.

The above hypothesis is probably the one which has prompted a few investigators to attempt to measure the relationship between experience designed to develop concepts and reading success. We need to have many more studies in this area. Some of the most pertinent ones which have been made are mentioned below.

Cantor [35] conducted a very interesting study to ascertain the value of excursions to kindergarten children as a means of preparing them for first grade reading. During the course of her investigation she used four methods of checking: (1) a critical summary of excursions taken according to previously established criteria, (2) an analysis of the concept-building characteristics of the excursions with relation to a standard vocabulary, (3) a comparison of the topical and vocabulary demands of primary readers with kindergarten preparation, (4) a check of primary work done by children during the first year who had had this excursion experience in their kindergarten year.

This investigator found that 204 concepts were given background in experience through nine excursions taken, and that a correlation had been effected between the vocabulary and concept demands of primary reading and the vocabulary and concept supply of nine typical kinder-

[35] Alma Cantor, *An Historical, Philosophical, and Scientific Study of Kindergarten Excursions as a Basis for Social Adaptation and Reading Readiness.* Master's Thesis (Cincinnati, Ohio: Teachers College, University of Cincinnati, 1935).

garten excursions. The children who had taken these excursions in kindergarten were also checked for reading readiness and reading achievement in first grade. Cantor's conclusion in regard to the effect of the excursions on learning to read was:

From results of scientific tests administered in the primary year and the comparisons made with reading readiness in other schools, it seems probable that the children [who had the excursions] definitely profited from the comprehensive program of kindergarten excursions experienced in their kindergarten year.

Hilliard and Troxell [36] and McWhorter [37] conducted studies showing that enriched background was beneficial to school achievement. (See page 43.)

Experimental evidence in regard to the relationship of concept development to reading success is too meager for us to draw any decisive conclusions at this time. What data we do have, however, are favorable. As previously indicated their implications to kindergarten and first grade teachers in so far as reading is concerned are two fold: (1) analyze the early books which children will use for vocabulary and concepts; (2) provide enriching experiences which will acquaint pupils with this vocabulary orally, and which will equip them with necessary concepts ahead of the time that they will meet these particular words and concepts in reading text. Some studies have shown that building experiential background is even more effective in later grades than in first grade.

Improving Reading Interpretation Through Concept Building

So much for the nature of concept building and the different types of word meanings for which concept building must be done. There is still left for discussion the very practical consideration of how to meet these problems in the classroom. The remainder of this chapter will be devoted to suggestions of mediums and procedures for use in improving reading interpretation through concept building.

First-Hand Experience

The semanticists tell us with repeated emphasis that "the word is not the thing," that at best the word is simply an abstract symbol which stands for experience. This being the case, one of the most basic functions

[36] George H. Hilliard and Eleanor Troxell, "Informational Background as a Factor in Reading Readiness and Progress," *Elementary School Journal*, Vol. 38 (Dec. 1937), 255.

[37] Opal A. McWhorter, *Building Reading Interests and Skills by Utilizing Children's First-Hand Experiences*, Master's Thesis. (Athens, Ohio: Ohio University, 1935).

of a teacher of reading is to ensure experiences for her pupils that will equip them to interpret symbols which in turn stand for these experiences. To some, such a statement may seem trite, indeed. Yet, up to this time, we have barely tapped the possibilities of utilizing experiential background in the teaching of reading.

As one example, consider the case of the teacher who, upon a certain occasion, placed this sentence on the bulletin board: "This is a chilly morning." Her pupils, who came from Mexican homes, gathered around the bulletin board and tried to read the message. The teacher helped them with the pronunciation of the new word *chilly*. Then she asked what the sentence meant. All of them thought that the sentence told them in effect that this was a morning on which they should eat food seasoned with Chili peppers. The teacher then explained that *chilly*, when spelled as it was in this sentence and when used to describe a morning, meant cold. She took them to the door and momentarily let them experience the sensation of cool, crisp air as it rushed against their bare faces and through their clothing. Undoubtedly, after this experience, these children sensed the full and correct meaning of the symbol for *chilly* whenever they encountered it in a phrase pertaining to temperature.

As teachers become increasingly sensitive to the part which experience plays in establishing meaningful concepts to use in filling in word symbols, they will more frequently take the time and trouble to provide experiences "on the spot" which will equip children to bring to new word symbols clear and accurate understandings of meanings. The use of first-hand experience as an aid to reading interpretation should receive a tremendous impetus as semantic implications "take hold."

Relating to Personal Experience

When class experiences are not feasible the practice of having a discussion, recalling and relating personal experiences, has proved beneficial. One third grade class read a poem in which the poet spoke of "the melancholy sky." Different children were asked to express their opinions as to the meaning of the word "melancholy." One or two were able to define the word acceptably. They and several of the other children were asked to recall and relate instances in which they had felt "melancholy." By guided discussion the teacher then brought out the point that the sky, of course, could not feel "melancholy," but that it had the effect of making people who looked at it feel "melancholy"; that it was a dark, gray, somber sky which caused one to feel sad, rather than a light, bright, sunny sky which had the effect of making people feel glad and happy.

Models and Construction Projects

Reading content is so broad in scope that it isn't possible, of course, to give children first-hand contacts with all the things that they will read about. At this juncture, models and construction projects serve very well in building accurate concepts. A modern child reading a story about medieval life in Europe might not have the slightest idea of the meaning of *moat, drawbridge, parapet,* and so on. Constructing a representation of an ancient castle and its surroundings under the skillful guidance of a teacher who is "concept conscious" would substitute for a first-hand experience in a very realistic way. The use of models and construction projects is all to the good in concept building.

Dramatization

An effective but simple medium to use in developing concepts of new words is that of dramatization. For example, the children in one classroom were reading a story which contained the sentence, "The pool was surrounded by tall grass." Questions revealed that some children were confused about the meaning of "surrounded." The teacher clarified their concept by having a group of children "surround" one of the tables in the classroom. Such an informal performance requires no preparation and very little time. This technique should be used more often.

Exhibits

Using an exhibit of objects pertaining to some new topic in a book serves a useful purpose in concept building. In one classroom the children were about to read a series of stories with settings in jungles. Preceding the reading of the stories, they talked about jungle life, and each pupil was asked to bring in something which might have come from a jungle. A table, set aside for the purpose, was soon covered with such articles as coconuts, bananas, Brazil nuts, palm leaf fans, a reptile-skin bag, and pictures galore. Discussions of these objects as they affected or contributed to the lives of the people provided these children with many meaningful concepts to bring to their reading of jungle stories. Even the simplest exhibits are valuable in building concepts.

Films and Film Strips

Those who have the facilities and films available for showing moving pictures are fortunate, indeed, in having this strong ally to assist in concept building. Consider how much more meaningful an informative selection on the bulb industry in Holland could be to children if the reading of this selection were preceded or accompanied by a moving picture showing all the steps involved, from planting the bulbs to harvesting and shipping them. For those experiences which cannot be provided first hand because of remoteness in distance or time, the instructional film probably is next best. Guidance and discussion are still necessary, of course, and for concept-building purposes great care must be taken to choose films which convey accurate information.

Chalkboard Sketches

Chalkboard sketches require no material other than chalk and chalkboard, and the teacher doesn't necessarily have to be an artist in order to draw a simple sketch or diagram which will help children to understand the meaning of a word or phrase. Some third grade children were reading a selection on astronomy, in which the constellation commonly known as "The Big Dipper" was featured prominently. Since the utensil known as a "dipper" passed away with the pump and water bucket, very few children today know what a "dipper" is. In this case, the teacher drew a picture of a "dipper" on the chalkboard and explained its use; then she drew a representation of the constellation, placing the stars appropriately, and called to the children's attention the similarity in the shape of the constellation to that of a "dipper."

Pictures

Undoubtedly, teachers could make much greater use of still pictures in building concepts than is usually done. One illustration will be given to show the usefulness of still pictures in reading interpretation.

A fifth grade class in California was about to read a story which had as its underlying theme the conservation of wild flowers. The "Spring Beauty" was the particular wild flower which was dealt with throughout the story, yet at no time was it called a flower. Spring Beauty grows profusely in the Middle West and East, but it does not grow in California. The children in California, who were not acquainted with this particular flower, might have deduced an abstract meaning from the phrase "Spring

Beauty," interpreting it as "the beauty of the season of spring" or "the beauty of spring water bubbling from the ground." Their wise teacher, anticipating this possible mental confusion, procured several colored pictures of Spring Beauties which she showed preceding the reading of the story. The children then had a clear mental concept of "Spring Beauty" as it was used in this story, and their interpretation of the entire selection benefitted accordingly.

More abundant use should be made of the excellent illustrations which are provided in modern textbooks. Careful study and discussion of these illustrations yield rich returns in concept building. In addition to pictures in texts, every teacher should make her own collection of pictures, adding to it continuously and drawing from it whenever concept building can be served.

As we become increasingly sensitive to the function of experience, real or vicarious, in teaching the interpretation of reading symbols, we shall provide in much greater abundance and use with much greater frequency all types of visual aids as integral parts of our instructional program in reading. Pictures in texts, photographs, mounted pictures, slides, motion pictures, models, maps, graphs, diagrams, dioramas—all will be drawn upon extensively in building the vivid concepts which are needed in converting combinations of reading symbols into clear, accurate, and dynamic thought units.

Context

Giving more attention to contextual influences is a *must* in the improvement of interpretation in reading. Words have the chameleon-like property of changing their color according to their contextual setting. The meaning of any one word symbol can be derived only from a study of the other words which surround it in context. Consider the word *people* for instance. If *people* were written on the chalkboard by itself and children were asked to tell its meaning, the response might be "just a lot of folks." The word would be abstract—not colored with any particular meaning. But if the teacher should write on the chalkboard a sentence containing *people*, then this word would immediately take on meaning from its neighboring words. Suppose the sentence were, "The old people of the tribe, in rags and tatters, bent and emaciated, followed in the rear." Upon reading this entire group of words, in which the one word *people* is embedded, the word itself immediately bristles with lively meaning and becomes a vivid and picturable concept.

As word relationships and their influences upon interpretation in reading are brought more sharply to the attention of teachers, they rightly will devote larger portions of their pupils' reading time to the study of contextual effects upon word meanings. Some of them will also come to realize more fully why modern methodology points a finger of disapproval at the once very prevalent practice of starting each reading lesson by having the children pronounce a list of new words which had been written on the chalkboard, or by having them say words in isolation as these words were flashed before them one by one on cards.

Abstract Meanings

The discussion on pages 277–87 stressed the imperative need for devoting increased amounts of time to discussion of word meanings. This is particularly necessary in developing understandings of the more abstract meanings of words.

When a child meets a word in text in its first, plain, sense signification, the word usually represents a fairly concrete meaning to him, particularly if it is one which he has previously encountered experientially. If he has not encountered such a word in his experiences, it is relatively easy to help him build its concept through some of the mediums and procedures which we have been discussing. The more difficult phase of concept building has to do with the abstract meanings of a word, which are far removed from its primary meaning, and which the child meets as he progresses through the grades.

As an example, consider the word *capital*. The child may have his first experience with this word while playing with his ABC blocks when someone calls to his attention "capital H" on one side of the block and "small h" on the other side. He soon learns the difference between "capital" letters and "small" letters, and in this sense *capital* has a real, concrete meaning for him. A little later in his life, he may take a trip to the capital of the state with his father and mother. Here he sees a building with a large round dome and many steps leading up to it, and is told that this is the capitol building where the law-making bodies sit while discussing the affairs of state. After this, when he reads that a certain city is the capital of a state, he has a fairly concrete idea of the meaning of the sentence. As he passes the local bank he reads on the window, "Capital $600,000." Now he associates *capital* with a bank and money. In all of these cases *capital* has been tied to a concrete object—a letter, a city, a bank—and while the child needs some additional help in getting the complete meaning of a capital city or the capital of a bank, he usually is not puzzled and confused when he encounters these terms in print. But the real trouble begins when in his more advanced reading he finds *capital* used in describing more generalized and abstract nouns, as "a capital error," "capital goods," "capital punishment." The most remote level of abstraction is reached when he meets the word as part of a term which represents an idea embracing a vast expanse of territory, that is, "capital and labor." The shift to this highly generalized use of the word *capital* is quite a long stride to take. If left alone to struggle with the interpretation of this meaning of *capital*, unaided by mental interaction and clarifying discussion, the pupil may leave his reading with only a vague or partial understanding of the meanings involved; or his understanding may be definitely erroneous; or it may be highly colored by emotive language with which the word was surrounded. Yet the word used in this sense has much to do with the structure, thought, and feeling of American society, and as such deserves careful study and interpretation.

The teacher of reading needs to cultivate a keen awareness of different levels of abstraction and she should be ever on the alert for shifts from one level to another as children meet such words in their reading. She should invite the class as a whole to study such a word and to tell what it means to them in terms of their individual experience. Out of all their experiences and their combined mental reactions, they should then attempt to construct a common meaning for the word as used in the particular situation which is acceptable to everyone in the group.

Discussion, then, would seem to be the best medium to use in regard to the interpretation of abstractions. One of the most important responsibilities of teachers is to develop clear and straight thinkers. Abundant discussion of words and terms having abstract meanings will contribute greatly to this goal.

Perhaps there is no better way of summing up the essence of this discussion on word meanings than to quote from *Alice in Wonderland*—that fanciful classic with a world of wisdom shining through the speeches of its whimsical characters. The quotations are taken from a conversation between Alice and Humpty Dumpty:

"The question is," said Alice, "whether you *can* make words mean so many different things."
"The question is," said Humpty Dumpty, "which is to be master—that's all."

Evaluation of Achievement in Getting Meanings

Informal Checks

As suggested in the discussion of evaluation of achievement in word identification (Chapter 8, pages 248–49), the teacher's own informal observations of growth are more significant than any other measures. As the teacher herself becomes increasingly sensitive to opportunities for giving practice in interpretation and in critical reading and makes the most of these opportunities, she will note that Bill, for example, is becoming more apt in interpreting and that Katie is developing in ability to react critically to reading content. At the same time she may notice that Sam and Sue are still reading largely at the literal comprehension level. She will then give more attention to these children in an attempt to help them to attain higher levels of understanding meanings.

In addition to observations, informal tests based on material with which the children are working in the classroom may be used at times to check understanding of meaning. Some of the suggestions given for "Additional Activities," pages 559–61 may be useful in preparing informal tests.

Standardized Tests

Almost all the standardized tests check understanding of meanings as well as vocabulary and word identification. Several of the standardized tests mentioned in Chapter 8, pages 250–51, check both meanings and word identification. Among these tests are: *California Achievement Tests, Gates Primary Test, Gates Advanced Primary Test, Gates Basic Tests, SRA Achievement Tests, Stroud-Hieromynus Primary Reading Profiles.* (See pages 250–51 for descriptions and publishers.) Among these tests *Gates Basic Reading Tests* deserve special mention in connection with evaluating meanings since they check several aspects of meaning as follows: Type A, Reading to Appreciate General Significance; Type B, Reading to Predict Outcomes of Given Events; Type C, Reading to Understand Precise Directions; Type D, Reading to Note Details.

In addition to the previously mentioned standardized tests, the following are valuable for use in checking meanings.

Stanford achievement tests

The *Primary Battery*, grades 1.9–3.5, checks paragraph meaning, word meaning, spelling, arithmetic reasoning, and arithmetic computation. The *Elementary Reading Test*, grades 3.0–4.9, and the *Intermediate Reading Test*, grades 5–6, include tests of paragraph meaning and of word meaning. (Harcourt, Brace & World, Inc.)

Iowa silent reading tests

The *Elementary Test*, grades 4–8, provides analytic silent reading tests including rate, comprehension, word meaning, and location skills. (Harcourt, Brace & World, Inc.)

Iowa every-pupil tests of basic skills

The *Elementary Test,* grades 3–5, and the *Advanced Test,* grades 5–9 are silent reading tests designed to check comprehension, including paragraph comprehension and vocabulary. (Houghton Mifflin Co.)

Durrell-Sullivan reading achievement test

There are two sections of this test, one for grades 2–4, the other for grades 3–6. Both of these tests check word meanings and paragraph meaning. (Harcourt, Brace & World, Inc.)

Coordinated scales of attainment

These Scales for grades 1–3 include tests which call for matching words with pictures, pictures with words, vocabulary recognition, and paragraph comprehension checked by multiple-choice questions. The Scales for the upper grades include tests of literature and language. (Education Test Bureau.)

The most complete reference for reading tests is Oscar K. Buros' *Mental Measurement Yearbook,* published periodically by Gryphon Press, Highland Park, New Jersey. All available reading tests, as well as tests in other subjects, are described in detail and evaluated in this book.

Additional Readings

Books

Betts, Emmett A., *Foundations of Reading Instruction,* rev. ed., pp. 556–76. New York: American Book Company, 1954.

Bond, Guy L. and Eva Wagner Bond, *Teaching the Child to Read,* rev. ed., pp. 345–76. New York: The Macmillan Co., 1950.

Bruner, Jerome S., J. J. Goodnow, and G. A. Austin, *A Study of Thinking.* New York: John Wiley & Sons, Inc., 1956.

Burton, William H., *Reading in Child Development,* pp. 310–46. Indianapolis: The Bobbs-Merrill Company, Inc., 1956.

Cobb, Jacob E., *A Study of Functional Reading,* Contributions to Education, No. 388. Nashville, Tenn.: George Peabody College for Teachers, 1947.

Curti, Margaret W., *Child Psychology,* 2nd ed. New York: Longmans, Green & Co., Inc., 1938.

Hendrickson, Dale, *Correlates of the Critical Thinking Abilities of Fifth-Grade Children.* Doctoral dissertation. Berkeley: University of California, 1960.

Dawson, Mildred A., and Henry A. Bamman, *Fundamentals of Basic Reading Instruction,* pp. 173–93. New York: Longmans, Green & Co., Inc., 1959.

DeBoer, John J., and Martha Dallmann, *The Teaching of Reading,* pp. 131–51. New York: Holt, Rinehart & Winston, Inc., 1960.

Deutsche, Jean M., *The Development of Children's Concepts of Causal Relations.* Minneapolis: University of Minnesota Press, 1937.

Dewey, John, *How We Think.* Boston: D. C. Heath & Company, 1933.

Durrell, Donald D., *Improving Reading Instruction,* pp. 285–308. New York: Harcourt, Brace & World, Inc., 1956.

Eller, William, and Dykstra Eller, "Persuasion and Personality: Reader's Predisposition as a Factor in Critical Reading," *Critical Reading,* Bulletin of the National Conference on Research in English. Champagne, Ill.: National Council of Teachers of English, 1959.

Gans, Roma, A *Study of Critical Reading Comprehension in the Intermediate Grades.* Teachers College Contributions to Education, No. 811. New York: Bureau of Publications, Teachers College, Columbia University, 1940.

Gates, A. I., *The Improvement of Reading,* pp. 356–79. New York: The millan Co., 1956.

Glaser, Edward M., *An Experiment in the Development of Critical Thinking.* Teachers College Contributions to Education, No. 843. New York: Bureau of Publications, Teachers College, Columbia University, 1941.

Gray, William S., ed., *Promoting Growth Toward Maturity in Interpreting What is Read.* Supplementary Educational Monographs, No. 74. Chicago: University of Chicago Press, 1951.

————, and Eleanor Holmes, *The Development of Meaning Vocabularies in Reading: An Experimental Study,* p. 140. Publication No. 6 of the laboratory schools of the University of Chicago. Chicago: Department of Education, University of Chicago, 1938.

————, "The Nature and Types of Reading," *The Teaching of Reading: A Second Report,* Thirty-sixth Yearbook, Part I, Chap. 2, pp. 23–38, National Society for the Study of Education. Chicago: University of Chicago Press, 1937.

Harris, Albert J., *How to Increase Reading Ability,* 3rd ed., pp. 458–67. New York: Longmans, Green & Co., Inc., 1956.

Hildreth, Gertrude, *Teaching Reading,* pp. 72–75, 239–40, 308–309, 454–57. New York: Holt, Rinehart & Winston, Inc., 1958.

Hurlock, Elizabeth B., "The Development of Understanding," *Child Development,* rev. ed., Chap. II. New York: McGraw-Hill Book Co., Inc., 1956.

Inhelder, Barbel, and Jean Piaget, *The Growth of Logical Thinking from Childhood to Adolescence.* New York: Basic Books, 1958.

Jersild, Arthur T., "The Growth of Understanding," *Child Psychology,* 4th ed., Chaps. 13, 14. Englewood Cliffs, N. J.: Prentice-Hall, Inc., 1954.

Johnson, Donald M., *The Psychology of Thought and Judgment.* New York: Harper & Row, Publishers, 1955.

McKee, Paul A., *The Teaching of Reading in the Elementary School,* pp. 385–552. Boston: Houghton Mifflin Co., 1943.

Miller, Clyde R., "What Everybody Should Know About Propaganda," *The Commission for Propaganda Analysis,* pp. 23–27. New York: Methodist Federation for Social Action, 1930.

Moore, Thomas V., *The Reasoning Ability of Children in the First Years of School Life.* Baltimore, Md.: The Williams & Wilkins Co., 1929.

Piaget, Jean, and others, *The Moral Judgment of the Child.* New York: Harcourt, Brace & World, Inc., 1932.

Piaget, Jean, and others, *The Child's Conception of Number*. London: Routledge & Kegan Paul, Inc., 1952.

————, *The Psychology of Intelligence*. New York: Harcourt, Brace & World, Inc., 1950.

————, *Judgment and Reasoning in the Child*. New York: Harcourt, Brace & World, Inc., 1928.

————, *The Language and Thought of the Child*. New York: Harcourt, Brace & World, Inc. 1926.

Russell, David H., *Children Learn to Read*, pp. 106–110, 115–19, 454–88. Boston: Ginn & Company, 1960.

————, *Children's Thinking*. Boston: Ginn & Company, 1950.

Vinacke, Edgar W., *The Psychology of Thinking*. New York: McGraw-Hill Book Co., Inc., 1952.

Periodicals

Artley, A. Sterl, "General and Specific Factors in Reading Comprehension," *Journal of Experimental Education*, Vol. 16 (Mar. 1948), 181–86.

Bedell, Ralph C., "The Relationship Between the Ability to Recall and the Ability to Infer in Special Learning Situations," *Science Education*, Vol. 18 (1934), 158–62.

Betts, Emmett A., "Guidance in the Critical Interpretation of Language," *Elementary English*, Vol. 27 (Jan. 1950), 9–18, 22.

————, "Reading Is Thinking," *The Reading Teacher*, Vol. 12 (Feb. 1959), 146–51.

Davis, Frederick B., "Fundamental Factors of Comprehension," *Psychometrika*, Vol. 9 (Sept. 1944), 185–97.

DeBoer, John, "Teaching Critical Reading," *Elementary English*, Vol. 23 (Oct. 1946), 251–54.

Filbin, Robert, and Stefan Vogel, "Semantics for American Schools," *Elementary English*, Vol. 36 (Dec. 1959), 567–70.

Friedman, Kapple C., "Time Concepts of Elementary School Children," *Elementary School Journal*, Vol. 44 (Feb. 1944), 337–42.

Gainsberg, Joseph C., "Critical Reading is Creative Reading and Needs Creative Teaching," *The Reading Teacher*, Vol. 6 (Mar. 1953), 19–26.

Gammon, Agnes L., "Comprehension of Words With Multiple Meanings," *California Journal of Educational Research*, III (Nov. 1952), 228–32.

Gray, William S., "New Approaches to the Study of Interpretation in Reading," *Journal of Educational Research*, Vol. 52 (Oct. 1958), 65–67.

Guilford, J. P., "Frontiers in Thinking that Teachers Should Know About," *The Reading Teacher*, Vol. 13 (Feb. 1960), 176–82.

Hall, G. Stanley, "The Content of Children's Minds on Entering School," *Pedagogical Seminary*, I, 2 (1891), 139–73.

————, and C. E. Brown, "Children's Ideas of Fire, Heat, Frost and Cold," *Pedagogical Seminary*, Vol. 10, (Mar. 1903), 27–85.

Heidbreder, Edna F., "Problem Solving in Children and Adults," *Journal of Genetic Psychology,* Vol. 35 (Dec. 1928), 522–45.

Krebs, Stephen O., "Teaching Critical Thinking," *Education,* Vol. 81 (Nov. 1960), 153–57.

McCullough, Constance M., "Responses of Elementary School Children to Common Types of Reading Comprehension Questions," *Journal of Educational Research,* Vol. 51 (Sept. 1957), 65–70.

———, "Implications of Research on Children's Concepts," *The Reading Teacher,* Vol. 13 (Dec. 1959), 100–107.

Oppenheim, June, "Teaching Reading as a Thinking Process," *The Reading Teacher,* Vol. 13 (Feb. 1960), 188–93.

Petty, Walter, "Critical Reading in the Primary Grades," *Elementary English,* Vol. 33 (May 1956), 298–302.

Robinson, Francis P., and Prudence Hall, "Studies of Higher Level Reading Abilities," *Journal of Educational Psychology,* Vol. 32 (Apr. 1941), 241–52.

Reichard, S., M. Schneider, and D. Rappaport, "The Development of Concept Formation in Children," *American Journal of Orthopsychiatry,* Vol. 14 (Jan. 1944), 156–62.

Seegers, J. C., "Reading for Meaning," *Elementary English Review,* Vol. 23 (Oct. 1946), 247–50, 261.

Serra, M. C., "A Study of Fourth Grade Children's Comprehension of Certain Verbal Abstractions," *Journal of Experimental Education,* XXII (Dec. 1953), 103–18.

———, "The Concept Burden of Instructional Materials," *Elementary School Journal,* LIII (May 1953), 508–12.

———, "How to Develop Concepts and Their Verbal Representations," *Elementary School Journal,* LIII (Jan. 1953), 275–85.

Smith, Nila B., "Levels of Discussion in Reading," *Education,* Vol. 80 (May 1960), 540–42.

———, "The Good Reader Thinks Critically," *The Reading Teacher,* Vol. 7 (Feb. 1954), 160–69.

———, "What is Critical Reading?" *Elementary English,* XXXX (Apr. 1963), 409–10.

Stauffer, Russell G., "Productive Reading-Thinking at the First-Grade Level," *The Reading Teacher,* Vol. 13 (Feb. 1960), 183–87.

Taba, Hilda, "Problems in Developing Critical Thinking," *Progressive Education,* Vol. 28 (Nov. 1950), 45–48.

Tyler, Ralph W., "Measuring the Ability to Infer," *Educational Research Bulletin,* Vol. 9 (1930), 475–80.

Webb, Ruth, "All Children Think and Plan," *Childhood Education,* Vol. 23 (Mar. 1947), 315–21.

Werner, Heinz, "Change of Meaning: A Study of Semantic Processes Through the Experimental Method," *Journal of General Psychology,* L (Apr. 1954), 181–208.

10

Study Skills Needed in Reading Content Subjects

Sometime during the course of transmission of opinions, beliefs, and customs from one generation of teachers to another, there evolved a legend to the effect that reading should be taught during special periods set aside for the express purpose of giving the child control over the skills of reading. Likewise legend dictated that arithmetic, science, geography, and history should be taught at specific times in the daily program to develop distinctive skills or implant characteristic knowledge in each of these fields, usually with little or no consideration being given to reading development as one aspect of this specialized instruction.

In the modern elementary curriculum the child reads more widely than ever before, and his functional needs, interests, and assignments compel him to read in the specialized content fields. It is true that much of his needed information in these areas comes to him through such mediums as experience, experimentation, visual aids, listening, and discussing. These other mediums of enrichment, however, furnish new drives and motives for delving widely and deeply into books; and the content of these books still represents each and all of the subject areas. Even the first grade child has his reading contacts with science, social studies, and to some extent, with that specialized text associated with arithmetic.

Regardless of whether the child reads content subject matter through his research in connection with a problem or special interest or whether he reads it as a result of assignments, the fundamental differences in the specialized subject matter itself remain unchanged. Artley [1] attributes these differences "to the fact that each kind of material has its own body of concepts and vocabulary, its unique relationships, logic, and form of presentation, and its distinctive assumptions and basic principles."

These differences of course become more clear-cut at the higher levels, but their roots are found even in materials intended for the early grades. The elementary teacher should recognize these differences and she should be willing to stop her ongoing activities long enough to utilize learning situations for reading as needs arise while children are working in these other subject fields. Reading proficiency could be improved immeasurably if pupils in the elementary grades might become as familiar with reading techniques needed in reading different types of subject matter at their respective levels as they are with techniques necessary in reading narrative material.

What Are Study Skills?

The phrase *study skills* is a fairly recent addition to the nomenclature of reading instruction. Terms like *word recognition* and *comprehension* have been used for years. Unlike these expressions, *study skills* is a comparatively new term, and it labels a fairly new concept.

Perhaps because our recognition of the study skills area of reading instruction is recent, we are not yet sure exactly what skills belong under this heading. This fact may explain why, at the present time, there is so much confusion in regard to what the study skills are. An attempt will be made to clarify this matter.

Some people define study skills broadly as habits, attitudes, and states of mind that are conducive to study, for example, working in a quiet place, budgeting time, attacking an assignment efficiently, concentrating during study. While these habits and attitudes are conducive to the best

[1] Sterl A. Artley, "General and Specific Factors in Reading Comprehension," *Journal of Experimental Education*, Vol. 45 (Mar. 1948), 181–88.

use of reading skills, it does not seem appropriate to consider them as *reading study skills.*

Some think of comprehension—literal comprehension—and interpretation as study skills. By study skills, others mean rapid reading, skimming, scanning, and various other speed skills. It is true that we use comprehension skills and speed skills in studying. But do we not also use these skills in other kinds of reading? Are these skills confined only to study?

The writer finds it helpful to think of reading study skills as those skills that form an integral part of the reading process, but that are used especially when application of the content is desired. Thus conceived, study skills in reading may be broadly defined as skills used when there is intention to *do something with* the content read.

As an illustration, consider an example outside of school. A busy housewife has an hour of leisure before she prepares the evening meal. She decides to devote this time to the perusal of a household periodical. She picks up a magazine and reads a story for entertainment. Then she reads an article because it interests her. She does nothing with the reading content of either feature. In neither case has she been using study skills in reading.

After devoting a good share of her hour to casual reading for entertainment or passing interest, she decides to look for a recipe for a new dish to add zest to the evening meal. Turning to the table of contents, she searches for a page that might have recipes. She finds a possibility, turns to the page, glances over it selectively, and finds an appealing recipe. She reads the recipe carefully and perhaps rereads it to make sure that she has all the ingredients and that the dish is easy to prepare. Then she puts the information to work in preparing the dish for dinner. She has done something with the reading content. She has used study skills in reading.

A child in the elementary school may read a story in a reader because he enjoys it. He may read a story on space travel in a trade book because it intrigues him. If he does nothing with the content of either story, he is not using study skills in reading.

However, he *is* using study skills when he reads in science and social studies for the purpose of gathering facts to use in class discussion, in experimentation, in demonstration, in making a report, in preparing a summary, in taking a test. He uses reading study skills in arithmetic when he reads a problem and applies information gained from his reading to work the problem, or when he reads directions that tell him how to perform the process. When he reads and does something with what he reads in situations such as these, he uses study skills.

Research

Research in regard to skills used in reading in content fields was late in entering the educational scene. A sprinkling of investigations appeared between 1940 and 1950; many more were conducted between 1950 and 1960. At the present time interest in study skills is high and numberless investigations are under way.[2] As a result investigators of reading now have gathered considerable significant research on this topic, and are in the process of gathering much more. The findings of some of these studies will be summarized in answer to salient questions before proceeding with further discussion of reading in the content areas.

Are Specialized Study Skills Needed in Different Subject Fields?

Are there really special skills in addition to the common reading skills? Does research confirm the assumption that different skills are used in different subject fields in addition to this common core of skills? Reference will be made to a few studies which have to do with this aspect of the topic.

Fay[3] conducted a study with sixth grade pupils for the purpose of finding relationships between achievement in five specific reading skills in three school subjects: arithmetic, social studies, and science. Shores[4] attempted to determine the relationships between certain study and reading skills and reading comprehension of scientific and historical materials. Artley[5] investigated the relationship between general comprehension and comprehension in the social studies area. McMahon[6] gave fifth grade pupils reading tests in four different fields: arithmetic, literature, social studies, and science. Robinson and Hall[7] tested rate and comprehension in art, geology, fiction, and history. Stone[8] studied eye-movements in reading psychology, physical science, and social science; Sochor[9] gave

[2] See Nila B. Smith, "What Have We Accomplished in Reading? A Review of the Past Fifty Years," *Elementary English*, Vol. 38 (Mar. 1961), 141–50.

[3] Leo C. Fay, "The Relationship Between Specific Reading Skills and Selected Areas of Sixth Grade Achievement," *Journal of Educational Research*, Vol. 43 (Mar. 1950), 541–47.

[4] Harlan J. Shores, "Skills Related to the Ability to Read History and Science," *Journal of Educational Research*, Vol. 36 (Apr. 1943), 584–93.

[5] Sterl A. Artley, "General and Specific Factors in Reading Comprehension," *Journal of Experimental Education*, Vol. 45 (Mar. 1948), 181–88.

[6] Ottis McMahon, "A Study of the Ability of Fifth Grade Pupils to Read Various Types of Material," *Peabody Journal of Education*, Vol. 20 (Jan. 1943), 228–33.

[7] Francis P. Robinson and Prudence E. Hall, "Studies of Higher-Level Reading Abilities," *Journal of Educational Psychology*, Vol. 32 (Apr. 1941), 241–52.

[8] Lewis Gordon Stone, "Reading Reactions for Different Types of Subject Matter," *Journal of Experimental Education*, Vol. 10 (Sept. 1941), 64–77.

[9] Elona Sochor, "Special Skills Are Needed in Social Studies, Science, Arithmetic," *The Reading Teacher*, Vol. 6 (Mar. 1953), 4–11.

tests in social studies, science, and arithmetic; and Traxler [10] summarized research in regard to reading in the content fields.

The conclusions of these investigators are: Fay, "that reading skills related to subject matter achievement differ from one achievement area to another"; Shores, "general reading ability does not apply . . . students must be equipped with specific skills"; Artley, "there is much overlapping in ability to read in different subject areas, but there are also many striking differences"; McMahon, "merely because a child reads efficiently one type of subject matter is not assurance that he will read efficiently other types of subject matter"; Robinson and Hall, ". . . reading in different fields is not highly related even though the selections are prepared under one editorship and tested by similar techniques"; Stone, "the reading of different types of material makes varied demands on the reader and is accompanied by different patterns of mental activity"; Sochor (stressed), ". . . the need for teachers to supplement general reading skills by teaching specific reading skills systematically in the subject matter areas"; Traxler and Townsend, ". . . it seems clear that in addition to training in general reading skill, there is a definite need for instruction in the reading skills peculiar to each field."

The results of these studies seem to indicate rather clearly that there are unique differences in skills used in different subject matter fields; and that while "general reading ability" is operative in all reading to a certain extent, there is also definite need for the development of specific skills to use in the different curricular areas.

Can Specialized Skills Be Improved?

Our next inquiry might well be, Do specialized skills yield to instruction? Can they be improved if we single them out and give them practice? Research revealed by the studies mentioned below gives an affirmative answer to these questions.

McKinnon and Burton [11] measured the effects of providing definite instruction in the use of certain skills in history. Rudolf [12] gave special reading instruction to a group in social studies. Sayre [13] conducted an experiment to determine the effect of devoting part or all of one period

[10] Arthur Traxler and Agatha Townsend, *Another Five Years of Research in Reading*, Bulletin No. 16 (New York: Educational Records Bureau, 1946), p. 21.

[11] Nettie J. McKinnon and William H. Burton, "An Evaluation of Certain Study Procedures in History," *Elementary School Journal*, Vol. 11 (Jan. 1940), 371–79.

[12] Kathleen B. Rudolf, "The Effect of Reading Instruction on Achievement in Eighth Grade Social Studies," *Teachers College Contribution to Education*, No. 945 (New York: Bureau of Publications, Columbia University, 1949).

[13] Harrison M. Sayre, "Teaching Reading in the Current Events Class," *Journal of Educational Research*, Vol. 33 (Apr. 1940).

per week to the development of basic reading skills in conjunction with the study of current events. Howell [14] checked results of training pupils in the study skills used in map reading. Leggitt [15] gave practice on certain working skills used in social science material. Jacobson [16] conducted a study in the field of science; Stevens [17] and Monroe and Englehart [18] in arithmetic; and French [19] in geography.

All these investigators found that improvement resulted when special attention was given to certain reading skills deemed necessary in working in a particular subject field. Jacobson [20] summarized many research studies in this area, and his conclusion was that "giving reading instruction in the field in which the content is to be mastered is superior to giving it in another subject field and expecting the abilities to transfer to the content field."

From these and similar investigations we are justified in concluding that study skills yield to improvement when they are pulled out and given special practice.

Is Vocabulary a Significant Factor?

Does vocabulary have anything to do with success in reading in the content fields? Some researches pertinent to this question will be reviewed briefly.

Pressey and Moore [21] conducted a study to determine the familiarity of children in third grade through high school with 106 technical terms in arithmetic. They concluded that 89 of these terms are never mastered by more than fifty per cent of the students at any level, and only thirty-six are ever mastered by as many as ninety-five per cent. Eagle [22] conducted a study in which he found that mathematics vocabulary was

14 Wallace J. Howell, "Work-Study Skills of Children in Grades IV to VIII," *Elementary School Journal*, Vol. 50 (Mar. 1950), 384–89.

15 Dorothy Leggitt, "Measuring Progress in Working Skills in Ninth-Grade Civics," *School Review*, Vol. 42 (Nov. 1934), 676–87.

16 Paul B. Jacobson, *Two Experiments with Work-Type Reading Exercises in Ninth Grade*, University of Iowa Studies in Education, Vol. 8, No. 5 (1933), 85.

17 B. A. Stevens, "Problem-Solving in Arithmetic," *Journal of Educational Research*, Vol. 25 (Apr., May 1932), 253–260.

18 Walter S. Monroe and Max D. Englehart, "The Effectiveness of Systematic Instruction in Reading Verbal Problems in Arithmetic," *Elementary School Journal*, Vol. 33 (Jan. 1933), 377–81.

19 Charles Lloyd French, "The Effect on Achievement in Geography of Special Training in Vocabulary; the Reading of Maps, Graphs, and Tables; Organization," *University of Pittsburgh Bulletin*, Vol. 29 (Jan. 1933), 83–92.

20 Jacobson, *op. cit.*, p. 85.

21 L. S. Pressey and W. S. Moore, "Growth of Mathematical Vocabulary from the Third Grade Through High School," *School Review*, Vol. 10 (June 1932), 449–54.

22 Edwin Eagle, "The Relationship of Certain Reading Abilities to Success in Mathematics," *The Mathematics Teacher*, Vol. 41 (Apr. 1948), 175–79.

closely related to mathematics achievement. Dresher [23] found that special training caused students to make greater advances in knowledge of mathematical vocabulary than were made by those who were given only the usual instruction. He found that students receiving such training improved in problem solving, also. Artley [24] found that a command of specialized vocabulary is at least as important as a knowledge of facts on a test of ability to comprehend social studies material. Phipps [25] attempted to improve the reading of history material in sixth grade by developing facility in the language of history. Among his several conclusions he stated: "The ability to read history can be improved by giving attention to the development of history vocabulary." French [26] conducted a study to ascertain the effect on achievement in geography of special training in vocabulary. The group having the specialized training was superior in results obtained.

Cole [27] has made a careful analysis of specialized words used in the different subject fields at different grade levels. The number and type of technical words listed is impressive. Still more technical words might well be added to these lists in terms of recent developments. Her report of this analysis provides an excellent prospective of the elementary teacher's job in teaching specialized vocabulary. The chapter on "General and Technical Vocabulary" in her book [28] on elementary school subjects is very pertinent to the present discussion.

From these and similar investigations, we are justified in concluding that familiarizing children with specialized vocabulary is an important aspect of reading development in the content fields.

Thus, research points the way to needs. The real problem with which we must come to grips is one of practical application. How can the elementary teacher strengthen the reading growth of her pupils through skillful guidance while they are working in these other fields? The remainder of this chapter will be devoted to practical suggestions for implementing the inferences so clearly delineated by research.

[23] Richard Dresher, "Training in Mathematics Vocabulary," *Educational Research Bulletin* (Ohio State University), Vol. 13 (Nov. 14, 1934), 201–204.

[24] Sterl A. Artley, "General and Specific Factors in Reading Comprehension," *Journal of Experimental Education,* Vol. 45 (Mar. 1948), 181–88.

[25] William Rodgers Phipps, "An Experimental Study in Developing History Reading Ability with Sixth Grade Children Through Development of History Vocabulary," *The Johns Hopkins University Studies in Education,* Vol. 24 (Baltimore, Md.: The Johns Hopkins Press, 1940).

[26] Charles Lloyd French, "The Effect on Achievement in Geography of Special Training in Vocabulary," *University of Pittsburgh Bulletin,* Vol. 29 (Jan. 1933), 83–92.

[27] Luella Cole, *Handbook of Technical Vocabulary* (Bloomington, Ill.: Public School Publishing Company, 1945).

[28] Luella Cole, "General and Technical Vocabulary," *The Elementary School Subjects* (New York: Holt, Rinehart & Winston, Inc., 1946), Chap. 2.

What study skills are needed in working successfully in the different content areas? Due to the intricate interweaving and overlapping of reading skills in all situations, it may add to clarification if some of the skill areas are classified.

Three categories of skills are needed to study effectually in content subjects: (1) common reading skills, (2) common study skills, and (3) specialized factors, including vocabulary and skills peculiar to certain subjects.

The *common reading skills* are those used in all types of reading regardless of whether or not the individual is studying. The pronunciation techniques, the meaning-gathering techniques, the rate techniques, and the eye-adjustment techniques are used in reading, irrespective of purpose or content. All these skills are used in study situations, as they are in all other reading situations. For this reason, there is no justification in designating these skills specifically as study skills. (*Common reading skills* are discussed in Chapters 8, 9, and 11.) Pupils most certainly need to use these common reading skills while studying, but they also need to make use of some "plus" skills in study situations. These "plus" skills are classified in this chapter as "Common Study Skills" and "Specialized Factors." The diagram below may aid the reader in visualizing the classification of study skills as they will be discussed.

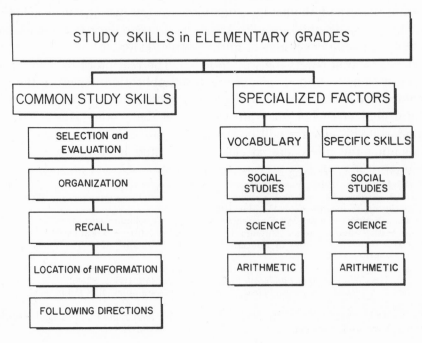

The Common Study Skills

There are certain study skills that are common to all study situations, skills we use only when we are *studying* reading content. These skills are needed in reading in all content fields. Regardless of whether a child is working with text in science, geography, history, health, or arithmetic, he needs to:

Select and evaluate—or pick out important parts of the text.
Organize—or put together ideas that belong together.
Recall what he has read—or fix it so he can bring it back when he wants it.
Locate information in textbooks, reference books, and periodicals.
Follow directions.

Selection and Evaluation

The skills of *selection* and *evaluation* team up together to make one important composite study skill. This skill is of significance because of the frequency with which it is needed and also because it is basic to other study skills, particularly *organization* and *recall.*

In using the selection and evaluation process, the child needs to select a certain item from many other items in context and evaluate it in terms of some condition imposed in a question or direction; in other words, he must pick out some item and judge its worth in meeting the specifications of an activity that he is asked to carry forward. For example, the child may be asked to find the answer to the question, "In what way do bees help farmers?" The chapter in his science text in which he is to find this answer contains many statements about the helpfulness of bees, several of which pertain to their helpfulness to man in general, some to flowers and plants, and one in particular to the farmer. In finding the answer to this question the child finds and reads several statements, mentally evaluating the pertinency of each to the farmer and his needs, and through this process finally selects the one that answers the question. Thus, he does more than recognize words and interpret meanings. In addition to using these common reading skills, he goes further and *works* with meanings derived from the symbols in accordance with the question which he has been asked.

Examples from Textbooks

Textbooks in the content subjects and their accompanying workbooks contain many questions and directions that call for the use of the selection and evaluation skills. A limited sampling of examples will be given to indicate the type of *selection and evaluation* responses which authors of textbooks in the specialized content fields expect elementary pupils to make. It will be noted that these responses include multiple-choice and completion activities and finding a specific item, specific parts of a selection, or the most important statement in a selection.

The very popular technique of finding the main idea in a paragraph is definitely a selection and evaluation study skill. When a child is told to "Find and write the main idea in each of the first five paragraphs," he must *evaluate* all the ideas in each paragraph and *select* the one that is most important in each case. This technique is called for more frequently in recent content books than it was a few years ago.

SCIENCE SAMPLES

1. An animal that hunts in packs is the

   wolf   rabbit   beaver

2. Which of these can Peter see all year round?

   High mountains
   Snow on high mountain peaks
   Snow in the village

3. In order to see an object, light must be _____ into our eyes.

   placed   sent   put   reflected

4. What is the main idea in the paragraph about fossils?

SOCIAL STUDIES SAMPLES

1. What two words tell about summer weather near the coast of Ireland?
2. (After several activities of Columbus have been mentioned, children are asked) "Which of all these things were most important?"
3. What useful trees are found in Southern forests?
4. Find on page 40 a sentence telling one way in which control of the Mississippi River helped Pioneers in the Ohio Valley.

LANGUAGE SAMPLES

1. Choose from the list of topics one that you would like to write about.
2. Read the composition below. Find any mistakes that have been made and correct them.

ARITHMETIC SAMPLES

1. Find the number that you need in working this problem. Find the one that you don't need.
2. How many parts does this problem have?

What Can the Teacher Do to Develop
Selection and Evaluation Skills?

Development

In order to meet study situations adequately, children should be given experience in using the selection and evaluation process at all levels of the elementary school. The teacher, of course, should not depend solely upon textbook exercises to develop this skill. Many occasions present themselves during discussion periods for giving instruction and practice in the use of this skill.

The alert teacher will sense and take advantage of opportunities to have children select pictures, words, phrases, sentences, paragraphs, stories, informative selections, and so on as needed in meeting the prerequisite of evaluation for some particular purpose. Functional practice in selection and evaluation is of very great value.

Selection and evaluation skills are basic to the higher level skills of critical reading when used in study situations involving subject matter in the content fields. Thus, we see possibilities for continuity of development, practice, and growth in applying these skills. Children who are provided with a rich succession of experiences of this type will most certainly be able to tackle study material with greater ease and success than if this study skill had been given but incidental or passing notice.

Direct Practice

The teacher may follow up class discussions and activities by providing materials of her own preparation. These may consist of oral, chalkboard, or duplicated instructions or exercises prepared in connection with the subject matter being studied. Such supplemental activities are particularly valuable in giving practice to children who are especially in need of help in the use of this study skill.

Several samples for types of activities to use in giving practice in selection and evaluation are presented in the section entitled "Maintenance and Practice Activities," pages 563–64. These activities are organized according to those which are most appropriate for first grade, second and third grades, and middle grades, respectively.

Organizing What is Read

Another study situation frequently encountered calls for organization of information gained through reading, that is, putting together systematically those things that belong to a whole. Grouping or listing items that belong to one classification or that occur in a certain order, outlining, and summarizing are the procedures most often used in making organization responses.

The *pre-view* technique, used so often in connection with content-subject books, is primarily one of organization. According to this procedure the individual skims through an entire selection or chapter noting only titles of sections, or topical sentences or main ideas. This results in an organized "picture" of the structure and topics discussed.

All the organizing techniques require selection and evaluation as a first step—to pull out the items to be organized. Therefore, organization is a complex skill; it is really a hierarchy involving the common reading skills, making basic use of the common study skill of selection and evaluation, and finally arriving at an organized whole.

In the interest of concreteness two examples of the organization process will be given and explained: In third grade, after reading a chapter on butterflies, the children were asked to give the life-cycle of a Monarch Butterfly. Because there was no one place in the chapter in which this information was given, they had to assemble the information by picking out pertinent bits here and there and organizing them into the entire life-cycle.

In fourth grade geography, the children were asked, "What are the land features of the Atlantic Coastal Plain?" In order to answer this question, they had to turn back to several paragraphs of text which discussed climate, land features, occupations, crops—and out of it all they sorted out those things which had to do only with land features and pieced them together to make a total "picture," thus using selection, evaluation, and organization.

Examples from Textbooks

Responses calling for organization appear very freqently in subject matter textbooks and workbooks. A small sampling of different types of textbook responses calling for organization is given below:

SCIENCE EXAMPLES

1. Pick out all the names of trees. Make a list of the trees.
2. Write the names of all the animals that sleep all winter.
3. Make a list of things that change the earth's surface.
4. Study the outline below and see if the items under each heading are correct. If not, change the items to come under the headings to which they belong.

1. Choose a scene from the experiences of Columbus to act. Plan what the characters should do and say.

2. List facts which prove the statement: "When the Pilgrims first came to America they knew very little about living in a new, wild country."

3. What are the advantages of an ocean front location for Korea? Write these advantages in one paragraph.

4. Outline the selection, "Eli Whitney's Jigs." Select the main points and include as subtopics under each main point any statements you think important in the story.

LANGUAGE EXAMPLES

1. Write the heading "Questions About Seeds." Beneath the heading write as many questions as you care to ask about seeds.

2. Prepare a form for your Reading Record. Write three headings: *Title, Author, Date.* Each time you read a book write the information asked for under each heading.

3. Here are the main headings of an outline. Write the details that are necessary in giving information about each heading (headings were given in the text).

ARITHMETIC EXAMPLES

1. In a first grade arithmetic book:
Draw a line from the big candy bar to each of the small candy bars. How many small candy bars are there all together?

2. Divide this list of numbers into two groups. Put all of the tens in one group and all of the 100's in another (list of numbers follows).

3. Make a list of the clothes in the picture on page 8, and write the price of each. Put the things that cost most first on your list and those that cost least at the end of the list.

What Can the Teacher Do to Develop Skill in Organization?

Development

While exercises in textbooks frequently call for organization responses, the teacher of reading is not relieved of the responsibility of *developing* this important skill and helping children to apply it in connection with their daily reading. If she is keenly aware of this skill and its significance, she will find many opportunities to discuss it and to have her pupils make use of it.

In the first grade, children may organize pictures and words according to certain classifications, arrange sentences to reproduce chart stories, classify ideas gained from reading, find stories concerning a given topic, and so on. In second and third grades, pupils may engage in more complicated organization activities in which they classify items according to headings, organize items in a certain order, and have beginning experiences in summarizing. In the middle grades, children are ready to take more advanced steps in organizing items in terms of sequence, outlining, note-taking, summarizing, bringing together information from several sources, preparing graphs and charts, and so on.

The wise teacher will watch for opportunities for children to have such organizing experiences as those indicated above, as these experiences serve some purpose in connection with their current study and classroom reading activities.

Practice Activities

Many suggestions for organization activities are given in the section entitled "Maintenance and Practice Activities," pages 564–65. These suggestions are grouped according to grade levels. Almost all the activities suggested may be conducted in conjunction with the content being studied currently in the different subject fields without the preparation of extra material.

Recalling What Is Read

Recalling what is read, fixing content in mind so that it can be brought back when wanted, is a very important study skill and one commonly needed in all subject fields. The present emphasis upon learning how to locate facts that we need at the time that they are needed, rather than memorizing a multitude of items is excellent. This emphasis has relieved the strain of memorizing numberless isolated items which children were required to remember in the old school. Nevertheless, there still is a large place in present-day education for recalling facts. The best student is usually the one who can most accurately recall what he has read in his text and reference books. This is especially true in science, history, geography, and often in mathematics.

In life outside of school, adults have many occasions and purposes for recalling what they read in connection with their professions, vocations, club work, and so on. Furthermore, from the personal standpoint, all of us enjoy being with an informed person, and the person who is well-informed usually is one who can accurately recall facts from his reading.

Unfortunately, the most common complaint of adults who come to a reading center to improve their reading is, "I can't remember what I read." Perhaps this reflects the fact that in the past practically nothing has been done to teach children how to fix in mind reading content which they were supposed to remember. Remembering what we read still is an important and useful skill both in school and in life. Since this is the case, teachers should give much more attention to this study skill all through the grades.

Examples from Textbooks

Responses calling for recall of facts in subject matter texts and workbooks are exceedingly numerous. The questions and directions used for this purpose are almost wholly of the type used in literal comprehension: questions based upon a statement in the text, true-false, multiple-choice, and completion exercises. These particular responses, however, differ from the checking of literal comprehension and the skill of selection and evaluation in that the fact which is being checked must be *remembered*. The child is supposed not only to understand the statement but also to fix it in his mind for recall purposes.

In all the examples given below the *responses were to be given without reference to the text*.

SCIENCE EXAMPLES

1. How does sleeping all the time help some animals to live all winter? Answer this question without looking it up.
2. Do you remember what are some of the plants that are used for making clothing? Write their names.
3. What did the book tell you about the way in which electricity is carried to our homes?

SOCIAL STUDIES EXAMPLES

1. Do you remember what is done with much of the milk sold by farmers in the Netherlands?
2. Can you recall where the first successful oil well was drilled?
3. Fill in the blanks below without rereading the chapter:
   The homeland of the Vikings was _____.
   (Other completion sentences follow)

ARITHMETIC EXAMPLES

1. Learn this multiplication table. Repeat it until you can remember all answers correctly.
2. Write the table for measurement of weight on a paper. Check with your book. Learn the correct number to any part you missed. Repeat until you can remember all parts of the table correctly.

What Can the Teachers Do to Develop Ability to Recall Reading Content?

As in the case of the other study skills, learning how to remember what one reads should not be left to chance. Just because children are frequently asked to give memory responses in textbooks doesn't necessarily mean that they know the best ways of fixing in mind the facts called for.

First Grade

Once children begin working with printed symbols, the teacher may provide frequent opportunities for them to fix in mind what they read during the process of reading, and to make simple explanations of what to do in trying to remember a certain item or certain items. For example, during the process of oral reading, the teacher may say something like this: "Now, *that* sentence is important. Let's think about it for a second and try to remember it. I'm going to ask you about it later."

The too frequent practice of questioning children verbally in order to check their remembrance of content may be supplemented by other interesting activities which serve the same purpose. One way to vary the question-answer response is for the teacher to place words or phrases in the wall chart which answer questions based on the selection. She then asks the questions one by one and requests different children to answer different questions by finding and reading the appropriate word or phrase in the wall chart. Cards may contain the words *swim, fly, run, crawl;* the pupils are asked to hold up the right card in answer to such questions as "What do fishes do?" To add variety the teacher may write the answers on the chalkboard and call upon different children to underline the correct answer to each question asked.

For additional recall activities suitable for first grade see "Maintenance and Practice Activities," page 566.

Second and Third Grades

In second and third grades there are numerous ways of giving children experience in remembering what they have read. At this level they may continue many of the activities initiated during the first grade period but applied to more difficult content.

In addition, pupils may engage in recall activities in which they give oral or written reports based on facts remembered, compile facts from memory, verify recall of facts, and so on.

See page 566, "Maintenance and Practice Activities," for additional suggestions suitable for second and third grades.

Fourth, Fifth, and Sixth Grades

It is in the middle grades that teachers should actually establish procedures that will serve the individual through his high school and college days in fixing the quantities of information that he will wish to grasp and hold clearly in mind as he prepares himself for his life's profession or vocation. Children should be given experiences in using different methods of remembering what is read, until each one finds the method which personally serves him best.

MEMORIZING TECHNIQUES

As a teacher or prospective teacher, you, the reader, probably were never given instruction in how to remember what you read. As you passed through high school or college, however, you very likely developed techniques of your own for, let us say, fixing in mind information that you thought you might need in passing a test. Perhaps you began using some one or a combination of these procedures: picking out important points as you read and pausing to fix them in mind, outlining and memorizing the outline, taking notes and fixing them in mind, writing a summary and memorizing the summary, underlining sections of text and reviewing the underlined sections.

A canvas of techniques which adults successfully use in preparing to remember information gleaned from the printed page reveals the procedures indicated above. Since such techniques are helpful to adults, why shouldn't children be taught to use them? After having practice in using all these procedures, they may later choose the technique of their personal preference or the one that they find most suitable for a particular purpose and a particular type of subject matter.

PSYCHOLOGICAL AIDS

Another aid to middle grade children is that of informing them about some of the things that psychologists have learned concerning recall: association, delayed recall, and the "whole" method versus the "parts" method of memorizing.

ASSOCIATION. First, what advantage can some simple information about the use of association have? It may be explained to children that it is much easier to remember a fact that has "handles on it" than one that is entirely bare. Facts in reading text are surrounded with "handles"— that is, with details associated with the facts. The explanation might be followed with an application; for example, the pupils in one class were asked to read two paragraphs which contained details about limestone. They were told to read for the purpose of fixing in their minds the principal ingredient of limestone. The first paragraph in the text told how limestone can be formed from corals and tiny shells which turn into *minerals* resulting in limestone. The second paragraph told about the limestone "icicles" in a cave, and that these were formed by *minerals* washed in at these spots by water. Through careful reading and discussion, associations were built up with details about the *mineral* ingredient that the children could turn to mentally in recalling information to answer the question, "What is the chief material in limestone?" The answer *minerals* had been fundamentally embedded in and surrounded with "handles" in both paragraphs, and these handles could be very useful in pulling the main fact back into mind.

DELAYED RECALL. The effect of delayed recall may be discussed with upper grade children also, and experiments may be tried out; for example, the teacher may ask the pupils to try recalling something they have just learned, then test them on it a week later, a month later, and so on until recall is perfect. The conclusion to be reached is that information which they wish to remember should be recalled periodically and not "crammed in" just one night before an examination.

THE "WHOLE" VERSUS "PARTS" METHOD. Children in upper grades might also be told about psychological experiments with the "whole" and "parts" methods of memorizing. Which method is better was controversial for a long time, but the majority of recent studies favor the "whole" method. In using the "whole" method, the individual repeats an entire poem or block of information, or outline or summary, rather than repeating one line or one fact at a time.

The pupils may experiment by using a different method in memorizing each of two comparable blocks of information, as in the example below:

Vitamin B₂	*Vitamin C*
Helps me grow	Helps me grow
Helps keep me strong	Helps keep me healthy
Helps me build strong body cells	Keeps my gums and teeth healthy
Helps me have steady nerves	Keeps my blood vessels strong and healthy

Pupils may time themselves in the use of each method and test themselves at that time—and later for delayed recall—to decide which method was most effective.

Suggestions for additional recall activities for the middle grades as well as for the primary grades will be found under "Maintenance and Practice Activities," pages 566–67. These are samples only for the teachers' use in reconverting them to the needs of her pupils and the materials with which they are working.

Locating Information

This growth area is better known than any of the other study skill areas. Even so, much improvement can be made in equipping elementary children with the various skills in the location constellation.

The reader no doubt has heard of such incidents as the one in which the college librarian announced that she and her staff had to spend most of their time during the first month of the fall semester in teaching freshmen how to find things in the library; or of the social studies teacher who had to stop teaching his own subject for a week while he taught his high school students how to use the location skills. Much evidence of inadequacies at higher levels points to the fact that a better job could be done in teaching the location skills in the elementary grades.

In this day of wide reading, both the prospective teacher and the teacher in service are well aware of the fact that authors of books in all content fields, as well as present-day teachers themselves, frequently ask pupils to search for information in many different sources. No examples are needed to reinforce this point.

The study-skill area of locating information is very complex. The constellation of location skills embraces many items, such as those enumerated under the headings below. And all of these items need to be developed and practiced.

Primary Grades

Foundation should be laid in the primary grades for the use of all location skills. The skills listed below are appropriate at this level. Many advanced third graders, however, will be able to participate in some of the activities suggested for children in the later grades.

Finding Page Numbers

Location skills should be introduced functionally and given functional practice in so far as possible. The need for finding page numbers usually occurs several times each day and is the easiest of the location skills to introduce. In beginning first grade, the teacher may write the number of the page to be found on the chalkboard as she says it, and then ask the children to match the number in their books. This procedure may also be used later when the number of the page is of a higher denomination than the children are able to read.

While in the early stages, pupils enjoy seeing how quickly they can find each of a series of numbers which the teacher reads orally and if necessary writes on the chalkboard for matching purposes.

In second and third grades a variation in practice may be provided by writing on the chalkboard several numbers, which the children then write in a column on the left side of their papers. The class is divided into two groups, and asked to see how quickly they can find and write on their papers the name of the story that begins on each of these pages. The group whose members finish writing all the titles first wins.

As pupils become increasingly proficient in reading numbers they should be encouraged continuously to make use of numbers on pages in all their reading, study, and reference activities.

Finding Specific Phrases or Sentences in Context

A specific phrase or sentence may be found quickly to prove an answer, to settle a disagreement, to emphasize a particular fact, or to take a quick look again at something to be remembered.

Children enjoy the activity of finding a word or phrase in answer to "Who, What, and Where" questions, as "Who was Happy?" (A little black dog.) "What did Judy give to Happy?" (A bone.) "Where did Happy bury the bone?" (Behind the garage.)

Using Titles

The concept of titles may be introduced during chart work. Sometimes before, sometimes after reading a chart the teacher may say something to this effect, "Let's give this story a title. What would be a good name for it?" Thus children may have opportunities to compose titles before reading them in a book. In working with content in books the word *title* should always be used, as "Read the title of the story." After a selection has been read, the teacher may take time occasionally to discuss the appropriateness of the title, and to ask the children if they can think of a better one.

Recognizing Chapters

Learning to recognize chapters or units in a book should be introduced as early as these subdivisions occur in books with which the children are working. Early readers, science books, and social studies books often mark the introduction of a new topic by an entire introductory page, a double-page illustration, or a page of colored paper bearing the title of the new topic. In all such cases it is advisable for the teacher to take time to have the children read the name of the new topic and to explain why it is so marked.

Using Tables of Contents

The table of contents may be introduced when the children meet a new topical division in a book they are reading. After having pupils read the title of the new unit, the teacher may have them turn to the table of contents, find the title there, and then read the names of the selections that come under the title. They may check the page number given for the title and some of the selections by turning to the pages indicated to see if the selections really are on the pages as stated.

Whenever the children are about to read a new chapter or unit they may be asked to examine the section heading, discuss what they might expect to find under this heading, turn back to the table of contents and read the titles under the heading. The table of contents should also be used whenever pupils are searching for stories or informative selections about a topic.

Alphabetizing

The first grade teacher usually has pupils in her class who are at different stages of development in their familiarity with the alphabet. Some know the alphabet in order. Others do not even know the names of the letters. The letter names are usually picked up by those who do not know them as the teacher incidentally calls attention to letters in numerous situations: "There is a *c* at the beginning of *cap* and also at the beginning of *cat*." "Jack's name begins with *J* and Jane's name begins with *J* also" (writing *Jack* and *Jane* on the chalkboard), and so forth. Most authorities believe that pupils should learn all the letters by name during first grade.

The sequence of letters in the alphabet must be taught as a readiness activity for dictionary work. Perhaps some functional situation can be used in introducing sequence. For example, the teacher might ask help in preparing an alphabetical list of the names of children absent during the past month to send to the principal. As they have difficulty, she may ask a pupil who knows the alphabet to say it in order as she writes the letters on the chalkboard. The names of children who have been absent are then arranged through reference to the alphabet on the chalkboard. The teacher may show the children a telephone directory, a dictionary, her classbook, and so forth and explain the use of an alphabetical arrangement.

Practice Activities

Skill in using an alphabetical arrangement requires a variety of competencies, and much practice. If students can locate words in a dictionary quickly and easily, they will use a dictionary freely. If they have difficulty in finding words they probably won't bother to look them up. The most basic and most important dictionary skill is that of using an alphabetical arrangement rapidly and accurately. This requires much practice throughout the elementary grades.

Suggestions are given for many practice activities in the use of alphabetical arrangement at both primary and elementary levels in the latter section of this book, entitled "Maintenance and Practice Activities." See pages 567–69.

Picture Dictionaries

Dictionaries in which the entry words are pictured are useful in the primary grades. These are of two kinds, those prepared by the children in the classroom and those commercially prepared.

PICTURE DICTIONARIES PREPARED IN THE CLASSROOM

1. Teacher and pupils may make a wall dictionary for use in recognizing new words met in early reading material. (See page 179.)

2. They may make a class dictionary book. The teacher binds together large sheets of paper and attaches alphabet tabs to the edges of the sheets. As the children meet new picturable words the teacher has them find the place in the class dictionary where the word should appear and the teacher manuscripts it on the page. The children then draw or find a picture to illustrate the word, and this is pasted in the dictionary at the appropriate place. The book is left in a readily available place, and the pupils refer to it for help in word recognition and spelling. This plan may be used also in connection with the special vocabulary of a unit or textbook topic, such as "Farm Animals" or "The Sky Above Us."

3. Pupils may make individual dictionaries. Each child may provide himself with a loose-leaf notebook with alphabetical tabs pasted on the leaf-edges. He keeps a record in this book of words that he does not recall in reading or know how to spell in writing. The nouns and verbs are illustrated with drawings or pictures cut from magazines. A pictured label is used for unpicturable words; for example, if *are* is the troublesome word a picture showing children skipping rope may be accompanied with the label, "These children are skipping rope." When the child looks for *are* in the *a* section of this dictionary, he finds the labelled picture, reads through the label, and finds *are* which he identifies from the label.

4. Alphabetical card files may be built up by the children as a group or individually. A cheese box makes a good container for 3 x 5 cards, some of which may be indexed by pasting alphabet tabs on them. An individual child or a group may write troublesome words on the cards, picture them, and insert them in their respective alphabetical positions in the file for future reference.

PICTURE DICTIONARIES PREPARED COMMERCIALLY

Commercially prepared picture dictionaries are having wide usage in primary grades. If such a dictionary is available, the teacher should explain its use to the children, use it for some of the alphabetical practice activities, and encourage children to turn to it frequently for self-help reference.

Many picture dictionaries are published. A few of them are mentioned below.

Courtis, Stuart, and Garnette Watters, *Illustrated Golden Dictionary*. New York: Simon & Schuster, Inc., 1951.

Guild, Marion, and Ruth Leder, *My Picture Dictionary*. New York: Maxton Publishers, Inc., 1949.

MacBean, Dilla W., *Picture Book Dictionary*. Chicago: Children's Press, Inc., 1952.

Moore, Lilian, *A Child's First Picture Dictionary*. New York: Wonder Books, 1948.

Oftedahl, Laura, and Nina Jacobs, *My First Dictionary*. Grosset & Dunlap, Inc., 1948.

O'Donnell, Mabel, and Willmina Townes, *Words I Like to Read and Write*. White Plains, N. Y.: Harper & Row, Publishers, 1954.

Parke, Margaret B., *Young Reader's Color-Picture Dictionary for Reading, Writing and Spelling*. Illustrated by Cynthia and Alvin Koehler. New York: Grosset & Dunlap, Inc., 1958.

Reed, Mary, and Edith Osswald, *My Little Golden Dictionary*. New York: Simon & Schuster, Inc., 1949.

Scott, Alice, and Stella Center, *A Picture Dictionary for Boys and Girls*. Garden City, N. Y.: Garden City Publishing Co., Inc., 1949.

Walpole, Ellen Wales, and Mary Reed, *The Golden Dictionary*. New York: Simon & Schuster, Inc., 1944.

Watters, Garnette, and Stuart Courtis, *The Picture Dictionary for Children*. New York: Grosset & Dunlap, Inc., 1939, 1945, 1948.

Wright, Wendell W., and Helene Laird, *The Rainbow Dictionary*. New York: The World Publishing Company, 1949.

Contacts with Encyclopedias, Atlases, World Almanacs

Children at the primary level are not expected to make direct use of these general sources of information. They should, however, become acquainted with the nature of such references and with their respective uses. Contacts with these references frequently may be provided through teacher demonstration when a need arises. For example, Tom brought in an amphibian which he said was a frog. Some of the children said it was a toad. Miss Drake borrowed two encyclopedias from an upper grade classroom, one with *F* on the shelfback and the other with *T*. She explained the function of encyclopedias, demonstrated how she could find *toads* and *frogs*, respectively, read the information to the children, showed them the pictures, and let them arrive at their own conclusion in the light of the encyclopedic information. Frequent contacts with atlases and world almanacs may be given in a similar fashion.

Intermediate Grades

In the fourth, fifth, and sixth grades pupils should use all skills developed in the primary grades with high proficiency. In addition, they should learn at this time to use with ease all location skills that are needed by high school and college students, and to develop permanent habits of using these skills whenever they may serve a purpose.

Using Parts of Books

The use of parts of books, usually taught in the middle grades, embraces recognition of copyright data, preface, introduction, glossary, and index.

With the present emphasis upon critical reading the *date that a book was copyrighted* often is an important item to know.

1. When the occasion arises show the children where the copyright date can be found in a book. Follow with practice in which they find

and report orally or in writing the latest copyright date of several books. They may also report the name of the individual or company who holds the copyright in each case.

2. When a new book is used for the first time, call attention to the *preface* or *foreword*. Explain that if a preface or foreword is written by the author its purposes usually are to give an overview of the book, to set forth its objectives from the author's viewpoint, and, sometimes, to give acknowledgments. If the preface is written by the editor or a person other than the editor it usually presents an evaluation of the book.

Have the children read the preface or foreword at hand to check and discuss the information given above. Practice may follow by using a similar procedure with other books.

3. Glossary and index procedures will be discussed below under "Dictionary skills." Index also will be discussed under a separate heading.

Using Dictionary Skills

The most extensive achievement in location skills to be realized at this level is the thorough establishment of the entire constellation of dictionary skills. These skills should be introduced through functional situations, if possible. Each different skill, however, should be given planned practice.

ALPHABETIZING

Alphabetizing skills should be extended to include: (1) locating a letter quickly by its position in the alphabet, rather than going through the alphabet one letter at a time; (2) locating words by examining the total alphabetical arrangement within the word.

Additional activities for use in giving practice in locating a letter quickly by its position in the alphabet are given on pages 568–69. These activities are extensions of those suggested for primary grades.

Working with the alphabetical arrangement within a word is a new skill. It may be introduced as suggested below.

After the children have had some practice in finding words by the use of the initial letter, the next step is to develop the short cuts of (first) the ability *to find a word in glossary or dictionary by use of the first two letters* and (later) by the *use of the first three letters,* and so on until the alphabetical arrangement within an entire word is noted. These are factors in the ability *to use a glossary and dictionary effectively.*

For example, in looking up the word *guitar,* the children should be told not to search all the way through the *g's* but to look at once through the section where *g* is followed by *u.*

Following this—as with a word like *strait*—the children may be told to turn immediately to the section of *s* words in which *s* is followed by *t* and then to turn quickly to the section of *st* words where the *st* is followed by *r*.

After introduction, practice activities may be used. The teacher will, of course, use these suggestions merely as examples for preparing activities of her own based on content with which the children are working. See pages 568–69 for suggestions.

USING GUIDE WORDS

It is usually advisable to introduce guide words in connection with the glossary of one of the textbooks that the children are using and then transfer the skill to dictionary practice.

As an example of an introduction, consider that *ridge* and *Sweden* are guide words on a glossary page of a reader which the children are using. The teacher may call the children's attention to the guide words at the top of each page in the glossary. Finally she may pause to discuss a certain page with *ridge* at the top of the left hand column and the word *Sweden* at the top of the right hand column. Through discussion she may lead the children to discover that the left hand guide word represents the first word which appears on a page, and that the right hand guide word represents the last word which appears on a page. They may then check this information by examining several pages.

Practice activities for use in improving skill in using Guide Words will be found on page 569.

USING PRONUNCIATION AIDS

Using diacritical markings, a key to pronunciation, syllabication, and accent marks were discussed in Chapter 8 on pages 229–40. Children's attention should be called to the use of all of these aids in working out pronunciations.

Respellings. Respelled words in a dictionary should be explained at the intermediate grade level, and, if necessary, practice in using respellings should be given.

In introducing respellings the teacher may explain to the children that when they look up a word in a dictionary they will find, after the word, a second spelling in parentheses. This second spelling tells them how to pronounce the word, by showing the syllables, the accent mark, and the sounds of the vowels. But in some cases the second spelling is different from the one used in the text of the story, for example, *English* (ing′ glish), *pygmy* (pig′ mi), *dense* (dens), *curds* (kurds). The children should be urged always to look for the spelling in parentheses as an aid in working out the pronunciation.

Practice activities for use in working with respellings will be found on page 569.

Preferred spelling. The teacher may explain that when there are two acceptable spellings of a word, both are listed in the dictionary. The first one, however, is the *preferred* spelling. Have the pupils find the *preferred* spelling for several words, such as *center, counselor, honor, meager, visor.*

USING MEANING AIDS

Finding definitions. Children need to be given considerable practice in choosing the right definition of a word as used in a certain context. Introduce the use of this skill when confusion arises concerning a new multiple-meaning word met in an immediate reading situation. As an example, the children in one group read that "The Colonists used candles to illuminate their homes." There was disagreement in regard to the meaning of illuminate. The teacher explained that several definitions of a word are often given in dictionaries, and that they need to select the one that best fits the sentence in which it is used. She then had the children turn to the dictionary definitions for *illuminate* where they found five numbered definitions. All the definitions were read, discussion followed, and the definition "to make light" was selected as the most appropriate one.

Activities to use in practicing the selection of the right definition will be found on pages 569–70.

Finding synonyms and antonyms. Locating and understanding synonyms in the dictionary might be introduced by the teacher in some such way as this: Frequently you will find the abbreviation "Syn." following the definitions of a word. This abbreviation stands for "Synonym," or another word or words which mean the same or nearly the same as the word being defined. It will help you to build your vocabulary if you note these synonyms.

The teacher may have the children look up a word such as *fortunate* and find its synonym *lucky.* They may then be asked to give a sentence containing *fortunate.* The sentence is written on the chalkboard. *Fortunate* is erased and *lucky* is written in its place. The teacher has the sentence read and discussed in terms of meaning when one word has replaced another.

331

A suggestion for giving practice in working with synonyms and antonyms will be found on page 570.

A suggestion for giving practice in working with synonyms and antonyms will be found on page 570.

USING AN INDEX

Introduction. This is a rather complicated skill. Its introduction should probably be delayed until most of the other skills discussed so far have been initiated and practiced.

In introducing this skill the teacher might use an index in the back of a textbook which the children are using. She might show them the index and give an explanation of this sort:

Most textbooks have an index. If you are looking for information in a textbook, you will save yourself a lot of time by using the index. You will also be able to find much more information through the use of the index. Usually not *all* information is given in any one chapter. Bits of information about a topic may be found here and there throughout the book, and only the index will tell you where.

Following this explanation the children may be asked questions in regard to different sections of the index which call their attention to its nature and use.

A sampling section of an index together with questions is offered as a suggestion.[29]

Rennet, 81
Reproduction, 290–298
  asexual, 295
  bisexual, 295
  budding, 290–291
  fertilization, 294
  fission or cell division, 290
  in flowering plants, 293–295
  mammals, 298
  by regeneration, 292–293
  sexual, 295
  with spores, 291, 292
  vegetative, 292
Reptiles, 280–281
Revolution of the earth, 31
Rhinoceros, 283
Rickets, 66
Rings of Saturn, 30
Rivers, "lost," 311
River systems, 331–333
Rockets, 10, 17
  Nike, 214
Rock extrusions, 309
Rock intrusion, 309
Rocks, 305, 306

Rocks (*cont.*)
  anthracite, 313
  bending and breaking of, 323–324
  collection of, 306
  cut by waves, 334
  hot springs and geysers, 313–315
  igneous, 307
  metamorphic, 312–313
  meteors (*see* Meteors)
  sedimentary, 309–311
  strata, 310
  using, 315–316
  weathering of, 333–334
Rock salt, 57
Rodents, 283
Root cuttings, 292
Roots of plants, 54
Rotation of the earth, 30–31
Rubber, synthetic, 246
Rubbish disposal, 121, 122
Rubies, 316
Ruminants, 284–285
Rural areas:
  disposal of wastes in, 114–115
  water supply in, 112

[29] From Ames, Maurice, Arthur O. Baker, and Joseph F. Leahy, *Science for Your Needs* (Englewood Cliffs, N. J.: Prentice-Hall, Inc., 1956), p. 361.

S

1. On what pages would you expect to find a general discussion of rocks?
2. How many subtopics are discussed under the general topic of *Rocks?*
3. Are the subtopics listed in order of their importance? In the order in which they appear in the book?
4. The authors had some plan in mind in listing the subtopics in a certain order. What do you think this plan was?
5. Write in order the first letter of the first word in each of the subtopics. Are these letters in alphabetic order?
6. Is there any reason why *metamorphic* should come before meteors? What is the reason?
7. If you are surprised to find *anthracite* listed under *Rocks,* where would you look to find out whether or not *anthracite* is a rock?
8. You read about sedimentary rocks on page 92. If you wish to find out more about sedimentary rocks in this book, where would you look?
9. In case you were interested in making a collection of rocks yourself where would you look?
10. After the subheading *meteors,* it says "*see* Meteors." Where would you look to "see Meteors"?
11. In the upper left-hand column you will find the general heading of *Salt.* Under this heading is the subheading *rock.* Do you think this heading is one you should look up if you were trying to find all information in the book about rocks? If you're not sure, how could you find out?

Practice suggestions for additional work with indexes are given on page 570.

Finding key words. A more advanced skill in using an index is to select key words under which to look for information about a topic. The teacher may introduce this skill by writing a topic such as the following on the chalkboard: "How is cheese made in Switzerland?" She may then ask the children to find two words under which they might look to find the information asked for. Explanation may follow to the effect that words in a topic, such as *cheese* and *Switzerland,* which lead to information are called *key words.* The pupils should follow through by actually searching for information under these heads. (See additional suggestions, page 570.)

Dictionaries for the Intermediate Grades

Every elementary classroom should be equipped with one unabridged dictionary which catalogs all the words and their important uses in the English language. Webster's *New International Dictionary* and Funk and Wagnall's *New Standard Dictionary* are the most widely used of the unabridged dictionaries.

It is advantageous for each pupil to have in his possession one of the abridged dictionaries prepared especially for the middle grades. If he has a dictionary at his seat he is more apt to use it frequently.

It is advisable to use the same unabridged dictionary with all children. There is considerable difference in the diacritical marking of words and in the manner of representing the *schwa* sound. For teaching purposes, the particular system advocated in the dictionary that the children have should be the one explained and used. If, however, the children have access to an unabridged dictionary published by a different publisher they will encounter a system of markings that differ from their abridged dictionaries. This would offer a good opportunity to have them examine the pronunciation key in each of the two types of dictionaries and note their differences.

Some of the several dictionaries appropriate for elementary and junior high school grades are:

Elementary Dictionary for Boys and Girls. New York: American Book Company.

Funk and Wagnalls Standard Junior School Dictionary, Charles B. Funk, ed. New York: Harper & Row, Publishers.

Thorndike-Barnhart Beginning Dictionary, Edward L. Thorndike and Clarence L. Barnhart, eds. Chicago: Scott, Foresman & Company.

Thorndike-Barnhart Junior Dictionary, Edward L. Thorndike and Clarence L. Barnhart, eds. Chicago: Scott, Foresman & Company.

Webster's Elementary Dictionary. Springfield, Mass.: G. & C. Merriam Co.

Webster Junior Dictionary, Springfield, Mass : G. & C. Merriam Co.

The Winston Dictionary for Schools, Thomas K. Brown and William D. Lewis, eds. Philadelphia: The John C. Winston Co.

Pubished Aids in Teaching Dictionary Skills

The dictionary skills are so important that several aids have been published to help teachers teach these skills and to help children learn them. Helpful dictionary references for the teacher are:

Dolch, E. W., *Building the Dictionary Habit.* Chicago: Scott, Foresman & Company.

Hobbs, Valerie, "The Dictionary as a Spelling Aid," *Elementary English Review,* Vol. 15 (1938), 268–69.

Kelly, V. H., "The Use of the Dictionary in the Elementary Grades," *Elementary English Review,* Vol. 13 (1936), 17–24.

Trabue, M. R., "Special Tools that Facilitate Expression: Use of the Dictionary," *Forty-third Yearbook of the National Society for the Study of Education,* Part II, pp. 187–93. Chicago: University of Chicago Press, 1944.

How to Use Your Dictionary. Bulletin to accompany the *Thorndike-Century Beginning Dictionary.* Chicago: Scott, Foresman & Company. This bulletin contains seventy lessons on how to use the dictionary. These are in two levels for Grades 4 and 5.

Murray, C. Merrill, "Selecting an Elementary School Dictionary," *Elementary English,* Vol. 34 (May 1957), 293–97.

Using an Encyclopedia

Beginning at fourth grade level children should learn to use encyclopedias independently in research work. It is advisable to introduce and give practice on encyclopedia skills at a time when information which an encyclopedia contains is needed. At such a time some such procedure as the one described below may be used.

The teacher may show the children a set of encyclopedias and explain somewhat as follows:

An encyclopedia, like the dictionary, is a book of facts. But whereas the dictionary or a glossary gives facts about *words*—their pronunciation, meaning, and so on—the encyclopedia gives facts about *topics*—that is, about the things we talk about and need to know about. Encylopedias are very valuable sources of information that you will need to use all your lives.

In the encyclopedia, as in the dictionary, the topics are arranged in alphabetical order. To find out about anything, one must know under what topic to look for it. The work you have just done in finding the key word in a sentence or question will help you in using the encyclopedia.

The teacher may let the children handle an encyclopedia, noticing its use of topical headings, the alphabetical arrangement, and so on. The teacher may suggest topics in the individual volumes being examined by different children which may be located.

The teacher may explain guide letters as follows:

Because the encyclopedia contains so much information, it usually is made into a set of books rather than into just one book. Each book is called a "volume" in the set.

To make it easy to find the volume in which a topic appears, the guide letters are printed on the back of each volume. (If you have a set of encyclopedias, show the children the first volume, calling their attention to the letter or letters on the shelfback.) For example, if you saw the letters *A–E* on the back of a volume, you would know that topics beginning with *A, B, C, D,* and *E* were included in that volume. (Show another volume and discuss the guide letters. Let the children suggest some topics that might be found in that volume.) Sometimes a volume includes only topics beginning with a single letter. In that case, only one letter appears on the back.

If a set of encyclopedias is available, have the children see how quickly they can find such words as *lions, coyote, insects, goatherd, turtles, raccoons,* and so on, using the guide letters.

GUIDE WORDS ON A PAGE

The teacher may say something like this:

After you have found the right volume, you want to be able to find the topic quickly. To help you do this, encyclopedias have guide words at the top of each page. (Show the children pages with guide words, and let them scan the pages hastily.) How do these compare with the guide words in a Glossary? In the dictionary?

Have the children practice finding topics that you suggest, using the guide words. This gives additional practice in the ability to make use of topical headings, which is one of the essential factors in using encyclopedias.

Following this preliminary experience, expanded practice may be given in finding and using information needed in furthering individual and group interests.

The index in the back of encyclopedias should be introduced and practice in its use given after children have had some experience in using an index in some of their textbooks.

A suggestion for practice in deciding upon the volume in which to look for a topic will be found on page 571.

Available Encyclopedias

Several suitable encyclopedias for use in elementary grades are available. *The Golden Book Encyclopedia* [30] is an eight-volume set designed for use in developing readiness for using the more complete reference sets. The publishers claim that it can be used as early as third grade.

Other widely-used junior encyclopedias in elementary and high schools are Compton's *Pictured Encyclopedia*,[31] *Britannica Junior*,[32] and *The World Book*.[33] Each of these contains a complete set of volumes and embraces all of the characteristics of a set of adult encyclopedias.

Our Wonderful World [34] and the *Book of Knowledge* [35] are useful reference books for elementary children. The content of these books, however, is organized by topics rather than alphabetically. These books are accompanied with complete indexes which, of course, are valuable in learning reference skills.

A helpful film strip to show the pupils is entitled *How to Use an Encyclopedia*, published by Popular Science Publishing Company, New York.

Library Skills

The library is serving a greater function now than ever before, both in connection with school activities and with life activities outside of school. Realizing the current values of libraries to children, many school systems are at present providing a central library with a trained librarian in each of their elementary schools. Such a provision, among its many advantages, offers elementary pupils an opportunity to learn about library skills and to use them often enough so that these skills may become firmly established before entrance into junior high school.

Even if a teacher is not fortunate enough to have a school library available to her pupils, she usually can have a library in her classroom and also can make use of a public library. Regardless of the situation every effort should be made to establish strong library skills which will enable pupils to make effective use of library facilities.

[30] New York: Simon and Schuster, Inc.
[31] F. E. Compton Company, Compton Building, 1000 N. Dearborn St., Chicago 10, Ill.
[32] *Britannica Junior*, 425 N. Michigan Ave., Chicago 11, Ill.
[33] Field Enterprises, Educational Division, Merchandise Mart Plaza, Chicago 54, Ill.
[34] *Our Wonderful World*, Chicago: Spencer Press, Inc.
[35] *Book of Knowledge*, New York: Grolier Society.

Care of Books

Early in first grade the teacher may show children how to open a new book and how to turn the pages. She may lead a discussion designed to instill an attitude of respect for books and to develop a desire to keep books clean and unmarked. This type of discussion will bear repeating many times throughout all the elementary grades.

Behavior in a Library

It is desirable to take children on trips to the public library, and in later grades, to send them to the library in groups or as individuals. While the younger children may do no more than listen to story-telling and look at picture books, the older ones may do some selecting, reading, and withdrawing of books. In any of these cases they should be taught to practice good library behavior.

Many teachers have found it helpful to have the pupils compose a chart of library rules which they read to refresh their memories before each trip to the library. An example of such a chart is as follows:

OUR LIBRARY RULES
Wash your hands before going to the library.
Enter the library quietly.
Listen carefully if the librarian talks to you.
Do not talk, whisper, or read aloud while in the library.
Handle books carefully.
If you take a book out be sure to return it on time.

Organization of Books

Children should learn early that books are grouped in libraries. Some activities directed toward this end are as follows:

1. They may group books in their own classroom by topics, such as fairy stories, true stories about people, animal stories, science books, history books, health books and so on.

2. They may prepare labels for the different classifications.

3. They may draw a floor diagram of their school library or the children's room in a public library and show where different kinds of books are kept.

4. They may read and discuss the Dewey Decimal System and its function from a listing of numbers representing ten classes of this system which the teacher writes on the chalkboard or on a chart.

000–099 General Works	500–599 Science
100–199 Philosophy	600–699 Useful Arts
200–299 Religion	700–799 Fine Arts
300–399 Social Science	800–899 Literature
400–499 Language	900–999 History

(Note: Some school and public libraries do not use the Dewey Decimal System, but the majority of them and almost all college libraries do, so children may as well become acquainted with it in the elementary grades.)

5. Perhaps advanced children can label groups of books in their classrooms with appropriate designations.

Using a Card Catalog

The teacher may find a chalkboard diagram, similar to the one below, useful in introducing a card catalog.

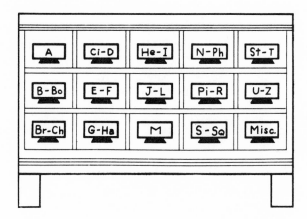

The nature of the card catalog and its use may be described in some such way as this:

You might think of a card catalog as a huge encyclopedia, each drawer representing a volume. Instead of containing pages, however, each drawer contains cards. Instead of giving you the information itself, the cards tell you in what book you can find the information.

The letter or letters on each of the drawers shown in the diagram tell you in which drawer you can find cards with names of authors, books, or topics beginning with the letter or letters shown.

If you wish to find the names of some books on the topic of *atoms,* you would of course look in the *A* drawer. If you wish to look up the names of books on *opossums,* you would look in the drawer marked *N–Ph* because the letter *O* comes between *N* and *P* and cards representing that letter would be included in the *N–Ph* drawer. If you are looking for the name of a person, you look for the first letter of his last name; for example, if you were looking for John Bakeless, you would look in the second drawer which contains cards falling between *B* and *Bo*.

The teacher should have the pupils write the letter or letters of the drawer in which they would find cards having to do with certain topics or persons as:

a. lumber _____
b. conservation _____
c. Panama _____
d. humus _____
e. sugar _____
f. Sam Houston _____

g. desert _____
h. furs _____
i. glaciers _____
j. weather _____
k. David Crockett _____
l. Daniel Boone _____

Reading Cards in a Card Catalog

This skill may be introduced through the use of a chalkboard diagram representing the three types of cards to be found in a card catalog.

Author Card	*Title Card*	*Subject Card*
532:4 Putnam, John A.	532:4 Cosmos rays.	532:4 Science
Cosmos rays.	Putnam, John A.	Putnam, John A.
Holton 1954	Holton 1954	Cosmos rays.
		Holton 1954

The teacher may explain each type of card and call attention to the name of the publisher and the date.

She may then erase the content of all three cards and have the pupils tell her what to write on each card using information given for other books, such as:

Library number—921.3; author—Mary Louise Strong; title—The Second World War; publisher—Southwick; Date 1948.

Additional activities in reading cards in a card catalog are as follows:

1. Take the children to a library. Show them a card catalog. Give them turns in finding the different types of cards for several books whose titles and authors are given to them.

2. Have the pupils write the different kinds of cards for certain books selected from the class supply.

3. Have the pupils catalog the library-type books in their classroom.

References Pertaining to Library Skills

Huus, Helen, "Libraries Bolster the Reading Program," *The Reading Teacher,* Vol. 14 (March 1961), 236–40.

Mott, Carolyn, and Leo B. Baisden, *The Children's Book on How to Use Books and Libraries*. New York: Charles Scribner's Sons, 1937.

Following Directions

Reading to follow directions is a fundamental skill needed in studying the content of all subjects. In arithmetic children must follow detailed and intricate directions for performing new processes, checking answers, and doing various things with examples and processes. In science they must read and carry out experiments and observations with high accuracy. In geography and history they are given directions for finding locations, tracing routes on maps, preparing time lines, reading graphs, and so on. In addition, practically all assignments in all subjects are given in the form of directions, most of which are printed.

Directions become even more prevalent, detailed, and complicated as children pass through high school and college. Many an assignment has been carried out incorrectly and many a test has been failed because a student has not read and carried out directions accurately.

Reading and following printed directions is a skill which lends itself to development as surely as do the other study skills. The development of this skill, however, often is more or less left to chance. Teachers would do well to work more directly for the development of this skill.

In early primary grades the teacher may frequently write directions for classroom work on the chalkboard, have the children read the directions orally, and tell in their own words exactly what they are going to do. At other times the pupils themselves may make up directions which the teacher writes on a chart. In either case, decision should be made later through group discussion in regard to how well the directions have been carried out.

As children encounter more complicated directions in textbooks, it is often advisable to have the directions read orally and discussed before carrying them out. If some children are having considerable trouble in carrying out directions, the textbook directions may be written on the chalkboard and read and discussed before the pupils read and follow the directions in their textbook itself.

In all situations in which children follow printed directions it is of the utmost importance that the work resulting from reading these directions be checked carefully, often through discussion and evaluation by the group. Children who have persistent trouble in following directions should have special practice in reading and carrying out sets of directions prepared by the teacher in keeping with their level of reading ability.

Some additional suggestions for giving help in following directions are provided on page 571.

Specialized Factors in Reading in
Different Subject Areas

The preceding pages have dealt with the common study skills with which pupils need to be equipped in order to do successful work in all content areas.

Now what about specialized factors, factors indigenous to different subjects? Are there particular factors to be considered in teaching pupils to read in each specific subject? The research summarized on pages 308–11 indicates that there are specialized factors, which include: (1) vocabulary, (2) special study skills.

Specialized Vocabulary

Every subject carries its own specialized vocabulary with it. This specialized vocabulary in each case seems to break down into four types of words. First, there are the readily identifiable words which all of us would agree have special significance in a certain subject matter field; for example, probably no one would dispute the fact that *magnets, terrarium, velocity* are peculiar to the subject of science; that *abolition, fortress, proclamation, allies* belong particularly to the field of history; that *fraction, cancellation,* and *divisor* are definitely arithmetic words; and that *hemisphere, continent,* and *equator* are special geography words. Special subject words of this type are not ordinarily met by children in reader stories. One reason why many children find reading in other subject fields difficult is because of their lack of concepts for these specialized meanings. Large numbers of children would profit by guided class discussion of such words in connection with their reading and study in the content fields.

Another type of special vocabulary word is the overlap word, the one which may be claimed in two subject fields. "Rain" and "rainfall" for example are very important words in geography, yet they also belong to the weather vocabulary, which is definitely in the realm of science. "Group" is important in social studies referring to a social group of people. "Group" may also be claimed in the arithmetic vocabulary because of its significance in giving the concept of an assemblage of numbers.

These overlap words which do not vary too much in their fundamental meaning from one subject to another give very little trouble. The real trouble-makers are the polysemantic words which mean something entirely different when used in different subject contexts. For example, consider the word *check*. In arithmetic, *check* may mean a blank form which

342   SKILL DEVELOPMENT

one fills in and presents at the bank when he wishes to draw some money on his account. In science, the child may be told to "check his experiment," meaning to prove it. In history he reads that a certain group of soldiers were able to "check the enemy," meaning that they were able to stop the progress of an oncoming attack. In geography he may read that the fields on a hillside look like "a great checkerboard"; and in literature he may read about a girl with "a checked gingham dress." While many children pick up these changed meanings incidentally as they occur in different subject contexts, others do not. The teacher who cultivates a sensitivity in herself to shifts of word meanings from one subject to another and who takes the trouble to inquire into her pupils' understanding of these words in different contexts will discover that much confusion exists in their minds, and that it is very worthwhile to help them to understand these distinctions.

Such work is particularly needed with multiple-meaning words whose meanings range from something very concrete to something very abstract. The word *bar* may be used to illustrate this type of word. Perhaps the first time the child encounters the word *bar* in print is when he reads an arithmetic problem such as this: "Mary bought a candy bar for 5 cents and Sue bought a candy bar for 5 cents. How much did the girls pay for the two bars of candy?" He has no difficulty in understanding this meaning because he has had much experience with candy bars, and to him, in this instance, *bar* means a long, narrow piece of candy.

Next the child may read a story in which some other child put a basket on "the handle bars of his bicycle" and used the basket as a receptacle for carrying his puppy. Again, the child will have no trouble with the word *bar,* for "handle bars" are concrete objects which he has seen and probably has used. In reading a selection on farming, he may have his first contact with the primary meaning of the noun *bar* when he reads that "the farmer pried up a large rock with a long iron bar." As a result of first-hand experiences, pictures, and context, he arrives at the generalization that a bar is a piece of material that has greater length in proportion to its breadth and thickness, and he easily grasps the meaning of *bar* when he meets it in text in which the word is used in this concept.

He may even understand the term "bar of music" when he encounters this phrase in a book, particularly if he has been well instructed in the subject of music. A "bar of music," however, is a bit less concrete than "a bar of candy" or "handle bars." Finally as the child progresses through the grades he reads in geography about a "sand bar"; in science, about a "bar magnet"; in arithmetic, about "a bar graph." In all these instances *bar* is becoming farther and farther removed from its primary meaning.

Finally, in social studies the child reads that someone was "behind the bars"; that a certain group "was barred because of religious prejudice"; that a thief was brought "to the bar of justice"; and eventually in literature at higher levels he reads Tennyson's "When I Have Crossed the Bar."

Who is going to help the pupil make the transition from one level of abstraction to another if it isn't the teacher—the teacher who is on the lookout for these different levels as they occur in all subject fields?

A fourth class of word meanings which should be considered in teaching reading in connection with different subject contexts are those innocuous little words which at first sight appear to have no specialized meanings whatsoever, but which suddenly bristle with a highly distinctive connotation when appearing in the context of some specific subject field. Consider *and* and *are* for example. In their reader, primary children may read that "Tom and Nan are in the car." In such common usage *and* is used as a simple connective and *are* means that the children exist in a certain place at that time. But when these same primary children turn to arithmetic text, they are immediately confronted with sentences like this: "2 and 2 are 4." In these arithmetic sentences "and" means "plus" and "are" means "equal." These common little words which take specialized meaning are snares and pitfalls in children's reading of books in the different subject areas.

The context of social studies, science, arithmetic, and even literature abound with specialized word meanings of these types. The skillful teaching of reading in the various areas demands abundant explanation of the meanings of words which are specialized in their primary meaning, and also of those which suddenly become specialized when they appear in different subject contexts.

Special Skills in Different Content Areas

As indicated on pages 308–309, research indicates that the reader uses distinctive skills when he reads different kinds of material for different purposes. Just what does this mean to the elementary teacher? The significance and application of this truth should be elucidated if its full impact is to be felt in the elementary school. While there are a few notable exceptions, by and large the elementary teacher of the past discharged her responsibility in teaching reading when she had taught her pupils to read stories in a reader and perhaps to use a workbook with exercises based on these stories. This is just a beginning in so far as skill development in reading is concerned. Basic instruction in reading serves well to develop the common elements of the reading process which are needed in all types of reading. This foundation is essential, but it remains for the teacher to provide additional direct and careful guidance in developing the specialized skills pupils need in reading in the different subject fields.

A few concrete examples will be given to illustrate the point made above. These examples are taken from books at the third or fourth grade levels as being representative of content which is of interest both to primary and intermediate teachers.

The first example was excerpted from a reader. It represents the interesting running-narrative type of material which makes up the bulk of content in the usual basic reader.

"The warm spring sunshine was coming in through the window of Sandy's room. Sandy opened his sleepy eyes and looked around.

He heard his father and mother talking downstairs. Then he heard his father get a pail of water from the well."

The story goes on to tell that this is Sandy's birthday; it tells about his presents, eliciting suspense in regard to a surprise present the nature of which is not revealed until the end of the story.

In pursuing such content a child reads on continuously and pleasantly just for the fun of following the plot of the story. In order to do this he needs to use appropriate eye-movements; to identify the word symbols; to glean meanings from groups of word symbols; to hold these meanings in mind, weaving all of them together into a total pattern aimed at story enjoyment. All these skills are important and basic, but the pupil needs to approach his science and geography and arithmetic reading in a different way.

In contrast to story content let's examine a typical sample of text in a third grade science book.

AIR HAS PRESSURE

This experiment will show that air has pressure.
1. Put one-half cup of water in a syrup can.
2. Heat the water until steam comes out of the opening for about one minute.
3. Remove the can from the stove.
4. Quickly put in the cork.
5. Set the can in a stream of cold air. What happens? Can you explain why it happened?

The child reads this text for the purpose of finding out how to conduct an experiment. It requires exact detailed reading. The pupil must recognize the pronunciation and meaning of every word. If he should confuse *steam* and *stream*, for example, this error alone would negate the entire experiment.

In this science text, the child must not only recognize words and meanings but must do something with the meanings after he gleans them from the printed symbols. He must hold the meaning of each direction in mind while he is performing it. When he has carried out all the directions, he is asked two questions in the text—not in regard to an incident described in a story but questions which cause him to reason, to summarize the results of his experiment, and to explain why those results took place.

Several processes are used here which are not required in narrative reading. The brighter children may make the adjustment independently, but the majority of children need to have explanations of differences concerning how they should work with this type of content and with other types of science text.

Geography text is different from narrative, also. Consider this sample paragraph:

Southwest of Philadelphia, areas of dense population are centered around two cities, Baltimore and Washington. You can see these cities best on the map on this page. Like the other great cities you have studied, Baltimore is a seaport. On page 62 is a picture of part of its harbor, which is the wide mouth of a little river flowing into Chesapeake Bay. It is an old city, started by a group of early settlers who came from England. Turn back to the map on page 45 and look at the land which had been settled in this region by the year 1700. There was a fringe of settlement all around the shores of Chesapeake Bay.

Even this limited sample gives indication of the fact that geography text has its own characteristics in so far as reading is concerned. In reading such text, the child must not only grasp detailed facts as he goes along but he must frequently leave the text which he is reading to carry out a direction to examine a map or picture elsewhere in the book. These examinations in turn involve the use of a cluster of skills needed in picture reading and of another cluster of skills needed in reading and interpreting maps. To complicate the situation further, the problem of a time concept enters into the total situation. After finding the references in each case, making use of the required set of skills in examining it, contrasting information obtained in terms of two time settings—after all this, the child must return to the text which he was originally reading and fit his newly found ideas into the total import of the paragraph. Quite different is this from reading stories in readers!

When children first begin to make use of content in geographies and social studies books, the teacher should conduct reading lessons with them until they become accustomed to the skills required in working effectively with this new and different kind of text. Such reading lessons should be initiated at any level with children who have not mastered the techniques of working successfully with such text, and they should be continued throughout the grades with children who are especially in need of such help.

Arithmetic text is unique in that it embraces types of reading content which differ markedly from narrative reading and from the text of geography, history, and science. It is more compact than text in any of the other fields. It is complicated also by having numerical symbols woven into the sentence along with word symbols, and every one of these symbols, whether word or numerical, must be taken into consideration. Detailed directions and exact explanations must be understood and used; and problems, calling for a careful weighing of relationships and a high level of reasoning, must be solved.

One type of arithmetic content—the problem-solving type—will be used as an example for discussion.

Four of Edith's friends will help her make things for a party. The five girls have 100 paper lanterns, 36 paper hats, and 36 baskets to make. This is an average of how many things for each girl?

This type of content requires a first reading for the purpose of visualizing the scene or situation as a whole—for getting the picture of the girls working together to prepare paper lanterns, hats, and baskets for a party. The reading skills used in this first reading are comparable to those which the child has been accustomed to using in reading and understanding a narrative paragraph in a story book. This will not be difficult for the child, but he should have his attention called to the need of getting the mental picture of a problem first of all, and should be given some guidance in doing this through such questions as: "What did you see when you read that paragraph?" "If you were to paint a picture to illustrate the paragraph, what would you put in the picture?"

Concentrating on the significance of a question at the end of a problem paragraph is a distinctive skill needed in solving arithmetic problems. Seldom does a child encounter a question in the text while reading narrative material; if he does, the question has probably been asked for rhetorical effect, and it doesn't matter much whether he answers it or not. In problem solving everything depends upon the question. Children need to have considerable experience in reading problems just for the purpose of finding out "What the question asks you?" and telling in their own words what the question directs them to do.

Other distinct and more complex skills are involved in rereading the problem to analyze it into elements necessary for solution. This process involves selection and evaluation in picking out facts and relationships pertinent to a "frame of reference," which in this case is the question. The question must be held in mind while rereading the entire paragraph and used as the guide in determining the relevancy and relationships of details. The reading skills needed in this aspect of problem solving can be developed and strengthened by experience in rereading problems for the purpose indicated above, accompanied by pointed discussion and skillful questions on the part of a teacher, who is herself aware of the distinctive reading skills involved.

Finally, the arithmetical process must be selected, again in terms of "what the question asks you to do" and of the various other considerations which were "weighed in the balance" during the rereading of the problem. Then the child is ready to write the numbers on paper and do the computation.

Up to this very last step, the work has been concerned largely with reading skills, and many of these reading skills are of a type that are not taught in connection with basic reading instruction or with any of the other subjects.

Of course the best preparation for solving concrete arithmetic problems is that of having many first-hand experiences in which such problems arise. Experiences in the use of the thinking processes necessary in solving problems are of fundamental importance. Regardless of such experiences, however, the majority of children have trouble when they encounter the more abstract situation of working problems in which word and number symbols replace first-hand experience. When such difficulty arises, probably children would profit by reading problems without making computations. Such reading, however, should proceed under skillful guidance directed toward development and continuous growth in skills of the type suggested above.

Adjusting to Different Patterns of Content

Different patterns of content call for different approaches and skills. The major patterns found in elementary textbooks in content areas are mentioned below. Teachers would be able to improve both the reading achievement and the content achievement of their pupils greatly if they would help them to identify these patterns, to adjust to the different patterns, and to develop the reading skills necessary in working with each one of them.

LITERATURE

Reading short stories
Reading novels (Example: *Lad, A Dog* by Albert Payson Terhune)
Reading drama
Reading biography

Reading well-written, interesting, informative material (Example: *Book of Marvels* by Richard Halliburton)

Reading poems of different types: lyric, elegiac, ballads, light-verse, free verse

SCIENCE

Reading the classification pattern in which certain likenesses and differences are pointed out in regard to certain things classified by scientists under one heading (rocks, animals, minerals, and so on)

Reading the explanation of a technical process (How the telephone works, for example)

Reading and interpreting diagrams

Reading and carrying out directions for an experiment

Reading content giving several examples leading up to a principle or generalization

Reading problem-solving information to find out how a problem was solved scientifically

Reading detailed information heavily packed with science facts

SOCIAL STUDIES

Reading pictures

Reading maps, globes, atlases

Reading cause and effect content

Reading content in which comparisons are made

Reading content in which sequence of events is given

Reading content in which dates are associated with events

Reading critically material in which (a) different viewpoints are expressed, (b) facts are mixed with opinions, (c) propaganda is used

ARITHMETIC

Reading numbers

Reading graphs

Reading tables

Interpreting detailed explanations of new processes

Following directions for using a new process

Reading problems for the following purposes: (a) to visualize the setting, (b) to answer the question, "What am I to find?" (c) to answer the question, "What facts am I given to work with?" (d) to answer the question "What process or processes do I need to use?"

Measuring Achievement in the Study Skills

Informal Tests

Informal tests which the teacher prepares herself in connection with children's daily reading in the content subjects are extremely valuable.

Many patterns for preparing tests to check pupils' ability to make use of the common study skills will be found among the practice activities suggested on pages 563–71. Some of the patterns found in practice activities given on pages 569–70 may be used in testing understanding of specialized vocabulary in a special subject.

After explaining different patterns of writing in a particular subject field, children's ability to identify these patterns may be checked by having them write the name of different patterns, and opposite each name, the pages in a subject book on which this pattern appears, as:

Classification: 101–106; 162–68; 201–205.
Technical Process: 92–96; 126–30; 176–80.

The teacher may prepare upon different occasions a ten-question test of content on a few pages representing each of two patterns of text in a certain subject, and compare the results to find in which pattern more instruction and practice is needed. Following instruction and practice in reading the pattern on which help was needed, a similar test may be given in reading that particular pattern and results again compared.

Standardized Tests

Very few standardized tests have been devised for use in measuring growth in study skills at the elementary level. With the present emphasis upon study skills in reading, many additional tests of these types will probably be forthcoming in the future.

At present two standardized tests which assess achievement in some of the study skills are:

Work Study Skills: Iowa Every-Pupil Tests of Basic Skills, Test B, New Edition. The elementary battery covers grades 3 to 5; the advanced battery covers grades 6 to 9. This test includes map reading, use of references, use of index, use of dictionary, alphabetizing. The advanced battery also includes graphing. (Houghton.)

SRA Achievement Series. One section of these tests is designed for grades 2 to 4, another is intended for grades 4 to 6. There are more advanced sections, also. Each battery of the tests as a whole covers language, perception, arithmetic, language arts, reading, and reading work-skills. The work-study skills section of the battery for grades 4 to 6 tests use of a table of contents, use of an index, knowledge of reference sources, and ability to interpret charts, tables, and graphs. This section dealing with work-study skills is available separately. (Science Research Associates.)

Summary of the Chapter

This chapter has presented research showing that special approaches and skills are needed in reading content in different subject areas and that improvement takes place when instruction and practice are provided to strengthen a special skill. Research has also shown the need for attention to specialized vocabulary in different subjects and has indicated that improvement takes place when such attention is directed toward the pronunciation and understanding of technical words in different content areas.

The *common* study skills were discussed: selection and evaluation, organization, recall, locating information, and following directions. Samples of activities were presented for use in giving practice on these common skills in the section titled "Maintenance and Practice Activities," pages 563–71.

The *specialized* factors to be considered in teaching children to read in different subject areas were discussed: specialized vocabulary, special patterns in the content of particular subjects. Standardized and informal tests of study skills were suggested.

In conclusion it might be said that the development of study skills in reading presents a vast frontier to those who wish to develop more fully the ability of children to read specialized types of content for a variety of purposes. The challenge is urgent and compelling; the opportunities are rich and boundless!

Additional Readings

Books

Dawson, Mildred A., and Henry A. Bamman, *Fundamentals of Basic Reading Instruction*, Chaps. 14 and 15. New York: Longmans, Green & Co., Inc., 1963.

DeBoer, John J., and Martha Dallmann, *The Teaching of Reading*, Chaps. 9A and 9B. New York: Holt, Rinehart & Winston, Inc., 1960.

Gates, Arthur I., *The Improvement of Reading*, 3rd ed., Chaps. 11–15. New York: The Macmillan Co., 1947.

——, "The Nature and Function of Reading in the Content Areas," *New Frontiers in Reading*, pp. 149–52. International Reading Association, Conference Proceedings. New York: Scholastic Magazines, 1960.

Gray, William S., comp. and ed., *Improving Reading in All Curricular Areas*. Supplementary Educational Monographs, No. 76. Chicago: University of Chicago Press, 1952.

Harris, Albert J., *How to Increase Reading Ability*, rev. ed., Chaps. 15 and 16. New York: Longmans, Green & Co., Inc., 1956.

Lodge, William J., *Reading and the Content Subjects*. Contributions in Reading, No. 17. Boston: Ginn & Company, 1957.

Morgan, Clifford E., and James Deese, *How to Study*. New York: McGraw-Hill Book Company, Inc., 1957.

National Society for Study of Education, *Development in and through Reading*, Sixtieth Yearbook, Part I, Chap. IV. Chicago: University of Chicago Press, 1961.

Russell, David H., *Children Learn to Read*, rev. ed., Chap. 11. Boston: Ginn & Company, 1961.

Somerville, John, *The Enjoyment of Study at Home or on your Own*. New York: Abelard-Schuman Limited, 1954.

Strang, Ruth M., *Study Type of Reading Exercises*, rev. ed. New York: Bureau of Publications, Teachers College, Columbia University, 1956.

Periodicals

Campanella, Thomas C., "Reading Techniques for Teachers of Content Subjects," *Catholic School Journal*, Vol. 53 (September 1953), 213–17.

Fay, Leo, "How Can We Develop Study Skills for the Different Curriculum Areas," *Reading Teacher*, Vol. 6 (1953), 12–18.

——, "Patterns of Grouping in the Content Areas," *Conference on Reading: Chicago University* (1959), 63–68.

Foote, Marie M., "Using Content Subjects to Promote Reading Interests in Grades Seven Through Nine," *Conference on Reading: Chicago University* (1956), 149–53.

Horn, T. Darrough, "Work-Study Skills: Some Neglected Areas," *Education*, Vol. 81 (May 1961), 521–23.

Kerfoot, James F., "The Vocabulary in Primary Arithmetic Texts," *The Reading Teacher*, Vol. 14 (January 1961), 177–80.

Romano, Michael J., "Reading and Science: A Symbiotic Relationship," *Education*, Vol. 81 (January 1961), 273–76.

Schwartz, Marvin, "Transfer of Reading Training from Nontechnical to Technical Material," *Journal of Educational Psychology*, Vol. 48 (1957), 498–504.

Scott, Helen Elizabeth, "Preparation of a File of Exercises for Developing Study Skills in the Middle Grades," *Journal of Education*, Vol. 136 (November 1953), 40–43.

Shores, J. Harland, "Reading of Science for Two Separate Purposes as Perceived by Sixth Grade Students and Able Adult Readers," *Elementary English*, Vol. 37 (November 1960), 461–68.

Smith, Nila B., "Teaching Study Skills in Reading," *Elementary School Journal*, Vol. 60 (December 1959), 158–62.

Spache, George D., "Types and Purposes of Reading in Various Curricular Fields," *The Reading Teacher*, Vol. 11 (February 1958), 158–64.

Stearns, Gertrude B., "Reading Techniques for the Content Subjects," *Journal of Education*, Vol. 134 (December 1954), 7–10.

Whipple, Gertrude, "Sequence in Reading in the Content Areas," *Conference on Reading: Chicago University* (1960), 124–29.

11

Reading Rate: An Important Growth Area

The teacher of yesteryear did not include rate as one of the basic skills to be developed in her reading program. In fact she didn't give a thought to rate improvement except to urge her pupils to "read smoothly" in their oral reading. Now all that has changed. Thousands of adults, parents of children throughout the country, are rushing back to reading centers to take speed reading courses. These and other parents who are hearing about speed reading are asking teachers what they are doing to teach their children to read fast. And teachers are asking "Why all this present interest in rapid reading?" and "What *can* the teacher do about it?"

Let's discuss the first question first: This is an age of speed —speed in transportation, communication; celerity in office equipment, factory machinery, and household appliances. We are in the midst of a speed revolution!

As for reading, we are living in a reading environment. Tremendous amounts of reading material are produced daily, speeded up by technological invention. Yet no one has time to read as much as he wants to. The business or professional man finds his desk piled high with memos, reports, correspondence, advertising material which he does not have time to read. The housewife would also like to read her household magazines and a novel or two but she doesn't have time to read either. The student is bogged down with reams of reading, and he too, complains that he does not have time to cover his assignments.

It would appear that this situation in the future will become increasingly burdensome and frustrating unless more attention is devoted to reading improvement in general, including a special consideration of rate in reading as a very important skill area to be cultivated. The elementary grade period is none too early to begin nurturing growth in faster rates of reading together with greater flexibility in using different rates when reading different materials for different purposes.

The Beginning of Interest in Rapid Reading

Interest in reading rate had its inception in studies of eye-movements which began in the late 1800's. The theory that a reader perceives words letter by letter had been an accepted fact throughout the centuries. The whole methodology of reading was based for many years on the assumption that a person looks at each separate letter as he reads. Hence children were always taught their ABC's as a first step in learning to read.

In 1879 a Frenchman by the name of Javal [1] became interested in investigating eye movements. He thought that ascertaining exactly how the eye behaves when a person is reading would afford some insight into the mental activities that go on as reading takes place.

First he tried observing the eyes of people who were reading just by looking at them with his own naked eyes. But the eyes of the readers moved so fleetingly that Javal couldn't tell what took place. He then tried placing a mirror in front of the reader, watching the reader's eyes in the mirror. But this didn't work either. Finally Javal concluded that the movements of the eyes could not be detected accurately by another pair of naked eyes.

He continued to work on the problem for some time. His thought was that it might be possible to rig up some sort of contrivance which could be used in obtaining objective evidence in regard to movements of the eyes. He consulted his friends, asking them to help him invent some way of checking the eye movements of a person reading. "Nonsense," said

[1] Emile Javal, "Essai sur la physiologie de la lecture," *Annales d'oculistique,* LXXXII (Nov.–Dec. 1879), 242–53.

they. "Why bother about something that everybody already knows? The eyes have to look at each letter in every word as they move across a line of print. Otherwise, how could the reader tell one word from another?"

Javal, however, doubted that a person recognized printed sentences letter by letter, so he persisted in trying to figure out some method by which he could detect and record the movements of the eyes under reading conditions. At last he hit upon it—a stick and a drumhead!

In developing his experimental equipment, Javal first fashioned a cup of plaster of Paris which was to fit over the eyeball of the person reading. He made an aperture in the middle of the cup through which the page could be seen.

While the plaster of Paris was still damp and pliable, Javal inserted one end of a long, slender stick into the outer side of the cup. When the cup dried, of course, the stick was securely rooted in the plaster of Paris.

Next, Javal smoked a drumhead as people sometimes prepare a piece of glass for use in looking at an eclipse of the sun. The smoke left a heavy black coating on the drumhead.

When this equipment was ready, Javal asked a man to sit close to the drumhead and read. The plaster of Paris cup was placed over one eye of the subject, and as he read the stick traced a design in the smoke coating on the drumhead.

What did this design reveal? That the eyes did not look at one letter at a time or even at one word at a time. Rather, they proceeded in a series of pauses and jerks, stopping only three or four times in covering an entire line. Thus it was that a startling discovery about reading was made, one that is the very foundation of modern speed reading—namely, that the good reader quickly moves his eyes along over the lines of print, grasping whole meaningful units at each glance, rather than stopping to scrutinize each letter or even each word.

A few years later Ahrens [2] improved upon the plaster of Paris cup in that he used an ivory cup to which he attached a bristle. The bristle recorded the eye-movements on a smoked drumhead.

Other investigators, stimulated by the experiments of Javal and Ahrens, began to make studies of their own using different kinds of equipment. Finally a huge camera was devised which would actually take photographs of eye movements. This camera was designed by a professor who devoted a year's time to its perfection, and it cost $6,000.

When using this camera, a bead of mercury was placed on the eyelid of the reader. If the reader has ever dropped a thermometer and broken its glass he has seen that little beads of mercury, almost as light as air

---

[2] A. Ahrens describes this method in *Untersuchringen über die Bewegung der Rugen beim Schreiben*. Rostac, 1891.

and as round as balls, rolled about here and there in response to the slightest movement. Because of these properties, mercury was a highly satisfactory medium for this experimental work with eye movements. Furthermore, rays of light were reflected from these bright mercury beads. These rays were photographed as they were reflected on the lines of print while the reader was in the act of reading.

Once this thoroughly scientific procedure for detecting and recording eye movements had been developed, hundreds of studies were made with all kinds of readers at various age levels. Voluminous evidence piled up, showing beyond the shadow of a doubt that there were decided differences between the way poor readers read and the way excellent readers pursue the printed page. These studies revealed that the poor reader perceives just one word or perhaps a part of a word at a time, while the excellent reader takes in an entire group of words at a glance.

Camera reproductions of the eye movements of a beginning reader and of a mature reader are shown below. The vertical lines indicate the eye fixations; the numbers above the lines show the order in which the eyes paused; those below the lines indicate the duration of each pause in sixteenths of a second.

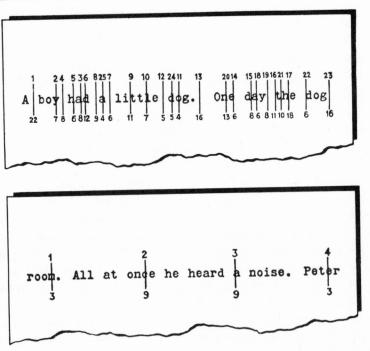

Source: G. T. Buswell, *Fundamental Reading Habits: A Study of Their Development*, Supplementary Educational Monograph, No. 21 (Chicago: The University of Chicago Press), pp. 2–3. Copyright 1922 by The University of Chicago.

Obviously, the person whose eyes swept along over the line with but four orderly pauses read much faster than the child whose eyes paused twenty-five times with many regressive movements in between. With such photographic reproductions of eye-movements, differences in rates of reading became startlingly apparent.

The Fallacy of Treating Symptoms

Following these scientific studies, instructors in some quarters began striving to train people to change their eye movements. For a time, this was considered the chief panacea for slow reading.

The writer recalls watching Dr. R., a psychiatrist, while under instruction designed to increase his reading speed. Since Dr. R.'s professional field was developing so rapidly that it was impossible for him to do all the necessary reading and also take care of his patients, he had entered a reading laboratory. He was told over and over again that he "must widen his eye span" and was put through the routine of exercises designed to "increase his span." He sat in a tense position, clutching a book and and straining every effort to widen his eye span. His eyelids were opened wide, and his eyes were fairly bulging out of their sockets. He soon became fatigued and remarked, "Well, I think I forced a pretty good span. The only trouble is, I was concentrating so hard on making my eyes work right that I don't know what I was reading about."

There you have in a nutshell the fallacy of striving to change the physical movement of the eyes only. When a patient is ill, the doctor takes his temperature and his pulse. If the temperature is high and the pulse rapid, he notes these as symptoms of the degree of illness. However, he looks for the cause of the illness and treats that rather than the symptoms.

So with reading. The eye movements are simply symptoms of the mental processes which a person uses while reading. The eyes are the servants of the mind and do its bidding in reading, just as the hands do the bidding of the mind when you tell them to "shell those peas rapidly and get it over with."

So as an elementary teacher, don't make the mistake of concentrating on the mechanics of changing the eye span of pupils to accomplish faster and better reading. In other words, don't try to treat the symptom; work on the fundamentals that contribute to the mental process of reading itself.

Perhaps a brief review of more recent research findings in regard to this reading skill which has suddenly gained wide acclaim will be helpful to the teacher in answering questions of the layman, and what is more important, perhaps it will give the teacher or prospective teacher guidance in offering a sound instructional program in developing appropriate rates in her pupils.

Research in Reading Rate

Since the early eye-movement studies, numerous investigations have been carried on for the purpose of learning more about rates in reading. Most of these studies have been conducted with adults, but the resulting information is useful for an elementary teacher to know.

Studies Made With Adults

Some of the most important facts revealed by investigations with adults are listed below:

1. Speed can be increased with training. Speed evidently is a skill that responds readily to instruction and practice. Reports of almost all studies in which systematic training was given to increase speed indicate that rate was increased.

2. The fast reader reads with the best understanding of content. Many of the earlier investigators of reading rate arrived at this conclusion without qualification. Later studies impose some restrictions on this generalization. Stroud,[3] for example, reviewed the literature on speed and comprehension and concluded that "published coefficients between speed and comprehension were spuriously high." Carlson[4] concluded that intelligence made a difference, and Flanagan[5] found that when reading is very rapid, comprehension is sacrificed and that difficulty of material also makes a difference in speed.

The studies mentioned above and similar ones lead us to believe that discretion should be used in interpreting the widely accepted inference that speed and comprehension always go together. Usually they do; sometimes they do not.

3. Many factors affect rate in reading. Intelligence, purpose, and relative difficulty of material all have their effects on rate of reading as indicated, for example, in the studies of Carlson and Flanagan, already men-

---

[3] J. B. Stroud, "A Critical Note on Reading," *Psychological Bulletin*, Vol. 39 (Mar. 1942), 173–78.

[4] Thorsten R. Carlson, "The Relationship Between Speed and Accuracy of Comprehension," *Journal of Educational Research*, Vol. 42 (Mar. 1949), 500–12.

[5] John C. Flanagan, "A Study of the Effect on Comprehension of Varying Speeds of Reading," *Research on the Foundations of American Education*. Official Report of the American Educational Research Association (1939), pp. 43–50.

tioned, and several others: Roesch,[6] Reed and Pepper,[7] Bell,[8] and Langsam.[9]

4. The use of mechanical devices at higher levels is controversial. Traxler and Jungleblut,[10] in summarizing recent research on the use of speed instruments of various types, arrive at this conclusion: "As was true of a good deal of earlier research, these studies do not indicate that any greater improvement in either speed or comprehension can be obtained through the use of mechanical devices than can be secured with more informal procedures."

Studies Made With Elementary Pupils

Recently a few studies of reading rate have been made with children in the elementary grades. The results of these studies are of special significance in this chapter.

The Stage at Which Systematic Speed Training Is Advisable.

At what stage in the elementary grades is it advisable to provide systematic practice to increase speed? More research is needed in answering this question. A few very significant studies, however, have been made.

Gray,[11] as early as 1925, reported as a result of research done up to that time that rate of silent reading increases rapidly throughout the first four or five grades after which gains in rate begin to taper off. This would indicate that rate grows along with other aspects of the reading process while children are mastering the mechanics of reading.

A significant study was conducted by Bridges [12] with comparable groups of pupils in fourth, fifth, and sixth grades. She concluded that

[6] Raymond A. Roesch, "Teaching Desirable Study Habits Through Experimentation," *Catholic Education Review*, LI (Mar. 1953), 152–62.

[7] James C. Reed and Roger S. Pepper, "The Inter-Relationship of Vocabulary, Comprehension, and Rate Among Disabled Readers," *Journal of Experimental Education*, Vol. 25 (June 1957), 331–37.

[8] Harry Bell, "Comprehension in Silent Reading," *British Journal of Educational Psychology*, XII (Feb. 1942), 47–55.

[9] Rosaline Streep Langsam, "A Factoral Analysis of Reading Ability," *Journal of Experimental Education*, X (Sept. 1941), 57–63.

[10] Arthur E. Traxler and Ann Jungleblut, *Research in Reading During Another Four Years* (New York: Educational Records Bureau, 1960).

[11] William Scott Gray, *Summary of Investigations Relating to Reading*, Supplemental Educational Monographs, No. 28 (Chicago: University of Chicago Press, 1925).

[12] Lucile Hudson Bridges, "Speed Versus Comprehension in Elementary Reading," *Journal of Educational Psychology*, Vol. 32 (Apr. 1941), 314–20.

". . . overemphasis upon speed tended to inhibit growth in reading at this level. With the better readers at about sixth grade level this did not seem to hold true."

Baranyai [13] conducted an elaborate study with 238 pupils. As one of her results she stated that "the development of the mechanical factors reaches their plateau somewhere between the ages of ten to fourteen."

A later study which offers clues in regard to levels of maturity was conducted by Ballantine.[14] This investigator checked the eye-movements of children in grades 2, 4, 6, 8, 10, and 12. One of the important facts revealed by his study was that growth was much more pronounced beyond the fourth grade than had been reported in earlier findings.

These studies would indicate that up through the fourth grade pupils are still perfecting their control over the mechanics of reading. It appears that it is not until they have reached fifth or sixth grade and have gained sufficient control over the mechanics that they are freed to make substantial gains in speed. These, then, are the elementary grades in which it would appear to be appropriate to give systematic training in rapid reading.

Use of Mechanical Devices

Several studies have been conducted in regard to the use of mechanical devices in teaching reading in the elementary grades, some with positive results, some with negative results. Very few of these studies have involved a control group using some other method. One such study which did involve a control group was conducted by Cason,[15] who set up four comparable groups of third grade pupils and evaluated phrase reading, extensive free-reading in the library, and training on the metronoscope. She concluded that extensive free library reading was as effective as mechanical techniques in increasing reading rate at this level.

The use of the tachistoscope in teaching pupils in the elementary grades has been the subject of many studies. In reviewing these studies Bormuth and Aker [16] stated in 1961: "None of these studies (preceding tachistoscopic studies with children) attempted to control the variables

[13] Erzsebet I. Baranyai, "Relation of Comprehension to Technique in Reading," *Journal of Genetic Psychology*, LIX (Sept. 1941), 3–26.

[14] Francis A. Ballantine, "Age Changes in Measures of Eye-Movements in Silent Reading," *Studies in the Psychology of Reading*, University of Michigan Monographs in Education, No. 4 (Ann Arbor, Mich.: University of Michigan Press, Apr. 1957), 65–111.

[15] Eloise Boeker Cason, "Mechanical Methods for Increasing the Speed of Reading," *Contributions to Education*, No. 878 (New York: Teachers College, Columbia University, 1943).

[16] John R. Bormuth and Cleatus C. Aker, "Is the Tachistoscope a Worthwhile Teaching Tool?" *The Reading Teacher*, Vol. 14 (Jan. 1961), 172–76.

of sex, age, visual acuity, intelligence, or reading ability, and they tended to overlook that motivation is a prime factor in all learning." In the light of this consideration these authors conducted a very carefully controlled experiment with sixth-grade pupils in which the tachistoscope was used with the experimental group. Their data revealed "that there were only chance differences between groups in comprehension, rate, and vocabulary."

Health May Affect Speed

Several studies made with remedial cases at the elementary level have revealed that physical disabilities and poor health affect reading achievement in general. One study at least has been made in regard to the effect of lowered vitality on speed. Parkins [17] made a study of fifth and sixth grade pupils which showed, among other things, that the reduction of physical vitality resulting from influenza was definitely reflected in reduced speed of reading.

Skimming

Grayum [18] made a study of skimming involving six different age groups varying from fourth grade pupils to adults. He found wide differences in ability to skim at each grade level. The chief processes used were: "skipping in various degrees," "marked changes in the regular reading rate," "pausing," "regressing," "looking back," "looking ahead." In addition, each subject who ranked high in skimming ability made use of detailed procedures "of their own devise."

Relationship Between Speed and Comprehension

The results of a recent study with sixth grade pupils has several implications for elementary teachers, particularly. This study was conducted by Shores [19] in an attempt to answer the questions, "Are Fast Readers

[17] George A. Parkins, "Influenza Epidemic of 1940–41 and its Apparent Effect on Reading Speed and Comprehension of 5th and 6th Grade Students in Pomona Public Schools, Pomona, California," American Research Council of Optometry Bulletin No. 26 (Ord, Neb.: American Research Council of Optometry, 1941), 5 (mimeographed).

[18] Helen Stolte Grayum, "An Analytic Description of Skimming: Its Purpose and Place as an Ability in Reading," Studies in Education (Bloomington, Ind.: School of Education, Indiana University, 1952), pp. 137–43.

[19] J. Harlan Shores, "Are Fast Readers the Best Readers?—A Second Report," Elementary English, Vol. 38 (Apr. 1961), 236–45. Reprinted with the permission of the National Council of Teachers of English and J. Harlan Shores.

the Best Readers?" Comparisons were made between the reading of sixth grade pupils and that of adults. The investigator's conclusions are so pertinent to this discussion that they will be quoted *in toto*.

1. Fast readers are the good readers when reading some kinds of materials for some purposes. When reading other kinds of materials for other purposes there is no relationship between speed of reading and ability to comprehend. In general the fast readers are the good readers on the reading tasks presented in the standardized tests of general reading ability. There is no relationship between speed of reading and comprehension for either sixth grade children or well-educated adults when reading scientific materials for the purpose of solving a problem, getting the main idea, or for keeping a series of ideas in mind in sequence.

2. When either adults or sixth grade children read the same materials for two different purposes and when the purpose for reading is set for the reader in advance of the reading, the purpose for reading influences the speed with which the reading is done. This finding is supported in Roossinck's study of the reading of scientists and sixth grade children.

3. There is no relationship for either adults or sixth grade students between comprehension and rate of the work-study reading involved in responding to the comprehension questions. In other words those who work rapidly on the rereading and question answering are not necessarily the best readers.

4. Efficient adult readers are much more flexible in adjusting reading rate to the demands of the task than are sixth grade students. In comparison to the adults, the children read relatively more rapidly as the task becomes more demanding with a consequent loss in relative comprehension. The efficient adult slows his rate and rereads as necessary in keeping with the demands of the task. Sixth grade students need to develop this type of rate flexibility.

5. Inasmuch as there are different relationships between rate and comprehension when rate is measured as an original reading time and when rate is measured to include rereading and question-answering time, it is important to define what is meant by reading rate. This finding also suggests that authorities in the field of reading would do well to attempt to standardize a practice for measuring reading rate. Since rereading and reorganizing what is read is both necessary and time consuming when reading for some purposes, the most meaningful measure of rate would be one which offered both an original reading time and a time for rereading and answering questions. The total time, which is a sum of these two, destroys some of the specificity of the composite parts and is useful only as an indication of the total amount of time taken to complete a work-study reading task.

Flexibility in the Use of Rate

There is a current misconception on the part of many people in regard to rate of reading. This misconception is that an individual should have *one* fixed rate of reading. When adults come to a reading center they almost invariably ask "How many words per minute should I read?" or "How many words per minute will I be able to read when I finish this course?" or "I hear that people can learn to read 1,000 words per minute." All such statements are indicative of the much too prevalent fallacy—the assumption that an individual has just one reading rate that he uses in *all* situations. As a matter of fact, the expert reader uses many different rates as they accommodate his reading of different kinds of content for different purposes. All of a person's rates can be improved, but improvement in speed alone should not be the goal; flexibility in adjusting speed to different situations is the achievement toward which learner and teacher alike should direct their efforts.

Three different categories of rate are represented in the diagram below.

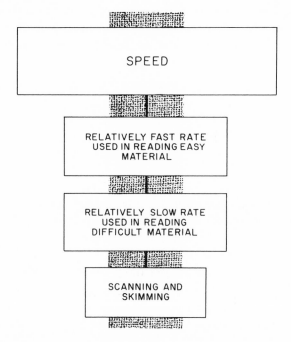

SPEED

RELATIVELY FAST RATE USED IN READING EASY MATERIAL

RELATIVELY SLOW RATE USED IN READING DIFFICULT MATERIAL

SCANNING AND SKIMMING

While the above diagram represents major categories of rate, no individual should have just one fixed speed for each category. There should be wide variations in each person within each category, again in terms of the material and the purpose for which it is read.

The relatively fast rate of reading material of average difficulty includes rate used in reading fictional selections and novels for recreational purposes, or in reading informative articles in popular magazines or non-fictional books for the purpose of pursuing a special interest or becoming broadly informed on some topic. Most of the reading material in the primary grades is of this type, and a considerable amount of the material in middle grade textbooks and supplemental books falls in this category.

A slower rate is used in reading or studying difficult material with a heavy burden of detailed facts. This is the kind of reading that a teacher does in reading and interpreting a technically phrased report of a scientific investigation, or in reading a technical article on space travel so that she can understand it well enough to relate its contents to her pupils. In the middle grades, pupils increasingly come in contact with material of this kind which they study for the purpose of entering into class discussion, making a report, or taking a test. For example, in a science textbook they may encounter this kind of material in an explanation of how the telephone works, or in an arithmetic book they may work with such text in reading directions for dividing a whole number by a fraction. Examples in many other situations of this kind might be given.

Rate for use in the two categories described above is developed in the same general way but applied differently. The third category requires different techniques. Scanning and skimming are extremely fast rates of covering reading content, and to be fully effective these techniques should be taught and not left to chance.

The term *scanning* is generally used to designate the process of quickly locating a particular word, phrase, sentence, fact, or figure within a selection, while *skimming* is used for the process of quickly passing over an entire selection or passage to get a general impression of it. A person *scans* when he sweeps his eyes over the list of items in a television schedule to find the time of a particular show. He *skims* when he glances through a short article on "How to Increase Your Energy" to catch a few phrases now and then that will give him a general idea of what suggestions the article holds.

Scanning may be given incidental practice in the first grade and continued practice throughout the grades. Skimming should be delayed until the mechanics of reading are well under control—probably until the latter part of the elementary period.

Laying Rate Foundations in the Primary Grades

We have evidence to the effect that rate in reading grows along with the other reading skills during the years in which the mechanics of reading are being mastered. As a child gains control over mechanics of reading, he is freed to cover the pages of print more rapidly. The cornerstones of speed are facility in: (1) recognizing words, (2) gathering meanings, (3) using study skills. Whatever a teacher does to improve these fundamental abilities will contribute also to an increase in rate.

In addition to her efforts to improve these basic skills, however, there are many specific things that a teacher can do to develop faster rates of reading and flexibility in using them.

Most authorities are agreed that it is not advisable to have primary children undergo speed pressure. Accuracy in pronouncing printed words and getting meanings should come first in reading skill. Also, pressure to read faster might have unfortunate effects both on a child's physical and mental well-being.

Establishing Phrasing

Word-reading impedes speed. The teacher should try from the beginning to develop ability to read in phrases by doing some of these things:

1. In all chalkboard and chart work divide runover sentences between phrases, as:

> *The big black dog came running*
> *down the road.*

2. In all chalkboard or chart work assist pupils to read in phrase units by sweeping a pointer or your hand under each complete phrase as it is read, rather than by pointing to each word separately.

3. When the children themselves are using a pointer, remind them to "keep the pointer sliding," thereby preventing the habit of pointing to and seeing just one word at a time.

4. Ask children to read as they "talk" when reading orally, rather than reading one word at a time.

5. Read orally in phrases to the pupils occasionally as an example of how they should read.

Breaking Habits of Bodily Movements

The mind of the good reader can leap far ahead of the rate at which physical movements can take place. Many children develop habits of using physical movements during beginning reading stages. If these are permitted to go unchecked they become fixed, and the individual undoubtedly will be a slow reader throughout his life.

Lip-reading is natural at beginning stages when the child is making the transition from the use of oral language to the silent reading of printed symbols. Normally, it disappears at second grade level. If it persists at this time, concentrated attention should be directed toward breaking the habit.

1. Make children themselves conscious of the desirability of eliminating lip movement as a means of helping them to become better readers.

2. Watch the children during study periods and frequently remind the lip-readers to "read with your eyes."

3. Place printed slogans around the room, such as "Fast readers use their eyes not their lips," "Eyes are for reading; lips are for talking."

4. Have the persistent lip-readers place a finger or a pencil over their lips

while reading. Instruct them to press down on the lips when they feel them moving and hold them still.

5. For variety have the lip-readers hold a piece of paper between the lips while reading. When lip-reading begins the paper drops and the pupil becomes conscious that he is moving his lips.

Finger-pointing holds the reader down to reading one word at a time so that only a very slow rate of reading can be attained.

1. In first grade provide pupils with a cardboard marker, about an inch wide and as long as the width of the page. Have them place this marker under the first line of print and move it down line by line as they read. (Do not continue the use of markers beyond first grade.)

2. Ask pupils to hold each side of the book with one hand. If they keep both hands in use holding the book, they will not have a free finger with which to point.

Head-moving prevents fast reading. Some children (and many adults) move their heads from left to right and back again from right to left each time they read a line and return their eyes to the beginning of another line.

Have children with head movements place their chins in one of their hands while reading. Instruct them to "make your hand keep your head from moving."

Setting Purposes

It has been found that adults and children read more rapidly when they are motivated by a well-defined purpose. Try to work out purposes with the children for reading selections in their daily work.

Wide Reading

One of the best ways to promote growth in reading rate at the primary level is to encourage wide reading of easy, interesting material.

Scanning

Ordinarily children in the primary grades are not ready for skimming as it is technically defined on page 364. They can, however, develop considerable skill in scanning during this period.

At the very beginning of reading experience, pupils want to read *every single word*. In the interest of accuracy, and meanings, they certainly should be permitted to do so. As they continue to read, however, they may be made aware of situations in which it is not necessary to read every word. During a chart lesson, for example, the teacher may explain that "when you are looking for one particular thing in a story you don't have to read every single word." She may then demonstrate by showing how quickly she can find some one word that she may name in a chart at hand. The children may then see how quickly they can find in the chart context words that she names.

Throughout the primary grades, many functional opportunities will arise to give practice in scanning. Usually such practice should be given during rereading rather than during the first reading of a selection.

Here are a few scanning activities which children can do appropriately at this level:

1. Find a new word in book text that has previously been developed on the chalkboard.
2. Find a sentence, phrase, or word to answer a specific question.
3. Find a phrase or sentence giving specific information.
4. Find a certain speech of a speaker in a story.
5. Locate names of speakers when their quotations have been written on the chalkboard.
6. Find characters needed in giving a dramatization.
7. Prove or disprove a statement as indicated in a particular sentence given orally or written on the chalkboard.
8. Find the page on which a chapter or story begins, first from chalkboard, later in table of contents.
9. Find a sentence that gives a word picture.
10. Find items to list under a heading.

Informal Procedures for Increasing Rates in the Middle Grades

While the development of rates in the primary grades should consist largely of incidental and functional activities, more direct work may be done in the middle grades. As previously pointed out, results of research indicate that the appropriate time to begin direct instruction in and practice to speed up reading rates is in the middle grades, more particularly the fifth and sixth grades. Many things can be done at the fourth grade level, however, which not only continue primary procedures but advance them.

Continuance of Primary Practices

The following practices used in laying the foundations for speed in the primary grades should be continued and emphasized:

1. Copious reading of easy material.
2. *Purposeful* reading.
3. Discontinuance of any bodily movements which persist while reading.

Develop An Awareness of Personal Rates

At the beginning of the year the teacher may give the pupils an informal test of speed and content. Prepare for this test by making up ten questions on the content of three or four pages of a story in a basic reader which they have not read.

Have the children find the page on which the story begins, keeping a finger in the place and immediately closing the book. Provide yourself with a stop-watch if one is available; if not, use an ordinary watch with a second hand. When the second hand is at 12:00 or 6:00 (for convenience in time-keeping) give the children the signal to start reading. Allow them to read silently for three minutes, then give them the signal to stop. Each child may make a faint lead-pencil dot (which later can be erased) at the point he has reached when the "stop" signal was given.

Place on the chalkboard the ten questions which you had prepared. Ask the children to write the answers to the questions with their books closed.

After the answers are written each pupil checks his own paper as you give the answers orally. A score of ten should be allowed for each correct answer.

Following the checking of the answers, ask each pupil to count the number of words he read and divide the number by three. This will indicate the number of words per minute that he read. Have this number written on the answer paper along with the score on questions relating to the content.

Gather up the papers and without giving the names of the pupils write the rate scores on the board, ranging from the highest to the lowest, with the question score to the right of the rate score in each case.

Use the scores as the basis for discussion. Point out the variation in both speed and grasp of content. Call attention particularly to the relationships between speed and grasp of content. Some scores will show that pupils read very fast and still answer all the questions correctly. This should be held up as a desired standard, but one that can still be improved in speed. Others will have a high speed score but a lower content score. This may mean that these pupils were reading too fast and also that they need to give more attention to getting meanings. Some will have read slowly but have high scores on understanding of content. They should be encouraged to read faster. Some probably will have low scores both in rate and content. They probably should work harder on grasping content, before trying to read faster.

Following the discussion return the papers so that each child may place himself in the total distribution.

Discussion of Advantages of Rapid Reading

The teacher may discuss with the children the reasons why it is an advantage to be able to read more rapidly. Give them some of the information presented on pages 353–54. Assure them that rapid reading is an easy skill to develop, but that much depends upon their own desire to improve and their efforts in doing so.

Develop the Concept of Reading in Thought Units

The teacher may give the pupils information similar to that presented below.

Investigations of eye-movements have shown that the rapid reader's eyes move fleetingly across the lines, pausing briefly two or three times on each line, picking up an "eyeful" of words at each pause, while the eyes of the poor reader pause on every word or on small word units. (Reproduce on the chalkboard the two diagrams on page 356, and explain their significance.)

It is the mind, of course, that controls the eye-movements. The great value of eye-movement investigations is that they furnish us a picture of the different ways in which the mind works in perceiving reading symbols. They tell us that the mind of the poor reader loafs along, picking up very small units at a time, while the eyes of the excellent reader race over the lines, gathering an entire, meaningful idea at a glance.

Cultivating the habit of reading for *ideas* not only increases speed but also increases undertanding. A person who reads one word at a time thinks in terms of the meanings of these separate words and thus "can't see the woods for the trees." The synthesis of important meanings is lost in any meticulous perception of the meanings of separate words or small units.

The first and most important instruction is, "Read for Ideas!" If you can cultivate the habit of rapidly picking up one complete thought unit after another, the eye movements will take care of themselves.

This explanation may be followed by writing a paragraph on the chalkboard, dividing it into thought groups, and letting the children try to read it for ideas. An example of a paragraph so marked is as follows:

OLD BET [20]

The pioneer elephant/in our country/was imported/by a sea captain./
She was named "Old Bet,"/and she arrived/in New York/about 1815./
She was sold/to a Mr. John Sloat./He sold her again/to a man/named Bailey.
The big old elephant/was transported/on a sloop/to Ossining-on-the-Hudson./
She was driven/from there/back into the country,/where she/was exhibited/
in a barn./

Write other paragraphs on the chalkboard. Ask the children to mark them into thought units.

[20] Adapted from George S. Bryan, "The First American Circus," *The Mentor* (Apr. 1922), p. 34.

Reproduce paragraphs or short selections and give them to the class to divide into thought units.

Continuously remind the children to read in thought units.

Develop Habits of Reading for a Purpose

The teacher may inform children of the desirability of setting up purposes for reading. Perhaps the advice below will be useful in making such suggestions.

In increasing your speed, and in fact in developing all of the other skills in reading, decide upon your purpose for reading a selection *before* you start to read it. Is it to get information about some special topic that you will need in class discussion? To find out how something works? To get an answer to some problem? To find out how to do something? To review for a test? To gather news about what others are doing? To find out how to improve yourself personally? To be entertained by some light reading? To follow the plot of a story? Or what?

Phrase your purpose concisely, and keep it uppermost in your mind throughout the reading of the entire selection. A well defined purpose pulls your eyes along more rapidly, and it gives you something to tie to in selecting and organizing ideas gathered from the text. In fact your purpose hastens your eyes along and acts as a pilot which guides you over the sea of print and leaves you with a well-filled dragnet of ideas at the end of your reading journey.[21]

Discuss with the children the possibility of a purpose for their next assignment. Work with them to set up a definite purpose, and urge them to try to keep the purpose in mind while they read.

Frequently set up a purpose for reading a selection or ask the children to do so. Help them to develop the habit of setting up their own purposes.

Develop the Preview Technique

The technique of previewing a selection or a chapter before reading it is a valuable one for middle grade children to learn. Skillful previewing contributes both to increased rate and comprehension.

There is a basic reason why a person "window shops" before buying a garment or a car or a new gadget. He wants to "size up" certain characteristics of articles in which he is interested as a whole. If it's a coat, he first evaluates it in terms of material and color. Then he looks at the style of the garment and notes the cut of the collar and the flare of the cuffs. No doubt he compares this piece of merchandise with others in price. In short, he gathers as much information as possible about characteristics which are important to him before he actually buys. Likewise,

21 Nila Banton Smith, *Read Faster and Get More from Your Reading* (Englewood Cliffs, N. J.: Prentice-Hall, Inc., 1958), p. 35.

it is possible and advisable to glean as much information as possible about an article, a chapter, or a book before reading it.

A preview aids a pupil by "whetting his appetite," arousing his interest in the subject and strengthening his personal motive for reading about it. It acquaints him with the general subject matter of the text to be read and its structure or organization. When he actually begins to read after previewing, he finds that his prereading insight has paved the way for speedier and more comprehensive coverage of the printed page.

Introducing Previewing

The steps usually used in previewing are: (1) studying the title, (2) examining visual materials, (3) reading subheads. All this is done without reading into the text of the printed matter at all.

The introduction to the technique may be accompanied by explanations containing information similar to that given below:

1. *Study the Title.* The first step to take always is to study the title. The title holds a world of information for you. It tells you concisely what the selection is about. It gives you a quick cue as to the topic of discussion. It provides you with advanced information in regard to the subject to be discussed and enables you to read in terms of the promise that the title holds out to you.

2. *Examine Visual Aids.* If any visual aids are furnished, turn your attention to them and study these visual aids for their meaning significance. Illustrations may accompany the selection. If so, look at them carefully. They will aid your comprehension by giving you a vivid mental picture of the people, things, and locale dealt with in the context. If maps are provided, study them. Your reading will be more meaningful if you have precise geographical locations in mind. Often graphs, charts, or diagrams are provided. If so, study these carefully before you read. They will give you a quick grasp of relationships and proportions among information which will be discussed in the text.

3. *Glance at the Subheads.* Next, glance through the selection to see if subheads are used. If so, you will find that a quick survey of these subheadings will be very valuable to you. You should consider each one for the information which it actually gives or which it implies. These subheads are the major topics in the author's outline. They reveal to you the heads of discourse in the structure of the article as a whole.

There will be occasions in reading light articles when a preview of subtitles will tell you all you want to know. At other times, especially when studying in the content subjects, they will serve as interest-leads to reading the different sections, and as door-openers to better understanding of the text that follows.

After explaining the preview technique the children should be asked to try it out step by step in reading a chapter or a section of a chapter in a science, geography, or history textbook.

Following the preview, the teacher may give a test based on information which could be gotten alone from the title, visual aids, and subheads. The test may contain ten questions or true-false statements for ease of scoring. The pupils will be surprised to find how much information they have gotten solely from previewing.

The habit of previewing should be firmly established during the middle grades. Repeated experiences similar to the one described above, together with frequent reminders, should accomplish this goal.

Systematic Practice in the Middle Grades

Timed Reading Practice

At the sixth grade level, pupils who are working up to their grade level or above in reading may be given systematic timed practice to increase their rate. Some fifth grade pupils who are excellent readers may be ready for such practice, also. This is a matter to be decided at the discretion of the teacher.

Children who are still having difficulty in recognizing words or getting meanings, or who are nervous when subjected to timed-exercises, should not be included in the practice-period activities at any level.

Materials

Materials used for timed reading practice may be either commercially prepared or they may consist of selections which the teacher chooses from readers, textbooks in the content areas, or trade books with which the children are working.

Easy material should be used while pupils are breaking their old tempo and establishing new habits. Later they may try increasing their rate in reading more difficult material.

Instructions for Giving Timed Practice

Instructions for giving timed reading practice with commercially prepared materials usually accompany the material itself. The procedures suggested below are provided for the use of teachers who use the regular reading materials available in the classroom.

Timed reading tests may be given from two to five times per week. The procedure described on page 368 may be used in working with materials available in the classroom. Three minutes per period is a desirable length for a practice period at the beginning of timed reading practice. Two or three repetitions of practice periods of three minutes each may take place at one sitting, with time being allowed between each practice period for scoring speed and grasp of content. The length of the practice period may be increased when in the judgment of the teacher it is desirable to do so.

Comprehension questions should, of course, be prepared in advance of each practice period. Checking speed without comprehension is quite valueless. Ten comprehension questions is a desirable number to prepare in the interest of scoring, a score of ten being allowed for each correct answer.

Ascertaining Rate and Grasp of Content

Checks of speed and content should *always* accompany one another following timed reading practice. Each pupil may check his own answers to questions, or papers may be exchanged and pupils may check each other's papers, as the teacher reads the answers to the questions orally. If ten questions have been used, a score of ten should be given for each correct answer, the total being the sum of all of the correct answers scored.

Speed is ascertained by counting the number of words read during a given time and dividing this number by the number of minutes or number of minutes plus seconds consumed in the reading.

For checking purposes it isn't necessary to count each word on the page individually. An estimate of the number of words on one page of the total number of pages covered may serve as an estimate for all pages in the same selection. In making such an estimate, the number of words in six or seven lines are counted. As a result three or four of the lines may turn out to have the same number of words, let us say thirteen. If this doesn't happen, then words may be counted in several lines and the average number found by dividing the total number of words by the number of lines in which words are counted.

Once the average number of words in a line has been ascertained, then pupils can quickly count the average number of lines covered during a practice period and multiply by the average number of words per line, as:

$$75 \times 13 = 975 \qquad \text{Total number of words}$$

This number divided by the number of minutes used in the practice yields the number of words per minute read, commonly designated as WPM. As an example, if three minutes were used for the practice period, the computation would be:

$$975 \div 3 = 325 \text{ WPM}$$

The above suggestions apply when the teacher holds the time of the practice period to the same number of minutes for all pupils. The time is constant but the number of words read by each individual varies within that time. An alternate procedure is one in which all pupils start reading at the same time and each one keeps a record of the time at which he individually finishes reading an entire selection or section of a selection which they have been asked to read for practice purposes. One way of conducting such a practice period is for the teacher to flash time cards for the pupils' use in recording their respective finishing times.

File cards, 3 x 5 in size, may be used for timing. A number is written on each card. This number should be large enough in size so that all children in the group can see it easily from where they are sitting. India ink or strong black crayon strokes should be used in making the number easily legible.

Usually 60 is used as a beginning number; then five is added for the number on each additional card, as 65, 70, 75, 80, 85, 90, 95, 100, and so on. The cards are held up at intervals of five seconds, beginning with the number that represents the number of seconds that have elapsed since the students started, until all have finished reading.

As in the other timing procedures described above, the teacher makes sure that all pupils wait to start reading until she gives the signal. It is easier for the teacher to keep time if she gives the signal when the second hand is either at 12 or at 6.

When some of the students have nearly finished with their reading, at the expiration of each five seconds the teacher should flash a card with a figure on it representing the total number of seconds that have elapsed since they began reading. As soon as a student finishes he looks up at the card the teacher is holding and writes down the number on the card as representing the number of seconds which it took him to read the selection. For example, if the number on the card is 125 when Tom finishes, he makes a note of 125, which indicates that it took him 125 seconds or two minutes and five seconds to read the article.

When computing rates involving seconds as well as whole minutes the following formula is useful:

$$\text{No. words} \qquad \frac{a}{b} \times 60 = \underline{\qquad} \text{WPM}$$
$$\text{No. seconds}$$

If a pupil read 320 words in 140 seconds his completed formula would be:

$$\text{No. words} \qquad \frac{320}{140} \times 60 = 138 \text{ WPM}$$
$$\text{No. seconds}$$

Keeping Personal Records

A strong motivating force in rate and content improvement is that of keeping records of personal progress. Individual records are better than group records in which students compete with each other for gains in spite of personal limitations. Trying to beat one's own record is the best kind of competition.

Various kinds of graphs, charts, and tables may be used for this purpose. In keeping records of growth it is very important that material of comparable difficulty be used for each successive recording. Growth in grasping content should always be recorded along with rate growth.

One sample of a graph that can be used for recording growth in rate is presented below as well as one for recording growth in understanding of content.

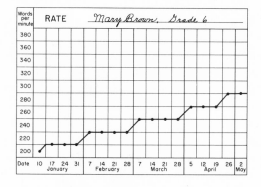

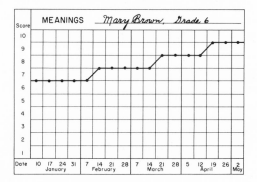

Controlled Reading

Types of Instruments Available

Several mechanical aids are on the market for use in regulating the rate at which reading content is exposed. There are group and individual tachistoscopes which flash numbers, words, phrases, and sentences at different speeds, such as Keystone Tachistoscope (Keystone View Company, Meadville, Pennsylvania); Timex (Educational Development Laboratories, New York) and Renshaw Tachistoscopic Trainer (Stereo Optical Company, Chicago).

There are pacers of several kinds. In using these pacers, reading material is placed within the frame of the instrument. A metal arm or shadow can then be moved down over the reading material covering a line at a time, and the reader has to read fast enough to read the line before it is covered. Rate can be regulated to different speeds. Some of the pacers available are: SRA Reading Accelerator (Science Research Associates, Chicago); Shadowscope Pacer (Lafayette Instrument Company, Lafayette, Indiana); Reading Rate Controller (Stereo Optical Company, Chicago); Reading Pacer (Keystone View Company, Meadville, Pennsylvania).

Instruments using film strips are also available for rate practice. One of these appropriate for use at the elementary level is the Controlled Reader (Educational Development Laboratories, New York). The Perceptascope (Perceptual Development Laboratories, St. Louis, Missouri) combines films with tachistoscopic techniques.

Evaluation of the Use of Instruments

Some believe that instruments are very beneficial; others think their importance has been overrated by many people. As mentioned on pages 359–61, research indicates that high speed can be achieved without the use of instruments. Probably the chief value of instruments is twofold: they motivate attempts to read faster, and they show a person how fast he really can read when he is forced to proceed at a rapid rate.

In regard to motivation, DeBoer and Dallman [22] state: "Quite possibly the machines have an initial advantage in that they provide novelty and interest in the improvement of reading. Unfortunately, after a time the novelty may wear off, and consequently, one of the chief reasons for success reported with instruments of this type may no longer operate."

More scientific evidence is needed in regard to transfer of the results of instrument training to natural reading situations, and retention of the speed attained with such practice. If instruments are used, care should be taken to insure that the speed achieved while reading with the use of the instruments is transferred to natural reading. After the use of an instrument the teacher should give some such directive as this: "You

[22] John J. DeBoer and Martha Dallmann, *The Teaching of Reading* (New York: Holt, Rinehart and Winston, Inc., 1960), p. 161.

have found out how fast you can read when the instrument is forcing you. Now, do the same thing without the instrument. Force your own eyes along over the next article and see if you can keep up to the instrument speed." By far the larger portion of the practice should be done while reading material under natural conditions, otherwise the speed attained during instrument work may not carry over and remain.

The instruments, of course, are limited in the types of skills in which they give practice. They do not provide help in developing word identification ability, critical evaluation of what is read, study-skills of specific types, flexibility in the use of speed in reading different materials for different purposes, and so on. Their chief function is to increase speed with accompanying checks on meanings. Gains in meanings usually are not outstanding. In other words, instruments should not be looked upon as a cure-all for children who are not doing well in reading, nor as a substitute for a complete, well-rounded developmental program for those who are up to their achievement level.

Developing the Concept of Flexibility

Flexibility in the use of rate is a skill in itself. Instead of adjusting rate to different purposes and different materials, many students in high school and college as well as in the grades use the same rate in all situations.

The need for developing the concept of flexibility in rate is pointed up in studies mentioned below.

It has been mentioned that Shores [23] indicated in the conclusions resulting from his study that "Efficient adult readers are much more flexible in adjusting reading rate to the demands of the task than are sixth grade students."

Sister Herculane [24] conducted a study to ascertain the extent to which 102 eighth grade students actually varied their rate and techniques of reading and appeared to understand the concept of flexibility according to purpose. She found that the students had no verbal or functional understanding of the concept.

Suggestions for Developing Awareness of the Need for Flexibility

At the beginning of the year the teacher may give timed reading tests to pupils in reading different types of material for different purposes: a

[23] Shores, *op. cit.*, p. 245.
[24] Sister M. Herculane, "A Survey of the Flexibility of Rates and Techniques According to Purpose," *Journal of Developmental Reading*, IV (Spring 1961), 207–10.

story to follow the plot; a geography or history selection to get general information; a science selection to get detailed facts. The pupils should read for a period of three to five minutes in each case, and then each should determine his average rate per minute. In every case the teacher should test comprehension with ten questions designed to check the kind of information for which the pupils were reading. All three speed scores and all three comprehension scores by subjects for a few of the pupils should be placed on the chalkboard and used as a basis for discussion. Many needs may be pointed out by examining these sample scores. Some pupils may have used the same rate in three situations and gotten poor comprehension scores in the science and geography tests, indicating that they were reading too fast in these subjects for the purpose assigned. Some may have used the same rate for all three and gotten perfect comprehension scores, which would indicate that they probably could have read the story at a rate that was much more rapid, and that they might be able safely to improve their rate in reading in the other two fields. Some might have adjusted their rates, reading the story very rapidly, the geography or history material less rapidly, and the science materials more slowly than either of the others—making high comprehension scores in all of them. Such a set of scores should be held up as an example of the desirable thing to do.

After background discussion, each pupil should compare his own scores and arrive at conclusions in regard to how he, personally, can develop desired flexibility.

While the above procedure may be used in fourth and fifth grades for developing the *concept* of flexibility, probably little more than this should be done at these grade levels. At sixth grade level, however, checks of flexibility similar to the above may be given periodically throughout the year, and records kept of improvement.

It is useful, occasionally, also to list purposes for which pupils might read and to determine the possible speed of reading for each purpose.

Frequent reminders should be given to pupils for the purpose of maintaining in them a vigorous awareness of their present individual rates of reading in the different subject fields and the need for using different speeds in reading different kinds of content for different purposes.

Developing Ability to Skim

There is no greater asset to the reader of today than highly developed skill in skimming. Skimming enables a person quickly to select content which he wants to read and to discard that in which he is not interested or which is inconsequential to his purpose.

Most adults develop some skill in skimming newspapers and magazines. This skill can be further developed to a very high degree and used profitably in doing all kinds of reading. Such development, however, requires instruction and practice if it is to function in the best capacity.

The middle grade period is none too early a time to make pupils aware of the skill of skimming and its uses and advantages. Informal, functional practice in skimming can be given safely to children in the fourth and fifth grades who are not having word recognition difficulties or trouble in getting meanings. Good readers in the sixth grade may be given timed practice in skimming.

Introducing Skimming

At a time when children are about to read an easy selection or chapter in a book, the teacher may discuss skimming as being a separate skill in itself, point out many of its uses, and ask the children to add to the list. Strong emphasis should be placed on the fact that skimming should be used only when a person wants to get a general overview or general impression of a selection or chapter—not for careful study to grasp details or factual information.

The pupils may also be given information in regard to the nature of the skimming process as follows: (1) it makes use of all of the reading skills they have previously had; (2) it necessitates a willingness to "break loose" and cover quantities of material without reading every word; (3) it calls for the development of new patterns of eye-movements—going from the top to the bottom of a page rather than following each line carefully from left to right across the page.

The teacher may demonstrate skimming with a newspaper in which she rapidly glances at headlines to see if there are some about which she would like more information. She may then glance only at the first sentence in each one, and perhaps at the main idea in additional paragraphs under some one of the topics. She may then tell what she found out.

The pupils may be asked to do the same with sample pages from newspapers which the teacher has brought in.

Follow-Up Practice

For follow-up practice pupils may be asked to see how quickly they can:

1. Skim a table of contents to find out on what page a chapter begins or a topic is treated.
2. Skim parts of an article in an encyclopedia to find a particular bit of information.
3. Skim to find a word in the dictionary.
4. Skim an index to find an entry pertinent to a certain topic.
5. Skim a selection to find one particular bit of information.

6. Skim a table to find one particular statistic.
7. Skim to find and read orally the most exciting part of a story or the part that describes the prettiest picture.
8. Skim to find the answer to each of a series of questions which the teacher writes on the chalkboard, placing at the end of each question the page number on which the answer may be found.
9. Skim to find sentences that portray the character of a person in a story.
10. Skim selections to get the main ideas.
11. Skim selections by previewing before reading.
12. Skim a chapter in reviewing for a quiz or test.
13. Skim a book to decide whether or not to read it.
14. Skim with the use of key words only—looking chiefly at nouns and verbs and ignoring the unimportant words.
15. Skim to make an outline.
16. Skim to write a summary.

Sample Procedures for Practice

Sample procedures for conducting practice on skimming will be found under "Maintenance and Practices Activities" on pages 573–80. These practice activities illustrate the use of the following techniques: skimming for main ideas, skimming for details, grasping key words, using the vertical field of vision.

In order that each set of procedures may be concrete, a selection to be used as the basis for practice and an accompanying checking exercise are presented, as well as possible explanations and directions to pupils. The chief purpose for presenting these helps, is that of suggesting to teachers procedures which can be used in giving skimming practice in connection with content in the books which the pupils are currently using or which are available to them in the classroom. These procedures are advisable only for good readers in fifth or sixth grades.

Evaluation of Growth in Reading Rates

Informal Checks

The teacher's observation of individual children can reveal much information concerning rate and habits affecting rate. Lip and head movements, finger-pointing, word reading, and dawdling while reading are undesirable habits that are easily detected through observation. A pupil's flexibility or lack of flexibility in rate may be noted by a keen observer, also.

Personal, dated notes jotted down at intervals while observing individual children may yield indication of growth in regard to these matters. Some teachers prepare check lists of factors pertaining to rate and check pupils on these items at intervals.

Informal tests of rates used in reading different kinds of materials yield the best evidence of a child's present status and later growth. Several suggestions were made for the teacher's use in preparing and administering informal tests of rates on pages 372–74. In order that comparisons of growth may be as accurate as possible, the teacher should strive to use material of approximately the same difficulty and the same type in checking rates of reading. Furthermore, checks should be made over a fairly long period of time, for growth in rates of reading usually doesn't take place in a week or two.

Charts, graphs, and tables are useful mediums for recording growth in rates and in understanding meanings. Each child should keep his own personal record rather than having it shown on a large class graph or chart in which he is compared with others. Beating one's own record is the best motive.

Standardized Tests

Standardized tests of rate are useful but they have their limitations in that rate of reading one selection of a certain type and difficulty only is tested. Each pupil should develop different rates to use with different materials and for different purposes as indicated in this chapter. Because of this need, standardized tests should be supplemented with informal tests based on materials which the children are using in the classroom.

Not many of the standardized tests for the elementary grades check rate. The following tests do check rate as well as some other aspects of reading ability: Iowa Silent Reading Tests, grades 4 to 8; Gates Basic Reading Tests, grades 3–8. The latter test is especially noteworthy in regard to rate for it checks rate in reading for four different purposes. Both of these tests were described on page 299.

Some additional standardized tests which check rate at the elementary level are:

Gates reading survey

This test, designed for grades 3 to 10, provides a separate measure of rate as well as of vocabulary, level of comprehension, and accuracy of comprehension. (Bureau of Publications, Teachers College, Columbia University.)

Diagnostic reading tests

The lower level of these tests is for grades 4 to 6. There are booklets which check reading skills as follows: Booklet 1, comprehension and word attack; Booklet 2, vocabulary and rate; Section IV of the lower level checks word attack and oral reading. (Committee on Diagnostic Testing.)

Reading tests for New York elementary schools

One set of these tests begins at grade 3 and tests word recognition and paragraph comprehension. The set beginning at grade 6 tests rate as well as the other two skills checked in the set beginning at grade 3. (New York State Education Department.)

Sangren-Woody reading test

This test is planned for grades 4 to 8. It tests rate as well as word meaning, fact material, total meaning, central thought, following directions and organization. (Harcourt-World Book.)

Reading versatility test

This test is made up of two separate booklets, the Basic Test and the Advanced Test. The Basic Test can be used with sixth grade children. The test is designed to check flexibility of comprehension and rate in reading for different purposes. (Educational Development Laboratories.)

Summary

Some of the research findings discussed in this chapter were: speed can be increased with training; the fast reader usually reads with the best grasp of content but not always; many different factors affect rate in reading; instruments are not a necessity in improving rate; provision for systematic training in speed is usually not advisable until fifth or sixth grade and then only with good readers.

Suggestions were given for laying rate foundations in the primary grades by developing accuracy in word identification and in getting meanings; developing habits of reading in phrases; breaking habits of bodily movement when reading; and encouraging wide, purposeful reading.

In discussing intermediate grades, suggestions were given for making pupils aware of their various rates, developing the concept of reading in thought units, establishing habits of reading for a purpose, and teaching the technique of previewing. Rather full procedures were described for conducting timed reading practice; controlled reading with instruments was discussed and evaluated; development of flexibility while reading was urged. The special skill of skimming was treated and many suggestions were given for use in developing this ability.

The general conclusion which might be drawn in regard to reading rate is that it is an important and complex skill which deserves special consideration, and that fostering growth in this skill should be one of the strong objectives of elementary teachers.

Additional Readings

Books

DeBoer, John J. and Martha Dallmann, *The Teaching of Reading*, Chaps. 8A, 8B. New York: Holt, Rinehart and Winston, Inc., 1960.

Durrell, Donald, *Improving Reading Instruction,* rev. ed., pp. 190–92. New York: Harcourt, Brace & World, Inc., 1956.

Harris, Albert J., *How to Increase Reading Ability,* rev. ed., Chap. XVIII. New York: Longmans, Green & Co., Inc., 1956.

Russell, David H., *Children Learn to Read,* rev. ed., pp. 132–33. Boston: Ginn & Company, 1961.

Smith, Nila Banton, *Read Faster and Get More from Your Reading.* Englewood Cliffs, N. J.: Prentice-Hall, Inc., 1958.

Periodicals

Bushwell, G. T., "Relationship Between Rate of Thinking and Rate of Reading," *School Review,* Vol. 59 (Sept. 1951), 339, 346.

Carrillo, Lawrence W., and William D. Sheldon, "Flexibility of Reading Rate," *Journal of Educational Psychology,* Vol. 43 (May 1952), 299–305.

Dolch, Edward William, "Rapid Reading with a Purpose," *School Review,* Vol. 59 (Oct. 1951), 410–13.

Fitzpatrick, E. A., "Speed and Comprehension in Reading," *Catholic School Journal,* Vol. 58 (June 1958), 20.

Haswell, Elizabeth F., "Accuracy Before Speed," *Peabody Journal of Education,* Vol. 28 (July 1950), 9–16.

Leeds, J. P., "Speed Reading and Visual Training," *Education,* Vol. 81 (May 1961), 554–56.

McCracken, Robert A., "Accelerating the Reading Speed of Sixth Grade Gifted Children," *Exceptional Children,* Vol. 27 (Sept. 1960), 27–28.

Simpson, Elizabeth Addis, "Reading Rate and Its Relationship to Good Reading," *Education,* Vol. 70 (May 1950), 565–69.

Smith, Nila B., "You Can Read Faster and Better," *Business Education World,* Vol. 36 (Mar. 1956), 17–18; (Apr. 1956), 28–29; (May 1956), 18–20; (June 1956), 29–31; Vol. 37 (Sept. 1956), 37–41; (Oct. 1956), 38–43; (Nov. 1956), 25–27; (Dec. 1956), 32–35.

Stolarz, T., "How Important is Speed in Reading?" *Chicago School Journal,* Vol. 43 (Nov. 1961), 71–77.

Stroud, James Bart, "Rate of Visual Perception as a Factor in Rate of Reading," *Journal of Educational Psychology,* Vol. 36 (Nov. 1945), 487–98.

Witty, Paul Andrew, "Evaluation of Methods and Devices to Improve Reading Rate and Comprehension," *Elementary English,* Vol. 31 (May 1954), 260–67.

PART 3

Developing Interest
and Taste
in Reading Literature

12

Literature in the Space Age: Status and Values

The development of interest in reading is a growth area of grave importance. Of what value are all our efforts to establish proficiency in the basic skills of reading if children do not make the fullest use of these skills to enrich their lives, both as children at present and as adults later on? Permanent carry-over interest in reading has long been stated as the ultimate goal of all reading instruction. This goal is more urgent now than ever before because of the many competing communication agencies with which reading is confronted.

In addition to the goal of developing permanent interest in reading per se, we need to develop desirable attitudes and habits in reading *selectively*. Our concern should not be simply to develop interest in reading anything and everything. We need to develop discriminating readers; readers who will choose to read those things which will contribute most to their lives culturally, socially, and informatively. The development of interest and taste should proceed hand-in-hand. In this chapter these two aspects of reading instruction are treated as interlocking and integrated factors.

Can Reading Withstand the Competition?

As previously indicated, reading in the world of today is challenged by several competing agencies. The cinema, television, radio, and comics have taken a strong hold on American life. These mediums of communication are attractively serving many of the purposes which reading previously served. As a result, one occasionally meets an individual who states, "Why all the fuss about teaching reading? In the future reading may become a lost art. All our recreational and informative needs will probably be met through mechanized communication in which we listen and look rather than read."

What is the answer to such a pronouncement? *Is* reading in danger of becoming a lost art, or does reading have some special advantages so compelling as to ensure its perpetuation? We think the latter is the case, and here are some of the advantages.

1. Reading embraces a greater range and variety of material than is available through any other communication agency. The heritage of the ages is stored up in reading as it never can be stored in radio or movies or television.

2. Reading material is more accessible at the time it is needed; in other words in reading we can put our fingers on what we want at the time we want it.

3. For an efficient reader, reading is more economical of time than radio or pictures. The rapid reader, for example, could probably gather as much information by skimming a newspaper for five minutes as he could obtain from a fifteen-minute broadcast slowed down to the rate of the commentator's oral speech and interspersed with commercials, station identification, and other radio conventionalities. Try it and see!

4. The reading process is more adjustable to our individual purposes, interests, and rates of assimilation than any other medium. In reading the individual may proceed at his own speed, he may choose that to which he wishes to give attention and skip that in which he is not interested, and he may turn back and go over certain sections again as many times as he likes.

These are particular advantages which it seems will always be inherent in reading. Because of their individual appeal and usefulness and because of the abundance and prevalence of reading materials, it would appear likely that reading will survive as the most fundamental of the communication agencies.

Of What Value Is Literature to the
Child of Today? [1]

The child of today lives in a mechanized world. His toys are miniature representations of rockets, jets, and space ships. His home is filled with gadgets for cleaning, cooking, washing, heating, and air-conditioning. He travels by automobile, train, or airplane. Much of his entertainment comes to him over television, radio, and cinema.

In this age of mechanized living, literature is an exigency. The child, immersed in his mechanized surroundings, must have an opportunity to obtain the wholesome recreation and aesthetic satisfaction that comes from exploring the fascinating world of stories and poems. He must have an opportunity to enjoy and interpret human experience as portrayed by master writers. Truly this nourishing refreshment is necessary to offset the mechanistic effects of machines, gadgets, and speed.

Why does literature hold so much promise for children in the space age? What specific values accrue from literature in a child-growth program at the present time? The remainder of this section will be concerned with a discussion of these questions.

Personality Development

Personality is an integration of social, emotional, and behavioral characteristics. These characteristics emerge as natural endowments which interact with experience. Literature provides an inexhaustible well of human experience, from which children may take deep draughts of life and living. It follows, then, that one of the most important functions of literature is to help children relive the experiences of others and thus to deepen and broaden their own personal experiences.

Literature affords an opportunity to participate sympathetically in the viewpoints, problems, and difficulties of others. It helps the child to understand culture patterns, both those which are currently in existence and those of the past. It enables him to interpret his own needs for security, love, companionship, success.

In addition, literature aids therapeutically in solving personal problems. As the child reads literary selections, he is bound to encounter characters who have had problems similar to his and who have successfully solved these similar problems.

[1] Reprinted from Nila Banton Smith, "Literature for Space Age Children," *Education*, Vol. 81 (Oct. 1960), 100–105.

Literature also contributes to the improvement of attitudes and behavior toward people, animals, cultures, creeds, beliefs, occupations, institutions, country. As evidences of some of the personality values heretofore mentioned, the writer submits a few quotations resulting from a study entitled "Some Effects of Reading on Children." [2]

Cynthia, Grade 6, wrote:

The story of *The Blind Colt* impressed me very much. I never thought that blind animals could get around or play tricks. I thought they should be killed. But now I know that with patience some blind animals can be taught to do the things they need in order to get along in life. They must have companions, though, who are interested in helping them.

Animals are something like people.

This summer when I was on a trip I saw a blind man playing a violin and traveling by himself and I thought of the little blind colt.

Whenever I see a blind person again I'm going to act the same way as if he wasn't blind. Instead of feeling sorry for him, I'm going to admire him for his courage in learning to do things.

Janice, Grade 7, in writing about "America For Me" said simply:

This poem made me realize how nice it is to be an American.

Richard, Grade 8, wrote:

I didn't realize very much what my country meant to me or what it meant to other people until I read *The Man Without A Country.*

When I read this, I realized that I was lucky to live here in this free land and am thankful that I don't have to live on a boat.

Roger, Grade 6, wrote:

I had always heard that Sitting Bull was a terrible Indian and that he was always killing people. Then I read the book *Sitting Bull.* It told how he had held back from fighting as long as he could but at last he had to fight and when he did he was a terror. After he made a treaty someone accused him of trying to start a war and he was killed in a cowardly way.

I learned that Indians have honor and now I have a greater respect for them than I did before.

Cynthia changed her attitude and behavior toward blind people. Janice and Richard developed a deeper love for their country, and Roger came to have better attitudes toward another race. Surely literature greatly helped these children to improve their personalities.

Creative self-expression which often buds out of communication with literature is a salutary agent in developing personality. Two important elements of creativity are, first, uniqueness, inventiveness, making something new and different; and second, integration, weaving personal feel-

2 Nila Banton Smith, "Some Effects of Reading on Children," *Elementary English Review,* Vol. 25, No. 5 (May 1948), 271–79.

ings, attitudes, and generalizations into some form of expression. Creative experiences involving these elements lead to discovery of dormant powers, draw upon reserves of untouched artistic emotion, develop a capacity for clarifying concepts and for arriving at basic generalizations. These new powers summoned to the surface through the medium of literary experiences release tensions, bring satisfactions, and induce personalities to unfold and to bloom.

As children derive pleasure from reading literary materials, they naturally feel compelled to prolong this pleasure through other arts closely akin to literature. For instance, they may wish to dramatize a story. They may want to draw, paint, or sculpture characters and scenery. They may want to write other stories and poems of their own, and even to set their poems to music.

The reading of literature in itself is a creative experience. Even so, however, it serves as a springboard for creative activities expressed in several other forms of symbolization.

To summarize: literature contributes to personality development by promoting understandings, by improving attitudes and behavior, by helping to solve personal problems, and by stimulating creative powers. No other type of material offers such rich and varied possibilities for nurturing and unfolding and shaping of personality!

The Stimulation of Interests

One of the most important areas of growth in reading is the area of interests. Without interests all the laborious work of developing reading skills would be of no avail. Unfortunately, many children and adults *can* read, but never *do* read. What good are reading skills if persons do not use them to enrich their living? Growth in skill proficiency is important, but of equal significance is the development of permanent, carry-over interests. These interests are necessary to impel an individual to make efficient use of reading skills in serving his life needs.

At present, we must strive as we have never striven before to develop wide, permanent, carry-over interests in reading. Mechanized communication agencies are striding across the reading habits of America with a heavy tread. Reading is faced with strong competition. As already indicated, radio, television, and movies almost completely satisfy many persons' desires for entertainment and information. If reading is to continue to function as the most valuable means of tapping our inexhaustible supplies of printed communication, then we must put forth far greater effort than ever before to establish abiding interests.

One of our best allies in achieving this goal is literature. Literature is entertaining. Entertainment is enjoyable. That which is enjoyable is interesting. When a child first experiences pleasure in literature, his appetite is whetted for more literature. Providing him with stories and poems geared to his interests, chronological maturity, and reading ability is one of the surest ways of encouraging him to delve ever more deeply into his literary inheritance.

Interests developed through literary experiences are likely to continue throughout elementary school, secondary school, college, and even throughout life. If literature had no function other than helping a person to establish life-time interests in reading, this value alone would place it close to the apex of curricular offerings.

Providing Functional Information

Children have many intellectual curiosities. Their quest for knowledge leads them to seek information about bugs, snakes, birds; stars, sun, moon; seaweed, shells, fish. They want to know about airplanes, rockets, trains, boats, and automobiles. They are eager for enlightenment about human beings, events, relationships, occupations, ways of living, castles, heroes, battles, and wars. This thirst for information is satisfied in many ways through the medium of literature.

One of the unique characteristics of literature is its diversity of content. It doesn't confine itself to one specialized area of knowledge. The writers of literature do not pour their stories and poems into subject-matter compartments. They write about things that touch them deeply at the moment, things that they feel impelled to share with others.

Authors write on topics as broad as life itself—as all-inclusive as children's searches for knowledge. In view of this fact, children find literary content a very satisfying source of information to answer numerous questions that prompt them to read.

Literature does far more, however, than provide information in the factual sense. It presents information in meaningful situations, rather than in organized subject-matter categories. For this reason it has a special advantage in broadening concepts, deepening insights, clarifying human relationships, arriving at social and philosophical truths. In other words, it provides knowledge far beyond facts—it enables facts to live and to function.

Another informative value inherent in literature is that knowledge is presented in interesting, dramatic, and colorful settings which appeal to children's interests. Many children, who are reluctant to read books designed to provide direct instruction, become completely absorbed in stories and poems that indirectly provide information and insights.

Trickling interests born in these integrated situations, if carefully guided, may well lead to the purposeful reading of textbooks or encyclopedic materials.

Thus literature serves in many ways, not only to provide facts, but also to stimulate and satisfy the child's quest for knowledge and wisdom.

Curricular Enrichment

Although literature never should be used for teaching subject matter directly, it may serve admirably to supplement, extend, and reveal content in the various curricular areas. I have already spoken of the close relationship of literature to art, music, drama, and creative writing and have indicated its overflow possibilities in these artistic areas. Social studies and science are also particularly benefited through literature.

The subject matter of literature is the subject matter of life, and life's subject matter lies almost entirely within the content areas of social studies and science. Consequently, literature, social studies, and science have a great deal in common.

Let us examine briefly how literature may serve to enrich the social-studies area. Literature deals with people, their work and recreation, their sorrows and joys, their relationships and individual problems. Consider Mother Goose, for example. In listening to or reading Mother Goose, children learn about planting and reaping, grinding flour, milking cows, shearing sheep, tending garden, making cheese and butter, and many other activities. They visit farms, villages, cities, markets, mills, fairs, and shops. They meet kings, queens, farmers, fishermen, shepherds, black-smiths, and milkmaids—all as they laugh or weep, talk or sing, work or play together in harmonious interpersonal relationships.

Mother Goose, of course, occupies but one tiny niche in the great world of literature. Many different types of literary materials—folktales, legends, modern fanciful tales, realistic stories, poetry—all have potentialities for social-studies enrichment.

Children studying the lumber industry, for instance, gain invaluable insights by reading about legendary Paul Bunyan and his blue ox. Children studying pioneer life gain rich understandings by reading such stories as "Mr. Meeker and the Indians" by Miriam E. Mason, and those studying transportation by reading "The Locomotive and the Horse" (story of the first run of the Baltimore and Ohio Railroad) by Thomas Bowles. Children studying city life certainly should have an opportunity to read the delightful little poem, "The Buildings," by Rose Fyleman. One could go on endlessly in giving such examples. Perhaps enough has been said to establish the point that literature is an inexhaustible source of enrichment for the varied subject-matter areas in the social-studies curriculum.

Science is equally fortunate in having strong reinforcements in literature. Consider Mother Goose again. In listening to or reading Mother Goose, children make repeated visits to farm, lane, field, seashore, and stream. They meet and learn about bird-life and barnyard fowl, fish and turtles, spiders and flies. They witness a fascinating procession of farm animals, such as lambs, sheep, colts, horses, calves, cows, and donkeys. Truly, Mother Goose may be called the child's first "Natural History."

The whole world of literature, of course, is pregnant with possibilities for enriching science. The child can greatly enrich his science learnings about animals by reading "Paddle Tail and Water Baby" by Jane Tompkins. He can enrich his appreciation and understanding of insects by reading "Firefly" by Elizabeth Madox Roberts; of wind and weather conditions by reading "Bumbershoot Wind" by Mary Calhoun; of modern inventions by reading "The Airplane" by Annette Wynne, "My Rocket Ship" by Frances Gorman Risser, and "David Makes a TV" by Vera Pickard. These, of course, are merely random samplings of the abundant and fruitful materials that literature affords to supplement and enrich the area of science.

As previously indicated, literature never should be used for the purpose of teaching subject matter in the various curricular areas. On the other hand it serves as a deft and subtle accompaniment to subject matter and provides immeasurable aid in supplying additional information, broadening concepts, and deepening appreciations.

Indirect Contribution to Skills

A child learns to read by reading somewhat as the swimmer learns to swim by swimming. The more enjoyable reading he does, the more proficient he becomes in using reading skills. No teacher should use literature solely as a basis for teaching reading skills, but she certainly should use literature as a medium for applying skills in joyful, purposeful reading. Care must be taken, however, to make certain that all literature falls within the readability level of the children for whom it is provided. The frustrating experience of trying to read literature that is "too hard" may discourage a child from making attempts to read at all. Any literature which is written above the reading level of children should be read or told to them by the teacher.

The interest factor in literature is especially conducive to fluency and speed in reading. Even the word reader forgets to loiter over each symbol when he becomes absorbed in a story. Instead, he races over the pages to find what will happen next, and in his eagerness he takes in whole meaningful groups of words.

Folklore is particularly valuable for reluctant readers. Repetition of phrases, simplicity of characterization, swiftness of plot make for easy reading. Too, the simple conversation in folklore helps to bridge the gap between oral reading and silent reading, a gap that the retarded reader often finds difficult to bridge.

Thus literature serves children in inestimable ways. Many people today, realizing the intrinsic worth of literature in this mechanized and troubled era of history, are combining their efforts to make the beneficent influences of literature more widely available. Educators are urging more abundant supplies of literature for classrooms and more skillful use of literature by teachers. Publishers are making available excellent story books for children and graded anthologies filled with fascinating selections for classroom use. Trained librarians, literary people, and childhood specialists are cooperating wholeheartedly in advancing and disseminating literary values. All these efforts are evidences of a growing realization of the unlimited values of literature. The present literary movement deserves our hearty support!

13

Guiding Children's Interest in Television, Comics, Newspapers, and Magazines

Is Television Beneficial or Harmful to Reading?

When television first appeared in American homes in 1949 to 1950, it was looked upon as a serious threat to reading. In the meantime many studies have been conducted to find out what effect television is having upon the reading interests of boys and girls, and what effect it is having upon their attitudes and behavior. A few of these studies and their results will be mentioned.

Time Spent in Televiewing

In a summary of studies concerning children and television, Witty [1] found that in 1950 the amount of time given to television by elementary pupils was, on the average, twenty-one hours per week. In 1957 the average was twenty-six hours in one experiment and twenty hours in another.

[1] Paul Witty, "Children, TV and Reading," *The Reading Teacher*, Vol. 11 (Nov. 1957), 15–16.

A recent study [2] of 2,000 junior high school students in Texas revealed that the *average* time they spent per year viewing television was 1,216 hours and the maximum time spent per year in classrooms was 1,144 hours. In other words, the average number of hours that these children spent in viewing television exceeded the maximum number of hours that they spent in school. The investigators concluded, "Any medium which absorbs as much of a student's time as television is almost certain to have some effect on his sense of values and on his sensitivity to his environment."

In the light of these studies and others, it would appear that children still are spending nearly as much or more time in televiewing than in classroom activities.

Many teachers and parents question the advisability of children spending such a large proportion of their free time in viewing television. These people would like to see a better distribution of free time among televiewing, sports, and recreational interests involving physical activities, artistic pursuits, hobbies, reading, and homework.

Televiewing and Amount of Reading Done

Witty [3] indicates that there appeared to be a slight drop in the amount of reading done as revealed by his early surveys made with parents, teachers, and children themselves. He concludes, however, that there is a recent trend toward slightly higher amounts of reading.

Wells and Lynch [4] found no significant correlation of hours of televiewing with hours of free reading. A study [5] of elementary school pupils' responses revealed that the pupils themselves believed that they were reading more since they had television. Forty-five per cent thought they read more, twenty-nine per cent less, and twenty-six per cent the same amount.

Many parents and teachers, however, are strong in their convictions that television interferes with children's recreational reading. We must face the fact that altogether too many children are reading very little or not at all outside of school. We need also to take note of evidence showing that elementary children on the average are devoting about one hour

[2] Zell Sorello and Jack Walker, "What is Television Doing to Our Children," *The Journal of Educational Research*, Vol. 55 (Feb. 1962), 236–37.
[3] Paul Witty, *op. cit.*, p. 13.
[4] Charles A. Wells and Timothy I. Lynch, "The Amount of Free Reading Engaged in by Intermediate Grade Pupils Who Have Viewed Television for One Year or More," *Journal of Educational Research*, Vol. 47 (Feb. 1954), 473–76.
[5] Paul Witty, "A Report on Televiewing in 1961," *Elementary English*, Vol. 29 (Jan. 1962), 31.

per day to voluntary reading as compared with three hours to viewing television.

The situation is one that should spur teachers on to intensify their efforts to increase interest in reading as a voluntary, free-time activity.

The Effect of Television on Achievement

Several studies have indicated that there is little or no relationship between school achievement and the amount of time devoted to viewing. Wells and Lynch [6] found no significant relationship between hours of television viewing with average reading achievement of fifth and sixth grade pupils. Greenstein [7] found a lack of close relationship between school grades and amount of televiewing.

On the other hand, Scott [8] and Witty [9] found lower achievements for children who spend an unusually large amount of time in televiewing. Kinsella [10] found differences in the amount of time that pupils in upper groups and lower groups of achievement devoted to viewing. Both boys and girls in the upper achievement groups devoted less time to televiewing than did those in the lower achievement groups.

Many children themselves seem to think that television is helpful to them in their studies. As a result of a questionnaire study, Witty [11] found that seventy-eight per cent of the elementary pupils, but only forty-seven per cent of the high school students, thought television was helpful. Elementary pupils thought television helped them in reading, geography, history, science, arithmetic, music appreciation, and knowledge of people around them. This study is interesting, but of course the validity of data resulting from a questionnaire based upon children's opinions is questionable.

Program Interests of Children

While children view all types of programs, they seem to have strong favorites. According to Witty's studies,[12] the types of programs that are

[6] Wells and Lynch, *op. cit.*

[7] Jack Greenstein, "Effect of Television upon Elementary School Grades," *Journal of Educational Research*, Vol. 48 (Nov. 1954), 161–76.

[8] Lloyd F. Scott, "Television and School Achievement," *Phi Delta Kappan*, Vol. 38 (Oct. 1956), 25–28.

[9] Paul Witty, "Televiewing by Children and Youth," *Elementary English*, Vol. 38 (Feb. 1961), 112.

[10] Paul J. Kinsella, *A Comparison of Mass Media Usage by Junior High School Pupils of Extreme Educational Achievement and Mental Ability.* Ph.D. Dissertation (Evanston, Ill.: Northwestern University, 1961).

[11] Witty, *op. cit.*

[12] Paul Witty, "A Report on Televiewing in 1962," *Elementary English*, Vol. 39 (Jan. 1962), 26–27.

most popular with primary children are the cartoon and the cartoon-comedy types. Mystery drama is most popular with intermediate grade children. More generally, in the elementary grades, Schramm [13] reports the favorite programs to be those representing variety, adventure, Westerns, and science fiction. As children approach adolescence, crime dramas and popular music claim much of their viewing time. Most people deplore the vast amount of violence, hate, and destruction shown on the screen in programs that are attractive to children.

Is Television Beneficial or Harmful?

The brief review of data given above would indicate rather clearly that there is no one definite answer to the above question. The medium of communication which is so attractive to children has both limitations and values. Teachers and parents can help to overcome the former and extend the latter.

What Can Teachers Do About Television?

Television undoubtedly has the strongest universal appeal of any of the many mediums of communication. We as teachers must learn to make the most of this interest in the educational development of children with whom we work. How can this be done?

1. View current programs which are popular with children. Thoroughly familiarize yourself with the characters and their typical activities.

2. Set times aside for frequent discussion of these programs. Express your own approvals and subtle criticisms, explaining why.

3. Encourage children to select programs with careful discrimination.

4. Aid children in developing a set of standards to use in evaluating programs.

5. Extend television interest to reading in which the children's purpose is to find out more about the same subject, or to enjoy a book containing the complete story from which a television play was taken.

6. Extend knowledge gained from television programs to the use of encyclopedias, demonstration of scientific principles, development of worthwhile hobbies.

7. Help parents to evaluate programs viewed by children.

8. Counsel parents whose children are spending an excessive amount of time in viewing. Suggest that they limit the viewing time and encourage other types of recreational activities.

---

13 Wilbur Schramm, Jack Lyle, and Edwin B. Parker, *Television in the Lives of Our Children* (Stanford, Cal.: Stanford University Press, 1961), p. 93.

9. Join other teachers and parents in a campaign to encourage the development of better television programs and the reduction or abandonment of the undesirable types of programs.

10. Study the particular interests of different children. Try to provide for these interests through reading or other recreational activities.

11. Study the possibilities of recreational activities for children in your school and community. Encourage children to avail themselves of these opportunities.

Uses of Television in Teaching Reading Skills

Before closing the discussion concerning the relationships of reading and television, mention should be made of ways in which this powerful medium of communication is being harnessed as an aid to the actual teaching of the reading skills.

Television has now entered the classroom as a teaching agent. Some schools are using television not only to stimulate interest in books but to teach such fundamental skills as phonics, comprehension, and speed. Controlled investigations on the effectiveness of television teaching of reading are not sufficient in number or quality to be conclusive, but they are promising.

Television is serving another purpose aimed at the improvement of reading instruction. It is being used as a teacher-training medium. Some college professors have prepared video tapes which they use in their methods courses in reading. Several large cities have prepared video tapes for a series of presentations designed to improve the teaching of reading by teachers in service.

What About the Comics?

The comics received much attention in professional literature between 1940 and 1950. With the advent of television in homes, anxiety then became transferred to this new threat to reading, and the comics receded in both public and professional interest. Television, however, did not substitute for children's interest in comics as we shall see in the results of research which are presented below.

Research in Regard to Comics

An extensive summary of investigations [14] reported in 1955 led to several conclusions of importance. Some of these conclusions are as follows:

[14] Paul A. Witty and Robert A. Sizemore, "Reading the Comics: A Summary of Studies and An Evaluation," *Elementary English,* Vols. 31 and 32 (Dec. 1934), 501–506; (Jan. 1955), 43–49; (Feb. 1955), 109–14.

1. At the time of the summary, studies indicated that over ninety per cent of children between eight and thirteen years of age read comic books regularly.

2. It was found that interest in comics begins with young children, continues in the primary grades, and reaches its height in fourth, fifth, and sixth grades. Children in junior high school, however, continue to read comics with intense interest. Students in senior high read, on an average, a distinctly lower number of comic strips than do those in junior high.

3. Many studies revealed that the amount of comic book reading was not related to school grades or achievement.

4. The effect of comics on children's behavior is controversial. Wertham [15] and others have blamed the comics for much juvenile delinquency and bad behavior. On the other hand, many studies have shown little difference between the amount of comic reading and delinquency. The investigators of these later studies, however, point out that comic books presenting violence, hate, and aggression might lead a child to a distorted and unwholesome view of the world around him.

What Can Teachers Do About Comics?

Comics are definitely entrenched in American life. Adults as well as children read them. Watch the tired business or professional man as he settles down in a bus or suburban train to return home at the end of a day's work. As he unfolds his newspaper he is very likely to turn to the "funnies" to enjoy a chuckle and a moment of relaxation after a tense day in the office. Before he arrives at his destination, however, he probably will turn to the front page news, the sports, the editorials, the stock market, the book and theater reviews. In other words, the comics have only a small and momentary place in his total repertory of reading interests pursued within a given time. That is as it should be.

Teachers' efforts then should not be directed toward keeping children from reading the comics but rather toward broadening their interests and tastes in reading other worthwhile things until the lush grass crowds out the weeds.

1. Guidance may be given in the selection of comics by inviting children to compare different comic magazines in regard to such matters as art, paper, and typography. The content may also be discussed in regard to realistic versus unrealistic situations, speeches, and action, and good English versus poor English.

2. Comics may be used as the first step in building interest in read-

15 Frederic Wertham, *Seduction of the Innocent* (New York: Holt, Rinehart & Winston, Inc., 1954).

ing desirable stories and books that possess the same elements of appeal as those found in the comics. These elements seem to be: (1) they are easy to read—the pictures carry the plot; (2) the content is compatible to children's stage of development: they have action, suspense, mystery, adventure—all of which appeal especially to children at elementary and junior high levels; (3) they offer escape from routine; (4) wordy descriptions and backgrounds are omitted; (5) the episodes are short; (6) they are inexpensive.

With the above characteristics in mind, the teacher may surround children with books that also possess these elements of appeal and thus use the comics as a springboard to better reading.

Carr [16] prepared a list of books called "Substitutes for the Comic Book." Book titles in this list are grouped according to elements of appeal in the comics. This list may be suggestive to teachers.

3. Teachers may have interesting children's magazines in the classroom and encourage parents to subscribe to magazines for their children. Magazines with attractive pictures and fresh stories, articles, and novel features offer strong competition to the comics.

Magazine and Newspaper Reading

Newspaper Reading

It appears that large numbers of children in the second and third grades are reading newspapers and continue to do so in substantial amounts throughout the remaining grades. This reading leaves much to be desired, however, in regard to choice of subjects and features.

Lyness' [17] study revealed that eighty-five per cent of third graders, and from ninety-seven to ninety-nine per cent of pupils in all other grades, read newspapers. The three top choices of the boys were found to be sports, crime-police-gangsters, and auto wrecks. The top choices of the girls were "Hollywood, sports, and Des Moines (local) news." The favorite section of newspapers for all pupils studied were comics, sports, and movie-radio news. Small interest was shown in public affairs, editorials, columns, book reviews, and other newspaper features.

Witty and Kopel reported as a result of their investigations that almost all children were reading local newspapers. At the primary levels their newspaper reading was confined to the comics, and in second grade

[16] Constance Carr, "Substitutes for the Comic Book," *Elementary English,* Vol. 28 (Apr. 1951), 194–200.

[17] Paul I. Lyness, "What Boys and Girls Like in the Newspaper," *Editor and Publisher,* Vol. 83 (Nov. 1950), 18.

eighty per cent reported that they liked to "read" this part of the paper and no other part. This interest continued throughout the grades but was supplemented somewhat by the reading of other features. The ranking of the most popular sections in order were: comics, sports, photographic part, and news. It will be noted that news has fourth place. The investigators warn that even this "does not show the entire picture, since only one fourth of the children in the upper grades like to read the newspaper, and their reading is usually restricted to scanning headlines or a hurried glance at appealing or lurid news items." [18]

Magazine Reading

Magazines are read by large numbers of children, beginning with the second grade and increasing throughout the grades.

In one of the earlier studies, Lazar found that boys turned to magazines more frequently than girls, and that boys preferred detective and mystery stories, while the girls chose selections of the "general story-types." [19]

Children's magazines can lend much to the establishment of interests in and habits of reading. The novelty of having a new magazine arrive each month fulfills pleasant anticipation and is a refreshing experience. The articles or stories are usually short, and the format of a magazine places reading content in a different container than a book. These qualities are especially attractive to a reluctant reader.

Interesting magazines placed on the browsing table in school invite young readers to pick them up, reading here and there bits of their own choice.

A magazine subscribed to by a parent for his child is the child's own possession, something that comes to him from the outside world—not a part of school work. When his parents are reading their adult magazines he can read *his* magazine and feel the satisfaction of participating in the same type of reading which the adults in the family enjoy. Thus, he has status in the family circle.

A study by Witty and Kopel [20] indicated that the most popular magazine with boys in the first four grades was *Child Life*. In the fifth grade,

18 Paul Witty and David Kopel, "Studies of the Activities and Preferences of School Children," *Educational Administration and Supervision*, Vol. 24 (1938), 429–41; "The Dreams and Wishes of Elementary School Children," *Journal of Educational Psychology*, Vol. 30 (1939), 199–205.

19 May Lazar, *Reading Interests, Activities and Opportunities of Bright, Average and Dull Children*, Contributions to Education, No. 707 (New York: Teachers College, Columbia University, 1939).

20 Paul Witty and David Kopel, *op. cit.*

Popular Mechanics had first place. *Boys' Life* had first place from sixth grade on, although *Popular Mechanics* continued to be very popular. *Child Life* was the most popular periodical with girls in every grade.

Although only the top choices resulting from this study are mentioned above, it should be pointed out that the range of choices over other periodicals was very wide, wider for the boys than for the girls. Forty-two magazines were mentioned as favorites by the boys, and only twenty-four by the girls.

This study also indicated that *news* magazines in the home were rarely read by children. A later study by Peterson,[21] however, revealed that the picture magazines *Life* and *Look* were popular with older pupils in the elementary grades. In order of rank, the choices for boys were *Life, Look, Boys' Life;* and for girls, *Look, Life, The American Girl.* Peterson drew the general conclusion that girls preferred magazines about home-making and fashions, while boys most frequently chose those concerned with science and mechanics.

These studies indicate differences in the interests in magazine reading between boys and girls. It should be further emphasized that there are many individual interests among boys and many individual interests among girls. The wisest course to pursue is to surround children with good magazines of several types. Several magazines should be provided in the classroom, and parents should be advised to subscribe to children's magazines for their reading pleasure at home.

A list of recommended magazines for children follows.

Children's Magazines

American Childhood. Published monthly except July and August. 74 Park Street, Springfield, Mass. $4.00. Ages 5–10.

The American Girl. Published monthly by Girl Scouts of the U.S.A., 830 Third Avenue, New York 22. $3.00. Girls, ages 10 up.

American Junior Red Cross News. Published monthly (October–May) by Junior Red Cross, American Red Cross, Washington, D. C. $1.00 per classroom.

Animal Kingdom. Published bimonthly by New York Zoological Society, 30 East 40th Street, New York. $3.50. Written for adults but interesting to children.

Arts and Activities. Published monthly except July and August. 8150 No. Central Park Avenue, Skokie, Ill. Ages 5–12.

Boys' Life. Published monthly by Boy Scouts of America, New Brunswick, N. J. $3.00. Boys, ages 10 up.

[21] Miriam Peterson, *Reading Preferences and Interests of Pupils in the Chicago Public Elementary Schools, Grades IV through VII.* Ph.D. Dissertation. (Evanston, Ill.: Northwestern University, August 1955).

Audubon. Published bimonthly by National Audubon Society, 1130 Fifth Avenue, New York 28. $5.00.

Children's Digest. Published by Parents' Institute of Parents' Magazine, 52 Vanderbilt Avenue, New York 17. $4.00. Elementary ages.

Children's Playmate. Published monthly (10 issues) by Children's Playmate Magazine, Inc., Cleveland 5. $1.50. Elementary ages.

Highlights for Children (combined with *Treasure Trails*). Published at 37 East Long Street, Columbus. Sold nationally by bonded representatives; not sold on newsstands. 30 issues (3 years), $15; 50 issues (5 years), $23.50. Ages 2–12. Wide variety of materials, some original work of children; general effect is average but pedantic.

Humpty Dumpty's Magazine for Little Children. Published by Parents' Institute of Parents' Magazine, 52 Vanderbilt Avenue, New York 17. $5.00. Ages 3–7. Nature stories, read-aloud stories, and stories for beginning readers; would be improved by creative art suggestions in place of "coloring fun."

Jack and Jill. Published monthly by Curtis Publishing Company, Independence Square, Philadelphia 5. $3.95. Ages 3–10. One of the more attractive magazines—good format and interesting materials.

National Geographic Society School Bulletins. Published weekly (except June–September) by National Geographic Society, 1146 16th Street, N. W., Washington, D. C. $2.00. *National Geographic,* the adult magazine, same address, $8.00.

Nature Magazine, 1216 16th Street, N. W., Washington, D. C. An adult publication but subscribed to by thousands of elementary schools throughout the country.

Pack-O-Fun. Published at 14 Main Street, Park Ridge, Ill. 10 issues. $2.00. Elementary ages. A "scrap" craft magazine in the "Handy Boy" tradition. Children would get ideas for new uses for easily available materials.

Popular Mechanics. Published monthly in Chicago. Subscription office: 250 W. 55th Street, New York 19. $3.50. A great favorite with boys. Has many pictures, short articles, and projects which can actually be done and which will work when finished.

Read Magazine (incorporating *Young America*). Published twice a month during the school year by American Education.

Wee Wisdom. Published monthly by Unity School of Christianity, Lee's Summit, Missouri. $2.00. Ages 6–11. (Braille subscription free to those blind reading Grade II materials.) Rather didactic. Parents should check religious views before subscribing. Materials are adequate.

News Magazines for Classroom Use

My Weekly Reader. Published weekly during school year by American Education Publications, 1250 Fairwood Avenue, Columbus 16. $1.00 per school year in quantities of five or more. Edition for each grade. There is also one intended for kindergarten use.

Scholastic Magazines. Published weekly during school year by Scholastic Magazines, 33 West 42nd Street, New York 36. 80 cents per school year in lots of five or more. One paper for each grade, first through fifth; *Junior Scholastic* for grades 6–8 ($1.20); *World Week* for grades 8–10 ($1.30).

Summary

In this chapter the dangers of television and the comics were minimized somewhat in the light of research that has been conducted in regard to these communication agencies. Most teachers and parents, however, consider these agencies to be threats to the amount of voluntary reading which they would like children to do, and particularly to the development of good tastes in reading. Suggestions were given to assist teachers in guiding children's interests in selecting the better television programs and the better comics, and in extending their interests generated by these agencies to reading.

Research in regard to magazine and newspaper reading also reveals a need for guidance in children's selection of what they read. It was urged that schools and parents provide children with magazines of the better type.

Additional Readings

Books and Pamphlets

Children and TV: Making the Most of It. Washington, D. C.: Association for Childhood Education.

Dale, Bryant N., "The Effectiveness of Television in Teaching a Reading Skill and Motivating Students to Practice It," *Reading in a Changing Society*, Vol. 4, 86–88. International Reading Association Conference Proceedings, 1959.

Flierl, Nina T., "Using Television Interests to Building Reading," *New Frontiers in Reading*, Vol. 5, 121–23. International Reading Association Conference Proceedings, 1960.

Frank, Josette, *Comics, T.V., Radio, Movies—What Do They Offer Children?* New York: Public Affairs Pamphlets, 22 E. 38th St.

Miriam, Sister O. P., "Can the Teacher Improve Pupil Discrimination in Television and Reading?", *New Frontiers in Reading*, Vol. 5, 124–26. International Reading Association Conference Proceedings, 1960.

Witty, Paul, *Reading in Modern Education*, pp. 32–42. Boston: D. C. Heath & Co., 1949.

Periodicals

Evans, Clara, "Tots and TV," *Childhood Education*, Vol. 33 (Mar. 1957).

Garner, Richard F., "The Effect of Televised Reading Instruction on Attitudes Toward Reading," *Elementary English*, Vol. 39 (Mar. 1962), 234–36.

McCutcheon, Constance Carr, "Coping with Comics," *Literature for Children*, pp. 52–56. Washington, D. C.: Association for Childhood Education International, 1961.

Murray, Walter I., and Karel Newman Rose, "Utilizing Television in Teaching Children's Literature," *Education*, Vol. 82 (Jan. 1962), 309–11.

Smith, Nila B., ed. "Television and Reading," *The Reading Teacher*, Oct. 1957 (Entire issue).

———, "A Tenth Yearly Study and Comments on a Decade of Televiewing," *Elementary English*, Vol. 36 (Dec. 1959), 581–86.

14

Establishing Lifetime
Interests and Tastes

Interest Inducing Activities

Interest is the touchstone to reading achievement, reading
enjoyment, and reading usefulness. It is the generator of all
voluntary reading activity. Everyone is acquainted with students and adults who possess the skills of reading but who
rarely ever do reading unless they have to as a result of some
extraneous pressure. Lack of interest in reading prevents
these people from capitalizing fully on the skill assets which
elementary teachers have striven so arduously to build in
them.

Psychologists have long recognized interest as a basic
factor in the learning process. Thorndike,[1] in formulating
his laws of learning as early as 1913, placed strong emphasis
upon *readiness*, that is, being in a state of readiness to undertake a learning experience. Thorndike's laws of learning have

[1] E. L. Thorndike, *Educational Psychology, II. The Psychology of Learning,* Introduction (New York: Teachers College, Columbia University,
1913).

been criticized in some respects by recent psychologists. All schools of modern psychology, however, include in their statements of conditions which are favorable to learning something that is comparable to or that springs from interest. The stimuli to action are variously called desire, purpose, motive, incentive, drive, goal seeking. Regardless of terminology, we must recognize that the child's attitude toward reading is of extreme significance in his learning to read and in establishing permanent, carry-over habits of reading. Attitude toward reading lends itself to development as truly as do other aspects of reading achievement. A teacher has to work at it though, as hard as she works at phonics, understanding meanings, or study skills. Interest in reading must be nurtured with the substance of appropriate content and guided by a teacher with tact and understanding. Materials and guidance when skillfully integrated by an enthusiastic teacher can tap dormant springs of interest and keep them flowing in ever widening streams of reading enjoyment and usefulness.

First, a brief review of studies of children's interests in reading literature will be presented. This will be followed by practical suggestions of activities to use in stimulating interests in this area.

Facts About Children's Interests in Reading Stories and Books

Hundreds of studies of children's interests in reading were made between 1930 and 1950. With the advent of television, however, major concern was directed toward ascertaining more information about children's interests in this newer medium of communication. In spite of the increase in the number of studies dealing with television interests and the corresponding decrease in the number dealing with reading interests, some very significant studies of children's reading interests are still being made. In this age, in which reading is competing with other attractive mass media of communication, it is of vital importance that teachers and prospective teachers be informed of the facts revealed by both former and recent studies of children's interests in reading. These facts offer basic guidance in planning and carrying out an effective program in developing interest and taste in reading. Toward the end of providing such guidance, several of the most significant studies will be summarized on the next few pages.

Children's Preferences According to Age and Sex

A recent study conducted by Norvell[2] with 24,000 children in grades 3 to 6 revealed that boys preferred adventurous action, physical struggle,

[2] George W. Norvell, *What Boys and Girls Like to Read* (Morristown, N. J.: Silver Burdett Company, 1959).

human characters, animals, humor, courage and heroism, patriotism. The unfavorable items mentioned for boys were description, didacticism, fairies, romantic love, sentiments, girls or women as leading characters, and physical weakness in male characters.

Girls favored lively adventure, home and school life, human characters, domestic animals and pets, romantic love, sentiment, mystery, the supernatural, and patriotism. These items were disapproved by girls: violent action, description, didacticism, boys and girls younger than the reader (except babies), and fierce animals.

According to this same study, many Mother Goose rhymes were enjoyed as late as grade 6, and others were rejected as early as grade 3. *Aesop's Fables* and fairy tales were especially popular in grades 3 to 5. Myths, legends, and hero and folk tales were most popular in grades 5 to 7.

This study also revealed that sex differences in children's interests appear early. Girls were found to enjoy many boy's books, but boys rejected almost all girl's books. This finding has been corroborated by several other studies. Terman and Lima,[3] for example, found that girls liked fairy tales, poetry, and sentimental fiction while boys preferred adventure and vigorous action. Lazar [4] found that mystery stories were ranked first by both boys and girls. Boys chose next, in this order, adventure, detective, history, invention, science, nature and animal, fairy tales, biography, novels, stories about home and school, and poetry. After mystery stories girls chose stories related to activities of home and school.

Jordan,[5] in a summary of several interest studies, reported the following as characteristic favorites of children: "plenty of action," "adventure," "thrills," "mystery," "excitement," "hair-raising escapes," "lots of shooting," "keeps you guessing," "funny." That teachers have an important work to do in improving tastes is a significant inference to be drawn from the results of the above summary.

A study which points out subjects of preferred reading more specifically was conducted by Rudman,[6] who found that children as a group prefer stories of mystery, adventure, children, horses, and dogs. This study revealed also that from grades 4 through 8 interest in mystery

---

[3] Lewis M. Terman and Margaret Lima, *Children's Reading: A Guide for Parents and Teachers,* rev. ed. (New York: Appleton-Century-Crofts, Inc., 1931), p. 131.

[4] May Lazar, *Reading Interests, Activities and Opportunities of Bright, Average and Dull Children,* Teachers College Contributions to Education, No. 707 (New York: Teachers College, Columbia University, 1937).

[5] A. M. Jordan, "Children's Interests in Reading," *The High School Journal,* Vol. 25 (Nov.–Dec. 1942), 323–30.

[6] Herbert C. Rudman, "The Informational Needs and Reading Interests of Children in Grades IV through VII," *The Elementary School Journal,* Vol. 55 (May 1958), 502–12.

stories, recreation, and sports increased, while interest in cowboy stories and fairy tales decreased.

A recent study[7] of the book choices of preschool children revealed interesting data in regard to the influence of certain characteristics of art. The research population in this study consisted of sixty children aged 3 to 5 years. Some of the findings were: light tints in illustrations are significantly preferred to bright saturated colors; a photograph is significantly preferred to a black and white line drawing; three-year-old children significantly prefer a modified realistic drawing, while five-year-old children prefer a true-to-life drawing; when the two are compared, illustrations with more colors are significantly preferred to those with fewer colors.

Reading Interests and Intelligence

The effect of intelligence upon interest in reading has been studied by some investigators. Lazar[8] found that titles chosen did not vary much with bright, average, and dull children. Terman and Lima[9] found that bright children read three or four times as many books as average children. Witty and Lehman[10] reported that "the voluntary reading of gifted children is extensive and exceeds greatly the amount which mentally average children do."

Stone[11] found as a result of his study that the types of reading preferred by dull children vary only slightly from those preferred by average or bright children, except that dull children apparently care less for humorous items than do the other groups. They also frequently choose books that are too difficult for them, and so need special guidance.

Teacher Enthusiasm and Presentation

Several studies have shown that a teacher's enthusiasm for literature is contagious. Wightman,[12] in his study of sixty-four elementary classes in New York, found that in nearly every class children preferred the same book that the teacher was enthusiastic about. Coast[13] conducted

[7] Ruth Helen Amoden, "Children's Preferences in Picture Story Book Variables," *Journal of Educational Research*, Vol. 53 (Apr. 1960), 309–14.

[8] Lazar, *op. cit.*

[9] Terman and Lima, *op. cit.*

[10] Paul A. Witty and Harvey C. Lehman, "A Study of the Reading and Reading Interests of Gifted Children," *Journal of Genetic Psychology*, XL (June 1932), 473–85.

[11] C. R. Stone, "Grading Reading Selections on the Basis of Interests," *Educational Method*, Vol. 10 (1931), 225–30.

[12] H. J. Wightman, "A Study of Reading Appreciation," *American School Board Journal*, Vol. 50 (June 1915), 42.

[13] Alice B. Coast, "Children's Choices of Poetry as Affected by Teachers' Choices," *Elementary English Review*, Vol. 5 (May 1928), 145–47.

a study in grades 1–5 to find out what poems appeal to children and how the teacher's choices influence pupil's tastes. She concluded that "The teacher's influence upon the literary taste of her pupils is even more powerful than we can realize."

Cappa [14] reported reactions to storybooks read by their teachers to kindergarten children. The response in rank order were: desire to look at the book the teacher had read (38.2 per cent), request to have the story read or told again by the teacher (27.3 per cent), drawing (10.7 per cent), and block play (2.2 per cent). Other lesser responses were dramatic play, painting, clay modeling, and so on. This study gives evidence of the teacher's influence on interest in so far as actual contact with the book, or having an opportunity to hear the story again, is concerned.

Pupil's Reasons for Choosing Books

The recommendations of others seem to have a salutary effect upon children's choices of books. Humphreys [15] asked 607 intermediate grade pupils to give their reasons for choosing a favorite book. The reasons given were as follows:

REASON FOR SELECTION	GRADE	PER CENT OF CHILDREN			
		IV	V	VI	AVERAGE
1. Recommended by personal friends or classmates		10	24	23	19
2. Found the book in library		19	9	9	12
3. Looked like a good book		14	11	6	10
4. Personal property of child (usually a gift from some member of the family)		10	8	9	9
5. Recommended by teacher personally		9	6	6	7
6. Selected on basis of content or authorship		3	7	10	7
7. Recommended by librarian personally		7	4	4	5
8. Recommended by members of the family		5	7	8	7
9. Found the preface, a few lines, or a chapter interesting		3	3	2	3
10. Had to make a book report		2	2	2	2
11. Was attracted by title		5	1	5	2
12. Was attracted by illustrations		1	4	1	2
13. Heard a report on the book in class		—	2	4	2
14. Saw a movie of the story		2	1	2	2
15. Story was related to school activities		2	3	1	2
16. Was attracted by cover		—	2	2	1
17. Story was mentioned in My Weekly Reader		0.5	0.5	—	0.3
18. Story was dramatized in class		—	—	0.5	0.2
19. Was attracted by illustration of story made by a pupil		—	0.5	—	0.2
Total number of children		211	183	213	607

14 Dan Cappa, "Kindergarten Children's Spontaneous Responses to Story Books Read by Teachers," *Journal of Educational Research*, Vol. 52 (Oct. 1958), 75.

15 Phila Humphreys, "The Reading Interests and Habits of Six Hundred Children in the Intermediate Grades," *Language Arts in the Elementary School*, Twentieth Yearbook of Department of Elementary School Principals, Vol. 20, No. 6 (1941), 421–28.

A glance at this table reveals the potency of the personal recommendations of friends, classmates, teachers, members of the family, and the librarian. In this respect the findings of this study correspond with those of Rankin [16] who found that forty-one per cent of children from twelve to fourteen years old read as a result of recommendations of others. Some recent studies, however, have indicated that the teachers' recommendations are not favored as much as recommendations from others. Perhaps the influence of the teacher's recommendation depends upon the way in which it is given. If the teacher says, "This is a good book that you should read," the children might regard her recommendation as an assignment and would shy away from it for pleasure purposes. On the other hand, if she suggests a book to meet a need or interest which a child feels at the moment, her recommendation would probably be welcomed.

Classroom Activities to Stimulate Interest in Reading

Interest in reading may be stimulated in many ways, some of which will be suggested below.

Making Materials Available

In reviewing the studies of children's interests, it was noted that their interests vary widely in terms of age, sex, intelligence, home influences, and teacher enthusiasm and presentation. Research has shown also that the reading achievement level of children in most elementary classrooms varies from three to as much as ten or twelve grade levels. Betts [17] found that children at the end of first grade commonly ranged from reading readiness level to about third grade in reading ability, and that this range increased with each successive year of school life.

Because of the extensive scope of interests and abilities within any one classroom, the best assurance of nurturing reading interests is to make available to children a wide enough variety of reading materials so that each pupil can find something that will pique his curiosity and challenge his interest, and that is suitable for his level of reading achievement.

Every classroom should have a collection of books covering a wide range of subjects. A school library and a nearby public library are strong assets, but in addition, classrooms should have their own libraries. It is fortunate if a school budget will permit the purchase of a large variety of books

---

[16] Marie Rankin, *Children's Interests in Library Books of Fiction*, Contributions to Education, No. 906 (New York: Bureau of Publications, Teachers College, Columbia University, 1944).

[17] Emmett A. Betts, "Differences in Readiness for Reading," *Visual Digest*, Vol. 6, No. 1 (Summer Issue, 1942), 5–8.

and some children's magazines for classroom use. In addition some school systems have bookmobiles, which go from school to school and loan books to teachers and children. This is an excellent provision.

There are many schools, however, in which the supply of classroom books is extremely limited, and which are not served by bookmobiles or other facilities of this type. Nevertheless, teachers in such schools often find ways of providing their pupils with a variety of books. Some teachers invite children to bring their books from home for other children to share. The teacher herself often increases and contributes to an ever-changing supply by getting as many children's books from the public library as she is permitted to check out on her own library card. Pupils are encouraged to take out library cards in the public library and to bring to the classroom books which they check out. Parent-teacher associations, upon the appeal of the principal or the teacher, frequently conduct coat-hanger or newspaper drives or candy sales as money-raising projects for the purpose of buying more books for the school. Children of individual classrooms often exercise their ingenuity in contriving ways to raise money for a book fund.

Ingenious teachers will think of other ways of supplementing the school's supply of books in case the school cannot supply the abundance and variety in reading materials that are desirable. In order to keep the variety fresh, the classroom supply of books should have some of the old titles replaced with new ones at intervals throughout the year.

Generating Enthusiasm

We noted that research points out the strong influence of a teacher's enthusiasm. The teacher who is most successful in developing an interest in literature is undoubtedly the one who, herself, loves literature, lives literature, appreciates literature, and conveys her enthusiasm to the pupils whom she teaches.

If teacher enthusiasm is such a potent factor in developing children's interest, then this is a quality which teachers should cultivate in themselves. Many teachers already possess this quality. They are fortunate and so are their pupils. For those who would like to become more interested, appreciative, and enthusiastic about children's literature, it is suggested that they *do* something about it. Here is some advice: take courses in children's literature, in appreciation of literature at the adult level, and perhaps in the appreciation of art or music. Furthermore, acquaint yourself thoroughly with books in the whole realm of children's literature; read widely in this area. Permit yourself to escape real life and live in fantasy as when you were a child; let tears moisten your eyes at sad parts and chuckles come to your throat at funny parts; identify with the little realistic heroes and heroines as they surmount obstacles and solve problems; give yourself freely to the emotions of sympathy and admiration as animal characters bear suffering and emerge triumphant; *feel* the beat and music of a poem and *see* the pictures which the poet paints with his words. Do these things frequently as you delve into the wonderful storehouse of children's literature—and lo—you soon will be an enthusiast! The glow that you feel will become infectious, and your pupils will begin to feel that way, too.

Counseling Parents

Another strong factor in the development of interest in reading is concerned with the situation in the child's home. Dovey [18] made a study of the effect of preschool background on the growth and appreciation of poetry upon children's entrance to first grade. Among her findings she concluded that a favorable home background served as a good foundation for later refinement and that children from literary homes showed greater interest in poetry than others. This interest was indicated by the children's requests, voluntary memorization, and discriminating comments.

In a study reported by Keshian [19] on the characteristics of good readers, it was found, as one would expect, that the best achievers in reading read the most books. What is especially pertinent to the discussion of the home as a factor are three other conclusions of this study: (1) the parents of good achievers read to their children often during early childhood, (2) the children came from homes where there was a great variety of reading materials, (3) 7.6 per cent of the children had their own subscription to a magazine.

Teachers might contribute to home influences which affect reading interests in the following ways:

1. Encourage parents to supply their child with an abundance of books selected in terms of the child's interest and his level of readability. (See pages 533–34, Chapter 20.)

2. Encourage parents to read aloud often to their younger children.

3. Encourage parents to work out a time budget with children which

[18] Irma Dovey, "The Relation Between the Literary Background of Young Children and Their Appreciation of Poetry." Unpublished Master's Thesis (Greeley, Colo.: Colorado State Teachers College, 1934).

[19] Jerry G. Keshian, *Studies of Reading Skills.* Paper presented at the Annual Meeting of the American Educational Research Association, Atlantic City, N. J., Feb. 20, 1962.

allows for physical recreation, studying (if the child is at the age at which he has homework), television viewing, and *reading*.

4. Suggest to the parents that they devote a stated period each evening to their own reading, with the child also participating by reading in *his* books and magazines at the same time.

Reading Orally and Telling Stories

Any appreciation experience is deepened by sharing with others. If we see a beautiful sunset, we call others in the family to come and share its beauty with us. If we have just procured an exquisite recording for our hi-fi and a friend drops in we say, "Sit down a minute. I want you to hear this beautiful recording." Appreciation of literature, in common with other appreciation experiences, is deepened through sharing. Oral reading and story-telling are the most natural mediums for sharing enjoyment of literature.

The telling of stories is most useful in kindergarten and first grade, at which stage of development children are unable to read stories in literature which they are entirely capable of understanding or enjoying when the story is given to them orally.

Reading orally to children has a place all through the elementary grades. Do you, the reader, recall experiences in which you came to love a piece of literature that the teacher read to you orally? I still remember when, as a beginning third grade pupil, I looked forward with thrilled expectancy to a ten-minute period each morning in which the teacher read *Heidi* in installments. In the fourth grade I discovered that I could read the book myself, which I did, reliving and re-enjoying the experiences of this lovable character. I'm sure that my stimulus for enjoying and reading this book arose from hearing the teacher read the story orally and with the feeling and expression that only a master teacher who loved literature could convey.

The amount of oral reading by the teacher should decrease rapidly as children pass through the grades because the goal, of course, is to develop permanent interests in children to seek enjoyment and satisfaction through their *own* reading of literature. But even in the upper grades a very effective interest-arousing technique is to tell the children a little about a story or read a preliminary part from the book—not enough to give away the climax, but just enough to serve as a "teaser" of interest. If the members of the Swiss Family Robinson are left in a despairing predicament on their wrecked ship after the crew has shoved off in the last life boat, few children can resist the desire to find out more about this story which promises to be so adventuresome; or, hardly more than a mere suggestion of the fascinating life of the butterfly need be told by the teacher to stir within a child a desire to discover the untold wonders of its full life story.

Planning for Specific Periods of Sharing

Extending reading interests is such an important objective in the elementary grades that definite periods should be set aside for group activities in connection with voluntary reading, regardless of whether the teacher is using basal readers, individualized instruction, or some other method. Many teachers use the last hour on Friday afternoons for this purpose. Others devote a little time at the beginning of morning sessions, two or three times a week, to discussion of school, library, and home books which have been read.

Different arrangements and frequency of times for sharing voluntary reading will vary from teacher to teacher. The important consideration is to plan definitely for periods of sharing and to be sure that other subjects and activities do not encroach upon these planned times.

An example of the use to which a weekly sharing period was put is described below.

The teacher of one fifth grade class wished to develop library habits in her pupils and to link up school, home, and library reading. She wished also to develop new tastes for different types of reading content, as well as to aid her pupils in reading along the line of already established interests. In order to provide for such growth, some library activity was sponsored each year. This particular year it took the form of a Reading Club. As several of the pupils received books for Christmas, the Reading Club was organized in January for the purpose of sharing books and interesting some members of the class who did not care for reading. It was decided that the qualifications for admission to the club would be twofold: (1) The candidate must have read and reported on four books and satisfactorily answered the questions put to him on the books by the group. (2) He must take a prominent part in contributing news items and discussing them during the weekly period devoted to current events.

The Reading Club conducted all its own activities. It had a president and a secretary. At its weekly meetings, reports on reading were given and other matters were discussed.

During one of these meetings it was decided that the books in the school library were stale, and that new books were needed which were wider in variety of content and more attractive in form. The teacher

417

told the club that the principal would not be able to provide any new books that year. The group then decided to earn enough to buy some books. This plan resulted in preparations for a fair. The children made favors, tea towels, clown's suits, grab bags, and so on, and planned various forms of entertainment. The fair was successful and netted the sum of forty-five dollars.

The next problem was that of selecting books. In class discussion, the children decided that they would like to have books of the following types: stories about other countries, interesting history stories, stories about great persons of our day, and stories of adventure. They immediately began to bring in book catalogs and reviews from the Sunday newspapers, all of which were read and discussed with a view to selecting suitable books for their class library. Many of the pupils also read books in the children's department of the city library and wrote reviews, which were read to the class in order to acquaint the other children with the books found there so that they might decide if they wished to buy any of these.

Recommending Books to Children

In reviewing research, we noted that the recommendation of others was the decisive factor in causing many children to make their choices. The teacher's recommendation no doubt is very effective *if* it is given at the right time and under the right conditions. The import of this to the teacher is that she should read books which are available to her pupils and be ready with instant information about them at any time. Of course, she must take the greatest care not to say, "Here is a book for you to read, John." For John's reading of the book, then, would not be voluntary; it would be *assigned* reading. Rather she should observe her pupils' interests and listen to their requests, and have such complete knowledge of the books at hand that she is in a position to say without hesitation, "This book has a chapter in it about engines, John, which would answer the question you just asked"; or, "You enjoyed that book about Colonial girls so much, Lucille, you might like to read another one about Colonial times. There are two very good Colonial books on that shelf over there if you would care to look at them before choosing your next book to read." Thus, in several indirect ways the teacher may recommend books to meet individual interests and needs, but *never* should she press her recommendation, for to do so might blight rather than excite the interest that she is striving to cultivate.

Using Table or Shelf Arrangements

One successful device for awakening interests in new books will be found in arranging attractive displays. Two or three new books may be placed on a table against a novel tapestry or wallpaper panel. The new books may be casually laid on a table with gay bookmarks indicating particularly alluring pages or illustrations. Perhaps new books may be placed in a background setting suggestive of the subject matter of the books, such as a small serape utilized as a hanging behind the table which displays new books on Mexico, and at the side a sombrero and a figurine of a burro carrying his pack. One teacher had a shelf placed on the wall of her classroom. She then prepared several miniature three-wing screens, each wing being about 12 x 6 inches. Each screen was covered with wallpaper of an attractive design taken from a page of a discarded wallpaper sample book. When she wanted to stimulate interest in a new book she would place it on the shelf with one of the colorful screens behind it. A different screen would be used each time a new book was displayed.

Using Bulletin Board Displays

The resourceful teacher will recognize the value of the bulletin board in displaying materials to stimulate an interest in free-choice reading. On one occasion a brilliant illustration of Chinese boys participating in a kite festival aroused such curiosity that the five books which the classroom library contained on the subject of Chinese customs were in constant demand until everyone in the class had read them. A magazine reproduction in colors depicting Long John Silver, with his wooden leg and black patch cocked over one eye and a parrot obviously screeching over his shoulder, caused an instant demand for *Treasure Island*. Colorful book jackets of new books usually create a number of inquiries on the day they are displayed. Sometimes teachers place lists of new books on the bulletin board. Children read these lists and call for certain books whose titles appeal to them. Comments and reviews about books when placed on the bulletin board disclose elements of interest which are not apparent to the children from a mere title. Beautiful poems placed on the bulletin board now and then may spur some laggard minds to voluntary reading of poetry.

If displays on the bulletin board are changed frequently, the teacher will soon find that the children glance eagerly toward the board each morning to see what new interests it may reveal. Children also enjoy contributing to and arranging the bulletin board display themselves, and such responsibility should frequently be given to them.

Preparing for Assembly, Television, or Community Programs

Searching for appropriate content to use in preparing for an assembly program motivates wide and discriminating reading. The program may be a dramatization of a series of scenes from one book or one scene each from several books. In either case, one or more children may give the titles of the books, the names of the authors, and tell why they recommend the book or books to others.

Many schools are now making it possible for children to dramatize stories over a closed television circuit. This is a splendid medium for developing interest in literature.

Preparing to participate in a community acitvity, such as a "Book Week" program, offers a motive for reading many stories in order to find appropriate ones to review, describe, re-enact, and discuss.

Holding Book Fairs

Book Fairs, or Book Bazaars as they are sometimes called, are becoming popular. These are really book exhibits with added interest-arousing features.

Local book fairs are usually sponsored by a combination of community groups, such as schools, parent organizations, and libraries. Sometimes churches and civic groups join in the project. A local bookstore or representatives from publishers of children's books usually furnish the books, which are placed in a centrally located school or some other community center. The exhibit often is accompanied with a display of attractive posters and other visual materials. Librarians or other qualified persons are usually in attendance to tell stories, discuss certain books, and answer questions. The book-seller or company providing the exhibit usually turns over a commission on sales made to some worthy project, often to schools for use in purchasing more books.[20]

[20] Information about organizing book fairs may be obtained from Children's Book Council, 50 W. 53rd Street, New York, N. Y. A *Book Bazaar Packet* is also available for those who wish to hold a book fair. This packet contains many excellent suggestions. Its cost is $2.00. The publisher is Scholastic Magazines, 33 West Forty-Second Street, New York, N. Y.

Grouping Books by Subjects

Children in the fourth, fifth, and sixth grades may add to their interest in reading different kinds of stories by grouping the books in their classroom into categories according to types, as: fairy stories, old folk-tales, fables and myths, animals, people, historical fiction, regional fiction, plants, science, miscellaneous.

In the sixth grade, pupils should be able to classify their books by the Dewey decimal plan as described on page 339.

Children's interests may be broadened by suggesting that each pupil decide in which categories he has been doing little or no reading and encouraging each one to round out his reading "diet."

Encouraging Creative Activities Related to Literature

Literature is closely related to other creative arts, and both interest in and appreciation of literature can be deepened by extension into other fields. Dramatization has already been mentioned. Other possibilities are choral reading, recording stories or plays on tape or wire, puppet shows, peep shows, shadow shows, dioramas, murals painted by the children, clay modeling. And, of course, experiences in writing stories and creating poems make a major contribution to interest in stories and poems that others have written.

Selecting, Recording, and Checking

Selecting Books in Terms of Difficulty

If teachers are to develop children's interest in literature, then the child should be allowed to select the book *he* wants to read during his voluntary reading activities. He often needs guidance, however, in regard to the difficulty of the reading content. If he should make the mistake of choosing a book upon two or three successive occasions which is too difficult for him to read with enjoyment, he may become frustrated and give up. Some guidance is often desirable, but it should be given in subtle ways still leaving the child free to make *his* choice.

Some suggestions of guidance in the selection of books have already been given in the section, "Interest Provoking Activities," but there are additional and more direct ways of meeting this problem. One way is to place the responsibility on the child for deciding whether the book is easy enough for him. If he chooses a book which the teacher suspects is above his reading level, she might say something like this, "I wonder if this book is easy enough for you to enjoy reading it. Why don't you try it out a little and see? Suppose you read a few paragraphs here and there in the book and see if you know most of the words and can understand what the author is talking about." The child may then try reading a paragraph orally in two or three different places in the book. If it is too difficult he no doubt will come to realize this himself, and will decide to choose another book. Furthermore, he is learning a technique which he himself can use in deciding upon difficulty before he takes a book away with him to read.

Some teachers meet the problem of difficulty by placing together books which are at about the same readability level. Books of fifth grade level may be placed on one shelf or table, those at fourth grade level on another, those of third grade level on another, and so on, in as many groupings as there are readability levels in the class. The children are not told the grade level of the books in any of the groups.

Bands of colored paper are sometimes attached to book covers to indicate their levels of difficulty. Pink bands, for example, may be attached to books of second grade level, blue bands to those of third grade level, and so on.

The teacher carefully observes children as they are about to make a selection, and if a child of second grade reading level is about to select a book of fourth grade level, she suggests that this book would probably be too hard for him to read just at present, and that he would get more pleasure out of it a little later. She then calls his attention to the group of books of the second grade level, and suggests that he can find any number of fine books in this group which he is sure to be able to enjoy immediately.

In the upper grades, lists of books grouped according to difficulty may be used in the same way in guiding children in terms of their present reading abilities.

Keeping Records of Voluntary Reading

One of the most fascinating and strongly motivating activities in which any child can engage is that of watching himself grow by means of a record of some sort in which he observes upward increments of achievement taking place week by week or month by month as he progresses through the school year.

Book reading in the elementary grades lends itself very readily to record keeping in so far as the number of books read is concerned. Some suggestions for record-keeping follow:

1. In the primary grades, pocket charts are favorites with pupils. The teacher may prepare a pocket chart using as its base a strip of tagboard three to four feet long and twelve to four inches wide, which is to be hung vertically on the wall. To this base the teacher attaches pieces of tagboard to make a series of pockets.

Such a pocket chart can be used in various ways. One way particularly liked by first-graders is as follows: The teacher writes a number on each pocket, such as 1 to 3 on the lowest one, 4 to 8 on the next higher pocket, and so forth. Each child places a picture of himself in a pocket that represents the number of books he has read. He moves his picture to a higher pocket when he has read more books than is indicated by the highest number on the pocket in which his picture is reposing. The pictures may be snapshots which the children bring from home, pictures which each one has found in a magazine or catalog which he thinks resembles himself, or a paper doll which each child makes to represent himself.

2. In classes in which children are able to write, the teacher may prepare a large pocket chart with a pocket for each pupil with his name written upon it. As each pupil finishes a book he places a card in his pocket on the chart, bearing the title of the book, author, and a sentence or two, perhaps a paragraph in higher grades, telling his personal reaction to the book.

3. In later grades, it adds to interest and helps develop balanced reading tastes if colored cards are used for the pocket charts, each card representing a certain type of literature, as: pink for fiction, blue for poetry, red for science, green for biography, and so on. A glance at the colors of cards in his pocket will tell a pupil to what kind of books he is devoting the most time and what kinds he is neglecting.

The cards in various pockets may be used also to aid children in selecting books to read. A child may read the cards in the pockets of several other children in deciding which book he will choose to read next.

4. Another simple form of chart is one which contains the pupils' names listed vertically on the left side. Opposite each name there appears a long horizontal line extending across the chart. Vertical lines are also drawn, making a series of squares opposite each pupil's name. As soon as a child finishes a book, he is permitted to color in a square opposite his name. He may use any color he chooses; or he may use a color each time which is the same as the color of the binding of the book which he has read. This form of chart is especially suitable at first grade level.

5. A very interesting chart is one which is called "Our Book Shelf." The foundation is the same as the one for the chart described above, except that the vertical lines are not drawn. The horizontal line opposite each child's name constitutes his individual "book shelf." As soon as he completes a book, he draws a book shelf replica of the book he has read, letters it if he is able to do so, colors it, and then pastes it on his "book shelf." The little "books" on his "book shelf" at any one time show at a glance how many and what books he has read. Children take great interest in building up their "book shelves" in this way.

6. Charts giving the names of pupils and names of books they have read also have been used with success. Each pupil writes the name of the book he has finished reading in one of the squares after his name.

7. Individual reading charts or booklets are effective. An individual record chart may consist of a piece of brightly colored paper for a foundation; or if it is to be developed into a booklet, several pieces of colored paper may be bound together and confined in an attractive cover. "Books I Have Read," or some other appropriate title may then be placed on the chart or booklet. In the case of either a chart or booklet, the child may write on a foundation sheet of paper the name of each book he has read, and then paste above or below the name a picture which he has made to illustrate some scene in the book.

8. In the intermediate grades, the keeping of a simple reading diary is an interesting reading activity for most children. In this case the pupils buy or prepare a small notebook. Upon completing the reading of each book, they write in the notebook the date, the name of the book, and the name of the author. Then they make a note of anything personal which they wish to say about the book. Many children keep these diaries as prized possessions in later years.

9. A personal file may be kept by each child. Such a file may consist of an ordinary box, perhaps a shoe box or a cheese box, or a small file case bought at a ten cent store. As a pupil completes a book, he writes on a file card the name of the author and book, together with a note giving his personal reactions to the book. The cards are then arranged in the file box in alphabetical order.

10. A large class notebook may be used for record keeping. This notebook should be placed somewhere near the classroom supply of books. It should contain as many pages as there are books available. The title and author of each book should be written at the top of one of the pages. When a pupil finishes one of the books whose title is in the notebook, he writes his name in the notebook under the title. He then prepares a card for the teacher giving the title and author of the book, a brief sum-

mary, and personal reaction. Both the class notebook and the cards serve as records of personal reading. A second class notebook may be prepared for use in recording library books read, the titles being added cumulatively as pupils finish the books.

11. Preparing bibliographies for other children to use may become a record-keeping activity as well as a valuable reading experience. A bibliography on Alaska, for example, might be prepared on 3 x 5 inch cards. Each pupil may write the title and author of each reference he reads on a card, adding the pages if the reference is a part of a book. He may then write a summary telling what kind of information the book contains and whether he thinks the reference is worthwhile. He then signs his name to the card. The bibliography may be given to another class of pupils who are or soon will be studying the same subject or it may be left for the next class that will occupy the classroom in which the bibliography was prepared.

Checking Voluntary Reading

One of the problems most frequently voiced by teachers in regard to the conduct of voluntary reading is how to check the child on his reading to be sure that he has read the book and that its readability is within his maturity level. It is neither desirable nor feasible for the teacher to listen as each child reads each book orally to her, or to ask a series of corresponding questions on the book he has read. Yet it is generally conceded that some check is necessary in order to make sure that the pupil really has read the book and that the vocabulary and depth of comprehension are not beyond his reading capabilities.

Granting that it is desirable to check voluntary reading, then we must think of pleasant ways to accomplish this, ways which will give the teacher the information she needs in determining how much of the book the child has assimilated, but ways which are tactfully concealed behind the cloak of informality so that the child will not realize he is being checked. We, as adults, would not enjoy a novel if we knew that someone was going to give us a comprehension test after we were through reading it. Children feel the same way. Their voluntary reading should be motivated entirely by their personal interests, curiosity, pleasure, and satisfaction, with no thought of testing activities.

Suggestions for Checking

Several of the suggestions given under "Keeping Records" result in evidence of the child's grasp of the book on which he reports and they are not obviously "tests." Some additional suggestions follow which are so natural and subtle that the child won't realize that he is being checked when one of them is used.

1. The child may discuss his story or book in an informal chat with the teacher in which the teacher uses his conversation as a check.

2. He may read or tell a part of the story that he has been reading during an hour set aside for reading club activities.

3. He may show two or three pictures in a book and tell what was happening in each one of them.

4. He may make illustrated maps or pictures to illustrate some scene from the book.

5. He may give an illustrated talk on the book read, as a "travel talk."

6. He may make a poster with a brief review of interesting quotations from the book.

7. He may tell something about a book read to other children in order to "sell them" (get them interested in reading) the book.

8. He may read aloud for the other children's enjoyment the funniest parts of the book or the parts describing the most beautiful pictures.

9. He may join other children in a "quiz show" in which different pupils take turns in quizzing each other about books they have read.

10. He may rewrite or give interpretations of his reading in dramatic form, pantomime, or tableau, depicting characters or scenes. In this case the child should work with others who have read the same book.

Library Activities

Library experience is an essential part of a well-rounded instructional program in reading—essential to skill development, refinement of tastes, and establishment of permanent, carry-over interests and habits in reading.

Library activities may take place in three different locales—in the classroom library, the school library, and the public library.

The Classroom Library Setting

The favorite setting for a classroom library seems to be a corner of the room. Around the wall in this corner there usually are low shelves filled with books. Two or more tables surrounded with chairs are set in the corner space. In case there is not a central school library to loan books, the library corner may contain a child's desk in which library cards and files are kept.

Some teachers prefer to arrange books and magazines in two groups, either in two separate sets of bookcases or on two different sets of tables.

In one group are placed all books and other materials that pertain to a center of interest or unit topic which the pupils are pursuing as a group.

Assuming that the center of interest is pioneer life, in this group there might be readers and trade books containing Indian stories, a life of Daniel Boone, tales of the covered wagon; a pamphlet of songs and dances of the pioneers; informative material, such as "How to Make a Loom," "Preparation of Flax for Spinning"; perhaps colored illustrations depicting pioneer subjects, such as the operation of a spinning wheel, the pony express, and so on, mounted on cardboard and bound into book form; puzzles and question games utilizing pioneer vocabulary; magazines and newspapers with marked pictures or articles bearing on pioneer subjects.

The second group of tables or bookcases should be given over to a great variety of materials which have nothing to do with the center of interest and which may be used by the children in forwarding their individual preferences.

The books on this table should cover a wide range: picture books, stories of animal life, fairy stories, biographies, books of science, books of adventure, books of travel, history subjects, books of poetry, and children's magazines.

While every effort should be made to maintain a high literary standard in the reading content used in connection with a center of interest, the fact remains that in the elementary grades the reading materials found on the center of interest table are apt to be concerned more largely with informative content used for research problems. For this reason it is a good plan to place strong emphasis upon literary quality in selecting the reading materials for this second group of books, which are to be read for the sheer enjoyment and the pleasure they afford. Hence this second group acts as a supplement to the center of interest tables, both in variety and in literary value.

The teacher should be sure to include in her classroom library materials that represent several different levels of reading difficulty. In a fourth grade classroom, for example, there should be some books easy enough for a second grade child to read and possibly others difficult enough for a seventh grade pupil to read. Such an assortment makes it possible to provide reading that will meet the individual abilities of all children in the class.

Use of the Classroom Library

The classroom library may be used in several different ways. A committee or individuals may do research reading to obtain information about a group topic being studied. An individual child may be prompted by a desire to walk over to the library, take down a book whose cover, perhaps, has attracted him, and sit down and browse solely for pleasure. At another time he may go to the library for the definite purpose of referring to an article on buffaloes, for example, in order to make sure of his accuracy in completing a painting on prairie animal life. Upon another occasion he may utilize these classroom facilities in true public library fashion by "taking out" on a library card the book of his choice, either to carry home or to keep at his seat until he has finished reading it. In classrooms using individualized instruction, books chosen from the classroom library usually serve as the basic materials of reading instruction.

Examples of Classroom Library Activities

Descriptions of activities that have taken place in actual classroom situations are often helpful in visualizing possibilities. The two accounts below are accurate reports of how a classroom library was used in a first grade classroom and in a third grade classroom.

Library Activities in a First Grade Classroom

The particular group of children dealt with in this report were second-semester first grade pupils who were unusually slow in reading. They didn't possess sufficient skill to be able to read entirely through any one preprimer or primer. Their reading was confined to the early pages only in these beginning books. Therefore, the teacher used her own resourcefulness in providing some small, easy books to be read in connection with classroom library activites.

Finding some primers which had been discarded by the school, the teacher cut out of them a large number of complete easy stories. Out of yellow, blue, and red heavy paper she made folders, one for each story. For record-keeping purposes a number was placed on the back of each folder. Fortunately, for some time previously she had been collecting attractive colored pictures from magazines. These now were used to good advantage on the folder covers. For a story bearing on the theme of a boy's kindness to his dog, she found just the right illustration—that of a boy leading his dog across a busy thoroughfare held close to his master's side by means of a leash. For an article on home life, she pasted on the cover a scene of a cheerful fireside around which a family group was reading, while on the floor a young child was fondling a cat.

These charming booklets were kept on the library table where all might see and use them at their leisure or take them home if they wished. The children's interest in these booklets was well worth the effort of preparing them. During the regular library hour each Friday, the children were encouraged by the teacher to tell which of all the stories read that week they had enjoyed the most and to give their reasons for the selection. The response was gratifying. One little boy liked the story about the white rat, "Because," he said, "I have a little white rat just like that at home." Another child asked if he could read to the group a small portion of the story he liked best, and he was allowed to do so, and so on.

Before long it was found that the children were reading so many of the books that the discussion period did not afford all of them an opportunity to contribute their reports. Since a definite check was needed, the teacher made it a point to call individual children to her between bells in the morning or during the first ten minutes of recess to discuss their books with them.

Furthermore, the teacher made a chart for use in recording the books similar to the one described in number 4, page 423. As soon as a child finished a book and proved by discussion that he had understood it, he colored the square opposite his name with the color which corresponded with the book he had read.

A plan somewhat similar to this had been used successfully by this teacher during a preceding term, except that primers were used instead of booklets. The group of children described above, however, did not seem to be ready for primers. Only one little girl at this time was reading easy primers, while the rest were still reading the shorter and simpler booklets containing one story each. Through this library activity, however, the entire group seemed to gain rapidly in reading interests and abilities.

Library Activities in a Third Grade Classroom

When the school semester began in this third grade classroom there were twenty books on the library table. These were from a collection furnished by the school, and the room was allowed to keep them throughout the entire year. As the children required many more books to satisfy their needs, a visit was made to the nearest branch library every Friday afternoon, and children and teacher brought back to the classroom fresh books that had been loaned to them by the library.

The teacher recognized the need for some definite plan in regard to the library reading in order to make it a successful and happy experience. She therefore asked the class president to call a special meeting to discuss library books. When all were seated in a circle, the teacher said, "So that we might let others know what we find out when we read our library books, I wonder if it would be desirable for us to make some kind of a plan to show how we can share our information." She then wrote the heading on the blackboard, "How can we let others know what we found out."

Herbert's quick response, "Just tell them the story," was used as the first suggestion, and after a further discussion, the children arrived at the following:

1. Tell the story.
2. Read the story.
3. Read a part and tell a part.
4. Tell the most interesting part.
5. Read or tell the funniest part.
6. Dramatize a part of the story.
7. Read the part of a character.

The teacher showed the children some utility boxes she had purchased. When stood up on end, these resembled tiny book shelves. It became necessary for her to suggest this idea to the class, after which Edith said, "Why can't we each have a shelf for our books and see who can read the most?" The class immediately accepted the idea, which led to the organization of "Our Bookshelf Club."

A chart was then made, similar to the illustration below. On it appeared all the children's names, with a number placed to the left of each one. The chart was hung up on the blackboard and the utility boxes placed on the chalk ledge beneath it. A space in this set of "bookshelves" was given to each child, and was designated by a number corresponding to the number opposite his name on the chart. As soon as a child had made an acceptable oral report on a book, he wrote the title and the author on a card and placed it in his "bookshelf."

BOOKSHELF CLUB
Our rules to join

Read and report on at least one book.
Follow our book report plan when you write.

Your number is beside your name.

1. Jean Sinder   6. Tom Sheldon
2. Doyle Masin   7. Louise Jones
3. Harold Fussell   8. Russell Green

The Bookshelf Club proceeded under high interest for quite a while, but eventually the novelty of making oral reports as planned originally wore off.

"May I write my report, instead of telling about the book?" one girl asked.

"I think that is a good suggestion," the teacher agreed. "How many others would prefer to do that too?"

The majority assented; therefore, it was arranged to work out a plan to follow in writing a brief report on each book read. After the plans were completed on the chalkboard, they were then printed on a chart for ready reference when writing book reports. They were listed as follows:

PLAN FOR OUR REPORTS

1. Tell the name of the book.
2. Tell the author's name.
3. Tell what the book is about.
4. Tell the most interesting part.
5. Did you enjoy the book? If you did, tell a *good reason* why.
6. Use your best writing.
7. Make complete sentences.

The teacher explained further, "When your report is accepted by the class, as well as by me, then you may make a book and place it on your own bookshelf."

This amused the children, and the addition of each red-, or green-, or orange-colored paper book on the individual shelves was watched with eager interest.

In concluding the discussion of the classroom library, it may be said that pupils in every elementary classroom profit by having a room library, one which they feel actually belongs to them as a group and one to which any child may turn whenever he has free time during the day. In classrooms where the individualized plan of instruction is used, a classroom library is essential as the basic source of reading material to use in the teaching of reading.

The School Library

At last, widespread recognition is being given to the salutary contribution of a central library in the elementary school. Elementary schools throughout the country are rapidly installing libraries staffed by trained librarians. This movement should result in substantial improvement of reading ability and reading interest.

Value of the School Library

The school library serves many worthy purposes. It is closer to the life situation, in so far as libraries are concerned, than is the classroom library. It contains card catalogs and reference materials which facilitate children's research reading. It contains the wide range of reading materials necessary to meet the interest and ability levels of all children in the public school.

If adequately conducted under the guidance of a skilled librarian, activities will be planned so that within the library many services may be rendered. Reading materials will be made easily accessible to a child who comes to the library looking for an answer to a question raised in the classroom. The librarian can artfully assist the pupil in making the transition from supervised to independent reading by arousing in him a genuine interest so that he will voluntarily seek out reading as a pleasurable pastime in later life. She can help him in developing the skills that he needs in making the best use of a library.

The librarian can render a great service in helping to build tastes for good literature by showing the child that the simplest way to satisfy his natural curiosities is through reading, and by giving him an attractive, inviting atmosphere in which to enjoy it. Many a child has lost his earlier tendencies toward reaching for a book of hair-raising comics by his surprised discovery in the library that "thrillers" can be found in real literature of a much more satisfying quality than that depicted in comics.

And last, but by no means least, such library activities develop in children a knowledge and appreciation of the valuable services that a library and a librarian can offer, sources of assistance which can be extremely valuable throughout life.

Physical Setting of the School Library

The ideal school library is a large, light attractive room with walls painted in soft colors, from which no glare will be reflected. It contains different sized tables and chairs, so that children of all ages and stature may be accommodated. Here and there a cozy corner invites the occupancy of the young readers. There are bulletin boards containing brightly colored book jackets and posters and interesting notices; there are attractive displays of books in conspicuous places; and there are lovely arrangements of flowers and plants to add to the beauty of the room. Thus, when Tommy enters this attractive room there will be many challenges to his interests. Perhaps he will first walk over to the bulletin board to examine more closely the brightly illustrated book jacket or glamorous poster that has caught his eye. He scans a notice which he finds tacked beside it and mentally notes that next Wednesday during a certain hour Miss Allen will tell the story of *Black Beauty*. He must be sure to arrive early enough to get a good seat so that he won't miss a word of the story.

Conspicuously displayed on a table near the entrance there may be some books on ducks and rabbits and one particularly on taking care of rabbits. This appeals to Tommy because he has just been given two rabbits for Easter, and the problem of arranging a proper environment for them has worried him a bit. Before picking up the book on rabbits, he lingers for a moment over a captivating arrangement of marigolds which has obviously been set up by a hand practiced in the art of modern flower arrangement. Then he settles down in this happy, bright environment for a half-hour or so of satisfying reading, the kind that will cause him to repeat the experience again and again. The influence of environment is exceedingly significant in building permanent library habits. This should be a matter of special concern to the elementary school librarian.[21]

Use of the School Library

The central library should become an integral part of the child's daily living in school. The most common plan of scheduling is one which provides for a daily allotment of time in the library for each class. This time may be used for research, pleasure reading, or for one of the other types of activities mentioned under the heading, "How the Librarian Works with Children."

Individual children use the library, also. In most schools individuals may go to the library at any time for special work. Children are also permitted to borrow books to take to their respective classrooms or homes for study or recreation.

How the Librarian Works with Children

The librarian plans her work with different classes just as a good teacher plans her work. Her activities with pupils include story telling,

[21] A helpful filmstrip of sixty-three frames has been published. It is titled *Remodeling the Elementary School Library*. The price is $7.50. It may be obtained from American Library Association, Chicago 11, Illinois.

discussion of books, instruction in library skills, supervision of reference reading, stimulation of recreational reading, guidance in regard to readability levels and in raising tastes to higher levels, and the extension of interests to a greater variety of subjects and literary types.

Cooperation between the Classroom Teacher and the Librarian

The classroom teacher and the librarian need to work together closely. The classroom teacher should give information to the librarian about the reading needs and the reading abilities of different children. She should also keep the librarian informed concerning group interest or unit topics being pursued in the classroom.

The librarian should promptly fulfill requests from the teacher for supplies of books relating to certain topics. She should keep the classroom teacher informed concerning the interests, habits, and needs of children as she observes them in the library. She should make herself familiar with all courses of study used in the school in order to choose books for the library that have to do with topics studied and in order to have these books available at appropriate times. Occasionally, the librarian may go into a classroom to show a new book or magazine and to tell something about it.

Administrative Cooperation

In order to realize the fullest benefits of a school library, the principal has a strong role to play. He needs to make administrative policies concerning the use of the library so that all may share its benefits equally. It is he who establishes the time schedules for classes and decides upon the length of time during which an individual may keep a book at home or that a teacher may keep a set of books in her classroom. He makes exceptions of time limits when he sees fit. If two or more classes at the same grade level are planning to study the same topic at the same time, he may change the order of topics for one of them so that the children in both classes may have a good supply of reference books from the library while working with the topic.

The astute principal also invites the librarian to participate in committee work in preparing courses of study. The librarian may be the materials specialist. She knows books old and new and is aware of resource lists from which books may be chosen. She is familiar with children's interests at various ages, and she knows the readability level of different books. Because of this specialized knowledge, she can make a splendid contribution in preparing bibliographies for courses of study.

In summary, it might be said that a central library in an elementary school is one of the strongest possible provisions for insuring the development of reading interests and life-long habits of library usage. Its greatest value can be derived only when it becomes fully integrated with the life of the school as a whole. Very close cooperation is needed among the librarian, the teachers, and the principal.

Public Library Activities

Whether or not a school has a central school library, children should have opportunities to engage in some activities in connection with the local public library or with one of its branches. Becoming acquainted with the public library and its services is one of the best assurances of promoting life-time usage of books.

Some suggestions are given below of activities in which children may participate in a public library. If the school does not have a central school library, then such activities should take place frequently at the public library. If the school does have a central library, contacts with the public library may be much less frequent, but they should still take place on occasion.

Taking Excursions to the Library

An excellent way to acquaint children with the services and benefits of a public library is to take them on excursions to the nearest library. The librarian should be notified in advance when the class will pay its visit to the library, and the teacher should also give the librarian some advance information about the children's grade levels, reading levels, and interests.

During visits to the library, the librarian may show the children certain books which may be of special interest to them; she may show them where different kinds of books may be found on the open shelves; she may acquaint them with the card catalog and teach them how to use it; she may encourage them to apply for a library card and to take out books for home reading. Most librarians in public libraries are very cooperative in working with teachers to further such activities as those mentioned.

Story Hours

The children's department in many libraries regularly holds a "story hour." This event is usually scheduled for some period in the late afternoon or Saturday. These story-telling activities are conducted by a librarian who enjoys and understands children and their needs. The group usually is held enthralled by the unfolding of a tale dear to their hearts, told or read in a delightfully realistic manner, and accompanied by the showing of cleverly characterized illustrations which are found in the book containing the story.

Reading Clubs

Very successful reading clubs are conducted by some librarians. At the beginning of a semester notices are sent to schools in the vicinity of the library, inviting the children to join the club and to help plan its program for the semester.

With the guidance of the librarian, the plan usually includes one meeting each week. Each meeting is concerned with a different field of interest which is agreed upon in advance by the members of the club.

In arriving at the subject to be reviewed, the children are usually influenced by some recent happening or outstanding contact which has impressed them. For example, Henry had recently seen in a museum one of the earliest models of phonographs, and his inquiries had disclosed that it was invented by Thomas A. Edison. In relating this experience for the enlightenment of the club, it was suggested by one of the members that information about Edison be the subject of their next meeting.

It has been found that in the late spring when attention is turned toward approaching vacations, travel stories usually are the most popular subjects brought up for discussion.

Often a specific event in history is chosen. A varied collection of poems dealing with a certain topic is decided upon if there is a sufficient number who are interested in poetry or who can be carefully guided by the librarian to become interested in having a poetry hour. Sometimes stories are taken from the old but ever-new treasures of literature and dramatized by a group; or demonstrations of puppet shows, artcraft, and so on are shown to accompany discussions.

Certain committees of children are made responsible for planning the entertainment at each meeting. Since reading must be done on the subject in order to present it, these clubs accomplish much toward exciting the interest of many heretofore dormant-minded readers.

School Representative Clubs

An excellent medium for bringing about a closer relationship between the classroom and public library is a school-representative club. In organizing such a club, a child from each room in the school is asked to represent his class at a series of monthly meetings in the library. One activity of this type which met with encouraging results is described below:

Edward was chosen to be the representative of the A-5 class. During the course of the first meeting in the library he was asked to inform the group of the special reading activities, discussions, programs, or other book projects that his own class at school was carrying on at the time. His report disclosed that his classmates were now deeply engrossed in a study of desert life. He told briefly a few of the most interesting aspects of the study and gave the names of some of the books the children had been reading as their needs developed.

When Edward came back to his classroom, he in turn brought with him a report consisting of items which representatives from other classrooms had contributed to the group regarding the reading activities, book reviews and so on in which their respective classmates had participated. He also had included in his notes news about recent books which the librarian had introduced to the club by giving a brief but enticing synopsis, as well as telling about books he had noticed on display and reporting other items of information which he had gained at the meeting.

Through the medium of such a club, the librarian may assist the teacher in many ways. Knowing, for example, that the A-5 class is studying desert life, the librarian may prepare and send to the teacher a list of references which she has available at the library that pertain to various forms of desert plants, desert animals, climate conditions of the desert, information on attempts made to reclaim certain portions, old desert tales, and so on; the list branching out from any one of these topics is endless.

Supplying Teachers with Book Lists

As another service, the librarian may send to the teacher at the beginning of each month a list of new books accompanied by comments concerning their content, grade placement, and interest features. Likewise she may provide the teacher with lists of books and appropriate comments for distribution to the children in order to arouse their interest in summer reading.

In these and various other ways the librarian of a public library and teachers in nearby schools may cooperate. Such cooperation will contribute much to laying a foundation in childhood for a life-long reading enrichment through the use of public library facilities.

Summary

Studies of children's interests have revealed facts which are important for teachers and prospective teachers to know, and several of these facts were reviewed in this chapter. Suggestions were given concerning classroom activities to use in developing interest in reading such as: making classroom materials available; the teacher generating enthusiasm; counseling with parents; reading orally and telling stories to children; planning for periods of sharing; recommending books to children; using table, shelf, and bulletin board arrangements for displaying books; preparing for assemblies and community programs; holding book fairs; and encouraging creative activities in connection with stories read.

Suggestions were also given in regard to the selection of books in regard to difficulty, keeping records of books read, and checking voluntary reading.

In summing up the discussion of the classroom library, the central elementary school library, and the public library, the point stressed was that all three types of libraries are desirable and needed, each one reinforcing the other in their many benefits to children.

In schools which do not have a central elementary library, the room library assumes major importance. In schools having a central library, children have opportunities to extend their interests and skills far beyond the possibilities of a room library by working also in the school library. In this case the central school library may cooperate with the room library, loaning books to the room as needed for unit topics and class interests. Activities in connection with the public library should supplement both classroom and school libraries by acquainting children with the larger supply of books available in a public library and by establishing habits in using public libraries.

Book-List Sources

Several excellent book lists have been prepared for teachers' reference. A few of the sources of such lists are given below:

A *Teacher's Guide to Children's Books,* by Nancy Larrick. Columbus, Ohio: Charles E. Merrill, 1960.

Adventuring with Books. Champaign, Ill.: National Council of Teachers of English, 1960.

A Basic Book Collection for the Elementary Grades, 6th ed. Chicago: The American Library Association, 1956.

Bibilograpy of Books for Children. Washington, D. C.: Association for Childhood Education.

Catalog of the Best Books for Children (2000 books classified by age and subject). Wellesley Hills, Mass.: Junior Reviewers, 1956.

Children's Books for $1.25 or Less. Washington, D. C.: Association for Childhood Education, 1961.

Children's Books Too Good to Miss, prepared by May Hill Arbuthnot, Elizabeth D. Briggs, Margaret M. Clark, Harriet G. Long, and Margaret L. White. Cleveland, Ohio: Western Reserve University Press, 1953.

Good Books for Children by Mary K. Eakin. Chicago: University of Chicago Press, 1960.

The Elementary School Science Library. Washington, D. C., American Association for the Advancement of Science, 1959.

Trade Books for Beginning Readers, by Martha Olson Condit. New York: Wilson, 1960. Reprinted from December 1959, Wilson Library Bulletin.

Additional Readings

Books and Pamphlets

Arbuthnot, May Hill, *Children and Books,* rev. ed. Chicago: Scott Foresman & Company, 1957.

———, "Literature" (In the Primary Grades), *Reading for Effective Living,* International Reading Association Conference Proceedings, Vol. 2 (1958), 60–63.

Association for Childhood Education International, A *Bibliography of Books for Children,* 1962 ed. Washington, D. C.

Dawson, Mildred A., and Henry Baumann, *Fundamentals of Basic Reading Instruction,* Chap. 8. New York: Longmans, Green & Co., Inc., 1959.

DeBoer, John J., and Martha Dallmann, *The Teaching of Reading,* Chaps. 11A and 11B. New York: Holt, Rinehart and Winston, Inc., 1961.

Grambs, Jean D., *Lifetime Reading Habits,* New York: National Book Committee, 1962.

Hildreth, Gertrude, *Teaching Reading,* Chaps. 1, 18, 21, 22. New York: Holt, Rinehart and Winston, Inc., 1958.

Jacobs, Leland B., "Literature" (In The Intermediate Grades), *Reading for Effective Living,* International Reading Association Conference Proceedings, Vol. 2 (1958), 72–75.

Rudman, Herbert C., "What We Know About Children's Interests," *Reading in Action,* International Reading Association Conference Proceedings, Vol. 2 (1957), 23–25.

Russell, David H., *Children Learn to Read,* rev. ed., Chaps. 12, 13. Boston: Ginn & Company, 1961.

Spiegler, Charles G., *The Library—Lifelong University*. Pleasantville, N. Y.: Reader's Digest Services, 1962.

Williams, Mary U., ed., *Significant Values in Literature*, Vol. 2. Sacramento, Cal.: Fourth Annual Reading Conference Proceedings, Sacramento State College Council and International Reading Association, 1959.

Periodicals

Archer, Marguerite P., "Library Opportunities for Children in the Primary Grades," *Elementary English*, Vol. 39 (Feb. 1962), 109–13.

Cleland, Donald L., "Psychological Basis for Children's Interests," *Education*, Vol. 79 (Apr. 1959), 465–69.

Corliss, William S., "Elementary School Libraries," *Elementary English*, Vol. 38 (Nov. 1961), 494–96.

Eller, William, "Reading Interest: A Function of the Law of Effect," *The Reading Teacher*, Vol. 13 (Dec. 1959), 115–20.

Fjeldsted, Lillian W., "Broadening Reading Interest Through Creative Expression," *Elementary English*, Vol. 35 (Oct. 1958), 391–94.

Frank, Josette, *Your Child's Reading Today*. Garden City, N. Y.: Doubleday & Company, Inc., 1954.

Gaver, Mary V., "Needed: More and Better Elementary School Libraries," *Journal of the American Association of University Women*, Vol. 53 (Jan. 1960), 96–100.

Gilbert, Christine B., "The Librarian and the Literature Program," *Literature for Children*, pp. 19–23. Washington, D. C.: Association for Childhood Education International, 1961.

Hogenson, Dennis L., "The Role of Interest in Improving Reading Skills," *Elementary English*, Vol. 37 (Apr. 1960), 244–45.

Huus, Helen, "How a TV Program Can Be Used as a Springboard for Further Reading," *Elementary English*, Vol. 34 (Feb. 1957), 81–84.

———, "Libraries Bolster the Reading Program," *The Reading Teacher*, Vol. 14 (Mar. 1961), 236–40.

———, "Developing Taste in Literature in the Elementary Grades," *Elementary English*, Part I, Vol. 39 (Dec. 1962), 780–89; Part II, Vol. 40 (Jan. 1963), 56–67.

Krary, Agnes, "Libraries: Motivation for Learning," *Education*, Vol. 79 (Apr. 1959), 491–94.

Mackintosh, Helen K., "Children's Interests in Reading and the Literature Program," *The Reading Teacher*, Vol. 10 (Feb. 1957), 138–49.

Schubert, Delwyn G., "Inviting Book Reporting," *Education*, Vol. 81 (Jan. 1961), 264–65.

Silver, Evelyn F., "A School Library for Every Child," *Elementary English*, Vol. 37 (Mar. 1960), 164–65.

Smith, John Steel, "Children's Literature: Form or Formula?" *Elementary English*, Vol. 35 (Feb. 1958), 92–94.

Strickland, Ruth, "Building and Expanding Worthwhile Interests," *Education,* Vol. 79 (Apr. 1959), 460–64.

Townsend, Agatha, "Another Look at Reading Interests," *The Reading Teacher,* Vol. 13 (Apr. 1960), 297–304.

Wenzel, Evelyn, "Extending Creative Experiences Through Literature, *Literature for Children,* pp. 43–47. Washington, D. C.: Association for Childhood Education International, 1961.

Witty, Paul, "Interest, Effort and Success-Bases for Effective Reading," *Education,* Vol. 79 (Apr. 1959), 480–86.

Today is Devon's birthday.
Bernie!
The Big Day
The big day is here at last.
Today we will have our play.
We will all have a part.
Tuesday.

PART 4

Beginning Reading
Instruction

15

Changing Concepts of Beginning Reading

The reader may wonder why the beginning stages of reading were not discussed early in this book rather than being postponed to a later section. The reason for this delay is that beginning reading is tied to almost everything else that has been said thus far: "Reading Instuction Unfolds" and "What's Ahead in Reading" have their bearings on beginning reading. Certainly child psychology, as discussed in Chapter 4, and the integration of reading with the entire constellation of language arts, as discussed in Chapter 5, are very significant areas to consider in regard to initiating the child into the art of reading. A thorough knowledge of the basic skill areas of word identification, getting meanings, study skills, and rate is absolutely necessary if the foundation for these skills is to be adequately laid during preparatory stages. Interest in reading and enjoyment of literature can be cultivated long before reading is taught systematically. Since full information about all these growth areas is highly significant in preparing children for the time when they are actually given instruction in reading per se, it seems advisable not to attempt a discussion of early reading activities until the reader has become thoroughly familiar with the research procedures and varied practices described in all the preceding chapters.

History Reveals Changing Practices

Tots Read in Early American Schools

In the early decades of American reading instruction, children were sent to school at two or three years of age. At this time they were immediately taught the alphabet and inducted into the intricacies of the reading process.

The charming account below tells what happened when a two-and-a-half-year-old entered school in 1863.

"Come and read," says the mistress to the little flaxen-headed creature of doubtful gender, for the child is in petticoats and sits on the female side as close as possible to its guardian sister. But then those coarser features, tanned complexion, and close-clipped hair, with other minutiae of aspect, are somewhat contradictory to the feminine dress. "Come and read." It is the first time that he-or-she was ever inside of a school-house and in the presence of a schoolma'am, according to recollection; and the order is heard with shrinking timidity. But the sister whispers an encouraging word and helps "tot" down from the seat, who creeps out into the aisle, and hesitates along down to the teacher, biting his fingers, or scratching his head, perhaps both, to relieve the embarrassment of the novel situation.

"What is your name, dear?" "Tholomon Icherthon," lisps the now discovered he, in a choken voice scarce above a whisper. "Put your hands down by your side, Solomon, and make a bow." He obeys, if a short and hasty jerk of the head is a bow.

The alphabetical page of the spelling-book is presented and he is asked, "What's that?" But he cannot tell. He is but two years and a half old, and has been sent to school to relieve his mother from trouble, rather than to learn. No one at home has yet shown or named a letter for him. He has never had even that celebrated character, round o, pointed out to his notice. It was an older beginner, most probably, who being asked a similar question about the first letter of the alphabet, replied, "I know him by sight, but can't call him by name." But our namesake of the wise man, does not know the gentleman even by sight, nor any of his twenty-five companions.

Solomon Richardson has at length said A, B, C, for the first time in his life. He has *read*. "That's a nice boy; make another bow and go to your seat." He gives another jerk of the head and whirls on his heel and trots back to his seat, meeting the congratulatory smile of his sister with a satisfied grin, which, put into language would be, "There I've read—ha'n't I." [1]

[1] J. H. and E. B. Buckingham, *The New England Magazine*, Vol. 2 (Feb. 1832), 519.

And thus it was that mere infants were started on their prilgrimage along the weary road to reading a century and a half ago. And a weary road it certainly must have been!

The Reading Readiness Concept Developed

Eventually, as state support of public education took on added importance, most states passed a law to the effect that public school support would be provided to children at six years of age. This fixed the age of beginning reading at six.

During the 1920's, however, school people became greatly concerned about the large number of failures in first grade. As they [2] studied this problem, they arrived at the conclusion that all children were not ready for reading at six years. Studies then ensued to find out what factors contributed to readiness for undertaking reading instruction.

The period between 1920 and 1940 was a period of great intensity in regard to research in the area of reading readiness. [3] The first doctoral dissertation on readiness was reported in 1927. From that time on, the number of master and doctoral studies increased, reaching its peak in the years 1937 to 1940. Fourteen such studies were completed in 1937, fifteen in 1938, fourteen in 1939, and twelve in 1940. Since that time only two or three academic studies on readiness have been reported each year.

A similar trend is seen in published articles on reading readiness. Periodicals abounded with discussions on readiness topics from 1930 to 1940. Articles on this subject rarely appear in current literature.

In the light of this evidence, it may be concluded that this was the period of most vigorous emphasis, both on investigations of reading readiness and applications of the readiness theory. The concept of individual differences in regard to children's maturity for reading instruction has now been accepted generally and little is heard about it at the present time.

As the newness of the innovation of the readiness concept wore off, American schools settled down to the generally accepted practice of postponing organized reading instruction in the first grade for large numbers of children. The postponement has been effected in consideration of many factors but chiefly on the basis of these two: (1) the results of

[2] "Pupils' Readiness for Reading Instruction upon Entrance to First Grade," *City School Leaflet No. 23* (Washington, D. C.: United States Department of the Interior, Bureau of Education, Dec. 1926). Mary Maud Reed, *An Investigation of Practice for the Admission of Children and the Promotion of Children from the First Grade.* Doctor's Dissertation (New York: Teachers College, Columbia University, 1927).

[3] Nila Banton Smith, "What Have We Accomplished in Reading?—A Review of the Past Fifty Years," *Elementary English* XXXVIII (Mar. 1961), 141–50.

447

reading readiness tests, and (2) the results of early investigations [4] which pointed to a mental age of six to six and one-half years as being essential for success in beginning reading.

Tots Are Being Taught Again

At the present time some people are urging that reading be taught to two-, three- and four-year-olds, a practice long since abandoned in American schools. With the present pressures to raise all phases of American life to higher levels of achievement, it is perhaps a natural corollary that some educators are turning their attention to the teaching of reading at earlier levels. Those who advocate the formal teaching of reading to young children are disregarding many theories in regard to reading readiness which have been so carefully built up in the past. Such practices call for careful evaluation. Such an evaluation is given on pages 451–52.

Reading By Preschool Children Today

The learning and teaching of children to read before school entrance is a topic of considerable interest at the present time. Even the author of the recent Pulitzer Prize-winning novel, *To Kill A Mocking Bird* [5] amusingly portrays the experiences of a preschool reader. At one point in this book Jem said of his four-and-a-half-year-old sister, ". . . Scout there's been readin' since she was born, and she ain't even been to school yet." Then upon entrance in first grade, Scout, whose real name was Jean Louise, was asked to read something that Miss Caroline wrote on the chalkboard, and she read it so well that Miss Caroline was really vexed. Miss Caroline then had her read most of the first reader and stock market quotations in the *Mobile Register*. All this time Miss Caroline's irritation was building up, and she finally exploded, "Tell your father to stop teaching you. It will interfere with your learning to read in school." Jean Louise said that her father wasn't teaching her and then she began soliloquizing to herself on how she did learn to read and finally decided that it just came like learning to fasten the flap on the back of her union suit without looking around. Her troubles continued, however, as her school days went by. Miss Caroline became increasingly annoyed and frequently

[4] M. V. Morphett and C. Washburne,"When Should Children Begin to Read," *Elementary School Journal*, Vol. 31 (Mar. 1931), 496–503. W. D. Rice, *Some of the Educational Gains and Losses to Childern Who Start at School at Different Ages.* Unpublished Master's Thesis (Chapel Hill, N. C.: Duke University, 1934). Wendell W. Wright, "Reading Readiness: A Prognostic Study," *Indiana University Bulletin,* XII (Bloomington: Indiana University, 1936).

[5] Harper Lee, *To Kill A Mocking Bird* (New York: Popular Library, Inc., 1962).

snapped out such sharp reprimands as "Stop it. You're not supposed to know that until next grade!"

The attitude of Miss Caroline toward Jean Louise's preschool reading ability is somewhat caricatured, but it does serve to point up the skepticism that many teachers have expressed in regard to children learning to read at home lest such learning would interfere with the method used in school—a tradition which is direly in need of reconsideration.

This topic of teaching young children to read before school is controversial at present and calls for careful evaluation. In making this evaluation two main categories of children will be considered: (1) those who seek reading of their own accord and learn to read informally at home, and (2) those who are given systematic instruction at the initiative of an adult who wishes to hasten them along their educational way. Each of these categories requires separate evaluation.

Preschool Children Who Seek Help in Reading

An example of the first category will be given as a basis for later discussion. This example is concerned with Cathy, the young daughter of a friend of the writer. When Cathy was three, the writer together with other guests, frequently spent an evening in her home. As the guests arrived, Cathy would gather up a half dozen books, seat herself under a lamp, and sit there oblivious to conversation of the guests, literally devouring her books for long periods of time.

When turning four, Cathy began asking what certain words were; she would now sit by herself and read orally from books, largely from memory but recognizing a word here and there. When she was about four and a half she was in a ten-cent store with her mother one day. While the mother was busy shopping, Cathy amused herself at a counter covered with books. Suddenly she discovered a paper-covered booklet with pictures in it and a word under each picture. She ran to her mother, begging her to buy this book. With the use of the book Cathy taught herself to read all the words under the pictures. When she entered the kindergarten at five, she was reading fluently.

Wondering whether Cathy's skill was being recognized by the kindergarten teacher, Cathy was asked, "Does your teacher let you read at school?" "Oh, yes," replied Cathy. "I read every day to her and sometimes to the other children." Again curious to know if the kindergarten teacher was actually teaching reading to *all* her pupils, another question was asked, "Does your teacher have all the children read each day?" "Oh, no," answered Cathy. "Just me and another girl. But I read better'n she does." Cathy was not only progressing in reading but she had evolved an evaluative process which she used in appraising reading quality and applied it quite immodestly.

The points to be made with the use of this illustration are: (1) Cathy learned to read as a result of her own questions and requests, which were answered and granted by a sympathetic mother. She didn't read because some adult decided to teach her to read and flashed word cards for her to memorize or told her that *b* said "buh" and *c* said "cuh." She taught herself to read whole words which were meaningful to her because they were pictured. (2) Cathy was not denied reading experience in kindergarten and told that she would have to wait until first grade. The kindergarten teacher nurtured Cathy's reading interest and ability but she did not formally teach reading either to Cathy or to the other kindergarten children who had not yet reached beginning reading maturity. It is hoped, however, that she provided rich informal contacts with reading for all her pupils in such ways as those mentioned on pages 468–70.

To return to the more general discussion of preschool readers: we have evidence that many children learn to read by informal methods, as illustrated in the example of Cathy. Terman [6] found that over one per cent of his subjects learned to read before they were three years old, and that two and a half per cent read before they were five. Most of them received only incidental assistance, and some surprised their parents by suddenly reading to them when their parents were not aware that they could read.

Durkin,[7] in her study of forty-nine children before grade one, states that some of these children began reading at two years of age. An important and common factor in the homes of these children was that there was at least one person in each home who took the time and had the patience to answer the children's questions about words and reading, and that such questions were usually constant.

Early Readers Who Are *Taught* to Read

In contrast to the informal procedures which young children use in learning to read as a result of their own initiative, some current experiments are being conducted in which young children are taught to read through an adult-planned, systematic method. Examples of such experiments are: the Yale experiment, in which Omar Moore is teaching children from two to five to read with the use of an electric typewriter; the Denver, Colorado experiment, in which parents are directed by television

[6] Lewis M. Terman, *Genetic Studies of Genius* (Stanford, Cal.: Stanford University Press), Vol. I (1925), 271–72; Vol. II (1926), 247–55.

[7] Dolores Durkin, "Children Who Read Before Grade One," *The Reading Teacher,* Vol. 14 (Jan. 1961), 163–66.

in teaching their preschool children with the use of a phonics book; the experiment of the Whitby School in Connecticut, which has been using the Montessori method; [8] and the experiment of the social psychology laboratory at the University of Chicago, in which it is hoped to teach four-year-old underprivileged children to read.

Such experiments await further longitudinal measurement before a valid evaluation can be made. It has been proved many times that an adult *can* teach a young child to read. The important question that many people are asking is, "Is this desirable?"

Specialists in early childhood education believe that these children are not sufficiently mature, physically and emotionally, to withstand systematic teaching. They inquire whether these children will develop antagonistic attitudes toward reading and a distaste for reading. Reading specialists wonder if these children will be at any advantage over other children in later primary grades. Also, they inquire if these children become fluent readers far beyond the usual grade-age achievement, will they be able to understand the concepts in the more advanced reading which they can do.

Evaluation

Children of today are sophisticated far beyond those of a generation ago. They talk glibly about rockets and jets and space flights. They know what country looks like in the snowy wastes of the Arctic, the scorched deserts of Africa, and the teeming jungles of the Amazon. Along with informative sophistication it is reasonable to expect that they are more sophisticated in regard to reading symbols.

They live in an environment of printed symbols. They see words on practically every package that is brought into the house, on the television screen, in the movies, on signboards, and in window displays. Possibly the present environment is conducive to the development of ripeness for reading in many children at an age earlier than we have heretofore recognized. On the other hand, there are many other children who, in spite of the environment, are not sufficiently mature to take on the reading process easily and happily until they are six, seven, or even eight years old. So it certainly is a mistake to assume that reading can be taught to *all* two-year-olds, or *all* four-year-olds, or to *all* children of any other age level. Ripeness for beginning reading is an individual matter. No dogmatic age can be set for reading maturity.

Another point to be made is that there is a vast difference between feeding the young child's own expressed interests in reading and an

[8] These methods were described more fully on pages 96–97.

adult-initiated program of instruction. When a child is eager to learn to read, asks what words are, requests help as Cathy did, then we can be fairly certain that he or she has attained maturity for beginning reading, and his requested help should be given freely. Members of the family should show interest in the child's achievement and should listen attentively when he or she wants to read to them. Certainly the opportunity to learn to read should not be withheld from such a child.

On the other hand, if a parent decides that her three-year-old should be taught to read so that she will have a head-start for school, and starts an organized program of instruction with him even though the child resists this instruction, she may do more harm than good. (See Chapter 20, pages 520–30.)

Summary

In summary, it might be said that young children, who, themselves, show an interest in learning to read and request help in reading at an early age should not be deprived of the assistance which they seek. Society needs the contributions of the gifted too much for these children to sit around and wait until the average or slow children are ready to read. More than this, probably most kindergarten teachers should be exposing their pupils to many more *informal* reading experiences than they now are doing.

The practice, however, of having an adult engage in some systematized form of instruction with young children irrespective of their beginning reading maturity is questioned quite generally by educators in the field of childhood education. Until the benefits and dangers are known, most school people are not willing to place themselves among the backers of this movement. In the meantime, let's keep an open mind and wait and see.

Additional Readings

Books and Pamphlets

Almy, Millie C., *Children's Experiences Prior to First Grade and Success in Beginning Reading.* Teachers College Contributions to Education, No. 954. New York: Bureau of Publications, Teachers College, Columbia University, 1949.

Fuller, Elizabeth Mechem, "Readiness Narrowly and Broadly Conceived," *About the Kindergarten,* pp. 8–10. Washington, D. C., National Education Association, 1961.

Periodicals

Bain, Winifred, "With Life So Long, Why Shorten Childhood?", *Childhood Education,* Vol. 38 (Sept. 1961), 15–18.

Barclay, Dorothy, "Readying Them to Read," *New York Times Magazine* (Dec. 3, 1961), 138.

Butler, Annie L. "Hurry! Hurry! Hurry! Why?" *Childhood Education,* Vol. 39 (Sept. 1962), 10–13.

Cohan, Mayme, "Two and a Half Reading," *Elementary English,* XXXVIII (Nov. 1961), 506–508.

Crain, R. E., "Home Centered Reading Readiness Program," *National Elementary Principal,* Vol. 35 (Sept. 1955), 34–37.

Durkin, Dolores, "Children Who Learn to Read at Home," *Elementary School Journal,* Vol. 62 (Oct. 1961), 14–18.

Herr, Selma, "Uses and Abuses of the Readiness Concept," *Reading in Action,* pp. 82–83. International Reading Association Conference Proceedings. New York: Scholastic Magazines, 1957.

Hooper, Laura, "Building on Sound Beginnings in Pre-Primary Education," *Childhood Education,* Vol. 39 (Sept. 1962), 423–24.

Smith, Gretel D., "Is Your 5-Year-Old Ready for School?" *Elementary English,* XXXV (Dec. 1958), 532–33.

Smith, Nila Banton, "What Have We Accomplished in Reading?" *Elementary English,* XXXVIII (Mar. 1961), 144–45.

16

Appraising Beginning Reading Maturity

The reader will note that the term "reading readiness" is not used in the title of this chapter. It will not be used whenever it can be avoided within this chapter or in additional chapters dealing with beginning reading.[1]

The original concept of "reading readiness" was certainly a sound one. However, the phrase which has been used to name this concept for a period of years has become formalized and interpreted too narrowly by many people. Perhaps dropping the term will pave the way for breaking from a too-narrow concept and for developing broader and more flexible considerations.

Many people narrowly consider "reading readiness" as something that suddenly bursts forth at the age of six to six-and-a-half, mentally. Truly, getting ready to read is a developmental process that proceeds all through the early years. It doesn't just happen at a certain age point in a child's

[1] The commonly accepted term "reading readiness" will be used of course when discussing published materials, studies, and reports in which this phraseology is used by the author whose materials, results, or viewpoints are being discussed.

life. Reading growth begins when the child speaks his first word; it proceeds as he sits in mother's lap watching the pictures and printed page as she reads; as he watches a large characteristically formed word when it appears nightly in a television ad; as he first realizes that he can identify a word in the title of a favorite story book; as he finds his name on packages under the Christmas tree. Thus maturation in the use of the reading process develops gradually all through the early years and it differs widely from child to child. We should begin to think about developmental stages in reading rather than to concentrate attention on just one point which we now consider as *the time* at which "reading readiness" appears.

Factors Related to Reading Maturation

In Chapter 3 the relationships between reading growth and other aspects of child growth were discussed. This discussion had to do more generally with factors related to reading success in the grades than with the development of reading maturation before school. Many studies, however, have shown that these same factors are operative in developing children's ability to undertake reading in the first place. These factors will be mentioned again very briefly and others will be presented as they pertain especially to *beginning* reading maturity.

Intelligence

A child's intelligence is one of the strongest contributory factors to beginning reading maturity. This has been proved repeatedly.[2]

Another fact, and a very significant one, is that no one mental age can be named as *the* mental age at which all children are able to undertake reading. Several studies have pointed to this conclusion. One of these studies, conducted by Gates,[3] is especially interesting.

Gates made a study of four different groups who were taught by different methods and materials. It was found that in one group, a mental age of five years was sufficient; in a second group, it was a half-year higher;

[2] Charles D. Dean, "Predicting First Grade Reading Achievement," *Elementary School Journal*, Vol. 39 (Apr. 1938), 609–16. Arthur I. Gates and Guy L. Bond, "Reading Readiness: A Study of Factors Determining Success and Failure in Beginning Reading," *Teachers College Record*, Vol. 37 (May 1936), 679–85. W. W. Theisen, "Factors Affecting Results in Primary Reading," Report of the Society's Committee on Silent Reading, *Twentieth Yearbook of the National Society for the Study of Education*, Part II (Bloomington, Ill.: Public School Publishing Company, 1921). George Isaiah Thomas, "A Study of Reading Achievement in Terms of Mental Ability," *The Elementary School Journal*, Vol. 27 (Sept. 1946), 28–33.

[3] Arthur I. Gates, "The Necessary Mental Age for Beginning Reading," *Elementary School Journal*, Vol. 37 (Mar. 1937), 497–508.

the third group required a mental age of about six years; in the fourth group, children with a mental age of six years and five months fared none too well, and some of those with mental ages of seven years or above had difficulty. Gates concluded that "statements concerning necessary mental age at which a pupil can be entrusted to learn to read are essentially meaningless."

Physical Fitness

There is some evidence that the physical maturation of a child has a relationship to his development of ripeness for reading. There is also a mass of evidence that reveals close relationships between specific physical deficiencies, diseases, and illnesses and reading development.[4] See pages 33–35 for references and further discussion.

It stands to reason that, other things being equal, a child who is free from visual and hearing defects, and who enjoys excellent health, will naturally have been more alert to reading situations before coming to school than a child who has been hampered by physical handicaps.

Cultural Background of the Home

Homes rich in cultural atmosphere, with shelves of good books, with the better magazines and newspapers, and with an abundance of good music and pictures—all of these are of immeasurable advantage to the child. In such homes, children usually are provided with collections of picture books and story books of their own, and they are encouraged by their parents in their initial reading interests. They are supplied with educational toys which provide mediums for matching, constructing, and experimentation of various kinds. Children in such homes come in contact with visitors who have interesting things to tell and to show.

These and many other influences too obvious to bear recording give the child of a cultured family a definite prereading supremacy over the child whose home influences are barren of cultural background.

Home and Community Experience

Children who have opportunities for rich first-hand experiences in their environment have a fund of meaningful concepts to bring to their first

[4] Thomas H. Eames, "A Frequency Study of Physical Handicaps in Reading Disability and Unselected Groups," *Journal of Educational Research*, Vol. 29 (Sept. 1935), 1–5. Elizabeth Mechem Fuller, "Peas in a Pod," *Educational Leadership*, Vol. 3 (Apr. 1946), 302–307. Willard C. Olsen, "Reading as a Function of the Total Growth of the Child," in William S. Gray, ed., *Reading and Pupil Development*, "Supplementary Educational Monographs," No. 51 (Chicago: University of Chicago Press, 1940). For a summary of such evidence, see Nila Banton Smith, *Readiness of Reading and Related Language Arts* (Chicago: National Conference of Teachers of English, 1950), pp. 8–14.

reading experiences. Beginning reading books, on the whole, devote their content to stories based on home and community experiences. If the child has had these same experiences he will understand and appreciate the vicarious experiences of the characters in his reading books.

Cantor [5] provided kindergarten children with excursions designed to develop concepts which they would meet in their first grade readers. As a result of "comparisons made with reading readiness in other schools, it seemed probable that children (who had the excursions) definitely profited . . . from excursions experienced in their kindergarten year." See a more complete discussion of this study on page 291. For references to similar studies see page 43.

Social Experiences

Exceedingly important are the child's social contacts with others of his own age, and even with those older and younger.[6] The social adjustments necessary in getting along well with the little girl next door and the little boy across the street, as well as with adults, are important contributions in preparing children for the social activities which are necessary in undertaking the activities involved in learning beginning reading.

Emotional Development

Well-rounded emotional development contributes much to the learning of beginning reading.[7] The child's attitude toward undertakings, his habits, his interests in the things about him and in the various phases of school life, his reactions to requests, to suggestions, and to criticisms, are all important factors in the undertaking of beginning reading. The importance of poised emotional stability cannot be overestimated. See Chapter 3, pages 44–46 for a discussion of emotional maturity.

Language Ability

As indicated in Chapter 4, language facility and reading ability are closely related. Facility in the use of spoken language is the most important skill stock-in-trade which the child brings to beginning reading. Facility in expressing himself, familiarity with the order of sentence struc-

[5] Alma Cantor, *An Historical, Philosophical, and Scientific Study of Kindergarten Excursions as a Basis for Social Adaptation and Reading Readiness.* Master's Thesis (Cincinnati, Ohio: Teachers College, University of Cincinnati, 1935).

[6] For a summary of studies dealing with "Social Readiness," see Nila B. Smith, *Readiness for Beginning Reading and Related Language Arts* (Chicago: The National Council of Teachers of English, 1950), pp. 19–22.

[7] *Ibid.*, pp. 17–19.

ture and common idiomatic expressions, grasp of a vocabulary sufficiently rich to enable him to understand stories for children—these acquirements contribute greatly to ripeness for beginning reading.

There is real need for a preparatory period directed toward language development for children who come from homes where a foreign language is spoken.

Attendance at Kindergarten

Children who have attended kindergarten, and have engaged in all the rich experiences in companionship and learning which kindergarten environment and activities afford, are better equipped for beginning reading than those who have not had this advantage. There is a considerable body of evidence to indicate that this is the case.

Studies made by MacLatchey,[8] Pratt[9] and Fast[10] and many others have revealed that children who have attended kindergarten made significantly higher scores on readiness tests, and later, on reading tests, than children who had not attended kindergarten. With the present trend toward providing more informal contacts with reading in the kindergarten, the contributions of the kindergarten to first grade reading maturity should be increased substantially.

Informal Reading Experiences

The informal reading of young children was discussed on pages 448–52. Naturally one would expect that a preschool child who had taken an interest in reading and who, of his own volition, had learned some reading symbols would be at an advantage when undertaking reading in school.

One of the most significant studies in regard to early reading experience was conducted by Almy,[11] who explored the possible relationships between success in beginning reading and reading experiences before first grade. She found a significant, positive relationship between success in beginning reading and the child's responses to opportunities for reading prior to first grade. She stated that such experiences as looking at books and magazines, or being read to, contributed to the positive relationship, and also that interests in words, letters, numbers, wherever

8 Josephine MacLatchey, *Attendance at Kindergarten and Progress in the Primary Grades,* Ohio State University, 1928.
9 Willis E. Pratt, "A Study in the Differences in the Prediction of Reading Success of Kindergarten and Non-Kindergarten Children," *Journal of Educational Research,* XLII (Mar. 1949), 525–33.
10 Irene Fast, "Kindergarten Training and Grade 1 Reading," *Journal of Education Psychology,* XLVIII (Jan. 1957), 52–57.
11 Millie Corrine Almy, *Children's Experiences Prior to First Grade and Success in Beginning Reading.* Ph.D. Dissertation (New York: Teachers College, Columbia University, 1949).

they may be found, as on signs, cans, packages, and table games, were important factors in the relationship.

Ascertaining Reading Maturity

How can a teacher tell when a child is sufficiently mature to undertake systematic reading instruction happily and successfully? Usually, a combination of facilities offer the best guidance: standardized tests, plus teachers' interviews and observations.

Intelligence Tests

The two types of standardized tests most widely used to check certain aspects of reading maturity are intelligence tests and reading readiness tests. Several studies [12] have been made concerning the reliability of certain intelligence and readiness tests, and the conclusion most generally reached is that intelligence tests and reading tests used together give a more accurate prediction of reading success than one test used alone.

There are two types of tests which may be used in ascertaining the intelligence quotient of young children: individual intelligence tests and group intelligence tests. The former must be given to each child individually, whereas the latter may be given to a group of ten or twelve children at a time. Most of the individual tests should be administered by a person specially trained to give them, while a group test may be administered by the classroom teacher if she follows instructions carefully.

Among the individual intelligence tests, the following have been found valuable to use with kindergarten and first grade children:

Stanford Binet Intelligence Scales, Third Division, 1960, Houghton Mifflin Company, Boston, Mass.

Wechsler Intelligence Scale for Children, The Psychological Corporation, 304 East 45th Street, New York 10, N. Y.

Some of the group intelligence tests frequently used are:

California Tests of Mental Maturity, 1957 Edition (Preprimary), California Test Bureau, 5916 Hollywood Boulevard, Los Angeles 28, Cal.

Detroit Beginning First Grade Intelligence Test, Revised, Harcourt, Brace and World, Inc., 750 Third Avenue, New York 17, N. Y.

[12] A. I. Gates and others, "Methods of Determining Reading Readiness," *Elementary School Journal*, Vol. 39 (Nov. 1939), 164–67. A. J. Huggers, "An Experiment in Reading Readiness," *Journal of Educational Research*, XLII (Dec. 1938), 263–70. P. Fendrick and C. A. McGlade, "A Validation of Two Prognostic Tests of Reading Aptitude," *Elementary School Journal*, XXXIX (1938), 187–94.

Kuhlman-Anderson Intelligence Test, 6th ed. (kindergarten and first grade levels), The Psychological Corporation, 304 East 45th Street, New York 10, N. Y.

Pintner-Cunningham Primary Test (kindergarten–grade 2), Harcourt, Brace and World, Inc., 750 Third Avenue, New York 17, N. Y.

Reading Readiness Tests

Reading readiness tests are widely used in assessing beginning reading maturity. While a readiness test is useful in giving some indication as to whether or not a child is ready for systematic reading instruction, it should not be relied upon as a sole criterion in making this decision. As indicated on the preceding pages, several different factors contribute to a child's ripeness in development for reading instruction. Many of these factors cannot be measured by a paper and pencil test. Therefore, the advisable course to pursue is to give a readiness test to obtain *one* indication of beginning reading maturation but to supplement the results of this test by many other measures, observations, and judgments.

Some of the most widely used group readiness tests are:

Gates Reading Readiness Tests, Bureau of Publications, Teachers College, Columbia University, 525 West 120th Street, New York 27, N. Y.

Lee-Clark Reading Readiness Test, Revised, California Test Bureau, 5916 Hollywood Boulevard, Los Angeles 28, Cal.

Metropolitan Readiness Tests, Harcourt, Brace and World, Inc., 750 Third Avenue, New York 17, N. Y.

Teacher Observation and Interview

Teacher judgment is probably the most reliable of all criteria for deciding when a child has arrived at a stage appropriate for undertaking reading instruction. If the teacher provides the child with many informal contacts with reading (as described on pages 468–70) he will demonstrate his readiness in his responses or lack of responses. All children in the group should be given repeated exposures to reading through informal activities. As a result of observing their reactions the teacher will come to know quite well which ones can take systematic reading instruction safely and which ones need to continue for awhile longer with informal activities.

If there are borderline children or children who show no disposition at all toward reading, the teacher should probe deeper to find in what areas of development they may need the most help.

Some items for use in conducting informal interviews and in making observations are suggested on the pages that follow. The teacher, however, will probably wish to make up her own list of questions or points for use with special cases. She may wish to prepare a chart for convenience in checking.

Interview Concerning Background Experiences

The richness or meagerness of a child's background experiences has a direct bearing on his understanding and enjoyment of the content in his first reading books. The teacher may obtain such information incidentally by listening to children's spontaneous conversation, and in noting what they talk about in class discussions or while telling personal experiences. If she is doubtful about certain children and wishes to obtain more direct information about their background experiences the questions below may be suggestive.

It is highly desirable to base these questions on the vicarious experiences which characters have in the first preprimer or other reading books pupils will use. This will reveal whether children should be given certain experiences designed to acquaint them with concepts needed in meaningful first reading.

What toys do you have at home? (doll, ball, toy train)
What pets do you have? (dog and cat are in most preprimer stories)
Do you play with other children? What do you play? (playing house, hide-and-seek, playing ball are prominent in the preprimer stories)
Do you help at home? What do you do?
Do you ever go to a store? What kind of a store? What do you see there?
Have you ever seen a train? Have you ever ridden on a train? Have you ever ridden on an airplane?
Do you have a garden? Is it a vegetable garden or a flower garden? What are the different plants that grow in it?
Do you ever go on trips with your Daddy and Mother? How do you travel? Where do you go?
Have you ever visited a farm? What did you see there? (In case of a farm child ask: Have you ever visited a city? What did you see there?)
What stores have you been in, other than a grocery store? What did you see there?
Have you ever been to a beach? What did you see there? What did you do there?

Interview in Regard to Reading Experiences

If the teacher wishes to ascertain the extent of reading experience which certain individuals have had at home, she may use such interview questions as these:

Do you have books of your own at home?

How many books do you have?

Do you look at your books by yourself?

Can you read any words in your books?

Do you have some books with old, old stories in them? What are they?

Do you have books with stories in them about children like you? What are they?

Does anyone read to you? What does she (or he) read to you? Do you ever look at the lines of print as she (or he) reads?

Do you know your name when you see it in writing?

Can you write your name?

Can you tell when the Stop-Go signal says *Stop*? When it says *Go*?

Do you know any words on the grocery packages in your mother's cupboard? What words?

Observation of Reading Interests and Abilities

Does the child voluntarily look at informal reading materials and try to find out what the symbols say?

Does he voluntarily choose books from the library table to look at?

Does he ask the teacher to read from some of these books?

Does he notice signs and advertisements when taking walks or going on excursions? Does he ask or try to read what these advertisements say?

Can he readily identify the picture of an object named by the teacher?

Is he able to match pictures of objects, letters, words?

Is he able to classify pictures of objects according to a common source?

Can he readily locate and select a picture of an object named by the teacher when it appears in a group of other pictured objects?

Can he supply a word in oral context?

Can he detect words that sound alike—rhyme words?

Can he interpret details in pictures?

Can he understand directions, explanations, stories?

Can he retain oral directions?

Can he retell stories?

Can he remember objects seen in a picture?

Can he give an oral interpretation of a single composite picture? Of a series of sequential pictures?

Does he enjoy all types of literature: old tales, realistic stories, poetry, and rhymes?

Can he follow lines of pictures from left to right across the line, then accurately down and back to the next line?

Can he associate a few words with their symbols?

For enrichment activities see the next section, pages 468–87.

Observation of Physical Condition

Physical defects and deficiencies should of course be given professional attention by a physician, eye-specialist, or otologist according to the nature of the difficulty. The teacher, however, *must* be alert to certain obvious indications of health or lack of health among the children in her classroom, and then promptly call upon the specialized service in the case of children who need attention.

A complete list of symptoms which a teacher might observe in regard to general health conditions should be obtained from a medical doctor. A few of the more easily discernible ones are as follows: bodily tension, strained expression, restlessness, hyperactivity, nervousness, fatigue, lack of energy, postural slumping, overweight, underweight, frequent colds, listlessness, inattention, lack of concentration while reading.

In regard to vision, see page 38 for indications of deficiencies to look for.

The keen observation of the teacher often leads to the detection of a child with a hearing defect. See page 40 for symptoms of hearing difficulty.

Observation of Language Facility

As we have noted, facility in language expression is closely related to facility in reading. The points below might well be considered in a teacher's observation of language expression:

Does the child have an adequate vocabulary with which to express himself intelligently?
Is he able to tell a story from a composite picture?
Is he able to tell a story in sequence with the aid of pictures?
Is he able to tell a story in sequence without the aid of pictures?
Is he able to relate a personal experience clearly enough so that other children understand it and enjoy it?
Can he anticipate what happens next in a story?
Can he supply a preceding incident in a story?
Can he supply conversation in a story?
Can he supply missing words or phrases in a sentence given orally by the teacher?
Can he take the part of a character in dramatizing a story?
Does he possess facility in saying words containing difficult speech sounds?
Does he enunciate distinctly?
Is he free from speech defects?

For stages of development see "Language and Child Development," pages 56–59.

Observing Indications of Intelligence

A careful study of the results of a standardized intelligence test is, of course, the teacher's most reliable guide in ascertaining the mental maturity of her pupils. As a supplement to a standardized intelligence test the teacher may wish to make some observations of her own in regard to indications of mental ability. The following abilities may be noted as some indication of the status of mental maturation.

Does he grasp the point readily in stories and simple jokes?
Does he follow directions accurately?
Does he ask intelligent questions?
Does he do logical thinking in helping to solve a problem in group discussion?
Does he choose material wisely in carrying out a plan?
Does he concentrate on a task for a reasonable length of time?
Is he able to evaluate group and individual work?

For a discussion of intelligence see "As the Child Grows Mentally," pages 28–33.

Observation of Social Adjustment

The disposition and ability to make certain social adjustments are necessary in learning to read. Some items of social adjustment which are worthy of observation in this respect are:

Does he enter into group play and work freely and of his own accord?
Does he cooperate well with other children?
Do other children have a friendly attitude toward him?
Does he assume his share of responsibilities as they contribute to the good of the group?
Does he sometimes take the initiative in group undertakings?
Does he follow well upon occasion?
Does he show self-control in cases in which he has to take his turn, or in which some other child is permitted to do something he wants to do?
Does he make contributions during discussion periods?
Is he interested in the work and in the welfare of other children?

For discussion of social implications see "Social Experiences," page 457.

Observation of Emotional Maturity

Certain emotional characteristics contribute to the child's success in beginning reading. The questions below are suggestive of points to look for in regard to emotional development.

Does the child respond to requests readily?
Does he take criticisms and suggestions pleasantly?
Is he timid?
Is he aggressive?

Is he well-poised?
Does he seem nervous?
Is he worried about something?
Is he willing to undertake new tasks?
Does he have confidence in himself?
Does he show interest in the various school activities?
Does he seem to experience satisfaction in achievement?
Can his general disposition be characterized as happy?

For enrichment activities see "As the Child Grows Emotionally," pages 44–50. Some children of course need the professional attention of a psychologist or psychiatrist.

Summary

In this chapter it was pointed out that the term "reading readiness" has been too narrowly interpreted and applied, and a broader viewpoint of developmental stages in the reading maturation of young children and factors contributing to such maturation was urged. The following factors were discussed as contributing to maturation: intelligence, physical fitness, cultural background, emotional development, language ability, home and community experiences, social experiences, attendance at kindergarten, and informal reading activities. Suggestions for ascertaining beginning reading maturation embraced a suggested list of intelligence tests and of reading readiness tests. Lists of items were also suggested for use in observation and interview of factors contributing to reading maturation.

Additional Readings

Books and Pamphlets

Betts, Emmett Albert, *Foundations of Reading Instruction*, rev. ed., Part 3, New York: American Book, 1957.

Dawson, Mildred A., and Henry A. Bamman, *Fundamentals of Basic Reading Instruction*, Chap. 3. New York: Longmans, Green & Co., Inc., 1959.

DeBoer, John J., and Martha Dallmann, *The Teaching of Reading*, Chap. 5A. New York: Holt, Rinehart & Winston, Inc., 1960.

Fuller, Elizabeth Mechem, "Readiness—Narrowingly and Broadly Conceived," *About the Kindergarten*, pp. 8–9. Washington, D. C.: National Education Association, 1961.

Harris, Albert J., *Effective Teaching of Reading*, Chap. 2. New York: David McKay Co., Inc., 1962.

Hildreth, Gertrude, *Readiness for School Beginners*, Chaps. 3, 4. New York: Harcourt, Brace and World, Inc., 1950.

Russell, David H., *Children Learn to Read*, pp. 169–79. Boston: Ginn & Company, 1961.

Smith, Nila Banton, *Readiness for Reading and Related Language Arts*. Chicago: The National Council of Teachers of English, 1950.

Periodicals

Baker, Emily, "Reading Readiness Is Still Important," *Elementary English*, Vol. 32 (Jan. 1955), 17–23.

Bradley, Beatrice E., "An Experimental Study of the Readiness Approach to Reading," *Elementary School Journal*, Vol. 56 (1956), 262–67.

Carpenter, Ethelouise, "Reading Is Being," *Childhood Education*, Vol. 38 (Nov. 1961), 114–16.

Karlin, R., "Prediction of Reading Success and Reading Readiness Tests," *Elementary English*, Vol. 34 (May 1957), 320–22.

Sutton, R. S., "Study of Certain Factors Associated with Reading Readiness in the Kindergarten," *Journal of Educational Research*, Vol. 48 (Mar. 1955), 531–38.

Zirbes, Laura, "Appraising Our Practices," *Childhood Education*, Vol. 37 (Mar. 1961), 306–307.

17

Laying Skill Foundations in Kindergarten and First Grade

With the increased interest and effort which is being directed toward the improvement of reading in American schools, attention is being turned toward kindergarten and prereading first grade periods as times in which more might be done in regard to reading development. Preschool reading was discussed in Chapter 15, and some guidance was given in regard to this matter. The present chapter, however, is concerned with children's reading development *after* they enter school—not with the systematic and formal teaching of reading, but with many *informal* activities which teachers of kindergarten children and prereading first graders may use in laying foundations for the reading skills without actually teaching reading itself.

In general, kindergarten and first grade teachers have done a good job during prereading periods in developing their pupils physically, mentally, emotionally, culturally, socially, experientially, and linguistically. And this is very important, for reading growth is intertwined with and dependent upon all these factors.

There is a strong trend of thought at present, however, toward the assumption that most kindergarten teachers could do much more about reading per se. As for first grade teachers, a complaint is frequently voiced against a too-common practice of holding *all* children for a prereading preparatory period upon entrance in first grade, when many of them are ready to start reading immediately. The most common complaint, however, is directed toward the nature of the work done with children who have to be held in a prereading group for a considerable period of time. The complaint is that there is not enough substance in the prereading curriculum, and particularly that not enough is done for these children in actually furthering their *reading* maturation.

This chapter will suggest many informal, functional types of *contacts* which children may have with reading in the kindergarten and in a prereading first grade period (if they need to have such a period). It is hoped that the concrete suggestions on the following pages will be helpful to those who don't know what to do in developing reading ability when they are not supposed actually to teach reading itself.

The major and original contribution of this chapter is the section devoted to suggestions for *laying the foundation for skills in all of the major growth areas* during the prereading period. These activities do not involve reading itself, but they develop habits and make use of thinking processes of the same specific types as those needed in each of these growth areas: word identification, getting meanings, study skills, rate, and interest in reading.

It was largely because of need for laying foundation skills that Part Four, "Beginnings of Reading Instruction," was delayed until the latter part of this book. Kindergarten teachers and teachers of beginning reading should be thoroughly acquainted with reading skill areas so that they may be alert to possibilities of doing something specific about developing skill foundations in these areas before children read at all, and while reading preparation is under way.

Informal, Functional Contacts

Informal, functional reading contacts will arise largely as the exigency of the occasion presents itself. The kindergarten teacher who is watching for such opportunities will find many of them as the daily activities ensue. Similarly, the first grade teacher discovers such opportunities while dealing with a group of children who are very immature in their qualifications for undertaking systematic reading instruction.

In these informal contacts with symbols, kindergarten children and immature first graders should simply be *exposed* to the symbols. If some of them start reading the content, whatever it may be, all right. Such children should not be denied this privilege. It should be encouraged. For those with whom the exposures do not "take," be content with the exposures only; eventually they will "take."

A few suggestions of possibilities for informal and functional contacts are given below.

Manuscript name cards and let each child, if he so desires, wear his card pinned to his clothing for a time. Invite each one to hold up his name card when his name is called to check attendance; or he may place his name in a pocket chart when it is called during attendance taking. Later some children might like to group together all names that begin with the same letter.

After discussion with the children, when a need arises place labels on objects in the room when they may serve some functional purpose; for example, if difficulty arises in finding the scissors, label the cupboard where the scissors are kept; place *in* and *out* signs on swinging doors to prevent an accident; label hooks in the hall with the children's names; and so on. The children themselves may prepare simple labels for their construction work on large paintings and drawings, as *City Airport, Tom's Home*.

Frequently, manuscript memorandums on the chalkboard; for example, orders for school lunches, as "Milk 6, Cocoa 8, Crackers 10, Apples 3"; names of committees and their members, as "Plant Committee—Tom, Alice, and Sue"; simple rules, as "Work quietly"; simple directions for some activity, such as making applesauce—"Pare. Wash. Cook. Sweeten."

Place "surprise" sentences on the bulletin board each morning, as "Susan will bring her pet rabbit this afternoon." Let the children gather around the bulletin board and try to guess what the surprise is; then read it to them.

When taking a walk or going on an excursion, call attention to the names on packages in a grocery store window; signs on store buildings; names of streets; names on trucks, street cars, and buses; danger signs; and so on.

Provide a very large book with blank pages. Attach alphabet tabs to the edges of the pages. Ask children to place their unfinished work between the leaves in this book, locating the place by matching the first letter of their first name with the letter on the appropriate alphabet tab.

The children may make class or individual scrap books, each page of which contains a picture or a collection of pictures which they have cut from magazines. The teacher may pass out labels typed on a typewriter with a primer-sized type, and place them under the pictures. The children may then paste these labels under the pictures on the pages of their scrap books.

During the entire kindergarten period and during any necessary preparatory period in first grade the teacher should frequently let children see their own words flow into printed symbols as she manuscripts them on the chalkboard or on tagboard. Advantage should be taken of every opportunity to manuscript, as the children watch, notices, plans, suggestions, directions which they, themselves, have composed. While the children should not be required to *read* the words, phrases, or sentences, they will have had the valuable experience of seeing meanings put into reading symbols, meanings which grow out of their own experiences, and some of them probably will begin to read words or sentences of their own accord. If words cut from a duplicate chart are placed under a pocket chart, perhaps some of them will try building in the pocket chart a composition like the one in the chart that is intact. (See pages 489–504, "Preparing and Using Experience Charts.")

Planned Activities for Skill Development

Word Identification Activities

Using Context Clues

As discussed in Chapter 8, pages 181–87, the use of context clues is a very useful method of attack in working out the pronunciation of unrecognized words while reading. A foundation for the use of this technique can readily be laid in working with prereading children by inviting them to see if they can supply a word in oral context.

The teacher might begin her activities with the use of an appropriate picture, a collection of which should be kept available for this purpose. One plan might be to show a picture of an object, such as an apple, the teacher saying, "This is an _____." Let the pupils supply the word *apple*. Another plan is to place two pictures on the chalk ledge, the name of one of which would be appropriate in completing a certain sentence, the other of which would not. For example, a picture of a boat and one of a cake might be placed on the chalk ledge. The teacher may say, "Boys and girls like to eat _____." A child is then called upon to pick up the right picture (the picture of the cake), hold it before the group, and say, "Cake." All the children are then asked to repeat the complete sentence, "All boys and girls like to eat cake."

A later procedure to use in furthering this development is for the teacher to tell the children that she is going to state a sentence, leaving out a word, and see if they can tell what the word should be. She then states an easy sentence, such as, "Apples grow on _____," leaving out the last word. The children who know what the word is will be asked to show hands or stand. Those who don't know what the word is should be given special help; the teacher may repeat the sentence, and ask questions such as, "Do apples grow on vines, or stalks, or what?"

Laying a Foundation for Phonics

As discussed in Chapter 8, pages 201–202, there are four distinct processes involved in the effective use of phonics: (1) visual discrimination, (2) auditory discrimination, (3) blending, and (4) contextual application. We cannot expect prereading children to work with the blending and the contextual application processes, but it is entirely appropriate for them to have many experiences in visual and auditory discrimination. Some suggestions for activities of these types are given below.

Visual Discrimination

Practice in matching colors is an easy beginning in visual discrimination. Scrutinizing pictures, words, and letters to detect their likenesses and differences should help the children later in recognizing sight words and in identifying phonic elements within words.

MATCHING COLORS

Matching colors is the simplest and one of the most attractive activities for prereading children.

1. Let children group any colored objects which are available according to color, naming the color of each group; for example:

   a. Group flowers according to color.
   b. Group marbles according to color.
   c. Group toys according to color.
   d. Group girls in the class according to the colors of their dresses.
   e. Group boys in the class according to the colors of their sweaters.
   f. Group painted paper mâché or clay fruits or vegetables according to color.

Later the children may match one object of a certain color with any other object in the room which is of that same color; for example, a child may match a red airplane with a red dress or sweater which another child is wearing; a red circle or square on the color chart with a red block or with a red crayon in his crayon box; and so on.

2. In using the activities described below, it will be necessary for the teacher to have on hand a large color chart on which the several colors appear in consistent forms.

Prepare a set of cards on which are pasted or drawn color forms which correspond with those on the color chart: that is, if circles are used on the color chart, a colored circle should appear on each of the cards. Pass out the cards, giving one to each child. Give different children a turn at matching the circle on his card with the circle of the same color on the chart. If the child is unable to match the color, give any assistance that is necessary.

Pass out several cards, upon each of which appears a colored picture of an object. For example, one card may have a picture of a red wagon pasted or drawn on it; another may have a picture of a blue boat on it; another may have a picture of a bunch of purple grapes on it; another may have a picture of a brown pony on it; and so on.

When ready to play the game, ask the child with the blue boat, for instance, to find blue on the color chart and place his boat over it. Ask him to tell the color of his boat, and also to tell the color of the figure on the color chart with which he matches it. This procedure should be repeated until all the children have had a chance to find the color of the object pictures on their respective cards.

A variation of the above activity may be conducted in this way:

Teacher: "Betty, what is your picture?"
Betty: "I have some purple grapes."
Teacher: "Will you show us on the color chart the color of your grapes?"

Or, perhaps the child does not know the color of the picture on his card, but he does know the picture:

Teacher: "John, tell us what the picture is on your card."
John: "I have a pony."
Teacher: "Can you tell us what color your pony is?"
John: (Hesitates, and is not sure.)
Teacher: "Would you like to come to the color chart and match your pony with the color up here?"

John comes up and matches his pony correctly; then the teacher or children tell John that the color is *brown.*

Teacher: "Now what is the color of your pony, John?"
John: "My pony is brown."

3. The teacher gives each child in the group a section of a magazine

containing colored pictures. The children cut out all the pictures which they can find of a certain color and paste these pictures on a sheet of paper or in a little booklet. This may be done for quiet period work. Some teachers write in manuscript on the bottom of the sheet the name of the color in that color; for example, blue would be written with a blue crayon. This activity may be used for quiet period work and then followed with evaluation, providing for additional experience in matching and discussing colors.

MATCHING PICTURES

Matching pictures is a step ahead of matching colors. Prepare a folder containing attractive sets of duplicate pictures. These may be cut from magazine covers or from dime-store booklets. Place several pictures in a row on the chalk ledge. To the left and clearly apart from the row of pictures, place one picture which is similar to one of the pictures in the row.

Ask a child to pick up one picture on the left and hold it above the similar picture in the row to the right, being sure that he proceeds from left to right across the row. When the child has placed the picture, he is supposed to respond in this way: "This ball is like that ball."

MATCHING LETTERS

After some experience in matching, similar to those activities suggested above, children should be ready to engage in matching activities in which letters are used.

1. The letters may be written on the chalkboard in duplicate arrangements similar to those suggested below, and the children may be asked to circle or indicate in some other way the two letters which are alike in each row.

c	l	v	x	c	r
a	k	u	s	w	a
b	l	p	b	d	g

For quiet period work the rows of letters may be mimeographed in large type and children requested to draw a circle around the two letters in each row which are alike.

According to an investigation conducted by the author, the order of difficulty in matching the letters of the alphabet is as follows:

a   c   u   o   w   s   g—Easiest letters to match

e   v   x   y   k   t   z   l—More difficult to match than the letters in the first row

r h f i j n m—Still more difficult to match than letters in the two
rows above

b p q d—The most difficult letters to match

2. Variation may be given to the matching activities involving letters by writing the letters on different mediums. Alphabet blocks may be used, or each letter may be written on a square of tagboard or other heavy paper. In each of these cases the teacher may hold up one of the alphabet blocks, or one of the squares on which the letter appears, and ask the children to find the same letter among other blocks or squares of paper to which they have access.

MATCHING WORDS

The ability to match words is, of course, very close to the reading process; in fact, word recognition cannot take place until the child reaches the stage in which he recognizes a particular word form as being the same every time he sees it. Large, characteristically formed words are easier for children to match than small words which are similar in appearance. Therefore, in any practice which is given in matching words, it would be well to begin with the large words which have a distinctive configuration and gradually proceed to the small words which are less characteristic in form.

In providing children matching experiences with words, it is suggested that several different mediums be used, as suggested in preceding matching activities: pictures with words clipped underneath them, word cards detached from the pictures, words written in manuscript on the chalkboard, words mimeographed in large type on sheets of paper.

1. It is desirable that children's first matching experiences with words be associated with pictures. One suggestion is to paste a picture on each of several large cards about 4" x 9" in size. Write in manuscript the name of the picture at the bottom of the card. On another card about 4" x 2½", write the name of the picture only.

Place several of the picture cards on the chalk ledge. Give one of the matching word cards to each of the children. Ask a child to place the card which he holds under the word of one of the picture cards which looks just like the word he holds. Continue until all the children have had a chance to match their words.

2. Words not associated with pictures may be matched. Words written in groups similar to those below may first be matched on the chalkboard; later they may be matched on paper on which they have been dittoed in large primer type.

Suggested gradations according to difficulty:

Group 1	Group 2
grandmother/girl, thank, grandmother	girl/dime, house, girl
airplane/candy, airplane, horn	yellow/dinner, yellow, mouse
blackboard/pie, picture, blackboard	carrot/carrot, milk, tomato
Christmas/Christmas, shoe, candle	stone/rabbit, stone, marble
elephant/lion, elephant, tiger	toast/window, engine, toast

Group 3	Group 4	Group 5
rat/fox, cat, rat	boy/day, boy, pig	in/it, is, at, in
hill/will, hill, kite	dog/box, pin, dog	me/my, we, me
fox/fox, can, sit	pet/pet, get, dot	to/it, at, to
nest/sing, nest, tail	queen/piano, green, queen	on/no, on, in
man/fan, eat,man		was/saw, has, was

Auditory Discrimination

Developing ability to discriminate between likenesses and differences of sounds in words is just as fundamental to word recognition as is the development of ability to see likenesses and differences in the shapes of words.

A part of the work in laying the foundation for later work in phonics may well be that of providing experiences in recognizing and discriminating between the spoken sound of word wholes, and possibly some recognition of and discrimination between the sounds of letters at the beginnings of words.

LISTENING FOR RHYME WORDS

One of the most enjoyable of the auditory discrimination experiences which can be provided to prereading pupils is that of listening for words that sound alike in rhymes and jingles which the teacher recites to the children, and later in rhymes which the children themselves make up. Couplets of this sort are suitable for this purpose:

Little Bo Peep	Little Miss Muffet
She lost her sheep.	Sat on a tuffet.
What does little birdie say,	A rat and a mouse
In her nest at peep of day?	Both dwelt in one house.

LISTENING FOR THE SAME WORD

An auditory discrimination experience which is a little more difficult than that of recognizing rhyme words in couplets is that of recognizing two words which are alike in a list of words named by the teacher.

The procedure is as follows. The teacher says, "I am going to say several words. One word I will say twice. Listen carefully and see if you can tell me which word you hear two times. You may raise your hand as soon as you know what the word is."

The children listen as the teacher says a list of words, such as, "boy, tree, girl, dress, boy"; they then make the appropriate response.

Here are some sample lists:

doll, fun, play, *doll.*   *cat,* pig, tree, *cat*
girl, *boy,* run, *boy,* play.   tree, *duck,* girl, *duck.*
tree, fish, *tree,* boy.   *car,* frog, ball, *car,* duck.
ball, girl, fork, *ball.*   *dog,* bee, *dog,* box.

Word Structure Activities

The plural form of nouns nearly always causes trouble during the period of early reading. If the teacher of prereading groups would keep herself alert to the possibilities of this difficulty, and would make direct effort to lay the foundation for recognition of plural forms during the prereading period, a great deal could be done to avoid this difficulty later on.

One way in which a beginning can be made is that of having children find pictures representing singular and plural forms of the same noun. The teacher may place several pictures on the chalk ledge, some of which represent the singular form of certain objects, and others of which represent the plural form of the same objects, such as dog, dogs; girl, girls; tree, trees; and so on. She may then ask different children to get the picture of the object she names, saying merely, "Dogs," "girls," "trees," and so on. All children should be given the same number of chances, and each one tries to see how many pictures he can obtain by the end of the game.

A similar activity may be carried on with *ing* forms, in which the pictures represent such activities as "a boy running," "a girl eating," and so on.

The resourceful teacher will devise many ways of varying these activities which will awaken in children a sensitivity to different endings of words.

Working with Meanings

In Chapter 9, "Getting Meanings from Reading," four different processes were discussed: literal comprehension, interpretation, critical reading, and understanding specific word meanings. Foundations for the use of each of these processes can be laid as a part of the prereading curriculum.

Literal Comprehension

Asking questions based upon direct statements in context probably doesn't need any special emphasis because most teachers do a great deal of this, both in connection with pictures and with stories read or told to the children.

In discussing a picture a teacher may ask: "What does this girl have in her hands?" "On what is she sitting?" "What pet is lying beside her?" In discussing a story which has been read to the children, the teacher may ask, "What was the name of the girl in the story?" "Where was she going?" "Whom did she meet on the way?" and so on.

All such questions are of the literal comprehension type. Those questions having to do with the picture simply required naming objects seen; those asked in connection with the story required only reproduction of statements made directly in the story context. Literal comprehension is necessary and important in working with some phases of content in the special subject areas. It should not be overemphasized, however, at the expense of interpretation, which has a much wider service to render.

Interpretation

Giving children experiences in *thinking* in connection with reading content is too important to be delayed. Thinking, of course, should be encouraged in connection with all activities of the day. "Why didn't the wheels on Bill's wagon work?" "What can we use for a big rock in our play?" and so on.

Picture Interpretation

Coming closer to reading skills, considerable experience may be given in interpreting pictured situations. The teacher may make a collection of thought provoking pictures; for example, one picture may show a little girl peeling onions, and she is crying; another may show three puzzled, brown kittens gathered around a large, black, china cat used as an ornament on a table; another may show a little boy eating spinach with his eyes turned toward his dessert.

The children may be invited to discuss the details of each picture and be encouraged to think about why certain things are happening, as "Why is the little girl crying?" "Can you think why the yellow kittens look so puzzled?" "Why isn't the boy looking at the spinach that he is eating?" In interpreting these picture situations, children are using the same thinking processes in "reading between the lines" as they will need to use in interpreting contextual situations.

Story Interpretation

Teachers of young children should frequently guide them in interpreting deeper meanings in stories. For example while reading the story of Bambi, a teacher read that "*Bambi* was in an open space in the forest that was really screened in on all sides." She paused to ask, "How could this space be 'screened in' on all sides?" In reading *The Lively Little Rabbit,* another teacher came to this sentence: "But, like practically all owls, he did not like to travel in the day time." To stimulate thinking about what was said in the text, this teacher asked, "Why don't owls like to travel in the day time?" If all teachers of prereading children would very frequently grasp such opportunities to give children experiences in interpreting reading content, perhaps we wouldn't have so many children in the grades who are "poor in comprehension."

Critical Reading

Young children are encouraged these days to evaluate, judge, and give friendly criticism in regard to all their school activities. In so doing they are using the same mental processes which we expect them to use when reacting to printed material. To bring the use of these processes a little closer to the reading situation, it is suggested that children be commended for good thinking when they pass judgment upon picture situations. Edith remarked "A kitten wouldn't ride in a wagon behind a tricycle like that. He'd jump out." Jim asked "Why do they always show a witch riding on a broomstick; that wouldn't be comfortable." In both cases they were told, "You are right. You are doing good thinking. Everything you see in pictures isn't necessarily true."

Still closer to the reading situation are the opportunities in which children are guided by the teacher to evaluate some incident or statement in a story. "Do you think it was fair for Peter Rabbit's mother to put Peter to bed with only a dose of camomile tea while his brothers and sisters had bread and milk and blackberries?" asked a teacher during a discussion after she had read *Peter Rabbit* to the children. Some children did think it was fair and gave their reasons; others didn't think it was fair and gave their reasons. All had an opportunity to express personal reactions to something read from a book.

Specific Word Meanings

This again is a matter of incidental teaching by a teacher who realizes how important a rich vocabulary is to a beginning reader. In addition, it may be said that in reading or telling stories words are often used that do not occur in the ordinary conversation of children. These should be noted and explained—not lightly passed over. In reading the "fox lived in a shady glade in the woods," the vocabulary-conscious teacher paused for discussion and explanation of "glade." After reading about a poor mother and child who "drank from the cool spring," the teacher remarked, "This season is called the *spring* of the year. We talked about spring flowers this morning. Yet it says here that the mother and child drank out of a *spring*. Could this same word mean two different things?" The children, through discussion, arrived at the two different meanings for *spring*. In other words they were noting multiple word meanings.

In such ways as these, much can be done in clarifying specific word meanings for later reading.

Laying the Foundation for Study Skills in Reading

This possibility may seem the most remote of all reading skill development possibilities with the prereader. How can you do anything about study skills with children who can't even read—let alone study?

In Chapter 10 the "common" study skills discussed were: selection and evaluation, organization, recall, locating information, following directions. It is entirely possible for children in prereading groups to experience the beginnings of each of these skills in so far as the use of their thinking processes are concerned.

Selection and Evaluation

The ability to pick out of a printed passage the sentence, word, or thought that is most pertinent to a certain purpose is but one step beyond selecting pictures or verbal ideas which fulfill a request, interest, or need during prereading activities. "Find the smallest cat in the picture." "Here are two new books. One is about Mr. Glenn going around the earth in a rocket and the other is about a boy who had an exciting experience in a sailboat. Which do you wish me to read?" "What part of this story was most exciting?" "What part gave us the prettiest picture?" All such questions lead to selection and evaluation of reading content.

Organization

Many incidental opportunities arise for children to assemble things that belong to a certain classification, as placing all the roses in one vase and the pansies in another; placing all blocks of a certain size and shape together at the end of the construction period; placing all books of a certain size on a shelf; placing all scissors, paint brushes, or paint jars of a certain kind together; and so on.

In picture activities, children may place together all pictures of things we ride in, of animals, of birds, of toys, of buildings, of musical instruments, and so on.

In working with words and letters, pupils may place together all cards with the same word on them, with words that begin alike, with words that end alike, with letters that are the same, and so on. The same idea may be used in working with dittoed material, except that the children may circle, box, or underline like items rather than grouping them on the chalk ledge.

Recall

The ability to recall printed material may be cultivated through incidental experiences of this type:

Memorizing rhymes or short poems through repeated incidental oral contacts.
Reproducing a short story from one told by the teacher.
Reproducing a short story interpreted from a series of pictures.
Remembering directions in connection with classroom activities.

Locating Information

The very useful cluster of skills needed in finding information in books should not be overlooked by the teacher of prereading groups. Some opportunities which may be utilized in laying the foundation for this skill area are:

Finding a new page in a book by matching it with a picture or number in an identical book held by the teacher.
Finding pictures of specific objects in books.
Identifying the content of a book by the picture on the cover.
Having attention called to the titles of books and stories.
Having attention called to the numbers on the pages of books as the teacher names them.

Turning pages in a picture book to find continuous developments in a pictured story.

Making booklets in which definite sections are devoted to different topics (pictures of dogs, pictures of cats, pictures of pet birds). The teacher should give children experience in finding the different sections.

Having attention called to books as a source of information and pleasure: the teacher finds information and reads from a book or encyclopedia to answer children's questions; or perhaps she looks through a book, reading titles of stories to the children until she finds one which she thinks they will like to hear.

Turning to a "library corner" in the classroom for pleasure and information to be gleaned by looking at the pictures in self-chosen books.

Following Directions

Of course children in the school situation have many experiences in following oral directions. They should be exposed also to situations in which they follow printed directions exactly, even though the teacher reads these directions to them. For the most part, however, they should participate in composing the directions which are to be used in making something, going somewhere, conducting room activities, and so on, such as:

MAKING A VALENTINE
Draw a picture.
Color it.
Cut it out.
Paste it on the heart.

ROOM DUTIES
_____: water the plant
_____: feed the fish
_____: get the crayons out
_____: put the crayons away
(A different child's name is written
in the blank space each day)

HANDLING BOOKS
Have clean hands.
Turn the pages carefully.
Hold the book with both hands.

Laying the Foundation for Reading Rate

We know that good eye movements are essential to desired rates of reading. The rapid reader focuses his eyes accurately at the beginning of each line of print, moves them from left to right across the line, pausing three or four times to "pick up" groups of words, then sweeps his eyes back to the left and focuses them at just the right place to begin their travels again to the right in reading the next line, and so on.

Beginning readers must make a tremendous adjustment in learning the mechanics of eye movements in reading. Previous to reading, the child has looked at people, airplanes, automobiles, buses, toys, trees, houses, and other objects which are fairly large, and he has looked at these objects in whatever arrangement they happened to appear before him. He usually has had no experience in following words across a page, starting at the left side, moving to the right, then bringing his eyes in one full sweep back to the left and lowering them to a new line. When he begins to read, it would make no difference to him whether the characters were arranged in our conventional form, or whether they were arranged in vertical columns in which the reader begins at the lower right-hand corner and reads up, then back down again, and so on.

A tremendously heavy load is placed upon the eyes of children when they first undertake reading. Investigation [1] has shown that the eyes of a first-grade child may make as many as twenty-three fixations in moving across one line of print, that they make many regressive movements, and that the return sweep is usually inaccurate.

Developing a Sense of Leftness and Rightness

These considerations impress us with the desirability of giving some attention during the prereading period to developing a sense of leftness to rightness, and rightness to leftness, with experience in following objects or pictures in lines from left to right and back again. The teacher will find many incidental opportunities for contributing to this growth.

Incidental Activities

After an art period, children often display their pictures. These pictures might be grouped in the following ways:

1. The characters who are walking or moving toward the right.
2. The characters who are going toward the left.
3. The characters who are looking toward the right.
4. The characters who are looking toward the left.

During discussion periods, the teacher and the children might note the border designs on books, tablets, and pictures, and observe whether the

[1] Guy T. Buswell, "Fundamental Reading Habits: A Study of Their Development," *Supplemental Educational Monograph No. 21* (Chicago: University of Chicago Press), Chaps. 1, 2, and 3.

objects are going in a certain direction. The figures in fancy wrapping paper, such as used for gift packages, may be used for this purpose also.

The teacher may show pictures in large picture books while she is telling stories represented by these pictures. As she proceeds, the children incidentally may be asked to name the objects which are going toward the right and the objects which are going toward the left.

If the children are solving jig-saw puzzles, they may be directed to note the position of objects on the cover picture of the box and to observe the left or right position in the picture. Leftness and rightness may be discussed also in connection with construction work.

Games

Children enjoy playing games which involve left and right orientations. A few examples are given.

TOUCHING GAME

Have a group discussion of right and left. Help each child to associate his right or left hand (whichever one appears to be the dominant one) with something on himself: a ring he wears, a pocket, a new tooth, and so on.

Following this discussion, blindfold one of the children, and have him stand or sit with his back to the others so that all left and right sides are corresponding. Touch the left shoulder of the blindfolded child. The child is expected to answer in a sentence similar to this: "You touched my left shoulder."

LOOBY-LOO

The children stand in a circle. The teacher directs them to do such things as these:

Put your left hand in the circle.
Put your right hand in the circle.
Put your left foot in the circle.
Put your right foot in the circle.

The goal of the game is for the children to see how quickly they can respond in each case and to avoid "getting caught."

DIRECTION GAME

In playing this game, all children should face in the same direction so that the right and left sides of all of them will be corresponding.

483

After the children are arranged in this way, blindfold one of the pupils, ask him to turn to the left or to the right, and raise his left or right arm as the case may be.

Additional directions might be: Put your right hand on your head, lift your left knee, look down, look up, turn your head to the right, and so on.

After one child has had a turn, choose another child to play the game. When the children have become familiar with the general procedure, then the pupils may be given turns in giving the directions for other children to follow.

Picture Activities

Activities involving the use of pictures are closer to the reading situation than those mentioned above. After the children have had sufficient experience of the above type to develop a sense of leftness and rightness, picture activities similar to those described below will be useful.

USING A WALL POCKET CHART

Place pictures in the pockets of a wall pocket chart. Ask a child to name these pictures, picking up each picture as he does so. Watch carefully that he proceeds in an orderly manner from left to right across the first line of pictures; then guide him in returning accurately back to the line and down to the beginning of the next line, and so on. Then give other children opportunities to engage in this same type of activity.

The children, of course, think that they are just playing a game of naming pictures, but in reality they are having the valuable experience of following lines from left to right and from top to bottom, just as they will do in their actual reading.

A variation of the above activity is to arrange pictures which accompany a story in sequence in the pocket chart and then let a child or different children hold up the pictures in order as you or one of the children tells the story.

At another time have different children arrange pictures in the chart into two groups according to the direction in which objects are facing, one group facing to the right, the other to the left.

FINDING PICTURES OF OBJECTS GOING IN DIFFERENT DIRECTIONS

The teacher prepares a set of pictures of objects in which direction is clearly indicated. She places several of these pictures before the children and asks a child to find the picture which shows something:

	going to the left	going down
	going to the right	going away
	going up	
or	looking up	looking away
	looking down	looking back
or	climbing up	and so on. . . .
	climbing down	

Be sure to encourage each child to tell about the picture which he selects, using such responses as: "This car is going to the left," "This boy is climbing up," and so on. This activity has an added value in that it acquaints children with meanings of adverbs and prepositions, which usually give difficulty in beginning reading.

MAKING PICTURE CHARTS

The children may be organized into committees, each committee to be responsible for making a picture chart. The teacher supplies each of the committees with a magazine and instructs the children to cut out all pictures in which the objects are going to the right or left.

After each committee has finished its work, the teacher pastes the pictures which the children have cut out on a chart in horizontal rows, letting the children tell in which group to place each picture.

The teacher displays each chart upon its completion, and lets the children in all the committees engage in discussion for the purpose of evaluating the chart made by each committee.

At another time all the children might search for one particular kind of a picture to prepare a left-right chart consisting entirely of pictures organized about one subject. Suitable subjects are things to ride in, people, animals, birds, and so on, all headed in one way or the other.

Laying the Foundation for Interest in Literature

An abiding interest and a full and satisfying appreciation and enjoyment of different types of literature is a life-time contribution which reading instruction can make to the individual. The period of early childhood is none too soon a time in which to begin laying the foundation for the full measure of satisfaction which reading can bring to girls and boys of school age, as well as to adults.

Realistic Stories

Young children should have ample opportunities to hear stories about boys and girls of their own age living in their own world. Their vision

485

of life would become quite distorted if they were told only fanciful tales. They need to have realistic stories, not only as a means of developing their taste for this kind of literature, but also as a means of helping them grasp relationships and clarify concepts concerning present-day living.

Appreciation for realistic stories can be developed easily in young children. Great care, however, should be taken in the choice of a realistic story for listening purposes. It *must* be related directly to the interest and experiences of the children at their particular level of development. The teacher should study the environment and out-of-school activities of the group of children with whom she is working in order to choose realistic stories which will be most satisfying to them.

Before presenting a story to the children, the teacher should thoroughly familiarize herself with it. If she is saturated with the story, and loves it herself, the chances are that she will present it in such a vivid way that the spirit of the selection will be felt and the desired appeal made.

An excellent method of introducing a realistic story is by means of discussion. This discussion should be concerned with the children's own interests and experiences as related to those of the characters in the story. Identifying oneself with the main character in a story is one of the surest avenues to appreciation.

Some motive for listening to the story often aids appreciation. Have the children listen to find out what happened to a certain character or why he behaved in a certain way or why the story was given a certain title. Such a motive also provides a good lead for discussion at the end of the story. This discussion should, of course, be kept free and spontaneous and enjoyable and should never degenerate to a quiz on remembrance of facts or events.

If the teacher can tell realistic stories and guide discussion concerning them in a way which will "throw back upon actual life a glow of art," then she will have taken a long step forward in developing appreciation in young children for this particular type of literature.

Fanciful Tales

Folk tales and fairy tales are the heritage of every child, and all young children should have an opportunity to listen to such stories, to retell them, to dramatize them if they like.

The same procedures suggested for presenting realistic stories also apply to the telling of the old tales. Relating personal experiences relevant to the subject of the fanciful tale, listening with a motive in mind, engaging in pleasant discussion after the story is told—all of these are procedures which contribute to the children's enjoyment of a story, regardless of whether it is realistic or fanciful.

Showing pictures which accompany a fanciful tale contributes much to children's appreciation of it. Calling their attention to an attractive book in which an old tale is found will help to awaken within them a desire to read such stories for themselves.

Poetry

Rhymes, jingles, and short poems are greatly enjoyed by children of this age. The rhythm, the cadence, the pat collocations of syllables are all pleasing to little children. Let us preserve this natural love for poetry and further develop it!

The teacher should keep choice collections of rhymes, jingles, and poems always at hand. She should memorize many of them to use upon spontaneous occasions, for enjoyment of poetry often reaches its greatest depth when the teacher recites a stanza or two of some appropriate poem just at the time that the children are having an interesting experience related to the subject of the poem.

Rhymes, jingles, and poems should not be left, however, entirely to incidental presentations. Plan a definite poetry program and read or recite poems to the children during the language or appreciation period rather regularly throughout the year.

Children should not be required to memorize poems. They will ask to hear their favorite poems read over and over again and they will join the teacher in saying these poems of their own accord. Through this natural and spontaneous repetition, many children will memorize several poems. Such memorization leaves the child with happy emotional attitudes toward poetry, whereas forced memorization is quite apt to thwart the very purpose of developing appreciation, and, instead, set up a dislike for poetry.

So keep teaching of poetry free, happy, joyous! Don't ever let it become a task or a chore!

Through such activities as those suggested above, children develop increased interest in literature, and this interest furnishes a strong motive for them to *read* stories and poems by themselves.

Summary

An important point stressed in this chapter was that kindergarten teachers and teachers of immature first grade children could and should be doing much more than many of them are doing in laying foundations for reading skills through informal, incidental, and game-like activities during the prereading period. Informal, functional contacts with reading were recommended strongly, but teachers were warned to let these reading activities "take" or not according to the state of reading maturation of individual children. The major contribution of the chapter was that of suggesting many planned and incidental activities to be used for the specific purpose of laying foundations for skills in each of the major growth areas: word identification, getting meanings, study skills, rate, and interest in reading.

Additional Readings

Books and Pamphlets

Association for Childhood Education, *Reading in the Kindergarten?* Washington, D. C., 1962.

Betts, Emmett Albert, *Foundations of Reading Instruction*, rev. ed., Part 4. New York: American Book, 1957.

Dawson, Mildred A., and Henry A. Bamman, *Fundamentals of Basic Reading Instruction*, pp. 44–49. New York: Longmans, Green & Co., 1959.

DeBoer, John J., and Martha Dallmann, *The Teaching of Reading*, Chap. 5B. New York: Holt, Rinehart and Winston, Inc., 1960.

Fuller, Elizabeth Mechem, *About the Kindergarten*. Washington, D. C., National Education Association, 1961.

Harris, Albert J., *Effective Teaching of Reading*, pp. 35–41. New York: David McKay & Co., Inc., 1962.

Hester, Kathleen, *Teaching Every Child to Read*, pp. 17–135. New York: Harper & Row, Publishers, 1955.

Hildreth, Gertrude, *Readiness for School Beginners*, Chap. 14. New York: Harcourt, Brace & World, Inc., 1960.

Russell, David H., *Children Learn to Read*, pp. 180–85. Boston: Ginn & Company, 1961.

Periodicals

Brazziel, William F., and Mary Terrell, "For First Graders: A Good Start in School," *The Elementary School Journal*, Vol. 62 (Apr. 1962), 352–55.

Bresnahan, M. M., "Reading Readiness in the Kindergarten," *Journal of Education*, Vol. 136 (Oct. 1953), 4–7.

Crosby, Muriel Estelle, "Experience and the Reading Process," *Elementary English*, Vol. 36 (Dec. 1959), 552–55.

Grau, M. L., "Approach to Beginning Reading," *Education*, Vol. 78 (Jan. 1958), 273–80.

Van Wie, Ethel K., and Donald M. Lammers, "Are We Being Fair to Our Kindergarten?" *The Elementary School Journal*, Vol. 62 (Apr. 1962), 348–51.

18

Preparing and Using
Experience Charts

Charts based upon the experiences of children and prepared cooperatively by teacher and children provide valuable reading material during beginning stages of reading
instruction. The effective preparation and use of such charts
involve many special techniques. Both beginning and experienced teachers usually welcome suggestions in regard
to these matters.

In so far as function is concerned, experience charts fall
into two categories: (1) *contactual* charts, and (2) *practice* charts. In working with contactual charts, children have
contacts only with the symbols on the charts; they are not
expected actually to read the charts. They compose the
charts with the guidance of the teacher and watch as the
teacher manuscripts their sentences on chart paper or the
chalkboard. The function of the contactual chart is that of
giving children experience in seeing their spoken words con-
verted into printed symbols, which say the same things that
they have said but in a different medium. Some children

who are more advanced in reading maturity will probably learn some words just from these reading contacts. Some may even want to read the entire chart, and they should certainly be permitted to do so. The main purpose of this type of chart, however, is simply to given children meaningful contacts with reading symbols. This is the kind of chart work most appropriate for use in the kindergarten and with children who are very immature in reading development in beginning first grade.

The *practice* chart, on the other hand, is prepared for the purpose of giving actual practice in reading. In preparing a contactual chart, long sentences and a comparatively heavy vocabulary load may be used. However, when preparing a practice chart, the teacher will try to guide the composition so that sentence structure is simple (but still natural) and the vocabulary load is light enough to promise successful reading by beginners. If the children are being prepared to read in a basic pre-primer, the teacher will keep in mind the words which appear on the early pages of this preprimer and try adroitly to work them into the chart composition. Regardless of the nature of the first material that the children are to read, the teacher should look ahead to the vocabulary in this material and plan to give repeated practice on the high frequency words by weaving them into chart stories.

Suggestions for giving children practice in actually reading charts will be found on pages 495–96.

Principles of Chart Construction

Charts Should Be Attractive

If we would lay a foundation for permanent interest in reading in the earlier years, we must do everything possible to make children's beginning reading experiences pleasurable to them. Colorful pictures have a strong appeal to young children. In building charts based upon children's experiences, we must not ignore the principle of attractiveness. Experience reading materials are ever so much more pleasing and interesting if decorated with brightly colored pictures which have been collected from magazines by the children or teachers, or which have been painted or crayoned by the children themselves.

As an example, a description is given of a chart which was based on the experience of going to a farm and getting a pumpkin. This chart was decorated by placing the picture of a large yellow pumpkin in the middle of the space at the top of the chart. A cluster of brightly colored leaves was drawn on each side of the pumpkin, and individual autumn leaves trailed across the bottom of the chart in an artistic manner. Another chart, containing statements in regard to different articles which the children had brought to school, was illustrated by pasting an appropriate picture made by the children opposite the name of each article. For example, the first statement read, "Janet brought some flowers"; to the right of the word *flowers* a bunch of flowers was drawn with colored crayons by the children. Each of the statements was decorated in similar fashion.

Another consideration which contributes greatly to the attractiveness of a chart is its typographical features. Letters should be large, black, and clear. The printing should be placed as nearly as possible in the middle of the chart, leaving a pleasing margin on each side and sufficient space at the top and bottom to permit an artistic arrangement of the decorations.

Charts Should Have a Measure of Literary Quality

Chart stories often consist of a dry, singsong list of statements which recount some experience the children have had. Their expressions concerning this experience are molded into terse statements to meet the teacher's requirements of preparing a set of short, complete sentences for reading purposes. There is no reason at all why these little chart stories should always be cast in a standardized, uninteresting form. First grade children have not lived long enough to fall into the hackneyed channels of expression which have become habitual with adults. They look upon the world from a fresh viewpoint and often express themselves in unique and interesting ways. If the teacher has an ear attuned to listening for these original bits as they come from the children, she will be sure to hear them. Incorporation of such expressions into the body of the story will greatly improve the literary quality of the chart.

In addition to utilizing the original expressions of children, monotony may be avoided by weaving in an occasional exclamatory sentence or question. Such sentences will come naturally during the composition of the chart if the teacher is on the lookout for them.

Modern writers of children's literature recognize the necessity of making a strong sense appeal to young children. Hence their stories are made vivid with sound, color, movement, and rhythm. This sense-appeal technique should be more widely employed in the preparation of experience reading materials in the classroom.

491

Examples of children's oral compositions which make use of sense appeal are:

1. *Sound*
Honk! Honk! came the automobile.
Clippity-clap! Clippity-clap! came the horse.

2. *Color*
Jean had a big, yellow orange.
She had some brown chocolate cake.

3. *Movement*
The chickens ran.
The cows ran.
The dog ran.
They all ran.

4. *Rhythm*
The airplane flew over the house.
It flew over the trees.
It flew over the meadow.

Charts Should Make Use of our Knowledge of Perceptual Clues

According to the old concept of teaching reading, one should proceed from the simple to the complex. This meant that the teacher was to ask the children to read two-letter words first. After these were mastered, she would proceed to three-letter words, then four-letter words, and so on. This theory has been entirely exploded as the result of recent experimentation. Research in the field of reading perception has disclosed evidence to the effect that a long word, such as *automobile,* is often more easily recognized by a child than a short one, such as *in.* There are probably two reasons for this. One reason is that children often recognize a word by its configuration; the general contour of a long word, such as *airplane,* is more strikingly characteristic than that of a short word, such as *in,* which closely resembles the contour of many other words, such as *is.* The other reason is that words such as *airplane* are rich in meaningful concepts for children, while words such as *in* are abstract, and for that reason, less vivid.

Another perception difficulty for young children is offered by words which look so much alike as to be mistaken for identical words. Such words as *them—then, these—those,* which differ only in one letter, are particularly troublesome.

Experience stories should be liberally sprinkled with the longer words having distinctly characteristic forms, vivid interest clues, and concrete, meaningful backgrounds. The pronouns, prepositions, and adverbs which resemble each other closely in contour should be carefully distributed so that they do not occur too frequently or too closely together.

Charts Should Give Consideration to Phrasing

Perhaps the cardinal error which a first grade teacher can make in preparing charts is to divide sentences at places other than between phrases. If we are going to build good eye-movement habits, then we must take care in the first grade to group words into meaningful phrases, to put together those words which belong together. This goal cannot be accomplished when the teacher breaks a sentence in such a way as this:

> We went to the farm in the
> bus.

In order to give the children the best assistance in seeing a group of words as a meaningful whole, the sentence should be divided like this:

> We went to the farm
> in the bus.

Charts Should Provide for Repetition

Repetition is necessary in fixing words occurring in children's early reading vocabulary. If the teacher has this principle in mind, she can readily guide children's compositions in such a way that the same words recur several times in a chart, and so that many of them will recur in succeeding charts. Compositions arising from the recounting of experiences or making plans are naturally repetitious in character because they simply enumerate a list of things that the children saw, did, or made, or things that they are going to see, do, or make. Every effort should be made to utilize these naturally repetitious situations in giving children the necessary practice on new words.

Making and Using the Chart

Composing the Chart

The first essential in the preparation of reading materials for use in beginning reading is that the children must have had some vivid, interesting experience, real or vicarious (preferably real), which fills their minds with ideas and stirs them to active discussion concerning it. In other words the subject must be something that is vital to them and something which they wish to talk about.

Once this prerequisite has been fulfilled, the teacher should proceed to give the children an opportunity to engage in free discussion concerning this event of mutual interest; and to let them talk it over spontaneously and happily, just as we adults talk over an exciting automobile trip which we have had, a gripping play which we have seen, or a new idea which we have worked out in solving some one of our problems.

The second essential of chart construction is that the children have some motive for recording their expressions. It may be interesting to talk over experiences, but why should they be written down and read?

There are several ways in which chart work may be made purposeful to children. Perhaps they will wish to record an experience so that the principal or other visitors coming to the room may know what they have been doing. Perhaps they will wish to record an experience to be read as part of a program which they are preparing on some general topic. Perhaps they will wish to record plans and rules and directions as guides to themselves in future work. Perhaps they will wish to prepare a series of stories to make a booklet. The children may suggest other motives, such as making a chart on a certain topic to have a mimeographed copy of it to take home to their mothers. These are but a few of the ways in which chart compositions may be made purposeful to children. The alert teacher will constantly sense other possibilities as she works with her group.

After the children have expressed themselves freely and pleasurably on the topic of mutual interest and have decided to write it down for some purpose, the teacher proceeds to ask a series of organizing questions to guide the children in making a composition which will have unity and interest, which will be simple enough to read, and which will include necessary vocabulary words. All this does not mean that the teacher will lead the children to give to her some predetermined chart story which she has already formulated. Nothing of the sort! Every question she asks should stimulate a variety of answers, and the children should have the privilege of selecting the sentence which they think is best in each case. Thus it is that teacher and children work together suggesting, weighing, considering, evaluating, and revising until a creditable but childlike composition is prepared.

The first draft of the chart may be manuscripted on the chalkboard. If the teacher is so expert in manuscript writing that she can do it very rapidly and well, the first draft may be made directly on lined chart paper as the children compose it.

Preparing the Chart

Materials

If the chart is to be used for practice, the next step is to manuscript it in duplicate copies on chart paper if the first draft has been written on the chalkboard, or preparing one duplicate copy if the first draft was written directly on chart paper. In either case there should be two duplicate copies of the chart, one to remain intact, the other to be cut up and used for practice purposes.

The following materials will be needed:

1. A broad-edge pen and black India ink or a crayon pencil prepared especially for this purpose.
2. A supply of lined chart paper. If this is not available, then oaktag or light cream-colored wrapping paper may be used. In this later case a chart liner to use in drawing lines across the chart should be used.
3. A wall pocket container in which the children may place sentences, phrases, and words in connection with their practice work in reading charts.

Procedure

Put the title about three inches from the top of the chart and equidistant from the right and left sides of the chart.

Begin the first sentence about three inches below the title.

Leave a left-hand margin of one and a half or two inches throughout the body of the chart.

Leave a space of about three-fourths of an inch between words.

Leave a space of about two inches between lines.

Use capitals only where they would be used in any ordinary writing.

Make lines as nearly uniform in length as possible.

When it is necessary to divide sentences always break them between phrases.

Reading Practice Charts

A Suggested Procedure

Chart reading offers a variety of possibilities. This is fortunate since meeting the same words in many different and pleasurable situations is one of the first principles of effective practice.

Each teacher will work out interesting ways of varying her own procedure as she becomes more and more experienced in chart work. It might be of value, however, to suggest a set of fundamental steps which are frequently used:

1. Calling upon different children to read the entire story by sentences as the teacher places her marker under each line.
2. Calling upon different children to read a single sentence at a time as the teacher places her marker under each, first indicating the sentences in order, then out of order.
3. Cutting a duplicate chart into sentences and letting the children read each sentence as it is cut off.
4. Calling upon different children to match a sentence from the cut-up chart with one on the intact chart, and to read it.
5. Building up a duplicate chart by matching and then placing the sentences in a container in such a position as to represent the story on the intact chart.
6. Cutting the sentences of the duplicate chart into phrases and words and letting the children read them as this is done.
7. Building up a duplicate chart with phrases and words, first in reference to the original chart, later without it.
8. Playing various recognition games in which the children read the words and phrases as they build up or tear down the chart story or certain sentences in it. (See pages 174–78 for suggestions of recognition games which may be used for this purpose.)
9. Giving each child a mimeographed or typed copy of the chart story to place in a story book which he is making or to take home and read to his parents.

Illustration of a Chart Lesson

There was a fire in the immediate neighborhood. The fire apparatus, with the siren blowing and bells clanging, went rushing by the schoolhouse. Excitement ran high in the first grade classroom. This was the big, vital, interesting, all-important event of the day. The stage was all set for developing a reading lesson based on an immediate experience.

Discussion

During and after the passing of the fire apparatus, all other school activities were laid aside, and the time was given over to discussion in which each child had an opportunity to express his viewpoint and to give his interpretation of the various phases of this experience. These were the different topics touched upon:

The fire	The thrill
The fire truck	The long ladder
The toys	The long hose
The speed	The firemen

Exclamations such as these were heard:

"I love to see the fire engines!"
"I like to hear the bell!"
"I like the siren!"
"What a long ladder!"
"What a long hose!"
"How fast they turn the corners!"
"I would like to be a fireman."
"See the smoke?"
"Now the fire is out, they are coming back."

Motive for Recording

The children were making a book of stories and pictures for a Mother's Day gift. One child suggested that they draw a fire truck in their book and another one said, "I have a big fire truck at home that I can bring for us to look at so that we'll draw it right." Another said, "There is a picture of a fire truck in a book we have; we could look at that."

The next period happened to be the art period, and so, when the art teacher came to the classroom, she was asked to give the children assistance in drawing a picture of a fire truck to put in their books.

All other pictures in their books were accompanied with stories which the children had composed; therefore, as soon as they had finished the picture of their fire truck, they asked to compose a story to go with that picture.

Composing the Chart

The following conversation took place while the teacher guided the children with questions and suggestions and wrote their responses on the chalkboard:

Teacher: What shall we have to do, children, if we are going to make a story for our book?
Ruth: Write the words—or I guess we'll say them and you write them on the board.
Teacher: We want this to be an interesting story, so let's think of the very best things that we can say about the fire truck.
Teacher: (Calls on individual children, suggesting with questions what she wishes as a response.) Can you tell us what you heard, Rose?
Rose: I heard the bell.
Teacher: What do you wish to say, Louis?
Louis: I like the way they turn the corners.
Teacher: How do they turn the corners, Louis?

Louis: Very fast.

Teacher: But you tell us, so that when Mother reads the book she will understand.

Louis: The fire engine turns the corner fast!

Teacher: All right, Louis. That is interesting. I think Shirley has something interesting for us too.

Shirley: I'd like to have something in our story about the siren, but I can't make the noise. (Several children raised their hands.)

Teacher: All right, Irvin, you may show us how.

Irvin: Ooooo! Ooooo!

Teacher: Shall I write that?

Tom: Yes, that is fun.

Teacher: What did you tell us this morning, James?

James: I guess I said, "Fire! Fire!"

Teacher: Daniel.

Daniel: I liked the long hose best.

Teacher: Mary.

Mary: And I liked the long ladder.

Teacher: I liked them, too, but what would you say if you wanted someone else to see the hose and the ladder?

Billy: Oh, I'd say, "See the long hose and the long ladder."

Eliminating and Selecting from the
Hit-or-Miss Story

Teacher: You have told me many nice things about this fire engine, but our story is such a long one that I'm afraid I won't have time to print so many sentences tonight. What do you think we should do about it?

Jane: You could print half tonight and half tomorrow night.

Teacher: I think that would be a fine plan. We will make two stories. I have room for only five or six lines on my paper, so let's look over our story carefully and decide which are the best sentences to put on the chart.

Discussion followed, guided by the teacher's questions and suggestions. Eventually the childen voted on which were the best sentences for the story. The rearranged story which resulted from this discussion was as follows:

Ooooo! Ooooo!
Fire! Fire!
Here comes the fire engine!
See the long hose.
See the long ladder.
The fire engine goes fast!

Reading the Chart from the Chalkboard

Teacher: Now let's read the whole story. Harriet, you may read. (Teacher aided Harriet by asking questions.) What did James say when he heard the siren? What did Frances say? (Harriet reads the sentences in response to the teacher's questions as the teacher places her marker under each one.)

The teacher called on others to read, aiding them when necessary. Several of the children read the chart all the way through without help.

Reading the Chart from Lined Chart Paper

The next morning the teacher showed the class the completed story which she had written in manuscript on lined chart paper. Upon showing the chart to the class she said, "Here's your story all ready to read. When you can read it well enough so you are sure that you can read it to your mother, then I will give each of you a copy to paste in your books."

The teacher then continued, "We are going to begin reading right here (placing her hand under the first word in the first sentence) and read right across to here (placing her hand under the last word in the first sentence). Then we are going to start here (placing her hand under the first word in the second sentence) and read across to here (placing her hand under the last word in the second sentence)."

The teacher continued in this way until she had covered all the sentences on the chart, aiding the children in the process of adjusting their eyes from left to right across the chart and from the end of a line to the beginning of the next line, until the entire story was read.

She then picked up a marker made of a piece of oaktag 4" x 27" and placed it under the first sentence of the chart.

Teacher: This is what the siren said. Can you read it, Bella?
Bella: Ooooo! Ooooo!
Teacher: This is your sentence, James. Can you read it to us?
James: Fire! Fire!
Teacher: Who can tell me what the next part says? (Hands raise.) Sylvia.
Sylvia: See the hose.
Teacher: What kind of hose?
Sylvia: See the long hose.
John (voluntarily): The next is easy! See the long ladder.
Teacher: How does a fire truck go, Jack?
Jack: The fire truck goes fast.

The teacher continued to give aids by asking questions until several children had read individual sentences and some had read the entire story.

Building a Duplicate Chart

On the third day after the story was composed, the teacher brought out duplicate sentences of the chart manuscripted on 4″ x 27″ strips of tagboard. This is the conversation that ensued:

Teacher: Today we are going to play some games with our story of the fire truck. First we will play the matching game. Who can put this sentence on the sentence that is just like it on the big chart?
Louis: (Matches the sentence on the chart.)
Teacher: What does it say, Louis?
Louis: Ooooo! Ooooo!

The teacher continued in this way until several children had an opportunity to match the different sentences and to read them. The teacher then cut each duplicate sentence into smaller units, phrasing each as indicated below:

1. Ooooo!/Ooooo!
2. See/the long hose.
3. See/the long ladder.
4. The fire engine/goes fast.

Teacher: (Cuts off Ooooo! and holds it up.)
Rose: Oh, I know! That's Ooooo!
Teacher: That's right. I guess you all know that word. (She then cut *see* off the second sentence.) Mary, find this word on the other chart and tell us what it is.
Mary: (Places the card with *see* on it under the *see* on the other chart and reads it.)

This procedure continued until the words and phrases were matched and read, both in order and out of order. The teacher then introduced the "Building Up and Tearing Down Game," in which the children named the words as they built up the chart and took it apart again.

Reading the Story in Preprimer Type

The next day the teacher had mimeographed copies of the story in great primer type ready to hand out to the children. They eagerly pored over the copies, and nearly all of them were able to read the story. The children who read the story fluently were allowed to paste it in their Mother's Day Book. The few children who could not read it well were given additional practice in another period, in which they read again in response to several questions and suggestions and played word-recognition games. As soon as one of these children learned to read the story well, he was permitted to paste it in his book.

This concrete illustration of chart teaching is typical of a series of lessons which some first grade teachers use as a part of their procedure in preparing their pupils for reading from books, and which they continue to use as the children have interesting experiences throughout the year.

Examples of Different Types of Charts

Experience materials lend themselves to a variety of forms. A few of these different types of materials will be described and illustrated with examples taken from typical first grade classrooms. The teacher is urged to make use of several of these different forms rather than confining practically all of her charts to the commonly used narrative accounts shown in the first example.

The Narrative Chart

The type of chart most commonly used in the first grade is the narrative chart. It contains a running account of some group or individual experience. The narrative chart below was written by a class who had just returned from an excursion to a farm:

We went to a farm.
We played in the barn.
We found some eggs.
We ate lunch under the big apple tree.

The Question Chart

The question chart is useful as a means of recording or capitalizing interests shown by children's own questions. The teacher jots down questions the children ask about any topic, and manuscripts them on a chart. These questions are then used as a nucleus of research and are checked off one by one as the children find the answers to them.

An example of a question chart is given below. It was prepared by some first grade children who had become interested in the postman. The teacher had invited him to come to the room, and these were the questions the children planned to ask him:

What did you do with our letter to Marie?
Where did you get your mail bag?

Charts Recording Children's Suggestions

Recording suggestions which children make when discussing a new activity is useful and profitable from the reading standpoint. One group insisted on making a stage in their classroom. "What could you do with a stage in here?" asked the teacher. Suggestions came thick and fast. The teacher recorded them on the board, and they were carried out later. Here is the list:

1. Tell stories.
2. Read from the stage.
3. Invite our mothers and have a play.
4. Do stunts.
5. Play instruments.
6. Make moving pictures and show them.
7. Make up stories.
8. Make up poems.
9. Make up songs.

Charts Recording Class Rules

Rules made up by the class to be observed by them form the basis of another kind of chart. A group had not been working very profitably during the workshop period. Discussion followed and the following rules were formulated by the class for future observance:

Plan our work.
Help each other.
Share our tools.
Finish our work.
Stop on time.
Clean up.

Charts Recording Plans

Plans are quite necessary in the active primary classroom of today, and may well form the content of a chart to be hung up in the room and reviewed from time to time so that the children can discover how well the plans for an activity are progressing. Some first grade children who were planning to build a library formulated this chart:

Bring in boxes.
Bring in spare lumber.
Pull out all old nails.

Another first grade planned its activities for the year as follows:

Learn to read.
Draw pictures.
Work with clay.
Make things out of wood.
Tell stories.
Paint pictures.
Play on slide.
Make a train.
Make a farm.
Bring materials for others to use.
Make chairs strong enough to sit on.

Diary Charts

Diary charts are favored in many schools as a means of recording the progress of a prolonged activity. A first grade who planted a garden kept this chart:

April 18. We wrote for our seeds.
April 25. We planted our garden.
May 14. The cucumbers came up.
May 21. All the seeds are up.
May 26. Our garden is growing fine.
June 10. We picked some lettuce today.
            We made sandwiches with the lettuce.

Direction Charts

Direction charts are necessary at times. For example, one first grade was making a frieze of circus animals for their room. Some of the children were coloring the bears green and the elephants lavender. A discussion was held concerning the color of each animal. As a result the following chart was formulated by the children for their reference in future coloring work:

Color the bears black or brown.
Color the elephants gray.
Color the seals black.
Color the lions brown.
Color the camels brown.
Color the tiger yellow with black stripes.

Charts Recording Fanciful Stories

Fanciful stories made up by the group provide interesting chart material. Here is an example:

Once there was a little fairy.
She lived in a buttercup.
She played in the woods every day.
At night she would go back to the buttercup to sleep.

Charts Recording Poems

Recording on a chart a particularly good poem which some child has composed is an excellent means of recognizing children's creative efforts. The following chart will illustrate this idea:

Jane's Poem

Miss Spencer had some violets.
Jane was looking at them.
She said,
   "Little violet so blue,
   Did the sky fall down on you?"

The examples given above illustrate only a few of the possible varieties of chart content. Many, many other types of charts will be suggested to the teacher as she works with children.

Summary

Discussion in this chapter distinguished between *contactual* charts with which children merely have contacts, and *practice* charts which are prepared for the purpose of actually giving practice in reading. Principles of chart construction which were presented included the need for attention to attractiveness, literary quality, perceptual clues, phrasing, and repetition. Suggestions were made for composing, preparing, and reading charts, and a stenographic report of a chart lesson was presented. Many examples of different types of charts were given and teachers were urged to use different types rather than to confine their charts mostly to narrative accounts as is commonly done.

Additional Readings

Books

Betts, Emmett Albert, *Foundations of Reading Instruction*, rev. ed., pp. 394–427. New York: American Book, 1957.

Dawson, Mildred A., and Henry A. Bamman, *Fundamentals of Basic Reading Instruction*, pp. 52–56. New York: Longmans, Green & Co., 1959.

DeBoer, John J., and Martha Dallmann, *The Teaching of Reading*, pp. 70–75. New York: Holt, Rinehart and Winston, Inc., 1960.

Lamoreaux, Lillian, and Doris Lee, *Learning to Read Through Experience*, pp. 145–81. New York: Appleton-Century-Crofts, Inc., 1943.

Russell, David H., *Children Learn to Read*, pp. 191–94, 353–54. Boston: Ginn & Company, 1961.

Periodical

Sister Mary Venard, "Experience Charts Teach Reading," *Catholic School Journal*, Vol. 61 (Sept. 1961), 80–81.

PART 5

Teacher-Parent Partnerships

chapter 19

Working with Parents

Parents Are People

Parents are people. Perhaps the most consuming interest of people, now and always, has been the welfare of their off-spring. In so far as school is concerned, the prime considera-tion of people for the welfare of their children is that they should learn to read well. With this double-edged interest the school has little difficulty in getting parents to participate in or to respond to any form of communication that they think will help them better to understand the teaching of reading and their children's needs. This highly favorable attention-getting situation opens a wide avenue of approach to the teacher who would avail herself of profitable commu-nication with parents. This should not be a one-way thor-oughfare, however. It should be a two-way road on which parents travel to teachers as easily as teachers travel to parents.

In years gone by about the only contact that parents and

teachers had with one another was when a mother came to school to complain because the teacher "shook Tom and made his nose bleed," or when a father was summoned to be told that he must make his son "behave himself."

Eventually teachers were required to take special training—one year, two years, then four years. They learned many things about children's physical growth, their emotional development, their learning capacities. Child psychology, mental hygiene, and personality development all came within their college curriculum, and withal they accumulated a stock of teaching methods. All this set a teacher apart from the parents. She now became a trained specialist. She couldn't explain her learnings to parents. They were just "laymen." "They wouldn't understand."

As a matter of fact it was the teacher who didn't understand. She didn't realize that parents were people; that each parent was a person—a person with an intellect, a capacity to think and feel; a person with his own goals and aspirations, his own problems and pleasures. She learned in college about the individual differences in children, but she didn't realize that there are individual differences in parents also. Instead of worrying about parents understanding her, the teacher should have been concerned about understanding parents.

In current times things have changed. Any speaker who recently has given a speech to a group of parents on present school practices or who has talked about modern methods over the backyard fence with his neighbors has been impressed with their thirst for information, especially about the teaching of reading. Even though the speech is over and the hour is late, the parent group will hold the speaker for question after question; and even at the risk of a late dinner for her family, the neighbor will linger on to have him tell her "a little bit more." Is there any other topic in which *people* are more interested?

Through such experiences as these we have come to realize that parents *are* people and *can* "understand" what we are talking about when we tell them how and why we teach reading as we do, and why certain things in a child's family life affect his reading. Too, they readily grasp the basic design of an experiment when it is described to them and are impressed when informed about the resulting data. Yes, parents are people and we had better be people, too, talking and working together with parents as people talk and work with people.

When a teacher as a person first begins to talk with a parent as a person, the parent may think that the two of them are just "visiting." But this of course is not the case. The conversation from the teacher's standpoint is not just idle chatter. All the time the parent is talking the teacher is asking depth questions, making interpretations, and seeking clues to situations which may be improved to the benefit of the child.

When the parent comes fully to realize that the teacher *is* deeply interested, that she *wants* to help, and that she *can* help, the flood gates are opened and information flows freely from one to the other and back and forth. Warm commendation is due the teacher who can truly be a person when talking with a parent. Let teachers be people for parents are people, too.

Parents' Attitudes Toward Reading Instruction

For background purposes it is worthwhile for a teacher to know, in general, what the attitudes of parents are toward reading instruction in our schools. Do they think we are doing a good job on the whole or are they dissatisfied?

We have some data in answer to this question. Two studies have polled parents' opinions. Larrick [1] investigated this subject and found that, in general, parents expressed satisfaction with progress that children are making in reading. They indicated some concern over failure to teach phonics although criticisms of this type represented only a small percentage of total respondents.

Presnall [2] found that parents generally supported the practice of keeping a child of low reading ability with his age group, and of grouping pupils of similar ability for reading instruction. His study also indicated that parents expressed a desire for more emphasis on phonics, more help on syllabication, and more oral reading in class.

While these studies show a wholesome attitude toward reading practices in general, they indicate some points of method about which parents should be given more information.

What Parents Want to Know

To the end of working in closer cooperation with parents, it is enlightening for the teacher to have a general perspective of parents' interests and of the things they want to know about their children.

One study has been made which gives some data on this subject. Mc-

[1] Nancy Larrick, "What Parents Think about Children's Reading," *Elementary English*, XXXIII (Apr. 1956), 206–209.
[2] Hugo E. Presnall, "Parents' Opinions of Reading Instruction," *Elementary English*, XXXIII (Jan. 1956), 29–33.

Connell [3] sent out questionnaire forms to parents of first, second, and third graders in a large urban community. The replies, which indicated in what areas parents wished more information, fell into categories and frequencies as follows: personal and classroom behavior, 27 per cent; academic progress, 26 per cent; social behavior, 22 per cent; home-school relations, 13 per cent; individual aptitude or ability, 9 per cent; and, health and physical conditions, 3 per cent.

More specifically, the types of questions under each category were reported as follows:

Parents indicated that they wanted to know about classroom behavior in relation to (1) the child's personal behavior and (2) his relation with the teachers and the principal and his attitude toward them and the classroom situation. Some of the parents' specific questions that were related to the child's personal behavior were: "Is he troublesome?" "Is he impudent?" "Does he show temper?" "How does he behave?" "Does he like to talk?" "Does he show self-confidence, self-control, self-reliance?" "Is he cooperative, courteous, considerate?"

Questions related to the child's school behavior were: "Does he do as the teacher says?" "What is his attitude toward the teacher and the principal?" "Does he take care of school property?" "Does he pay attention?" "Does he listen to the teacher when she talks to him?" "Will he take correction?" "How does he react to it?"

Questions concerning academic progress related, in general, to two areas: (1) progress in schoolwork, specifically in reading, writing, arithmetic, and speech (two direct questions often asked were: "How are his marks?" "Will he pass?"); (2) reaction to, and attitudes toward, schoolwork. In the last category were such questions as: "Does he study?" "Does he try?" "Is he doing his best?" "Is he improving?" "Is he interested in school?" "Does he understand his work?" "Does he volunteer or show initiative?" "Does he ask questions?" "Does he express his opinion?" "What is his best subject?"

In the field of social behavior, the question asked by the overwhelming majority of parents was the direct, "Does he (or how does he) get along with other children?" Other questions in this group were: "Is he a good sport?" "Is he fair with his classmates?" "Do they like him?" "Does he make friends?" "Does he participate in school activities?" "Is he selfish?" "Is he aggressive?" "Is he well adjusted?" "Does he seem happy with others?"

The most frequent responses dealing with home-school relations were: "How can I help at home?" "Let me know what he isn't doing and how I can help you?" "In what subject does he need the most help at home?"

Less frequently asked questions were concerned with the length of home study and the amount of homework assigned. Some parents said they would like a better understanding of methods of marking and teaching. A few in each school expressed a desire to visit the teacher or have a conference about specific

[3] Reprinted from Gaither McConnell, "What Do Parents Want to Know," *The Elementary School Journal*, LIII (November 1957), 88–90, by permission of The University of Chicago Press. Copyright 1957 by The University of Chicago Press.

or personal problems. One parent asked, "What would you like to know about my child from me?"

A small per cent of parents, ranging from 5 to 12 per cent in the various groups, asked about individual aptitudes and abilities of their children, the greatest per cent being those of the higher socio-economic group. The one question most frequently asked concerned the ability of the child in relation to other children: "Is he slow, fast, or average as compared with others?"

Some parents said they would like to know their child's intelligence quotient. Some were interested in results of achievement tests. A number of parents in the schools in the higher socio-economic group said that they would like to be told if their children had any special abilities or talents or showed qualities of a leader.

Only 2 to 5 per cent of the parents wanted the school to tell them about the health or physical conditions of their children. Parents in the lower social group asked more questions in this category than did the upper-group parents. Questions in this area were few and varied. The three most frequent were: "Does he have good health habits?" "Does he eat his lunch?" "Does he seem nervous or ill to you?" A few questions concerned the condition of eyes, ears, and speech mechanism.

The types of questions asked tend to show that parents want specific and detailed information about their children. Parents want concrete evidence of the status, progress, and development of their children, whether the information is given by report cards, by letters, or by conferences. Parents indicate that they want the school to accept responsibility for the improvement of personal and social behavior of their children as well as for their intellectual growth. One parent summed up her idea of the function of the school in reporting to parents in this statement: "I think you should tell parents anything that they should know about their children, whether you think they would like it or not."

Techniques of Working with Parents

During recent years teachers and parents have developed many useful techniques for working together in exchanging information and promoting mutual understanding beneficial to the children with whom both parties are concerned. Some of these techniques will be described.

Use of Interview

The interview is perhaps the most effective technique to use in cooperative parent-teacher work. The interview may be initiated by the teacher or by a parent; it may be long or short; it may be in the classroom or in the home; it may be planned or spontaneous. These things don't matter too much, but there are a few very important considerations that do matter: (1) both the parent and teacher should feel perfectly at ease; (2) the teacher should be a good listener; (3) she should keep herself highly alert to anything the parent says which might be significant; (4) she should interject questions unobtrusively, tactfully, delicately, and in some instances not at all; (5) she should make constructive suggestions to the parent in regard to any matter that needs attention; (6) she should follow up any significant information she obtains from the parent with applications in her own work with the child.

Sample Interviews

Two samples of parent-teacher interviews will be presented and evaluated in terms of their significance to the teacher of reading.

Jenny (8), Third Grade, Public School.[4]

The parents came to the school by appointment. The father was voluble and talkative, the mother shy and quiet. The talk together was principally about Jenny's schoolwork, in which the father particularly is very much interested. He said that he had had little education himself and that he wants all of his children to get to college. He spoke of being very proud of Jenny's reading and said that he has her read to him every evening. It is comic books now she wants to read most and he doesn't think much of them for reading. However, he said, "That's what she wants so we read them." He spoke of his concern that she does not seem to be much of a speller and that all of her writing is printing. The teacher explained that work in spelling was just beginning and told why manuscript writing is taught. She mentioned that a great deal of informal spelling has been going on for some time but that now there would be more and more of the drill which the father said he had when he learned to spell. He said he guessed it was a good idea not to make so much fuss about it as they used to. There was talk, too, about Jenny's drawing, which is mostly of cowboys. Then the mother spoke up, saying that the drawing and the comics interfered with helping with the cooking and ironing and that she has to keep after Jenny to sew on her buttons and to wash the dishes, but that those things are just as important as school and that it was time the child should be learning to do things in the house. The father said, "She can do both." The teacher spoke of her interest in hearing about Jenny's home doings and of what she liked to do besides play cowboy. The mother told about the chores that she insisted must be done before there could be any play: making her own bed, wiping the dishes, bringing in the eggs, setting the table. The father laughed and said, "But she's a cowboy all the time she does those things and her mother's always after her to be a lady." Then the mother said that she had had to work hard always and didn't have much bringing up and that she wants her girl to learn to do things right.

Here were two parents, each wanting in a different way the best that could be had for their Jenny, and only by listening quietly and letting them feel her interest and respect and understanding could the teacher ever hope to

[4] Grace Langdon and Irving W. Stout, *Teacher-Parent Interviews*, © 1954 by Prentice-Hall, Inc., Englewood Cliffs, N. J. By permission.

even glimpse the depth of the feeling about it. Yet, how it would help in working with that child to know the way the parents looked at things.

In this situation the teacher could do little about settling the conflict between the father and mother. It did help her, though, better to understand Jenny. Perhaps during the school year the teacher would be able to help Jenny more clearly to realize that everybody has to do things that he doesn't enjoy as well as things that are fun. There has to be a balance.

In this interview the teacher had an opportunity to explain the school's practices in regard to manuscript writing and spelling. In so doing, she promoted better understanding on the part of a parent and subdued his worries in regard to these matters.

In so far as reading itself was concerned, it would appear that Jenny was having no difficulty with skill development in this subject. There was an opening, however, for encouraging continued home reading and for extending interest beyond the comic strips. The father might well have been praised for being proud of Jenny's reading and for having her read to him every evening. This evidently was a happy experience in which the father showed his approval of Jenny's achievement and in which he and Jenny shared her accomplishments together with pleasure.

In the course of the interview the father also should have been commended warmly when he said that it was comic books now that she wants to read most, that he didn't think much of them for reading, but "That's what she wants so we read them." This bit of information from the father opened up several possibilities for the teacher to give worthwhile information; for example, the father might have been told that it is extremely important for children to establish the habit of reading at home at an early age, that it is better to let them read anything at home in which they are interested than to force them to read something of a parent's choice, that none of us think much of the comics for reading but that Jenny is at the age in which the comic interest is at its height and comic interest is something to be expected.

Perhaps at a later conference, after the teacher had had time to explore library possibilities, she might have invited the parents to come to see her again. This time she might have inquired about and engaged in some conversation with the mother concerning the work Jenny was doing to help at home, and explained that she was trying to get Jenny to realize in school that doing work is as important as doing the special things a person likes to do.

After recognizing the mother's point of view, the teacher might then have inquired of the father if Jenny was still drawing cowboy pictures and if she was still reading the comics with him every night. Using his answers as a point of departure, she might then have suggested that he use Jenny's cowboy interest in helping her to make a beginning transition, at least, to reading from books. At this point the teacher might have pulled from her desk a few attractive books that she had gotten at the library—books about cowboys, easy enough for Jenny to read—and offered to let the father take them home to surprise Jenny with when it was reading time that night.

Having found that Jenny was fascinated with these cowboy books, the father might have gotten other cowboy books from the library and the bookstore. Eventually the teacher might have suggested that he extend Jenny's reading interests by getting books for her on subjects related to the cowboy interest—horse stories, cow or calf stories, shepherd dog stories, stories about jack rabbits, coyotes, prairie dogs, rattlesnakes, or other animals that cowboys encounter, and so on. And Jenny might gradually have been weaned away from her exclusive interests in comics and cowboys to new horizons of reading interest.

All this could have happened as a result of a teacher-parent interview.

Stanley (11), Fourth Grade, Public School.[5]
The teacher went for the interview to the small café which the mother owns and runs, since she could not leave it. The teacher had talked with the mother twice before. This time he came because Stanley had been doing very poor schoolwork, had been showing little interest, and was always in trouble with other children. On two days he had been absent and the teacher wondered if the mother knew it. The school is a small one in a small rural town, and there is no visiting teacher, social worker, or psychologist. Each teacher does whatever is done himself, with such help as the superintendent has time to give.

The mother had been very reticent in previous talks, and the teacher felt that he had been able to get hold of very little to work on. This time, however, she was so disturbed by the absences, of which she had not known, that she began to talk more freely. She told how she has been the sole support of the family. She divorced the father when this boy was five and his brother three. There are three step-sisters whom she raised, all of them married and away. There has always been trouble with Stanley, and the mother said that he has been getting out of hand and that she had been able to do very little with him for several weeks. He wants to stop school and earn money. The teacher asked if there was any special reason that he wanted to earn money. She said that he didn't want to take money from her and, when the teacher commented that this showed a fine spirit, the mother said, "No, it is because he is always mad at me." The teacher asked if she knew why and she said, "Oh, I guess it is still that calf." Then she went on to tell that Stanley had always wanted a calf, and that when the children were little she made them save money by

5 Grace Langdon and Irving W. Stout, *Teacher-Parent Interviews,* © 1954 by Prentice-Hall, Inc., Englewood Cliffs, N. J. By permission.

telling them if they did they could buy a calf. They did save the money but they never got the calf. This boy had always held it against her, saying she cheated them. The teacher had not heard of this before and asked if she thought it was too late to still get the calf and if she thought it might help. She said she wouldn't have a calf around, that there was no place for it, and that she could not afford it. The teacher suggested that they both think about what might be done and said that he would drop in the next day after school. He did so, having meanwhile located a calf, just in case. When the teacher came in the mother began to cry and said she had thought about it and had stayed up the night before until Stanley came in late, and she had told him she would get him a calf. He was so excited that he cried, and she said he kissed her for the first time in two years. As she told the story she said, "You hear the pounding out back? It's him building a shed." At least a first step had been taken, because a teacher cared enough to talk things over.

Sometimes significant things do not come out in the first interview as in the case of Jenny. It took three interviews on the part of Stanley's teacher before the momentous bit of information came through.

Stanley was at a disadvantage to begin with. He came from a broken home, and the break had occurred at the strategic time in life when he began school. No doubt he was emotionally upset about this family situation, not only in kindergarten, but all through first grade where the foundations of reading are laid. Records of children who fail in reading, particularly at the beginning reading level, very often reveal a break in the family.

In addition to having the misfortune of a broken home befall him at beginning school age, Stanley had been frustrated in the realization of a childish longing—to possess a calf. In addition to all this, he had developed an antagonistic attitude toward his mother because she hadn't played fair with him. He was unhappy in school because he was doing so poorly and there was no pleasure for him in being home with his mother. Therefore, he sought amusement elsewhere and wanted to quit school and earn money so that he could buy things he wanted, himself.

In this state of mind, no teacher, regardless of how competent, could have taught Stanley reading or anything else. In lumbering, when a key log is removed from a log jam the whole pile straightens out and moves along. It is hoped that getting the calf for Stanley loosened the "key log" which permitted all his emotional tensions to move on. Released from these, he might once more become receptive to reading instruction and other school work.

Group Activities

Interview involves only a teacher and one or both parents. There are many types of group activities, however, through which parents may be

517

informed and understandings developed. Usually these group activities are conducted at Parent-Teacher Association meetings. Sometimes, however, a teacher invites the parents of the children in her classroom to come in for a get-acquainted tea or to hear an explanation of some new method or plan which will be or already has been put into effect.

Some types of activities which take place at group meetings are as follows:

Talks on Reading

A speaker talks on some aspect of reading, and the talk is followed by parent questions and discussion. The speaker may be a university or college professor who specializes in reading, a reading consultant in the public schools, the principal or superintendent (especially if some new plan is being put into effect in the school), the guidance counselor, the school psychologist, the librarian, or a parent or other prominent citizen who may have a worthwhile message to give about reading.

Some topics appropriate for such talks are:

1. How sound are the arguments of the critics concerning our present methods of teaching reading?
2. How is reading taught in our new plan (whatever the new plan is in the particular school—individualized instructed, ungraded school, Joplin plan, integrated language arts plan, and so on)?
3. How can parents help the child with reading at home?
4. Where and how is phonics usually taught?
5. Why are experience charts used for beginning reading?
6. Should we teach preschool children to read?
7. Why don't the schools do more oral reading?
8. Why is it that many children are not learning to read well?
9. What about the new methods of teaching speed in reading?

Panel Discussions

Panel discussions may be conducted in which the panel consists of:

1. Teachers
2. Parents
3. Parents and teachers together
4. Pupils in more advanced grades
5. Special service personnel: reading consultant, librarian, school psychologist, guidance counselor, school nurse, social worker, and so on.

Demonstrations

Demonstrations of teaching methods with children never fail to evoke a high degree of interest. Demonstrations of reading methods may be conducted before an entire PTA group, or they may be given in separate classrooms on a "Visiting Night," at which time parents visit classrooms in which their children are being taught. Demonstrations should be preceded with explanations and followed with discussion.

Demonstrations may be conducted by:

1. A teacher demonstrating with children procedures by which some aspect of reading is taught.
2. A parent demonstrating with her own child some effective procedure in regard to home reading.

Films, Tapes, and Slides

Several films have been prepared on the teaching of reading. Parents enjoy viewing these films and they can be informative, too, especially when supplemented by explanations of a reading consultant or teacher.

Some films and moving pictures appropriate for group meetings have been prepared by public school systems. Among these are:

Gregory Learns to Read (Detroit Public Schools); available for purchase or rental from the Audio-Visual Materials Consultation Bureau, College of Education, Wayne State University, Detroit 2, Michigan.

Reading (Los Angeles Public Schools); available from Jam Handy Organization, 281 East Grand Boulevard, Detroit 11, Michigan.

How Your Child Learns to Read (Salt Lake City Public Schools); available from the Director of Audio-Visual Education, Board of Education, 440 East First South, Salt Lake City 2, Utah.

Other excellent films are:

They All Learn to Read, B & W Sound, Syracuse University. This film shows teaching in a third grade in which there are four different groups reading at different levels.

Encyclopaedia Brittanica Primary Reading Series, color, $50.00 each; 6 for $270. Set I of 6 films, showing rich background in home and family living; first grade.

Background for Reading and Expression Films, Coronet, B & W, $55.00; color, $110.00.

Recordings are sometimes used at meetings with parent groups. Sprout [6] reports success in presenting to parents a series of recorded sections of reading lessons dealing with phonics in grades one through six. A set of slides accompanied by tape has been developed by Percy Bruce of Roslyn Heights, New York, and used with success at parent meetings.

[6] Janet E. Sprout, "Using Tape Recordings of Reading Lessons with Parents," *International Reading Association Conference Proceedings*, Vol. 3 (1958), 144–46.

No doubt, many other people in school systems have prepared and are preparing film and tape materials to use in giving information. The use of such media lends variety and interest, especially when a series of meetings are held.

Television

Some school systems are using the television medium for informing parents at teacher meetings. For example, the public schools of New York City prepared a television presentation for parents in which parents asked questions of a reading specialist from a local university. The questions had to do with controversial issues in reading and were particularly significant in clarifying current practices, which were being criticized and misunderstood by laymen. This was a novel and effective way of getting important information across to parents at parent-teacher meetings.

Materials for Informing Parents

Letters are effective. These may be personal letters written by a teacher, reading consultant, or principal to the parent concerning a certain child, telling his strengths and needs in reading and suggesting things that the parent may do. Other letters may be in the nature of a school bulletin sent to all parents of children at a certain level, such as primary or intermediate grades. Such a letter may inform parents concerning the over-all program in reading in the school or give information concerning the way in which a certain aspect of reading is taught and why.

The school newspaper is often used in giving small but related bits of reading information at intervals of time.

If it is possible to get articles on reading into a local newspaper, this is a very desirable thing to do. A newspaper article often assumes special importance to the public.

Exhibits of children's work growing out of reading, their records of books read, their book reviews, and so on are viewed with interest by parents. Exhibits of books recommended for children to read at different ages and levels of achievement are helpful to parents. Usually exhibits are used to accompany a general meeting rather than to constitute the entire substance of an evening meeting. If, however, the exhibit is accompanied by talks and personal explanations it may well furnish content for a profitable evening in itself.

Printed pamphlets have been prepared by many school systems for use in giving parents information about reading.

Some professional organizations have also published such pamphlets. Among the most popular of these are *Janie Learns to Read* [7] and *Sailing Into Reading*,[8] published by the Elementary School Principals and National School Public Relations Association of the National Education Association.

There are some excellent books which have been prepared expressly for parents and which may be recommended strongly to them. Some of these books are devoted entirely to the subject of reading; others contain sections in which reading is discussed. See "Additional Readings" at the end of Part Five, pages 536–37, for references to these books.

Summary

Emphasis in this chapter was placed upon the need for free intercommunication between parents and teachers. Researches were presented for the teacher's enlightenment, one indicating parents' attitudes toward reading; one listing things parents want to know about their children in school, and related topics. Techniques of working with parents included a discussion of interview procedures together with examples; group activities with suggestions for giving talks to parents; conducting panel discussions; giving demonstrations; and using films, tapes and slides. Suggestions of materials to use in informing parents concerning reading practices included a discussion of letters from the teacher, reading consultant, or principal; school newspaper; local newspaper; exhibits of children's work; printed pamphlets and books written especially for parents.

[7] Edith Stull, *Janie Learns to Read* (Washington, D. C.: National Education Association, 1953).

[8] Nila Banton Smith, *Sailing Into Reading* (Washington, D.C.: National Education Association, 1956).

Some paragraph impressions have also published sentences through the glass ... from the Louis Zserts to these ... into Reading ... at that Phonograph School. This is done ... and School ... you ... the nature of the nature ...

chapter **20**

Giving Advice to Parents

"What can I do to help Tom with his reading?" "Nothing. Don't try to teach him at all. It will interfere with the method I am using in school." Such a conversation occurred very frequently between parents and teachers not too many years ago. Parents went away feeling helpless and frustrated because they were blocked from doing something that might contribute to the well-being of their children.

Now-a-days teachers answer such questions in some such way as this: "Yes, Mrs. Brown. There are some things you can do to help. Studies have shown that growth in reading depends upon many aspects of child development. My job is concerned largely with *teaching* your child to read, but you have a major role to play in developing him in many other ways that will help my teaching to be successful. He is with me only five or six hours a day. He is with you or under your supervision seventeen or eighteen hours a day, so you have a better chance than I do to develop him in many important phases of his growth, which in turn will contribute to his ability to learn to read. You have a very great contribution to make to Tom's reading success."

What Are Some Conditions of Successful Readers

As a point of departure in discussing home conditions related to reading, the teacher might find it advisable to tell a parent about a study which was recently conducted with successful readers. Keshian [1] reported an investigation which he made with 72 fifth graders who were selected because they were successful readers. All these children had a reading age at or above their mental age.

Among his findings Keshian reported the following characteristics which have a relationship to the homelife of the children:

There was no apparent relationship between reading success and socio-economic level. (This finding is also supported by Ladd.[2])
The children were well-adjusted in terms of personality. . . .
The parents of these children encouraged them to read. They provided stimulation to read by giving books as gifts, taking their children to the library, and by reading themselves. . . .
The parents indicated strong interest in their children's school work. Examples of this interest was their attendance at PTA meetings and participation in PTA work and other school functions.
All of the children were read to by their parents on a regular sustained basis throughout their early childhood.
General health of the youngsters was excellent. . . .
The children walked and talked at about the same time as the children in the population. . . .
Most of the children owned their own library cards, and made use of them. . . .
The families were strong units—they did things together, such as attending athletic events, going to movies, and working at hobbies. (The investigator suggested that this might be a very important factor in building a strong emotional basis for reading success.)
Twelve per cent of the children had memberships in book clubs, and 76 per cent had their own subscription to a magazine. . . .
These children came from homes where there was a great variety of reading materials. The parents subscribed to more magazines and read more newspapers than did the unselected population.

[1] Jerry G. Keshian, "The Social, Emotional, Physical and Environmental Characteristics and Experiences of Children Who Learn to Read Successfully." Paper presented at the Annual Meeting of the Educational Research Association, Atlantic City, N. J., Feb. 20, 1962.
[2] Margaret Ladd, "The Relation of Social, Economic and Personal Characteristics to Reading Ability," *Teachers College Contribution to Education*, No. 582 (New York: Bureau of Publications, Columbia University, 1933).

The investigator rightly concluded that "Factors operating singly, such as a lack of reading materials in the home, do not in themselves prevent a child from becoming a successful reader. Rather, a whole range of characteristics and environmental factors appearing in combination, enable a child to achieve success in reading."

How Can Parents Help with General Growth Factors?

What are some contributions that parents can make? What advice can we give them that will help them, their children, and the teacher? Some suggestions are given below.

Health

A child cannot profit fully from reading instruction in school if he isn't feeling well or if he is absent frequently.

Records of children who are having serious difficulty in reading very often contain statements such as these:

Bill often had sore throat when he was in primary grades. I finally took him to a doctor and the doctor said Bill's tonsils were badly infected and that they had been draining toxics into his system all through his early school years.

When Arnold was a year old, he had an illness that left him with ear trouble. He had frequent attacks during the years he was in first and second grades. Each attack usually lasted for about three weeks so that he was absent from school a good part of the time. When he returned to school after these attacks, he was so weak and listless, he didn't take much interest in what was going on. . . .

No wonder these children didn't learn to read well. They lacked the vitality that was necessary to give attention to reading instruction, which involves the mental processes of thinking and concentration.

Of course many physical illnesses and defects are beyond the parents' control. The parents can, however, keep themselves alert in noting symptoms of poor health in their child and take him to a physician at the first appearance of signs of ill-health. Some of these signs are: bodily tension, strained expression, restlessness, hyperactivity, nervousness, fatigue, lack of energy, slumping, overweight, underweight, frequent colds, listlessness, inattention, lack of concentration. Parents may obtain a more complete list from the family physician.

The first and best thing for a parent to do in nurturing physical fitness is, of course, to preserve and contribute to the good health the child already possesses and thus aid him to build resistance to disease.

During teacher-parent conferences, the child's needs in regard to fresh air, exercise, sleep, and relaxation should be discussed and followed up by check-ups of application.

Means of developing health habits in the child himself is a topic which may well be pursued. The mutual interest of parent and teacher in a child's physical well-being often results in improved health habits.

Diet may have a part to play in a child's success in reading, and that, of course, is almost entirely within a parent's control. Here is an example:

A frail eight-year-old youngster who had never learned to read was brought to the attention of the writer. He was pale, emaciated, and lacking in physical energy. While interviewing the mother, it was discovered that the child had been born a "blue baby." Along with this misfortune, it followed that he developed fastidious food tastes to such an extent that there were only three foods which he would eat. While he ate acceptable quantities of these three foods, still, he was being starved because of a lack of nutritional elements. It was suggested that the mother enlist the help of a pediatrician or dietician in recommending supplements to the child's restricted diet which would provide him with all necessary food elements. Such elements were, in turn, prescribed by a specialist in the form of tablets and condensed foods which could be taken in dosages. The boy was given the food supplements regularly. Within a few weeks he came to the reading clinic with more vitality, energy, and interest. He entered into reading activities with enjoyment and his progress was very rapid.

The mother of another boy who was having great difficulty in reading gave these menus as samples of the boy's three meals:

Breakfast: bread, cheese, coffee
Lunch: bread and cheese sandwiches
Dinner: bread, meat, potatoes, and pie

In this diet there was a conspicuous lack of fruit and vegetables. These lacks conceivably might have had something to do with his reading failure. At any rate, several studies have shown that learning ability in all school subjects has been improved by adding to children's diet some food elements which were previously not included.

One very interesting study of this type was reported by Harrell.[3] This investigator studied the possibilities of a step-up in learning taking place

[3] Ruth Flinn Harrell, *The Effect of Added Thiamin on Learning.* Ph.D. Dissertation (New York: Teachers College, Columbia University, 1942).

as a result of increased intake of Vitamin B1. She used as her subjects two matched groups, ranging from 4 to 20 years of age, following the same diet in an orphanage in which the subjects were meagerly fed. Two mg. of thiamin were added daily to the diet of the experimental group, while each of the subjects in the control group was given a pill of no therapeutic value. The experimental group consistently made higher gains in learning, ranging from 7 per cent to 87 per cent. In general, the thiamin group learned more than the control group by about 24 per cent.

Several investigators have found that many children who are having difficulty in reading are also suffering from malnutrition. Most of these children are not hungry. They eat sufficient amounts of food, but their diet is poorly balanced. We have sufficient evidence of this type to point strongly to a relationship between malnutrition and reading disability. The two are associated frequently. This information may well be given to a parent in cases in which interview reveals the possibility of an inadequate diet.

Vision and Hearing

The capacity to see well and to hear well should be discussed with parents, and the importance of these capacities in learning to read should be emphasized. For information and symptoms of visual and hearing difficulties see Chapter 3, pages 36–40.

Sex Differences

Parents should realize that many more boys than girls have difficulty in learning to read. This, of course, is a matter of individual differences. Many boys are excellent readers. The fact remains, however, that the great preponderance of pupils so seriously retarded in reading that they wind up in a clinic are boys. Data in regard to this matter usually indicates that about ninety per cent of such cases are boys.

For further discussion of this topic see Chapter 3, pages 35–36.

Summary

In summary, parents should be given the following advice in regard to their child's physical well-being as a factor contributing to his reading success:

See that he gets plenty of fresh air, exercise, sleep, and relaxation.
Provide him with a well-balanced diet.
Have his vision checked in his third, fourth and fifth year, at the time of beginning first grade, and promptly thereafter at the first appearance of symptoms indicating difficulty.

If there are symptoms of hearing difficulty, take the child to an otologist as soon as they are observed.

Take him to a physician immediately if he shows signs of ill health.

If he misses school for long or frequent absences, talk the matter over with his principal and teacher. If they advise it, get a tutor for him, or put him in a reading clinic where he will have a chance to catch up with his class.

Emotional Stability

The child who has no fears or tensions about reading will probably be at an advantage in acquiring skill.

Parents often do not realize that little remarks they make and little things they do have a profound effect upon their children emotionally. Frequently, parents unconsciously set up attitudes, fears, tensions, and inferiority feelings in regard to their child's reading which actually stand in the way of his achieving success in learning this skill.

One investigator [4] who made a study of 30 children of normal intelligence with reading difficulties found that a third of the children had over-hostile mothers, four suffered from "acute sibling jealousy reaction," two others were "indulged, then neglected or rejected as they reached school age," and two were "over-indulged." Practically all the children tested were "insecure," "restless," and "emotionally ill."

Some parents whose child is not learning to read well ascribe the difficulty either to obstinacy or to lack of intelligence. They are disgusted with him and turn to scolding, reproaches, pressures, nagging, and sometimes punishment as a means of curing the trouble. These are the very worst things that a parent can do. Not only do such tactics militate against learning to read, but they are apt to contribute to other undesirable forms of behavior.

A child who is not doing well in reading is in trouble. His reading difficulty often stems from something entirely outside his realm of control. He needs sympathy, kindness, understanding. One wouldn't scold a child who had tuberculosis because he doesn't get well faster! Often a child's difficulty in reading is due to factors which he can't help any more than he can help having tuberculosis. He needs the parents' encouragement, not reproaches or pressures which may cause him to be so resentful or discouraged that he won't even try to read.

Another warning which is tremendously important to parents is that they should refrain from making comparisons between a child in the family who isn't learning to read too well and his brother or sister or other

[4] W. H. Missildine, "The Emotional Background of Thirty Children with Reading Disabilities, With Emphasis on its Coercive Elements," *The Nervous Child*, Vol. 5 (July 1946), 263–72.

children who have quickly picked up the skill. Neither should they permit children to make these comparisons among themselves. Instead, advise parents to give the poor reader a chance to do things in which he excels. Maybe he can skip rope more times without tripping than the good readers, or paint better, or bat a ball more often. Praise should be given for these achievements as a means of preserving his personal dignity and self-esteem.

In summary here is some advice to give to parents who need it:

Don't become irritated and disgusted with your child if he isn't doing well in reading.
Don't tell him he should be ashamed of himself because he can't read.
Don't try to force him to read at home.
Don't tell him he *must* learn to read in school.
Don't talk about his reading difficulties before visitors or other members of the family.
Don't compare a child who isn't reading well with others who are.
Don't be over-indulgent in other ways because you are sorry for him due to the struggle he is having in reading.

For a more complete discussion of emotional maturity see pages 44–50 in Chapter 3.

Providing Broad Social Contacts and Rich Experiences

This aspect of child growth as related to reading was discussed in Chapter 3, pages 42–44. Much of this information might well be given to parents, especially if they have children who are beginning or about to begin reading.

Reading Itself—Do's and Don'ts

There are certain things which parents *can* do in helping their child with reading itself, and certain things they shouldn't do. Some warnings and some constructive suggestions in regard to possibilities of a parent working with reading are discussed below.

Warnings

Preschool Reading

There are two periods in a child's life when a parent often "takes over" and tries to teach him to read herself. One of these times is before he goes to school.

Many preschool children at the present time show an interest in learning to read. This interest may be initiated by the child in requesting the parent to tell him what a word on a grocery package says, or what a recurring word on the television screen says, or he may begin to pick out a word here and there in one of the story books from which his parents read to him. If a preschool child shows an interest in reading in such ways as these and asks for help then the parents should by all means give it to him. For a more complete discussion of preschool reading see Chapter 15, pages 448–52. Much of the information given on these pages would be helpful for a parent to have.

While responding to the child's requests for help with reading is desirable, the systematic teaching of reading to young children is questionable. If the preschool child is not interested in reading and resists or responds negatively to learning to read, the chances are strong that he is not sufficiently mature to have any reading instruction at all. Under such conditions the parent may do harm in persisting in attempts to teach him to read.

Here is an example of what happened in one case when an overly concerned mother began teaching her child to read before he was sufficiently mature to have such instruction.

When the writer met John, he was 12 years old, healthy, intelligent, emotionally stable. He could read just three words: *the, a,* and *boy.*

Mrs. M., John's mother, said that the family lived in Florida when he was four and a half years old. They expected to move to New York the following year. Someone told her that children in New York entered the first grade when they were five [5] and that, unless John were taught to read, he would be behind the others when he started school in New York. So Mrs. M. employed a tutor to work every afternoon with John on reading. She said that she (Mrs. M., herself) also tried to teach John to read evenings. "With all that effort he never learned a thing," she regretfully related. "There was something wrong with him from the very beginning. He took no interest in reading and paid no attention to us. He got sulky and pouty and stubborn. Finally he got so he'd scream and cry when we started to work with him and one day he threw the book at the tutor. A year and a half later he began attending school in New York and he behaved in the same way when the teacher tried to teach him to read. He's always been like this and never would learn all through the grades."

[5] Children do not enter first grade in New York when they are five. Mrs. M. had been misinformed.

And so John wound up at a remedial reading clinic, probably largely because he had formal reading instruction forced upon him before he had reached that stage of total maturation at which he could work readily with reading symbols.

Unfortunately, some other parents insist that their young children learn to read when they are not sufficiently mature for reading instruction and they try teaching these children themselves or having someone else do so. If the child is too immature for reading it is far better to provide him with an abundance of rich, happy experiences, to let him have opportunities for abundant physical activity out of doors, to surround him with a wealth of picture books, and to read to him frequently. Eventually he will ask: "What does it say on that package?" or "What does that flashing off-and-on sign say?" Then it's all right and highly desirable to answer his questions. But for a parent to take a book while the child is still too immature to read and sit down and make a job of teaching him is another matter and one that is highly questionable.

After School Reading Begins

The preschool period, then, is one critical stage at which ambitious parents sometimes try to teach their children to read, and they may do harm if the child is too immature for reading. Another critical period of parent-teaching often occurs when the parent discovers that a child is having trouble with reading as he progresses through the grades. In her anxiety the parent, herself, then attempts to teach the child to read.

Very frequently parent-teaching is highly charged with emotion on the part of both the parent and the child. The parent often is in a definite state of worry because the child isn't getting along well. She is annoyed because the child doesn't learn to read like other children of his acquaintance, and impatient because the child doesn't "remember the words" after being told once or twice. The child, on the other hand, probably comes to the situation with a distaste for reading, inferiority feelings, fear because he knows that he will fail to respond the way his parent wants him to do. Under these conditions "the lesson period usually blows up," and both parent and child are worse off than if the teaching attempt had not been made. So in the interest of developing sound emotional health and desirable attitudes toward reading, it is inadvisable for an over-anxious parent to attempt to teach reading to a child who is having difficulty.

Another reason why parents should refrain from actually teaching reading to underdeveloped readers is because they have not been trained in modern methods of teaching this skill.

For example, a parent was heard to say the other day, "I had him memorize all the words in the word-lists in the back of his reader, but he still can't read in the book at all. He doesn't know these words when he comes to them in sentences."

This parent was using the wrong approach. Teachers who have had recent training in reading wouldn't think of teaching a child to read by forcing him to memorize a list of isolated words. Teachers found out long ago that having children memorize isolated lists was no assurance that they would be able to read these words when woven together in sentences.

When parents attempt to teach reading they usually confine their instruction to word-recognition only, and as pointed out in Introduction to Part II, pages 164–65, there are many other phases of reading to be developed, phases which are equally as important as "calling words." There is a lot to the teaching of reading these days, and one has to be trained to this job well. Parents should be advised to leave the technical aspects of teaching reading to teachers who have been trained in this specialized field, just as they leave their child's health problems to a physician and his dental problems to a dentist.

What a Parent Can Do About Reading

Suggestions were given on page 450 concerning possibilities of parents giving informal help to preschool children who request or in some cases demand help. The suggestions below pertain to possibilities of parental help after school reading instruction begins.

Responding, Listening, and Encouraging

The parent should be advised to take advantage of every functional situation which offers the child an opportunity to use reading. If he has a new erector set, let her refrain from reading the instructions to him. Rather she should have him read the directions even if she has to tell him many of the words, and she should let him carry out each instruction one at a time as he reads it. If he wants to know the name of a picture on the movie marquis, the parent may have him figure out as much of it as he can for himself, and supply the rest for him. If he asks what an ad on the ad border in a bus says, the reply might be, "You know many of those words. The first one is 'Remember.' What's the next one?" etc. In other words, the parent should be advised to take advantage of every reading situation to help "put the child on his own" as he will have to be in his life's reading.

These are some of the ways in which a parent may help her child directly with reading, without attempting to enter into the technical process of actually *teaching* reading.

A strong recommendation should be made to parents concerning listening attentively to a child if he wishes to read from one of his school books. The parent might be told that regardless of whether she is in the midst of peeling potatoes or clearing the dinner table she should give the child her undivided attention when he wants to read to her. If he doesn't know a word the parent should just tell it to him. This is not a major calamity. Advise her, however, to jot down the words the child misses and give them to you, the teacher, for analysis of his phonics needs and let it go at that. The parent should not interrupt this enjoyable reading situation by trying to work on word recognition techniques with him, herself. Rather she should listen to the child's reading with interest, enter into enjoyable discussion with him concerning the content, and praise him for any part of the reading that he does especially well, such as figuring out the pronunciation of a new word by himself, reading smoothly, or showing during discussion that he understands perfectly what he has read. The parent shouldn't force the child to read, but if he voluntarily makes any gesture toward reading, she should handle the situation pleasurably and with interest, as discussed above.

Reading to the Child

It is advisable for parents to read to their children at preschool and early primary levels as well. When they read to a child from story books, comic strips of the better type, and children's magazines, he becomes aware that books, magazines, and newspapers hold something of interest and amusement for him. He also comes to realize that this "something" which he enjoys is tightly locked within black and white symbols, and that these symbols can be unlocked only when one knows how to read. This awareness and interest form a springboard from which he can leap into learning to read in school, and into voluntary reading of self-selected books.

Parents should be warned, however, not to continue reading to their child year after year as he passes through the elementary grades. Some parents have been known to continue reading to their child long after he has reached the point at which he should be reading for himself. If he can get his pleasure from reading through his parents' efforts, he may not have much motive for doing the reading himself. Parents should decrease their reading to the child as the child learns to read and put him on his own as soon as possible.

Selection of Books

Usually, parents who buy books for a child go to a bookstore preceding Christmas, the child's birthday, or similar occasions and choose a book which they think the child would like or which they think the child should read because of its cultural, exemplary, or informative value. A book chosen in this way often proves to be of little or no interest to the child and frequently is too difficult for him to read. Instead of being read and enjoyed, it becomes just a permanent fixture on the book shelf.

Results of a study made by Kolson, Robinson, and Zimmerman [6] reinforce the statements made above. In discussing their study of children's preferences of publisher's books they stated that clerks in book sections of stores reported that children's books were most frequently chosen by adults and that even though the children were with the adults, the adults still chose the books. Their study revealed further that adult's preferences for publisher's books which ranked high, ranked low in children's preferences.

It would be well to suggest to parents that they take their child with them to the bookstore and frequently to the library. Upon these occasions let him pick out his own book but with some guidance from them if necessary.

A further suggestion might be that as parent and child stand together looking over the book counter or bookshelves the parent might ask, "What kind of a book would you like?" Maybe he will reply, "One on rockets," and pick up an attractive book on this subject which at first sight appears to be too difficult for him. In such a case the parent should ask the child to read a paragraph or two orally from the book. If he misses so many words that it would seem he wouldn't enjoy the book, then she should look for other books on rockets, trying him out on each one until she finds one in which he can read easily and well. This is the one the parent should buy and take home for the child's enjoyment.

In case a child says he doesn't know what kind of a book he wants, the parent may show him several books, becoming enthusiastic about them herself, and calling attention to the characters and their vicarious ex-

[6] Clifford J. Kolson, Richard E. Robinson, and William G. Zimmerman, "Children's Preferences in Publishers," *Education*, Vol. 83 (Nov. 1962), 155–57.

periences in some of the appealing pictures. In such a situation, no doubt, the parent's enthusiasm will become contagious and the child will suddenly decide, "This is the book I want."

A word to parents about keeping a child's books at home is in order. Each child should have his own bookcase or set of low shelves on which he keeps his own books with plenty of space to challenge him to add more.

Selecting a Reading Clinic

If a child is seriously retarded in reading, the parent should be advised to take him to a reading clinic for diagnosis and treatment.

Some school systems have professional remedial reading services as a part of their own organizations. If the child is in a system that does have a reading clinic, then of course the teacher may recommend that the child be taken care of within his own school system.

Many school systems, however, do not have clinical facilities. In such situations the parent should be encouraged to take the child to some reading clinic in the neighborhood. This is the strategic point at which advice is necessary.

So-called "reading clinics," "reading centers," and "reading laboratories" are being established by private individuals throughout the country. In some cases the director and instructors in these centers are very well trained. In other cases, such centers are being conducted by people who never even had one college course in reading and perhaps no teaching experience.

Remedial reading is a highly specialized area of education. A parent should not entrust her child to a privately-run reading clinic without exploring the qualifications of the director and those who will be working with her child.

The International Reading Association has published a pamphlet entitled "Minimum Standards for Qualifications of Reading Specialists." It would be a good idea if teachers would ask their principals to send for a few copies of this pamphlet to have on hand for distribution to parents who contemplate sending their child to a clinic. The address of the International Reading Association is Box 119, Newark, Delaware.

Brief excerpts from this publication are quoted below.[7]

> I. A minimum of three years of successful teaching and/or clinical experience.

[7] Reprinted by permission of the International Reading Association.

II. A Master's Degree or its equivalent of a Bachelor's Degree plus 30 graduate hours in reading and related areas as indicated below:
A. A minimum of 12 semester hours in graduate-level reading courses
with at least one course in 1 and 2, and 3 or 4:
1. Foundations or survey of reading
2. Diagnosis and correction of reading disabilities
3. Clinical or laboratory practicum in reading
4. Supervision and Curriculum in Reading
B. At least one graduate-level course in each of the following content
areas:
1. Measurement and/or evaluation
2. Child and/or adolescent psychology or development
3. Personality and/or mental hygiene
4. Educational psychology
C. The remainder of semester hours in reading and/or related areas.
Courses recommended might include one or more of the following:
1. Literature for children and/or adolescents
2. Organization and supervision of reading programs
3. Research and the literature in reading
4. Foundations of education
5. Principles of guidance
6. Nature of language
7. Communications
8. Speech and hearing
9. Exceptional child
10. Or any additional courses under II A and II B

Parents looking for a clinic should find out whether the staff members
of the clinic possess these minimum qualifications. If not, they should
search for a clinic in which those who work with their child have professional competency in the way of training and experience.

Summary

In Chapter 20 suggestions were given in regard to advising parents concerning important aspects of child growth related to reading success:
health, vision, and hearing; sex differences; emotional stability; social
contacts; and rich experiences. Teachers were advised to express approval to parents for responding to their preschool children's requests for
help in reading but to warn them against forcing reading instruction upon
a young child who is not sufficiently mature to undergo such instruction.
It was suggested also that parents be discouraged from attempts to teach
reading directly to a child who is retarded in reading achievement. Con-

structive suggestions for parental work with reading were: respond, listen, and encourage; read to the child; let him select his own books. An important section provided the teacher with information to give parents who are seeking a reading clinic for a child needing special help.

Additional Readings

References for Teachers

D'Evelyn, Katherine E., *Individual Parent Teacher Conferences*. New York: Teachers College, Columbia University, 1945.

Frasure, Kenneth, "Parent and Teacher Partnership," *Education*, Vol. 82 (Mar. 1962), 406–409.

Himmel, Frank M., "Give Parents a Real Place in School," *Childhood Education*, Vol. 32 (Nov. 1955), 116–18.

Kindred, Leslie W., *School Public Relations*, Chap. 8, "Parent Relations," 125–47. Englewood Cliffs, N. J.: Prentice-Hall, Inc., 1957.

Langdon, Grace, and Irving W. Stout, *Helping Parents Understand Their Child's School*. Englewood Cliffs, N. J.: Prentice-Hall, Inc., 1957.

Larrick, Nancy, "How to Enlist Parents in the Reading Program," *International Reading Association Conference Proceedings*, Vol. 4 (1959), 165–68.

Martin, Kenneth A., and Harold J. Bienvenue, "The Parent Conference—Progress Report, Not Psychotherapy," *The Elementary School Journal*, LVII (Oct. 1956), 42–44.

Michael, Calvin B., "PTA Influence on Teachers," *The Elementary School Journal*, Vol. 62 (Mar. 1962), 321–31.

"Parents and the Reading Program," *The Reading Teacher*, VII (Apr. 1954).

Snyder, Agnes, *An Educator Substitutes for Parents*, Washington, D. C.: Association for Childhood Education, International, 1962.

Stout, Irving W., and Grace Langdon, *Parent-Teacher Relationships*. Washington, D. C.: National Education Association, 1958.

References for Parents

Ames, Louise Bates, and Frances L. Ilge, *Parents Ask*. New York: Harper and Row, Publishers, 1962.

Artley, Sterl A., *Your Child Learns to Read*. Chicago: Scott Foresman & Co., 1953.

Brown, Muriel W., *Partners in Education*, Bulletin 1950, No. 1. Washington, D. C.: Association for Childhood Education, International, 1950.

Frank, Josette, *Your Child's Reading Today*. Garden City, N. Y.: Doubleday & Company, 1954.

Frank, Lawrence K., and Mary Frank, *How to Help Your Child in School*. New York: Viking Press, Inc., 1950.

Gates, Doris, *Helping Children Discover Books*. Chicago: Science Research Associates, 1956.

Larrick, Nancy, *A Parent's Guide to Children's Reading*. New York: Doubleday & Company, 1958.

Ojemann, Ralph H., and Luella Fatland, "Parents and Teachers as Partners," *National Parent-Teacher,* Vol. 40 (Sept. 1945), 20–23. Condensed: Education Digest, Vol. 11 (Nov. 1945), 1–4.

PART 6

Practice and Maintenance Activities

Introduction

Activities were suggested in Chapters 8, 9, 10, and 11 for introducing the various reading skills in the four basic areas of skill growth. Most children, however, require special practice following the introduction of a reading skill, some requiring a great deal, others not so much. Furthermore, after a skill has been introduced and given practice at one school level, review is necessary to keep it alive and functioning at successive levels. Skill development doesn't end with introduction. Each skill should be maintained and increased year by year as the child passes through his school life.

Teachers in service and students doing practice teaching usually welcome suggestions for a variety of activities to use for these purposes, and the author felt that this book would be remiss if it did not offer many practical hints to serve these purposes. It was thought, however, that the inclusion of these numerous suggestions within the skill development chapters themselves would clutter the pages to such an extent as to interfere with the reader's train of thought as he or she pursued the more basic discussions. For this reason suggestions for the *introduction* of the skills only, was included within the skill development chapters, and the additional suggestions for *practice activities* were placed in this separate section at the back of the book where a teacher or student teacher might turn to them if and when he or she needs them.

Some of these suggestions are appropriate for beginning reading, some for second and third grade levels, and some for the higher elementary grades. The teacher or student teacher is left to choose certain ones at his or her own discretion as they are appropriate for the developmental level of the pupils under consideration.

These activities are not to be used as set exercises as they appear on these pages of suggestions. They are provided only as sample suggestions from which the creative teacher will obtain hints to use in preparing her own practice materials in connection with reading content with which her pupils are working.

21

Practice and Maintenance Activities
in Word Identification

Several suggestions are given in this chapter for additional practice and maintenance activities in the use of different methods of attack needed in finding out the pronunciation of unrecognized words. These suggestions are organized in categories to correspond to headings of sections in which discussions were presented in Chapter 8. These different categories contain suggestions for giving practice in the use of context clues, phonics, structional analysis (including prefixes, suffixes, contractions, syllabication, and accent), and dictionary aids to pronunciation.

Practice and Maintenance in Using
Context Clues

The use of context clues in pronouncing unrecognized words is valuable and it requires more than incidental attention if children learn to make the most of this skill.

The activities together with their accompanying sentences presented below are of course only suggestive. The teacher will make use of sentences which grow directly out of experiences and reading content of the particular children with whom she is working.

SUPPLYING WORDS IN CHALKBOARD SENTENCES

The teacher may write sentences on the chalkboard, including in each one a word which the children probably do not know and which can be supplied readily through the context in the rest of the sentence. The words *home* and *bed* are examples of such words in the sentences below.

When school is out we will go *home*.
At night we go to *bed*.

The children are asked to read the sentences to themselves. One child is then asked to read the first sentence orally but not to say the last word. The teacher asks, "How many know what the last word is? Raise your hand. Don't say it." If there are some children who cannot supply the word the teacher guides these children with comments and questions until they are able to deduce it from the context in the rest of the sentence. Work with the next sentence proceeds in the same way and so on.

SUPPLYING WORDS IN COMPLETION SENTENCES

The same plan as discussed above may be used, except that blanks appear where the children are to fill in words. At first separate words may be provided for them to use in making a selection of an appropriate word for each blank. There should always be a joker in the list of words provided. Later they may try filling in blanks without the accompaniment of word choices.

Examples of completion sentences to use in working with context clues are:

Squirrels like to climb _____.
Mary washed her face and _____.
Dick's wagon had four _____.
wheels   girl   hands   trees

Supplying a word at the end of a sentence is easier than supplying one within a sentence. A sample of sentences that may be used for the latter purpose is given below.

Ducks like to _____ in the water.
Alice asked Daddy to tell her a _____ before she went to bed.
Tommy gave the man in the store five _____ for some candy.
cents   story   toys   swim

The teacher may work with a group at the chalkboard while choosing and supplying words in such sentences; or if the children needing practice can write, the sentences may be duplicated and given to them for independent work at their seats.

MULTIPLE CHOICE SENTENCES

Sentences similar to those above may be used for practice purposes, except that two or three choices are provided for each sentence as:

Frank likes to play { cat / ball

Birds can fly in the { book / sky

Shirley wore a blue { dress / ribbon in / shoe } her hair.

Children are to cross out the wrong words in each sentence, leaving only the one that makes sense. The choices may be placed beneath each sentence instead of within the sentence if preferred. In this case blank lines are placed where the word belongs, and the teacher writes the children's choice in each sentence or they write it in themselves if they are able to do so.

ASSOCIATING BEGINNINGS AND ENDINGS OF SENTENCES

Prepare simple sentences, separate their beginnings and endings, and place the endings in mixed arrangement. Children are to draw a line from the beginning of each sentence to its appropriate ending. Such sentences may be used for chalkboard development or duplicated and passed out for independent seat work.

An example of content to use for this activity is:

Dorothy likes to help	for his dog.
Bill likes to fly	for her doll.
Dorothy made a dress	his toy airplane.
Paul made a house	her mother.

GUESSING RIDDLES

Simple riddles provide excellent content in developing ability to get a word from context because children have to supply a word in terms of the total meaning of three or perhaps several related sentences. The riddles may be written on the chalkboard and used for group or individual work with the teacher, or they may be duplicated and passed out, a copy for each child who needs such practice. The word which is the answer to each riddle may be written or illustrated with a drawing.

Here are some examples of riddles:

Mother gave me something for my birthday. I can read in it. What is it?

It has long ears and a short tail. It can hop. It likes to eat carrots. It has soft brown fur. What is it?

Children may make up their own sentences for context work. After they become acquainted with materials of the types suggested above, invite them to make up sentences leaving out one word for the other children to supply. The sentences may be given orally, and the children needing practice may supply the missing words orally. Riddles which the children make up may be used in a similar manner.

EXCHANGING SENTENCES WRITTEN BY PUPILS

In the more advanced grades each child may make up and write a set of sentences (whatever number the teacher thinks is advisable), leaving out one word in each. Then they may exchange papers and try to fill in the appropriate words in each other's sentences. A score of one should be given for each sentence in which the correct word was supplied. After the papers are returned the answers should be discussed and the children guided in deciding why the use of context clues worked in some cases and not in others.

BRINGING IN SENTENCES FROM OUTSIDE READING

Invite each pupil to bring in one sentence encountered in his outside reading in which he found an unrecognized word and figured it out from context. Each pupil reads his sentence to the group, and they discuss what was in the sentence that helped him to get the word.

DECIDING ON TYPES OF CONTEXTUAL AIDS

Perhaps some of the more advanced pupils in the upper elementary grades might profit by being acquainted with the different types of contextual aids presented on page 183. After explaining these types, the children might be asked to find examples of one of the types in their school texts or library books. Eventually, examples may be found for the other types, one by one. Discussion should always accompany or follow the children's search for examples of a particular type, and ways pointed out in which an awareness of that particular type might be helpful to them in supplying unrecognized words in their own individual reading situations.

Practice and Maintenance in Using Phonics

Samples of activities are given below for the purpose of suggesting a variety of possibilities to the teacher for use in providing additional phonics practice in accordance with the needs of certain individuals or groups. The teacher will adapt any particular activity that she chooses by selecting appropriate words which contain the type of phonic element on which pupils need practice. The suggestions are samples only which the teacher may use in preparing content for her own purposes.

PRACTICE IN VISUAL DISCRIMINATION

Children usually need less practice on visual discrimination than on any other phonics process. When such practice is needed it may be given through a variety of matching or comparing activities that the children look upon as puzzles which they do "just for fun."

In the interest of providing variety, several suggestions for this type of activity are given below.

1. Select three leaders and have them choose teams. Ask each leader to name a word. If the word begins with a blend do not accept it at beginning stages. Accept only words that begin with a single consonant. Write the words on the chalkboard, as:

bird   penny   soldier

Ask each child to turn to a page in the book he is reading and see how many words he can find that start with the same letter as the word selected by his team leader. Write the words under the key words on the chalkboard as they are found. The team that finds the most words wins the game.

2. In beginning stages children may find words in advertisements (with large type faces) which begin in the same way as a word that the teacher has written in manuscript on the chalkboard. They may circle all such words with crayon, or if the type face is large enough to permit, they may cut out the words and paste them in a column on a piece of tagboard.

3. A visual discrimination technique that lends itself to many variations in phonic content is that of writing two columns of words on the chalkboard and having children underline, circle, or connect with a line those letters or words that are similar in some respect. Samples of some uses for this technique are given below.

Write on the chalkboard the names of children in the classroom whose names begin with the same letter. Choose names to represent two initial consonants upon which practice is needed, as *m* and *h*. This technique is especially appropriate for practice in matching capital letters. As an example in working with the content below children might be given turns to find and draw a circle around a word that begins like *Mary;* similarly, with a word that begins like *Henry.*

Mary	*Henry*
Harold	Maurice
Marie	Harriet
Harvey	Mildred

Similarly, this activity may be used for words frequently confused because of similar configuration; for example, children may box each copy of *was* and draw a line under each copy of *saw,* and so on.

was	*saw*
saw	was
was	was
saw	saw
was	was

Another activity is one in which children connect with a line all words that begin with a certain phonic element, such as *st,* and similarly connect all words that end with the same element, as:

stand	*most*
story	test
best	stop
start	past
last	still
stem	stamp
toast	west

4. The teacher may place in the wall chart three different sets of known words, containing three phonic elements each, on which she wishes to give matching practice. For example, if she wishes to give practice in noting the final consonants of *t, g,* and *m,* she might place these known words in the pockets of the wall chart, one set in mixed arrangement in each pocket: *dog, coat, pig, farm, feet,* *room; want, big, drum, not, leg, swim;* *warm, bug, eat, him, frog, hat.*

Have the children place all words ending with *t* in one pocket, those ending with *g* in another, and those ending with *m* in another.

5. Children may draw a circle around pairs of words that are alike in some respect, according to the phonic elements upon which they need practice. The pairs may be alike or unlike in terms of whole-word configurations or in beginning, medial, or final phonic elements.

As an example, let us suppose that the teacher wishes to give practice in noting the final speech sound, *ck;* the words below might be placed on the chalkboard and children asked to circle each pair of words that end with *ck.*

pick	creep	lick	spend
black	speak	crack	blade
chick	slick	sick	prick
chill	pack	pack	proof

6. To provide practice in very careful scrutiny the children may be asked to note certain exceptions. Examples:

Draw a line under all words in the list which are exactly alike except for the first letter as:

cook, take, coat, make, cold, bake

Draw a line under all words that are like the first word except that the letter at the end is different:

him   not   hit   hat   his   have

PRACTICE IN AUDITORY DISCRIMINATION

The ability to distinguish the sounds of letters and letter combinations often requires considerable practice for certain children. The suggestions below should be of special value in working with such pupils.

1. After a common experience, such as taking an excursion or build-

ing and equipping a playhouse, the teacher may say, "Let's think of all the things we saw" or "all the things we have in our playhouse that begin like *Ted*." Such lists as *turtle, turkey, toad, tools* or *table, telephone, tub, tack* may result. These are written on the chalkboard and attention is called to the sameness of the appearance and sound of the beginning letter.

2. Riddles may be used to give practice in auditory discrimination, as:

I am round.
Children play with me.
My name begins like *book* and *baby*.
What am I?

3. Dramatizing action words offers an opportunity for auditory discrimination. Tell the children that you are going to ask one of them to do something that starts with the sound of *r* and that you want them to guess the word. Whisper the word *run* to a child and have him carry out the action. Let the other children supply the word.

Continue with action words beginning with other initial consonants, as *c:cut; d:dance; f:fall; g:go; h:hop; j:jump; l:laugh; m:march; p:push; r:ride; s:sing; t:talk; w:walk.*

4. A description word activity is especially desirable for auditory practice since the recognition of an initial consonant sound takes place in a contextual setting.

Write on the chalkboard a sentence containing a noun which begins with a consonant on which you wish to give practice, as: I have a *book*. Ask the children to add other words that start with the sound of *b* that might be used to describe the book, as:

I have a beautiful book.
I have a big book.
I have a blue book.

Use the same activity for other consonants.

5. Identifying sounds similar to two known words written on the chalkboard may be used in giving auditory practice. Write two known words such as *fall* and *sing* on the chalkboard. Have some of the children represent the sound of *f* in *fall*, and the rest represent the sound of *s* in *sing*. Pronounce several words in mixed arrangement beginning with these consonants, as *soon, father, funny, sell, see, find, send, for, said*. When you say a word beginning like *fall*, have all children representing the sound of *f* as in *fall* stand; similarly, have the other group of children stand whenever you mention a word beginning with the sound of *s* as in *sing*.

6. To provide more practice on initial consonants the teacher may have pupils supply missing letters in incomplete sentences as indicated below:

b c n f d

The robin has a _____est.
Billy drank water from a _____up.
Alice put her doll to _____ed.
Playing ball is _____un.

7. Completion sentences may be used for review purposes. If the teacher wishes to review the sound of *n* when used as a final consonant, she might write on the chalkboard completion sentences similar to those below. Then she would have the children supply the missing words in response to such directions as: "We need another word in the first sentence. It should end with the sound of *n* as in *fan*. Read the sentence, tell me what the missing word is, and I'll write it in the blank space."

Mother baked the cake in a _____.
The farmer kept his pig in a _____.

Jim had _____ playing the game.
Harold's sister can count to _____.
Mother said, "Tom, _____ to the store."
Father and some other _____ went fishing.

8. Writing a requested phonic element each time a word containing the element is pronounced can be used for practice with children who are able to write. An example is as follows: if the teacher wishes to give practice in recognizing the sounds of final *r* and final *p* she would ask the pupils to write as headings on a piece of paper two key words such as *car* and *hop*. She would then direct them to write the letter *r* under *car* each time she says a word that ends with *r*, and *p* under *hop* each time she says a word that ends with *p*. Some words to pronounce might be: *jump, chair, door, deep, four, stop, ship, deer, bear, help, for, sleep, pair, skip.*

9. Working with rhyme words is enjoyed by beginners. They may tell what words rhyme in Mother Goose rhymes as the teacher recites them; they may supply a rhyme word which she omits; they may make up rhyming couplets; they may tell which words sound alike when the teacher pronounces several words, such as *stick, stem, thick, spring, friend, sick, kick;* they may supply more words to rhyme with one that the teacher gives, such as *cake.*

10. Illustrating words containing a certain phonic element is enjoyed by children. The teacher may write a word such as *ball* on the chalkboard and draw a picture of a ball opposite the word. The children are told to think of other words that begin with the sound of *b* as in *ball* and draw a picture of each one. If they can write, they may write the name of each word, also. The list of pictured words

might be: *boy, baby, bird, book, bear, bell, bed, bag,* and so on.

PRACTICE IN BLENDING

1. Write some words on the chalkboard which can be changed by substituting different initial consonants, and some that can be changed by substituting different final consonants. Let the children erase the preceding consonant, add the new one, and pronounce the resulting word as the teacher gives instruction; for example:

> Change *cat* to *bat*
> Change *cat* to *cap*
> Change *fan* to *ant*
> Change *see* to *bee*
> Change *see* to *seek*
> Change *real* to *reach*

Have the children read sentences containing the new words they have made, as:

> A *bat* can see at night.
> Ted has a new *cap*.
> Louise saw a large black *ant* in the garden.
> Harry was stung by a *bee*.
> The children played a game of hide and *seek*.
> Sarah had to *reach* to get the dish from the shelf.

2. Place sentences on the chalkboard containing words representing elements that you wish to review. Have children find and read words in the sentences that begin like a word you mention. For example, if you wish to review *st, bl,* and *cr,* write sentences something like the ones given below. Then give such directions as "Find a word that begins with the same sound as *cheese*. Show the word. Then read the sentence."

> Janice saw a bright star.
> Michael has red cheeks.
> Marie built a house with her blocks.

Every Sunday Ray goes to church.
Sam put a stamp on the letter.
John heard the little lamb bleat.

PRACTICE ON VOWEL SOUNDS

1. If children need practice on the vowel sounds, have them substitute vowels in words similar except for the vowel sound. They should pronounce each new word that they make and read it in a sentence. As an example of content for such activity, the key words *big* and *hat* are given, together with words which the children might make by substituting vowels. Sample context sentences are also given.

big: *bag, beg, bug*

The man put candy in a *bag.*
My dog will sit up and *beg* for a bone.
Jack found a *bug* on the plant.

hat: *hit, hot, hut*

Bill couldn't *hit* the ball.
The soup was too *hot.*
The old man lived in a little *hut.*

2. After developing a certain sound, such as the sound of *a* followed by *r,* the children may be invited to blend different beginnings and endings with *a* followed by *r* to see how many words they can make in which *a* has that sound. Write the words on the chalkboard as they are given. The lists may look something like this:

arm	carton	hard	march
ark	carbon	harm	park
art	dark	harbor	part
artist	dart	jar	parcel
bark	garden	large	tart
barber	garbage	lark	target
car	garlic	mark	varnish
cart			

Immediately after listing, write sentences on the chalkboard containing the words and have them read. A few examples of sentences are given:

It was a *dark* night.
Mr. White has a *large car.*
John found a *lark's* nest.
Tom couldn't hit the *target.*
Mary bought some milk in a *carton.*

3. When a child confuses two words, such as *these* and *those,* write the two words on the chalkboard pointing out the letter or letters responsible for a difference in pronunciation and explaining this difference. In some cases manuscript the two words on separate strips of tagboard. Let the child trace one word on transparent paper and place the tracing over the other word to note differences in the two words.

4. Children may write the vowels to be practiced on separate slips of paper. As the teacher names a word containing one of the vowels, they hold up the slip of paper with that vowel on it. For example, the teacher wishes to give practice on the long and short sounds of *a,* so she has the children write on one slip of paper *long a* and on another slip, *short a.* She then names words that contain either one sound or the other. The children hold up their slips of paper accordingly. The words named might be: bake, back, cane, ate, sat, name, clay, pan, cape.

5. A team game, in which long and short sounds are identified in context, may be played. Divide the group into two teams with a captain for each team. Write a number of sentences on the chalkboard which contain long and short vowels on which you wish to give practice. For example, in the case of long and short *i,* one team would be the long *i* team, and the other the short *i* team. The sentences might be:

Jimmy liked to ride in a wagon.
Katie did not like mice.

The children had ice cream for dinner.
The big pile of leaves was in the yard.
Jimmy put the stick on the fire.

Have all the children read the first
sentence silently, then have the captain of the long *i* team indicate the
long *i* words in the sentence, as "long
i—liked, ride." If he misses a word,
the next child in his team becomes
captain. Use the same procedure with
the short *i* team, beginning with the
first sentence, and so on.

5. Filling words in with vowels
provides extra practice on the vowel
sounds. A sample of sentences to be
used for this purpose is:

Sylvia has a new h__t.
It is r__d.
It has a b__nd of ribbon on it.
Her aunt s__nt it to her.

PRACTICE IN APPLYING A PRINCIPLE

Finding words to which a principle
applies affords practice in associating
principles with word pronunciations.
After children have generalized a
principle from known words, they
may put words to which the principle
applies in sentences on the chalkboard
or find words on pages in a book.
Sentences appropriate for chalkboard
practice in finding words to illustrate
the principle of final *e* are as follows:

Our bird's *name* is Susan.
We put her in a *cage.*
The cage is made of *wire.*

A sample appropriate for finding
words to illustrate the principle of
two vowels coming together might
be:

Susan likes to *eat* often.
We gave her some *wheat* seed.
She has never *laid* an egg.

PRACTICE IN RECOGNIZING SILENT LETTERS

After the concepts of silent vowels
and silent consonants have been developed, as mentioned on page 198,
additional practice in detecting silent
letters may be given by writing on the
chalkboard words similar to those
suggested in the sample below and
asking children to cross out the silent
letter or letters in each one.
A sample of the content for each
activity is given.

Cross out the silent vowels:

fail	apple	reason
people	afraid	hoarse
really	lay	raise
date	throat	ridge
health	beetle	tube
foam	plain	crate
brake	wise	reef
aid	soap	float
feel	heat	leak
fairly	taste	speed
meals	seize	

Cross out the silent consonants:

weight	answer	borough
yellow	blight	main
own	climbing	anti-knock
wrist	thought	tight
knuckle	sign	insight
half	wreck	knelt
check	stuck	bomb
wrapped	catch	through
sought	might	two
struck	often	patch
knife	vehicle	packed
pick	chestnut	frighten
although	foreign	height
stretch		

CHECKING VISUAL AND AUDITORY DISCRIMINATION

If there are children in the classroom whose ability to recognize any
or all of the classifications of phonic
elements and their respective sounds
is doubtful, the teacher may wish to
test these children individually. Sug-

gestions are given for the content and conduct of tests for this purpose.

If a test of initial consonants is desired, write on the chalkboard the following groups of consonants:

h g p f d
c t r w k
s m b n l

Read the words below one at a time and have the child select the consonant with which each word begins: *bed, cow, dog, fish, goat, horse, kite, leaves, monkey, nuts, pen, rake, soldier, top, window, hill, log, past, dishes, side, wait, tiger, rest, basket, feather, go, kick, mop, nest.*

In checking the final consonants, pronounce a word. Ask the child to listen to the beginning sound and then name one or more words that end with the same sound. Suggested words to use are: *bell, dig, far, girl, keep, late, move, nest, pill, race, same, told.*

In checking blends, speech sounds, and hard and soft *c* and *g* write on the chalkboard the following speech sounds and consonant blends: *th, ch, qu, sp, sn, sh, wh, st, sm, sw, thr, spr, str.* Read to the child words that begin with the different sounds. After you read each word, ask the child to select from the chalkboard the blend or speech sound with which that word begins. Repeat with the other words. Suggested words to use are: *chore, think, shirt, wheel, quick, swim, snow, stove, smart, spin, spread, throw, straight.*

Proceed similarly with the initial blends *dr, tr, gr, pr, cl, pl, br, fr, cr, sl, bl.* Suggested words to use are: *bridge, trick, drop, crab, freckle, great, proud, cloud, play, plow, slip, blaze.*

Check in the same way these final speech sounds: *th, sh, ch, nk, ng, ck.* Suggested words to use are: *song, teeth, catch, drink, pick, bush.*

Proceed similarly in reviewing hard and soft *g* and *c*. These words may be used: *giant, game, gentleman, go, get, coast, carry, cent, city, cabin, cup.*

If the teacher wishes to test a group of children who can write, she can check their recognition of blends, speech sounds, hard and soft *g* and *c* as described below:

Have the children write four headings on their papers:

First two letters   First three letters   g   c

Ask them to write under the first heading the two letters of the first sound in words which you will read to them. Read all the words listed above for review which would come under this heading.

Ask them to write under the second heading the three letters of the first sound in each of these words as you pronounce them: *strange, spread, throw.*

Then pronounce the words with hard and soft *g*, having them write *hard g* or *soft g* under the appropriate heading according to the sound of the *g* in the word.

Proceed similarly in testing *hard c* and *soft c*.

Practice and Maintenance in Using Structural Analysis

The words used within the descriptions of the various procedures below are, of course, listed simply for illustrative purposes only. The teacher who selects any of these procedures for use with a particular group of children will use words that the children are meeting functionally in their own daily reading.

COMPOUND WORDS

1. *Using cards.* One of the most effective ways of giving practice in identifying whole word units within compound words is through the use of cards containing the compound words and cards containing their separate components.

Select eight or ten compound words to which the children have been introduced. Manuscript duplicate copies of each compound word in large letters on strips of cardboard about 18 x 4 inches.

Hold up one of the copies saying, "This is *fireman.* I am going to cut the word into two parts and see what we have." Cut the card, holding up the two parts of the word, which the children read separately. There are now three separate cards for the compound word:

> fireman
> fire man

Pass out to the children the smaller cards upon which are printed the single words, such as *fire, man, cow, boy,* and so on. Hold up a large card upon which is printed one of the compound words, such as *fireman* or *cowboy.* As the compound words are held up, each pupil who has one of the smaller words runs up, says his word, and holds it in the appropriate place under the large card. The class then tells what the entire word is. The activity continues in this way.

As a later step, dispense with the large cards, on which the compound words are written as a whole, and use only the smaller cards containing the component words of the compound.

Distribute these cards, one to each child. Ask a child to stand and hold his card up before the other children. The other children look at their cards and the one who finds that he has a word to go with the word held up, comes and places his card by the side of the other card. (It may go before or after the word held up.) For example, the child who first holds up a card may have the word *with;* the child who has *out* comes up and places his card beside the other card, thus making the word *without.* Each child reads his word and the class tells what the "big" word is. The children should, of course, understand that the two words they put together must make a real word—it must make sense.

This activity may well serve the double purpose of aiding in the identification of words in compound words in general and of giving practice on troublesome sight words in particular. As an example: The teacher passes out the separate cards for *some, body, time, thing, where, my, him, her, self.* A child holds up the word *some;* four other children may come up, each having one of these cards: *time, thing, body, where.* Each in turn holds his card beside *some,* making the words *sometime, something, somebody, somewhere.* The children looking on read the words as they are made.

2. *Dividing compound words with marks.* A variety of marking techniques may be used in giving practice in the analysis of compound words. Select the words from material that is being read or that is about to be read. Write the words on the chalkboard and call upon different children to indicate the two words by some marking plan described below. Different plans may be used upon different occasions, or a variety of marking plans may be used upon any one occasion.

Have the children:

Draw a box around each of the words as ⬚sail⬚ ⬚boat.⬚

Draw a circle around each word as ⟨pop⟩⟨corn⟩

Underline each word separately as <u>side</u> <u>walk.</u>

Draw a line between the two words as bee | hive.

Connect the parts of compound words in opposite columns by drawing a line from one part to the part that goes with it, as:

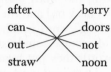

after   berry
can   doors
out   not
straw   noon

INFLECTIONAL ENDINGS

In conducting any of the activities below the teacher should make up her own list of words consisting of those that the children are meeting and with which they need help. In case of word activities not accompanied by sentences, it is suggested that the children make up sentences using the words with inflectional endings that are given practice.

1. Have children compare pairs of words, telling how they are different and how their meanings are changed.

toy   hen   boat   cat   girl
toys   hens boats cats girls

2. Place two headings and a mixed list of words on the chalkboard:

ing   ed

picked, pushed, chewing, looking showing, opened, crossing, marched.

Have the children organize the words under the appropriate headings.

3. Place a list of modified words on the chalkboard and ask the children to box "the main word" in each one; or have children circle the endings that have been added.

4. Place different headings on the chalkboard, together with a list of root words. Children are to say (or write) each word under each heading, adding the ending in the heading to the word. Example:

ing   ed   s
walk, play, jump, call, work

5. Write a list of variants on the chalkboard. Have the children read them and tell what the root word is in each one. The teacher may write the root words, or ask the children to do so if they are able.

sending _____
roared _____
boxes _____
pointed _____
galloping _____
barrels _____

PREFIXES AND SUFFIXES

As in all other cases the particular prefixes and suffixes on which the children are given practice should be chosen from their current reading material.

1. Pupils may add prefixes or suffixes to words and tell or write how the added element changes the meaning of the word. Examples are given below.

Prefixes:

happy _____ happy   not happy
successful _____ successful   not successful
willing _____ willing   not willing
true _____ true   not true
wise _____ wise   not wise
fair _____ fair   not fair

Suffixes:

art	art _____	one who practices art
organ	organ _____	one who plays an organ
balloon	balloon _____	one who flies a balloon
real	real _____	one who thinks realistically
harp	harp _____	one who plays a harp
humor	humor _____	one who has humor
special	special _____	one who specializes in something
journal	journal _____	one who writes for a journal

2. Children may give orally or write prefixed or suffixed words to match definitions, as:

Prefixes:

un—not

trans—across

mis—wrong or wrongly

much too bold _____

not sold for enough _____

across the continent _____

out—beyond or to be removed

over—too or too much

under—under or not enough

not able _____

a wrong deed _____

a view over something _____

Suffixes:

ful—full of

ment—result or process of

less—without

er—one who

one who plants _____

without a father _____

in a close manner _____

pail filled with water _____

en—to make or to be made of

ness—state of being

ist—one who does a certain thing

ly—in a manner

one who plays a harp _____

made of wood _____

state of being sweet _____

process of governing _____

3. The above activity may be varied by asking children to add a prefix or suffix to a word to make it convey the meaning of a given definition, as:

Prefixes:

in—into, not

circum—around

ex—out of, from

_____port: to send out of the port

_____press: to send out, away

_____navigate: to sail around

_____debtedness: to be in debt

_____scribe: to write or draw around

      something

_____ability: not having ability

Suffixes:

al—pertaining to

ward—turning to, direction of

able—given to, tending toward

fraction_____: pertaining to fractions

west_____: toward the west

home_____: toward home

intention_____: pertaining to an intention

change_____: given to change

peace_____: tending toward peace

4. Filling in blanks in sentences with prefixed or suffixed words is a meaningful activity. Examples are given:

un, mis, trans, out, over, under

fed	wit	time	planted
formed	laid	view	ground
current	directed		

The horse was very thin. It was because he had been _____.
Many plants in the desert will not live when _____ to other parts of the country.
The swift stream had a deep _____.
The soldiers made their way into the city through an _____ passage.
Hal went to the top of the mountain where he could get a good _____ of the country.
Tom's letter never reached the person to whom he wrote, because it was _____.
Jack's father was late getting home last night. He worked _____.
In many of the old fables, one animal tried to _____ another.

5. Changing a root word by adding to it as many prefixes or suffixes as possible is an activity enjoyed by children. Examples are given:

reload	imitates	imitation
unload	imitated	imitative
preload	imitating	imitatively
	imitator	imitativeness
	imitable	

Children should be asked to give orally or write sentences containing each of the changed forms.

CONTRACTIONS

In reviewing the contraction *he's*, a teacher wrote on the chalkboard a sentence that had something to do with a story the children had been reading: *The little bird will think he is in a tree.* She then asked the children for a shorter way to say *he is* and replaced *he is* with *he's*. She then had them match these phrases and contractions:

| it's | that is | he's | how is |
| that's | it is | how's | he is |

Finally, she wrote on the chalkboard the words and sentences below and had the children substitute a contraction for each of the italicized phrases.

how's   he's   it's   that's
Pat said, "*It is* a very good nest."
Janet said, "*That is* a mockingbird."
Pat said, "*He is* a nice pet."
Janet said, "*How is* the little bird going to eat?"

Another way in which practice can be given is to have children match contractions and the words for which they stand in a mixed list of this type:

could not	wasn't
had not	haven't
was not	couldn't
have not	hadn't
is not	isn't
does not	shouldn't
would not	aren't
must not	wouldn't
should not	mustn't
are not	doesn't

After drawing lines connecting phrases and contractions that belong together, the children may be asked to read sentences connected with their experiences or reading material in which they replace phrases with contractions. The following sentences were written after the children had visited a farm where there was a donkey, and phrases were replaced with contractions.

At first the boys *could not* ride Tricky.
Susan *did not* fall from Tricky.
Tricky *is not* a beautiful beast.
The children *have not* been sorry they visited Tricky.
Tom said, "Tricky *is not* a bad donkey."

In working with older children the teacher may read contractions and ask the children to write the words for which they stand, and vice versa.

SYLLABICATION

Recognizing Syllabic Units

The teacher may use these patterns in giving as much practice as is necessary. She will of course use words with which the children are working currently in reading and other subjects.

1. Have children respond to questions and lists as indicated.

	How Many Sounded Vowels?	How Many Syllables?
main	_____	_____
twins	_____	_____
branch	_____	_____
Benjamin	_____	_____
complete	_____	_____
historical	_____	_____

How many syllables can you hear?

get _____	dipper _____	grownup _____
happen _____	crack _____	handful _____
multiply _____	Columbus _____	paragraph _____

Do silent vowels count?

	How many vowels are silent?	How many vowels are sounded?	How many syllables are in the word?
rose	_____	_____	_____
wave	_____	_____	_____
huge	_____	_____	_____
sail	_____	_____	_____
coast	_____	_____	_____
beam	_____	_____	_____

Write the right word in the sentence below:
The only vowel that counts when you are deciding on the number of syllables is the vowel that is _____.

2. The riddle technique in auditory identification of syllables is enjoyed by children. Teacher and children may make up such riddles as this:

There are two syllables in my name. I am a bird. I come early in the spring. I have a red breast. What am I?

Children supply the answer.

Dividing Between Words in Compounds

The teacher may initiate practice in using this technique in some such manner as this:

"Now we are going to learn to divide words into syllables. There are several guides that you can use in deciding where to divide a word. One of the easiest guides is the one that can be used in working with compound words. You always divide compound words between the two words. Each word is a syllable. Sometimes one or perhaps two of the words in a compound word is made up of two or more syllables within itself. But you are always safe in dividing between the complete words as a starting point.

Here are some words from a story that you have just been reading. I am going to divide the first word by drawing a line between the two words, which really are two syllables. You may divide the other words in the same way."

bake|shop	township	runaways
horseback	withdrawn	upset
nowadays	halfway	within
watchman	northwest	snowshoes

Continued practice of this type can be given with compound words selected from the children's reading.

Children may also be given duplicated lists of compound words to divide.

Upon occasion they may select compound words from books they are using, copy them and divide them into syllables.

Dividing Between Double Letters

One teacher began practice on this procedure as follows:

"Another easy guide is one that works with double-letter words. When a word has double consonants within it, you always break it into syllables between the double consonants. The second consonant is always silent. So we just cross off the second consonant."

She continued, "I have written some words that I took out of something you have been reading. I have divided the first word and crossed out the silent second consonant in the double-letter group. You may do the same thing with the rest of the words." The words used in this case were:

message	current	suppose
differ	saddle	correct
happen	carry	support
appeal	success	oppose

Repeated practice of this type may be given at the chalkboard or through the use of duplicated lists containing words which children will meet in reading which they will do in the immediate future.

Frequently invite children to compile their own lists of double-consonant words from current reading material, and divide the words into syllables.

Dividing Prefixed Words

In one case a teacher introduced practice on the use of this technique as follows:

"If a word has a prefix, your starting point is to divide the word between the prefix and the root. The prefix must contain a sounded vowel, and the root must contain a sounded vowel. So you may be sure that each of these parts of the word is a syllable. I have placed some words on the chalkboard that contain prefixes. I have divided the first word between the prefix and the root. You may divide the others in the same way.

The words used in this situation were: *discuss, explain, unless, exchange, receive, inquire, enlarge.*

Additional practice may be given functionally whenever an occasion presents itself, and also through the use of duplicated lists or lists which the children compile.

Dividing Suffixed Words

Practice in the use of this technique was initiated by one teacher in this manner:

The teacher explained that "In words that have a suffix, a syllable division may be made between the root word and the suffix. The root word has one or more sounded vowels and the suffix has a sounded vowel. So of course the root word has one or more syllables and the suffix is a syllable. If there are two or three suffixes in a word, each one of them is a syllable, so in that case you divide between each of the suffixes as well as between the root word and the first suffix.

She continued, "I have divided the first word in the list on the chalkboard. You may divide the others, just at the suffixes, nowhere else." The words used in this particular development were *different, dangerous, government, blockade, freedom, statement.*[1]

As in all of the other cases, additional practice may be given through chalkboard work, duplicated lists, and pupil-compiled lists.

ACCENT

Usually additional practice is necessary after the initial development of the concept of accent and interpretation of accent marks.

Application of the development both of primary and secondary accents should be made by direct work with the dictionary itself. Following development of the primary accent, children may look up several familiar words to note the accent mark and test its affect. They may then look up some *new* words to ascertain what help the accent mark gives them in pronouncing these words. Similarly, they may make dictionary application in looking up words containing both primary and secondary accents.

Children needing additional practice may be asked to place the accent mark on familiar words on the chalkboard or at their seats with the use of duplicated or pupil-compiled lists.

Pupils enjoy pronouncing words with the accent placed after different syllables. This helps them to see what effect the accent mark has on a syllable. In conducting such an activity the teacher may write pairs of two-syllable words on the chalkboard and

[1] The teacher should explain, however, that in some cases it is easier to pronounce a word when the preceding consonant is attached to the suffix as in *re al is tic.* In such cases exception should be made.

have pupils place the accent mark after different syllables and pronounce them according to the accent mark, as:

express′	num′ber	cir′cle	magnet′
ex′press	number′	circle′	mag′net

The youngsters might be informed that some words really are pronounced with the accent on different parts according to their usage in a sentence, such as: *per′fect, perfect′; in′crease, increase′; ex′pert, expert′; com′pact, compact′.* They may use these and other words of this type in sentences, giving the appropriate accent according to usage.

USING DICTIONARY AIDS IN PRONUNCIATION

Interpreting Diacritical Marks

Some teachers have found the procedures described below helpful in giving practice on the diacritical markings of a small group of sounds at one time.

The teacher explains the marks of, let us say for example, long *a*, short *a*, long *e*, short *e*, long *i*, and short *i* by writing a key for these particular sounds on the chalkboard, as:

long ā—a as in made
short ă—a as in cat
long ē—e as in me
short ĕ—e as in pen
long ī—i as in mile
short ĭ—i as in bit

She then may ask the children to give her a list of words that have either one or the other of the two sounds of *a*. She writes the words as the children give them and asks them to direct her in placing the right mark over the *a*.

Later the teacher may pronounce several words containing long or short sounds of *a*, *e*, and *i*, letting different children write and mark the words on the chalkboard one at a time.

At another time she may pronounce a list of words which the children are to write on paper; they later mark them and check their own markings by looking up the words in the dictionary.

Similarly, the teacher may proceed with the two sounds of *e* and *i*. On other occasions she may use like procedures with other sounds, such as *ă, â, ä, à;* the *schwa* sound of *a*, as in *another, amoeba* (marked differently in different dictionaries); and the other sounds of *e, i, o,* and *u.*

In all this work it is highly desirable, of course, that the words used should be selected from the children's immediate reading and that the results be applied directly in helping them with the pronunciation problems they are encountering at the time that the practice is given. Continuous application of these skills when looking up new words in the dictionary is, of course, the end point of all this practice.

22

Practice and Maintenance Activities in Getting Meanings

In Chapter 9, "Getting Meanings in Reading," an example of a procedure to use in introducing each of the growth areas is given. Children, of course, need much more practice than that offered by initial development. The most effective practice probably results from discussion concerning a selection in which the different skills are used naturally. Additional practice may be provided in more direct ways. For the teacher who wishes to vary her procedures, several additional suggestions are offered in this section.

Additional Literal Comprehension Activities

A variety of literal comprehension responses may be called for in connection with the same selection. Samples of various types of responses used in connection with four different selections are presented on page 560. In all cases the answers were given directly in the text on which the activities were based.

1. Responses asked for in connection with a story in which two children visited a jungle country with their mother and father were:

a. List the main characters in this story. You may use your book.
b. Write the names of four foods that grew in the clearing.
c. Write a sentence telling how far the talking drums could be heard.
d. Copy the sentence that tells how tall the pygmies were.
e. Complete the following:
The monkey played two very funny tricks. She _____ to the top of the window blind and sat there chattering as though she were at home in the _____. Later she opened Mother's box of _____ and dropped a great deal on the floor.

2. Requested responses in regard to the experiences of a boy and his mother in Switzerland were:

a. _____ and _____ were spending the summer in Switzerland.
b. Write a sentence telling the names of the sounds they heard one night.
c. Write on a paper summer, autumn, winter, spring. Under the name of each season write some kinds of work done by Swiss farmers during that particular season.
d. Write five ways in which electricity helps the Swiss people.
e. What sport did Sepp like best of all?
f. What four words help you to get a picture of the Alps?

3. A series of factual questions based on specific sentences were asked in connection with a selection concerning Leif the Lucky:

Find a sentence in the story that best answers each of these questions. Prepare to read each answer to the class.

a. Where did Leif live?
b. Why did King Olaf like Leif?
c. What did King Olaf ask Leif to tell the people of Greenland?
d. Why wouldn't Eric become a Christian?
e. Why did Leif want Eric to go with him to explore the new land?
f. What seemed strange to the Vikings in this new land?
g. Why did Leif call the country Vinland?
h. Why didn't Leif go back to Vinland?
i. Why were other settlers unsuccessful?
j. Why do many people think that Columbus was the first explorer to reach America?

4. Practice in literal comprehension was given in connection with a selection dealing with dinosaurs through drawing activities as suggested below.

a. Draw the dinosaur described in the story. Write a number above the dinosaur showing how many feet long it was.
b. Draw four other animals that lived at the same time that the dinosaur lived.
c. Draw a piece of land in which dinosaurs might have lived in early times. Draw a picture of the same land after it changed in ways that were not suitable for dinosaurs to live.

Additional Interpretation Activities

As in the case of "Additional Literal Comprehension Activities," space will not be given to present the text upon which the activities are based. The reader can probably grasp the nature of the text accompanying each question. The questions in themselves may suggest a few of the many different types of approaches which may be used to stimulate children's *thinking* in connection with their reading. The questions are unrelated, being based on several different selections.

Do you think the things mentioned in this story really happened? Why?

Do you think that this story would make a good play? Why?

What did Mr. Green mean when he said, "Sometimes accidents bring unlooked-for blessings"?

Do you think the boy's father should have been angry? Why?

Would you like to have had some other ending to the story? If so, what?

Why does the story say that Balmat's heart felt "as heavy as the heaviest cheese"? Have you ever felt this way? How would you describe your feelings?

What do you think the Indians did from the time they left Tom's house until they attacked Fort Hunter?

Which experience would you rather have had, Ted Brown's airplane flight or Peter Linton's dog-team trip? Why?

What qualities did Ted have that made him a good sportsman?

How would you describe Mr. Putnam's manner when he saw the twins?

What did Suzy do that showed that she was clever? That she had great strength?

Would you have wanted to go with the miners if you had been Otah? Why?

Was Thorpin faithful to his work? What makes you think so?

The story says Guy couldn't scream because there was no breath in his lungs. Was that the real reason? What do you think the real reason was?

At what point in the story do you think the pilot began to be sorry that he complained about Chip's ride? Why?

The story said that Lobo had no "trail experience." What did this mean?

What would you like to know about early locomotives that this story does not tell?

Compare the two birds, Sampson and Don Pedro. Which did you like better? Why?

How can you account for the change in Harsha's attitude toward the boys?

Luther Burbank was surprised when money came pouring in. What does this tell you about his purpose for carrying on experiments?

What did the author mean when he wrote about "the red monster that roared hungrily to the south"?

At what point did you realize that the spider was going to play a trick?

What is Jerry's purpose in telling the story, do you think? Is she sharing an experience with Grace? Or does she have some other motive? If so, what?

What are some of the features of this story that make it "a tall tale"?

Did you get a picture of Mary as you read the story? Describe the picture.

What did Stuart's discussion of Tom tell you about Tom's character?

Do you think there was any significance in mentioning that Bob had a little white scar near his left eyebrow? If so, what?

Can you give a reason why Steve and Jimmy lost track of each other a year or two after Bob left New York?

What is the significance of the title of this story?

Additional Critical Reading Activities

Some of the activities suggested below can be used effectively in the upper grades:

1. Ask the children to bring to class newspapers from different publishers; then have them compare several re-

ports of the same event and note the variations. Much worthwhile discussion will ensue. Guide them in evaluating the newspaper's reputation for containing "uncolored reports" and on the writer's reputation for presenting facts accurately. Encourage spirited discussion as the children pick out statements which they think are opinions and statements which they think are facts.

2. Invite the pupils to bring in articles from the various columnists, and discuss each one in terms of personal opinion versus facts, biases, radical ideas, and attempts at sensationalism. The same procedure can be used with magazine articles, pamphlets, and books.

3. Encourage a pupil to express an opinion on material read; then ask him to defend this opinion by showing how the material is related to it.

4. Find differing views on a subject and discuss which are most valid and why.

5. Develop an idea and have pupils find relevant and irrelevant information and valid and invalid information concerning the idea.

6. List authorities in specific areas and discuss whether their writing should be accepted or not. Determine why or why not.

7. Develop criteria with the class, such as author's background, position, experience with the subject, prejudices, style of writing, and date of publication for use in determining the competence of the author.

8. Hold panel discussions with students presenting various views on the validity of different opinions.

23

Practice and Maintenance Activities
for Use in Developing Study Skills
in Content Areas

Several suggestions are given below for practice activities to supplement class development and discussion. These suggestions are offered only as samples of possibilities. The teacher may glean ideas from these samples to use in preparing her own materials related to the content which the children are studying at any particular time.

Selection and Evaluation

FIRST GRADE

During the first grade period children may work both with pictures and with reading symbols. They may engage in activities of the following types:

1. Select from several pictures on the chalk ledge one that represents a word, phrase, or sentence held up by the teacher (or vice versa).

2. Select, upon request, specified words and phrases in context in their books.

3. Select words and phrases to answer questions and complete sentences.

4. Select statements on the basis of whether they are true or false.

5. Select from given lists the correct answers to riddles.

6. Select statements they should try to remember because they give such important information.

7. Select pertinent bits of information needed in connection with construction work or other class activities.

SECOND AND THIRD GRADES

As children pass on into the second and third grades, they are capable of participating in selection and evaluation experiences of higher levels. They may continue to select phrases, sentences, paragraphs, and stories of increasing difficulty in terms of a variety of specific purposes. In addition they may participate in activities of the types indicated below.

1. Select portions of context which express a specific idea.

2. Select a paragraph in terms of its importance.

3. Select the most important thought in an informative selection.

4. Find answers to specific questions in informative articles.

5. Select and read materials pertaining especially to certain problems or interests.

MIDDLE GRADES

In the fourth, fifth, and sixth grades, children should continue to have many selection and evaluation experiences of all the types previously mentioned in connection with the reading which they do in all of their subjects. In addition, they are now ready for, and should have specific development of and practice in more complex types of selection and evaluation such as indicated below.

1. Find the main idea of a paragraph together with its supporting details.
2. Select and evaluate statements which:
   a. support a conclusion or generalization
   b. prove a point
   c. answer a leading question requiring judgment
   d. lead to a decision in regard to statements of fact versus opinion.
3. Select ideas to evaluate critically:
   a. truth of statements
   b. significance of incidents
   c. validity of facts.

Organization

Practice in the skill of organizing what is read may be given in some of the ways suggested below, adapted by the teacher, of course, to meet her own situation.

FIRST GRADE

1. Pupils at this stage may arrange sentences in the wall chart in the order in which the events in a chart or reader story took place.

2. They may group together words representing a given classification, as *toys, animals, people.*

3. They may classify ideas; for example, after reading about a park, the teacher may place on the chalkledge the words birds, train, girls, baby, doll, boats, Mother, store, tree, chair, boys. Then she may write on the chalkboard, "In the Park," "Not in the Park." Pupils classify the words.

4. After reading an easy science book children may classify living things or objects as "Animals that Have Fur" and "Animals that Do Not Have Fur."

5. In addition to classifying words, phrases, and sentences for a variety of purposes, first grade children may retell science or social studies text they have read, being careful to observe the exact sequence of processes or events, as: "Tell just what the children did in their experiment in planting beans in the order in which they did the different things," or "Just how did the Indians make their headbands?"

6. They may search for as many selections as they can find about *boats* or *rabbits* or some other topic of interest.

SECOND AND THIRD GRADES

In second and third grades, experiences in organizing reading content should take on forms and purposes which are even closer to those found in study situations in content fields.

1. Children at this stage may select and organize simple bits of information under a specific heading or in answer to a question.

2. They may organize in sequence steps, events, and incidents selected from increasingly difficult content.

3. They may select words from given lists and classify them under appropriate headings.

4. They may select and organize in a written list all items in a given selection that belong under a particular heading.

5. They may classify in sequence the steps of some process described within an informative article.

6. With guidance they may begin summarizing activities, such as choosing for a short section of content an appropriate title from a list of three or four appropriate titles; formulating one, two, or three summarizing paragraphs giving the gist of a selection; formulating a summarizing sentence for each of several short parts of a selection.

MIDDLE GRADES

If the organization skills have been nurtured all through the primary grades, then children in the middle grades should have no trouble in taking several advanced steps of the type which will be needed in their future study activities. During this period the teacher should develop and give practice in such organizing activities as indicated below.

1. Listing in sequence the steps leading up to an event, climax, undertaking, or preparation of a finished product.

2. Placing events in the right sequence when reading historical materials.

3. Classifying products, industries, or land features in regard to certain locales when reading geographical material.

4. Organizing facts to support a conclusion.

5. Finding and bringing together information from several sources as it has a bearing on some specific topic or problem.

6. Taking notes and organizing them to give the gist of a selection.

7. Reading, making, and using outlines of material read.

8. Summarizing a selection in a paragraph or in a sentence.

9. Organizing facts gleaned from reading in tabular form, graphs, and charts.

Recall Activities

Samples of possible activities are given by grade levels. The teacher will of course use her judgment in adapting those which are appropriate for certain children.

FIRST GRADE

1. Drawing pictures to show items mentioned in text is useful in providing practice in recall. Children may be given help in selecting and remembering items in a short section of content for the purpose of drawing pictures, for example:

> You may draw pictures of all the things that Tommy got for his birthday. Glance through the story to find the names of all of the different presents (selection and evaluation) and tell me the names as you find them. Now close your books and see if you can tell the names of all of the presents. All right, now draw pictures of all Tommy's presents.

2. Pictures may be drawn to illustrate a question based on information, as "What kind of a boat did the Indians use?" Such a question gives practice in recalling details, and the resulting pictures indicate how well details have been grasped and retained.

3. Pupils may draw pictures to show how well they have understood and remembered concepts. After reading a section on *Wind* in their first-grade science book, discussion might take place in regard to how wind affects trees, bushes, leaves on the ground, kites, people, and other things mentioned in the text. The teacher may then suggest that the pupils draw a picture to show how the wind affects people and all the objects mentioned. Reference to the text may be necessary for practice in recalling the items before drawing the picture.

Some other types of activities which may be used to give first grade children experience in remembering what they read are as follows:

4. Picking out and fixing in mind the speeches of characters for a dramatization.

5. Recalling the events of a social studies story as the teacher writes the sentences which they dictate on the chalkboard.

6. Recalling directions for carrying out some class activity.

The directions may be written on the chalkboard, the children being asked to fix them in mind, and then to carry them out after the directions have been erased.

7. Selecting words or phrases to answer questions and recalling them.

SECOND AND THIRD GRADES

1. Recalling factual details, of science, social studies or health information, in answering questions or in making multiple-choice, completion, or true-false responses.

2. Recalling information needed in furthering a class project or needed in solving a class problem or in giving an oral report to the class.

3. Writing short informative reports based on something they have read.

4. Verifying exact recall of facts. After making recall responses they should frequently be asked to reread and check the accuracy of their statements.

MIDDLE GRADES

Give children directions such as these:

1. Reread the selection. Prepare to report to the class facts about "The Railroad Track." Try to pick out these facts as you read and memorize them.

2. Take notes on this selection. Use them to guide you as you practice reproducing the information in the selection. Do this until you can give an account of the information accurately and well.

3. Reread the selection on Hawaii and prepare to report to the class facts you have learned about a *luau*. Take notes, and underline the important words as an aid to memorizing points you wish to report.

4. Try memorizing the characteristics of the arteries and those of the veins. Use the "whole" method.

Arteries
Carry blood *from* the heart
Have thick, tough, elastic walls
Carry oxygen and food to cells
Force of heart and contracting of arteries keeps blood flowing forward
Are usually placed deep for protection

Veins
Carry blood *to* the heart
Have thinner walls than arteries
Carry waste materials from cells
Valves keep blood from flowing backward; contracting of body muscles helps push blood forward
Some are placed deep but many are close to surface

5. Make a list of important dates which you have come in contact with while reading about the Revolution. Arrange them in order and write the event which took place on each of these dates. Try to memorize these events and dates in order as one led to the other. Memorize by saying the entire group over and over and by thinking how one event led to another, rather than trying to memorize just one event and date at a time. Your teacher will call for these dates again within a week to see how many of them you have remembered. She will call for them again several times before the year is over.

Locating Information

ALPHABETICAL ORDER

Primary Grades

1. Working with sections of the alphabet in order: "Who can tell me what the first six letters are?" Write the letters *a, b, c, d, e, f,* on the chalkboard. Have children who need the practice read the letters. Erase and rearrange the letters. Ask children to tell in what order to put the letters. Erase one of the letters. Ask what letter goes in that space. Repeat with variation.

2. Children may find all the words in a mixed list that begin with *b*, all that begin with *f*, and so forth.

3. Arrange a mixed list of letters alphabetically; similarly a mixed list of words. Have the children tell you the order in which to write them.

house boy apple fat dog cat go every

apple, boy, cat, dog, every, fat, go, house

4. Crossing out of lists of words, those which are not in alphabetical order.

and, big, ~~hat~~, can, do, ~~man~~, eat, ~~long~~

5. Filling blanks with words in alphabetical sequence. Children may select from several words a particular word needed in filling in a blank space in lists of words alphabetically arranged, as:

animal	errand	ignite
bake	_____	_____
cobweb	garden	_____
_____	_____	lantern

feather, join, hustle, kindle, drug

567

1. Write the alphabet in groups of halves. In which half does each of the letters belong? Write *first* or *second* after each letter.

h_____ e_____ n_____ q_____
t_____ p_____ a_____ v_____
f_____ w_____ i_____ j_____
l_____ d_____ o_____ y_____
b_____ r_____ k_____ s_____
m_____ c_____ z_____ u_____
                        g_____

2. Write the alphabet in quarters with six letters in the first group, eight letters in each of the two middle groups, and six in the last group.

In which quarter of the alphabet does each of the following belong? Write the words first, second, third, or fourth after each letter.

r_____ b_____ e_____ v_____
k_____ y_____ u_____ j_____
g_____ s_____ c_____ m_____
n_____ u_____ t_____ f_____

3. Write the letters from *l* to *o*. Write the letters from *p* to *t*. Write the letters from *d* to *k*. Write the letters from *v* to *z*.

4. Write *Before* or *After*:

  a. Does *m* come before or after *l*?
  b. Does *t* come before or after *u*?
  c. Does *k* come before or after *r*?
  d. Does *s* come before or after *r*?
  e. Does *e* come before or after *f*?
  f. Does *n* come before or after *o*?
  g. Does *j* come before or after *i*?
  h. Does *r* come before or after *o*?
  i. Does *l* come before or after *k*?

5. Write in the blanks the letters as they come in the alphabet:

_____ _____ t
_____ d _____
w _____ _____
a _____ c
g h _____

_____ p
i _____ k
_____ m _____
_____ _____ g
_____ v _____

6. The children may play a game as follows: They may be told to hold the dictionary between their two hands, letting it rest on its back on the desk. The teacher names a letter, such as *s* or *d*. The children, judging by its position in the alphabet, try to open their books to the letter. If they find the letter without having to leaf through the pages they are allowed a score of 10. If they come within two letters they score 8, and so on. They may be allowed only a few seconds to find the letter, the time being shortened as they become more proficient. The game continues, each child trying to gain the highest number of points.

7. Another game for recognition of letter placement is a guessing game. One child says, "I am a letter of the alphabet between *f* and *h*. Which letter am I?" The child who first gives the correct answer then asks the others to guess some letter he has in mind.

ALPHABETICAL ARRANGEMENT WITHIN WORDS

1. The children may be asked to see how quickly they can find words in the dictionary by looking for the first two letters in each one as the teacher writes words on the chalkboard. Such words as these may be used: *Africa, emery, guariba, maniac, serpent, triple, shear, giraffe.*

This activity may be repeated as children locate words by examining the first three letters, the first four letters, and so on.

Children may carry out directions with words similar to those in (2) and (3) below.

2. Which word of each pair of

words should appear first in the dictionary:

dilute scientist chuck claw western den stampede chance clean wait

3. Arrange these words in the order in which they would come in the *d* section of the dictionary:

delegate	dynamite	dinosaur
double	dyspepsia	Darwin
Diesel	dabble	diction
donate	destroy	duct

GUIDE WORDS

1. Here are the guide words on page 471 and on page 472 of your glossary. Write the number of the page on which each word in the list appears.

Guide Words
Page 471   abyss carbon
Page 472   Canute Egypt

_____ bazaar _____ dense
_____ anaconda _____ custom
_____ chariot _____ eager
_____ bridle _____ Cabot

2. The guide words on a certain page are *damp* and *dead*. What words from the following list would be on that page?

dinosaurs, dying, darkness, dad, dashed, den, discovery, daylight, divide, discovered.

3. The guide words on page 230 of a glossary are *Egyptian* and *Gritti*. Follow these directions in working with these guide words.

First, list those words found on preceding pages
Second, list those words found on the same page
Third, list those words found on later pages
fiber, iceberg, coyote, hurl, English, afford, guitar, ivory, gamoose, bow, estate, hare, flute, current, graze

1. The teacher may write on the chalkboard dictionary respellings of new words in material that the children are reading currently, and ask them to pronounce the words from their respelled forms.

2. Have the children look up several words in the dictionary and pronounce them from the respellings.

3. Ask the pupils to make a list of difficult words selected from something they are reading, then to the right of each word write the word in its respelled dictionary form. Following this activity all words should be pronounced for checking by the teacher.

CHOOSING THE RIGHT DEFINITION

1. The teacher may have the pupils locate and choose the appropriate dictionary definition for several words which she and they select from pages of text with which they are working. Oral discussion should accompany or follow this activity.

2. Pupils may be asked to write the appropriate definition for each of several words as each appears in the context of a certain sentence.

3. They may also write the number of an appropriate dictionary definition on a blank line placed before a sentence containing an underlined word which is to be looked up as indicated below:

_____ a. Judith thought the new movie was very *tame.*
_____ b. Mr. Fowler grew some *tame* blackberries in his back yard.
_____ c. Sam had a pet owl that was very *tame.*
_____ d. After a long and bitter fight the inhabitants became quite *tame.*

569

4. Pupils may be asked to number their papers with as many numbers as there are definitions for a certain word, then to write a sentence using the word appropriately for each definition.

SYNONYMS AND ANTONYMS

The teacher may have the children copy several sentences, each of which contains a word that has a synonym, and then proceed as follows.

Directions: Find a synonym for the underlined word in each sentence. Cross out the word and write the synonym above it. Then read the sentence to see if there has been any noticeable change in meaning.

The tree surgeon put an application on the trunk of the tree to $\frac{\text{retard}}{\text{delay}}$ its decay.

The plant had a $\frac{\text{strong}}{\text{sturdy}}$ stalk.

Mr. Jones could hardly $\frac{\text{bear}}{\text{endure}}$ the pain in his leg.

Jocko was a very $\frac{\text{smart}}{\text{clever}}$ seal.

Proceed similarly in working with antonyms.

USING AN INDEX

1. Questions relating to items appearing in an index in an available text may be prepared by the teacher, preferably having to do with a topic concerning which the pupils wish to find information. They may be asked to write answers to the questions.

2. The pupils may be asked to arrange items in an index, as follows:

Direction to the pupils: Below you will find three main topics together with their substopics and the pages on which they are discussed. The subtopics are not arranged alphabetically. Write these subtopics under the heading to which they belong in alphabetical order as they would appear in an index.

Communication, 280–82
  printing press, 131, 133, 248, 301
  cable, 132, 305
  telegraph, 134, 302, 305, 309, 371, 406
  radio, 286, 320, 330, 419
  effects of development, 269, 270
  telephone, 131, 273, 376, 422
  wirephoto, 129, 341
Colonial Life in America, 137–48
  self-government in, 61–63, 66–67, 85–89, 95–99, 116–21
  taxation, 73–77, 119, 121
  agriculture, 65–67, 70
  trade, 114–15
  education in, 90–93
  unity among Colonists, 60, 83–84, 78–79
  religious freedom in, 62, 73, 81–82, 117
Canada, 172–82
  Second World War, 179
  War of 1812, 174
  Oregon Treaty, 173
  boundary line, 175, 179
  Sault Ste. Marie Canals, 179
  settled by French, 92–93
  Quebec Act, 68
  relations with United States, 205–209

FINDING KEY WORDS

1. The children may be asked to find and underline key words in several topic sentences, and then to try out their key words in searching for information.

Examples from geographies:

The mining of copper
Manufacturing in the Netherlands
Railroads in the British Isles

Examples from histories:

How Hendrick Hudson happened to

plant the flag of Holland in America

Spanish explorations in South America

Transportation in Colonial Times

Theodore Roosevelt, for President of the United States

Examples from science texts:

Exploring for minerals and rocks

The earth and space

Electricity and magnetism

FINDING AN ENCYCLOPEDIA VOLUME FOR A TOPIC

1. To provide practice in deciding upon the volume in which to look for a given topic, the teacher may draw a diagram of a set of volumes and ask children to locate lists of topics as indicated below.

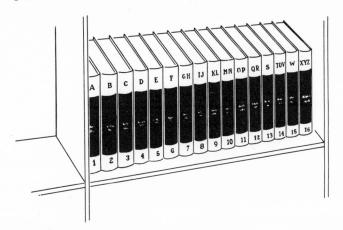

Directions to children: See how quickly you can find the right volume for each of the topics below. Write the number of the volume in which you think the topic would be discussed in the space to the right of each topic.

a. soil _____

b. England _____

c. forests _____

d. diet _____

e. shells _____

f. navigation _____

g. fish _____

h. oranges _____

i. zinc _____

j. weather _____

k. soap _____

l. boats _____

m. Daniel Boone _____

n. Jonathan Chapman _____

Following Directions

1. Require the pupils to number the consecutive steps when reading directions.

2. Discuss the reasons for the particular sequence indicated.

3. Point out to pupils the value of reading the *entire* set of directions first to obtain a general understanding of purpose and method.

4. Require the pupils in the second more deliberate reading of the directions to determine how the steps in sequence, if followed, will achieve the purpose.

24

Practice and Maintenance Activities
for Increasing Rate

Suggestions for Skimming Practice

Suggestions were given in Chapter 11 for testing rate of reading in working with different types of materials for different purposes, and suggestions were also given for initial practice to increase rate when reading both difficult and easy material for varied purposes. Systematic practice in the different techniques of skimming was not given much attention because such practice is not appropriate for most pupils at elementary level. If the teacher, however, has a few superior readers who would profit by such practice, she may find it helpful to have the suggestions given on the following pages.

These suggestions are given only for the purpose of illustrating procedures which the teacher may use with textbooks in her own classroom or with newspaper articles which she or the children may bring in. Usually children for whom such practice is appropriate can bring in the same copy of a newspaper to use for skimming practice. Articles, television or radio programs, and other types of practice material may also be duplicated for skimming practice.

EXAMPLE [1] OF SKIMMING FOR
MAIN IDEAS

Directions: In the following selection skim for main ideas only and omit everything else.

1. Preview the title.

2. Formulate your purpose for reading the article. For practice purposes, let's agree that you want to read to find the answer to the question, "What was the hoax?"

3. Grasp the main idea in each paragraph as quickly as you can, then sweep your eyes with high speed straight to the next paragraph, grasp the main idea in that paragraph, and so on. Pay no attention to anything but main ideas.

4. Allow yourself a total of one minute. Stop at the end of one minute whether or not you have finished.

5. Take a test based upon main ideas only.

The Famous Fossil Hoax

The hoax of the Wurzburg fossils, a far-reading piece of foolery perpetrated 200 years ago by German university students, ranks in ingenuity with the "Balloon Hoax," the New York Sun "Moon Hoax," and other celebrated practical jokes of history.

The butt of the fossil joke was a serious-minded old professor, Johann Beringer, who held an honorable position as a Doctor of Philosophy and Medicine at Wurzburg University. The doctor, highly respected for his learning and studious habits, was appointed private physician to the reigning Prince Bishop of the old university

---

[1] This example including directions, selection, and test is reproduced from Nila Banton Smith, *Read Faster and Get More From Your Reading* (Englewood Cliffs, N. J.: Prentice-Hall, Inc., 1958), pp. 244–47. The selection "The Famous Fossil Hoax" originally appeared in *The Mentor* (Feb. 1922), pp. 40–42, under the authorship of Leon Augustus Hausman.

---

town. He was distinguished as a scholar and writer in the fields of zoology, botany, and medicine.

Of all the problems then engaging scientific minds, none had caused more contention than the origin and meaning of fossils. It was claimed by some that the creation of fossils was due to an unknown influence of the stars. Another theory explained fossils as the remains of oceanic animals and plants stranded on the land by the Flood. It was not until about 1800 that it was determined that fossils were relics of animal and vegetable life that existed in prehistoric times and had become entombed in rock, in frozen mud, in the beds of rivers, even in the soft gum of cone-bearing trees.

The science of paleontology, or the knowledge of fossils, attracted Professor Beringer. He advanced an original theory that fossils were merely a capricious fabrication of the Creator, placed in the earth to test human faith. He was so keen about this pet notion that some of his pupils at the university could not forbear playing a trick on the old professor.

With the connivance of some of his own colleagues, the students prankishly fashioned "fossils" out of clay and hid them among the rocks of a hillside where they knew Beringer used to roam around on geological exploration. It was not long before the venerable professor chanced upon the fictitious deposits during one of his walks. Completely deceived, overjoyed at his discovery, Beringer hurried back to the university and exhibited the organisms he had found.

The jokers, perceiving with glee the success of their jest, now went further and buried the most fantastic figures their imaginations could suggest. Not content with these, they even buried inscriptions, worked out on "fossil" shells, one of them being the name of God Himself, in Hebrew!

Professor Beringer's elation upon the discovery of these forms knew no bounds. He was now completely convinced of the soundness of his doctrine, and made ready to publish the results.

The semi-religious fervor of the honest old scholar swept all before it. Despite the advice of level-headed friends, he hurried his ponderous work to completion.

And now for the strangest part of the story. The jesters came forward and confessed. They exposed all they had done. To their confusion, Beringer refused to listen. The hoaxers reiterated their statements that the whole thing was a colossal joke. Beringer could not be convinced. He conceived this as a base trick of his adversaries. He suspected them of trying to rob him of the glory of proclaiming his discoveries and establishing the truth of his theory. He hurried into print. His magnum opus appeared!

The entry of the volume into the world of learned literature was heralded by a shout of laughter! The author's name became a byword in the universities of Europe. Some declared his book was only an attempt to fool the scientific world, others set it down as the product of a mind diseased.

Copies of the weighty volume, printed in Latin, bore the title *The Figured Stones of Wurzburg,* and were illustrated with "marvelous likenesses of the hundred figures, or rather, insectiform stones." It was published in Wurzburg in 1726. The pompous dedication, nine pages long, is to Christopher Francis, Prince Bishop of Wurzburg. After the dedication and the preface comes the body of the work, descriptive of Beringer's discovery of the fossils, the manner of their exhumation and examination, the account of the attempt of his colleagues to dissuade him from the work, and the description and significance of the "fossils" themselves.

For a time there was question in some parts of the scholastic world whether or not Beringer's book was of value, a situation that spurred the deceived scientist to greater efforts in his own defense.

But, as the truth became generally established, Beringer himself was finally undeceived. The blow staggered him; he was overwhelmed.

From the pinnacle of learned dictatorship, which he had formerly occupied so securely, he beheld himself tumbled headlong, almost in a night.

In a frenzy he attempted to buy up all copies of his book that had been issued. His most assiduous efforts were futile, however. Finally he surrendered to despair. His life's work was treasured and exhibited by many as an object of ridicule.

The broken-hearted scientist fell ill under the strain and died shortly afterward, with the laughter of the scientific world ringing in his ears.

Even after Beringer's death there was no end to the tragic joke. A bookseller, one Hobhard of Hamburg, seeing an opportunity to make capital out of Beringer's misfortunes, bought up all available copies and not only reissued them, but compiled a second edition which achieved a large circulation.

Check of Understanding of Meaning

1. The hoax of Wurzburg (a) boomeranged on the perpetrators instead of hitting its mark, (b) ranks with the greatest practical jokes of history, (c) brought eventual fortune to the man at whom the joke was aimed, (d) was really not a hoax in the true sense of the word. _____

2. The butt of the joke was (a) a university student, (b) a professor, (c) an astronomer, (d) a minister. _____

3. The science of pal-

eontology is concerned with (a) bacteria, (b) the plants, (c) medicine, (d) fossils.

4. The jokers fashioned their fossils out of (a) soap, (b) wax, (c) clay, (d) wood.

5. The hoax was perpetrated by (a) Beringer's colleagues, (b) students with the connivance of his colleagues, (c) students without the knowledge of his colleagues, (d) none of the foregoing. _____

6. The jokers (a) placed their most fantastic figures on the professor's desk, (b) placed them on a stairway leading to his classroom, (c) buried them in a place where Beringer would discover them, (d) placed them in a glass case containing fossils. _____

7. When Beringer discovered the fossils he (a) was delighted, (b) ignored them, (c) returned them to the person he considered the rightful owner, (d) recognized them as fakes. _____

8. When Beringer was informed about the hoax, he (a) refused to believe it at first, (b) withdrew from the university staff, (c) wrote a public confession and apology, (d) went into seclusion. _____

9. After finding the fake fossils, Beringer (a) punished the jokers, (b) gave lectures on the discovery, (c) published a book, (d) sent articles to a newspaper. _____

10. In the end Beringer (a) convinced others that he was right, (b) received recognition from other scientists, (c) died from the strain that accompanied his discovery of the truth about the fossils, (d) tried to capitalize financially on the sale of his books. _____

Allow 10 points for each correct answer.

Score: _____

EXAMPLE [2] OF SKIMMING FOR DETAILS

Directions: In the next selection you will use a technique for grasping detailed facts about *one* item under a title, ignoring everything else in the article. Skim the pages from top to bottom until you find the paragraph or paragraphs that deal with the details in which you are interested.

Suppose you come across this informative article, "Stalking a Hurricane." You don't care about hurricanes in general, but you are interested in the phenomenon called "the eye of the hurricane," and you want some specific details about it. With this purpose in mind:

1. Skim through the article, using vertical eye movements at your highest speed, until you come upon mention of the "eye of the hurricane." Don't try to read any of the text until you find this section. And don't worry about skipping several paragraphs without knowing what they say.

2. When you find "the eye," slow

[2] This example including directions, selection, and test is reproduced from Nila Banton Smith, *Read Faster and Get More from Your Reading* (Englewood Cliffs, N. J.: Prentice-Hall, Inc., 1958), pp. 244–47. The selection "Stalking a Hurricane" previously appeared in *Science Digest*, Sept. 1953 (reprinted from *Nature*, Aug. 1953) under the authorship of E. John Long.

down, reading and absorbing each detail about the eye of the hurricane and fitting each detail into a pattern of relationships to the main idea and to one another. Do this as fast as you can, grasping all details.

3. Allow yourself no more than one minute for this exercise. If you can do it in less time, so much the better.

4. After you have read for the specified length of time, take the comprehension test which, in this case, is concerned *only* with the eye of a hurricane.

Stalking a Hurricane

Why are there fewer deaths and less property damage from hurriances? Are the "big winds" getting weaker? Or fewer in number?

Not at all. The hurricane remains one of the most powerful forces on earth. During the 1952 hurricane season, six of these colossal whirlwinds roared through the American tropics with momentum enough to carry several of them on into northern areas as the worst storms of the year. But property damage set no records, and no deaths could be attributed directly to any of them.

Yet in 1928 a Florida hurricane took 7,800 lives. At Galveston, Texas, in 1900, a hurricane killed more than 6,000; and as late as 1948 casualties from the big winds were still numbered in scores.

The explanation of reduced casualties and smaller property damage in recent years is, in three words, *better advance warning.* . . .

During the progress of a major hurricane, the Miami Hurricane-Warning Center, for example, issues four "advisories"—weather versions of a wartime communique—daily, based on reports received during the previous six hours. . . .

In the meantime, a search plane has made contact with the enemy. Far ahead through the rain squalls the pilot sees a dark, ominous-looking mass of whirling clouds, mist, and water that seems to reach up into the heavens and stretches fully 30 miles from side to side. . . .

Because a hurricane's safest point of entry is usually its westward side, the plane approaches from the west. And from now on, every 15 minutes information obtained from meteorological instruments and by radar will be radioed to Miami. . . .

After nearly an hour of sampling the air on the fringes of the hurricane, the pilot heads directly into it. The heavy, four-engined ship pitches and yaws, dives and soars again, until its creaking frame seems to be tearing apart. . . .

An interminable quarter hour of this—and suddenly the plane breaks through the storm into the clear. All pitching and tossing ceases, the howling gale quiets as if a valve had shut it off, and bright sunshine pours through the drenched windshield. Down below, the sea shows a few whitecaps, but the whole aspect is one of peace and calm. The transition is so sudden and unexpected that it comes as a shock, even to crews who have experienced it many times.

This strange world, called "the eye of the hurricane," is one of the weirdest, most awesome sights on earth. Its boundary is a vertical curtain of black, reaching from the ocean far up to the open sky above. It is difficult to believe that beyond this ebony cylinder, now 10 to 15 miles in diameter, is a watery chaos, revolving furiously in a counterclockwise direction as it is driven by gales of 180–200 mph.

Strange things have been observed by planes cruising "the eye." Flocks of birds sometimes take refuge there, moving along within the comparative safety of the storm's vortex, which may have a forward motion of only 10 to 15 mph. Ships sometimes seek the eye to ride out the worst of the storm's violence before resuming their course. One plane observed a fishing

boat, with the crew on deck sunbathing, within a hurricane's eye.

As the hurricane-stalking plane crashes around the eye, the "dropsonde" operator goes into action. As the dropsonde, an instrument dropped from the plane by parachute, slowly descends, it automatically records atmospheric pressure, temperature, and humidity of the air, and relays these to the plane by a radio transmitter.

But now the fuel is getting low, so the pilot plunges back into the black wall of the hurricane, choosing the western or "weak" side, where, experience has taught him, a hearty tailwind can be picked up. Fifteen minutes more of furious buffeting, and the tired crew heads for the barn, clipping through squalls that would be bypassed by ordinary pilots.

Check of Grasp of Details

1. The adjectives used to describe "the eye" in the article are (a) black, very dangerous, (b) windy, strange, treacherous, (c) weirdest, most awesome, (d) powerful, terrifying. _____

2. The shape of the eye is (a) square, (b) cylindrical, (c) elliptical, (d) conical. _____

3. The eye is bounded by (a) a black circular band, (b) horizontal black bands, (c) heavy orange lines, (d) a vertical curtain of black. _____

4. The diameter of the eye is (a) approximately 1 mile, (b) approximately 5 miles, (c) approximately 6 miles, (d) 10 to 15 miles. _____

5. The hurricane is driven by gales of (a) 180–200 mph, (b) 40–60 mph, (c) 400–500 mph, (d) 10–20 mph. _____

6. The eye is (a) furiously active, (b) drenched with rains, (c) calm enough so that birds or ships can take refuge in it, (d) cold and snowy. _____

7. The eye (a) has no motion, (b) moves around in circles, (c) moves forward at about 100 mph, (d) may move forward with a motion of only 10–15 mph. _____

8. The first thing the search plane does upon discovering the eye is to (a) fly through it and report its location, (b) fly into it and stay there, (c) avoid it, (d) cruise around it and put the dropsonde into action. _____

9. The functions of the dropsonde are to (a) record the direction and velocity of the wind, (b) record the diameter and height of the eye, (c) record the atmospheric pressure, temperature, and humidity, (d) record the size of the area the hurricane is covering. _____

10. When fuel gets low the search plane leaves the eye on the western side because (a) the plane is facing the sun, (b) the hurricane is strongest in the west, (c) the eye is in the western part of the hurricane, (d) experience has taught the pilot a hearty tailwind can be picked up there. _____

Score 10 points for each correct answer.

Score: _____

EXAMPLE [3] OF GRASPING KEY WORDS

Directions: Grasping key words is another shortcut to rapid skimming for general comprehension. Usually the important ideas are carried largely through nouns, verbs, adverbs, and adjectives. With practice, you can mentally supply less important words without stopping to read each one.

Examples of "less important" words are the articles (*the, an,* and *a*), pronouns (such as *you, your, it, they*), prepositions (such as *in, of, with, to*), and many other words that are not essential in putting across the import of a sentence.

In the following paragraph, the less important words have been omitted. Skim through the key words rapidly. You will find that you have little trouble following the trend of what the author is saying.

My Neighbor the Hippo

_____ mud hut _____ _____ I lived _____ five years _____ British East Africa _____ situated _____ two miles _____ Lake Elmenteita. _____ remote stretch _____ water remains _____ _____ _____ undisturbed _____ white men. Except _____ _____ _____ naked savage _____ spear _____ club, no human being troubles _____ lives _____ _____ _____ waterfowl _____ scarlet flamingoes. I used _____ wander _____ _____ _____ shores because _____ knew _____ _____ depths _____ inhabited _____ hippopotami. _____ certain seasons _____ sunrise _____ sunset _____air would resound _____ _____ _____ _____ bellows.

[3] This example including directions and selection is reproduced from Nila Banton Smith, *Read Faster and Get More from Your Reading* (Englewood Cliffs, N. J.: Prentice-Hall, Inc., 1958), pp. 252–53. The selection "My Neighbor the Hippo" originally appeared in *The Mentor* (June 1922), pp. 30–31, under the authorship of Llewellyn Powys.

Provide additional practice of this kind and urge pupils in their own reading of light material, to take the more advanced step of ignoring the less important words as they skim through, grasping key words only.

USING THE VERTICAL FIELD OF VISION [4]

Give an explanation similar to the following to the pupils. This will introduce you to the highest skill in skimming—using your vertical field of vision. This skill enables you to see two or three words, figures, or phrases above and below the point where your eyes are fixed without moving your eyes up or down. You simply hold your eyes in one place and take in everything within your range of vision, *vertically.*

With Column of Figures. Write the column of figures on the chalkboard and give instructions as follows: First try to see three sets of figures in a vertical column at one glance. (Teacher: Write the column of figures below on the chalkboard.)

In this vertical column look squarely at the middle figures, and read all three figures *without moving your eyes.*

12:15
12:30
12:45

Continue to give practice with other groups of figures, increasing the number of items in a column as it seems advisable.

With Radio or Television Schedules. Have the students bring in radio or television schedules found in

[4] This example including directions, selection, and test is reproduced from Nila Banton Smith, *Read Faster and Get More from Your Reading* (Englewood Cliffs, N. J.: Prentice-Hall, Inc., 1958), pp. 260–61.

their local newspaper. Proceed with instructions similar to the following.

Practice this skill on the radio schedule in your newspaper. This will require using vertical eye movements and vertical field of vision. But you will also have to switch to horizontal eye movements and to your horizontal field of vision.

Suppose you want to find a particular program—say, a news program at around noon. You turn to the radio column of your daily paper. Now, what is the quickest way to find the program?

1. First preview to find the heading that tells you which section is devoted to *daytime programs*.

2. Using the fewest possible vertical eye movements, glance down the columns until you find the time you want.

3. Next glance quickly at the words to the right of the time in search of the one word, *news*.

4. Then with one quick backward fixation, grasp the call letters of the station. All this should take about one second.

With Double-Column Material. To give practice in grasping groups of words and numbers in double-column material this example of instructions, selection, and answers is given.[5]

Directions: Now that you have had some experience in using your vertical field of vision in skimming groups of numbers and words, try using it in a selection consisting of sentences and paragraphs.

Increasing numbers of magazines are using double columns these days. This practice facilitates skimming with vertical eye movements and the vertical field of vision. Often it is possible to sweep the eyes straight down through the middle of a narrow column, taking in the center of two lines at a time. In the great majority of cases, the central section of the lines contains enough words to convey the information in the selection, even though you do not see the words at the sides. If you find that you aren't following the thought at a certain point, you can always glance quickly to the left or right to catch a key word that will complete this meaning. Even if you do have to take a side excursion now and then, you can still cover the selection much more rapidly this way than by reading horizontally, line by line.

1. In the selection below, sweep your eyes straight down through the middle of the column.

2. Gather all the important details you can by reading the center of two lines at one fixation.

3. If you lose the thought at any point, catch a key word with a fleeting left or right glance.

4. Allow yourself exactly five seconds to skim the article in this way.

5. Take the comprehension test after you have finished skimming the selection.

Facts About Hamsters

Hamsters have been increasing in favor as laboratory animals. They're also kept as pets.

Hamsters can be bought from the same sources as white mice. Price is $2.50–$3.00 a pair. Keep your hamsters in a room with a temperature between 55 and 70 F. Keep them in metal cages, or in wooden cages protected on the inside with hardware cloth, to keep them from gnawing their way out. A cage 12 x 15 x 12 inches will house a pair, while a cage 35 x 25 x 15 inches will take care of eight to ten animals. An adult ham-

---

[5] This example including directions, selection, and test is reproduced from Nila Banton Smith, *Read Faster and Get More from Your Reading* (Englewood Cliffs, N. J.: Prentice-Hall, Inc., 1958), pp. 266–67.

ster needs about 10–15 grams of food per day (⅓–½ ounce).

You can breed your animals throughout the year, but most litters are produced between November and May. A female will produce only five or six litters in her lifetime. The gestation period is about sixteen days. The number of young per litter averages about seven.

Hospitals, laboratories, biological-supply houses, schools, and certain other institutions offer the best market for the sale of hamsters. You should assure yourself of such a market before you raise many hamsters to be sold.

Check of Understanding of Meanings

Write "True" or "False" to the left of each statement.

_____ 1. Hamsters are decreasing in favor.

_____ 2. They are bought from the same source as white mice.

_____ 3. The price of a pair of hamsters is from $5.00 to $10.00 per pair.

_____ 4. They may be kept in a metal cage protected with hardware cloth.

_____ 5. One pair should have a cage 40 x 20 x 40.

_____ 6. A hamster needs 10 to 15 grams of food per day.

_____ 7. They produce litters in June and July.

_____ 8. The female produces ten to fifteen litters in a lifetime.

_____ 9. The gestation period is ten days.

_____ 10. You might be able to sell some hamsters to laboratories.

Check your answers with the article itself to find how well your vertical field of vision worked for you.

Index

Memorizing techniques, 321
Mental characteristics:
    of intermediate grade children, 31–33
    of primary children, 30–31
Mental growth, and reading, 28–33
Mental maturity test, 64
Mental Measurement Yearbook, 300
Metaphors, 283
Metronoscope, 360
Metropolitan Readiness Tests, 460
Misrepresentation of natural sounds, 202
Missildine, W. H., 48, 527
Missing words technique, in new-word introduction, 245
Misuses of basal readers, 99
Models and construction projects, in concept building, 294
Modern Montessori Approach, 96–97
Monitorial System, 109
Monroe, Walter S., 310
Montessori, Maria, 96
Montessori Method, 451
Moore, W. S., 310
Morphemes, 94–103
Morrison, Ida E., 64
Movements, body, 365–66
Multiplegrade grouping, 119–20
    in intermediate grades, 119
    in primary grades, 119

Narrative chart, 501
Natural sounds, misrepresentation of, 202
Navarra, John G., 262
Need, immediate, applying phonics to, 209–10
Need for new words, 286–87
Needs, integrative, and ego, 46
Neff, Neal, 117
Negative self-concept, 113
Nelson, Donald, 71
Newark Phonics Experiment, 212
New Castle, Pennsylvania, 87
Newell, Nancy, 47
New England Primer, 4, 189
Newhall, Sydney M., 193–94
New Natura Brevium, 28
News magazines for the classroom, 405–406
Newspaper reading, 402–403
New-word introduction, 73, 88, 96, 242–47
    children's experiences in, 243–44, 247
    direct-question technique, 246
    introductory pictures in, 244–45
    key-sentences technique, 245
    missing-words technique, 245
    phonics in, 247
    structural analysis in, 247
    teacher-prepared material in, 246–47
    teacher's experiences in, 245–46
New words, need for, 286–87
New York Elementary Reading Tests, 382
Nichols, Ralph G., 63
Nongrading, 117–19
    in intermediate grades, 117
    in primary grades, 117

Oaks, Ruth E., 197
O'Donnell, Mabel, 135
Office of Education, U. S., 12

Ohio State University Studies, 262
Olson, Willard C., 34, 134
One-grade classroom, flexibility in, 114
Oral composition, 56, 66, 81
Oral reading, 71, 93, 103
    and interest stimulation, 416–17
    and tape recordings, 15
Organization skills, 315, 564–65
    in arithmetic, 317
    development of, 317–18
    in language, 317
    practice in, 564–65
    in preparatory period, 480
    preview technique in, 316
    in science, 316
    in social studies, 317
Over-expectations:
    of parents, 120
    of peer groups, 120
    of teachers, 120
Overlap words, 342

Pacers, 376
Pacing, 134
Page numbers, finding, 323–24
Panel discussions for parents, 518
Parents, 11, 509–33
    counseling, and interest, 415–16
    demonstrations for, 518–19
    and emotional stability, 527–28
    films for, 519
    giving advice to, 522–33
    group activities with, 517–20
    and health, 524–26
    lectures for, 518
    methods for informing, 520–21
    panel discussions for, 518
    of preschool children, 12
    and preschool reading, 528–30
    and sex differences, 526
    slides for, 519
    tapes for, 519
    techniques of working with, 513–20
    television for, 520
Parker, Edwin B., 399
Parkhurst, Helen, 132–33
Parkins, George A., 361
Parts of books, in locational skills, 328–29
Patriotic emphasis, period of, 4–5
Patterns of speech, 89–93
Peake, Nellie L., 64
Pepper, Roger S., 359
Perception:
    auditory, 41–42
    and comprehension, 93
    visual, 41–42, 172–74
Perceptual cues:
    and experience charts, 492–93
    in word identification, 41
Perceptual growth, and reading, 40–42
Period of application of scientific investigations, 6–7
Period of cultural emphasis, 5–6
Period of German-Pestalozzian emphasis, 5
Periodic testing, 118
Period of patriotic emphasis, 4–5
Period of religious emphasis, 4

Reading instruction (*Cont.*)
  parents' attitude toward, 511
  at preschool age, 448–52
  and technology, 16–19
Reading intelligence tests, 30
Reading magazines, 403–406
Reading material:
  availability of, 413–14
  child-written stories as, 147
  in classroom library, 427–28
Reading maturation, 7, 11, 25, 26, 124, 454–66
  ascertaining, teacher observation and interview, 460–61
  and emotional maturation, 457, 464–65
  and environmental experience, 456–57, 461
  and health, 456, 462–63
  and individualized instruction, 148
  and informal reading experiences, 458, 461
  and intelligence, 455–56, 463–64
  and kindergarten, 458
  and language ability, 457–58, 463
  and social experiences, 457, 464
Reading maturity:
  ascertaining, 459–65
    and intelligence tests, 459–60
Reading newspapers, 402–403
Reading Pacer, 376
Reading program, conducting, in individualized instruction, 142–45
Reading Rate Controller, 376
Reading readiness (*See also* Reading maturation):
  history of concept, 447–48
Reading skills, and functional usage, 71, 72
Reading success:
  and basic needs, 46
  home conditions for, 523–24
  implications to teachers, 43
  relationship of background experience to, 43
Reading tests, development of, 130
Reading unit, planning, 72–75
Reading Versatility Test, 382
Realistic stories, for prereaders, 485–86
Recall, 318–23
  in arithmetic, 319
  and association, 321–22
  delayed, 322
  development of, 320–23
  practice in, 566–67
  in prereaders, 480
  psychological aids in, 320
  in science, 319
  in social studies, 319
  "whole" method in, 322
Recognition of correct usage, 63, 76
Recognizing chapters, 325
Recommending books, 418
Record-keeping, 118
  in checking rate and comprehension, 375
  in individualized instruction, 143–44
  and voluntary reading, 422–25
Recreational reading:
  in establishing interest and taste, 408–41
  in guiding children's interests, 396–407

Recreational reading (*Cont.*)
  in reading literature, 387–95
Reed, James C., 359
Rehwoldt, Walter, 119
Reichard, S., 290
Religious emphasis, period of, 4
Renshaw Tachistoscopic Trainer, 376
Repetition, and experience charts, 493
Representative clubs, library, 437
Research:
  in book interests, 409–13
  in child growth, 26–27, 30, 33–35, 37, 39, 41–43, 47
  in comics, 400–401
  in concept building, 290–92
  in effect of experience, 43
  in factors of maturation in reading, 355–58
  in grouping, 120, 123–25
  in individualized instruction, 155–56
  in language arts, 57–58, 59, 62–64
  in magazines and newspapers, 402–404
  in parent attitudes, 511–13
  in perception, 41–42
  in reading rate, 358–62 (*See also* Rate, research in)
  in study skills, 308–11
  in thinking skills, 259–60
  in word identification, 195, 197, 198–200, 212, 217, 219
  in word meanings, 280–81
Research activities, 75
Research skills, 74, 116 (*See also* Locational skills)
Respellings, 238–40, 569
  in intermediate grades, 330–31
Retardation, reducing, 126
Retarded readers:
  and listening, 57
  phonics instruction for, 214
  and picture cards, 170–71
Rhyme words, in prereading instruction, 475
Richards, T. A., 97
Richards-Gibson Approach, 97–99
Right and left, sense of, 482–85
Rittenhouse, Gloria G., 121–22
Robinson, Francis P., 308
Robinson, Helen M., 48
Roesch, Raymond A., 359
Root words, procedures for teaching, 221–22
Roswell-Chall Diagnostic Reading Test, 251
Rudman, Herbert C., 410–11
Rudolf, Kathleen B., 309
Rules chart, 502
Russell, David H., 48, 64, 262, 290

Safford, Alton L., 157
Sanderson, Marion, 280
San Diego, California, 81
San Francisco State Normal School, 131
Sangren-Woody Reading Test, 382
Sarason, Seymour B., 262
Sartain, Harry W., 158–59
Sayre, Harrison M., 309–10
Scales of attainment, coordinated, 300
Scanning, 364, 366
Schneider, M., 290
School librarian, 433–34